To my grandmother, Veronique Masang Nkweta, and to the Bamboutou highlands which she and my mother hoed to raise me.

Allan Afuah

About the Author

Allan Afuah holds a Ph.D. from the Massachusetts Institute of Technology. He is co-chair and associate professor of corporate strategy and international business, and a Hallman Faculty Fellow, at the University of Michigan, where he teaches the core course in strategy and an elective in strategies for technology and innovation management. He has also worked as an engineer in California's Silicon Valley.

Preface

Most firms are in business to make money, and business models are about making money. It is therefore no surprise that one of the most common phrases in the vocabulary of executives, entrepreneurs, consultants, venture capitalists, analysts, individual investors, and scholars of management is *business models.* It is also no surprise that in the functional areas of business schools—from accounting to finance, from entrepreneurship to marketing, from management information systems to strategy, from organizational behavior to operations management—the phrase *business models* is also common. Yet, until now, there has been no textbook that is dedicated to business models.

Business Models: A Strategic Management Approach focuses on business models. In it, I draw on research in strategic management to provide an integrative framework for exploring how to formulate and execute profitable business models. Existing strategy textbooks lack two essential ingredients for serving as texts for business models. First, their focus is on broad strategy concepts, and they do not give the money-making aspects of strategy the attention that they deserve. They do not focus on the linkages between strategy and profitability. Second, they do not explore some key factors that play a critical role in firm profitability. For example, pricing and its strategic significance are not explored in strategy texts despite their extremely important role in firm profitability. Nor are sources of revenues explored.

My fascination with firm profitability and business models dates back to when I worked in California's Silicon Valley. I was puzzled by why chip companies such as Intel were so much more profitable than their competitors despite the fact that employees at all these firms appeared to work very hard. When I went to graduate school to study business, I quickly realized that studying strategic management might help me find some answers to this puzzle. After graduate school, I carried my passion for the underpinnings of firm profitability with me to the University of Michigan, where, for the past six years, I have taught the core course in strategy and an elective in strategies for technology and innovation management. This book is the result of the years of trying to find an integrative framework for exploring why some firms are more profitable than others.

INTENDED AUDIENCE

This book is intended for master's-level and some advanced-level undergraduate courses in the following areas.

Strategic Management

In strategic management, the book can be used to teach an elective entitled "Business Models" in which strategic management concepts are explored from a money-making perspective in more detail than would be covered in a core course in strategy. The book can also be used in a core course in which the goal is to emphasize strategic thinking and the money-making aspects of strategy rather than inundating students with too many perspectives. In the electives that follow such a core course, students can then explore non-money-making aspects of strategy.

v

Entrepreneurship

Most entrepreneurs who start new ventures want to make money. Thus, a core course in entrepreneurship can focus on business models. *Business Models* is designed for such a course. Where the core or foundation course focuses on other aspects of entrepreneurship, *Business Models* can be used for an elective.

Other Courses

This book can be used by any other department that wants to focus on the money-making strategic aspects of the functional area. For example, rather than teach the traditional engineering economics course that many engineering schools offer, an engineering department (aeronautics and astronautics, chemical, electrical engineering and computer science, civil, industrial and operating, mechanical) may want to focus on teaching engineers how to better profit from their engineering inventions. *Business Models* could be used to teach such a class. Some marketing classes, especially those on new product development, could also benefit from the concepts of the book.

ACKNOWLEDGMENTS

I continue to owe a huge debt of gratitude to my mentors at MIT, in particular, Rebecca Henderson, James Utterback, and Tom Allen. Many of the concepts in this book were pretested on my students at the University of Michigan. Their demanding questions helped me tremendously in my efforts to shape and refine "connected activities" and the "seven C's." The cases in the second part of the book were written by some of the students under my supervision. I am grateful to all these students. I would also like to thank my colleagues at the University of Michigan, especially Prashant Kale and Sendil Ethiraj, for their feedback and suggestions. Courtney Loverman was an excellent reader for some of the cases and co-authored another.

I would also like to thank John Weimeister, senior editor for management books, whose professionalism convinced me to work with McGraw-Hill to publish this book. My thanks also go to Julie Daniels of McGraw-Hill for suggesting that I add a chapter on corporate governance and social responsibility. Working with Kari Geltemeyer, Trina Hauger, and Ellen Cleary of McGraw-Hill was a pleasure. Finally, it was an absolute joy to have Susan Gottfried as the copy editor for the book. Her copy-editing and suggestions made the book easier to read and the concepts of the text easier to understand.

Allan Afuah
Ann Arbor, Michigan

Brief Contents

Table of Contents

Positions, Activities, Resources, Industry Factors, and Cost

Chapter **One**

Introduction
and Overview

Over the past two decades, the performance of some U.S. firms has been remarkable. Microsoft has been profitable since 1981, when it went public. Wal-Mart not only has been profitable since it went public in 1972 but by the year 2000 had grown to become the world's largest company. The Internet company eBay survived the dot-com burst of 2001 and continued to perform well even in the general stock market slump that followed. In 2001, Southwest Airlines made a profit of $511 million, while AMR (the parent company of American Airlines) lost $1.76 billion, US Airways Group lost $1.969 billion, Delta Airlines lost $1.216 billion, and UAL (the parent company of United Airlines) lost $2.145 billion and filed for bankruptcy in December 2002. One factor that enables firms such as Microsoft, Wal-Mart, eBay, and Southwest Airlines to perform so remarkably well is their business models.

PRELIMINARY DEFINITION OF *BUSINESS MODEL*

A **business model** is a framework for making money.[1] It is the **set of activities** *which* a firm performs, *how* it performs them, and *when* it performs them so as to offer its customers benefits they want and to earn a profit. Since business models are about making money, let us first explore what determines a firm's profitability before we complete our definition of a business model.

DETERMINANTS OF PROFITABILITY

Table 1.1 shows the profitability of different U.S. industries over a 21-year period. The interesting thing to note about the data is that firms in the pharmaceuticals industry outperformed firms in the airline industry. The average return on equity (ROE) for pharmaceuticals was 25.87 percent compared to a meager 2.68 percent for the airline industry, while the return on assets (ROA) was, respectively, 10.27 percent compared to 2.05 percent. In fact, there are consistent differences between the profits earned in different industries, not just between those in pharmaceuticals and airlines. This suggests that *there is something about some industries that allows the firms within those industries to be more profitable, on average, than firms in other industries.*

Now look at Table 1.2, which shows the profitability of the individual firms *within* pharmaceuticals and *within* the airline industry. The interesting thing about these data is that within each industry there are significant differences between the profitability of firms. In pharmaceuticals, for example, Bristol Myers Squibb out-performed all its rivals, while in the airline industry Southwest Airlines outper-formed its rivals. Thus, within each industry, some firms can be consistently more profitable than others. This suggests that, *within each industry, there is something about some firms that makes them more profitable than their rivals.*

As shown in Table 1.2, Bristol Myers Squibb has the highest profitability of all the firms in both industries. Its superior profitability is due to two things: (1) There is something about pharmaceuticals—so-called *industry factors*—that makes firms within the industry more profitable, on average, than firms in other industries, and (2) there is something specific to Bristol Myers Squibb—so-called *firm-specific factors*—that enables Bristol Myers Squibb to outperform its rivals within pharmaceuticals. In general, a firm's profitability is determined by both industry and firm-specific factors.[2]

Industry Factors

The question here is, Why is it that firms in some industries are, on average, more profitable than firms in other industries? In other words, what factors determine whether firms in one industry are more profitable, on average, than those in other

TABLE 1.1
Industry Profitability, 1981–2001

Source: Compustat. My thanks to Paul Michaud for making these calculations. Grant explored ROEs for these industries for the years 1985–1997: R. M. Grant, *Contemporary Strategy Analysis: Concepts, Techniques, Applications* (Oxford, U.K.: Blackwell, 2002) p. 68.

	Industry	ROE	ROA
1	Pharmaceuticals	25.87%	10.27%
2	Chemicals and allied products	21.70	7.88
3	Food and kindred products	24.78	7.25
4	Printing and publishing	16.30	6.68
5	Rubber and miscellaneous plastic	15.07	6.25
6	Fabricated metal products	19.00	5.58
7	Paper and allied products	13.77	4.70
8	Electronics and electrical equipment (no computers)	9.63	4.67
9	Nonferrous metals	10.39	4.23
10	Machinery, except electrical	15.69	3.80
11	Petroleum and coal products	13.25	3.76
12	Textile mill products	5.11	3.71
13	Aircraft, guided missiles, and parts	14.02	3.57
14	Stone, clay, and glass products	9.16	3.44
15	Motor vehicles and equipment	11.91	3.16
16	Iron and steel	6.40	3.14
17	Airlines (transportation by air)	2.68	2.05

TABLE 1.2
Firm Profitability, 1981–2001

Source: Compustat. My thanks to Charlie Chung and Paul Michaud for making these calculations.

Firm	ROA	Firm	ROA
Pharmaceuticals		**Airlines**	
Bristol Myers Squibb	13.71%	Southwest Airlines	4.85%
Merck	13.37	AMR	1.51
Schering Plough	12.89	Delta Airlines	1.50
WYETH American Home Products	12.52	UAL	0.96
Eli Lilly	10.23	US Air	0.31
Pfizer	9.66	America West Holdings	−3.27
Pharmacia & Upjohn	7.98	Continental Airlines	−4.97
American Cyanamid	3.57	TWA	−5.37
		Northwest Airlines	−13.40

industries? There are three primary **industry factors** that influence the profitability of firms: competitive forces in the industry, the influence of the overarching macro environment on the industry, and the cooperative forces between the firms and their suppliers, customers, rivals, and potential new entrants (Figure 1.1).

Competitive Forces

Firms in every industry face **competitive forces** exerted by suppliers, customers, rivals, potential new entrants, complementors, and substitute products.[3] The stronger these competitive forces, the less profitable the industry's firms are likely to be.

- The competitive force exerted by *rivals* is high if, for example, there are many similar industry firms that sell identical products. High rivalry can, and often does, force down the prices that industry firms can charge for their products. This lowers profitability. High rivalry can also force industry firms to offer higher-quality products to customers at smaller price premiums than the quality would suggest, or it can force them to advertise more than is necessary in an attempt to differentiate themselves. In both cases, industry costs can go up unnecessarily, thereby decreasing profitability.

- The force exerted by *suppliers* is high if the suppliers have bargaining power over industry firms. Suppliers with bargaining power can extract high prices from industry firms, thereby raising their costs. These suppliers may be powerful enough to force industry firms to take lower-quality supplies (inputs), making it difficult for them to offer the type of quality that they would have liked to offer their customers.[4] And the higher the prices that industry firms have to pay for their supplies, the higher their costs. The higher a firm's costs and the lower the quality of its products, the lower the profits that the firm can make.

- The competitive force exerted by *customers* is high if customers have bargaining power over industry firms. When customers have bargaining power, they may be able to extract lower prices from industry firms or force these firms to ship higher-quality products than the prices that customers pay for the products warrant.

- The competitive force exerted by *potential new entrants* is high if barriers to entry in the industry are low. When it is easy to enter the competitive space in which firms are operating, these firms face the constant threat of entry

FIGURE 1.1
Determinants of Profitability

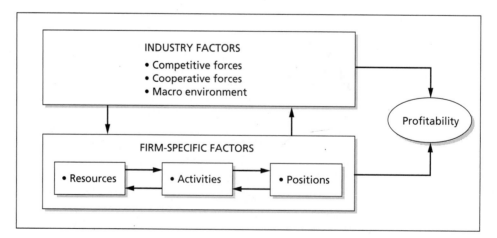

from other firms. This puts pressure on the prices that these firms can charge because higher prices tend to attract more entrants. Industry firms may also be forced to spend unnecessarily on attempts to raise entry barriers (e.g., advertising more than necessary). Both measures reduce industry profitability.

- A firm's *complementors* are the firms whose products complement the firm's products. The competitive force exerted by complementors is high if they have bargaining power over industry firms and therefore the interests of the complementors are reflected in the industry firms' actions.
- Finally, if the products that firms in an industry produce have viable *substitute products,* these firms are forced to keep their prices lower since charging higher prices can drive customers to the substitutes. Viable substitutes can also force industry firms to raise the quality of their products while keeping prices constant, for fear of driving customers to the viable substitutes. Lowering prices or increasing quality without charging a premium for the quality may decrease profits.

Where the competitive forces on industry firms are low, allowing these firms to be, on average, more profitable than firms in other industries, as is the case with pharmaceuticals, the industry is said to be an **attractive industry.** If these forces are high, as in the case of airlines, they lower the average profitability of the industry's firms and, therefore, the industry is said to be an **unattractive industry.**[5] In any case, any firm that formulates and executes a business model should pay attention to its competitive environment as it decides on the set of activities that it will perform to create and offer value to its customers and as it strategizes to profit from the value.

Cooperative Forces

Suppliers are not always adversarial, exercising whatever bargaining power they may have to extract high prices from firms and force them to accept low-quality inputs. Rather, suppliers can be allies with whom firms cooperate to create better value for the end customer and earn higher profits.[6] For example, in the automobile industry, cooperative relations with suppliers result in lower-cost and higher-quality products than do adversarial relations.[7] Customers and complementors are not always adversarial either, nor are all rivals. Alliances with customers can allow firms to offer these customers better value,[8] and cooperation with rivals, where legal, can lower firms' costs.

Macro Environment

The competitive environment in any region or country is also influenced by the region's or country's culture, government policies, fiscal and monetary policies, judicial and legal systems, and technological change.[9] For example, regulation and deregulation increase or decrease barriers to entry and, therefore, the profits that can be made. By issuing a limited number of taxicab licenses, for instance, a city is creating entry barriers to the taxicab market and thereby reducing competition in that market. National and international economic factors such as interest rates, exchange rates, employment, income, and productivity also impact industry competitiveness. For example, if a government limits the quantity of steel that can be imported into the country, the government is effectively decreasing competition and allowing local steel firms to make more money than they would have otherwise.

Critical Industry Value Drivers

In almost every industry, there are certain factors that have or are most likely to have a significant impact on cost or differentiation. We will call these factors **critical industry value drivers** since they have a large impact on the value—low cost or differentiation—that firms offer their customers (see below for more on customer value). In consulting, for example, capacity utilization is critical. Few firms can afford to have MBAs, who cost over a quarter of a million dollars each per year, idling around. Every day that they are not working is a day of billings down the drain, and they still have to be paid. In pharmaceuticals, two critical value drivers are the performance of research and development (R&D) and the ability to carry out clinical trials quickly and efficiently. Firms that discover lucrative drugs usually conduct a great amount of R&D.

Firm-Specific Factors

Recall from Table 1.2 that within each industry there can be vast differences in the performance of rival firms. In fact, some firms in unattractive industries can perform better than some in attractive industries. Consider Southwest Airlines: Although it is from the unattractive airline industry, it outperforms not only its rivals but also American Cyanamid, from the attractive pharmaceuticals industry (Table 1.2). The question here is, What is it about some firms that allows them to outperform their rivals? Three **firm-specific factors** determine whether a firm is more profitable than its industry rivals: the positions that it attains and maintains within the industry and the markets in which it competes, the activities that it performs to attain and maintain these positions, and the resources that enable it to perform the activities (Figure 1.1).

Positions of a Firm

A firm's positions within an industry consist of (1) the value that the firm offers its customers, (2) the market segments to which it offers value, (3) the sources of revenues within each market segment, (4) the firm's relative positioning vis-à-vis its suppliers, customers, rivals, potential new entrants, substitute products, and complementors, and (5) the prices that it charges its customers.

Customer Value   For a firm to keep making money, customers must prefer its products over those of competitors. For customers to prefer a firm's products over competitors' products, the firm's products must satisfy at least one of two conditions:

1. The products are **differentiated products.**[10] That is, there is something about the products that customers *perceive* as being different and better than what they perceive in competitors' products. For example, customers may prefer the firm's car because it has better gas mileage and performs better in government crash tests than competitors' cars. A customer may also prefer a cola from Coca-Cola because he or she perceives that company's drink as being better than the colas from competitors even though, in blind taste tests, many people cannot tell the difference between Coca-Cola's cola and its competitors' colas.

2. The firm's products are perceived as being the same as competitors' products but the price that the firm charges is lower than the price charged by competitors. For example, customers may buy one company's skim milk because it costs less than competitors' skim milk.

Effectively, for a firm's revenues to stay high, the firm must keep offering customers something that they value and that competitors cannot offer—differentiated or lower-priced products or services. The concept of differentiated or lower-priced products is sometimes referred to as **customer value.** Thus, we can say that customers will keep coming to a firm only if it offers them better customer value than its competitors.

Market Segments Since different customers often have different preferences, a firm may also need to target the right **market segments** with products or services that have the right mix of value for each segment if the firm is to keep attracting customers. For example, although one group of customers may want a car with high gas mileage and better crash test results, other segments may want different features in a car, such as acceleration from zero to 60 miles per hour, smooth handling, or roominess.

Sources of Revenues Within a market segment, a firm may have multiple **sources of revenues.** For example, most jet engine makers earn most of their profits not from selling new jet engines but from servicing older engines; most car dealers in the United States profit more from servicing cars than from selling new ones. Identifying the sources of revenues helps a firm decide what value to offer customers and what level of focus to apply in performing its value-adding activities.

Relative Positioning Even if a firm offers the right customer value to the right market segments and does so better than its rivals, it is still possible that the firm might not be profitable. That is, superior relative customer value offered to the right customer segments, while necessary, is not always a sufficient condition for profitability. Consider the hypothetical example of a firm that has invented an electronic fuel injector that improves the gas mileage of Ford Motor Company cars by 40 percent but can work only in Ford cars and uses microprocessors made only by Intel. Clearly, such a fuel injector offers Ford many benefits and is therefore highly valued by the firm. However, since the injector can work only in Ford cars, the inventor cannot sell it to any other firm. Therefore, Ford has the bargaining power and consequently does not have to pay a high price to the inventor. Moreover, Intel also has bargaining power over the inventor since only Intel can provide the microprocessor that the inventor needs. The competitive forces from its supplier and customer are too high. In other words, the inventor's relative positioning vis-à-vis its supplier and customer is not good. In fact, if customers have bargaining power over a firm, the firm is not likely to charge customers their reservation prices (discussed below). Effectively, it takes both superior relative customer value and an advantageous bargaining position to make money. In general, a firm's **relative positioning** vis-à-vis its suppliers, customers, rivals, potential new entrants, and substitutes plays an important role in a firm's profitability.

Price Offering the right value to the right customer segments and being positioned advantageously vis-à-vis suppliers, customers, rivals, potential new entrants, and substitute products may still not be enough for a firm to capture the revenues that its positions suggest it should. To profit from the superior value it offers customers and from its positions, a firm needs to **price** its products effectively. Every customer has a certain maximum price that he or she is willing to pay for a particular level of benefits he or she perceives in a product. This is the customer's **reservation price.** Pricing products below a customer's reservation price means leaving money on the table; pricing higher than a customer's reservation price means driving away the customer. A firm that can charge its customers their reservation prices for the benefits they perceive in its products is therefore more likely to be profitable than one that does not. For example, in 2000, Napster offered its customers great value in the selection of online music and the community of music lovers that belonged to the Napster network. However, it did not charge its customers for the music they downloaded from its servers and that may have contributed to its fall.

Activities of a Firm

To deliver the right value to the right market segments, price the product right, focus on the right sources of revenue, and position itself well in relation to suppliers, customers, rivals, new entrants, and competitors, a firm must perform the **activities** that underpin these positions. For example, if BMW is going to offer its customers cars that they perceive as having superior performance, it has to see to it that the cars are conceptualized, designed, manufactured, branded, promoted, delivered, and serviced appropriately. The extent to which a firm can attain and maintain profitable positions is a function of *which* activities it chooses to perform, *how* it performs them, and *when* it performs them.

Which In creating and offering value to its customers to earn a profit, a firm usually has many activities to choose from, and which ones it chooses to perform plays a major role in the positions that it can attain and maintain. For example, to create and offer value to its customers and earn a profit, a PC manufacturer must choose which activities it can perform. It can conduct extensive R&D or none at all; it can manufacture its own products or outsource the activity; it can target business customers or home users; it can sell its computers through the Internet using a build-to-order strategy or sell them through dealerships and its own retail stores; it can price its computers for outright sale or for lease; it can offer various types of after-sale service or none at all; and it can collect payments from customers well before paying suppliers or collect at about the same time that it pays. Dell Computers performs little R&D compared to Apple, targets both business customers and consumers, sells its products through the Internet rather than through dealerships, and usually collects payments before paying its suppliers for the components that go into the computers it has sold. These choices have played an important role in Dell's profitability.

How Once a firm chooses which activities it wants to perform, it usually must also decide *how* to perform the activities. In the PC example, if a firm chooses to design and manufacture its own computers, it may decide to work closely with customers and suppliers of key components when designing the PC or to have little consultation with these parties during the design phase. It also has the choice of whether to use the latest methods in lean manufacturing and total quality management. Cooperating with customers and suppliers and using total quality control or lean-manufacturing methods can keep defects low and increase the quality and reliability of products while also reducing their costs.

When The timing of a firm's performance of its activities relative to competitors or of an activity relative to its other activities can also be critical to the success of the activities. If a firm's activities are timed so that it can introduce its products before those of competitors, it may have a "first-mover" advantage. In pharmaceuticals, for example, once a firm introduces the first effective drug of its kind and gets doctors to start prescribing it, a competitor usually has difficulty dislodging the original drug with a new one unless the new drug demonstrates substantial advantages over the first mover's drug. However, being the first to introduce a product is no guarantee of success. That's because timing alone is not sufficient. A firm's decisions on which activities to perform and how to perform them also matter. And so do the resources that the firm needs to perform the activities, as we will see below. Firms that move later but do the right things well are more likely to be successful than those that move early but do the wrong things. Microsoft was not the first to introduce any of the major products that are the cornerstones of its business model—Word, Excel, Windows, Explorer, PowerPoint, and Outlook. The first PC makers, such as Altair, were in the market in the late 1970s but did not do very well; only when IBM entered in 1981 did the fledgling PC market gain credibility. The timing of a firm's performance of an activity relative to its other activities can have an impact on the effectiveness of its other activities. Intel has been known to introduce new generations of its microprocessors before unit sales of an older generation have peaked. Although in doing so it cannibalizes its own products, it is able to maintain its market advantage.

Resources of a Firm

Performing the activities that enable a firm to create and offer superior customer value and position itself to profit from the value requires resources.[11] A firm's **resources** are its assets and its abilities to use those assets to effectively perform the activities that its business model calls for. Assets can be *tangible,* such as plants and equipment, or *intangible,* such as patents, brands, copyrights, trade secrets, and market research findings. They can also be human, such as the skills and knowledge embodied in employees. For example, to conduct R&D and discover blockbuster drugs that allow a pharmaceutical company to make profits, the company needs laboratories, skilled scientists, equipment, and stocks of related knowledge. A firm's ability to turn its assets into customer value for different market segments and the right bargaining position is its **competence** or **capability.** For example, Honda Motor Company's ability to design light, high-performing, dependable engines is a capability (competence) that many of its automobile rivals envy.

COMPONENTS OF A BUSINESS MODEL

Two key points emerge from the above discussion of the determinants of profitability that will help us in our exploration of business models. The first is that a firm's profitability is determined by both industry factors and firm-specific factors (positions, activities, and resources). Thus, since business models are about making money, a business model must also depend on the factors that determine a firm's profitability. That is, a firm's business model is a function of its positions, activities, resources, and industry's factors. These four components are shown in Figure 1.2 together with a fifth component—cost. The rationale for adding the cost component to our business model is simple: Performing activities generates costs, regardless of whether a firm is pursuing a low-cost or differentiation strategy, and firms do not always minimize their costs, even when they are so-called low-cost producers. Therefore, since profits are the difference between revenues and costs, cost should be a component of business models.

The second key point is that a firm makes money when it uses its resources to perform activities, given its industry, to create superior customer value (low-cost or differentiated products) and put itself in a position to appropriate the value. (*Appropriate value* here means "earn a profit commensurate with the value created.") The extent to which a firm can offer superior customer value (relative to its competitors) and appropriate the value is a function of which activities the firm performs, how it performs them, and when it performs them. Thus, we can expand our earlier definition of *business model:*

A business model is the set of *which* activities a firm performs, *how* it performs them, and *when* it performs them as it uses its resources to perform activities, given its industry, to create superior customer value (low-cost or differentiated products) and put itself in a position to appropriate the value.

FIGURE 1.2
Components of a Business Model

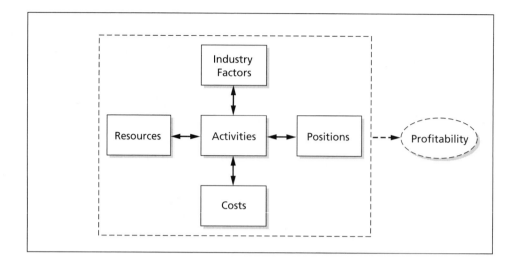

From these two key points, we can say that the profitability of a business model depends on which activities the firm performs, how it performs them, and when it performs them to better position the firm relative to its competitors, build and leverage its resources in performing activities, exploit industry factors, and keep costs low. We will have much more to say about this in Chapter 5 but provide some examples below.

Positions

Activities that are consistent with a firm's positions are better than those that are not.[12] For example, if a PC maker positions itself as a low-cost provider, spending a lot more money on basic R&D than its low-cost competitors would not be consistent with its low-cost position. Large spending on advertising by a maker of cola concentrate is consistent with a differentiation position if the firm's goal is to differentiate itself using its brand.

Resources

Activities that leverage a firm's existing resources or its ability to build such resources can help the firm create and appropriate customer value. For example, a semiconductor firm with dedicated scientists, engineers, a database of circuit design code, and an installed base of microprocessors is more likely to succeed in designing microprocessors that customers want than one without such a stock of resources. Honda designs and builds its own lawn mowers, cars, electric generators, motorcycles, off-terrain vehicles, and snowblowers largely because it has superior competencies in making internal combustion engines.

Industry Factors

The activities a firm performs can also influence the competitive forces that act on the firm. For example, when competitive forces are strong, firms perform activities that allow them to differentiate their products or lower their costs to levels below those of competitors. For companies that have built strong brands, such as the Coke brand, such brands can curb new entry and rivalry, thereby making the pressure from industry competitive forces less repressive on those firms. Activities that take advantage of industry value drivers are also likely to strengthen a firm's position. Take consulting, for example. Since utilization of consultants is a strong driver of costs, consulting firms should take steps to ensure that they do not have consultants idling around. This might entail, for example, engaging in longer-term assignments since a lot of idling occurs between engagements.

Costs

Engaging in activities such as total quality control and reengineering can keep a firm's costs low, regardless of whether the firm pursues a low-cost or differentiation strategy. Cooperating with suppliers can also improve a firm's position. For example, researchers have found that when automobile makers cooperate with their suppliers and work closely with them rather than treating them like adversaries, developing cars costs less and takes less time and the resulting cars are of better quality.[13]

TAXONOMY OF BUSINESS MODELS

During the dot-com boom of the late 1990s, it was not unusual for analysts, start-ups, and potential investors to refer to a firm as having an advertising, an auction, a markup, a production, or a subscription business model. These terms were largely a way of describing how firms obtained their revenues—they pertained to revenue models, not business models. For example, Yahoo! was described as having an advertising business model because it generated most of its revenues through advertising. By the time the bubble burst, there were over a hundred revenue models that were labeled "business models."[14] A business model is distinguished by how the firm earns a profit, not by how it generates revenues alone. Revenues are just one component of making money. Cost is the other. A **revenue model** is distinguished by the set of activities a firm performs that enable it to create value, offer the value to its targeted customers, and appropriate the value. Thus, two firms that generate revenues through advertising can have similar revenue models but very different business models.

RELATIONSHIP BETWEEN BUSINESS MODELS AND STRATEGY

By now, readers who know something about strategy must be wondering what the differences are between a business model and a strategy. Various definitions of *strategy* have been offered by scholars over the years. These include:

- "A firm's theory about how to compete successfully."[15]
- "A firm's theory of how it can gain superior performance in the markets within which it operates."[16]
- "The overall plan for deploying resources to establish a favorable position."[17]
- "The determination of basic long-term goals and objectives of an enterprise, and the adoption of courses of action and the allocation of resources necessary for carrying out these goals."[18]
- "A commitment to undertake one set of actions rather than another."[19]
- "The creation of a unique and valuable position, involving a different set of activities."[20]
- "The pattern of objectives, purposes or goals, and the major policies and plans for achieving these goals, stated in such a way as to define what business the company is in or should be in and the kind of company it is or should be."[21]

Phrases such as "compete successfully," "gain superior performance," "establish a favorable position," "carrying out these goals," and "unique and valuable position" in these definitions all suggest that strategy is about performance, about winning. To the extent that business models are about making money and strategy is about performance, the two should be highly related. The differences between the two start to emerge when the following three key aspects of strategy are considered.

Strategy and Operational Effectiveness

Differences have been identified between strategy and operational effectiveness. **Strategy** involves committing to undertake one set of actions rather than another and, in the process, creating a unique and valuable position that allows the firm to perform better than its competitors.[22] It is about *which* activities to perform and which ones not to perform. According to Professor Michael Porter, **operational effectiveness** entails "performing similar activities better than rivals perform them."[23] It is about *how* to, for example, perform the activities faster or with fewer mistakes using operational processes such as total quality management; in other words, it is about doing things right. Both strategy and operational effectiveness are critical to a firm's performance. Since a business model comprises *which* activities a firm performs, *how* it performs them, and *when* it performs them so as to earn a profit, a business model includes the profit-oriented aspects of strategy and operational effectiveness.

Strategy and Implementation

Effective implementation of a strategy is critical to its success. While strategy involves commitment to one set of activities rather than another, **implementation** entails executing those activities. A business model usually includes the elements of both business strategy and implementation that are oriented toward financial performance.

Corporate- and Business-Level Strategy

A diversified firm has three levels of strategy: corporate, business, and functional.[24] **Corporate strategy** involves deciding what businesses the firm should be in and how the businesses should be managed so as to ensure that the corporate whole is more than the sum of its parts.[25] By "the corporate whole is more than the sum of its parts," we mean that a firm's portfolio of businesses performs better than those businesses would perform if each were a separate company. For example, General Electric (GE) has many businesses, such as aircraft engines, plastics, broadcasting, and financial services. For GE, ensuring that the whole is more than the sum of its parts means that—as a portfolio of businesses—aircraft engines, plastics, broadcasting, financial services, and its other businesses should be more profitable under GE than if each of them were a separate company. Being successful at the corporate level often entails creating scarce, difficult-to-imitate resources that the businesses in the firm's portfolio can exploit to their advantages.[26] Each business in a portfolio has its own business model and is related to corporate-level strategy only to the extent that (1) there are corporate-level resources that can augment its business-level resources and (2) the corporate office sets the strategic direction for the business. For example, for GE to keep a business in its portfolio of businesses, one criteria was that the business must be number one or two in its market. Such a goal influences the type of business model that each business pursues.

Business strategy—also called **competitive strategy**—involves creating and offering better customer value than competitors do, with the objective of creating a competitive advantage for the firm in a particular business.[27] It usually entails offering customers lower-cost products than those of competitors or offering differentiated products that give customers better benefits than do competitors' products. Therefore, a firm's business model includes the profit-oriented aspects of its business strategies with the associated operational effectiveness and implementation. **Functional strategy** pertains to the set of functional activities that a firm performs—within functions such as R&D, manufacturing, marketing, and human resources—in support of a business's (or businesses') goal of attaining and maintaining a competitive advantage. Thus, a firm's business model also includes the functional strategies of the firm's different functional areas with the associated operational effectiveness.

ORGANIZATION OF THIS BOOK

The book is organized as shown in Figure 1.3. In Chapter 2, we explore in detail customer value and relative positioning vis-à-vis a firm's customers, rivals, substitute products, suppliers, potential new entrants, and complementors. In

FIGURE 1.3   **Organization and Flow of the Book**

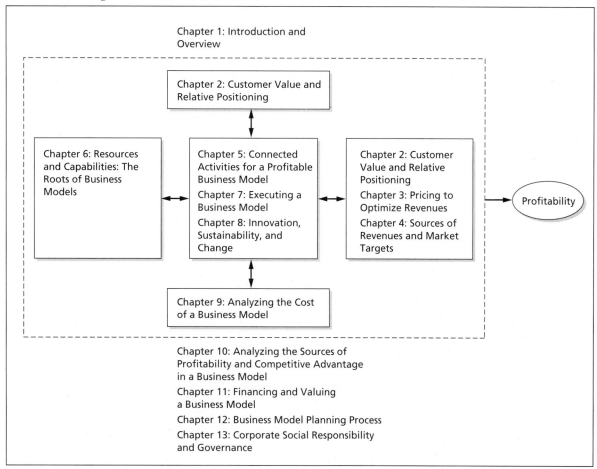

particular, we examine the benefits that customers usually value in products and the role that such benefits and a firm's relative positioning in its industry play in the firm's profitability. We recognize the fact that offering customers better value than competitors do is a necessary condition for profitability but not always a sufficient one; therefore, a business model should strive to improve the firm's relative positioning in addition to promoting superior customer value. In Chapter 3, we explore how firms price the value that they offer customers. We examine the different pricing strategies and methods that firms use to set prices as close to customers' reservation prices as possible in an effort to appropriate the value that they create for customers.

Since customers have different needs and preferences, what they value in a product can differ from customer to customer. Thus, a firm may need to target the right customers with the right value to increase its chances of having a profitable business model. In Chapter 4, we explore the revenue sources and revenue-generating models that are available to firms as they formulate and execute their business models. We also explore how firms target mass markets, individuals, and market segments in generating revenues.

In Chapter 5, we examine in detail the relationship between the three dimensions of a business model's activities—the *which, how,* and *when* of activities—as well as the other components of a business model—positions, resources, industry factors, and costs—and a firm's profitability. In Chapter 6, we argue that in order to perform the activities it chooses to perform, a firm must have the resources and capabilities that are required to perform such activities or must be able to build them. We describe a method for determining the profit-generating potential of resources and capabilities. Choosing which activities to perform, how to perform them, and when is one thing. Executing the activities is another. We explore the execution of a business model in Chapter 7. Firms that have formulated and executed their business models well make money. Making money attracts competitors who want a piece of the action. In Chapter 8, we explore innovation, sustainability, and change—in particular, what it takes for a firm to exploit change (through innovation) to sustain an existing advantage or gain a new one.

Chapter 9 examines the costs that a firm incurs as it performs the activities of a business model. It explores the relationship between the activities that are performed and the cost of those activities. In Chapter 10, we outline the steps necessary to analyze the sources of a firm's profitability or competitive advantage. We provide a detailed example of a step-by-step analysis using the case of Southwest Airlines. In Chapter 11, we explore the financing and valuation of a business model. We examine the different sources of finance for a business model and how capital markets value business models. Chapter 12 explores a business model planning process—the process through which a firm conceptualizes a new business model or fine-tunes an existing one to reflect important changes in its internal or external environment. Chapter 13 examines the corporate social responsibility issues that potentially have an impact on business models. We explore the fact that there are good ways and bad ways to make money.

Summary

A firm's business model is the set of activities *which* it performs, *how* it performs them, and *when* it performs them to earn a profit. It is a firm's framework for making money through the building of its resources and the transformation of those resources into products or services that customers want. Since a firm's profitability is determined by industry factors (competitive forces, cooperative forces, and macro-environmental forces) and firm-specific factors (positions, activities, and resources), a business model should depend on these factors because it is about making money. Thus a business model can be conceptualized as having five components: the positions that a firm occupies in its industry and markets, the activities that the firm performs to attain and maintain the desired positions, the resources that the firm needs to perform the activities, the industry factors that influence the activities that can be performed, and the cost of performing the activities. The extent to which a business model can give a firm a competitive advantage is a function of the extent to which the activities that the firm performs, how it performs them, and when it performs them allow the firm to attain and maintain the right positions, to build and exploit new resources and capabilities better than competitors do, to understand and exploit industry factors, and to keep the firm's costs low regardless of whether the firm pursues a low-cost or differentiation strategy. Business models embody the aspects of corporate-level strategy, business strategy, functional strategy, operational effectiveness, and implementation that are oriented toward financial performance.

Key Terms

activities, *8*
attractive industry, *5*
business model, *2*
business strategy, *13*
capability, *9*
competence, *9*
competitive forces, *4*
competitive strategy, *13*
corporate strategy, *12*
critical industry value drivers, *6*

customer value, *7*
differentiated products, *6*
firm-specific factors, *6*
functional strategy, *13*
implementation, *12*
industry factors, *4*
market segments, *7*
operational effectiveness, *12*
price, *7*
relative positioning, *7*
reservation price, *7*

resources, *9*
revenue model, *11*
set of activities, *2*
sources of revenues, *7*
strategy, *12*
unattractive industry, *5*

Study Questions

1. What are the differences between a business model and a strategy?
2. What is the difference between a business model and a revenue model?

Endnotes

1. This definition of a business model has the same money-making orientation as the following definitions:

   "A company's business model deals with the revenue-cost-profit economies of its strategy—the actual and projected revenue streams generated by the company's product offerings and competitive approaches, the associated cost structure and profit margins, and the resulting earnings stream and return on investment." A. A. Thompson and A. J. Strickland, *Strategic Management: Concepts and Cases* (New York: McGraw-Hill, 2003), p. 3.

   "Configurations of strategy relating to the sources of revenue and profits." R. M. Grant, *Contemporary Strategy Analysis: Concepts, Techniques, Applications* (Oxford, U.K.: Blackwell, 2002), p. 307.

   "A unique configuration of elements comprising the organization's goals, strategies, processes, technologies, and structure, conceived to create value for customers and thus compete successfully in a particular market." S. Ehiraj, I. Guler, and H. Singh, "E-Business Models: Value Creation and Competitive Advantage," working paper, The Wharton School, 2000, p. 2.

"A template or prototype comprising the core set of organizational processes and patterns of behavior that form the basis for continuing viability of the organization." S. Ethridge, P. Kale, and H. Singh, "Alliance Value Creation in E-Business—An Empirical Analysis," in *Cooperative Strategies and Alliances,* ed. Farok Contractor and P. Lorange (Amsterdam: Elsevier, 2002), p. 6.

"A viable business model is a strategy that has a reasonable probability of succeeding if well executed." G. Saloner, A. Shepard, and J. Podolny, *Strategic Management* (New York: Wiley, 2001), p. 279.

"A firm's business model is how it plans to make money long term." A. N. Afuah and C. L. Tucci, *Internet Business Models and Strategies: Text and Cases* (New York: McGraw-Hill, 2003).

"It is a hypothesis about how a company will make money over the long term: what the company will sell, and to whom; how the company will collect revenue; what technologies it will employ, when it will rely on partners, and, following from the last two points, how its costs will 'scale' with growth." T. R. Eisenmann, *Internet Business Models and Strategies: Text and Cases* (New York: McGraw-Hill, 2002).

2. R. Rumelt, "How Much Does Industry Matter?" *Strategic Management Journal* 12 (1991), pp. 167–185; A. M. McGahan and M. E. Porter, "How Much Does Industry Matter? Really?" *Strategic Management Journal* 18 (summer special issue, 1997), pp. 15–30; M. E. Porter, *On Competition* (Boston: Harvard Business School Press, 1998).

3. M. E. Porter, "How Competitive Forces Shape Strategy," *Harvard Business Review,* March–April 1979, pp. 137–156.

4. Sometimes, however, the relationship between suppliers and firms is more cooperative than adversarial.

5. M. E. Porter, *Competitive Strategy: Techniques for Analyzing Industries and Competitors* (New York: Free Press, 1980).

6. R. Gulati, "Alliances and Networks," *Strategic Management Journal* 19 (1998), pp. 293–317; R. Gulati, N. Nohria, and A. Zaheer, "Strategic Networks," *Strategic Management Journal* 21 (2000), pp. 203–215.

7. J. H. Dyer and K. Nobeoka, "Creating and Managing a High Performance Knowledge-Sharing Network: The Toyota Case," *Strategic Management Journal* 21 (2000), pp. 345–367; J. H. Dyer, "Specialized Supplier Networks as a Source of Competitive Advantage: Evidence from the Auto Industry," *Strategic Management Journal* 17 (1996), pp. 271–292.

8. E. Von Hippel, "Lead Users: A Source of Novel Product Concepts," *Management Science* 32 (1986), pp. 791–805.

9. M. E. Porter, *The Competitive Advantage of Nations* (New York: Free Press, 1990).

10. M. E. Porter, "Towards a Dynamic Theory of Strategy," *Strategic Management Journal* 12 (1991), pp. 95–117.

11. R. Priem and J. E. Butler, "Is the Resource-Based 'View' a Useful Perspective for Strategic Management Research?" *Academy of Management Review* 26 (2001), pp. 22–41; J. B. Barney, "Is the Resource-Based 'View' a Useful Perspective for Strategic Management Research? Yes," *Academy of Management Review* 26 (2001), pp. 41–57; R. Priem and J. E. Butler, "Tautology in the Resource-Based View and the Implications of Externally Determined Resource Value: Further Comments," *Academy of Management Review* 26 (2001), pp. 57–67.

12. M. E. Porter, "What Is Strategy?" *Harvard Business Review,* November–December 1996, p. 68.

13. K. B. Clark and K. Fujimoto, *Product Development Performance: Strategy, Organization, and Management in the World Automobile Industry* (Boston: Harvard Business School Press, 1991); Dyer and Nobeoka, "Creating and Managing a High Performance Knowledge-Sharing Network."

14. Afuah and Tucci, *Internet Business Models and Strategies;* T. R. Eisenmann, *Internet Business Models and Strategies.*

15. J. B. Barney, *Gaining and Sustaining Competitive Advantage* (Reading, MA: Addison-Wesley, 2002), p. 6; P. Drucker, "The Theory of Strategy," *Harvard Business Review,* September–October 1994, pp. 95–105.

16. Drucker, "The Theory of Strategy"; J. B. Barney and A. M. Arikan, "The Resource-Based View: Origins and Implications," working paper, Fisher College of Business, Ohio State University, 2001.

17. Grant, *Contemporary Strategy Analysis: Concepts, Techniques, Applications.*

18. A. D. Chandler, *Strategy and Structure: Chapters in the History of the Industrial Enterprise* (Cambridge, MA: MIT Press, 1962), p. 13.

19. S. Oster, *Modern Competitive Analysis* (New York: Oxford University Press, 1999), p. 2.

20. Porter, "What Is Strategy?" p. 68.

21. K. R. Andrews, *The Concept of Corporate Strategy* (Homewood, IL: Dow Jones–Irwin, 1971), p. 22.

22. Oster, *Modern Competitive Analysis;* P. Ghemawat, *Commitment: The Dynamics of Strategy* (New York: Free Press, 1991); Porter, "What Is Strategy?" pp. 61–78.

23. Porter, "What Is Strategy?" p. 62.

24. Grant, *Contemporary Strategy Analysis: Concepts, Techniques, Applications;* M. E. Porter, "From Competitive Advantage to Corporate Strategy," *Harvard Business Review,* May–June 1987, pp. 43–59.

25. E. H. Bowman and C. E. Helfat, "Does Corporate Strategy Matter?" *Strategic Management Journal* 22 (2001), pp. 1–23; Porter, "From Competitive Advantage to Corporate Strategy."

26. D. J. Collis and C. A. Montgomery, "Competing on Resources: Strategies for the 1990s," *Harvard Business Review,* July–August 1995, pp. 118–128.

27. Porter, "From Competitive Advantage to Corporate Strategy."

Chapter Two

Customer Value and Relative Positioning

In Chapter 1, we said that a business model is a framework for making money. Money comes from customers who pay for the benefits that they value in products or services. For a firm to make money, customers must prefer its products over competitors' products. Customers prefer one firm's products over competitors' products if they perceive the firm's products as offering them something that they need and that competitors' products do not offer. For instance, a customer may buy a product from one company rather than another because the product costs less or because there is something different about it that the customer wants. As an example, a customer may buy a car because it costs less than comparable cars or because it has superior handling on the road. Thus, a critical part of a business model is offering customers something that they value and that competitors cannot offer—that is, offering better *customer value*.

Offering customers better value than competitors offer allows a firm to charge premium prices for the superior value and generate revenues. But how much a firm charges for superior value depends on the bargaining power that the firm has over its customers and suppliers, the rivalry in its industry, the barriers to entry into its industry, and the viability of substitute products.[1] That is, the revenues that a firm generates depend on the value that it offers to customers and on its *relative positioning* vis-à-vis its customers, suppliers, rivals, potential new entrants, complementors, and viable substitute products. Additionally, since profits are the difference between revenues and costs, a firm's ability to profit from the superior value that it creates is a function of the costs that the firm incurs in generating revenues. As with how much a firm charges for value, these costs depend on the bargaining power that the firm has over its customers and suppliers, the rivalry in its industry, the barriers to entry into the industry, and the power of substitutes. Effectively, the costs that a firm incurs in generating revenues depend on the same factors the revenues depend on: the value that the firm offers and its relative positioning vis-à-vis its competitive forces.

In this chapter, we explore customer value and relative positioning. We start by defining customer benefits and value. Next, we explore how demand for customer benefits and value can be determined. Finally, we explore relative positioning.

CUSTOMER VALUE: LOW-COST OR DIFFERENTIATED PRODUCTS

Firms that want to make money in any market must compete for customers' dollars in that market. Customers choose one firm's product over its competitors' products if the firm's product offers benefits that customers need and that either:

- Are superior to benefits of competitors' products.
- Are identical to benefits of competitors' products but are offered at a lower cost than competitors' prices.
- Are superior to benefits of competitors' products *and* are offered at a lower cost than competitors' prices.

In other words, customers prefer one firm's products over its competitors' products if the firm offers a differentiated product, a low-cost product, or both. A product is *differentiated* if customers *perceive* it as offering benefits that are superior to those of competing products or as having benefits that competing products do not have. For example, one cell phone may be perceived as being differentiated from another because it is lighter and more durable than competing phones or because it embodies a camera and competing phones do not. Customers may see a BMW as differentiated from many other cars because it is perceived as being a high-performing car. Since the goal of a business model is to make money, it is important that customers value the difference in the benefits enough to pay a price premium that more than compensates for any extra costs the firm may have incurred in differentiating the product. That is, if BMW is going to make money, customers must be willing to pay a premium price that more than makes up for the extra costs the company incurs in convincing them that a BMW is a high-performing machine and more. Firms whose activities are designed to offer their customers differentiated products are said to pursue a **differentiation strategy.**

Customers in an industry may perceive products in that industry as having identical features. For example, firms in the bread industry may perceive all the wheat that they buy from different suppliers as having the same quality. Some consumers may perceive all PCs as offering them comparable software, microprocessor speed, amount of memory, and ease of use. In such cases, customers are likely to buy from the firm that has the lowest-cost product. A firm in this situation is able to offer its products to customers at a lower cost than competitors' prices if it can produce and deliver the products at a lower cost than its competitors can. Such a firm is able to pass some of its cost savings on to its customers in the form of lower prices. For example, Wal-Mart offers its customers shopping experiences comparable to those offered by its competitors but at lower costs than the competitors charge. Since its costs are lower, Wal-Mart can charge its customers lower prices. When a firm's activities are designed to offer its customers lower-cost benefits than its competitors offer, it is said to pursue a **low-cost strategy.** A firm that pursues a low-cost strategy is usually said to be *competing on price.*

DIFFERENTIATION

From the car and computer examples in the previous section, it might be tempting to conclude that customers value only product features. However, a number of factors influence customers' buying decisions, so product differentiation goes beyond product features. There are seven means by which a firm can differentiate its products and services: product features, brand-name reputation, network externalities, timing, location, service, and product mix.[2]

Product Features

As we saw above, a firm can make its products more valuable to customers than competitors' products by offering features that competitors' products do not have. An automaker can differentiate a car by the styling of the car, its gas mileage, how quickly the car can accelerate from 0 to 60 miles per hour, and the smoothness of the ride. A pharmaceutical company's cholesterol drug may be differentiated from competing drugs by the amount of bad cholesterol it reduces, the amount of good cholesterol it increases, or the extent to which it reduces the incidence of heart attacks. Using product features to differentiate one's products is probably the most familiar form of product differentiation, but there are other ways of making one's product valuable to customers.

Brand-Name Reputation

A firm's brand-name reputation can make customers perceive its products as being more valuable to them than the products' physical characteristics would suggest. In the BMW example, some customers may buy the car because it is a high-performing car, but others may buy it because over the years they have come to believe that a BMW is "the ultimate driving machine." That is, many people buy a BMW not so much because of its performance as because it *is* a BMW— because of its brand-name reputation. In blind taste tests, many people cannot tell the difference between Coca-Cola's cola drink and its competitors' colas. However, customers still buy Coke at premium prices because it is differentiated from competitors' drinks by Coke's brand-name reputation. Association with a reputable firm can also be a source of differentiation. For example, early in the life of the computer industry, many people bought Compaq personal computers because they were clones of IBM personal computers. Similarly, small start-up biotechnology firms that enter strategic alliances with more established pharmaceutical companies boost their status.[3]

Network Size

For some products or technologies, their value to customers increases with the number of customers who use the same product or technology. Such products are said to exhibit **network externalities**—that is, the greater the number of people who use the product, the more valuable it becomes to users.[4] Thus, a firm offering products that exhibit network externalities can differentiate its products by building a larger user base (network size). A good example of such a product is the telephone. If your telephone were connected only to the author of this book, the phone would not be as useful to you as it is when connected to members of your family and the rest of the world. As the number of people connected to a telephone system increases, it becomes more valuable to users. The phenomenon of network externalities also applies to products whose value to customers increases with complementary products. Computers are a good example. Software is critical to computer use, and software developers want to sell to large numbers of users. Therefore, if more and more people own computers of a particular standard, more software is likely to be developed for their computers. And the more software that is available for that computer standard, the more valuable the computers are to users. This causes more people to purchase those computers, and the additional users, in turn, mean even more software is developed for the computers.

Although estimates of the value of network size go as high as n^2 and n^n (where n is the number of nodes on the network),[5] a larger network size does not always mean more value for customers. The best way to determine whether size matters is to go back to the definition of network externalities and ask this simple question: "Does having more people in the network make the network more valuable to me as a customer?" Take the example of an online book retailer and an online auction firm, both of which have the same number of registered users. Which one enjoys the benefits of network externalities more? To answer this question, put yourself in the place of a customer and ask yourself: "Does it matter to me whether there are millions of other book buyers when I want to buy a book from Amazon.com?" Now, ask yourself this question: "Does it matter to me whether there are millions of other art enthusiasts on eBay when I want to buy art at eBay's online auction site?" Clearly, the greater the number of people who are registered to trade on eBay, the better your chances of finding someone who has the type of art you want. However, you will most likely find the book you want at Amazon whether the number of people who shop there is large or not. Thus, network size matters more in consumer-to-consumer (C2C) online auctions than in business-to-consumer (B2C) online retailing.

Timing

A firm can differentiate its products by being the first to introduce the products. When a firm is the first to introduce a product, that product is, by default, differentiated since no other firm's product has its features. A cell phone that is introduced in 2003 with identical physical characteristics to one introduced in 2004—durability, time between battery charges, and ease of use—is differentiated from the one introduced in 2004. A firm that brings out its products earlier than competitors' products and pursues the right strategies can gain first-mover advantages. In pharmaceuticals, for example, doctors are usually reluctant to drop a drug that they are used to prescribing until one that is dramatically better in performance is introduced. Thus, firms that can introduce their drugs first and get doctors to start prescribing them can be difficult to dislodge.

Location

Customers value physical location, so two products with identical features can be differentiated by virtue of their locations. One factor is product availability. To a customer in Paris, a croissant sandwich in Paris is more valuable than an identical sandwich in Chicago. Another differentiating factor is the ease of access to products. For example, a customer who needs gasoline is likely to go to the nearest gas station, especially if the prices of gas in the immediate vicinity are about the same. A third factor is a location's reputation. A customer may prefer to shop at a store because the store is located in a famous shopping mall.

Service

Another means of differentiation is the after-sale service a firm offers for its products. When consumers consider buying a product, they often value how quickly they can get the product repaired if it breaks down. For example, an automaker in a developing country can differentiate itself by assuring potential customers that if a car bought from it develops problems, the spare parts and service needed for its repair will be available.

Product Mix

A product may be more valuable to a customer when there are other products that the customer can purchase while buying that product. This is particularly true for customers who prefer one-stop shopping. A variety of products, or **product mix,** is characteristic of shopping malls and electronic marketplaces. One advantage of the latter is that they offer a tremendous amount of choice. Amazon.com, for example, offered 16 million items for sale at its website as of May 1999,[6] a mix differentiating it from other retailers.

DETERMINING DEMAND FOR DIFFERENTIATED BENEFITS

If a critical determinant of the profitability of a firm's business model is the firm's offering of better customer value than its competitors offer, a firm should be very interested in understanding which benefits customers are interested in so that it can provide them. An important question, then, is, How does a firm determine which benefits customers want in a product or service? In some markets, it is clear what type of benefits customers want in new products. Cell phone users, for example, would like phones that allow them to call anywhere at any time, with batteries that require little or infrequent recharging and allow fast Internet access. Computer makers are always looking for microprocessor chips that are very fast, consume little power, occupy very little "chip real estate," and do not cost much. In many other cases, however, it is much less clear what customers want, so firms must work with customers to find out what they need or to help them discover their needs. We explore three ways of determining what customers value in products and services: multidimensional scaling, hedonics, and technological progress.

Multidimensional Scaling

It is often important to find out from customers what they want in a product. One way to do so is to collect data via market research. The data collected are usually analyzed using multidimensional scaling. **Multidimensional scaling** is a technique whereby customers' perceptions of the benefits of competing products are represented graphically, showing the similarities and dissimilarities between the products.[7] Customers are asked to rate competing products according to how similar or dissimilar the products are to them with respect to key benefits that the products offer. The results of the survey are mapped, two variables at a time, with one benefit on the vertical axis and the other on the horizontal axis. A benefits map for passenger jet airplanes is shown in Figure 2.1. The vertical axis represents the typical speed at which a plane can cruise, while the horizontal axis represents the number of passengers that the plane can carry. Airlines consider cruise speed and capacity (number of passengers that a plane can carry) important variables. The faster the cruise speed, the more quickly an airplane can reach its destination. The more passengers a plane can carry, the lower its per-passenger costs can be. On the benefits map in Figure 2.1, the BAE/Concorde is the fastest plane, with a cruise speed of over 2,100 kilometers per hour, but the Boeing 747 has the largest capacity. Another variable that is important to airlines is the maximum range that a plane can fly before it has to refuel. The longer such a range, the more diverse the route options, such as flying over oceans. Another benefits map of passenger airlines is shown in Figure 2.2 with maximum range and passenger capacity as the two variables.

FIGURE 2.1
Benefits Map for Passenger Jet Airplanes
Cruise speed and number of passengers the plane can carry

Source: Data are from the Airbus and Boeing websites, www.airbus.com/dynamic/product/index_h.asp and www.boeing.com/commercial/flash.html (2002).

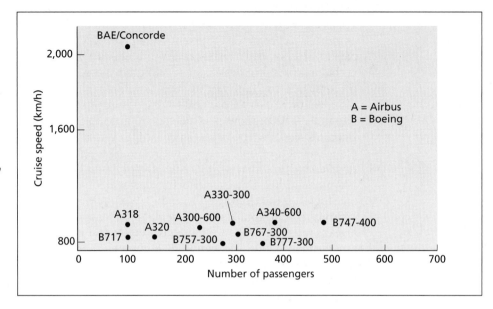

FIGURE 2.2
Benefits Map for Passenger Jet Airplanes
Range and number of passengers

Source: Data are from the Airbus and Boeing websites, www.airbus.com/dynamic/product/index_h.asp and www.boeing.com/commercial/flash.html (2002).

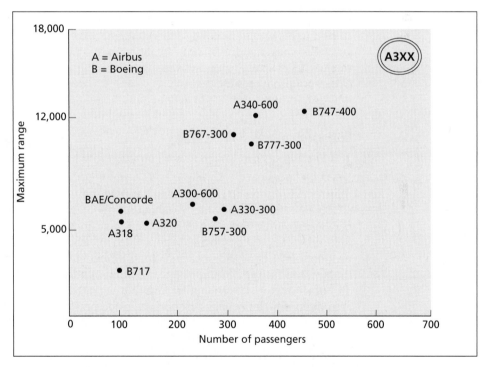

A multidimensional map provides useful information in several respects for a business model. First, it indicates which products are more differentiated than others. In Figure 2.2, the Boeing 747 is the most differentiated plane since it stands out alone, whereas all the other planes have closer competitors as far as range and passenger capacity are concerned. In Figure 2.1, the Concorde is the most differentiated with respect to cruise speed. Second, and more important, the map shows so-called **white spaces.** These are parts of a benefits map where there seems to be a need for a product that offers benefits customers want but where there is no existing product. In our airline example, a white space exists in the upper right quadrant of the Figure 2.1 benefits map, indicating what seems to be an unfulfilled need for a passenger airplane that ranks high on both the number of passengers it can carry and cruise speed. There also seems to be an unfulfilled need for a plane that ranks high on both maximum range and passenger capacity (Figure 2.2). In 2002, Airbus was developing the A3XX, a superjumbo jet airplane that will carry from 550 to 900 passengers and have a range of over 15,000 kilometers. This plane is indicated by a double circle in Figure 2.2. Originally, Boeing's response to Airbus's decision to build the superjumbo was to develop a plane called the Sonic Cruiser with a much higher cruise speed (20 percent faster than conventional jets) but with a much smaller capacity, 350 passengers. In November 2002, however, Boeing decided to scrap plans for the Sonic Cruiser and focus on developing a cheaper 250-seat conventional jet.

Multidimensional scaling, like most management tools, has both advantages and disadvantages. As we have just seen in the Boeing versus Airbus case, multidimensional scaling can be used to compare competitors' products on the basis of various benefits, as well as to identify white product spaces. In addition, its graphical display of key information on critical product benefits enables management to see and more easily understand what is going on. Like every useful tool, however, multidimensional scaling has to be used carefully. First, only a few benefits (dimensions)—usually two—at a time can be usefully compared. Second, since market researchers have to determine which benefits to include in the survey, they may overlook some benefits that customers really want. Third, customers do not always know what their needs are and may need help from producers to discover these needs.

Hedonics

Multidimensional scaling does not tell us how much customers are willing to pay for each of the benefits that they want in products. In the passenger jet plane case, for example, we do not know how much, in dollar terms, cruise speed is worth to customers, as compared to sitting capacity or maximum range. This is useful information that firms would like to have as they develop business models. The method of **hedonics** can be used to determine how much firms have paid per benefit in the past.[8] Although the past does not always predict the future, this information gives firms a good idea of how much customers have valued product benefits in the past and thus some idea of how much they might value them in the future. Hedonics assumes that products can be represented as bundles of characteristics (benefits) and that when customers pay for a product, they are paying for the benefits embodied in the product. Thus, when an airline pays for a plane, it is paying for the plane's cruise speed, maximum flying range, seating capacity, maximum thrust, maximum takeoff weight, maximum fuel capacity, and so on. By running a regression of price versus benefits, a firm can determine the price that customers pay for each benefit.[9] In a study of cholesterol drugs, for instance, it was determined that patients and their insurance companies paid more for each percentage decrease in LDL (so-called bad cholesterol) than they paid for each percentage increase in HDL (so-called good cholesterol).[10]

Like multidimensional scaling, the method of hedonics has its disadvantages. First, all the characteristics of a product that should matter to customers are often not known. For example, a group of drugs called *statins,* usually prescribed to lower cholesterol, have recently been shown to prevent heart attacks in people whose cholesterol levels were not considered high. Second, even when the key benefits in a product are known, it may be difficult to collect the necessary data for a hedonics study.

Technological Progress

Sometimes, customers do not know what they want in a product and therefore cannot articulate their needs without help from producers. Customers did not tell the inventor of the microwave oven that they needed one. Rather, Raytheon invented it and, together with the competitors that copied its invention, worked with customers to help them discover what they want in a microwave oven. Owners of horse-driven carts did not tell automobile start-ups that they wanted an internal combustion engine vehicle. The same is true of cell phones, computers, answering machines, videocassette recorders, the Internet, the World Wide Web, and the numerous other inventions that we enjoy today—their existence was not prompted by requests from customers. Instead, these advances were invented or discovered through R&D.

Firms conduct such R&D with a broad understanding of what customers want. For example, computer makers know that computer users want notebooks that are very light, have batteries that last for days, not hours, and are loaded with functional software. In pharmaceuticals, customers want drugs that are safe, have very few side effects, and are effective in curing all kinds of diseases, many of which presently have no known cures. In the automobile industry, customers want cars that pollute the air less, have better gas mileage, are safer, and are fun to drive. Underpinning all these specific needs are some fundamental needs, which span many industries and consumer groups, that R&D can focus on meeting:

- *Space:* People prefer more square footage per dollar in their homes and offices.
- *Time:* Customers prefer computers that turn on as soon as they flick the switch. Few people like waiting too long on a line.
- *Economy of size:* "Less" can also be better. Consumers prefer smaller notebook computers, handheld devices, and so on.
- *Economy of price:* Customers always want to pay less for any given set of benefits, and therefore firms keep finding newer and better ways to decrease costs.

Finally, many products that are used in homes started out at businesses or factories.[11] Videotape recorders, cameras, audiotape recorders, telephony, computers, and air conditioners are examples of such products. This suggests that if people like a product at work, there is a good chance that they might want it at home as technological progress makes home versions more feasible and affordable.

Sources of Differentiation

At the beginning of this chapter, we said that a firm will keep making money only if it can keep offering its customers benefits that its competitors cannot. An important question at this point is, What is it about some firms that allows them to keep offering these benefits while their competitors cannot? Why can't such a firm be imitated or leapfrogged? We will argue in Chapter 5 that firms that are in certain industries and take advantage of their industries' idiosyncrasies by performing difficult-to-imitate activities that allow them to position themselves well in their industries can keep offering superior benefits to customers and making money. In Chapter 6, we will also argue that firms with valuable, rare, difficult-to-imitate, and nonsubstitutable resources or capabilities can offer their customers better value than competitors and make money.

LOW COST AND ITS DETERMINANTS

As we stated earlier in this chapter, a firm has a low-cost strategy if its activities are designed to offer its customers the same benefits as its competitors offer but at a lower price than that charged by its competitors. The firm is able to charge a lower price because it performs its value-adding activities at lower cost than competitors do and it can therefore pass some of its cost savings to its customers. To successfully pursue a low-cost strategy, a firm needs to understand what determines its costs as it performs its value-adding activities. Since even firms that pursue differentiation strategies need to keep their costs low, such firms also need to understand what determines their costs. There are six primary determinants of a firm's per-unit costs: economies of scale, factor costs, industry-specific cost drivers, innovation, economies of learning, and agency costs.[12]

Economies of Scale

A firm's activities exhibit **economies of scale** if the firm's per-unit cost of the activities decreases as its output increases. Consider, for example, software that has been developed at a cost of $100 million and can be sold at an additional cost of $1 per copy by being posted on the Web for customers to download. If only 1 million copies are sold, the per-unit cost is $101 (see Table 2.1). If 10 million copies are sold, the per-unit cost is $11. If 100 million copies are sold, the per unit cost is $2. Since the per-unit cost decreases as more copies of the software are sold, the activities that underpin the creation and offering of software to customers are said to exhibit economies of scale. The main reason that offering software exhibits economies of scale is that it involves high fixed costs and low variable costs. **Fixed costs** are costs that must be expended no matter what the total output ends up being.[13] They do not change no matter how many units are sold. In our example, the $100 million had to be expended regardless of whether zero or 100 million units of the software were downloaded from the Web by customers. Therefore, the $100 million development costs are fixed costs. **Variable costs** are costs whose total increases with output. In our software example, $1 is the per-unit variable cost. When the number of units produced is 1 million, the total variable costs are $1 million ($1 × 1 million). When the units sold rise to 100 million, the total variable costs are $100 million ($1 × 100 million).

When offering a product entails very high up-front fixed costs and low variable costs, the product usually exhibits economies of scale. Most R&D involves costs that are expended irrespective of whether any units are sold or not. Thus, in R&D-intensive industries such as pharmaceuticals and semiconductors, R&D costs usually exhibit economies of scale.[14] Developing a medicinal drug, for example, costs about $500 million, but producing each capsule costs only a few cents. Thus, the higher the number of drug units sold, the lower the per-unit cost. Usually, advertising also exhibits economies of scale because no matter how many

TABLE 2.1 **Decreasing Per-Unit Costs from Economies of Scale**

Copies sold	1 mil	10 mil	100 mil
Fixed costs	$100 mil	$100 mil	$100 mil
Variable costs	$1 × 1 mil = $1 mil	$1 × 10 mil = $10 mil	$1 × 100 mil = $100 mil
Per-unit cost	$\dfrac{\$100\text{ mil} + \$1\text{ mil}}{1\text{ mil}} = \$101$	$\dfrac{\$100\text{ mil} + \$10\text{ mil}}{10\text{ mil}} = \$11$	$\dfrac{\$100\text{ mil} + \$100\text{ mil}}{100\text{ mil}} = \$2$

product units a firm sells, its costs for preparing the ad or promotion and buying advertising spots on television or in newspapers remain about the same. For example, a TV spot during the Super Bowl costs a beer company the same amount whether the company sells 10 million cans of beer per year or 20,000. However, the per-unit cost of the TV spot when the firm sells 10 million cans of beer is one-thousandth of the per-unit cost when it sells only 10,000 cans.

Factor Costs

To offer customers the value that they want, a firm usually has to translate inputs into products or services that contain value. If a firm finds a way to get its inputs cheaper than its competitors, it improves its chances of being able to offer value to its customers at lower cost than its competitors can. One factor in lowering the cost of inputs is location. Depending on what a firm's inputs are, it may locate where their costs are lowest. Early in its life, Wal-Mart located in rural parts of the southwestern United States. This gave it access to low-cost labor, inexpensive leases, and nonunion workers. Since the 1970s, many U.S. microchip makers have located labor-intensive activities in countries where labor is cheaper. Today, many U.S. companies have software development offices in Ireland and India, where software developers are not as expensive as they are in the United States.

Another factor in lowering input costs is a firm's bargaining power over suppliers. A firm has bargaining power over a supplier if it can extract lower prices or higher-quality inputs from the supplier. This would be the case, for example, when the quantities that the firm buys are very large compared to what any of the supplier's other customers buy. Such a firm can ask its supplier for discounts, and the supplier can afford to give the firm these discounts since it enjoys some economies of scale in serving the large customer. We will explore the concept of bargaining power in more detail later in this chapter.

Industry-Specific Cost Drivers

Sometimes, the factors that have a significant impact on costs in an industry are idiosyncratic to the industry. For example, in the cement industry, the cost of transporting cement is very high. In strategy consulting, MBAs are usually paid very high salaries, and their salaries constitute the firm's largest expense. Thus, capacity utilization is critical in consulting. That is, it is important to make sure that consultants are not idle because there is no work for them. Each hour that they have no work is an hour of forgone billings and accumulated salary expenses.

Innovation

Innovation occurs when firms use new knowledge to offer customers better value that they want.[15] This new knowledge can be used to augment existing ways of doing things or to create entirely different ways of doing things. In either case, the result can be a considerable reduction in costs. In the computer industry, for example, innovation has allowed chip makers to double the processing power of computers every year since 1969 while also drastically reducing costs. Firms can use the Internet to reduce both transaction and production costs.[16] Lean manufacturing, reengineering, the just-in-time approach, total quality control, and cooperation with suppliers are all innovations of one kind or another that firms have used to reduce their costs. Computer-aided design and other such tools have been used to produce designs easier and cheaper than ever before.

Economies of Learning

Most of what we do today, including walking and eating, had to be learned at some point. It should therefore come as no surprise that firms that have been doing certain things longer than other firms and have learned in the process, or made a greater effort to learn, can keep their costs lower than the costs of competitors that have not done so. A surgeon who has studied medicine and spent years practicing surgery should be better at performing surgery than one who has not. Quite simply, the more a firm learns to perform particular tasks, the less its costs of performing the tasks are likely to be. Such a firm exhibits **economies of learning.**

Agency Costs

Agency costs are the costs that a firm incurs because employees slack off and do not perform their duties.[17] For example, many companies incur very high agency costs because their employees waste company time and resources surfing the Internet, downloading music or videos, or performing other activities that have nothing to do with their jobs. The costs can go beyond the time being wasted by employees. Downloading music or videos from the Internet has been known to tie up company servers and slow down the company's legitimate activities. Elimination of such wastes can help keep company costs down.

DIFFERENTIATION VERSUS LOW COST

Figure 2.3 depicts a relationship between the **low-cost position** and the **differentiation position.**[18] In the figure, a firm that pursues a low-cost strategy gets a high market share (M1) since more customers can afford its products rather than higher-priced products. With this high market share, the low-cost leader is likely to have a high level of profitability (P1). If a firm pursues a differentiation strategy, fewer customers can afford its higher prices and so it ends up with a smaller unit market share (M3). However, it can still have a high level of profitability (P1) since it charges premium prices for its products. According to Professor Michael Porter,

FIGURE 2.3
Low-Cost versus Differentiation Positions

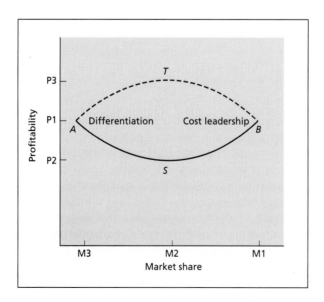

firms that try to be both low-cost and differentiation providers may be stuck in the middle (point S) because they cannot do either well and therefore may end up with low market share (M2) and lower profitability (P2).[19] According to this argument, the activities that a firm has to perform to be in a low-cost or differentiation leadership position are very different and require specialization. Trying to do everything lacks the type of focus that is needed to be in a leadership position. Thus low-cost and differentiation strategies are mutually exclusive.

While it is true that these positions are mutually exclusive in some industries, there are several reasons for believing that this may not be the case in other industries. First, in some industries, the nature of the technology on which offering products rests is such that cost reduction and differentiation rest on the same activities. Performing these activities well results in both low cost and differentiation. In semiconductors, for example, technological progress is such that more and more transistors can be fitted into smaller and smaller silicon real estate, thereby increasing speed while lowering costs. Intel can differentiate its products and lower costs at the same time. Second, as we pointed out above, product differentiation goes beyond product features. Timing, location, brand-name reputation, product mix, network externalities, and service can also be bases for differentiation. Thus it is difficult to find products or services that are not differentiated along one of these parameters. Consider Southwest Airlines, which has often been touted as a low-cost leader.[20] Although its primary attraction to customers is low cost, it can be argued that some customers prefer Southwest over its competitors because of its frequent flights from uncongested airports. The fact that its prices are lower than competitors' does not mean that its products are not differentiated. Third, the rate of technological change and imitation in many industries is high. This means that some products are going to be imitated sooner or later. Thus, if a firm in such an industry is not a cost leader when its products are imitated, it stands to incur even larger losses in its competitive edge if imitated by a low-cost firm. Finally, as we will see in Chapter 6, competitive advantage sometimes comes from owning valuable, rare, and inimitable resources, and this suggests that such resources can allow a firm to have both a low-cost and a differentiation leadership position. Since, effectively, a firm can be a low-cost leader and a differentiator at the same time, the possibility exists that such a firm would be at T (Figure 2.3) with a market share M2 and profitability P3. Thus, although many firms that try to be both differentiators and low-cost leaders may get stuck in the middle, there may be many cases where a firm needs to be both and can be both successfully.

CREATING CUSTOMER VALUE AND CAPTURING PROFITS FROM IT

In exploring customer value so far, we have often referred to a firm as creating and offering value to customers. Usually, the benefits that customers value in a firm's product stem from the combined efforts of the firm and its suppliers, complementors, and customers. (A firm's **complementors** are firms that offer products that are complementary to the firm's products—sales of their products increase demand for the firm's products. For example, sales of software increase sales of computers, and therefore software developers are complementors to computer makers.) Consider a customer who buys a computer from Apple because it is fast, easy to use, and reliable and enables the user to quickly put together excellent business presentations using PowerPoint and Excel. Even though the

FIGURE 2.4
Coopetitors

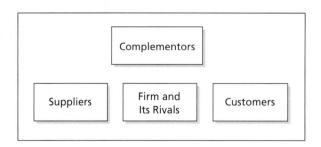

customer buys the computer from Apple, the benefits that he or she enjoys from it—putting together excellent business presentations using PowerPoint and Excel—come from the combined effect of the fast microprocessor from Motorola, Apple's ability to design computers, the application software (PowerPoint and Excel) from Microsoft, and the customer's own ability to use PowerPoint and Excel.

From a firm's point of view, there are usually two sides to suppliers, complementors, and customers. On the one hand, they can be important allies in creating value for customers.[21] For example, Intel, Microsoft, and the many PC makers, such as Dell, are allies in creating value for end users of PCs. On the other hand, they can pose a threat to a firm's profitability.[22] Intel decreases Dell's profits when it charges high prices for the microchips that it sells to Dell. Microsoft decreases Dell's profits if it charges such exorbitant prices for its software that firms refuse to purchase computers because they cannot afford to buy the software. Effectively, suppliers, complementors, rivals, and customers are sources of opportunities as well as threats. A firm's suppliers, rivals, complementors, and customers are called its **coopetitors** since it often must cooperate *and* compete with them (see Figure 2.4).[23]

Cooperating to Create Value

Since the value that customers perceive in a product is usually a combination of value from different coopetitors, one can expect that cooperation between partners during the creation of such value would help create better customer value. Several studies in the automobile industry have demonstrated that firms that collaborate with their *suppliers* during the development of cars shorten development times, reduce development costs, and produce cars with improved quality.[24] Cooperation with *complementors* can also help speed the adoption of products. For example, microprocessor makers that work with software developers can help developers understand the inner workings of the processors and thereby enable them to develop better software earlier than would be possible without such cooperation. Since the availability of more software means more customers are likely to buy computers, and since the increased demand for computers increases the demand for microprocessors, the maker of microprocessors will sell more of them. For many products, cooperating with coopetitors is critical to the success of firms in the industry. The more a firm can work with *customers* and understand what they need, the more it can offer the types of benefits that these customers want.[25] Where legal, a firm can work with its *rivals* to develop a new technology and standard. For example, the alliance between Sony and Toshiba is generally credited with establishing the compatible standard for the digital video disk (DVD) and bringing DVDs to customers. *New entrants* to an industry add new resources to the industry's stock of resources, and if the added resources are more efficient, they can increase industry growth and efficiency, thus increasing profits. This is particularly true when new entrants enter an industry by using a new technology. New brokerage firms used the Internet to enter the brokerage industry and, in the process, contributed online brokerage capabilities to the industry.

Customers, suppliers, and complementors can also be sources of innovations for firms.[26] For example, Alcoa and Reynolds Aluminum invented the two-piece aluminum can and gave the technology to aluminum-can makers such as Crown Cork and Seal, which makes the cans that Coca-Cola, PepsiCo and other firms use for their beverages.[27]

Competing to Appropriate Value

The revenues generated from the value that coopetitors create are shared among them. Customers pay firms for the benefits that they value in the firms' products and pay complementors for complementary products (Figure 2.4). Firms then pay suppliers for the benefits that they see in the inputs from the suppliers. In cooperating with coopetitors to create value, a firm faces two important questions:

1. How much of the revenues that customers pay for the created customer value can the firm capture or *appropriate*?
2. How much of the costs of creating and offering the value does the firm, rather than coopetitors, incur?

The extent to which a firm can realize profits from the value that it offers its customers is a function of who has power in the firm-coopetitor relationship. A *firm's power* over a coopetitor is the extent to which the firm's interests are reflected in the coopetitor's decisions or the extent to which the coopetitor is dependent on the firm.[28] In the firm-supplier relationship, for example, a *supplier's bargaining power* is the extent to which the supplier can effectively determine the price-cost relationship between itself and the firm. Suppliers with considerable power can charge higher prices and ship lower-quality supplies. Higher prices for suppliers mean higher costs for firms and therefore lower profitability. Effectively, the extent to which a firm can appropriate the value created in its value chain is a function of the firm's bargaining position vis-à-vis its coopetitors. In our example of the PC industry, Intel and Microsoft have bargaining power and therefore capture most of the profits from customers.

Impact of Bargaining Position on Ability to Appropriate Value

The impact of a firm's bargaining position—vis-à-vis its coopetitors—on its ability to appropriate the value that it creates can be understood by considering the rather simple relationship in Equation 2.1. The equation states that the profits a firm makes are equal to the revenues the firm receives from customers in exchange for its products or services minus the costs of offering them:

$$\text{Profits} = \text{revenues} - \text{costs} = P(Q) \times Q(P) - C(Q) \quad \textbf{(2.1)}$$

Relative Positioning vis-à-vis Suppliers

If a firm is more powerful than its suppliers, it can pay suppliers lower prices than the quality of the supplies would suggest. This keeps the firm's costs down in the relationship in Equation 2.1, increasing its chances of making money from the value that it offers customers. A powerful firm can also force its suppliers to deliver input components with higher quality and features than the prices paid for the components warrant. By using these superior components, the firm is more likely to deliver superior benefits to its customers. Delivering such products means that the firm is more likely to command a high premium price for its products. Its market share may even rise. Receiving higher-quality products from a supplier can also lower a firm's costs since the firm does not have to add as much value as it would with inferior components. In either case, the firm's chances of profiting from the value that it creates increase.

Relative Positioning vis-à-vis Customers

A firm that is more powerful than its buyers can keep its profits high since it can extract higher prices from its customers. Doing so increases its revenues in the relationship in Equation 2.1, thereby increasing its chances of making money from the superior value that it offers customers. A powerful firm can also force its customers to accept products with benefits inferior to what the prices paid for the products warrant. Remember the days when your local telephone or cable monopoly delivered terrible service and charged you an arm for it? By forcing customers to take inferior products, firms can lower their costs.

Relative Positioning vis-à-vis Complementors

A firm that is more powerful than its complementors can influence the quality and number of complements that are offered for its products. As the quality and number of complements that are offered for a firm's product increase, more customers are likely to value that product.

Impact of Rivalry, New Entry, and Substitutes on Ability to Appropriate Value

Potential new entry, rivalry, and viable substitutes can reduce a firm's bargaining power over customers and suppliers, and therefore its ability to appropriate the value that it created for customers.

Rivalry

In an attempt to increase their market shares or prevent rivals from increasing theirs, firms often engage in price wars, advertising, and unnecessary product introductions. This fighting for share is called **rivalry.** Price reductions—for example, as a result of innovations that allow firms to deliver better customer value at lower costs while maintaining their price-cost margins—are good for firms. But price wars, in which firms lower their prices in response to each other, thus reducing their price-cost margins, are not good. Steep and senseless price reductions can reduce revenues and profits. Advertising and product introductions are good, unless they become a war that firms wage as they jockey for market share. Such wars can result in unnecessary cost increases, which erode profitability. High rivalry reduces the power that industry firms have over customers since customers can play rival firms against each other. This allows customers to extract lower prices or higher quality from industry firms, thus reducing the ability of a rival firm to appropriate any of the value that it creates for customers. High rivalry also gives suppliers an opportunity to play firms against each other.

Potential New Entry

A rational firm or entrepreneur will enter an industry only if it believes that it will make money in that industry. One indicator of the chances of making money in an industry is the prices charged for products as compared to the costs of offering the products. The higher the prices are, relative to costs, the better the chances of making money and therefore the more likely that new entrants will want to enter. A high threat of entry forces firms to play into the hands of customers by charging lower prices for their products or offering products of higher quality than the prices being paid for them warrant. This reduces their revenues and profits. Firms may also be forced to take costly measures to create barriers to entry, such as advertising to differentiate their products. This increases costs. In either case, any profits that a firm might have earned from the value created by coopetitors can be dissipated by a high threat of new entry.

Substitutes

Substitute products can sap a firm's profits in two ways. First, they provide an alternative for products, thereby putting pressure on the prices that a firm can charge. Second, to make substitutes less attractive as an alternative to its products, a firm may have to boost its products' benefits or advertise, both of which can be costly. Thus, the more viable the substitutes are, the more difficult it is for a firm to appropriate the value that it creates.

DETERMINANTS OF RELATIVE POSITIONING AMONG COOPETITORS

A firm's bargaining position vis-à-vis its coopetitors is determined by two things: (1) the competitive forces that are exerted on industry firms by suppliers, customers, and complementors and (2) the decisions that the firm makes to influence these forces. In formulating and executing a business model, then, it is critical to determine the competitive forces that are exerted by coopetitors and find ways to counter those forces.

Competitive Forces Exerted by Coopetitors

In his seminal work, Professor Michael Porter of the Harvard Business School identified five forces that can sap an industry's profits if not identified and influenced.[29] A sixth force was identified and examined later by other researchers. We explore these forces below.

Suppliers

The extent to which suppliers have bargaining power over firms is a function of several factors.

Concentration and Dominance of Suppliers The more suppliers there are, the better off firms are since they can play suppliers against each other. If one supplier does not agree to their terms, the firms can go to another supplier. An industry is *concentrated* if it has only a few firms in it. Therefore, if the supplier industry is concentrated relative to the industry it supplies, suppliers are likely to have power. If the supplier market is not concentrated but has a few dominant players, these dominant suppliers are likely to have power over buyers.

Differentiated Products If the products that suppliers provide to firms are highly differentiated, firms are less likely to play suppliers against each other. This is particularly true if the product supplied can build up customer switching costs. *Customer switching costs* are the costs that a firm incurs when it switches from one supplier to another. For example, if a firm has been using a particular computer system for some time, it is likely to have learned the computer's operating system and to have accumulated application software that runs on that system. Switching to another computer system has high switching costs since doing so entails learning a new operating system and buying new application software to replace existing programs.

Credible Threat of Forward Integration If suppliers pose a credible threat of vertically integrating forward into industry firms' business, the firms are less likely to push for concessions for fear that suppliers will move in and become competitors. A threat of forward integration is credible if suppliers have demonstrated that they can integrate forward; for example, they may have integrated forward at some point in the past. This is the case with aluminum suppliers. Metal-can makers use lots of aluminum to make their cans, and they know that producers of aluminum can become can makers anytime they want to since they have done so before. Metal-can makers are therefore less likely to push for price concessions from aluminum makers.

Small Fraction of Costs If the products supplied are a small fraction of firms' costs, the firms are less likely to be sensitive to price increases by suppliers.

High Profits If suppliers are supplying to an industry that earns very high profits, industry firms are less likely to be price-sensitive.

Importance to the Quality of Industry Firms' Products In some industries, the quality of the firms' products is very dependent on inputs from suppliers. In such a case, industry firms basically cannot do without these components. They depend on suppliers, and therefore suppliers have power over them. For example, in the PC industry, the quality of PCs strongly depends on the microprocessor. Thus, suppliers of microprocessors have bargaining power over the PC makers that buy them.

Cost Savings If a product or service from suppliers can pay for itself many times over, industry firms are less likely to be price-sensitive about the supplied product. For example, thorough research and preanalysis before oil drilling can save tens or hundreds of millions of dollars in drilling costs. Therefore, oil companies are less sensitive to the pricing of such services.

Unavailability of Substitute Products If substitutes for suppliers' products do not exist, industry firms are less likely to be sensitive to any price increases requested by suppliers. Suppliers therefore have more power when there are fewer substitutes.

Lack of Information The more informed one is, the better prepared one is to bargain. For example, the more information you have about a car (its costs, suggested retail prices, performance relative to competing cars, etc.), the better off you are when you go to a dealership to buy the car. The same is true for firms. The more information industry firms have about suppliers and their costs and prices, the better the firms can bargain. Therefore, suppliers are more powerful when there is a lack of information about them and their products.

Buyers

The determinants of the power of buyers over firms are analogous to those we have just explored for suppliers. Effectively, the extent to which buyers have bargaining power over firms is a function of several factors.

Concentration and Dominance of Buyers The more buyers there are, the better off firms are since they can play buyers against each other. If one buyer does not agree to their terms, the firms can go to another buyer. Therefore, if the buyer industry is concentrated relative to the industry from which it buys, buyers are likely to have power. In some cases, the buyer industry may not be concentrated but may have one or more dominant buyers that can wield a lot of power by virtue of the large quantities of products they buy. For example, the retail market is not concentrated, yet the sheer volume of purchases that companies such as Wal-Mart make give those companies considerable bargaining power.

Undifferentiated Products If the products that buyers buy from firms are undifferentiated, buyers are more likely to play firms against each other. This is particularly likely when the product has no switching costs.

Credible Threat of Backward Integration If buyers pose a credible threat of vertically integrating backward into industry firms' business, the firms are less likely to push for higher prices or other concessions for fear that buyers will move in and become competitors. For example, IBM is one of the largest buyers of microchips but it has always produced a lot of its own chips. Since microchip makers know that IBM can produce more of its own chips if it had to, IBM has considerable buying power when it negotiates with a chip maker.

Large Fraction of Costs If the products being bought are a large fraction of buyers' costs, the buyers are more likely to be sensitive to price increases.

Low Profits If buyers earn very low profits, they are more likely to be price-sensitive.

Importance to the Quality of Buyers' Products In some industries, the quality of the buyers' products is not dependent on inputs from industry firms. In such a case, buyers basically can do without these components and therefore do not have to put up with demands from industry firms.

No Cost Savings If a product or service cannot pay for itself many times over, buyers are more likely to be price-sensitive about the product. Buyers are therefore more likely to have power in such cases.

Availability of Substitute Products If substitutes for a firm's products are readily available, buyers can switch to them if the firm's prices increase. Buyers are therefore more likely to be sensitive to any price increases requested by firms. Thus, buyers have more power when there are more substitutes.

More Information The more informed one is, the better prepared one is to bargain. As anyone who has used the Internet to buy a car lately can testify, the more information you have about a car (its costs, suggested retail prices, performance relative to competing cars, etc.), the better off you are when you go to a dealership to buy the car. The same is true about buyers. The more information buyers have about industry firms and their costs and prices, the better the buyers can bargain. Therefore, buyers are more powerful when there is more information about industry firms.

Rivalry

Rivalry in an industry is increased by several factors.

Number of Competitors and Their Similarity When allowed by law, coordination of activities among firms can increase industry profitability. In R&D, for example, coordination avoids duplication of efforts, thereby saving costs.[30] Coordination of prices can reduce price wars, thereby holding down erosion of profits. Such coordination is more likely when the number of firms in an industry is small. If there are many competitors in an industry, there is a higher likelihood that one of the firms is not happy with its market share or profits and would rather not participate in coordination but prefer, instead, to stir things up by starting a price, product, or advertising war. When there are a great many firms in an industry, many of them usually have a small market share and are likely to believe that when they change their prices, no one will notice. In industries where there are few large competitors, we can expect to see few real price wars. When such competitors cut their prices, the cuts are healthy reductions, not price wars. Coca-Cola and PepsiCo, for example, had so-called cola wars in the 1970s, 1980s, and 1990s in which they advertised heavily, introduced new products, and offered price cuts for bottled and canned colas. However, the price of their concentrate (their biggest money maker) actually went up during those years.

Small or Declining Industry Growth Most firms are under pressure from investors to increase earnings. When industry growth is slow or declining, firms may be tempted to try to steal market share from competitors. Firms that want to steal market share may resort to price, advertising, or product introduction wars, which sap industry profits.

Undifferentiated Products If industry products are highly differentiated and switching costs for customers are high, price decreases by a firm attempting to steal customers may not be very effective because the firm's products may still not be a close match to competitors' products. Moreover, if switching costs are high, it would take very deep price discounts to convince a customer to switch. With undifferentiated products that have low switching costs, products from all firms are similar and the temptation to steal customers is higher.

Excess Capacity In some industries, adding capacity has to be done in large increments, and this can result in excess capacity. Excess capacity can also result from a recession or other cyclicities. In any case, when there is excess capacity, the temptation to cut one's prices to fill up capacity is high.

High Exit Barriers Exit barriers are the costs that must be incurred in order to exit a business. Depending on the country, these costs can be high. In some countries, labor laws make it almost impossible to lay off workers. If exit costs are high compared to the losses that a firm can incur by staying in business and reducing its prices, the firm might decide to stay in business and take the losses.

High Fixed Costs, Low Variable Costs When fixed costs are high relative to variable costs, firms may sell products at a loss as long as the prices cover their variable costs, especially during recessions. When the product is perishable, there is even more of an incentive to do so. For example, airlines have very high fixed costs compared to the variable cost of carrying each passenger. Each passenger seat that is not filled when the plane takes off represents lost revenue that can never be regained. Thus, one can expect airlines to be very willing to discount empty seats.

Diverse Competitors If rivals have different cost structures, origins, strategies, and objectives, they are less likely to be able to coordinate their activities, thereby leaving more room for price, product, or advertising wars. In fact, a firm with a very low cost structure has a strong incentive to lower its prices since it can do so and still be very profitable. A firm in a country where sales are more important than profits may decide to lower its prices to increase sales even if that increase means an erosion of profits.

Threat of Entry

The threat of entry into an industry is high if barriers to entry into the industry are low. Several factors contribute to high barriers to entry.

High Economies of Scale (High Minimum Efficient Scale Relative to Market Share) As a firm produces more of a particular product, the cost per unit of the product usually falls. Beyond a certain volume, however, the decrease in unit cost stops. This volume is called the **minimum efficient scale (MES),** the minimum volume that a firm has to produce in order to attain the minimum per-unit cost possible in the market.[31] This means that an entrant must produce at least this volume if its costs are going to be competitive. If the MES is high, an entrant faces two problems. First, it has to gain a high market share to sell the large volume from the high MES that it has to attain. Second, producing that much means adding that much more product to the market. The larger the MES and therefore the more of the product that a new entrant must bring into the market, the lower the prices will be. Thus, if the minimum efficient scale is large, potential entrants are less likely to enter since they can expect the price to drop considerably given how much they have to add to the industry's capacity.

Product Differentiation Product differentiation can be a barrier to entry when the customer benefits of a product are difficult to replicate. Brand-name reputation is a good example. It takes time, effort, and money to build brand reputation and awareness. Thus new entrants that want to replicate such brands need time, money, and effort. The customer service that firms offer can also be a difficult-to-overcome barrier to entry.

Capital Requirements The sheer size of the financial investment that is needed to compete in some markets can limit the number of potential entrants. For example, in 2001, it was estimated that the Airbus A3XX would cost about $13 billion to develop.[32] Such a high cost suggests that the average entrepreneur is not going to start making passenger jets to compete with Airbus and Boeing. Likewise, it takes about $500 million to develop a successful pharmaceutical drug. This constitutes a barrier to entry for many entrepreneurs.

Access to Critical Inputs Potential new entrants may be prevented from entering because they do not have access to the kinds of inputs that will allow them to be competitive. These include distribution channels, technological know-how, location, and raw materials. One critical input to entering a market for consumer goods is distribution channels. For example, shelf space is critical to selling soda in the United States, but firms such as Coca-Cola and PepsiCo have dominated most of that space. Most blockbuster pharmaceutical drugs are protected by patents in the United States, and this reduces entry. A firm that is located in a developing country may not be able to enter the pharmaceutical industry because it cannot find the scientists to run ethical drug discovery laboratories. A country that wants to start producing aluminum may not be able to do so because it does not have a cheap supply of electricity, a critical input to producing aluminum.

Network Externalities As we saw earlier, a product or technology exhibits network externalities if an increase in the number of people who use it causes it to become more valuable to users.[33] A large network of users or an installed base that incumbent firms have built can deter entry. For example, Microsoft has not seen many challengers to its Windows operating system partly because of the large number of people who have learned to use the system and the large installed base of computers that use Windows.

Experience Curve In some industries, the more experience and know-how a firm accumulates in offering a product to customers, the lower the firm's costs of offering a unit of the product. In such industries, incumbents that have accumulated experience and know-how over the years have a cost advantage over new entrants. Anticipation of having a cost disadvantage relative to incumbent firms prevents some potential new entrants from entering.

Reputation for Retaliation If an incumbent has a history of retaliating (e.g., by lowering its prices or quickly offering similar products) against firms that have ventured into its product-market space, this may be an indication that it will retaliate against future entrants. Such a reputation signals to potential new entrants that they may be in for a big fight upon entry. For example, if entry into a route dominated by an airline carrier has been followed by drastic fare cuts by the carrier, it is likely that the carrier will cut its prices on other routes if another airline enters. Start-up airlines will think twice before venturing into that carrier's routes unless their cost structures or other factors suggest that they can make money at low prices. If incumbents have excess capacity, this may also be a sign that they will lower their prices when new firms enter.

Government Policies Governments often limit entry to some industries. In some cities, the number of taxicabs that can operate is limited by the number of taxi licenses that are issued. In some states or countries, there are idiosyncratic restrictions to commerce in one form or another. In the United States, for example, car companies are not allowed to sell cars directly to customers; they have to sell via dealerships. This creates a barrier to entry for new car companies since most dealers already have existing contracts with incumbents. Thus it is very difficult for a new entrant to establish a nationwide network of dealers—a critical success factor in the industry.

Substitutes

The extent to which firms offering substitute products have power over industry firms is determined by the following factors.

Availability of Key Substitutes and Willingness of Customers to Switch If substitutes are readily available and customers are willing to make the switch, firms may feel the pressure from substitutes. For example, in areas where clean water is readily available, soft-drink makers may feel a threat.

Benefits from Substitutes The more benefits per dollar customers can get from substitutes, the more power the makers of the substitutes have.

Price Elasticity of Demand The *price elasticity of demand* for an industry is a measure of the extent to which a decrease in price results in an increase in purchases of the product. When an industry's price elasticity is high, increases in price are likely to cause customers to turn to substitutes.[34]

Complementors

The extent to which complementors have power over industry firms is determined by the factors below.

Availability of Key Complements If complements are not readily available from many complementors, the complementors that do offer them have power over firms. For example, application software programs like Microsoft's Word and Excel are not easily available from other software developers. Microsoft dominates as far as these applications are concerned. Therefore, Microsoft has more power over PC makers, such as Dell.

Benefits from Complements The more benefits per dollar customers can get from complements, the more power the makers of the complements have.

Cross-Price Elasticity of Demand The *cross-price elasticity of demand* for complements is a measure of the extent to which a drop in the price of a complement results in disproportionate increase in purchases of complementary products. For example, the cross-price elasticity of demand for software is high if a drop in software prices results in a disproportionately high increase in sales of computers. The higher the cross-price elasticity of demand for complements, the higher the potential power of complementors.

Influencing Competitive Forces to Strengthen One's Relative Positioning

Given the role that competitive forces play in a firm's ability to appropriate the value that it creates for customers, an important question is, Can a firm influence the competitive forces that impinge on it? The answer is yes. The activities that a firm chooses to perform, when it performs them, and how it performs them, as well as the resources that allow the firm to perform these activities, can go a long way toward determining its position vis-à-vis its suppliers, customers, potential new entrants, substitutes, complementors, and rivals. In Chapters 5 and 6, we will explore the which, how, when, and whence of activities and how they improve a firm's relative positioning. For the moment, let us examine how a firm's low-cost or differentiation position can dampen the impact of all its competitive forces. We reserve a detailed exploration of the activities and resources that underpin a low-cost or differentiation position for Chapters 5 and 6.

Differentiation Position as Influencer

By offering a highly differentiated product, a firm is effectively reducing the level of the impact of its industry's competitive forces from the level it would have been if the product were not differentiated. When a product is differentiated, then, by definition, customers are less likely to find the same product elsewhere. Therefore, customers are less likely to switch from a differentiated product. Thus, when a firm offers its customers a differentiated product that they want, it effectively reduces customers' bargaining power. Also, since customers are less likely to switch from a differentiated product, rivals are less likely to lower their prices in an attempt to steal market share. Thus, the firm is also reducing the impact of rivalry on its competitive positioning.

For two reasons, offering a differentiated product also reduces the impact of the threat of new entry. First, there is less information available about a differentiated product and its costs since rivals do not offer the same product. Less available information means potential new entrants are less likely to have the information (such as how much it costs to offer the product) that they need to determine whether they can make money if they enter the industry. Second, a potential new entrant into an industry with incumbents that offer differentiated products faces an additional barrier to entry in the form of the extra costs of differentiation that it would take to compete effectively with the incumbents. These extra costs can deter entry. Consider the example of a potential new entrant into the cola market. It can enter the market but is not likely to steal significant market share from Coca-Cola, whose strong brand equity has allowed it to differentiate its colas.

Since there is less information available about a product and its costs when it is differentiated, suppliers have less information on which to base negotiations. Scarce information for a supplier means less bargaining power. Finally, by offering a differentiated product, a firm is making it more difficult for makers of substitutes to steal its customers by lowering their prices. Price drops are less likely to lure customers away from differentiated products as opposed to commodity products.

Low-Cost Position as Influencer

If a firm offers its customers low prices because it has the lowest cost in its industry and can afford to price lower than its competitors, the firm is likely to improve its relative position vis-à-vis all the competitive forces in the industry. A firm can have the lowest cost in its industry when, for example, it has valuable resources that are rare, difficult to imitate, and nonsubstitutable.[35] If a firm has such a dominant low-cost position, customers are less likely to go to competitors since, by definition, the firm offers the lowest prices. Even if new firms enter the industry, they cannot compete against the dominant firm because they cannot offer the low prices that only this firm can. Existing rivals cannot do much better either since their higher costs do not allow them to compete on price. Similarly, substitutes are less likely to lure the firm's customers away since its customers are already being offered very low prices.

Summary

An important component of a firm's business model is the positions that the firm occupies in the industry and markets in which it competes. Two of these positions are customer value—low-cost or differentiated products—and relative position vis-à-vis competitive forces. A firm makes more money than its competitors only if customers purchase the firm's products rather than competitors' products. But customers choose a firm's products over its competitors' only if the firm's products offer superior customer value relative to competitors' products. Superior customer value, while a necessary condition for making money, is not always sufficient. A firm also needs to be positioned well vis-à-vis customers, suppliers, rivals, potential new entrants, complementors, and viable substitutes. A firm that positions itself as a product differentiator can differentiate its products by their features, brand-name reputation, location, timing of product introductions, network size (if the product exhibits network externalities), and association with other products or mix of products offered. A firm that positions itself as a low-cost competitor usually can do so because its strategies allow it to have a low-cost structure that enables it to compete on price.

A firm's relative positioning within an industry is determined by the competitive forces in the industry that act on industry firms and by the activities that the firm performs to counter these forces. When a firm's business model offers superior customer value and positions the firm well in relation to its customers, suppliers, rivals, potential new entrants, complementors, and viable substitutes, this greatly improves the chances of the firm's business model being more profitable than competing business models.

Key Terms

agency costs, *28*
complementors, *29*
coopetitors, *30*
differentiation position, *28*
differentiation strategy, *19*
economies of learning, *28*
economies of scale, *26*

fixed costs, *26*
hedonics, *24*
low-cost position, *28*
low-cost strategy, *19*
minimum efficient scale
  (MES), *36*
multidimensional scaling, *22*

network externalities, *20*
product mix, *22*
rivalry, *32*
variable costs, *26*
white spaces, *23*

Study Questions

1. What does competing on price mean? Can you name some companies that compete on price?
2. In addition to customer value and relative positioning, what else is likely to impact a business model's profitability? Which of these factors can also be regarded as positions?

3. When a firm offers highly differentiated products or very low cost products, it is effectively improving its position vis-à-vis customers, rivals, potential new entrants, substitute products, and suppliers. What else can a firm do to influence its relative positioning?

Endnotes

1. M. E. Porter, "How Competitive Forces Shape Strategy," *Harvard Business Review,* March–April 1979, pp. 137–156.

2. M. E. Porter, *Competitive Strategy: Techniques for Analyzing Industries and Competitors* (New York: Free Press, 1980); J. B. Barney, *Gaining and Sustaining Competitive Advantage* (Reading, MA: Addison-Wesley, 2002).

3. T. E. Stuart, H. Hoang, and R. C. Hybels, "Interorganizational Endorsements and the Performance of Entrepreneurial Ventures," *Administrative Science Quarterly* 44 (1999), pp. 315–349.

4. M. L. Katz and C. Shapiro, "Technology Adoption in the Presence of Network Externalities," *Journal of Political Economy* 94 (1985), pp. 822–841.

5. See, for example, L. Downes and C. Mui, *Unleashing the Killer App: Digital Strategies for Market Dominance* (Cambridge, MA: Harvard Business School Press, 1998).

6. R. D. Hof and L. Himelstein, "eBay vs. Amazon.com," *Business Week,* May 31, 1997.

7. S. Shiffman, M. Reynolds, and F. Young, *Introduction to Multidimensional Scaling: Theory, Methods and Applications* (Cambridge, MA: Academic Press, 1981); G. L. Urban and J. R. Hauser, *Design and Marketing of New Products* (Englewood Cliffs, NJ: Prentice-Hall, 1993).

8. A. N. Afuah, "Mapping Technological Capabilities into Product Markets and Competitive Advantage," *Strategic Management Journal* 12 (2002), pp. 171–179; Z. Griliches, *Price Indexes and Quality Change: Studies in New Methods and Measurement* (Cambridge, MA: Harvard University Press, 1971).

9. Regressing prices on product characteristics to determine the implicit prices of the characteristics is not new. It dates back to the 1920s, when hedonics was used to estimate implicit prices for different features of asparagus, and has since then been used to study automobiles. See E. R. Berndt, *The Practice of Econometrics: Classic and Contemporary* (New York: Wiley, 1991).

10. Afuah, "Mapping Technological Capabilities into Product Markets and Competitive Advantage."

11. A. N. Afuah, *Innovation Management: Strategies, Implementation, and Profits* (New York: Oxford University Press, 2002), chap. 6.

12. For more details on costs, see R. S. Pindyk and D. L. Rubenfeld, *Microeconomics* (Upper Saddle River, NJ: Prentice-Hall, 2000); D. Besanko, D. Dranove, and M. Shanley, *Economics of Strategy* (New York: Wiley, 2002).

13. See, for example, Besanko, Dranove, and Shanley, *Economics of Strategy;* Pindyk and Rubenfeld, *Microeconomics.*

14. R. Henderson and I. Cockburn, "Scale, Scope, and Spillovers: The Determinants of Research Productivity in Drug Discovery," *Rand Journal of Economics* 27 (1996), pp. 32–59.

15. Afuah, *Innovation Management.*

16. A. N. Afuah, "Redefining Firm Boundaries in the Face of the Internet: Are Firms Really Shrinking?" *Academy of Management Review,* in press.

17. Besanko, Dranove, and Shanley, *Economics of Strategy.*

18. Porter, *Competitive Strategy;* Porter, *On Competition* (Boston: Harvard Business School Press, 1998).

19. M. E. Porter, "What Is Strategy?" *Harvard Business Review,* November–December 1996, pp. 61–78.

20. Ibid.

21. A. Brandenburger and B. Nalebuff, *Co-opetition* (New York: Doubleday, 1996); E. Von Hippel, *The Sources of Innovation* (New York: Oxford University Press, 1988).

22. Porter, *Competitive Strategy.*

23. A. N. Afuah, "Do Your Co-opetitors' Capabilities Matter in the Face of a Technological Change?" *Strategic Management Journal* 21 (2000), pp. 387–404; Brandenburger and Nalebuff, *Co-opetition.*

24. K. B. Clark and K. Fujimoto, *Product Development Performance: Strategy, Organization, and Management in the World Automobile Industry* (Boston: Harvard Business School Press, 1991); J. H. Dyer and K. Nobeoka, "Creating and Managing a High Performance Knowledge-Sharing Network: The Toyota Case," *Strategic Management Journal* 21 (2000), pp. 345–367.

25. R. Rothwell, C. Freeman, A. Horsley, V. T. P. Jervis, A. B. Robertson, and J. Townsend, "SAPPHO Updated—Project SAPPHO Phase II," *Research Policy* 3 (1974), pp. 258–291.

26. Von Hippel, *The Sources of Innovation;* Afuah, *Innovation Management,* chap. 4.

27. K. D. Gordon and R. Hamermesh, "Crown Cork and Seal Company, Inc. (condensed)," Harvard Business School case 9-388-096, p. 2, 1988.

28. J. Pfeffer, *Managing with Power: Politics and Influence in Organizations* (Boston: Harvard Business School Press, 1992); D. J. Brass and M. Burkhardt, "Centrality and Power in Organizations," in *Networks and Organizations,* ed. N. Nohria and R. G. Eccles (Boston: Harvard Business School Press, 1992).

29. This section draws heavily on Michael Porter's seminal article "How Competitive Forces Shape Strategy."

30. It is important to understand what type of coordination of effort is permitted by law. For a great summary of what U.S. antitrust laws permit for coordination, see S. Oster, *Modern Competitive Analysis* (New York: Oxford University Press, 1999), pp. 46–48.

31. Ibid.

32. M. Kane and B. Esty, "Airbus A3XX: Developing the World's Largest Commercial Jet (A)," Harvard Business School case 9-201-028, Aug. 24, 2001.

33. Katz and Shapiro, "Technology Adoption in the Presence of Network Externalities."

34. Besanko, Dranove, and Shanley, *Economics of Strategy.*

35. D. J. Collis and C. A. Montgomery, "Competing on Resources: Strategies for the 1990s," *Harvard Business Review,* July–August 1995, pp. 118–128.

Chapter Three

Pricing to Optimize Revenues

Offering customers better products than competitors do and taking the right strategic steps to be well positioned vis-à-vis coopetitors, as we saw in Chapter 2, are critical to the profitability of a business model. But a firm must also be able to price the products well enough to earn revenues that are commensurate with the value it has created and its positioning in relation to its customers, complementors, rivals, and potential new entrants, while keeping its costs down. As can be seen in Equation 3.1—which states that profits are equal to revenues minus the costs of generating the revenues—a key determinant of profitability is price:

$$\text{Profits} = \text{revenues} - \text{costs} = P \times Q - C \qquad \textbf{(3.1)}$$

Simply put, pricing is an extremely important component of a business model, and pricing decisions can have a tremendous effect on firm profitability. In 2001, for example, Polaroid went bankrupt, and one reason for its failure was its inability to price its digital photography products properly.[1] A computer simulation that examined why People Express—a very promising airline with a strategy strikingly similar to that of Southwest Airlines—was on the verge of bankruptcy in 1986 when acquired by Texas Air suggests that the company could have avoided failure by raising its prices, which were extremely low. The story of PepsiCo also illustrates how pricing can help a company get out of financial ruins. In 1931, the company was in its second bankruptcy when its president, Charles Guth, decided to sell 12-ounce bottles of Pepsi for the price of 6-ounce bottles of Coke—5 cents.[2] PepsiCo's profits increased, and by 1934 it was out of bankruptcy. According to Henry Vogel of the Boston Consulting Group, raising prices by 1 percent can boost profits by up to four times as much as a 1 percent cut in overhead and fixed costs. These examples are only the tip of the iceberg of some of the consequences that poor pricing can have on the success of a business model.

Successful pricing is determined by the answers to some important questions:

- How should prices be set relative to the benefits they offer customers and the cost of offering these benefits?
- When should a firm lower or raise its prices?
- What is the reaction of competitors and customers likely to be when a firm raises or lowers its prices? (PepsiCo's price decrease resulted in more profits because of Coca-Cola's reaction [or nonreaction], customers' response, and how much it cost PepsiCo to deliver the 12-ounce drink.)
- When can a firm give away its products?

In this chapter, we explore the fundamentals of pricing on which the answers to these questions rest. We start with a very brief and relevant description of the evolution of different forms of pricing. We then explore some of the methods that firms use to set prices. Next, we examine what is involved in changing one's prices. This is followed by an exploration of some of the pricing strategies that firms use to better position themselves. Finally, we discuss the management of the pricing process within firms.

A BRIEF HISTORY OF PRICING

The oldest form of pricing, used by our ancestors, was barter. In **barter,** goods are swapped for other goods. This was very practical in the early days of commerce, when there were no currencies. Today, barter is used sparingly. It is used by people in communities without a currency or with a currency that the community has little faith in, and it is sometimes used by start-up companies that are strapped for cash. For example, a start-up software company may develop software for a law firm in return for legal advice. However, barter has many problems, which stem from the fact that it does not entail the use of currency. In our example of the software start-up, barter prevents the firm from selling its software to anyone it chooses and buying legal services, or anything else, from anyone it chooses; rather, the start-up must find a law firm that needs the software it produces. This is very limiting.

Another very old form of pricing is **one-to-one bargaining,** in which the seller negotiates with each buyer to determine each one's **reservation price**—the maximum price that the buyer is willing to pay. Effectively, the seller can capture the value that each customer perceives in the seller's product or service. One-on-one bargaining is very common on the streets of most developing countries. Since, by definition, one-on-one pricing requires that the seller be able to bargain individually with every customer, this approach to pricing is difficult to implement in large brick-and-mortar stores. Imagine customers trying to negotiate separate prices on all the items in a supermarket. The store owner would, at the very least, need to hire numerous sellers, whose combined salaries could be an exorbitant cost. Moreover, customers who pay lower prices might brag about their abilities to win these prices, infuriating some of the higher-paying customers even though they were willing to pay the higher prices.

In **menu pricing,** or **fixed pricing,** there is no bargaining; the seller sets a price and buyers can either take it or leave it. It was introduced in the United States at the end of the nineteenth century by major department stores because they carried so many items that the number of employees required for one-on-one bargaining was impractical. Menu or fixed pricing is the most common pricing scheme in developed countries today,[3] although, as we will see later, information technology may be changing that. Fixed pricing has two major disadvantages. First, the price that a firm sets may be below or above the reservation prices of many customers. That is, many customers may be willing to pay more for the product than the fixed price set by the seller. Think of some products that you really like and how many of them you would pay more for if you had to. By asking and receiving less money than customers are willing to pay, a firm is leaving money on the table and thus reducing its profits. In contrast, the menu price may be too high for some customers, whose reservation prices fall below the fixed price. By losing out on sales to these customers, the firm is forgoing the extra revenue it could have received from this group. Second, prices are sticky—once set, it is difficult to change them. Two factors drive the stickiness of menu pricing. First, it is not easy to detect changes in consumer preferences quickly enough to respond with price changes since menu prices do not reveal much about how much customers value a product. Second, it is difficult to implement price changes. It takes time and costs money to change the labels on products, input the data into a computer system, and get new labels onto products that are already in stores. Imagine how costly it would be to keep changing all the prices in a supermarket as a function of the day of the week or time of the day.

In **auction pricing,** a seller solicits bids from many buyers and sells to the buyer with the highest bid. Ideally, buyers bid at their reservation prices. There are two major problems with auctions. First, buyers can collude to hold down the price of an item, and sellers can collude to limit the number of items up for bid at any one time. Second, it is difficult to bring together many sellers and buyers in a brick-and-mortar world. As we will see later, the Internet is alleviating some of these problems. In a **reverse auction,** many sellers "bid" on selling a product at a fixed price that the buyer offered. This contrasts with an auction, where many buyers bid on one item offered by the seller. Priceline.com is normally credited with pioneering reverse auctions. A Priceline client proposes a price he or she is willing to pay for, say, air transportation between cities A and B on a certain day. Priceline then presents this price to the airlines to see if any of them are interested. If an airline is willing to sell tickets at that price, the deal is consummated and Priceline gets a commission from the seller.[4]

SETTING PRICES FOR AN OPTIMAL REVENUE MODEL

Whether a firm uses fixed pricing, auctions, one-on-one bargaining, or reverse auctions, it still must set prices for its products. In setting a price, it is important to have an objective in mind and to find some way of tracking the extent to which the price that is set meets the goal.

Objective

Since the goal of a business model is to make money, a firm's objective in setting prices in its business model should be to maximize its profits. That is, it should set its prices such that the quantities it sells will result in the highest revenues and lowest costs. According to economic theory, if a firm wants to determine the quantities and prices at which it can maximize its profits, the firm needs to know its demand and cost functions.[5] Knowing a firm's *demand function* entails knowing the relationship between the quantity of a product that the firm can sell and the factors that influence this quantity. These factors include the price of the product, the benefits from the product, the price of complementary products, the price of substitutes, competitors' prices, customer needs, customers' ability to pay, the benefits from competitors' products, advertising, product promotion, and any other factors that can affect any of the "Four P's" of a firm's or competitor's marketing mix: product, price, promotion, and place. The sheer number of these variables, the interaction between them, and the fact that any one of them can change at any time suggests that it is very difficult to predict demand. For example, if a firm changes its prices or advertising expenditures, competitors may decide to change theirs. In response to these changes, customers may decide, if the prices have risen, not to buy the products again or, if the prices have dropped, to buy more products than expected.

Knowing a firm's *cost function* entails knowing the relationship between the firm's cost, the quantity produced, and all the factors that influence that quantity, such as the technology the firm uses, prices of materials, labor, and capital. These factors are also difficult to predict but less so than the factors that influence demand because firms have a little more control of their costs than they do of demand. In practice, since a firm's demand and cost functions are difficult to determine, prices are normally set with a less ambitious objective than profit maximization. Firms' objectives can vary from wanting to sell at prices that are high enough to cover variable costs and some fraction of fixed costs to wanting to appropriate all the value that the firm creates for customers. The methods commonly used for selecting prices embody some subset of these objectives. Whatever the price that is set, it is useful to track the extent to which the price makes a contribution to profitability since the purpose of business models is making money. For example, a firm may want to know how the expected profits from a product will vary with the quantity of the product sold.

Contribution of Price to Profitability

For a product to be profitable, the revenues from selling the product must cover both the variable and the fixed costs associated with the product. The price of each unit produced should cover the product's per-unit variable cost and make a contribution to recovering fixed costs. Recalling from Chapter 2 that fixed costs are the costs that a firm must incur irrespective of the total output produced, while variable costs are the costs whose total increases with the level of output, we can restate Equation 3.1 for a product as follows:

$$\text{Profits} = \text{revenues} - \text{variable costs} - \text{fixed costs} \qquad \textbf{(3.2)}$$
$$= PQ - V_cQ - F_c = (P - V_c)Q - F_c$$
$$= \text{contribution margin} - F_c = (\text{contribution margin per unit})Q - F_c$$

where P is the price per unit of the product, V_c is the per-unit variable cost, Q is the total number of units sold, and F_c is the up-front or fixed costs. The quantity $PQ - V_cQ$, or revenues minus variable costs, is called the **contribution margin** and represents the amount over variable costs that is contributed to recovering fixed costs. When enough units have been sold to recover all fixed costs, the contribution margin starts to contribute to profits. The quantity $P - V_c$, the difference between price and *per-unit* variable cost, is called the **contribution margin per unit.** Both contribution margin and contribution margin per unit are key concepts in understanding the implications of a product's price for the revenues and profits that can be generated by the product. To illustrate the concept, consider the following example.

Example

A company called MacroSoft has spent a total of $10 million in R&D, marketing, promotion, and other up-front fixed costs to offer a software package that it sells at $100 a copy. Since MacroSoft has posted the software on the Web for customers to download, each copy that it sells costs the company only $5. The company estimates that it can sell anywhere between 25,000 and 2,500,000 units in the first year.

If MacroSoft sells 25,000 units, its profits from the product are

$$\text{Profits} = \text{revenues} - \text{variable costs} - \text{fixed costs}$$
$$= PQ - V_cQ - F_c = (P - V_c)Q - F_c$$
$$= \$100 \times 25{,}000 - \$5 \times 25{,}000 - F_c = (\$100 - 5) \times 25{,}000 - F_c$$
$$= \$2{,}500{,}000 - \$125{,}000 - F_c = \$2{,}375{,}000 - F_c$$
$$= \$2{,}375{,}000 - F_c = \$2{,}375{,}000 - \$10{,}000{,}000 = -\$7{,}625{,}000$$

Thus, the contribution margin for MacroSoft's software when 25,000 units are sold is its revenues minus its variable costs: $PQ - V_cQ = \$2,375,000$. This is the amount that goes to cover fixed costs. Since fixed costs are $10,000,000, the $2,375,000 contribution margin falls short by $7,625,000; therefore, the losses generated by the product are $7,625,000. That is, profits $= \$2,375,000 - \$10,000,000 = -\$7,625,000$. This means that if the company sells only 25,000 units of the product, it will lose money. If the company sells 500,000 units, its contribution margin is $47,500,000 ($50,000,000 - $2,500,000). The contribution margin of $47,500,000 more than covers the fixed costs of $10,000,000. The $37,500,000 excess over fixed costs is the profit generated by the product. The contribution margin, and therefore profits, increases with the number of units that the firm can sell. Table 3.1 summarizes the changes in the contribution margin and profits as the number of units sold changes.

Since a business model is about making money, the process of setting prices or analyzing them should always keep in mind contribution margins and how much they contribute to profits.

COST-BASED PRICING

In **cost-based pricing,** a firm sets its prices by adding a markup to its costs or subtracting a markdown from the costs. Very little attention is given to how much customers value the product.

Markup over Cost

In **markup** or **cost-plus pricing,** a firm estimates its cost of offering a product or service and adds some percentage of the cost—a cost markup—to the cost for its profit. This markup can be a function of the firm's expected return on sales or return on investment.

TABLE 3.1   Contribution Margin and Profits as a Function of Number of Units Sold

The price (column A), per-unit variable cost (B), and quantity sold (C) are given. Revenues (E) are the product of price (A) and quantity sold (C). Variable costs (F) are the product of price (B) and quantity sold (C). As defined in the text, the contribution margin (G) is equal to the revenues (E) minus variable costs (F). The product's operating income is the contribution margin minus fixed costs.

A Price	B Per-Unit Variable Cost	C Quantity Sold	D Contribution Margin per Unit A − B	E Revenues A × C	F Variable Costs B × C	G Contribution Margin E − F	H Fixed Costs	I Operating Profits G − H
$100	$5	25,000	$95	$2,500,000	$125,000	$2,375,000	$10,000,000	$(7,625,000)
100	5	50,000	95	5,000,000	250,000	4,750,000	10,000,000	(5,250,000)
100	5	200,000	95	20,000,000	1,000,000	19,000,000	10,000,000	9,000,000
100	5	500,000	95	50,000,000	2,500,000	47,500,000	10,000,000	37,500,000
100	5	800,000	95	80,000,000	4,000,000	76,000,000	10,000,000	66,000,000
100	5	1,000,000	95	100,000,000	5,000,000	95,000,000	10,000,000	85,000,000
100	5	1,200,000	95	120,000,000	6,000,000	114,000,000	10,000,000	104,000,000
100	5	1,500,000	95	150,000,000	7,500,000	142,500,000	10,000,000	132,500,000
100	5	2,000,000	95	200,000,000	10,000,000	190,000,000	10,000,000	180,000,000
100	5	2,500,000	95	250,000,000	12,500,000	237,500,000	10,000,000	227,500,000

Return-on-Sales Markup

One measure of the profitability of a firm's business model is its *return on sales*—that is, profits divided by sales.[6] One price-setting practice is to set prices equal to cost, marked up by return on sales. Such a price is given by

$$\text{Price} = \frac{\text{per-unit cost}}{1 - \text{return on sales}}$$

Consider a microchip maker that spent $25 million on R&D in developing a chip that costs $7 per chip to produce. It believes that it can sell 5 million of the chips, and it wants to make a return on sales of 20 percent. Again, recall that fixed costs are the costs that a firm must spend irrespective of the total output produced, while variable costs are the costs that increase with the level of output. Also recall that the unit cost is given by the expression

$$\text{Per-unit cost} = \text{per-unit variable cost} + \frac{\text{fixed cost}}{\text{sales}}$$

Applying this relationship to the chip maker example,

$$\text{Per-unit cost} = \text{per-unit variable cost} + \frac{\text{fixed cost}}{\text{sales}} = \$7 + \frac{\$25,000,000}{5,000,000} = \$12$$

Since the chip maker wants to make a return on sales of 20 percent, it should price each chip at

$$\text{Chip price} = \frac{\text{per-unit cost}}{1 - \text{return on sales}} = \frac{12}{(1 - 0.20)} = \$15$$

Thus the chip maker will charge its customers $15 per microchip. Since the firm is projected to sell 5 million of these chips, its profits are $15 × 5,000,000 − $12 × 5,000,000 = $15,000,000. Since the 5 million sales figure is only an estimate, it is usually advisable for the firm to calculate the price and profits under different sales scenarios. Table 3.2 shows a spreadsheet of different prices and profits for each sales forecast.

The cost-markup method of setting prices has several disadvantages. First, it does not consider the benefits that are in the product and customers' willingness to pay for them. Second, it says very little about competitors.

TABLE 3.2 **Price and Profits as a Function of Forecasted Sales**

Sales (units)	Per-Unit Variable Cost	Fixed Costs	Per-Unit Cost	Price	Revenues	Total Cost	Profits
100,000	$7	$25,000,000	$257	$321	$32,125,000	$25,700,000	$6,425,000
500,000	7	25,000,000	57	71	35,625,000	28,500,000	7,125,000
1,000,000	7	25,000,000	32	40	40,000,000	32,000,000	8,000,000
4,000,000	7	25,000,000	13	17	66,250,000	53,000,000	13,250,000
5,000,000	**7**	**25,000,000**	**12**	**15**	**75,000,000**	**60,000,000**	**15,000,000**
7,500,000	7	25,000,000	10	13	96,875,000	77,500,000	19,375,000
10,000,000	7	25,000,000	10	12	118,750,000	95,000,000	23,750,000
12,000,000	7	25,000,000	9	11	136,250,000	109,000,000	27,250,000
15,000,000	7	25,000,000	9	11	162,500,000	130,000,000	32,500,000
17,500,000	7	25,000,000	8	11	184,375,000	147,500,000	36,875,000

Return-on-Investment Markup

If you were to invest your money in a company, say, by buying the company's stock, you would expect a certain return on your money. From the point of view of a firm, it must invest in the product that is being priced, and it wants a return on that investment. As such, the price of the product can be set as a function of what the firm expects its *return on investment (ROI)* to be. In this case, the price is set equal to the firm's cost per unit plus an ROI markup. Thus,

$$\text{Price} = \text{per-unit cost} + \frac{\text{return} \times \text{invested capital}}{\text{sales}}$$

Continuing with the above example of the microchip maker, suppose now that its cost of capital is 20 percent and that it invested a total of $50 million. Thus it expects profits of $10 million (0.20 × $50,000,000). In this case,

$$\text{Price} = \$12 + \frac{0.20 \times \$50,000,000}{5,000,000} = \$14$$

Again, the $14 price is based on the expectation that the firm will sell 5 million units. Prices under different sales scenarios can be calculated as shown in Table 3.3.

Contribution to Fixed Costs

Recall from earlier in the chapter that the excess of a product's price over its variable cost usually goes to recover fixed costs and that when the fixed costs have been recovered, the excess becomes the firm's profits. During a recession or other hard times when there is excess capacity, a firm may decide to sell its product at a price that is below its per-unit cost as long as the price covers its variable costs and makes a contribution to recovering some of the fixed costs. In the chip maker example, its variable costs are $7 per unit and its per-unit cost is $12. Thus, any price that is above $7 and below $12 will be okay since such a price covers the $7 variable costs and makes a contribution to recovering some of the estimated per-unit fixed cost of $5.

TABLE 3.3
Investment-Based Prices under Different Scenarios

Sales (units)	Per-Unit Variable Cost	Fixed Costs	Per-Unit Cost	Price	Profits
100,000	$7	$25,000,000	$257	$259	$10,000,000
500,000	7	25,000,000	57	59	10,000,000
1,000,000	7	25,000,000	32	34	10,000,000
4,000,000	7	25,000,000	13	15	10,000,000
5,000,000	**7**	**25,000,000**	**12**	**14**	**10,000,000**
7,500,000	7	25,000,000	10	12	10,000,000
10,000,000	7	25,000,000	10	12	10,000,000
12,000,000	7	25,000,000	9	11	10,000,000
15,000,000	7	25,000,000	9	11	10,000,000
17,500,000	7	25,000,000	8	10	10,000,000

CUSTOMER VALUE–BASED PRICING

As mentioned above, cost-based pricing ignores the value that customers perceive in a firm's products relative to those of competitors. The goal of customer value–based pricing is to *appropriate* the value created—that is, to price the product so as to earn a profit that reflects the value created. Ideally, a firm would like to charge each customer his or her reservation price. As we will see soon, doing so is a challenge.

Price and Performance: Value-Based Fixed Pricing

In some markets, the benefits that customers want in a product are clear. For example, in the market for cholesterol drugs, it is clear that the ability of a drug to reduce cholesterol levels is an important performance criteria. In the market for high-performing cars, performance and reliability are important features that customers look for; price may not be important to some customers, but others may prefer to get that high performance and reliability at lower prices. In such markets, three factors are important in setting prices:

1. *The benefits (product characteristics) that customers value in the firm's product.* The greater the value customers place on the benefits in a firm's product, the more the firm can charge for them. In setting prices, it is important to note the difference between perceived benefits and potential benefits. *Perceived benefits* are those that customers already value in a product. *Potential benefits* are those that a firm can get customers to value in the product through, for example, promotion and advertising.
2. *The benefits from competitors' products and their prices.*
3. *The firm's pricing strategy.* This is especially important when the firm decides to position itself in terms of benefits per dollar or price and performance. (We will explore pricing strategy in more detail later in this chapter.)

Two examples illustrate how firms can exploit these three factors to build successful business models. In the 1980s, Toyota, Honda, and Nissan decided to enter the high-performance car market, which had long been dominated by BMW, Mercedes-Benz, and Volkswagen's Audi. Toyota, Honda, and Nissan each developed a line of high-performing cars and priced them so that they offered customers much more in terms of performance and reliability per dollar (see Figure 3.1). Each also realized that, until deciding to enter this segment of the market, it had been known for low-cost reliable cars rather than high-performing cars. To prevent this image of low-cost, low-performing cars from tainting the image of its new products, each firm established a separate division to promote and sell the new cars. Toyota established the Lexus group to sell its Lexus high-performing cars, Honda established the Acura division to sell Acuras, and Nissan established the Infiniti group to sell Infinitis. By creating these new groups, promoting and advertising the new vehicles, and delivering high-performance, reliable products, these firms were able to turn Lexus, Acura, and Infiniti into new brands that customers value. In addition, by pricing the cars so that customers get more benefits for their dollar relative to competitors' offerings, Toyota, Honda, and Nissan were able to establish themselves as a major force in the U.S. luxury-car market by 2001.

The second example is Warner-Lambert's pricing of Lipitor, a cholesterol-reducing drug. Lipitor belongs to a group of drugs called *statins,* which are much more effective in reducing cholesterol levels than were previous generations of

FIGURE 3.1
Honda, Nissan, and
Toyota in the U.S.
Luxury-Car Market

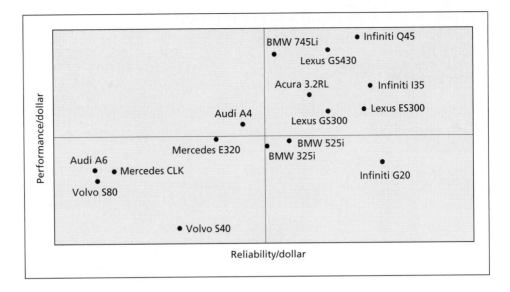

drugs. When Warner-Lambert introduced the drug, there were already four other statins in the market. The makers of these other drugs touted the effectiveness of the products in reducing total cholesterol in patients. Lipitor turned out to reduce so-called bad cholesterol, or LDL, and triglycerides much more than other statins. Warner-Lambert not only priced its drug to make sure the per-dollar reductions in total cholesterol, LDL, and triglycerides were larger than those of any statin competitor but also promoted and advertised LDL and triglyceride reduction as a desirable feature in a cholesterol drug. In 2002, Lipitor was the number-one selling drug in the world, with over $6 billion in sales.

Customer Reservation-Price Pricing

Setting a product's price as a function of the benefits that customers value in the product has one major problem: This approach does not reach the ultimate goal of having every customer pay her or his reservation price, a goal that allows the seller to fully profit from the value created. Recall that a customer's reservation price for a product is the maximum price that the customer is willing to pay for the product.

The Appropriability Challenge

Each customer has certain needs that he or she would like to fulfill with the product that he or she is buying. Each also has personal perceptions of the benefits in the different products that can fulfill these needs. Finally, each customer has a certain ability to pay. Thus, each customer's reservation price is a function of his or her needs, perception of the benefits in the product, and ability to pay. Since these factors vary from customer to customer and from group to group, the maximum price that one customer or group (i.e., market segment) is willing to pay is different from what another is willing to pay. To maximize profits from its business model, every firm would like to capture all the value it creates by charging each customer or segment the maximum price that each is willing to pay and by keeping costs low as it does so.

The primary problem is finding out how much customers or segments value the benefits that a firm has created and thereby determining their reservation prices. If a firm sets one price for all its customers or segments, it risks driving

FIGURE 3.A

The Appropriability Challenge

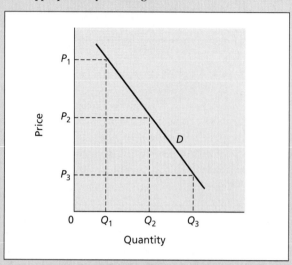

To understand the appropriability problem, consider a firm selling a product that has the demand line D in the accompanying figure, where prices and quantities are measured from the origin 0.* Although, as detailed in the text, demand depends on numerous factors, assume here that it depends on product price, with the other factors fixed. When the firm prices the product at P_1, it can sell only Q_1 units of it. If it decreases the price to P_2, some of the customers who did not buy the product at price P_1, because that price was above their reservation prices, will now buy it. Thus the total quantity the firm can sell rises to Q_2. At the even lower price P_3, even more customers want and can afford the product, and so the firm can sell Q_3 units. Thus, if the firm decided to set the price of the product at P_2 for all customers, it would lose the customers whose reservation prices are below P_2 and would let the customers whose reservation prices are above P_2 pocket the difference between P_2 and their reservation prices.

*Not all demand curves are linear and slope downward as in this example. Demand curves for luxury goods may slope upward since more people buy luxury items at higher prices.

away some customers or leaving money on the table. On the one hand, setting a price that is too high usually drives away the customers whose reservation prices are below the high price set by the company. The result is that the company ends up selling fewer units of the product than it would have otherwise. Selling fewer units deprives a firm of the benefits of economies of scale and therefore keeps its costs higher. An exception is luxury goods, where setting product prices high may result in more customers wanting the product and a larger quantity being sold. On the other hand, setting a price that is too low leaves money on the table as some customers' reservation prices are above the price set by the firm. These customers pocket the difference between the price they are willing to pay and the lower price they actually pay. With a low price, however, the firm may be able to benefit from the economies of scale that selling a large quantity can bestow.

The Practicality Challenge

By setting a price for each customer equal to his or her reservation price, a seller can, in theory, appropriate all the value that customers perceive. Charging each customer his or her reservation price for the same product is usually referred to as **first-degree price discrimination.** In general, **price discrimination** occurs when a firm charges different customers or groups of customers different prices that do not reflect proportional differences in product benefits or costs.[7] Although the word *discrimination* connotes a sense of wrongdoing, price discrimination is usually good for the firm since customers are willing to pay and the firm makes money. In practice, it is very difficult to charge every customer his or her reservation price. For one thing, customers will talk to each other and quickly discover that they are paying different prices for the same product or that the differences in products do not warrant the differences in the prices they pay.

Customers with high reservation prices, who would ordinarily be happy to pay the prices, may feel cheated when they find out that other customers are paying less for the same product. Another problem is that it is difficult to determine customers' reservation prices. It is not very practical, for example, to ask every customer what he or she wants and how much he or she values a product, and even if this could be done, the answers might not be reliable. Customers may not be willing to reveal their reservation prices, especially when their willingness to pay is high but they do not want to pay high prices.

While charging all customers their reservation prices is not very practical, there are, nevertheless, cases in which sellers may charge some customers prices close to their reservation prices. Such cases occur when two conditions exist: (1) Sellers know a lot about their customers, and (2) it is difficult for customers to tell if the product or service they are receiving is identical to that which other customers are receiving. The services performed by accountants, lawyers, architects, and doctors are characterized by these two conditions.[8] Lawyers can get to know their clients very well, and it is difficult to determine if the services they perform for clients are the same or different. (Only the lawyers know if there are really any differences in their services, but they would probably not tell.) Thus lawyers usually can charge according to their clients' reservation prices. A lawyer may decide to charge a rich client who is in trouble a lot more money than a poorer one for the same service. We usually have no idea how much doctors charge our insurance companies. They too can price discriminate.

Segment Pricing

Rather than go after the reservation price of every customer, a more practical method is to segment customers on the basis of customer characteristics and charge each group a different price for the same product or service or slight variations. For example, businesses are more willing to pay higher airfares than the average vacationer. Therefore, airlines separate business travelers from vacationers by instituting restrictions on low fares that vacationers are more likely to meet than business travelers. To get the low fares, customers must purchase tickets in advance (many business travelers do not know their travel plans until the last minute) and include a Saturday night stayover (most business travelers want to be at home with their families on the weekend). The end result is that business travelers pay more than vacationers for the same flights. Another example: Because their incomes are low, students and senior citizens are normally not as willing as others to pay high prices. Therefore, many services such as movies and museums charge students and seniors less than the rest of the population. In general, the practice of charging different market segments different prices for the same product is called **third-degree price discrimination.**

Quantity-Bought Pricing

For three reasons, a firm may set prices for customers who buy large quantities of its products lower than those for customers who buy smaller quantities. First, a customer who buys large quantities may have bargaining power over the seller, which allows the customer to extract lower prices from the seller. Effectively, this large buyer may expect to be charged lower prices, and therefore its reservation price is lower than the reservation prices of smaller competitors. Second, when a firm sells large quantities of a product to a particular customer, it is likely to enjoy economies of scale in selling to that customer. For example, a firm that delivers a generic product (also called *private brand*) to a larger retailer, such as

Wal-Mart, may need sales personnel dedicated to the retailer, equipment to brand the product using the retailer's generic (private) brand name, and a logistics setup to deliver the product on time. The costs of all these are predominantly fixed costs, so the larger the quantity sold to the customer, the lower will be the per-unit cost of the product. The cost savings can be passed on to the customer in the form of lower prices. Third, consumer demand for some products decreases with the number of units consumed. Classic examples are water and electricity. The willingness of customers to pay for such products decreases as the amount consumed increases. Thus, a seller may need to lower prices for larger quantities to encourage more consumption.

Setting prices by quantity bought consists of using one of the price-setting methods we explored earlier to set a price for the average quantity and then discounting that price for larger quantities. In general, when a firm charges different prices for different quantities of the same product or service, it is said to be practicing **second-degree price discrimination.** There is evidence of second-degree price discrimination in most stores. A 2-liter bottle of Coke, for example, costs less per liter than a 1-liter bottle.

Bundling

Bundling occurs when a firm sells two or more products as one product, charging a single price for the bundle that is usually less than the sum of the prices of the individual products. For example, rather than charge for leather seats, automatic transmission, global positioning, satellite radio, DVD, and tinted mirrors as separate items, an automaker can bundle them together and sell the bundle as one option in a car. When a restaurant offers a meal including salad, soup, appetizer, main course, dessert, and coffee all for one price that is less than the sum of the prices of the individual items, it is bundling different products since each of the items can be sold as a separate item. Many symphony orchestras in the United States offer a season-ticket package at a price that is less than the sum of the prices of the individual performances.[9] Bundling can also occur with products from different firms. Many U.S. airlines bundle frequent-flyer miles with credit cards. The customer receives airline miles for each purchase that he or she makes through the credit card service. The "price" the airline and credit card company receive is the yearly credit card fees that are charged to the customer or to the merchants whose products the card member buys. In 2002, this bundling was one of the most profitable sources of revenues for airlines.

The purpose of bundling is to attract customers who would otherwise buy only one product or none. For example, a customer may be attracted to a credit card solely because he or she gets frequent-flyer miles with each purchase. Bundling enables a seller to better tailor products to what individual customers perceive as valuable and therefore to better capture customer value. Consider the following example.[10]

Example

A software company has a word processing software product called Good and a spreadsheet product called Excellent, each of which it can sell separately. Let us assume that there are two kinds of customers, each of which has a different reservation price for the company's word processor and spreadsheet software (Table 3.4). The quantitative-type customers, who need spreadsheets for their number crunching but do not care much about word processors, have a reservation price of $70 for Excellent and $20 for Good. The verbal type, who need word processors for their jobs but do not care much about numbers, have a reservation price of $60 for Good and only $25 for Excellent. If the company sold each product separately, it would

TABLE 3.4
Bundling Example

Type of Customer	No. of Customers	Reservation Price			
		Good	Excellent	Good + Excellent	Firm's Bundle Price
Quantitative	20 mil	$20	$70	$90	$85
Verbal	30 mil	60	25	85	85
Revenues		**1.8 bil***	**1.4 bil***		
Total Revenues		**3.2 bil**		**4.25 bil**	

*For simplicity, we assume that when products are sold separately, each customer will buy only the product that he or she values most: Good = 30,000,000 × $60, Excellent = 20,000,000 × $70.

collect $1.4 billion from the 20 million quantitatives by charging them their reservation price of $70 for Excellent (20,000,000 × $70) and $1.8 billion from the 30 million verbal types by charging them their reservation price of $60 for Good. (We assume here that the company cannot price-discriminate by charging quantitatives $20 for Good and $70 for Excellent while charging verbals $25 for Excellent and $60 for Good.) The company's combined revenues are $3.2 billion ($1.4 billion + $1.8 billion).

Now suppose the company decides to bundle Excellent and Good and sell them as one product for one price. Quantitatives value the bundle at $90 ($20 + $70), while verbals value it at $85 ($60 + $25). If the company sets its price at $85, both groups of customers should buy the bundle since the price equals the reservation price (for the bundle) of the verbal type and is below that of the quantitatives. The company collects $1.7 billion from quantitatives (20,00,000 × $85) and $2.55 billion (30,000,000 × $85) from verbals for a total of $4.25 billion. That is, bundling brings in an extra $1.05 billion in revenues, most of which contributes directly to profits since software costs almost nothing to replicate once developed!

Two-Part-Tariff Pricing

The two-part-tariff pricing method is one more attempt to get closer to charging customers their reservation prices. In a **two-part tariff,** the seller sets two prices. The first price is for the right to use the product and the second one is for the number of units consumed.[11] Amusement parks usually charge an admission fee and, inside the park, a separate fee for each ride. There is a chance that your telephone company charges you a monthly fee for the right to use the phone and a per-minute price for every minute of usage. At some nightclubs, you pay an admission fee to go in and, once inside the club, pay for each drink that you want and can afford. Car rental agencies usually charge a daily fee for use of a car and another fee per mile driven. Makers of razors charge a price for the razor and a price for each blade that customers buy after buying the razor. When Rambus decided to license its memory chip technology to makers of dynamic random access memory, it charged them an up-front fixed fee for the right to use the technology and then a per-unit royalty for each microchip that the licensee sells.

In each of these examples, there are two sets of benefits, each of which is valued differently by each group of customers. In the amusement park example, some parents who go to an amusement park value getting into the park with their kids a lot more than going on the rides, but their kids love the rides. By charging an entry fee and a fee for rides, the amusement park can capture the value that the parents attach to entry and the value that the kids attach to the rides. Moreover, some people want to go on the rides all day, and it makes sense to charge them more money—no free rides. In the telephone example, some customers value having a phone just in case they need to make an emergency call; others like to make lots of calls. By using a two-part tariff, the phone company is able to capture more of the value from both types of customers. In the car rental example, some customers value the convenience of having a car for short rides, while others want to drive the cars over long distances. Again, the two-part tariff provides the company with the opportunity to appropriate the value offered to both types.

PRICING STRATEGY

A firm often must decide whether to exercise a price cut or price increase, charge high prices or low ones for new products, stick with one price over long periods or change prices regularly, use fixed-pricing schemes or an alternative such as auctions, and give away products or charge for them, as well as whether to use prices as strategic signals and where to position its prices relative to competitors' prices. A commitment to one set (or subset) of these pricing activities rather than another is the firm's **pricing strategy.** For most of its life, Southwest Airlines has been committed to simple "everyday low prices" rather than the frequently changing unpredictable prices of other major airlines. Swatch always offers its basic watch model at a constant price—$40 during most of the 1990s.[12]

The success of a pricing strategy is a function not only of the strategy itself but also of the business model, especially how the pricing strategy fits with the business model. For example, Southwest Airlines' everyday-low-prices pricing strategy fits very well with its low-cost business model, which allows it to perform its value-adding activities at low cost and therefore to pass some of its cost savings to customers in the form of everyday low prices. To understand how a firm's pricing strategy fits with its business model and strategy, it is important to understand the nature of some of the pricing activities that underpin a pricing strategy.

Price Cuts and Increases

A firm's ultimate goal in raising or cutting prices should be to increase the profitability of its business model. Whether a price cut or increase results in better profitability for a firm is a function of the elasticity of demand for the product, competitors' reaction, and the cost of producing the extra units demanded as a result of the lower prices.

Role of Price Elasticity of Demand

If a firm decreases the price of its product, it is likely to sell more units of the product. If the increase in units is substantial, the firm's revenues may actually go up. Specifically, if the percentage increase in the number of units sold is larger than the percentage decrease in price, the revenues will increase. One way of understanding the sensitivity of price changes is to consider the relationship in Equation 3.3:

$$\text{Profits} = \text{revenues} - \text{costs} = P(Q) \times Q - C(Q) \qquad \textbf{(3.3)}$$

If a firm cuts its prices, P in Equation 3.3 would drop, tending to decrease revenues. At the same time, a drop in P means that more people can now buy the firm's product, effectively increasing the quantity Q that the firm can sell. Whether the revenues generated by the lower price are higher than those that would have been generated by the higher price depends on whether the percentage increase in the quantity sold as a result of the price decrease exceeds the percentage decrease in price. That is, it depends on the price elasticity of demand.[13] The **price elasticity of demand** is the percentage change in quantity divided by the percentage change in price that brings about the change in quantity. Elasticity of demand, E_d, is given by

$$E_d = -\frac{\% \text{ change in quantity}}{\% \text{ change in price}} = -\frac{(Q_2 - Q_1)/Q_1}{(P_2 - P_1)/P_1} \qquad \textbf{(3.4)}$$

Given the differences in products and markets, it can be expected that the sensitivity of quantity to price changes would vary considerably. That is, price elasticity of demand can be expected to vary considerably from product to product and from market to market. To understand Equation 3.4, consider the following two examples.

Example 1

Product A is priced at $20 and sold in market M1. At this price, 5 units of the product are sold. If the price is reduced to $10, the quantity of units sold in market M1 increases to 25 units. Using Equation 3.4, price elasticity of demand in market M1 (Figure 3.2) is

$$E_{dA} = -\frac{(25 - 5)/5}{(10 - 20)/20} = -\frac{4}{-0.5} = 8$$

This is interpreted as follows: For every 1 percent decrease in the price of the product in market M1, there is an 8 percent increase in the quantity demanded. That is, the percentage decrease in price is less than the percentage increase in quantity demanded. When price elasticity of demand is more than 1, as is the case here, demand is said to be *elastic* since the percentage increase in the quantity demanded outstrips the percentage decrease in price. In markets with elastic demand, a price cut by a firm expands the market and takes market share from competitors if they do not react. The personal computer market offers a very good example. By cutting its prices, Dell has been able to increase demand for its PCs and increase its market share over the years. (It is important to emphasize again that an elastic market allows for an increase in market share. To be profitable, however, a firm must have a low-cost business model to back the low prices.)

Example 2

Product B is priced at $20 and sold in market M2. At this price, 12 units of the product are sold. If the price is now reduced to $10, the quantity of units sold in market M2 increases to only 16 units. Using Equation 3.4, price elasticity of demand in market M2 (Figure 3.3) is

$$E_{dB} = -\frac{(16 - 12)/12}{(10 - 20)/20} = -\frac{0.34}{-0.5} = 0.7$$

FIGURE 3.2
Elastic Market

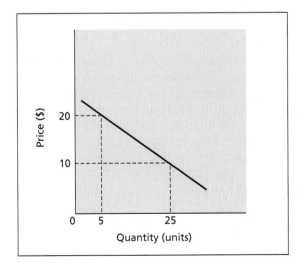

FIGURE 3.3
Inelastic Market

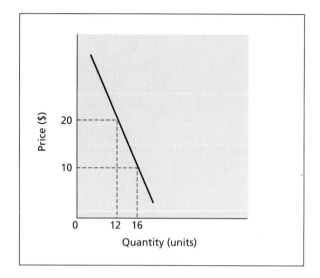

This is interpreted as follows: For every 1 percent decrease in the price of the product in market M2, there is only a 0.7 percent increase in the quantity demanded. That is, the percentage decrease in price is more than the percentage increase in quantity demanded. When price elasticity of demand is less than 1, demand is said to be *inelastic* since the percentage increase in the quantity demanded falls short of the percentage change in price. In markets with inelastic demand, a price cut by a firm shrinks its market share and may increase competitors' market shares. In contrast, a price increase in an inelastic market can increase the firm's revenues. This is because, although the price increase will decrease demand, the percentage decrease in quantity demanded will not be as much as the percentage increase in price.

From our examples, market M1 is more price-sensitive than market M2. An important question, then, is, What makes demand for one firm's products more sensitive to price changes than demand for others' products? Several factors affect price sensitivity:

1. *Presence of viable substitutes:* If there are viable substitutes that customers can turn to, price increases are more likely to drive customers to the substitutes. Conversely, price decreases will bring in customers who previously used viable substitutes. If airlines raise their prices too high, more people might opt to drive or take a train.

2. *High percentage of customer's cost:* If a firm's product constitutes a high percentage of a customer's expenditures, the customer is likely to be sensitive to price increases since such increases have a large impact on his or her expenditures. Thus, price increases may push customers to competitors or substitutes. If the product represents only a small fraction of the customer's costs, the customer is not likely to notice price increases or be very concerned about them.

3. *Low switching costs:* If the costs of switching from a product are low, users of the product are more likely to switch away from the product when there is a price increase and to the product when there is a price cut.

4. *Price-sensitive end market:* If the product is an important input to another product that is sold to a price-sensitive market, buyers of the product are likely to be sensitive to any price increases for the input.

Competitors' Reaction

Before a firm can cut or raise its prices, it must carefully consider the reaction of existing and potential competitors.[14] Two main factors affect how existing competitors react to price increases:

1. *Size:* If a firm is very small relative to major players in the industry, the chances are that they may not even notice what, to the firm, is a large gain in market share. Consider, for example, a firm that has a 2 percent market share of a $100 million business compared to an industry leader that has a 40 percent share. If the market is elastic and the small company cuts its prices and increases its market share by $0.2 million, this is a 10 percent increase in share for the small firm but an amount that is hardly noticeable to the large company, with its share of $40 million. Moreover, the large firm does not want to get into a price war with the small firm since price cuts during a price war result in reductions in revenues that are proportional to existing market shares and profits. (There is a price war if each firm keeps trying to beat the other's price with an even lower price, putting downward pressure on prices.) Investors generally do not like to see reductions in revenues and profits. Thus, price cuts are a more viable strategy for smaller firms than for larger firms.

2. *Cost position relative to competitors:* A firm with a cost-competitive advantage can afford to cut its prices deeper than less cost-efficient competitors can. If a firm's costs are too high, a price war may lead to a point where the firm is selling at prices that are below its costs, thereby losing money.

As far as new entrants are concerned, low prices may reduce entry. Why? Potential new entrants will enter an industry only if they believe that they can make money in the industry. If they believe that future prices will be low, this might reduce their willingness to enter. If an industry firm's prices are low today, those prices send a signal to potential new entrants that the firm has a low-cost structure and therefore its prices may be low in the future. This may discourage potential new entrants who do not believe that they can attain such a low-cost structure. A firm that holds down its prices to discourage entry is said to be practicing a **limit-pricing strategy**.[15]

Before pursuing a limit-pricing strategy, firms must consider the cost. Keeping prices low means leaving money on the table. Consider a firm that has introduced a new product whose unique features allow the firm to sell 10 million units at $9 per unit. If the firm decides to sell the product at $7 per unit to deter entry, it forgoes $20 million in revenues. One strategy is to charge high prices when there are no competitors but cut the prices when other firms start entering. A firm can also charge high prices now and, when entry has started, follow whatever prices competitors are charging. Another entry-deterring strategy is to establish a reputation as a retaliator. That is, a firm makes it a policy that whenever another company enters its market space, the firm retaliates by cutting its prices. Once this practice becomes known, new entrants will be afraid to enter for fear of similar retaliation.

Many airlines have been known to lower their prices significantly for specific routes when new entrants attack such routes. Depending on the country, some forms of this strategy may be considered illegal. In the United States, for example, antitrust laws frown on predatory pricing. In **predatory pricing,** a firm lowers it prices in an attempt to drive out competitors.[16] When competitors have been driven out of the market, the firm raises its prices again.

Cost of Producing Extra Units

If a firm cuts its prices in an elastic market and demand for its products increases, the firm must produce and sell the extra units needed to satisfy the demand. Thus, whether the demand generated by a price cut results in profits is a function of how much it costs to produce and sell these units. The extra demand may require the building of a new plant or the creation of a new sales force or distribution channel, each of whose per-unit cost may be too high. Such costs can be high, for example, if the addition adds too much capacity and large increases in fixed costs or if the price of adding such capacity has recently gone up.

Skimming

In **skimming,** a firm introduces a new product and, while there are no competing products in the market, sets its price high.[17] When competition sets in or is about to, the firm lowers its price. In setting the price high, the assumption is that demand for this early market is primarily inelastic and therefore pricing low is not likely to bring in enough additional customers to more than make up for the price decrease. Skimming works very well in markets with so-called lead users. *Lead users* are customers whose needs are similar to those of other customers except that they have these needs months or years before the bulk of the marketplace does and they stand to benefit significantly by fulfilling these needs earlier than the rest of the customers. In the PC market, for example, there are some customers who simply must have the latest PC, either because their jobs require the speed or because they have a personal need to own the faster machine. A major contributor to PC speed is the microprocessor. Thus, Intel, which in the 1990s produced more than 80 percent of the microprocessors for IBM-compatible PCs, usually sets the prices of its latest microprocessors very high. After skimming the profits from the early users—through PC makers—Intel drastically cuts its prices. By skimming, a firm is effectively dividing its customers into segments according to how soon customers stand to benefit from a product.

Penetration Pricing

Another option for a firm that is introducing a new product is to set prices very low or give the product away for free. Such a pricing strategy, known as **penetration pricing,** is usually used when the goal is to become a standard or attain a sustainable high market share. This is particularly true for products whose up-front costs are very high relative to the variable cost of producing and offering each unit to customers. Many so-called knowledge-based products fall into this category. *Knowledge products* are products that are heavy on know-how (rather than bulk material). For example, the cost of developing a software application can be hundreds of millions of dollars, but the cost of producing and selling each copy to customers is almost zero as the developer can post the software on a website for customers to download. Consequently, giving away software does not cost as much as giving away products with higher variable costs, such as automobiles. As we saw at the beginning of this chapter, when a firm sells a product, the *contribution margin*—the excess of revenues over variable costs—goes to cover fixed costs. When enough units have been sold to cover fixed costs, the contribution margin of any additional units sold accumulates as profit. Thus, when the contribution margin per unit is large, large increases in the number of units sold can result in rapid increases in profits. In this case, giving away a product (setting very low prices) early in the life of the product to secure large sales volumes in later years may be a good strategy.

To understand why and when a firm can price low or give away products and still make money in the long run, consider the following example:[18]

Example

Two firms, A and B, have each developed a proprietary software package in the year 2002 for a market in which only the two of them are competing. Each spends $500 million per year on R&D, marketing, and promotion, with the bulk of it going to R&D.[19] Since the software can be downloaded by customers, let's assume that it costs each firm $5 to sell each copy (for credit card verification and management of the marketing website). Firm A decides to give away its product in the first year (2002) but charge $200 per copy in 2003 and 2004. Firm B charges $200 from the day it introduces the product (in 2002). In 2002, each firm has a 50 percent market share. In 2003, because A charged nothing for its product in 2002, A's market share quickly rises to 80 percent of the unit market, where it remains in subsequent years. Suppose 1 million units are sold in 2002, 10 million in 2003, and 100 million in 2004. Which pricing strategy is better, firm A's or firm B's?

Recall Equation 3.2:

$$\text{Profits} = \text{revenues} - \text{variable costs} - \text{fixed costs}$$
$$= PQ - V_cQ - F_c = (P - V_c)Q - F_c$$

where P is the price per-unit of the product, V_c is the per-unit variable cost, Q is the total number of units sold, and F_c is the up-front or fixed costs. Using this relationship, we find the following:

In 2002:

$$\text{A's profits} = 0 - 500,000,000 = -\$500,000,000$$
$$\text{B's profits} = (200 - 5) \times 500,000 - 500,000,000$$
$$= 97,500,000 - 500,000,000 = -\$402,500,000$$

In 2003:

$$\text{A's profits} = (200 - 5) \times 8,000,000 - 500,000,000$$
$$= 1,560,000,000 - 500,000,000 = \$1,060,000,000$$
$$\text{B's profits} = (200 - 5) \times 2,000,000 - 500,000,000$$
$$= 390,000,000 - 500,000,000 = -\$110,000,000$$

In 2004:

$$\text{A's profits} = (200 - 5) \times 80,000,000 - 500,000,000$$
$$= 15,600,000,000 - 500,000,000 = \$15,100,000,000$$
$$\text{B's profits} = (200 - 5) \times 20,000,000 - 500,000,000$$
$$= 3,900,000,000 - 500,000,000 = \$3,400,000,000$$

The profits, losses, and market shares for each firm over the years are summarized in Table 3.5. In 2002, firm A loses more money ($500 million) than firm B ($402.5 million) largely because A gives away its product while B charges $200 per copy. In 2003, when A's market share rises to

TABLE 3.5   Market Share and Profitability for Knowledge-Based Products

	2002			2003			2004		
	Market Share	Market Share (1,000 units)	Profits (millions)	Market Share	Market Share (1,000 units)	Profits (millions)	Market Share	Market Share (1,000 units)	Profits (millions)
Firm A	50%	500	−$500	80%	8,000	$1,060	80%	80,000	$15,100
Firm B	50	500	−402.5	20	2,000	−110	20	20,000	3,400
Total	100	1,000	−902.5	100	10,000	950	100	100,000	18,500

80 percent and the market grows to 10 million units, A's profits rise to $1.06 billion, more than making up for the losses that it incurred in 2002, when it gave away its product at no charge. Also note that firm A makes a whopping $15.1 billion in 2004 even though its market share in 2003 and 2004 is the same—80 percent. The difference is that it sells 8 million units in 2003 and 80 million in 2004. Interestingly, firm B makes $3.4 billion in 2004 even though it lost $110 million in 2003 and its market share in both years is the same—20 percent. The fact that A makes more money than B even though they both have the same variable and fixed costs suggests that market share matters. The fact that B loses money in 2003 but makes money in 2004 even though its market share in both years is 20 percent suggests that the total number of units sold is the critical element. This is because the higher the number of units sold, the larger the contribution margin that can contribute to recovering fixed costs, with any excess over fixed costs going to profits. If variable costs were high, the contribution margin would not be as high, thus reducing potential profits that accrue from increased unit sales. Note that A could have lowered its prices in 2003 and 2004 and still have made money.

One assumption in this analysis is that there is something about firm A that allows it to maintain its market share over the years. For example, A might have patents or copyrights that exclude competitors from offering an identical product. Microsoft has its huge market share largely because its copyrights prevent competitors from copying its software and competing with the firm. In pharmaceuticals, firms often acquire patents for their products, thereby preventing competitors from making identical copies of their drugs during the life of the patents. Another assumption is that in 2003 and 2004, firm B cannot reduce its price low enough to take market share away from firm A. This would be the case, for example, when a product has very high switching costs or customers are locked into the product. Products that lock in customers usually exhibit the following characteristics:

1. *Using such products requires learning.* When users have learned how to use a product, switching to another means they have to learn how to use the new one. For example, a user who already learned how to use Microsoft's Windows operating system will be reluctant to switch to UNIX because he or she would then have to learn how to use UNIX. For many customers, the required new learning may not be worth the cost savings from a price cut.

2. *The product has complementary products that are not compatible with competing products.* In such a case, switching can mean having to buy new compatible products all over again. In our Windows example, switching to UNIX may mean having to abandon all the Windows application programs that the user has accumulated over the years.

3. *The product exhibits network externalities.* That is, the more users who own the product, the more valuable it is to users. If you and a great many other people already own an IBM-compatible PC, it makes sense to stay with such a PC when you need another computer. If you are a new user, you may want to join this large PC network to gain the benefits of its extensive installed base of machines, stores, and users, which enables you to share information and software with other users.

To summarize, the strategy of giving away one's product (or pricing low) in the early years of a product and raising prices later works best when:

1. *Variable costs are low compared to fixed costs.* Microsoft's operating systems offer a good example. It costs over $1 billion to develop an operating system but costs only a few dollars per copy to enable customers to download it from the Web.

2. *Something about the firm prevents competitors from replicating its product, leapfrogging it, or offering substitutes.* Microsoft's copyrights play a major role in preventing competitors from replicating and selling its software.

3. *Customers find it difficult to switch from the firm's products.* Switching from Microsoft's Windows, for example, may mean having to abandon many applications that one has used over the years and having to learn a new operating system and join a network that is not as large as the Windows network.

In fact, in the early days of the PC software industry, when Microsoft's DOS operating system was still competing with CPM, the company lowered its prices in addition to offering complementary software that could work only on its own operating system and not on CPM.[20]

Everyday Low Prices versus Changing Prices

Firms often must decide whether to set prices and leave them relatively the same for a while or keep changing them through advertising or promotions.[21] In everyday low prices (EDLPs), a firm sets its prices low and keeps them that way for some time.

Pricing to Avoid Confrontation

A firm's objective in pricing its products might be to avoid confrontation with competitors. One way to attain this objective is to construct a benefits-per-dollar map of the firm's products and try to locate the products in the empty spaces. This map is similar to the product benefits map discussed in Chapter 2 except that it adds the price element and depicts benefits *per dollar* rather than benefits.

Bundling and Two-Part-Tariff Pricing

Both bundling and the two-part-tariff technique, which we described earlier, are also pricing strategies. In bundling, a firm decides to sell two or more products as a bundle for one price rather than as individual products each of which has its own price. In a two-part tariff, a firm charges each customer twice, once for each type of customer value, rather than charging a single price per customer.

INFORMATION TECHNOLOGY AND PRICING (BACK TO THE FUTURE)

Recall that in an ideal pricing world for a firm, the firm would set as many prices for one product as there are individual customers, with the price for each customer set at his or her reservation price. That way, each customer pays what he or she is willing to pay, and the firm can capture most of the value that customers perceive in the product. There are two problems with capturing every customer's reservation price. First, it is very difficult to determine reservation prices. Second, customers who are happy paying their reservation prices may change their attitude toward the product if they find out that someone else is paying a lot less than they are for the same product benefits. The advent of information technology raises two questions on this issue: (1) Can information technology be used to solve these two problems and enable firms to better capture customer value? If not, (2) can it help existing pricing schemes, such as menu pricing, to inch toward the ideal of capturing customers' reservation prices?

Impact on Determining and Capturing Reservation Prices

In a way, determining customers' reservation prices is an information problem. It entails finding out which benefits people want in products and how much they are willing to pay for the benefits. Thus, information technology can help firms in their quest to determine customers' reservation prices. For example, the Internet allows firms to track the purchasing habits of customers, and from this information, firms can have a better idea of what a specific customer wants and is willing to pay. This means that, in theory and online at least, firms can more easily practice price discrimination and capture more customer value. The problem is that the same information technology that allows firms to price-discriminate better also allows more customers to communicate with each other and be in a better position to discover that they are paying different prices for the same product benefits. In fact, not only does the Internet provide forums in which consumers can discuss the values they attach to product benefits and the prices they pay, but it also enables customers to know a lot more about firms and their products. For these reasons, the Internet makes it even more difficult to maintain price differences that are not supported by proportionate differences in benefits.

Impact on Pricing Schemes

The pricing scheme on which the Internet promises to have the most impact is auctions. Recall that there are two major disadvantages of auctions in a brick-and-mortar world: (1) Buyers can collude to hold down the price of an item, and sellers can collude to limit the number of items up for bid at any one time, and (2) it is difficult to bring together many sellers and buyers in a brick-and-mortar world. The Internet makes more information available to more people and therefore can reduce instances of collusion. For example, eBay has developed programs that allow buyers and sellers to rate each other, and these ratings are available online to everyone. Such information can help customers avoid colluders, and it can also deter potential colluders from colluding. In addition, by bringing together millions of people, the larger communities of the Internet greatly enhance the likelihood of finding more potential buyers or sellers. At the beginning of 2002, for example, eBay had over 42 million registered users.[22]

Information technology can improve menu pricing by helping firms identify customer preferences so as to segment customers according to the benefits that they value in products. Many retailers have banks of information on customers— the types of products they buy, their buying habits and preferences—information that can be used for such segmentation. Thus, although it may be difficult to charge every customer his or her reservation price, information technology can enable firms to segment customers and charge a fixed price to each segment. Effectively, information technology may not help much with first-degree price discrimination, but it does facilitate third-degree price discrimination. Recall that first-degree price discrimination occurs when a firm charges each customer a different price that does not reflect proportional differences in product benefits or costs, whereas third-degree price discrimination occurs when a firm charges different market segments different prices for the same product.

Information technology can also enhance the ability of firms to track who is buying how much of which products from them, thereby allowing a firm to work with customers to give them price discounts that are proportional to the quantities they buy. In other words, information technology facilitates second-degree price discrimination. Recall that second-degree price discrimination occurs when a firm charges different prices for different quantities of the same product or service.

Summary

A business model that offers customers the right benefits and positions a firm well relative to its customers, suppliers, complementors, rivals, potential new entrants, and substitute products may still not make money if the firm does not price its products well. Customers will buy products that are priced at or below their reservation prices and will not buy when the prices are above their reservation prices. Ideally, a firm would like to charge each customer his or her reservation price. However, in practice, meeting this goal is not easy. For one thing, it is difficult to determine a customer's reservation price. Thus, the prices that firms set may or may not approach reservation prices. In fact, some firms set their prices without paying attention to customers' reservation prices at all. Such firms price their products by, for example, adding a margin to their costs. In rare cases, a firm can determine customers' reservation prices and set its prices accordingly. More often, a firm has to use indirect means to get closer to reservation prices. These include second-degree price discrimination, bundling, and two-part-tariff pricing. Sometimes, prices are used as a means or strategy to reach a larger goal such as becoming a standard. Some common pricing strategies include skimming, pricing to penetrate a market, using price cuts or price increases, changing everyday low prices, and pricing to avoid confrontation. The advent of digital networks such as the Internet promises to have a considerable impact on pricing schemes such as auctions and reverse auctions.

Key Terms

auction pricing, *45*
barter, *44*
bundling, *54*
contribution margin, *46*
contribution margin
  per unit, *46*
cost-based pricing, *47*
cost-plus pricing, *47*
first-degree price
  discrimination, *52*

fixed pricing, *44*
limit-pricing strategy, *59*
markup pricing, *47*
menu pricing, *44*
one-to-one bargaining, *44*
penetration pricing, *60*
predatory pricing, *59*
price discrimination, *52*
price elasticity of
  demand, *57*

pricing strategy, *56*
reservation price, *44*
reverse auction, *45*
second-degree price
  discrimination, *54*
skimming, *60*
third-degree price
  discrimination, *53*
two-part tariff, *55*

Study Questions

1. It has been argued that the Internet will render existing menu pricing schemes obsolete. Do you agree? Why or why not?
2. Is bundling illegal or not?

Endnotes

1. "Pricing Strategy: The Pricing Is Wrong," *The Economist,* May 25, 2002, pp. 59–60.
2. R. Tedlow, *New and Improved: The Story of Mass Marketing in America* (New York: Basic Books, 1990).
3. "The Heyday of the Auction," *The Economist,* July 24, 1999.
4. See A. Cortese, "E-Commerce: Good-Bye to Fixed Pricing?" *Business Week,* May 4, 1998, www.businessweek.com/1998/18/b3576023.htm.
5. See, for example, J. Tirole, *Industrial Organization* (Cambridge, MA: MIT Press, 1988).
6. See similar examples in P. Kotler, *Marketing Management* (Upper Saddle River, NJ: Prentice-Hall, 2002).
7. R. S. Pindyk and D. L. Rubenfeld, *Microeconomics* (Upper Saddle River, NJ: Prentice-Hall, 2000).
8. This example is from Pindyk and Rubenfeld, *Microeconomics.*
9. G. J. Tellis, "Beyond the Many Faces of Price: An Integration of Pricing Strategies," *Journal of Marketing,* October 1986, p. 155.

10. This example is very similar to the one in S. Oster, *Modern Competitive Analysis* (Oxford, England: Oxford University Press, 1999), p. 298.

11. W. Oi, "A Disneyland Dilemma: Two Part Tariffs for Mickey Mouse Monopoly," *Quarterly Journal of Economics,* February 1971, pp. 77–96; Pindyk and Rubenfeld, *Microeconomics.*

12. R. J. Dolan and H. Simon, "Power Pricers," *Across the Board,* May 1997, pp. 18–19.

13. For an outstanding treatment of price elasticity of demand, see Pindyk and Rubenfeld, *Microeconomics.*

14. Oster, *Modern Competitive Analysis.*

15. J. Bain, *Barriers to New Competition* (Cambridge, MA: Harvard University Press, 1956).

16. For a brief and to-the-point discussion of legal issues in pricing, see Oster, *Modern Competitive Analysis.*

17. T. T. Nagle and R. K. Hodlen, *The Strategy and Tactics of Pricing: A Guide to Profitable Decision Making,* 2d ed. (Englewood Cliffs, NJ: Prentice-Hall, 1995).

18. This example is similar to one from A. N. Afuah and C. L. Tucci, *Internet Business Models and Strategies: Text and Cases* (New York: McGraw-Hill, 2003).

19. For a related example, see A. James, "Give It Away and Get Rich," *Fortune,* June 10, 1996, pp. 90–98.

20. H. Goldblatt, "How We Did It: Paul Allen and Bill Gates," *Fortune,* Oct. 2, 1995.

21. G. Ortmeyer, J. Quelch, and W. Salmon, "Restoring Credibility to Retail Pricing," *Sloan Management Review* 33 (1991).

22. eBay's 2001 financial statement, published in 2002.

Chapter **Four**

Sources of Revenues and Market Targets

In Chapter 2, we said that for customers to keep buying from a firm rather than from its competitors, the firm must offer them better customer value than competitors do. An important question is, Which customers would want the value that a firm creates, and how much of it would the customers want? Not every customer wants the same benefits that other customers want in a product, nor can everyone afford to pay for these benefits. For example, not everyone wants to own a BMW or can afford one. Moreover, each customer who wants a BMW may want features that are very different from what other BMW customers want. Thus, an important part of a business model is targeting the right customers with the right value. That is, in creating and offering value to customers, it is important for a firm to decide which customers or groups of customers it wants to serve and how much of each one's needs it wants to serve. Also, many market targets have more than one source of revenue, some of which may be more profitable than others. For example, car dealers receive revenues from selling cars and from servicing cars, but the latter is often more profitable than the former. In this chapter, we explore both the sources of revenues that are available to firms and the different market targets in which firms can position themselves.

SOURCES OF REVENUES

Recall that the goal of a business model is to make money. Since profits are the difference between revenues and the costs of generating the revenues, an important part of a firm's formulation and execution of a business model is understanding the sources of revenues in the market in which the firm is competing. This is important for two reasons. First, by understanding its market's sources of revenues, especially the profitability of each source, a firm can make better choices about which activities to perform, how to perform them, and when to perform them so as to increase its chances of being profitable. For example, consider the online brokerage industry, which has three primary sources of revenues. The first source is the commissions that an online brokerage firm can charge for the stock trades it executes for its customers. The second source is the interest that it charges customers who want to borrow money (usually from the cash deposited with the broker by other customers) to pay for any securities that they buy on margin. The third source is the spread from the bid and ask prices of stocks. The profit margins for the first and third sources are very thin. Thus an online brokerage firm may decide to pursue rich clients who are more likely to deposit or borrow large amounts of cash, since this allows the firm to take advantage of the more profitable source of revenues, interest charges. With many such clients, a firm may decide not to charge any commissions at all for trades.

The second reason that it is important for a firm to understand its sources of revenues is that doing so puts the firm in a better position to understand the threats a technological change can pose to it. This is best illustrated with the example of a local newspaper versus the Internet. A local newspaper earns revenues from selling papers and from publishing the classified ads. With the Internet, an auction house such as eBay can use its auction capabilities to offer classifieds, without bundling them with news. A traditional competitive analysis that looks only for potential new entrants into the newspaper business is likely to miss the threat posed by a firm that attacks only one source of newspaper revenues. This can be especially bad for newspapers whose classifieds are their most profitable source of revenues. By understanding its sources of revenues well, a newspaper would be more aware of the threat that a firm such as eBay poses when it moves into regional markets.

In general, it is important to understand the choices of revenue sources that are possible in a market, how revenues can be generated at each source, and the profitability of each source to a firm. In other words, what is it about a firm and a source of revenues that will allow the firm to profit from the source better than competitors can?

Taxonomy of Revenue Sources and Revenue Models

Although it is common to think of a firm's revenues as coming from the sale of products or services, such sales are not the only source of revenues that a firm can profitably pursue in formulating and executing its business model. There are at least six primary sources of revenues that firms usually pursue in their business models: direct product sales; after-sales service; indirect content sales; product financing; collect-early, pay-later financing; and royalties on intellectual property. To generate revenues at each of these sources, a firm usually chooses from a number of revenue models. A **revenue model** is a framework for generating revenues. It is the choice of which revenue source to pursue, what value to offer, how to price the value, and who pays for the value. Table 4.1 presents the different sources of revenues and the associated revenue models.

Direct Product Sales

Many firms earn revenues from the **direct product or service sales** that they have created or to which they have added value of some kind. Customers pay for the value that they perceive in the product or service. The type of revenue model that

TABLE 4.1 Sources of Revenues and Associated Revenue Models

Source of Revenues	Revenue Model					
	Advertising	Commission	Fee-for-Service	Markup	Production	Subscription
Direct product or service sales		√	√	√	√	√
After-sales service			√			√
Indirect content sales	√					
Product financing		√	√			
Collect-early, pay-later financing		√				
Royalties on intellectual property		√	√			√

is available to a firm depends on the activities the firm performs to add value to the product or service. If a firm creates a product or service, it can pursue a production, subscription, fee-for-service, markup, or commission revenue model:[1]

- In a **production model,** the firm that creates the product or service sells it to a customer who values it and pays for it. This is the most common model. For example, an automaker makes cars and sells them to customers who pay for them and take them home.

- In a **subscription model,** a customer pays a flat fee for the right to use the product for a period of time. Whether the customer uses the product or not, he or she still pays the flat fee. Newspaper and magazine subscriptions fall into this category, as do flat-rate phone services. Leasing a computer, copier, or building for a flat fee is also an example of a subscription revenue model.

- In a **fee-for-service model,** customers pay only for the service that they use. In contrast to the subscription model, there is no flat fee involved. For example, some phone companies and Internet service providers (ISPs) charge their customers only for the time that they spend on their phones or online. If a firm does not create a product or service but, rather, acts as an intermediary or mediator between the creator and customer, the firm can use a markup or commission revenue model.

- In a **markup model,** a firm buys a product or service, marks up its price, and resells it to customers. This model characterizes wholesalers and retailers, who buy products from manufacturers, mark up their prices, and resell them to end customers.

- In a **commission model,** a firm charges a fee for a transaction that it mediates between two parties. This model is used, for example, by stock brokerage firms that charge customers a commission for selling stocks to those customers and by auction companies such as eBay that collect commissions on the sales that clients make in online auctions.

After-Sales Service

Selling a product is not the only way to make money from the product. Most complex products require **after-sales service,** and therefore a firm can generate revenues from providing such service. In some cases, after-sales service is more profitable than product sales. For example, GE makes more money from servicing jet engines than from selling them, and United Technologies makes more money from servicing elevators than from selling them. Firms that perform after-sales service can pursue either a fee-for-service or a subscription revenue model. Customers can pay for the service that they actually use or pay a flat fee that entitles them to some amount of service whether they use it or not.

Indirect Content Sales

Customers who watch TV, listen to radio, or read magazines or newspapers in the United States usually do not pay for most of the content that they value. Advertisers pay for most of the content (programming or news) in exchange for the right to have their ads or classifieds shown to the TV or newspaper audience. We will refer to this source of revenues, in which customers do not directly pay for the customer value, as indirect content sales. The primary revenue model in this case is the **advertising model.**

Product Financing

In addition to making money by selling a product or providing after-sales service for it, a firm can make money in financing the product. Some of the most profitable divisions of large firms are the ones that offer financing to customers who buy the firms' products. For example, in 2002 it was estimated that GE Capital was responsible for more than 42 percent of GE's total earnings even though it is known for its jet engines, plastics, gas turbines, and so on.[2] The revenues received in **product financing** are the interest charges and other fees collected by the company and can therefore be seen as elements of the commission revenue model. Since a customer who borrows money can end the interest payments whenever he or she decides to pay back the loan, the interest can also be seen as a fee for service.

Collect-Early, Pay-Late

When a firm buys a product, the terms of payment are usually such that the firm has 30 days to pay for the product. If a firm's operations and positioning relative to customers, suppliers, rivals, potential new entrants, and substitute products permit it, the firm can collect payments from its customers well before it has to pay its suppliers. While waiting to pay its suppliers, the firm can invest the money it has collected in other money-making opportunities. Effectively, **collect-early, pay-later** is a source of revenues. Dell Computers earns money this way through its Dell-Direct model. When a customer orders a Dell computer online, the customer usually pays for the computer at that time. Dell collects the cash almost immediately but does not pay for the components that it uses to assemble the customer's computer until some time later.

Royalties on Intellectual Property

When firms conduct research and development (R&D), they sometimes invent or discover items or processes for which they obtain patents or copyrights. Rather than commercialize an invention or discovery by turning it into a product, a firm (licenser) may decide to license other firms (licensees) to use the knowledge embodied in the patent or copyright. Licensees pay the licenser a fee for the right to use its intellectual property to create products. The licenser can charge a fixed up-front fee, a per-unit fee for every unit of product that a licensee sells, or both an up-front fee and a per-unit charge. Between 1987 and 1994, for example, Texas Instruments collected over $1.9 billion in such **royalties,** while its combined earnings from operations over that period were only $1.3. A major part of Qualcomm's profits are the royalties it collects from licensees that utilize its intellectual properties, such as its code-division multiple access (CDMA) technology.

Combinations

Although we have described each of the revenue sources separately, firms often use them in combination. Many firms that make money from product sales also make money from after-sales service. Texas Instruments sells many products stemming from some of the same intellectual properties that it licenses to licensees. So does Qualcomm.

Profitability of a Source of Revenues

Recall that the goal of a business model is to make money and that a firm's profitability depends on both industry factors (competitive forces, cooperative forces, and the macro environment) and firm-specific factors. Thus, one can explore the profitability of a source of revenues for a firm by analyzing industry factors—the attractiveness of the source—and the specific factors that would allow the firm to profit from the source.

Industry Factors: Attractiveness of a Revenue Source

There are two main steps in exploring the attractiveness of a source of revenues. The first is to establish the viability of the source as a revenue generator.[3] That is, it must be determined whether the revenue source comprises or will comprise enough customers who want and can afford the value that is being offered. Once a market has been established, the next step is to explore the competitive forces that act on the firms that are competing for revenue at the source of revenues. That is, the second step is to perform an analysis of the six competitive forces to determine whether the source is, on the average, profitable.

Firm-Specific Factors

Recall that a firm makes more money than its rivals if (1) the firm offers products or services at a lower cost than its rivals do or offers differentiated products at premium prices that more than compensate for the extra cost of differentiation[4] and (2) the firm is well positioned vis-à-vis its suppliers, customers, rivals, complementors, substitutes, and potential new entrants to appropriate the value it creates. There are two ways by which a firm can achieve both (1) and (2). First, a firm that performs a difficult-to-imitate system of activities that allows it to offer customers in the segment superior value that competitors cannot match is able to better position itself at the source of revenue vis-à-vis its competitive forces.[5] We will explore this in more detail in Chapter 5. Second, a firm that has valuable, rare, difficult-to-imitate, nonsubstitutable resources can also offer superior value to customers and position itself well within the segment in relation to its competitive forces. We will pursue this in more detail in Chapter 6.

EVALUATING REVENUE SOURCES AND REVENUE MODELS

If a firm earns revenues from more than one source, it often needs to evaluate the different sources and its performance at each in order to plan the next steps in its business model. Two popular frameworks that were developed for use in business portfolio analysis—the Growth-Share matrix and the GE/McKinsey matrix—can be used to analyze different sources of revenues.

Growth-Share Matrix

A firm that has more than one business has important considerations: Which businesses should it promote and which ones should it eliminate; how should it allocate resources to the different businesses; and how should it set performance targets and strategy for each business? Answering these questions starts with an assessment of how well each business is performing in its own market relative to its competitors and to the firm's other businesses. The **Growth-Share matrix** was developed by the Boston Consulting Group (BCG) as a framework for answering some of these questions.[6] In this matrix, the businesses are displayed in a two-by-two arrangement such as that shown in Figure 4.1, which analyzes four businesses. The gray circles show the positions of the businesses in 2003, while the blank circles show where the same businesses were in 2002. The area of each circle is proportional to the revenues earned by the business. Thus, in 2003, business 2 had the most revenues, and business 4 had the least revenues. The horizontal

FIGURE 4.1
The Growth-Share Matrix

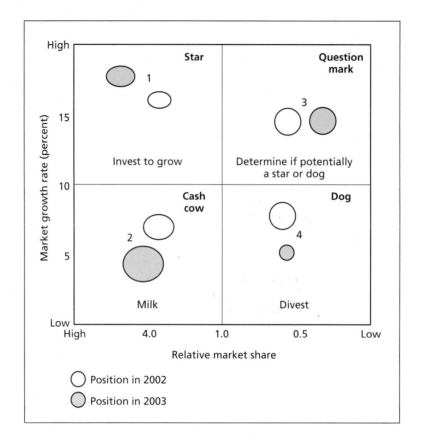

axis of the matrix depicts **relative market share,** which is a business's market share relative to that of the largest competitor in the market in which the business competes. Thus a relative market share of 0.5, such as the one that business 3 had in 2002, means that the business has 50 percent of the market share of the largest competitor in the market. A business with a relative market share of 4.0, such as that of business 2, has four times the market share of the closest competitor and is clearly the leader in the market. Since the vertical dividing line crosses the horizontal axis at 1.0, businesses that are located to the left of this line are market leaders while those to the right of the line are not. The vertical axis of the matrix depicts **market growth rate,** which is the rate at which the market is growing, adjusted for inflation. It is assumed that high-growth markets typically grow at a rate of 10 percent or higher, and therefore the horizontal dividing line crosses the vertical axis at 10 percent, with high-growth businesses above the line and low-growth businesses below. Since a firm's profitability depends on both industry and firm-specific factors, market growth rate reflects industry factors while relative market share reflects firm-specific factors.

Stars, Question Marks, Cash Cows, and Dogs

The matrix is divided into four quadrants: stars, question marks, cash cows, and dogs. *Cash cows,* located in the lower left-hand corner, have large market shares in markets with low growth rates and generate large amounts of cash. A firm's strategy for a cash cow is to "milk" the cow by investing some of the cash it generates in stars that need cash. *Stars,* located in the upper left-hand quadrant, are businesses with leading market shares in high-growth markets. Such a business often must invest heavily to maintain its leadership position in the growing market and therefore is not likely to have a positive cash flow. The strategy pursued here is to invest in the star and develop it into a future cash cow. *Dogs* are businesses with low market shares in low-growth markets. They generate little or no cash and have little potential for future growth. The strategy is to divest such businesses and focus attention on more viable businesses. *Question marks,* located in the upper right-hand corner, are in high-growth markets but have low market shares relative to the leader in the market. They are called question marks because it is not clear whether they will become stars or dogs. Such a business typically involves a new product with the potential for high sales volume, but it may need cash to gain enough market share to become a leader in the market and, thereby, a star for the firm. The strategy is to take a deep look at the question marks and determine whether they will become stars or dogs and then to place one's bets accordingly. The question mark in Figure 4.1, business 3, gained market share relative to its largest competitor between 2002 and 2003.

Strengths and Weaknesses of the Framework

Like any model, the Growth-Share matrix has both strengths and weaknesses that must be carefully considered by any firm that wants to use it as an analysis tool. The model has two main strengths. First, it can be used to analyze not only multiple businesses but also a single business's performance in different countries or regions; different products, technologies, or brands; major customers; revenue models; and sources of revenues. Second, the analysis uses only two simple but important variables that are easy to understand and that allow data on different businesses to be displayed in a format that managers can quickly comprehend. Because of these advantages, this framework has been used widely.

However, it is important for users of the model to understand its weaknesses. First, using only two variables to summarize a firm's performance may be an oversimplification. It is worthwhile exploring other variables. Second, the model assumes that an industry that is not growing today will not grow tomorrow. What we know about innovation suggests that a technological discontinuity can revive an industry, drastically increasing growth rates. Third, deciding to divest a business just because it is a dog may be discounting the effect of any synergies that may exist between the dog and stars or cash cows—synergies that may have allowed these other businesses to perform as well as they have. Fourth, labeling a business group as a dog or cow may not be a good idea. Who wants to be called a dog or cow?

GE/McKinsey Matrix

In the **GE/McKinsey matrix,** developed by General Electric and McKinsey and Company, the vertical dimension is *industry attractiveness,* and the horizontal dimension is *business strength or competitive position* (Figure 4.2).[7] Industry attractiveness is measured by a combination of several variables: market size and growth rate, intensity of competition, cyclicities, macro-environmental factors, barriers to entry and exit, industry profit margins, seasonality, technological and capital requirements, and emerging opportunities and threats. Business strength or competitive position is measured by a combination of relative market share, profit margins relative to competitors, relative cost position, technological capability, possession of desirable distinctive capabilities, ability to match or beat rivals on product quality and service, knowledge of customers and markets, and caliber of management.

FIGURE 4.2
The GE/McKinsey
Matrix

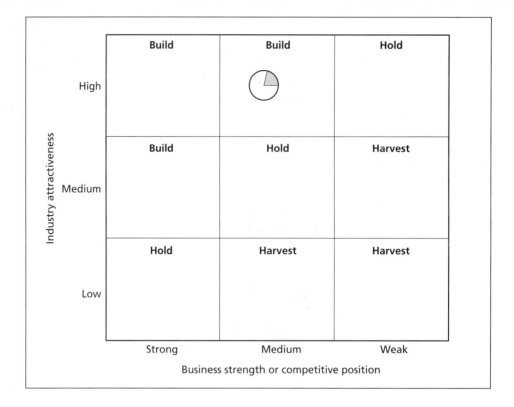

The size of each circle represents the size of the market for the business in question, while the shaded part of the circle represents the business's share in the market. (This contrasts with the Growth-Share matrix, where the size of the circle represents the size of the company's business.) The three-by-three matrix results in nine cells. Businesses that fall into the quadrant where industry attractiveness is high and the firm's business strength or competitive position is strong are very profitable businesses, and a firm ought to invest in them and take other strategic steps to build them. The firm should also invest in and build those businesses that are in industries whose attractiveness is medium and where the firm's business strength or competitive position is strong and those that are in industries whose attractiveness is high and where the firm's business strength or competitive position is medium. Businesses in industries whose attractiveness is low or medium and where a firm's business strength or competitive position is weak ought to be divested or harvested in some other way. So should businesses in industries whose attractiveness is low and where a firm's business strength or competitive position is average. The businesses that fall into the other quadrants should be held and different strategies explored to make them more profitable.

The GE/McKinsey Matrix has the same strengths and weaknesses as the BCG Growth-Share matrix except that by using a combination of variables to measure industry attractiveness and business strength or competitive position, the GE/McKinsey matrix more closely reflects the industry and firm-specific factors that underpin a firm's profitability. In doing so, however, the GE/McKinsey matrix is not as simple and elegant as the Growth-Share matrix.

Relationship between Business Model and Revenue Model

Recall that a business model is a framework for making a profit. As defined above, a revenue model is a framework for generating revenue. Thus the primary difference between the two has to do with cost. However, it is not unusual to hear managers and scholars alike refer to a revenue model as a business model.

TARGETING CUSTOMERS

In offering value to customers, a firm faces two important choices. First, it usually must decide which customers, in the market that it serves, it should target. It can target the entire market as if all customers had the same needs, target individual customers one to one, or target market segments. Both the way a firm identifies customers' needs and preferences and the approach the firm uses to create and deliver customer value depend on the customer targets that the firm chooses (Table 4.2). Second, a firm must usually also decide how much of the needs of its target market it wants to satisfy. Which one of these targets and how much of its needs a firm can profitably serve are a function of the firm's distinctive activities or resources.

Mass Market

Rather than create and deliver products that have the features customers *have ordered,* firms that target mass markets produce what they believe customers will want and then engage in mass marketing that is aimed at making customers perceive the products as items they want. Producing goods that are targeted not at any customer or group of customers in particular but, rather, at all customers with the hope that some customers may like them is sometimes referred to as **mass production** (see Table 4.2). The **mass marketing** that usually accompanies mass production to influence customers' perception of and preference for the product is also referred to as **one-to-all marketing.** (The "one" in this phrase refers to the fact that one company is doing the marketing, and the "all" refers to customers.) The automobile industry in the United States offers a good example of mass production and mass marketing. U.S. automakers usually build quantities of cars with the features that they believe customers want and then ship the vehicles to distributors all over the country and hope that the cars will sell at the suggested retail prices. When cars do not sell at the expected prices and locations, automakers resort to costly measures such as offering rebates or low-interest financing, redistributing cars to locations where they have a better chance of being sold, or holding on to finished-goods inventory longer.

TABLE 4.2
Targeting Different Customers

	Customer Target		
Activities of Firm	**Mass Market**	**Market Segment**	**Individuals**
Needs and preferences identification	One-to-all marketing	One-to-segment marketing	One-to-one marketing
Value creation and delivery approach	Mass production	Mass production Mass customization	Customization Mass customization

The mass-production and mass-marketing combination is sometimes referred to as **supply push** or **technology push** since a firm produces a product, sometimes using a new technology, and then tries to push it on customers through marketing. The supply- or technology-push approach is not limited to firms that produce for consumers; it is also practiced in business-to-business transactions. Microprocessor makers such as Intel produce faster and more functional generations of processors and work with makers of personal computers and video games to convince them that they need to offer new PCs and video game consoles that will run on the improved processors.

If a firm happens to produce what many customers want or convinces many of them that they want what it is mass producing, targeting a mass market can allow a firm to capture a larger market share than it could by targeting individuals or market segments. In turn, the large market share can result in economies of scale that lead to lower cost.

Individual Customers

Since individuals' needs, preferences, purchasing power, and buying habits differ, one can expect that the benefits individuals prefer in a product will also differ from person to person. Thus, the best way to offer superior value to some customers is to target each of them individually. When a firm targets individual customers, it treats each consumer as if he or she were its entire market, and it discovers each one's individual needs and preferences through **one-to-one marketing.**[8] After understanding what its customer wants, the firm can use customization or mass customization to offer the customer that product (see Table 4.2). In **customization,** a firm uses the information obtained from a customer about his or her needs and preferences to create and deliver the product that the customer wants. In **mass customization,** a firm also creates and delivers the product that a customer wants but it does so cost-effectively.[9]

Customization was around long before mass production. In earlier times, if a person wanted a suit or shirt or pair of pants, he or she went to a tailor who took the person's measurements and made a suit or shirt or pair of pants to fit the individual's body the way he or she wanted it to fit. Today, most clothing is mass produced and mass marketed. However, customization never went away—it has just been too expensive for most people. Those consumers who can afford it have always been able to have their clothes, houses, cars, jewelry, and so on custom-made. With the increasing proliferation of technologies such as the Internet, however, mass customization is becoming possible—that is, firms can more cost-effectively produce what each customer has asked for and thus meet each one's individual needs. For example, through the Lands' End online system, customers can input the information that the company needs to make jeans that can fit the many customers that mass-produced jeans cannot fit.[10] Customers pay more for the custom jeans but probably not as much as they would pay if they had to find their own tailors to custom make the jeans. Levi's also mass customizes jeans, and Nike also mass customizes sneakers. Some automobile companies have plans for offering made-to-order cars.

A customization approach, in which a firm finds out what customers want and then produces a product that meets the customers' needs, is sometimes referred to as a **demand-pull** approach (as opposed to *supply push,* in which a firm mass produces products and then pushes them on customers through marketing).

While technological change is making one-to-one marketing and mass customization more feasible for many products, these approaches may not be practical for all products. It is still very costly to determine, create, and offer what each individual customer wants in many products. For example, imagine a company that has to offer a soft drink to a population that has not had soft drinks before. The amount of sugar that each individual wants in his or her drink is likely to vary from person to person. So are the amount of caffeine, the texture of the drink, the temperature at which each customer prefers to drink it, the type of container that the drink comes in, the labeling on the container, the colors on the container, and so on. Finding out exactly what each individual wants and delivering it to him or her are likely to be very expensive. Where one-to-one marketing and mass customization are feasible, however, firms that move first can gain some advantages through the one-to-one interactions. For example, a customer who has provided a firm with personal information and helped teach the firm about himself or herself may not want to go through the process again with a competitor that the person hardly knows. Likewise, a customer may be reluctant to move personal and financial histories from one financial institution to another.

Our discussion so far has focused on consumers. In business-to-business commerce, businesses often have to target each of the businesses that they serve on a one-to-one basis. In the microchip business, for example, many of the chips offered by companies such as Xilinx, LSI Logic, and Altera are so-called semi-custom chips that are produced using mass customization in which both the customer and the firm work together to customize the chip for the customer.

Market Segments

Rather than target a single mass market or many markets of "one," firms sometimes divide the markets that they serve into groups in such a way that customers within each group have homogeneous needs and each group has little or no overlap with other groups. Each of these groups is called a **market segment.** When a firm targets a market segment, it usually pursues **one-to-segment marketing,** in which its efforts are directed toward identifying the needs and preferences of the customers within the segment (see Table 4.2). The approaches for creating and delivering value to a market segment vary from mass production to mass customization. Many firms mass produce their products and then use one-to-segment marketing techniques to try to convince customers that they need the products. For example, a beer manufacturer might target an ethnic group with advertising that convinces the group members that the beer is for them, but it might deliver the same beer that it mass produces for everyone else to this ethnic group. Sometimes, the product is modified for a market segment. For example, a car earmarked for the luxury-car segment is created and designed to have luxury features. Other firms use mass customization to address the market segments that they target. For example, a maker of jeans that targets teenagers might use the Internet to let teenagers have their jeans custom-made for them. Market segmentation depends on whether the target is businesses or consumers.

Business Segments

Businesses can be segmented as a function of the benefits that customers in the industry want in the products, the time that customers want the benefits, the industry demographics of customers, customer size, and customers' geographic locations.[11]

Benefits A firm can segment its business customers as a function of their needs. To the extent that the customers in a market the firm targets offer their own customers different value and have different strategies, their needs are likely to be different. Since being successful in a market requires offering better value than competitors, the firm may want to segment its market by need so that it can better focus on meeting the specific needs of each segment, thereby improving its chances of offering superior customer value. For example, aircraft manufacturers, aluminum-can manufacturers, automobile makers, chip makers, home appliance makers, and commercial builders all need aluminum of different qualities and quantities since their outputs are so different. The aluminum that chip makers use is of much higher purity than that used by the building and construction industries, while the quantities required by aircraft manufacturers are much larger than those needed by chip makers. Thus, a maker of aluminum may want to segment its market by need and create separate market segments for aircraft manufacturers, aluminum-can manufacturers, automobile makers, chip makers, home appliance makers, and commercial builders.

Timing of Needs When firms introduce new products, some of their customers are often lead users. **Lead users** are customers whose needs are similar to those of other customers except that they have these needs months or years before other customers and stand to benefit significantly by fulfilling these needs earlier than the other customers.[12] For example, in the microchip industry, the firms that need to be the first to produce smaller and faster chips often need essential equipment earlier than the bulk of the industry so that they can develop the chips sooner. A firm that markets to such industries may be better off targeting lead users as a separate market segment.

Industry By understanding how customers use its products in their own products, a firm can better provide the benefits those customers want in its products. For example, a maker of microprocessors that understands and interacts with computer makers is in a better position to understand what computer makers want in a microprocessor than a chip maker that does not. Thus, a firm selling products that can be used in more than one industry may want to segment its market by industry. For example, a type of microchip called a programmable logic array (PLA) is used in video games, PCs, servers, automobiles, machine tools and other industrial control equipment, telecommunications switches, airplanes, and so on. Customers in these industries often need some hand-holding, especially when they are introduced to PLAs for the first time. Thus PLA makers such as Xilinx target each industry as a separate market.

Customer Size Sizable customers that buy large quantities of a product usually have bargaining power. Firms usually assign an account manager or a program office to each large customer to ensure that the customer's needs are identified and met. Some firms may decide not to serve large customers at all but to pursue smaller ones instead.

Geography For two reasons, geography matters and can therefore be the basis for market segmentation. First, business practices, cultures, factor conditions, concentration of industries, government policies, fiscal and monetary policies, and judicial and legal systems often vary from country to country or region to region. Second, a firm's value-creating activities cannot always be profitably located close to all the customers that it serves. Thus, a firm can segment the business customers that it serves by region made up of more than one country, by country, or by region within each country.

Consumer Segments

If a firm's customers are consumers, the market segments that it targets are a function of demographics, psychographics, behavior of customers, and geography.

Demographics Firms often segment customers on the basis of **demographics:** age, family size, gender, income, occupation, education, race, nationality, and social class. In the United States, for example, firms used to target so-called baby boomers (those born between 1946 and 1964), but recently attention has shifted toward generation X. An underlying assumption in segmenting by demographic groups is that customers' needs, wants, and preferences are largely determined by their demographic group. One reason for the popularity of demographics as a basis for market segmentation is the availability of data that can be used for market research. The census data that are collected in the United States provide a vast amount of relatively inexpensive information.

Psychographics Customers can also be segmented on the basis of **psychographics:** lifestyles, personalities, and values. Thus, rather than assuming that just because people belong to one race they will all like a certain product, the psychographic view argues that customers' needs are more likely to depend on individuals' values, lifestyles, or personalities. People with the same lifestyle are more likely to buy the kinds of products that support that lifestyle. For example, people who like health foods may want to cook for themselves and may also like goods that have something to do with being physically active. A lifestyle may also be reflective of some underlying characteristics of the people with that lifestyle. For example, people who exercise regularly may do so because they are concerned about looking good. Such people may thus be interested in fashionable clothes, furniture, and shoes and in certain types of food, books, and so on.

Behavior One of the more popular ways of segmenting consumers to target with a product is to use behavioral variables such as the occasions on which the product is used, the benefits in the product, the user's status, usage rate, the extent to which users are loyal to the product, and the user's attitude toward the product.[13]

Geography Given the extent to which incomes, cultures, and government policies can vary from country to country and from region to region within a country, one can expect preferences to also vary from one such location to another. Moreover, some transactions are best carried out locally. Consider a consumer-to-consumer business such as online auctions: While many items can be cost-effectively shipped across the country, many others cannot. For example, not only are cars difficult to transport, but their value is better determined in person by, well, kicking the tires. An online auction house may thus be better off segmenting the market for auctioning products such as cars by region.

Multidimensional Segmentation Rather than use one criteria such as psychographics, demographics, or geography to segment a market, a firm can use two or more criteria. Figure 4.3 presents a segmentation approach that combines both geography and psychographics. Thus instead of trying to segment the entire U.S. market by values, lifestyles, or personalities, a firm can segment each region of the market by these three psychographic groups. Such an approach may show that even a so-called athletic lifestyle varies from region to region. Moreover, the type of athletic wear that someone in California might need is likely to be different from the type that someone in the eastern United States would need. What is considered a core value might also differ from region to region. The primary advantage of multidimensional segmentation is that it is one step closer to individual marketing. A segmentation approach that considered only psychographic information without geographic information would miss out on satisfying the needs of some regions.

FIGURE 4.3
Multidimensional
Segmentation

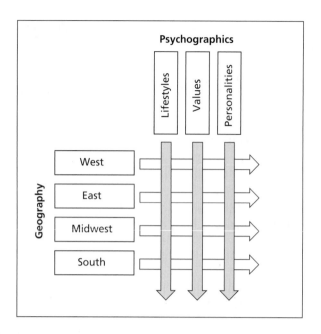

Mapping Value into Targeted Markets

In creating and offering value to a targeted market—whether individuals, mass market, or market segment—an important question for a firm is, How much of the targeted customers' needs should the firm position itself to meet? A firm can position itself to meet only a subset of the needs of a mass market rather than trying to meet all the needs of a segment of the market. For example, in the consulting industry, a firm may decide to pursue only strategy consulting for any customer that needs consulting services. Michael Porter calls this **variety-based positioning.**[14] In what Porter calls **needs-based positioning,** a firm positions itself to supply all the needs of a segment of the market. For example, another consulting firm may decide to provide not only strategy services but also operational efficiency consulting.

Evolution of Targets

For three reasons, customer preferences can change. First, customers often need to learn how to use a product when it is first introduced. As the product evolves, the features that customers need in it may also change. The PC is a good example. When it was first introduced, most users did not understand how it worked and therefore needed some hand-holding. Thus, firms such as Apple Computers offered complete systems: computer hardware and software and, sometimes, printers. Over the years, however, many customers understood more about computers. Consumers now know more about computer software and hardware. Some businesses have management information system (MIS) departments that are very knowledgeable about computers and therefore do not need any hand-holding from PC makers. Thus, many customers today may prefer not to buy complete solutions from one company but, rather, to buy components from different companies. Second, different customers who have different tastes may enter a market segment. For example, many Americans who graduate from college today are so used to the Internet that they may prefer to make many more purchases online than their parents do. Third, a technological change can drastically raise customers' expectations about firms' products and services, thereby altering their preferences. For example, as a result of the Internet, many customers expect that when they buy an airline ticket online, the process will take only a few minutes and they will be able to print out the ticket immediately and make hotel and rental-car reservations at the same time.

Selecting Customer Targets

Recall that the goal of a business model is to make money and that a firm makes profits if (1) it offers products or services at a lower cost than its competitors do or offers differentiated products at premium prices that more than compensate for the extra cost of differentiation[15] and (2) there are enough customers that want the product and can afford it. Thus, before moving into a market segment or focusing on a source of revenues, firms may find it worthwhile to explore the following characteristics of potential targets.

Market Size

The first question for a firm to ask is whether there are enough customers in the segment to allow the firm to generate the revenues it needs to be profitable. There may be people who want to fly the Concorde from Paris to New York, cutting their flight time by almost half, but that does not mean that there are enough of them to make the Concorde a profitable venture. If there are not enough customers, is there something the firm can do to increase the market size? Good market research can estimate the size of the market.

Affordability

If there are enough people in the market segment, the next question is whether they can afford the product that the firm wants to offer. There may be half a billion people in a country, but that does not mean that there is a large market there for all products. Again, good market research can estimate how many people in the segment can afford the firm's product.

Attractiveness of Target

Even if a market segment is large and has people that can afford the firm's product, that does not necessarily make it an attractive market segment. Therefore, it is important to analyze the competitive forces that suppliers, rivals, customers, substitute products, complementors, and potential new entrants exert on the segment.

Firm-Specific Factors

It is also important to make sure that the firm has the system of activities and resources to profit from the target.

Summary

A business model is about making money. A key component of making money is generating revenues, and a firm's framework for generating revenues is its revenue model. By understanding the sources of revenues that are available to it in the market that it serves, a firm can better target the customers in that market and better formulate its revenue model. Sources of revenues include direct product or service sales; after-sales service; indirect content sales; product financing; collect-early, pay-later financing; and royalties on intellectual properties. The revenue models that can be used to generate revenues at these sources include advertising, commission, fee for service, markup, production, and subscription. A firm can evaluate how well it is doing in generating revenues from its sources or through its revenue model by using the BCG Growth-Share matrix or the GE/McKinsey matrix. In using either one, however, it is important to pay attention to its shortcomings.

An important part of a revenue model is targeting the right customers with the right value. A firm can target either the mass market, segments within the market, or individuals as if each one were the entire market. Depending on the target that a firm chooses, it can (1) use one-to-all, one-to-segment, or one-to-one marketing to identify the needs and preferences of the target and (2) use mass production, mass customization, or customization to create and deliver value to the target. Business customers can be segmented on the basis of the benefits that customers want, the time that they need the benefits, industry demographics, customer size, and customers' location. Consumers can be segmented on the basis of demographics, psychographics, geography, and behavior. Which customers a firm chooses to target is a function of the market size, the extent to which the customers can afford the value that the firm offers, and the attractiveness of the target. Even an unattractive target can be profitable if the firm has a target-specific system of activities and/or target-specific distinctive resources and capabilities.

Key Terms

advertising model, *69*
after-sales service (revenue source), *69*
collect-early, pay-later (revenue source), *70*
commission model, *69*
customization, *76*
demand-pull, *76*
demographics, *79*
direct product or service sales (revenue source), *68*
fee-for-service model, *69*
GE/McKinsey matrix, *73*

Growth-Share matrix, *71*
lead users, *78*
market growth rate, *72*
market segment, *77*
markup model, *69*
mass customization, *76*
mass marketing, *75*
mass production, *75*
needs-based positioning, *80*
one-to-all marketing, *75*
one-to-one marketing, *76*
one-to-segment marketing, *77*

product financing (revenue source), *70*
production model, *69*
psychographics, *79*
relative market share, *72*
revenue model, *68*
royalties (revenue source), *70*
subscription model, *69*
supply push, *76*
technology push, *76*
variety-based positioning, *80*

Study Questions

1. What is the difference between customization and mass customization? What kinds of strategy are appropriate for each?

2. Choose an industry that you like. What are the major sources of revenue and market segments in the industry?

3. Which tool would you rather use for evaluating the different revenue sources or market segments of question 2: the BCG's Growth/Share matrix or the GE/McKinsey matrix? Why?

Endnotes

1. For more on revenue models, especially in an Internet context, see A. N. Afuah and C. L. Tucci, *Internet Business Models and Strategies: Text and Cases* (New York: McGraw-Hill/Irwin, 2003), chap. 6.

2. C. C. Williams, "GE Capital Still Expects Earnings to Climb 18% to 21% This Year," *Wall Street Journal,* May 15, 2002.

3. E. R. Biggadike, "The Contributions of Marketing to Strategic Management," *Academy of Management Review* 6 (1981), pp. 621–632.

4. M. E. Porter, "Towards a Dynamic Theory of Strategy," *Strategic Management Journal* 12 (1991), pp. 95–117.

5. Biggadike, "The Contributions of Marketing to Strategic Management."

6. Hax, "Strategic Planning."

7. Ibid.

8. Although I use "he or she" here, customers can be other firms.

9. B. J. Pine II, *Mass Customization* (Boston: Harvard Business School Press, 1993); B. J. Pine II, D. Peppers, and M. Rogers, "Do You Want to Keep Your Customers Forever?" *Harvard Business Review,* March–April 1995, pp. 103–112.

10. F. Keenan, S. Holmes, J. Greene, and R. O. Crockett, "A Mass Market of One: As Custom Online Ordering Moves into the Mainstream, Web Merchants Learn to Fine-Tune Their Trade," *Business Week,* Dec. 2, 2002, pp. 68–72.

11. T. V. Bonoma and B. P. Shapiro, *Segmenting the Industrial Market* (Lexington, MA: Lexington Books, 1983).

12. E. von Hippel, *The Sources of Innovation* (New York: Oxford University Press, 1998).

13. P. Kotler, *Marketing Management* (Upper Saddle River, NJ: Prentice-Hall, 2000).

14. M. E. Porter, "What Is Strategy?" *Harvard Business Review,* November–December 1996, pp. 61–78.

15. Porter, "Towards a Dynamic Theory of Strategy."

Connected Activities for a Profitable Business Model

Recall that a firm makes a profit when it offers products or services at a lower cost than its rivals do or offers differentiated products at premium prices that more than make up for the extra cost of differentiation and when it is well positioned to appropriate the value (earn a profit commensurate with the value) it creates.[1] Offering this value (low-cost or differentiated products) entails performing the value-adding activities that underpin the creation and delivery of the product or service. For example, if Toyota is going to offer high-performing Lexus cars to its customers and charge a premium price for them, the cars must be designed, manufactured, marketed, and distributed to customers who want them. In this chapter, we explore the activities that firms perform to offer value to their customers and put themselves in a position to appropriate the value. In particular, we explore how the choice of activities that a firm performs, as well as how and when it performs them, (1) impacts the firm's positions—its differentiation or low-cost position and its relative position vis-à-vis its coopetitors, (2) dampens industry competitive forces, (3) builds and exploits the firm's resources, and (4) keeps costs low, irrespective of whether the firm pursues a low-cost or differentiation strategy. To provide the background information for such an exploration, we begin the chapter with a description of business systems, value systems, and vertical linkages.

BUSINESS SYSTEMS

In every business, there is a sequence of activities that firms perform to produce goods and services, deliver them to customers, and make or lose money doing so. This sequence of activities, called a **business system,** differs from industry to industry.[2] For example, in offering its customers high-performance cars, BMW designs the cars, purchases components from suppliers, assembles the components according to the design, and markets and distributes the cars to dealers, who sell them to end customers. A commercial bank attracts both depositors and borrowers and pieces together the kinds of services that meet the needs of its different clients. A business school must attract both students and professors and piece together the kinds of activities that allow professors to generate knowledge and transfer that knowledge to students. Depending on the industry and the firm that is performing the activities—and, therefore, the interdependence of the activities that must be performed—the business system is called a value chain, value network, or value shop.[3]

Value Chains

Figure 5.1 presents a generic business system for a manufacturing firm. For reasons that will become apparent soon, the business system for a manufacturing company is called a **value chain.** Each of the stages in the system—R&D, product design, manufacturing/operations, marketing/sales, distribution, customer support/services—is usually a separate department, or **function,** within a firm. The activities performed by each function are sequentially interdependent. That is, the output of, say, Product Design is the input of Manufacturing, and therefore Manufacturing must depend on Product Design to finish designing a product before it can successfully carry out its primary manufacturing activities. Thus, although Marketing, Product Design, and R&D may work together early in the development of a new product that uses a new technology, full-scale performance of the primary activities of each stage of the value chain usually starts after the activities of the previous stage have been completed. That is, full-scale manufacturing does not start until product design is complete, major marketing and sales usually do not take place until there is some evidence of a new product to show customers, and distributors do not have much to deliver to customers until a product has been manufactured. Each stage of a business system has two important properties: (1) It adds value to the good or service being created, and (2) it usually gives a firm many options—as far as activities are concerned—to choose from.

Value Addition

Each stage of the business system usually adds value before turning its output to the next stage, which, in turn, adds more value. This is one reason that a manufacturing business system is referred to as a *value chain.*[4] Consider a computer

FIGURE 5.1   **Business System of a Manufacturing Company**

Human Resource Management					
R&D	Product Design	Manufacturing/ Operations	Marketing/ Sales	Distribution	Customer Support/ Services
Sophistication Patents Product technology Process technology	Function Physical characteristics Aesthetics Quality/ reliability	Assembly Location Technology Information Manufacturing Financial ops. Procurement Purchasing Vendor relations Inbound logistics Inventory holding Parts production	Pricing Advertising Promotion Sales force Packaging Brand	Channels Integration Inventory Warehousing Transport	Warranty Speed Captive/ independent Prices

← **Upstream**   **Downstream** →

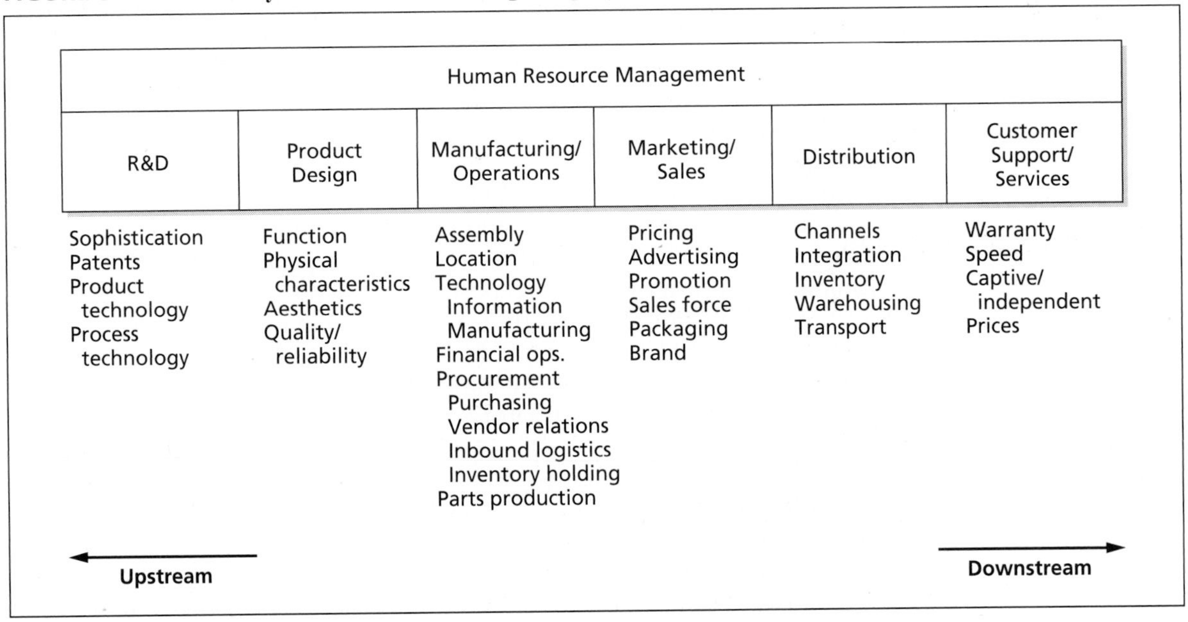

maker with a business system similar to the one in Figure 5.1 that wants to introduce a new 64-bit computer. R&D adds value by researching the differences between existing 32-bit technology and the new 64-bit technology and determining the implications of the new technology for new product design. The product design group adds value by using the information from R&D and its own knowledge of computer design to conceptualize and specify which components of the new computer will be used and how these components will be linked to each other to produce a computer with the desired characteristics. Manufacturing adds value by assembling the components in accordance with the design specifications. Marketing adds value by performing activities such as advertising and promotion that influence customers' perception of the benefits that the new 64-bit computer can endow on them.

One way to comprehend how value is added is to imagine a customer sitting downstream at the end of the value chain and looking upstream toward the design stage (Figure 5.1). Each time a value chain activity is performed, the value perceived by the customer is increased. When designers combine their knowledge of 64-bit processors and produce a design, they increase the value that customers perceive by specifying how components will be turned into a product. In fact, customers can look at a model of the design and begin to get a feel for some of the benefits that they can expect from the computer. By purchasing and assembling components, the manufacturing group brings the computer to life and customers can experience the benefits that the computer can endow on them. Through advertising and promotion, the marketing group can influence how customers perceive the 64-bit machine by making them believe that the product is valuable to them in ways that they may not have thought of on their own.

Options

At each stage of its business system, a firm usually has numerous activities to choose from as it performs its value-adding activities. At the manufacturing stage, for example, a firm may decide to manufacture the product itself or outsource the activity to another firm, perhaps in another country. If it decides to manufacture the product itself, it may choose to work closely with suppliers or to treat them more like adversaries. And so on. We will have much more to say about these options later in this chapter.

Value Network

The business system of commercial banks, dating services, investment banks, and employment services can be very different from that of manufacturing companies, such as those in the computer and automobile industries, which utilize the value chain.[5] At a commercial bank, for example, the primary value-adding activity is finding depositors who will deposit money with the bank and borrowers who will borrow the money and offering them the kind of service that will keep them coming to the bank rather than drive them to competitors. This is different from adding value in the automobile industry, where it is done by converting the input at each stage to an output that becomes the input to the next stage of the chain and so on. At a dating service, value is added primarily by bringing together people who want a date. Employment agencies add value primarily by bringing together employers who have positions to fill and job seekers who want jobs.

In such industries, firms act as mediators between clients. For example, commercial banks mediate between borrowers and depositors, investment banks mediate between issuers of equity and investors, dating agencies mediate between people who want dates, and employment agencies mediate between employers and job seekers. These industries have been classified as **mediating industries** since their primary value-adding activities mainly involve mediating.[6] A firm and the clients that it mediates make up a network called a **value network.** Value networks exhibit the property of network externalities. That is, the more clients the network has, the more valuable the network is to the clients. For example, as the number of clients at a dating agency increases, the chances that a client will find a date through that agency also increase. As the number of depositors at a commercial bank increases, so do the chances that a borrower will be able to get a loan from that bank.

Value Shop

The logic for creating and offering value at hospitals, consulting services, universities, R&D laboratories, and law firms is different from that for adding value in manufacturing and mediating firms. A hospital does not bring in patients and move all of them through the same predetermined series of activities, as firms in the automobile industry do with components. Nor do hospitals exist to act as mediators between patients. Hospitals, as well as consulting services, universities, and other such businesses, serve a variety of clients with different needs and thus require a business system that offers flexibility in meeting those needs. In these businesses, value is created through a set of activities called a **value shop.**

To understand a value shop, consider the system at a hospital. A patient (client) comes into the hospital to be cured. The hospital has resources such as diagnostics testing, doctors, nurses, surgery, anesthesiology, physical therapy, and a pharmacy at its disposal. At the hospital, the process of finding out what is wrong with the patient might start with an examination of the patient by a doctor. If the doctor finds nothing wrong with the patient, the curing process is complete and the patient is sent home. If the doctor determines that the patient needs more attention, he or she might send the patient for laboratory testing. If the test results convince the doctor that nothing is wrong with the patient, the patient will be sent home. The tests may also suggest that the patient needs some more value-adding activity, such as surgery. In general, in a value shop, a client brings a problem to the firm and, depending on the nature of the problem, the firm can use one or more of its resources to solve the problem. The first set of resources applied to the problem may solve it. If the first set of resources does not work, another set of resources is applied, and so on until the problem is solved.

Outsourcing

Firms do not always perform all the activities that make up their business systems. For example, a firm with a value chain that consists of design, procurement, manufacturing, marketing, and distribution may decide to contract out design and manufacturing to another firm and perform only procurement, marketing, and distribution internally. When a firm contracts out one of its value configuration activities to another firm, it is said to be **outsourcing** that activity. For convenience, let us call the firm that is outsourcing the activity the *outsourcer* and refer to the firm to which the activity is being outsourced as the *outsourcee.*

Why would a firm outsource an activity rather than perform it in-house? A firm will outsource a value-adding activity if doing so will enable it to deliver better customer value (low cost or product differentiation) than it could by performing the activity in-house. Whether this is the case depends on several factors: (1) the superiority of the outsourcee's capabilities relative to those of the outsourcer in performing the activity, (2) the market power of outsourcees with the relevant capability, (3) the outsourcer's integrative or architectural capability, and (4) the criticalness of the capability underpinning the particular activity to the outsourcer's competitive advantage.

1. *Outsourcee's capabilities:* If outsourcees possess superior capabilities in performing the activity and the outsourcer cannot match those capabilities, the outsourcer might be better off outsourcing the activity. The rationale here is that by going with the firm that has superior capabilities, the outsourcer will end up with lower cost or better differentiation. Lufthansa's capabilities in mechanical servicing of airplanes are generally considered to be superior to those of most other airlines, and therefore many airlines outsource the servicing of their planes to Lufthansa. In the 1980s and early 1990s, many U.S. firms outsourced manufacturing to firms in countries where labor costs were lower than in the United States. The practice was so common that it gave rise to the term *virtual corporation* in reference to a firm whose primary value-adding activity was coordinating the activities of contractors to which it outsourced everything from design to manufacturing and sometimes marketing.[7]

2. *Market power of outsourcees:* An outsourcee's superior capability in performing an activity is not a sufficient condition for outsourcing an activity to it. The market power of outsourcees is also important. The fewer the outsourcees with the relevant capability, the more power they are likely to have. As we saw in earlier chapters, suppliers with bargaining power can extract high prices from the buyer or force the buyer to accept lower-quality products. In outsourcing, the outsourcer is the buyer and the outsourcee is the supplier. Thus, an outsourcer may want to avoid outsourcing activities when there are only one or two outsourcees, especially if the activity is critical to the outsourcer's value creation.

3. *Outsourcer's integrative or architectural capability:* When a firm outsources an activity, the output of that activity still has to be integrated into the firm's value-adding activities. For example, if a firm outsources design, the design must be translated into finished products by the outsourcer's manufacturing group and marketed by its marketing group. The outsourcer must coordinate its activities with those of its contractors to offer a superior product. Thus, firms that have superior integrative or architectural capabilities may be better at outsourcing than other firms since they can better integrate their activities and those of contractors.

4. *Criticalness of activity's underpinning capability:* If the capability that underpins the activity being considered for outsourcing is critical to the outsourcer's competitive advantage, the outsourcer may want to try to build its own capabilities in that area rather than depend on an outsourcee that has the capability. If a microchip company considers product design to be a critical area in which it must build a competitive advantage, it may be better off performing design activities internally so that it can develop the design capabilities it needs.

Advantages and Disadvantages of Outsourcing

When carried out properly, outsourcing has several advantages. First, by having an outsourcee with superior resources perform an activity, the value created is likely to result in lower costs or more differentiation than would be the case if the outsourcer performed the activity. Second, by letting an outsourcee perform an activity that the outsourcer is not very good at, the outsourcer is free to concentrate on the cornerstones of its competitive advantage. Outsourcing also has some shortcomings, especially if it is not pursued properly. First, the outsourcee can hold the outsourcer hostage if the former suddenly finds out that it is performing a valuable service that no other firm can and thus that the outsourcer is dependent on it. Second, outsourcing too many functions can prevent a firm from seeing important synergies between its different functions. Third, outsourcing deprives a firm of learning and improving its chances of innovation.

Example

In the second and third quarters of 1999, eBay's website crashed a few times, leaving many anxious clients unable to access the site and conduct trade. Sometime after that, eBay announced that it was outsourcing its back-end Internet activities to two companies: Abovenet Communications and Exodus Communications. These two companies would be responsible for the maintenance and performance of web servers, database servers, Internet routers, and other technologies that were central to the availability of eBay's site for trading. Some analysts wondered loudly if eBay was doing the right thing by outsourcing such a critical part of its value-adding activities.

Whether eBay has done the right thing or not can be examined on the basis of the four factors listed above. First, Abovenet Communications and Exodus Communications specialize in back-end Internet activities. Since eBay's competitive advantage rests on its large number of registered users (large network size) and brand name, Abovenet and Exodus are more capable of running the back-end activities than eBay is. Second, there are many companies that can perform these activities. In fact, eBay was going to hire two companies (from the many available) to perform the same activities, giving it more bargaining power. Third, eBay's integrative capabilities or lack of them are not an issue since keeping a website up and running does not require a lot of integration. Fourth, learning how to run a website is not critical to the cornerstones of eBay's competitive advantage—its network size and brand name. Since keeping its website up and running well all the time is critical for eBay's business, the natural temptation is to argue that eBay should perform this activity internally. Nevertheless, on the basis of the reasons just outlined, eBay made the right decision. It will be important for eBay, however, to have an internal group working very closely with and learning from Abovenet and Exodus, just in case. Most important of all, by letting Abovenet and Exodus manage the back-end technology, eBay is free to concentrate on building the cornerstones of its competitive advantage: network size and brand name.

VALUE SYSTEMS, SUPPLY CHAINS, AND VERTICAL LINKAGES

In performing the activities of a business system—whether it is a value chain, value network, or value shop—a firm often must interact with suppliers, customers, complementors, and firms from other industries. These other firms have business systems of their own. What we really have, then, is a system of business systems. This system, known as a firm's **value system,** is the chain that stretches from end customers (consumers) to the firm to its suppliers to their own suppliers and so on. Figure 5.2 shows a value system for makers of the microprocessors that are used in PCs. Microprocessor makers such as Intel obtain their equipment and other materials from semiconductor equipment manufacturers such as Applied Materials, which obtain their own inputs from other firms, such as makers of steel, and so on. The microprocessor makers sell their chips to PC makers such as Dell, HP, IBM, and Gateway, which use them to build PCs. The PCs are sold, either direct or via distributors, to the end customers, the computer users.

In a value system, the direction of flow of the goods is usually referred to as *downstream.* Thus, in Figure 5.2, the direction from semiconductor equipment manufacturers to microprocessor makers to computer makers to distributors to computer users is the downstream direction. The opposite direction is usually referred to as *upstream.* Firms such as Dell that are downstream, close to the end of the value system, have two kinds of customers to whom they can offer value: businesses and consumers. Further upstream, firms usually create and offer value to other businesses. Although the activities of such firms are largely business to business, some marketing activities such as advertising can be business to consumer. For example, a firm that makes major components that are used by other firms to build and sell systems to consumers can advertise directly to consumers. By so doing, the firm can generate sales for the systems, thereby generating sales for its components. Intel Corporation's "Intel Inside" advertisement is a good example. The ad is targeted to consumers and businesses that buy PCs from Dell, HP, IBM, Gateway, and other PC makers since if these companies can sell more PCs that contain Intel microprocessors, Intel can sell more microprocessors.

The value system from raw materials to consumers is also called the **supply chain** since it consists of suppliers who supply their customers, who add value and then supply their own customers, and so on until the end customer.

Vertical Integration

In Figure 5.2, we have shown a computer maker as obtaining its microprocessors from microprocessor makers and having distributors sell its outputs to computer users. In this case, we say that the firm obtains its supplies and disposes of its outputs through **market exchanges** since it buys the inputs from and disposes of its outputs through independent firms in the market. This is similar to your going to a store, buying a book, paying for it, and leaving. However, the computer maker may decide to make its own microprocessors or dispose of its own outputs. Producing one's input or disposing of one's output is known as **vertical integration.**

When a computer maker produces its own microprocessors, we say that the firm is engaging in **backward vertical integration** into microprocessors; that is, the firm is vertically integrated into the upstream market. When the firm distributes its own computers directly to customers, we say that it is practicing **forward vertical integration** into disposing of its own outputs; that is, the firm is vertically integrated into the downstream market. In **tapered integration,** a firm produces only some of the quantity of the input that it needs and buys the rest of the

FIGURE 5.2   **Value System for Makers of PC Microprocessors**

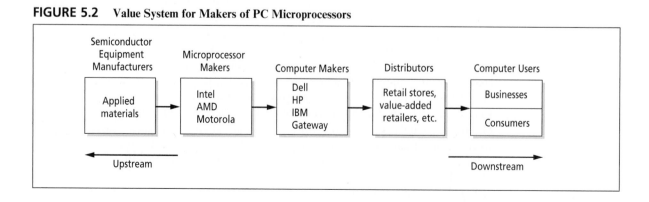

input from outside suppliers. If a firm uses the entire quantity of the input that it produces and does not sell any, the input that the firm produces is said to be **captive input.**

An important question for a business model is, When is a firm better off being vertically integrated? The guiding principle is simple: A firm should integrate vertically if, in doing so, it can offer its customers better value (low cost and differentiation) than its competitors offer and/or it can put itself in a better position to appropriate value.

Lower Cost

For several reasons, an external supplier's cost of producing an input can be lower than that of a firm that is vertically integrated into producing the input. First, if the external supplier produces only the input in question, it is more focused on producing that input than a vertically integrated firm that must not only produce the input but also combine it with other components to produce its own output. Such specialization can allow the external supplier to fine-tune its capabilities in producing the input and, thereby, can enable the supplier to offer a lower-cost input than could a vertically integrated firm. For example, Intel Corporation, which is focused on producing microchips, is more likely to produce microchips at a lower cost than Dell Computers could if Dell decided to integrate vertically into producing the chips it needs. Second, since an external supplier is likely to supply the input to more buyers than a vertically integrated firm would, it is likely to enjoy economies of scale that the vertically integrated firm does not. For example, Intel sells to many more computer companies than IBM, which is vertically integrated backward into making microprocessors. Thus Intel enjoys more economies of scale in microprocessor production than IBM does. For these two reasons, an external supplier is likely to produce a component at lower cost than that of a vertically integrated user.

The cost of producing an input is only one of two major input costs. The other is transaction costs. **Transaction costs** are the costs associated with buying and selling: the costs of searching for sellers and buyers; negotiating, writing, monitoring, and enforcing contracts; and transporting goods.[8] Transaction cost economic theory argues that a firm should integrate vertically to produce its input if the transaction costs of dealing with an external supplier are so high that they negate any production cost advantages that the external supplier may have enjoyed from specialization and scale.[9] When might this be the case? According to O. E. Williamson, a noted economist, the answer often depends on the cost of negotiating, writing, monitoring, and enforcing contracts. For many inputs, writing complete contracts that specify all possible contingencies can be prohibitively expensive, and therefore most contracts are incomplete.[10] Because the contracts are incomplete, they may have to be renegotiated over time. This leaves room for either the supplier or the buyer to be opportunistic—to lie, cheat, or hide information that is critical to their relationship. Opportunistic behavior can result in costly court battles between an external supplier and a firm that can drastically increase transaction costs. If a firm is vertically integrated, any disputes can be settled in-house without costly battles.

In general, transaction costs increase with the specificity of the assets needed to offer the input, the uncertainty involved in producing and delivering the input, and the frequency of the interactions needed between supplier and firm in producing and delivering the input. Thus, the higher the asset specificity and uncertainty and the more frequent the interactions in a relationship with an input supplier, the more a firm should think about integrating vertically to produce the input for itself.

Differentiation

A firm can differentiate its products by integrating vertically backward to produce a critical input if suppliers cannot offer the specific type of input that the firm needs to differentiate itself.[11] A seller of gourmet coffee may decide to buy and manage farms in developing countries if a steady supply of high-quality coffee cannot be ensured otherwise. Some U.S. companies had to integrate vertically backward into producing bananas to assure their customers of high-quality bananas all the time. This has differentiated these companies from those that depend on market exchanges.

Better Positioning

By integrating vertically backward or forward, a firm can demonstrate a credible threat of forward or backward integration to its suppliers or distributors. Such a threat can reduce a supplier's or buyer's bargaining power. Until the 1990s, IBM always made sure that it could produce any of the chips that it bought from external suppliers. During negotiations with IBM, suppliers always knew that the company could produce the same components that it was buying if it had to. This usually reduced the bargaining power of the suppliers. IBM usually reduced the bargaining power of suppliers even further by requiring that suppliers of certain components had to have a second source. That is, a supplier had to let a competitor learn how to produce its product, thereby reducing its bargaining power, if it was going to win an IBM contract.

Strategic Alliances

Buying an input from a supplier or integrating vertically backward to produce the input are not the only ways to get one's inputs. Neither are integrating vertically forward or depending on an intermediary the only ways to dispose of one's output. An alternative exists in strategic alliances. In a **strategic alliance,** or **strategic collaboration,** two or more firms agree to combine their resources to carry out a project. They agree to cooperate for a specific time and for specific operations. Thus, rather than buy an input from an external supplier or integrate vertically to produce the input, firms often form strategic alliances with suppliers, competitors, customers, or any other firm to produce the input. Toyota's success relative to other automobile companies has been attributed partly to strategic collaboration with its suppliers in which they team up to identify and solve problems associated with the development and use of the components that the company needs.[12] In the 1990s, Siemens, Toshiba, and IBM collaborated to develop a memory chip.

Strategic alliances range from casual agreements to joint ventures. In a **joint venture,** two or more firms pool resources to create a separate legal entity that is jointly owned by the collaborators. For example, General Mills and Nestlé pooled their resources in breakfast foods to create Cereal Partners Worldwide, a joint venture that both firms owned. The joint venture combined General Mills' strengths in cereal technology with Nestlé's distribution channels outside the United States to give the venture a presence in cereal in other countries.

Advantages and Disadvantages of Strategic Alliances

An alliance usually gives partners access to capabilities that either would have been very difficult to build or would have taken very long to build. It would have been very difficult for General Mills to develop the type of distribution channels outside the United States that Nestlé brought to the alliance. In many countries, the only way for foreign firms to have access to local markets is to form joint ventures with local partners. A strategic alliance can also allow participating firms to undertake a project that each firm, alone, may not have been able to undertake because of the cost, risk involved, or sheer difficulty of building the capabilities from scratch. For example, it is unlikely that Aerospeciale, MBB, Fokker, Casa, British Aerospace, or Belairbus alone would have been able to internally develop the capabilities that their joint venture, Airbus Industrie, was able to develop.[13] Finally, strategic alliances offer participants a chance to learn from each other.

Strategic alliances also have disadvantages. First, there is the free-rider problem, in which participating firms decide not to send their best people or resources to the joint venture, hoping that the other partner(s) will provide such resources. They save their best people and resources for firm-specific rather than alliance-specific tasks. Second, there is usually a clash of organizational cultures between firms. Third, during the formal and informal interactions that take place in an alliance, participants risk losing proprietary information that they would have preferred to see remain proprietary.

COMPETITIVE ADVANTAGE AND CONNECTED ACTIVITIES

Most firms are in business to make money, and their business models help them do so. A well-conceived and executed business model can give a firm a competitive advantage. Recall that a firm has a competitive advantage if it earns a higher rate of profits than its rivals earn in the markets in which it competes or if it has the potential to do so. Those characteristics of a firm's business model that allow it to earn a higher rate of profits than its rivals do are its **competitive advantage.** A firm's competitive advantage often rests in the activities which it performs, how it performs them, and when it performs them. The degree to which a firm's business model can give the firm a competitive advantage is a function of the extent to which the activities which the firm performs, how it performs them, and when it performs them allow the firm to create superior customer value and appropriate it. That is, competitive advantage is a function of the extent to which the activities allow the firm to (1) attain and maintain the right positions, (2) dampen industry competitive forces, (3) better build and exploit its resources, and (4) keep its costs low irrespective of whether the firm pursues a low-cost or differentiation strategy (Figure 5.3).

WHICH ACTIVITIES TO PERFORM

As a firm formulates and executes its business model, it usually has to choose which of the activities of its business system and value system it wants to perform and which ones it does *not* want to perform. Since creating and appropriating value are achieved through performing the activities of business and value systems, the choice of which activities to perform plays an important role in the profitability of the firm. The choice of the right activities allows a firm not only to offer superior customer value but also to address the negatives of its industry, thereby allowing it to be better positioned to appropriate the value created. In this section, we examine (1) the activity options that are available to a firm within its business system and value system, (2) criteria for choosing activities that can give a firm a competitive advantage, and (3) criteria for *not* choosing activities. In our discussion of item (3), we will be emphasizing the fact that the choice of which

FIGURE 5.3
Activities, Positions,
Resources, and
Industry Factors

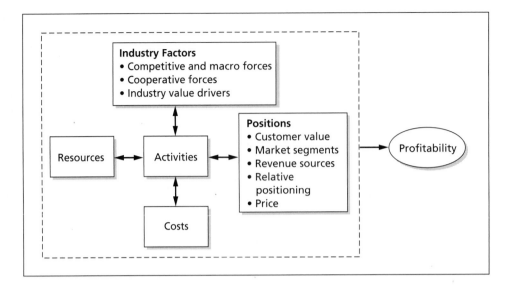

activities *not* to perform can be as important as the choice of which activities to perform since the opportunity cost of performing some activities can be very high.

Options

As our discussion of business systems and value systems suggests, a firm usually has many activities to choose from at each stage of its business system and value system in creating and offering customer value and appropriating the value.

Business System Activities

To illustrate the options that are usually available to a firm in its business system, we use the example of a manufacturing firm with the business system shown in Figure 5.1.

Research and Development At the R&D stage, a firm may choose not to be very sophisticated about its R&D and thus to pursue applied research only rather than in addition to basic research. (In *applied research,* firms perform R&D activities whose results are earmarked for use in targeted products; in *basic research,* firms usually pursue knowledge for knowledge's own sake, without immediate plans for using the results of the research in any specific product.) For example, Dell Computer does not pursue basic R&D. A firm also has the choice of patenting its new ideas or not doing so. Firms usually have the choice of different process technologies—different technologies for producing the same product. For example, Intel's commitment to metal oxide semiconductor (MOS) technology, rather than bipolar technology, early in its business life played a key role in the company's success. A firm may also choose to perform all its major R&D activities alone or team up with coopetitors through strategic alliances, joint ventures, or other forms of contracts or agreements.

Product Design If a firm decides to design its own product, it can design a product whose functionality, physical characteristics, aesthetics, quality, and reliability are either very different from or similar to the features of competitors' products. It may decide to trade off some features for others. For example, a car maker may decide to choose gas mileage, durability, and reliability over high performance.

Manufacturing/Operations A firm may decide to manufacture its designs by itself or to outsource some or all of the manufacturing to other firms. For example, in semiconductors, firms such as Xilinx design their own microchips but outsource fabrication to so-called foundries—companies such as Taiwan Semiconductor that perform contract microchip manufacturing. If a firm decides to manufacture its own designs, it often must decide which location is best for the plant. It also decides which of the manufacturing technologies, such as lean manufacturing, to include. In some industries, a firm may have to decide whether to use custom components or standard, off-the-shelf components. Its procurement group must decide which vendors to purchase components from: whether, for example, to have a few large suppliers or many small ones. A firm may also decide to make some of its own components, especially if the choice is made early in the face of certain types of technological changes.[14]

Marketing/Sales A software developer, an automobile maker, or an office equipment maker often must decide whether to lease its products, sell them, or do both. Which option it chooses depends on many factors, including whether it can find the money to finance the leases or not. Firms often must decide whether to advertise or not. If they decide to advertise, they often must also decide which medium to use for advertising and promotion—the Internet, TV, radio, or print media.

Distribution A firm usually has several choices of distribution channels for its products. Makers of digital products—products based on bits of ones and zeros—such as software, books, movies, music, and information (e.g., stock quotes and news) can distribute their products through the Internet. Others use the Internet to start the process of distribution and then ship the product themselves. In the computer industry, Dell sells directly to its customers, while HP, Apple, and Gateway use distributors. For nondigital products, a firm may decide to use dealers to distribute its products. Even within the dealer category, there are different kinds of dealers. PC dealers can vary from specialty stores to large retailers such as Wal-Mart.

Customer Support/Services For many firms, the question is whether to offer customer support and after-sales service at all. If service is an important source of profits for the firm, this question is often an easy one. Servicing jet engines is a very lucrative market for makers of jet engines, as is servicing elevators for makers of elevators. This is one reason that GE and United Technologies service jet engines and elevators, respectively.

Value System Activities

Within its value system, a firm usually has the option of integrating vertically backward to produce its components, integrating vertically forward to dispose of its own outputs, or forming joint ventures or other strategic alliances to produce its inputs or dispose of its outputs.

Deciding Which Activities to Perform

Having explored the options that firms can choose from in performing the activities of their business systems and value systems, the next question is, Which activities should a firm choose to perform? Our focus is on activities that have the potential to enable a firm to (1) attain and maintain the right positions, (2) take advantage of industry factors, (3) better build and exploit its resources, and (4) keep its costs low irrespective of whether the firm pursues a low-cost or differentiation strategy.

Attain and Maintain the Right Positions

Recall that attaining the right positions entails offering superior customer value in targeted market segments, pursuing the right sources of revenues within each market segment, positioning the firm more advantageously vis-à-vis its coopetitors, and charging the right prices for the value offered.

Offer Superior Value   Several factors influence the extent to which a firm's activities enable it to offer superior customer value.[15] First, the activities should be consistent with the type of value that the firm offers customers. If the value that a firm offers is low cost, each activity that it performs should be consistent with low cost. For example, in the 1980s and 1990s, the primary value that Southwest Airlines offered its customers was low cost. Each activity that the company performed—offering no meals, operating largely from uncongested airports, and the like—was either directly or indirectly cost-reducing. If some activities are low-cost-oriented while others are not, the effects from the two types of activities may neutralize themselves. If the value offered by a firm is differentiation, each activity should have a positive effect on differentiation. For example, many of the activities that Coca-Cola performs, such as advertising, are geared toward reinforcing or building its brand equity and thereby differentiating its products. Second, the activities that a firm performs should be different from those that its competitors perform; or, if the activities are similar to those performed by its competitors, the firm should perform them differently. The rationale here is that if a firm were to mimic a competitor both in the activities it performs and the way it performs them, the best the firm could do is offer the same value as that competitor, not superior value. It is difficult to beat a competitor by trying to be like the competitor. Third, the set of activities that the firm performs should constitute a system that is difficult to imitate.

Attain Superior Relative Positioning   In addition to offering low-cost or differentiated products, there may be other things that a firm can do to address the negative aspects of the industry in which it competes. For example, if suppliers of an input are very powerful, a firm may decide to eliminate the component from its future designs or integrate vertically backward to demonstrate a credible threat of backward integration. If distributors are very powerful, a firm can bypass them through innovation. A case in point is Dell. When Dell started out, PC dealers had power over the company, so Dell decided to use an 800 number so that customers could buy directly from it, bypassing the dealers. When the World Wide Web came along, Dell used the Internet to sell its computers directly to customers. The Wal-Mart case that we will explore at the end of this chapter offers another example of a firm countering competitive forces through its choices of which activities to perform.

Take Advantage of Industry Factors

Recall that every industry has some industry-specific factors that have the most impact on cost or differentiation. The activities that firms perform should be consistent with exploiting such factors. For example, in the airline industry, utilization of planes is critical. That is, planes should not be sitting at a terminal but, rather, should be flying, as full of passengers as possible. The reason is simple: When planes are waiting at a terminal, they are not transporting passengers and thus are not making money. Therefore, the activities that an airline performs should be consistent with making sure that its planes are flying full and not waiting at gates. For instance, if an airline chooses to fly out of uncongested airports, its planes can land and take off more quickly, thereby increasing utilization. For another example, consider the PC industry. Two characteristics of PCs have a large impact on the value that PC makers can deliver to customers: (1) The rate of change of technology is very fast and, as such, PCs that are sold through dealers can quickly become obsolete if they sit on dealers' shelves too long, and (2) prices of PCs usually drop rapidly. Dell Computer's build-to-order activities take advantage of these industry characteristics. By going directly to customers, rather than through distributors, Dell has been able to get its computers to customers fast enough for them to enjoy the latest microprocessor before expectations of its successor render the processor obsolete. Also, since prices of PCs drop very fast, the longer the PCs wait at distributors, the less the PC maker will get for the computers when they are eventually sold; bypassing distributors and selling directly to customers gets products to customers before prices drop too much and eliminates the cost of dealer commissions.

Build and Exploit Resources and Capabilities

As we will see in Chapter 6, some resources are scarce, difficult to imitate, and can make an unusually high contribution to the value that customers perceive in a firm's products. A firm may therefore want to pursue activities that rest on such resources. As an example, Honda Motor Company has a reputation for making high-performance, dependable, reliable engines and has taken advantage of this resource in developing and selling cars, motorcycles, lawn mowers, electric generators, off-terrain vehicles, winter recreation vehicles, and marine vehicles. If a firm does not have scarce resources to exploit, it may be able to create them. For example, eBay has built a large network of registered users through the Internet. Such a network is a scarce, difficult-to-imitate, valuable resource in the online auction business and has been central to eBay's business model.

Keep Costs Low

As we will explore in detail in Chapter 9, an important objective of any business model, irrespective of whether the firm offers differentiated or low-cost products, is to keep cost as low as possible while offering superior value. The activities that a firm chooses to perform should be geared toward satisfying this goal. Any activities that reduce agency costs, increase learning to gain economies of learning, or increase economies of scope are helpful.

Deciding Which Activities *Not* to Perform

Since offering superior customer value and being positioned well relative to suppliers, customers, potential new entrants, and substitute products are critical to making money, it is easy for a firm to focus only on activities that contribute to these goals when it is considering *which* activities to perform. For several reasons, it may also be important to take a look at how the activities that a firm is *not* performing can impact the success of its business model. First, each time a firm chooses to perform an activity, it is forgoing another activity. For example, by operating only 737s, Southwest Airlines is forgoing the opportunity to operate 747s, 757s, and so on. Second, firms usually have limited resources. Therefore, each time a firm chooses to perform an activity, some of its limited resources are tied up in that activity, causing the firm to forgo the opportunity of investing the resources in something else that is more valuable. Thus, by not performing certain activities, a firm may be freeing up precious resources that can be used to perform more valuable activities. Third, by not performing an activity, a firm may delegate the activity to another firm that is more efficient and effective in performing it. The eBay case that we explored under "Outsourcing" is a good example. Despite the fact that keeping its website up is critical to running its business, it chose to outsource its back-end technology to two firms that are more capable at back-end technology than eBay. This has allowed eBay to concentrate on building its difficult-to-imitate resources—its network of registered users and brand-name reputation.

HOW TO PERFORM ACTIVITIES

In deciding *which* activities the firm will perform, the focus is on *doing the right things.* In deciding *how* the activities will be performed, the focus is on *doing things right.* Two firms can perform the exact same activities, but the one that knows how to perform them better stands to be more profitable. How a firm is organized—who does what, how tasks are carried out—and which processes it uses can allow it to outperform competitors that perform similar activities differently. **Processes** are the "patterns of interaction, coordination, communication, and decision making" that a firm uses to perform the activities that transform its resources into customer value and position the firm to appropriate the value.[16] For each activity that a firm chooses to perform, there is usually more than one way for each stage of the firm's business system to interact with other stages, coordinate activities within and outside the stage, communicate within and outside the firm, and make decisions. A firm's choices as to who does what, how tasks are carried out, and how it communicates, interacts, coordinates activities, and makes decisions can be the difference between that firm and others that perform similar activities. In this section, we examine (1) the options that are available to a firm in performing each activity that it chooses to perform, and (2) criteria for choosing how to perform activities.

Options

Again, we use the business system of a manufacturing firm, as shown in Figure 5.1, to illustrate some of the options that are usually available to a firm in performing the activities that it has chosen to pursue.

Business System Activities

Research and Development In pursuing applied research, a firm that has decided to form a strategic alliance may choose to put some of its best employees to work on the alliance and create a separate group within the firm to focus on carrying out alliance activities. Another firm may choose to send its mediocre employees to work on the alliance and retain its more talented employees to work on firm-specific projects it considers more important than the alliance. Since product technology intellectual property is more difficult to protect than process technology intellectual property, a firm may decide to pursue aggressive patenting for product technology but not process technology.

Product Design In undertaking the design of its products, a firm may decide to have its manufacturing and marketing groups get involved in the design process rather than wait until the design is complete to begin their work. If the firm is not very familiar with the technology that underpins the design, it may decide to team up with a firm that is more familiar with the technology. If the design requires processes, methods, and a culture that are very different from the firm's existing ones, the technology may be disruptive and the firm might want to form a separate group outside its existing design organization to undertake the design.[17]

Manufacturing/Operations   If a firm has decided to do its own manufacturing, the way it interacts with vendors can impact its product's performance. In the automobile industry, for example, firms that work closely with their suppliers of key components (rather than, e.g., fighting over costs) are more successful at designing and manufacturing cars that are of better quality and cost less than cars from competitors whose relationships with suppliers are more antagonistic.[18]

Marketing/Sales   If a firm decides to lease its products rather than sell them, it has to decide on how to price and finance the leases. It also faces other decisions, such as whether to charge a high up-front cost and low monthly payments or a low up-front cost and high monthly payments. If it has access to cheap funding, the firm may want to finance the leases itself. A firm that lacks brand equity may want to team up with another firm to build its brand equity. When Pixar created its digital animation movies, it teamed up with Disney and co-branded movies such as *Toy Story I, Toy Story II,* and *A Bug's Life* to help build its brand equity in the animation movie business.[19] Firms also must decide how much to spend on sales and marketing relative to the other functions. Cola-concentrate makers such as Coca-Cola spend as much as 43 percent of their revenues on sales and marketing. In the 1990s, pharmaceutical companies spent more on sales and marketing than on R&D.

Distribution   If a firm chooses to use distribution, it often must decide whether to own the dealerships. Gateway owns many of the retail stores that sell its PCs.

Customer Support/Services   Often, firms are faced with the decision of whether to perform service on only their own products or on other firms' products as well. GE services more than just GE-made jet engines.

Cross-Functional and Cross-Firm Processes

The processes that firms use to perform the activities they have chosen to perform often involve more than one stage of the business system and, sometimes, more than one firm or country. Such processes include total quality management (TQM), benchmarking, and business process reengineering.

Total Quality Management   **Total quality management (TQM)** is a set of management practices and organizational processes designed to enable a firm to perform activities accurately and to continuously improve the quality of all of its processes, products, and services.[20] The idea is not only to "get things right the first time" but also to keep improving the things that one got right the first time. Although it started out with practices focusing on manufacturing products to meet customer requirements, TQM quickly spread to all the value-adding activities of firms. Many TQM concepts have their origins in the ideas of H. W. Edwards Deming, an American statistician who preached the importance of quality and continuous improvement. The concepts were implemented in Japan as early as the 1950s, but they were not applied in the United States until the late 1970s and early 1980s.

In the mid-1980s, the Malcolm Baldrige National Quality Award was established to recognize firms' efforts to improve quality.[21] The criteria on which firms are judged include customer focus and satisfaction, quality and operational results, management of process quality, human resource development and management, strategic quality planning, information and analysis, and senior executive leadership. A similar award, the European Quality Award, was established in Europe in 1992. Its criteria for awards include leadership, people management, policy and strategy, resources, processes, people satisfaction, customer satisfaction, impact on society, and business results.[22] The criteria for both awards indicate how organizationwide and how involved all the different stages of a business system are in TQM.

Benchmarking **Benchmarking** is a process in which a firm identifies best practices inside and outside its industry by performing a comparative evaluation of products and/or services and the underpinning value-adding activities. The idea is to find out which firm has the best processes, activities, and products or services. Products and services can be evaluated in terms of what customers want or profitability. Processes and activities can be evaluated using generally accepted measures such as costs, time, and so on. The main difficulty with benchmarking is that competitors usually do not want to release the type of data about their products, processes, and activities that effective benchmarking may require. Financial analysts sometimes have some of the information about publicly traded companies. Some product information can be obtained by *reverse engineering*—a process in which a firm tests another firm's product, opens it up, and takes it apart to understand its inner workings. Benchmarking allows a firm to compare how well it is doing relative to best practices and can be a good starting point for TQM and business process reengineering.

Business Process Reengineering Although its meaning has evolved over time, **reengineering** entails taking a fresh look at a firm's processes and redesigning them to be more efficient, especially by taking advantage of advances in technologies and other resources. The focus is on improving processes rather than just individual tasks. If, as defined earlier, *processes* are the "patterns of interaction, coordination, communication, and decision making" that a firm uses to perform the activities that transform its resources into customer value and position the firm to appropriate the value,[23] then advances in things such as information technology potentially can enable firms to communicate better, interact better, coordinate their activities better, and improve their decision making. Moreover, other determinants of the processes, such as the availability of resources, may change over time. Thus, by redesigning or reengineering these processes, a business can take advantage of these advances and gain high rewards in the form of lower costs, better products, and higher profits.[24]

The importance of taking a fresh look at problems and using the inductive, rather than the deductive, approach to problem solving is best illustrated by the story of the man who went fishing to catch his dinner: A woman observed that each time he caught a very big fish, he would throw it back into the water, but that when he caught a tiny one, he retained it. So the woman went up to the man and said, "Excuse me for being nosy, but I am curious as to why you throw back the big fish and keep only the little ones." The man replied, "That's simple. I have a small pot." In the deductive method of problem solving, a firm is so intent on finding a solution to a small pressing problem that it forgets about taking advantage of new solutions that could solve bigger problems, as well as the smaller one. In the inductive method, the firm takes the new solutions and tries to find problems that they can solve. Thus, if he had not focused solely on the size of his pot, the fisherman could have brought home a big fish and sold some of it, given some of it to hungry neighbors, or frozen some for future dinners. Similarly, if, in adopting the Internet, a person saw it only as a replacement for existing electronic data interchange (EDI) instead of as a new technology that allows individuals to do much more, the person would miss out on many benefits and opportunities.

Whereas reengineering is about internal processes, **x-engineering** examines the processes that link firms and their coopetitors and other stakeholders, such as shareholders, in the digital age.[25] Apart from the external orientation of x-engineering and the technique's greater attention to use of the Internet for process redesign, most of the concepts in x-engineering are the same as those in reengineering.

Choosing How to Perform Activities

The criteria for choosing how to perform activities are similar to those for choosing which activities to perform. That is, how a firm performs the activities that it chooses to perform should be consistent with helping the firm attain and maintain the right positions (customer value, market segments, price and revenue sources), exploit industry factors, build and exploit resources and capabilities better than competitors, and keep the firm's costs low irrespective of whether the firm pursues a low-cost or differentiation strategy.

WHEN TO PERFORM ACTIVITIES

Two firms can perform similar activities in similar ways but still end up with business models whose profitabilities are different if the timing of when they perform the activities is different. Such differences in performance can stem from the way firms take advantage of first-mover advantages or windows of opportunity in their business models.

First Movers

A **first-mover advantage** is an advantage held by virtue of being the first to perform an activity.[26] Performing certain activities first can give a firm advantages in its positions, its resources, the way it exploits industry factors, and its costs (see Figure 5.3).

Advantages

Positions By being the first to offer a product, a firm can build a brand and develop such a loyal following that customers keep buying its product even if later entrants offer products with identical features. A firm can also build a large installed base and establish relationships with customers that make these customers perceive the firm's products as being better than those from competitors that enter the market later. In industries where network externalities are important, a firm that introduces its products first can build a large network first. Since the larger a network is, the more people there are who want to join it, a firm that moves first can build a network that is difficult to match. Such a network would make the products of first movers more valuable.

Resources Some resources can be valuable, rare, and difficult to imitate or substitute. First movers can capture such resources, depriving later entrants of the opportunity to compete for them. For example, when Southwest Airlines moved to many uncongested U.S. airports and saturated them with frequent flights, it effectively built itself a network of uncongested airports. Later entrants did not have as much of an opportunity to build networks that cover as many uncongested airports. A pharmaceutical firm that discovers a new drug and takes a patent on it effectively preempts other companies from selling the exact same chemical compound. This can allow the firm to collect huge profits before its patent expires.

Industry Factors Sometimes the advantage that a firm gains by moving first is the contracts and other relationships that it builds along its value system to dampen the competitive forces in its industry. For example, by moving first, Coca-Cola and PepsiCo were able to sign exclusive contracts with bottlers that allowed them to cover most of the U.S. market. This effectively raised barriers to entry for potential new entrants. Television and radio stations that obtained licenses to broadcast have had an advantage because only a limited number of licenses are issued and they were all allocated by the time many potential new entrants were born.

Costs In addition to the cost advantages that a first mover can obtain from the resources it obtains by moving first, it can also establish a cost advantage from economies of learning and scale. A first mover has time to learn and move up the experience curve before new firms enter the industry. By accumulating experience and know-how, a first mover can produce its units at a much lower cost than can a newcomer that does not have such experience and know-how. If, in moving first, a firm is able to garner a high market share, it will be able to sell many more units than new entrants can sell. This gives the first mover an economy-of-scale cost advantage.

It is important to note two things about first-mover advantages. First, a firm usually has to earn them. They are not automatically endowed on whoever moves first. They are usually earned by firms that take the right strategic steps. If a firm does not invest well in R&D and obtain patents on new products when it discovers them, it cannot enjoy the temporary monopoly rights that patenting endows on firms that do so. If PepsiCo and Coca-Cola had not signed exclusive contracts with their bottlers and defended their rights to have the contracts, these contracts would not have become the barrier to entry that they have been. A company that moves first but makes no effort to build brand equity and earn customer loyalty will have little of both. Second, first-mover advantages usually do not last forever. In fact, many last only for a short while after challengers move in.

Disadvantages

Moving first can become a disadvantage when challengers arrive. If a challenger moves in using a new technology, some of the same resources that were first-mover advantages can become disadvantages. For example, when Compaq decided to use the Internet to have its customers order computers directly from it—in response to Dell's use of the Internet to sell directly to customers—its network of dealers, which had been one of its advantages from moving first as an "IBM PC cloner," became a handicap as the dealers fought Compaq's move. Also, a firm that wants to be the first to introduce a new product may end up with higher development costs since there is no other firm from which it can learn. Such a firm must bear all the costs associated with the experimentation, trial, error, and correction that are critical to new product development. Moreover, followers can benefit from its mistakes through, for example, reverse engineering its products or hiring away its employees.

Windows of Opportunity

Some activities have windows of opportunity—periods within which they are best performed.[27] Performing the activities outside such windows is not as rewarding. Consider the simple example of a firm whose management wants to introduce TQM or business process reengineering. For the adoption process to be successful, it may be necessary for management to prepare employees for the changes that are going to take place. For example, management might have to explain to employees why the firm needs the TQM or reengineering and might have to hire a consulting firm or individuals to facilitate the process. Doing these things takes time. Once the adoption process has been initiated, motivated employees are eager to perform well in adopting the change and will work hard to do so. In doing so, they expect some results. If, after doing what is expected of them for some period of time, they do not see any results or have not learned enough about the innovation to see its potential, their enthusiasm may wane. If that should happen, it would be very difficult to renew their motivation, without which it would be difficult to successfully adopt the TQM or reengineering. The window of opportunity would have closed.

Timing Options

As with choosing which activities to perform and how to perform them, a firm has many options as to when it can perform the activities of its business or value system.

Business System Activities

To illustrate the options that are available to firms as far as the timing of their value-adding activities is concerned, we again use the business system shown in Figure 5.1.

Research and Development In performing R&D activities, a firm may decide to pursue new technologies only after rivals with more sophisticated R&D have advanced the state of knowledge in the new technologies. It may decide that it will be aggressive about patenting only early in the life of a technology rather than later in the technology's life cycle.

Product Design A firm may decide to introduce new designs frequently even when doing so cannibalizes existing products. For example, in the 1980s and 1990s, Intel often introduced a new generation of its microprocessors before sales of an existing one had peaked. As to coordinating its activities with the manufacturing group, a firm may decide to do so well before the concept design stage or after conceptualization is done and all that is required is obtaining the right components for the design.

Manufacturing/Operations If a firm treats its vendors like allies, it must decide when, in the manufacturing process, to get them involved. Should the firm get vendors involved as early as the process development stage or just before manufacturing starts? If a firm decides to adopt the latest manufacturing technologies, such as lean manufacturing, when should it start training its manufacturing staff: weeks before its own plants start manufacturing or after its plants have started operations? If it decides that information technology is important to the manufacturing process and it wants to include manufacturing information systems, when should it start integrating such systems into its manufacturing?

Marketing/Sales When a new product is about to come out, a firm must often decide whether to start advertising the product before the product has been manufactured or after the product has gone into production. It may also have to decide on the intensity of the advertising—at what time during the product launch and postlaunch advertising is going to be most intense.

Distribution A technological change that impacts distribution channels can present opportunities to change distributions. For example, the Internet introduced a new channel for digital products, making it easier to switch distributors, especially for firms whose products are digital.

Value System Activities

Coopetition Since value is often created and captured through coopetition, the activities that a firm performs often anticipate or respond to coopetitors' activities. If Intel introduces a 64-bit microprocessor chip, Dell is probably better off developing a PC that uses the chip. Microsoft may also be better off developing software that takes advantage of the new chip's tremendous capabilities. Such cooperative activities would help all three firms create better value for the end customer. In many other cases, a firm's decision to engage in an activity comes in response to competitive moves.

Industry Changes Since industry characteristics often evolve, the timing of the activities that a firm performs in its business model can be a function of its industry's evolution. For example, one reason Dell's build-to-order strategy was so successful in the late 1990s was that the PC industry had evolved to a point where many businesses had management information system (MIS) groups that could better determine the PC needs of their firms without hand-holding from distributors.[28] Up to that point in the PC's life cycle, most customers needed hand-holding, some of which the dealers provided. A standard had also emerged, making it easier for firms to specify exactly what it was that they wanted in a PC. Finally, the Internet became easy to use and widely available to many potential build-to-order customers.

CASE EXAMPLE

We now present a short case and case analysis to illustrate some of the concepts discussed in this chapter.[29]

Case: Wal-Mart

The first Wal-Mart discount store was built in Rogers, Arkansas, in 1962; by 2003, Wal-Mart had become the largest company in the world, with sales of over $217,799 billion and an income of $6.67 billion.[30] Since going public in 1972, the company has never lost money. This success has generally been attributed to Sam Walton, the company's founder, and, more importantly, to the decisions that the company has taken over the years. While competitor Kmart, also founded in 1962, initially located its stores only in large population centers, Wal-Mart saw a need in small towns that was not being satisfied. As Sam Walton would later recall, "If we offered prices as good or better than stores in cities that were four hours away by car, people would shop at home. It was just that simple."[31] So Wal-Mart located its stores in small towns, with the first stores concentrating in areas with populations of 25,000,[32] what Sam called "little one-horse towns which everybody else was ignoring."[33] Wal-Mart also saw some other advantages of moving to small towns. According to Sidney McKnight, a Wal-Mart official, "occupancy fees, advertising costs, payroll and taxes are all lower than in the big cities. You get a work force that is likely to be more stable and the instant identity of being the biggest store around."[34]

In addition to having to contend with its competitors, Wal-Mart, like most retail start-ups, had to face major retailers, many of whom wielded a lot of power. As Sam Walton would later recall, "Sometimes it was difficult getting the bigger companies—the Procter & Gambles, Eastman Kodaks, whoever—to call on us at all, and when they did, they would dictate to us how much they would sell us and at what price."[35] By the late 1980s, however, that had changed. In 1987, Procter & Gamble (P&G), which once wouldn't talk to Wal-Mart, proposed setting up a "partnership" with Wal-Mart. An electronic data interchange (EDI) link was installed between the two firms for sharing information. P&G could instantaneously receive information on any of the hundreds of different items that it sold to Wal-Mart. This allowed P&G to better tailor its production to meet Wal-Mart's demand.[36] Wal-Mart also had access to the schedules and production flows of P&G. At some point in the P&G–Wal-Mart relationship, Wal-Mart was selling as much as 6 percent of P&G's output. It took the relationship further with other firms. Gitano, a maker of fashionable jeans, was responsible for the inventory in a specific area of Wal-Mart warehouse space, but Wal-Mart did not "buy" the merchandise until it had been moved into a store. In return, Wal-Mart told Gitano, for example, the rate and prices at which it was selling the jeans.[37]

Once the decision had been made to go after small towns, Wal-Mart expanded aggressively into neighboring small towns. For example, by 1979, it had opened 276 stores in 11 states in the southwestern United States. This expansion had an interesting pattern to it: "We are always pushing from the inside out. We never jump and then backfill," CEO David Glass would later say.[38] In addition to saturating contiguous small towns with stores, Wal-Mart built distribution centers and established an innovation called *cross-docking*.[39] In cross-docking, goods destined for all stores within a certain radius were centrally ordered and then delivered to different distribution centers, each of which covered a certain geographic region with many stores.[40] At each distribution center, merchandise was sorted and loaded into waiting trucks for delivery to individual stores. As early as the 1970s and 1980s, when most retailers were slow to embrace information technology, Wal-Mart was busily adopting information and communication technologies. In particular, it integrated them with such retail functions as logistics, purchasing, and inventory management. For example, in the early 1980s, it installed electronic point-of-sale systems (EPOSs) in all its stores to better manage store inventory and collect information on customers' buying trends—well before its competitors and well before the dot-com era. This information was then relayed by satellite communication systems to distribution warehouses. At the distribution centers, the data were consolidated and used to order merchandise as well as sort and direct merchandise to the right trucks for delivery to the stores within their distribution zones that needed the goods. Some of the trucks also picked up merchandise from manufacturers and returns from stores on their way back to the distribution centers—an activity that was also facilitated by the installed information and communication technologies. In 1991 alone, for example, Wal-Mart saved over $720 million in distribution costs.[41]

Over the years, Wal-Mart also built what would later be known as the "Wal-Mart culture." It gave all employees an opportunity to participate in the management of the firm, well before the word *empowerment* became popular in management literature. For example, managers of local stores had some freedom in pricing some items to respond to local conditions. Equally important was the fact that management was genuinely open to suggestions from employees. As Sam Glass, a Wal-Mart CEO, recalled, "I was talking with Sam the other day, and he was remarking about how 99 percent of the best ideas we ever had came from our employees."[42]

In 2003, Wal-Mart was still thriving, while Kmart had filed for bankruptcy. In May 2002 alone, Kmart had lost over $1 billion and its future was in doubt. The question that attracted the attention of many scholars and managers alike was why Wal-Mart had done so well compared to Kmart and other retailers. Did positioning have anything to do with a small Arkansas retail store's growing to become the world's largest company and one of the most profitable discount retailers?

Analysis: *Which, How,* and *When* in Wal-Mart's Success

The activities that Wal-Mart performed, how it performed them, and when it performed them played a critical role in the company's success. In particular, *how* it moved into small towns played a pivotal role in preventing competitors from moving in and eroding Wal-Mart's first-mover advantage.

Which

By moving into small towns that its competitors shunted for larger ones, Wal-Mart avoided early head-on confrontation. The move also gave Wal-Mart some economies of small-town operations such as lower taxes, lower lease expenses, lower advertising expenses, a stable workforce, and so on." By building its own distribution centers rather than depending on reluctant powerful suppliers, Wal-Mart could afford to keep its stores stocked, although at the cost of holding inventory longer. By adopting information technology and integrating it with store operations and logistics, the company was able to keep its costs low while offering its small-town customers the goods that they wanted when they wanted them. By building the so-called Wal-Mart culture, it had employees who truly cared about the company and who worked harder for less. This system of activities—moving into small towns, establishing the Wal-Mart culture, building distribution centers, adopting information technology, building an efficient logistics system, and integrating its information technology with store operations and logistics—constituted a business system that was difficult to imitate. The system enabled Wal-Mart to be better positioned relative to its competitors: It allowed the company to offer low-cost products to its customers and to reverse the direction of bargaining power between it and suppliers. The system also made it difficult for Wal-Mart's competitors to catch up or leapfrog the company. As the company grew larger, it gained more power in the relationship with its suppliers, until eventually it had bargaining power over the suppliers. Its well-earned bargaining power, the economies of scale from its size, and the various measures it took to keep agency costs low kept its per-unit costs low.

How

How Wal-Mart moved into small towns was also critical to its success. It saturated contiguous towns with its stores and built distribution centers and logistics systems to serve the areas. Recall David Glass's comment: "We are always pushing from the inside out. We never jump and then backfill." By saturating neighboring towns with stores rather than "jumping and backfilling," Wal-Mart made it more difficult for competitors to move in. If a rival such as Kmart wanted to enter an area saturated by Wal-Mart and profitably offer the same low prices that Wal-Mart offered, it would have to build the same number of stores, distribution centers, and logistics systems as Wal-Mart had. (In the language of economists, a new entrant would have to build a "plant" of the same minimum efficient scale, or MES.) Doing so would double the capacity in an area already saturated with stores, causing both firms to lose money. The realization that they would lose money prevented rational rivals and new entrants from entering the areas saturated with Wal-Mart stores. Effectively, Wal-Mart reduced rivalry in and potential new entry into the areas that it had saturated. With few rivals in these areas, Wal-Mart could charge high prices to customers, who had fewer choices. Overall, however, its prices were still very low compared to competitors' prices.

When

It was because Wal-Mart moved into small towns first that its strategy of saturating contiguous small towns worked. In addition, it built a first-mover advantage by capturing scarce resources such as store locations in contiguous towns and loyal small-town employees and customers.

Effectively, the types of activities *which* Wal-Mart chose to perform, *how* it performed them, and *when* it performed them allowed the firm to be better positioned vis-à-vis its coopetitors, capture scarce resources, keep its costs low, and make a relatively unattractive retail industry more attractive for itself.

Summary

A firm makes more money than its rivals if its business model offers products or services at a lower cost than do its rivals or offers differentiated products at premium prices that more than compensate for the extra cost of differentiation and the firm is well positioned vis-à-vis its suppliers, customers, rivals, complementors, substitute products, and potential new entrants to appropriate the value. To offer such customer value and appropriate it, firms perform the activities of their business systems in the context of their value systems. The extent to which a firm can offer superior value and appropriate the value, thereby earning a higher rate of profits than its rivals can, is a function of which activities the firm performs, how it performs them, and when it performs them. In particular, it is a function of how the activities that a firm performs offer lower-cost or more differentiated products than those of its competitors to the market segments it decides to serve, dampen industry competitive forces, exploit industry value drivers, leverage the firm's resources, and keep its costs lower regardless of whether the firm has a low-cost or differentiation advantage.

Activities that are consistent with low-cost or product differentiation are different from those performed by rivals, form a system that is difficult to imitate, and take advantage of industry value drivers are more likely to offer superior customer value and position a firm to appropriate the value, thereby increasing the chances that the firm will have a competitive advantage. How activities are performed (e.g., using TQM, reengineering, or benchmarking) can also increase a firm's ability to offer superior value and appropriate it. The timing of when to perform activities can be important, especially if first-mover advantages can be exploited. The Wal-Mart case analysis clearly shows the importance of which activities are performed, how they are performed, and when they are performed.

Key Terms

backward vertical integration, *90*
benchmarking, *100*
business system, *84*
captive input, *91*
competitive advantage, *93*
first-mover advantage, *101*
forward vertical integration, *90*
function, *85*

joint venture, *92*
market exchanges, *90*
mediating industries, *87*
outsourcing, *87*
processes, *98*
reengineering, *100*
strategic alliance, *92*
strategic collaboration, *92*
supply chain, *90*
tapered integration, *90*

total quality management (TQM), *99*
transaction costs, *91*
value chain, *85*
value network, *87*
value shop, *87*
value system, *89*
vertical integration, *90*
x-engineering, *100*

Study Questions

1. Choose your favorite industry and any firm in it you like. Draw the industry's value system and the firm's value chain, value network, or value shop.
2. List the different options that are available to the firm in question 1 as far as which activities it can perform, how it can perform them, and when it can perform them.
3. What are the value drivers in question 1 and how has your favorite firm taken advantage of them?

4. Does the firm in question 1 have a competitive advantage? Why or why not?

5. What are connected activities?

Endnotes

1. M. E. Porter, "Towards a Dynamic Theory of Strategy," *Strategic Management Journal* 12 (1991), pp. 95–117.

2. R. Buaron, "New-Game Strategies," *McKinsey Quarterly,* Spring 1981, pp. 24–40; C. B. Stabell and O. D. Fjeldstad, "Configuring Value for Competitive Advantage: On Chains, Shops, and Networks," *Strategic Management Journal* 19 (1998), pp. 413–437; M. E. Porter, *Competitive Strategy: Techniques for Analyzing Industries and Competitors* (New York: Free Press, 1980).

3. The idea that value also comes from value networks and value shops was developed by Stabell and Fjeldstad, "Configuring Value for Competitive Advantage"; the underpinnings of these value configurations are in J. D. Thompson, *Organizations in Action* (New York: McGraw-Hill, 1967).

4. The concept of a value chain was developed by M. E. Porter, *Competitive Advantage: Creating and Sustaining Superior Performance* (New York: Free Press, 1985).

5. Stabell and Fjeldstad, "Configuring Value for Competitive Advantage."

6. Thompson, *Organizations in Action.*

7. "The Virtual Corporation," *Business Week,* Feb. 8, 1993; W. H. Davidow and M. S. Malone, *The Virtual Corporation* (New York: HarperCollins, 1992).

8. R. H. Coase, "The Nature of the Firm," *Econometrica* 4 (1937), pp. 386–405; O. E. Williamson, *Markets and Hierarchies* (New York: Free Press, 1975).

9. O. E. Williamson, *The Economic Institutions of Capitalism* (New York: Free Press, 1985); A. N. Afuah, "Redefining Firm Boundaries in the Face of the Internet: Are Firms Really Shrinking?" *Academy of Management Review* 28 (2003), pp. 34–53.

10. Williamson, *The Economic Institutions of Capitalism.*

11. K. R. Harrigan, "Formulating Vertical Integration Strategies," *Academy of Management Review* 9 (1984), pp. 638–652.

12. J. H. Dyer and K. Nobeoka, "Creating and Managing a High Performance Knowledge-Sharing Network: The Toyota Case," *Strategic Management Journal* 21 (2000), pp. 345–367.

13. P. S. Dussauge, S. Hart, and B. Ramanantsoa, *Strategic Technology Management* (New York: Wiley, 1992).

14. A. N. Afuah, "Dynamic Boundaries of the Firm: Are Firms Better Off Being Vertically Integrated in the Face of a Technological Change?" *Academy of Management Journal* 44 (2001), pp. 1211–1228.

15. For more on these factors, see M. E. Porter, "What Is Strategy?" *Harvard Business Review,* November–December 1996, pp. 61–78.

16. C. M. Christensen and M. Overdorf, "Meeting the Challenge of Disruptive Change," *Harvard Business Review*, March–April 2000, pp. 67–76 (quote is on p. 68).

17. Ibid.

18. K. B. Clark and K. Fujimoto, *Product Development Performance: Strategy, Organization, and Management in the World Automobile Industry* (Boston: Harvard Business School Press, 1991).

19. A. Afuah, C. Crane, W. Johnson, K. Neumark, and C. Perrigo, "Pixar, 1996," University of Michigan Business School case, 1998.

20. T. C. Powell, "Total Quality Management as Competitive Advantage," *Strategic Management Journal* 16 (1995), pp. 15–37.

21. www.quality.nist.gov, accessed Jan. 6, 2003.

22. www.efqm.org/human_resources/about.htm, accessed Jan. 6, 2003.

23. Christensen and Overdorf, "Meeting the Challenge of Disruptive Change."

24. M. Hammer and J. Champy, *Reengineering the Corporation: A Manifesto for Business Revolution* (New York: HarperBusiness, 1993).

25. J. Champy, *X-Engineering the Corporation: Reinventing Your Business in the Digital Age* (New York: Warner Business, 2003).

26. M. Lieberman and D. Montgomery, "First-Mover (Dis)Advantages: Retrospective and Link with the Resource-Based View," *Strategic Management Journal* 19 (1998), pp. 1111–1125.

27. M. J. Tyre and W. J. Orlikowski, "Windows of Opportunity: Temporal Patterns of Technological Adaptation in Organizations," *Organization Science* 5 (1994), pp. 98–118.

28. D. B. Yoffie, J. Cohn, and D. Levy, "Apple Computer 1992," Harvard Business School case 9-792-081 (1995).

29. This section draws heavily on A. N. Afuah, *Innovation Management: Strategies, Implementation and Profits* (New York: Oxford University Press, 2003), chaps. 8 and 10.

30. "Wal-Mart Reports Record Sales and Earnings for 4th Quarter and Year," Wal-Mart financial statement, Feb. 19, 2002.

31. "Wal-Mart: A Discounter Sinks Deep Roots in Small Town, U.S.A.," *Business Week,* Nov. 5, 1979.

32. Ibid.

33. S. Walton and J. Huey, *Made in America: My Story* (New York: Doubleday, 1992).

34. "Wal-Mart: A Discounter Sinks Deep Roots in Small Town, U.S.A.," p. 145; W. Vlasic and K. Naughton, "Kmart: Who's in Charge Here?" *Business Week,* Dec. 4, 1995, p. 104.

35. "Change at the Check-Out: A Survey in Retailing," *The Economist,* Mar. 4, 1995.

36. Ibid.

37. B. Saporito and S. Kirsch, "Is Wal-Mart Unstoppable?" *Fortune,* May 6, 1991.

38. "Wal-Mart: A Discounter Sinks Deep Roots in Small Town, U.S.A.," p. 145; P. Gemawat, "Wal-Mart Stores' Discount Operations," Harvard Business School case 9-387-018, 1986; "Change at the Check-Out."

39. "Change at the Check-Out."

40. Stores frequently displayed locally made merchandise. *The Story of Wal-Mart,* 1992 Annual Financial Statement.

41. "Change at the Check-Out."

42. Saporito and Kirsch, "Is Wal-Mart Unstoppable?"; "Wal-Mart: A Discounter Sinks Deep Roots in Small Town, U.S.A."

Chapter **Six**

Resources and Capabilities: The Roots of Business Models

Recall that a firm makes more money than its rivals if its business model creates and offers superior customer value (lower-cost or more differentiated products than those of competitors) and positions the firm to appropriate the value. To perform the activities that enable a firm to offer superior customer value and appropriate the value, a firm needs resources. For example, for Southwest Airlines to offer its customers low fares and frequent flights, it needs to have the rights to operate in uncongested airports, a friendly culture, and airplanes. A pharmaceutical company such as Pfizer needs well-equipped R&D laboratories, scientists, and patents to be able to produce drugs such as Viagra that customers find valuable. To make its cola drinks readily available to customers whenever they want them, Coca-Cola needs shelf space at its distributors and needs contracts with its bottlers.

Resources in and of themselves do not, however, produce customer value and profits. Firms must also have the ability or capacity to turn resources into customer value and profits. For ExxonMobil to make money from oil, it needs not only resources such as exploration rights, sophisticated exploration equipment, and geologists but also the ability to find oil and turn it into something that its customers want. In short, resources and an ability to use them underpin the value-adding activities that a firm needs to perform so as to offer its customers the type of value they want.

In this chapter, we explore the central role that resources and an ability to use them play in business models, especially in the profitability of business models. We start the chapter by defining resources and capabilities. We then explore the characteristics of resources and capabilities that allow one firm to build a more profitable business model than its competitors' models. This is followed by an exploration of the link between resources and the other components of a business model, an exploration of how to build new resources, and an examination of some of the efforts that are under way to better quantify resources.

DEFINITION OF *RESOURCES* AND *CAPABILITIES*

Resources and Assets

Creating value for customers and making money from the value requires **resources** (or *assets*) such as plants, equipment, patents, skilled scientists, brand-name reputation, geographic location, client relations, distribution channels, and trade secrets. Assets or resources can be categorized as tangible, intangible, and human.[1] **Tangible assets** can be physical, such as plants and equipment, or financial, such as cash. These are the types of assets that are usually identified and accounted for in financial statements under the category "assets." **Intangible assets** are non-physical and nonfinancial assets such as patents, brands, copyrights, trade secrets, market research findings, relationships with customers, knowledge in databases, and relationships with vendors.[2] They are usually not identified in financial statements but can be excellent sources of profits. For example, a patent or trade secret that gives a firm exclusive access to a product or process may allow the firm to be the only one producing a product with certain characteristics, thereby making the product highly differentiated and profitable. For a while, the copyright for Intel's microcode allowed the firm to offer differentiated microprocessors to makers of personal computers. **Human assets** are the skills and knowledge that employees carry with them.

Capabilities and Competences

As important as assets are, it usually takes more than assets to offer value to customers. A firm needs to have the ability to convert its assets into customer value. Customers will not scramble to a firm's doors simply because the firm has modern plants, geniuses, and patents. The firm has to use the plants, the geniuses, and the knowledge embodied in the patents to offer customers something that they value. Patients do not buy patents or skilled scientists from pharmaceutical companies. They buy medicines that have been developed by skilled scientists using knowledge embodied in patents. Assets must be converted into something that customers want. A firm's ability or capacity to turn its resources into customer value and profits is usually called a **competence** or **capability**. Competences usually involve the use or integration of more than one asset.[3] LSI Logic's ability to quickly turn its "cores" into products that customers want is a competence. Intel's ability to develop microprocessors that exploit its copyrighted microcode and that are compatible with its installed base of microprocessors is a competence. So is Coca-Cola's ability to turn its secret formula and brand into a product that many customers perceive as being preferable to its rivals' products.

ASSESSING THE PROFITABILITY POTENTIAL OF RESOURCES

Since the goal of a business model is to make money, a question that must interest a firm as it pursues a business model is, What types of resources are most likely to make its business model profitable? This is a question that has interested strategy scholars for a long time. The profitability potential of a firm's resource can be assessed via a **VRISA analysis** (value, rareness, imitability, substitutability, appropriability analysis), as shown in Table 6.1. This analysis consists of answering five questions:[4]

1. Does the resource make a significant contribution toward the value that customers perceive?
2. Is the resource rare? That is, is the firm the only one with the resource; if not, is its level of the resource higher than that of competitors?
3. Is the resource difficult to imitate?
4. Is the resource difficult to substitute?
5. To what extent can the firm appropriate the value from the resource?

TABLE 6.1 **VRISA Analysis**

Attribute	Key Question
Value	Does the resource provide customers with something that they value?
Rareness (uniqueness)	Is your firm the only one with that capability? If not, is its level of capability higher than that of competitors?
Imitability	Is it easy for other firms to imitate the resource?
Substitutability	Can another resource offer customers the same value that your firm's resource does?
Appropriability	Who makes the money from the resource?

Customer Value

The first question that a firm must ask itself in assessing the extent to which a resource contributes to the profitability of its business model is, Does the resource make a significant contribution toward the value that customers perceive? Honda Motor Company is known for its ability to build internal combustion engines that are light, reliable, and high-performing. Customers recognize this, and that may be one reason that they buy Honda cars, motorcycles, lawn mowers, and portable electric generators. Thus Honda's capabilities in building internal combustion engines make a valuable contribution to the value that the company's customers perceive in its products. In the 1980s and 1990s Merck's R&D group developed a number of drugs that offered patients superior benefits. For example, it introduced the first of the statin drugs, a group of drugs that significantly reduce the level of cholesterol in patients. Thus, Merck's R&D capabilities made an important contribution to the value that customers perceived in the firm's products. Coca-Cola's brand-name reputation makes a significant contribution to the value that customers perceive in the company's colas.

Rareness

Making a significant contribution to the value that customers perceive is a necessary condition for a resource to earn its owner profits. But it is not a sufficient condition for making money. The contribution that the resource makes to customer value should be superior to that made by competitors' resources. This will be the case if (1) the resource is uniquely held by the firm or (2) if it is widely held, the firm's level of the resource is higher than that of competitors. In other words, the resource should be rare, or, if it is not rare, the firm's level of it should be higher than that of competitors. The most valuable substance to life on earth is water. But water is abundantly available to many people, and therefore it is difficult to make as much money from water as its value would suggest. Eli Lilly's formula for Prozac was rare during the life of the drug's patent, a period during which no one could legally duplicate Prozac's chemical structure. There were no other patents for the particular chemical compound that makes up Prozac. When the patent expired, competitors could offer generic versions of the drug, thereby matching a lot of the value that Prozac previously offered customers. Many firms have internal combustion engine capabilities that are comparable to Honda's capabilities, but Honda's level of the capabilities is higher than that of these competitors. Unless a firm's resource is unique or its level of it is superior to that of competitors, a firm cannot make money from the resource. Offering superior value requires having unique or superior resources.

Imitability

A rare resource that makes a valuable contribution to customer value is likely to make its owner money. How long the resource can keep making its owner money is a function of its **imitability**—the extent to which the resource can be imitated. If a resource can be copied, the owner of the resource will suddenly have many competitors whose resources make the same significant contribution to customer value as the owner's resource does. This decreases the prices that the owner of the resource can charge for the value created or the quantity of its product that is demanded. Inimitability is said to be high if the resource cannot be imitated or substituted. Many patents for drugs are protected by law until their expiration, thereby increasing their inimitability. Coca-Cola has kept its cola formula secret for decades, thereby limiting the extent to which it can be copied. There are at least six other reasons, discussed below, that imitating a resource might be difficult.[5]

Historical Context

It is often difficult to replicate the historical context in which a resource was acquired. Caterpillar's difficult-to-imitate and valuable worldwide service network of technicians trained to repair and service its earth-moving equipment can trace its roots to World War II.[6] During the war, Caterpillar's earth-moving vehicles were the machines of choice for allied forces in Europe, and many service personnel learned how to operate, repair, and service the equipment. After the war, many veterans who returned to the civilian work force had the skills and knowledge needed to repair and service Caterpillar equipment, making it easy for Caterpillar to organize the valuable network. Trying to replicate the context in which this network was built would be almost impossible.

Causal Ambiguity

It is not always clear exactly which of a firm's capabilities allow it to offer its customers better value, or to be more profitable, compared with its rivals. For example, it is difficult to place a finger on what it is about Honda that makes the firm so good at offering superior engines. When there is considerable uncertainty about which capability allows a firm to perform better than its competitors, we say that **causal ambiguity** exists. If a potential imitator cannot tell exactly what it is that it wants to imitate about an industry leader, it is difficult for the potential imitator to imitate the leader. How can one imitate something that one does not know? However, firms themselves often do not know what makes them perform better than their competitors. Thus, causal ambiguity is sometimes to blame for the failure of firms to extend their capabilities into different product markets.[7]

Success Breeds Success

The amount that can be added to some resources is proportional to the existing resource stock that the firm already has. Thus, an imitator that starts from scratch may never catch up since its initial addition to the nothing that it has is proportional to nothing and therefore close to zero. For example, the number of copies of a new operating system that Microsoft can sell is proportional to the firm's installed base of Windows operating systems that customers already have. A start-up that has a comparable operating system but no installed base is likely to sell a negligible amount compared to Microsoft. Therefore, the rate at which Microsoft can build its installed base is greater than that of the start-up.

Time Compression Difficulties

Building resources usually takes time and continuous reinforcement, thereby giving first movers an advantage that is difficult to overcome. Merck's R&D capabilities and ability to get its drugs through clinical testing and approval by the U.S. Food and Drug Administration (FDA) are outstanding. This is partly attributed to the relationships that the firm has created over the years with various doctors, research centers, and hospitals. Once doctors and hospitals have made a commitment to a particular company, switching to another firm is usually not an easy decision for them. Moreover, relationships with doctors and hospitals cannot be created overnight. It takes time, and even doubling the amount of effort put into building the capability will not necessarily cut the time in half.

Strategic Stemming of Erosion

The strategies that a firm can use to slow down imitation of its capabilities can also stem erosion. First, a firm can keep reinvesting in its resources to prevent them from depreciating. In the 1990s, Coca-Cola reinvested more than 40 percent of its revenues from concentrate in marketing and sales, largely to maintain the strength of its brand. Second, having a history of retaliating against imitators or new entrants into the firm's product market spaces can reduce the number of attempts to imitate the firm and thereby stem erosion. In the 1990s, for example, Intel Corporation sued any firm that copied the microcode in its microprocessors.

Interconnectedness of Resources

Toyota's superior product development and manufacturing capabilities are often associated with the network of relationships that it has with its suppliers.[8] A new entrant may not be able to develop such product capabilities without first building relationships with a network of suppliers. But such relationships take time and trust to develop. This may make it difficult to imitate Toyota.

Substitutability

If a resource cannot be imitated, the question becomes, Can it be substituted? Caterpillar's competitors found its worldwide service network very difficult to imitate, but one of them was able to substitute the resource. Komatsu developed products that were so reliable that they did not need to be repaired as often, and therefore the firm did not need the type of service network that Caterpillar needed. Effectively, Komatsu had substituted design capabilities for some of Caterpillar's service network. It is easy for a firm to be so focused on preventing imitability that it forgets about **substitutability.**

Appropriability

A resource that is valuable, rare, inimitable, and nonsubstitutable should create distinctive value for customers. But as we saw in Chapter 2, creating value for customers does not guarantee that the creator of the value will profit from it. Thus, it is not always the case that a firm is able to appropriate the value from its resources. Whether a firm that creates value profits from it is a function of the bargaining power that the firm has over its suppliers, customers, and complementors. If suppliers have bargaining power over the firm that creates the value, they can extract high prices for the inputs the firm needs, thereby reducing the profits the firm can earn from the value created. For example, if the valuable, rare, inimitable, and nonsubstitutable resource is an outstanding chip designer at a chip company or a Nobel laureate at a pharmaceutical company, this person can threaten to leave and start a new company. To convince him or her to stay, the company may have to spend so much to keep the person that its profits will be considerably reduced. If customers have bargaining power, they can force the firm to accept low prices. Since the goal of a business model is to make money, a firm should be able to appropriate the value that its resources and capabilities create.

EXAMPLES OF VRISA ANALYSIS

To illustrate how a VRISA analysis can be performed, we present sample analyses of Wal-Mart, Pfizer, and Southwest Airlines resources.

Wal-Mart Resource: Location in Small Towns

When Wal-Mart moved to small towns in the southwestern United States, it saturated contiguous towns with its stores and built distribution centers, logistics systems, and information technology to match. The analysis below is summarized in Table 6.2.

Value: Does Wal-Mart's location in small towns provide customers in these towns with something that they value? Customers in these areas can shop at low prices close to home instead of driving hundreds of miles to do so.

Rareness: Is Wal-Mart the only one with this resource? If not, is its level of the resource higher than that of competitors? In many of the contiguous towns that it has saturated with its stores, Wal-Mart is the only major discount retailer in town. There are only so many large discount retail stores that can be profitably located in these towns, and Wal-Mart is already in them. It has preempted competitors as far as the all-important retail resource of location is concerned. Where it faces competing discount retail stores, Wal-Mart offers lower prices than these competitors since its overall low-cost structure allows it to pass on some of its cost savings to its customers in the form of lower prices.

TABLE 6.2 **VRISA Analysis: Wal-Mart's Location in Small Towns**

Attribute	Key Question	Answer
Value	Does Wal-Mart's location in small towns provide customers in these towns with something that they value?	Yes. Customers can buy low-cost merchandise close to home.
Rareness (uniqueness)	Is Wal-Mart the only one with this resource? If not, is its level of the resource higher than that of competitors?	Yes. In many areas of the U.S. Southwest, Wal-Mart is the only large discount retailer; where it is not the only one, its prices are lower than competitors' prices.
Imitability	Is it easy for other firms to imitate Wal-Mart's location advantage?	No. It is difficult for competitors to come in and build similar stores and distribution centers in areas Wal-Mart has already saturated.
Substitutability	Can another resource offer customers the same value that Wal-Mart's saturation of small towns does?	Yes. A viable substitute for some products is an e-commerce capability.
Appropriability	Does Wal-Mart make money from its location in small towns?	Yes. The threat of entry into saturated areas is low, there are few close-by rivals, and Wal-Mart has power over suppliers.

Imitability: *Is it easy for other firms to imitate Wal-Mart's location advantage?* Imitating Wal-Mart in its saturated areas is not easy. For a potential competitor to benefit from the same economies of scale and efficiencies as Wal-Mart enjoys, the competitor would have to build the same number of stores, distribution centers, and logistics systems, and establish the same information technology and organization, as Wal-Mart has. But doing so would almost double capacity and would result in a price war in which both firms would lose money. Since rational potential new entrants will enter only if they expect to make money, new entrants are not likely to try to replicate Wal-Mart's activities in areas that it has already saturated with stores.

Substitutability: *Can another resource offer customers the same value that Wal-Mart's saturation of small towns does?* Business-to-consumer (B2C) capabilities such as those possessed by Amazon.com in books, CDs, videos, and so on can be substituted for Wal-Mart's location since customers in its areas can shop via the Internet. But Wal-Mart has developed e-commerce capabilities too.

Appropriability: *Does Wal-Mart make money from its location in small towns?* Since Wal-Mart has bargaining power over its suppliers, faces little threat of entry, and has few rivals in its areas, it appropriates most of the value that it creates for its customers. It has been very profitable in the areas that it saturated with stores.

Pfizer Resource: Knowledge for Making Lipitor

Our second VRISA example is an analysis of Pfizer's knowledge for making Lipitor, its blockbuster drug for reducing cholesterol levels (Table 6.3). Lipitor belongs to a class of drugs called statins that, as of 2003, were popular for their ability to reduce cholesterol levels and heart attacks in patients.[9] With sales of more than $6 billion, Lipitor was the best-selling drug in the world. To produce Lipitor, Pfizer needs knowledge of the chemical compound for the drug and knowledge of the technology that underpins statins.

TABLE 6.3 VRISA Analysis: Pfizer's Knowledge for Making Lipitor

Attribute	Key Question	Answer
Value	Does Pfizer's knowledge for making its Lipitor drug give customers something that they value?	Yes. Lipitor reduces bad cholesterol and increases good cholesterol in many customers and reduces heart attacks in some.
Rareness (uniqueness)	Is Pfizer the only one with the knowledge for making this type of cholesterol drug? If not, is Pfizer's level of the knowledge higher than that of competitors?	No. Other firms also have the knowledge for producing this type of drug. However, Pfizer's drug reduces bad cholesterol and increases good cholesterol better than competing products do.
Imitability	Is it easy for other firms to imitate Pfizer's knowledge?	No. Pfizer's Lipitor patent prohibits imitation during the life of the patent.
Substitutability	Can another resource offer customers the same value that Pfizer's customers get from this cholesterol drug?	Yes. Other capabilities for producing cholesterol drugs exist, but Pfizer's technology so far offers the best benefits for customers.
Appropriability	Does Pfizer make money from its knowledge of making Lipitor?	Yes. Suppliers and customers have not been very powerful.

Value: Does Pfizer's knowledge for making its Lipitor drug give customers something that they value? Pfizer's knowledge of the compound and knowledge of the related statin technology allow the firm to produce Lipitor, which reduces levels of bad cholesterol and increases levels of good cholesterol in many patients who take it and also reduces heart attacks in some patients.

Rareness: Is Pfizer the only one with the knowledge for making this type of cholesterol drug? If not, is Pfizer's level of the knowledge higher than that of competitors? Pfizer is not the only firm with knowledge of how to produce statins. In fact, in offering Lipitor, Pfizer was the fifth company to offer a statin cholesterol drug. However, its drug reduces bad cholesterol and increases good cholesterol better than competing products do.

Imitability: Is it easy for other firms to imitate Pfizer's knowledge? Since Pfizer's Lipitor is protected by U.S. patent laws, duplication of the product's chemical structure before the patent has expired is illegal.

Substitutability: Can another resource offer customers the same value that Pfizer's customers get from this cholesterol drug? Although competitors have similar capabilities for producing cholesterol drugs, Pfizer's capabilities offer customers the most benefits that customers value.

Appropriability: Does Pfizer make money from its knowledge of making Lipitor? As of 2003, suppliers and patients had little power over Pfizer when it came to Lipitor. Thus the company was able to appropriate much of the value that customers enjoyed in Lipitor. That is likely to change when the patent expires.

Southwest Airlines Resource: Network of Uncongested Airports

Our final VRISA example is an analysis of Southwest Airlines' network of uncongested airports (Table 6.4).

Value: Does Southwest Airlines' network of uncongested airports provide customers with something that they value? Since the airports within the network are uncongested, planes can land and take off with fewer delays than they could at more congested airports, thereby enabling Southwest to offer passengers more frequent flights that are also more likely to arrive on time. Because the airports are uncongested, landing fees are lower. Passengers are also more likely to find parking at such airports than at the more congested ones.

Rareness: Is Southwest Airlines the only one with this resource? If not, is its level of the resource higher than that of competitors? Other airlines fly to uncongested airports but do not have a network of such airports that is as large as Southwest Airlines' network. They also do not have as many landing slots or gates at each airport as Southwest does.

Imitability: Is it easy for other firms to acquire Southwest Airlines' network of uncongested airports and associated gates and landing slots? Competitors may be able to acquire access to a few uncongested airports, but they may find it difficult to replicate the entire network, with the associated gates and landing slots.

Substitutability: Can another resource offer customers the same value that Southwest Airlines' network of uncongested airports does? There is no clear substitute resource or capability for offering the type of low prices and frequent flights that Southwest does using its network of uncongested airports.

TABLE 6.4 **VRISA Analysis: Southwest Airlines' Network of Uncongested Airports**

Attribute	Key Question	Answer
Value	Does Southwest Airlines' network of uncongested airports provide customers with something that they value?	Yes. Passengers can choose from more frequent flights, which are more likely to arrive on time, at low prices. Landing fees are lower, and passengers are more likely to find parking at such airports than at the more congested ones.
Rareness (uniqueness)	Is Southwest Airlines the only one with this resource? If not, is its level of the resource higher than that of competitors?	Yes. Other airlines fly to uncongested airports but none has a network of uncongested airports that is as large as Southwest's network. Nor do they have the associated landing slots and gates.
Imitability	Is it easy for other firms to acquire Southwest Airlines' network of uncongested airports and associated gates and landing slots?	No. Competitors may be able to acquire access to a few uncongested airports, but to replicate Southwest's complete network is difficult.
Substitutability	Can another resource offer customers the same value that Southwest Airlines' network of uncongested airports does?	No. It is difficult to offer the type of low-cost, frequent flights that this network provides by any means other than this network.
Appropriability	Does Southwest Airlines make money from its network of uncongested airports?	Yes. Suppliers and customers do not have much power.

Appropriability: Does Southwest Airlines make money from its network of uncongested airports? As of 2003, Southwest Airlines had good relationships with its employees and unions, and there were plenty of planes available. Southwest was therefore able to appropriate the value from its network of uncongested airports.

COMPETITIVE CONSEQUENCES

The characteristics of a firm's resources and capabilities have competitive consequences for the firm and the type of strategy that it may want to pursue to stay profitable.[10] Table 6.5 shows six different cases and the competitive consequence for each:

- *Case 1:* The firm's resources are valuable, rare, inimitable, and nonsubstitutable and the firm can appropriate them. The firm is thus said to have a *sustainable competitive advantage.* (For many industries, however, the more common situations are cases 2, 3, and 4, where the firm has a *temporary competitive advantage.*)

- *Case 2:* The firm has resources that are valuable, rare, and nonsubstitutable and the firm makes money from them, but the resources can be imitated. During the time that it takes to imitate the resources, the firm has a competitive advantage. Patents fall into this group since they usually give pharmaceutical companies a competitive advantage for the duration of the patent. When the patent expires, however, imitators are allowed to produce generic versions of the drug, eroding the advantage of the original patent owner.

TABLE 6.5   **Competitive Consequence of Resource Characteristics**

	Characteristics of Resources					Competitive Consequence
Case	Valuable	Rare	Difficult to Imitate	Nonsubstitutable	Appropriable	
1	Yes	Yes	Yes	Yes	Yes	Sustainable competitive advantage
2	Yes	Yes	No	Yes	Yes	Temporary competitive advantage
3	Yes	Yes	Yes	No	Yes	Temporary competitive advantage
4	Yes	Yes	No	No	Yes	Temporary competitive advantage
5	Yes	No	No	No	No	Competitive parity
6	No	No	No	No	No	Competitive disadvantage

- *Case 3:* The firm's resources are valuable, rare, and difficult to imitate but are substitutable. Again, such a firm can have a competitive advantage during the period in which competitors are developing substitutes for the advantage. In the 1970s and 1980s, Xerox had a network of trained technicians who could repair its large installed base of copiers. Competitors such as Canon substituted the capability by building machines that did not fail as often and therefore did not require the type of technician network that had been Xerox's advantage.

- *Case 4:* The firm's valuable and rare resources are neither nonsubstitutable nor imitatable. Until its resources are imitated or substituted, the firm has a competitive advantage.

- *Case 5:* If a firm's resources are valuable but are not rare, difficult to imitate, nonsubstitutable, or appropriable, the firm is said to have *competitive parity* with imitators since just about every imitator has the same level of the resources as the firm has. For example, most wheat growers in the United States have competitive parity in growing quality wheat since just about all of them are capable of producing the same quality of wheat.

- *Case 6:* The firm has resources that are not valuable, rare, difficult to imitate, nonsubstitutable, or appropriable. In such a case, the firm and its imitators are at a *competitive disadvantage.*

In general, many competitive advantages are temporary, and there are several reasons for this. First, many competitive advantages can be overturned by technological change. In the video game industry, for example, competitors have used the introduction of new generations of microprocessors to overturn advantages held by incumbent video console makers: Nintendo took over from Atari, Sega took over from Nintendo, Sony took over from Sega, and so on. Second, the proliferation of information technology means that firms can use it to imitate or substitute competitors' capabilities. For example, a software developer whose advantage in the early 1990s rested in having well-functioning teams of software developers in the United States is likely to see that advantage threatened by software development teams in Ireland and India who can work via the Internet. Third, globalization, privatization, and deregulation can also erode existing advantages. For example, globalization often means that a local company that was protected by high tariffs or quotas may now have to face foreign competitors with deep pockets that can allow them to build better local capabilities.

BUILDING NEW INTANGIBLE RESOURCES

One challenge that firms often face is deciding how to acquire new intangible resources. The familiarity matrix framework offers some guidelines.[11]

Familiarity Matrix Framework

The **familiarity matrix** is based on the assumption that the more familiar a firm is with the knowledge that underpins new resources it wants to acquire, the more the firm should contemplate developing the resources internally rather than through outside avenues such as alliances (Figure 6.1).[12] The rationale behind this matrix is that it takes related knowledge to absorb knowledge.[13] For example, it is much easier for a medical doctor to understand the latest developments in treating heart disease than it is for an electrical engineer to do so. Conversely, it is much easier for an electrical engineer to understand the latest microchip developments than for a medical doctor to do so. Thus, acquiring new resources that are largely knowledge-based is easier if the firm already has related knowledge.

For convenience, in the familiarity matrix framework the knowledge needed to offer customer value and appropriate it is divided into technological and market knowledge. *Technological knowledge* is knowledge of components, linkages between components, methods, processes, and techniques that are used to create a product.[14] *Market knowledge* is knowledge of distribution channels, product applications, and customer expectations, preferences, needs, and wants. As shown in Figure 6.1, the familiarity matrix expresses the extent to which the technological knowledge and market knowledge underpinning the new resources needed by a firm differ from the firm's existing knowledge.[15]

FIGURE 6.1
Familiarity Matrix

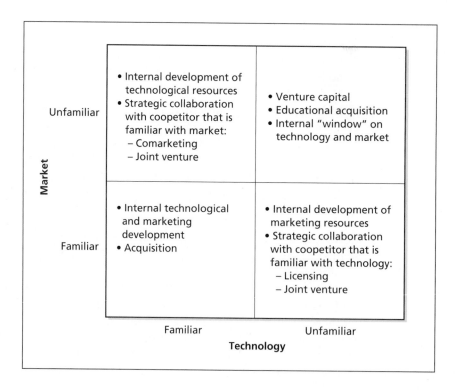

Familiar Technology and Market

If both the technology and the market are familiar to a firm, the firm can develop both technological and marketing resources internally. For example, if General Mills wants to offer a new cereal in the United States, it should be able to develop the capabilities internally since it is very familiar with corn technology and the U.S. market for cereal. A firm can also acquire new resources through an acquisition when it is familiar with the technology and market. The idea here is that since the firm is familiar with both the technology and the market, it can better evaluate candidates for purchase and more easily integrate the purchased technological and marketing resources into existing ones.

Familiar Technology, Unfamiliar Market

If the technology is familiar but the market is not, a firm can develop the technological resources internally and acquire marketing resources through some form of strategic collaboration. Strategic collaboration includes comarketing agreements and joint ventures. In a *comarketing agreement,* a firm that needs marketing resources signs an agreement with one that has them to comarket a product that the firm has produced or plans to produce. For example, in the late 1990s, Warner-Lambert entered into a comarketing agreement with Pfizer to sell Lipitor, Warner's cholesterol-reducing drug, since Pfizer had a superior sales force for cardiovascular drugs (of which Lipitor is one) compared to Warner-Lambert's (Pfizer bought Warner-Lambert in 2000).

Rather than participating in a comarketing agreement, a firm can pursue a joint venture. In a *joint venture,* two or more firms usually pool their resources to form a separate legal entity, with each firm having an equity share that is proportional to its equity investment in the venture. A firm that is familiar with the technology but not the market can form a joint venture with one that is familiar with the market. For example, General Mills wanted to enter the European market for cereal, but although it was very familiar with cereal technology, it was not familiar with the European market for cereal. In contrast, Nestlé was very familiar with the European market for breakfast foods, but had no cereal technology. Both companies formed a joint venture called Cereal Partners Worldwide that combined technology resources from General Mills with European marketing and distribution channels from Nestlé.

Familiar Market, Unfamiliar Technology

If the market is familiar but the technology is not, a firm can develop the marketing resources internally and acquire technology resources through licensing or a joint venture. In *licensing,* a firm (the licensee) pays a fee to another firm (the licensor) for the right to use the technological knowledge that is embodied in the licensor's intellectual property. Firms with superior marketing resources that are difficult to imitate can license technology from other firms to exploit these resources. For example, one of Pfizer's best-selling drugs, Procardia, used for treating high blood pressure, was licensed from the German drug company Bayer AG. Licensing allows a firm to have instant access to the licensor's technology. For a firm that may never be able to develop the technology on its own, licensing can be a means of participating in a market. Licensing has two major disadvantages. First, unless a firm has some scarce, inimitable, complementary resources, it may not be able to gain and maintain a competitive advantage through licensing, especially if it keeps depending on such arrangements. Second, firms that have a "not-invented-here (NIH) syndrome" may face the wrath of their scientists, who may not be very enthusiastic about accepting a licensed technology.

Instead of licensing a technology from another company, a firm can form a joint venture to have access to the technology. The Cereal Partners Worldwide example illustrates how a firm that is familiar with the market but not the technology (Nestlé) can gain access to technology resources via a joint venture.

Unfamiliar Market and Technology

When the technology *and* the market are unfamiliar, a firm is better off getting help from another firm that is more familiar with both. This can be achieved through (1) venture capital, (2) educational acquisition, and (3) an internal "window" on the technology and market (Figure 6.1). In *venture capital,* a firm takes a minority position in a start-up that has the capabilities the firm is interested in acquiring. As a venture capitalist investing in a start-up, a firm usually goes through a rigorous process of evaluating the technology, industry, and market of the start-up. Once it invests in the start-up, it also monitors the start-up, technology, and market as both the industry and the start-up evolve. These evaluation and monitoring processes give the firm a chance to learn more about the technology and market as well as to build capabilities in them.

Rather than take a minority equity position in a start-up, a firm may decide to buy the start-up outright. If a firm buys a start-up not to keep it as a subsidiary but primarily to learn from it, the acquisition is said to be an *educational acquisition.* Such an acquisition can be seen as the reverse engineering of an organization in which the acquirer buys, opens up, and learns from its acquisition.

Instead of taking a minority position in a start-up or buying one for educational purposes, a firm may decide to nurture a small group within itself that keeps tabs on new technologies and markets. This avoids the need to make heavy investments right away, and it enables the firm to increase its knowledge while still remaining focused on delivering products through its existing technologies to its existing markets. When a firm uses this approach, it is said to be trying to *maintain a "window"* on potentially important technologies and markets. In the 1970s, 1980s, and 1990s, for example, Sharp Corporation focused its efforts on technologies such as flat-panel-display technology that cut across many applications. At the same time, it also maintained a window on other technologies by having internal groups keep tabs on them. Mechanisms for maintaining windows on technologies also include forming strategic alliances, joining technology consortia, working closely with customers, participating in conferences, being close to or allying with universities, and constantly collecting information about other firms.

Dynamic Capabilities

One of the biggest threats to resources is change. Change can render valuable, rare, difficult-to-imitate, difficult-to-substitute, and appropriable capabilities obsolete or less valuable, thereby eroding any competitive advantage that the capabilities may have endowed on their owner. For example, Digital Equipment Corporation's abilities to design, introduce, and service minicomputers were valuable, rare, difficult to imitate, and appropriable until personal computers and small servers considerably reduced their value, thereby eroding the company's competitive advantage. **Dynamic capabilities** are a firm's abilities to quickly reconfigure its resources and capabilities and to build whatever resources and capabilities are needed to cope with rapidly changing environments.[16] Firms with such capabilities would be able to cope with change and thereby always maintain their competitive advantages. Thus, Digital Equipment Corporation would have retained its advantage in computers if it had dynamic capabilities.

EXTENDABILITY OF RESOURCES

A firm that uses its valuable, rare, and inimitable resources to offer products in one market may decide to use the same resources to offer products in another market. Honda Motor Company comes to mind again. Honda uses its superior resources in internal combustion engine technology to offer engines not only for its cars but also for motorcycles, lawn mowers, marine vehicles, small electric generators, ground tillers, pumps, and chain saws. The Disney Company is another example. Its Mickey Mouse character and theme park resources have been leveraged into numerous businesses. Thus, an important question for a firm with distinctive resources is, When can the firm extend such capabilities into other businesses and make money in doing so? The fact that a firm's valuable resources can be extended to another product market does not mean that the firm is going to make money in that market. Answering the following four questions can be helpful to a firm, as it develops its business model, in extending its capabilities into a new business:[17]

1. Is the market for the new product an attractive market? If not, can the firm, in moving in, make it attractive for itself?
2. If complementary assets are needed, can the firm get them?
3. How much will it cost the firm to get into the new business?
4. Will the firm's capabilities really help the firm gain a competitive advantage in the new business? If not, is there anything in the new business that can help the existing business reinforce its existing competitive advantage or gain one?

Attractiveness of New Industry Test

A firm that wants to use its capabilities to enter a new business may want to first analyze the attractiveness of the new business or industry. As we saw in Chapter 3, the profits that firms in an industry make depend on the competitive forces that suppliers, customers, potential new entrants, rivals, and substitute products exert on them. For example, the competitive forces exerted on firms are low if the firms have bargaining power over their suppliers and customers, rivalry is low, barriers to entry are high, and the threat of substitutes is low. Firms in such an industry are, on average, profitable, and the industry is said to be attractive. However, although an attractive industry is attractive to firms that are already in the industry, it may not be attractive to a potential new entrant, especially if barriers to entry are high. A firm that wants to use its capabilities to enter a new business is a new entrant, so an analysis of the competitive forces that act on industry firms can provide the firm with useful information. For example, if the industry is attractive because barriers to entry are high and the firm's capabilities can allow it to overcome these barriers, the firm has a better chance of entering the industry and taking advantage of its attractive features. When Honda, for instance, extended its engine capabilities in the United States from motorcycles to cars, customers at the time wanted dependable cars with good gas mileage. Honda's engine capabilities allowed it to offer these benefits better than the major U.S. car makers could. This made Honda's extension of its capabilities easier.

Complementary Resources

The capabilities that a firm wants to bring into a new business are often not enough to offer superior customer value in the new market. Complementary resources are often required. For example, although Honda's engine capabilities can be used to produce cars, motorcycles, and lawn mowers, each product requires different distribution channels and somewhat different manufacturing and marketing processes. Thus, in extending its capabilities from offering only motorcycles in the United States to offering cars as well, the company had to establish car dealerships and build the manufacturing and marketing capabilities that would offer car buyers the type of value they wanted. Honda might not be as successful as it is in the United States had it not built the car dealerships and the manufacturing and marketing capabilities it needed when it decided to extend its capabilities from motorcycles to cars.

Cost of Entry Test

It costs money to enter a new business. Product development, manufacturing plants, capital equipment, and complementary resources can cost a lot of money in some industries, thereby raising the cost of entry into those industries. For example, it was estimated that Microsoft spent $2.5 billion to enter the video game business. If the costs of entering a new business are too high, whatever revenues the firm collects from the new business may all go to cover these costs, leaving the firm with no profits. For example, if the new business is in an attractive industry and one reason it is attractive is that barriers to entry are high, a firm that incurs high costs in overcoming these barriers to enter the business may spend so much doing so that it finds it difficult to make a profit. If a market is attractive, the chances are that other firms may be interested in entering the same market. This is likely to bid up the price of complementary resources, making it even more difficult for a firm to make money when it buys its way into the business.

Better-Off Test

In extending its capabilities into a different business, a firm must ask itself if its capabilities will allow it to offer better value than its competitors offer in the new business or will give it a better position vis-à-vis suppliers, customers, new entrants, and substitutes in the new business. If the capabilities do not give the firm an advantage in the new business, the question becomes, Is there anything in the new business that will give the firm an advantage in the old business? In short, is the firm better off moving into the new business? When a firm extends its capabilities into a new business, it must pay attention to the new business as well as its old one, instead of focusing only on the old one. If, in doing so, the profitability of both businesses is less than that of the old business, the firm would have been better off not expanding into the new business.

In general, there are several reasons that extending a firm's capabilities into another business may not be profitable. First, the new market into which a firm moves may be so different that the firm may overestimate its ability to craft and execute a business model in the industry. In the 1960s Philip Morris successfully competed in the cigarette business by building and exploiting its Marlboro brand. In the 1970s, it bought Miller Beer and very successfully exploited its marketing capabilities to build the Miller Beer brand and profit from it. However, it failed in the 1980s when it bought 7-Up and tried to apply the same marketing capabilities that had worked in the beer and cigarette industries to the soda industry. It could not replicate or outdo Coca-Cola's or PepsiCo's business model. Second, if a firm's resources are inimitable, the firm itself may not be able to replicate them in the new business. While it is a good thing that no other firm can imitate the resources, it is not good when the firm itself cannot replicate them in a different business.

QUANTIFYING INTANGIBLE RESOURCES

Earlier in the chapter, we showed how a firm can use a VRISA analysis to assess the profitability potential of its business model. This analysis is, however, qualitative since we cannot associate a numerical value to each asset. That is, a VRISA analysis enables us to determine whether a patent is potentially very profitable but not how much, say, in dollars, the patent is worth. Company financial statements tell us the worth of tangible assets such as plants, equipment, cash, marketable securities, and inventories (Figure 6.2) but say nothing about intangible assets such as patents, copyrights, trade secrets, installed base, client relations, and government relations, which can be critical to a firm's profitability. For firms that depend on such intangible assets for their revenues and profits, valuing them is important but difficult. Attempts to measure them have led to the term *intellectual capital.*

Intellectual Capital

Intellectual capital has been defined as "knowledge and knowing,"[18] "knowledge that exists in an organization that can be used to create differential advantage,"[19] and "knowledge that can be converted into value."[20] The common denominator in these definitions is "knowledge"—whether embedded in organizational routines, spelled out in patents, expressed in copyrights, embodied in employees' heads, or encoded in some other physical form such as drawings or computer programs.

FIGURE 6.2
Balance-Sheet Context

Source: Adapted from A. N. Afuah, *Innovation Management: Strategies, Implementation, and Profits* (New York: Oxford University Press, 2003).

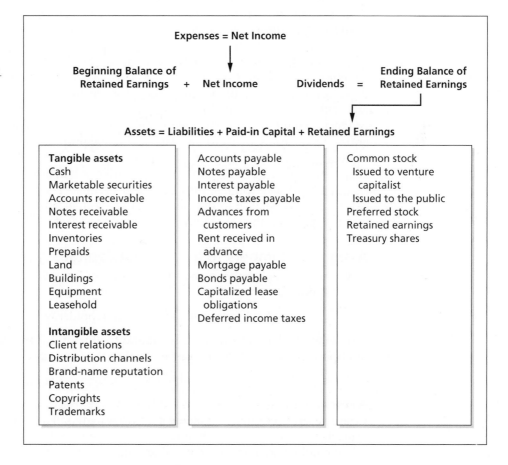

Intellectual capital can be divided into three components that differ in terms of where knowledge resides and how it can be converted into customer value: intellectual property, human capital, and organizational capital.[21]

Intellectual Property

As a component of intellectual capital, **intellectual property** is knowledge that is codified in a form that a company can claim ownership of. It includes patents, copyrights, trademarks, brand names, databases, microcodes, engineering drawings, contracts, trade secrets, documents, and semiconductor masks, as well as intangibles such as reputation, network size, installed base, client relationships, and special licenses.[22]

Human Capital

Intellectual property alone does not give a firm a competitive advantage. A firm also needs human beings: employees with the skill, know-how, experience, and ability to translate intellectual property into customer value or create intellectual property.[23] The specialized knowledge and abilities of employees are collectively called **human capital.** A basketball player's skill and knowledge of how to dribble, pass, and score points in a basketball game are an example. So is a design engineer's knowledge of semiconductor physics.

Organizational Capital

For a pharmaceutical company, having the largest number of patents and Nobel laureates in its industry may not be enough to give the firm a competitive advantage. That is, intellectual property and human capital alone may not be sufficient to give its owner a competitive advantage. The factors, external and internal to a firm, that allow the firm to translate intellectual property and human capital into customer value are collectively called **organizational capital.** Factors internal to a firm are structure, systems, strategy, people, and environment. As we will see in Chapter 8, these factors allow a firm to create, share, coordinate, and integrate the knowledge and skills of individual employees to create intellectual property and convert it into products and services that customers want.[24] Factors external to a firm can also be critical to the firm's ability to translate intellectual property and human capital. For example, firms in environments with a culture that tolerates failure, with relevant suppliers, customers, and complementors, with research institutions such as universities, and with a system that provides financial support and rewards for innovation can be more conducive to the creation of intellectual property and its conversion into new products than environments without these factors.[25]

Assigning Numbers to Intellectual Capital

Consider the simple balance-sheet relationship of Equation 6.1, which is obtained from Figure 6.2:

$$\text{Assets} = \text{liabilities} + \text{shareholder equity} \qquad \textbf{(6.1)}$$

This suggests that, at any time, the market value of a firm (shares outstanding multiplied by share price) should be equal to the firm's assets minus liabilities:

$$\text{Assets} - \text{liabilities} = \text{shareholder equity} \qquad \textbf{(6.2)}$$

Assets minus liabilities is also called **book value.** Book value is the amount that would be left over for shareholders if a firm were to sell its assets and pay its creditors. This implies that, at any given time, a firm's book value should be equal to its shareholder equity or market value. That is not always the case, however.

TABLE 6.6   Book versus Market Values (millions of dollars), Various Companies

Firm	3/15/94		3/15/97		3/15/99	
	Book Value	Market Value	Book Value	Market Value	Book Value	Market Value
Intel	9,267	35,172	19,295	125,741	23,371	196,616
Microsoft	4,450	41,339	10,777	199,046	16,627	418,579
General Motors	12,823	33,188	17,506	54,243	14,984	63,839
General Electric	26,387	92,321	34,438	260,147	38,880	360,251
Dell			1,293	41,294	2,321	111,322

As Table 6.6 shows, in 1994 Microsoft's book value was $4.45 billion, while its market value was almost 10 times as much, $41.34 billion. In 1997, it had a book value of $10.78 billion and a market value of $199.05 billion, almost 20 times the book value. Compare this to General Motors' book value of $17.51 billion and market value of $54.24 billion. In 1999, Microsoft's market value was about 25 times its book value. While the differences in other firms' book and market values are not as astounding as those in Microsoft's, they are still very large.

For each firm, the difference between its book value and market value suggests two possibilities: (1) that there is something else about the firm, something other than the assets on its books, that makes investors believe that they will keep generating free cash flows or earnings, or (2) that the stock market overvalues the firm's stock. If we assume that the market does not overvalue the firm's stock, the difference between book value and market value must be a measure of *intellectual capital* since it represents the intangible assets that are not captured by financial statements.

Using the difference between book value and market value to measure intellectual capital has several shortcomings. First, firms that have not gone public and business units cannot use the measure since they have no market value. Second, it is an aggregate measure since it estimates a value for all of a firm's intellectual capital. While it highlights the extent to which a firm's value depends on its intellectual capital, it reveals nothing about the different components of the capital and their relative contributions to the value. Thus while the measure can tell us whether Merck depends more on intellectual capital than its competitors do, it does not tell us how much of Merck's value is from its cholesterol or hypertension technology.

Summary

To perform the activities that enable a firm to create value and position itself to appropriate the value, a firm needs resources (assets) and capabilities. Since a business model is about making money, an important question for a firm is, What types of resources are likely to make a business model profitable? The VRISA (value, rareness, imitability, substitutability, and appropriability) framework can be used to explore the profitability potential of resources. Firms with valuable, rare, difficult-to-imitate, difficult-to-substitute, and appropriable resources are likely to have a competitive advantage. That is, such firms can have a higher rate of profitability than competitors have. Sometimes, a firm has to build its resources from scratch. How a firm does this depends on whether the knowledge underpinning the resources is technological or market knowledge and how familiar the firm is with either. The more unfamiliar the technology or market, or both, the more a firm should consider teaming up with a firm that has greater familiarity with the resources and capabilities.

Resources that are valuable, rare, difficult to imitate, difficult to substitute, and appropriable in one market may not be easily extended to another market. To determine whether resources are extendable to a new market, a firm should analyze the new market on the basis of industry attractiveness, complementary asset availability, cost of entry, and whether the firm will be better off by extending. Although it is easy to tell from a VRISA analysis if intangible assets can or do give a firm a competitive advantage, it is still very difficult to quantify intangibles.

Key Terms

better-off test, *124*	familiarity matrix, *120*	organizational capital, *126*
book value, *126*	human assets, *111*	resources, *110*
capability, *111*	human capital, *126*	substitutability, *114*
causal ambiguity, *113*	imitability, *113*	tangible assets, *111*
competence, *111*	intangible assets, *111*	VRISA analysis, *111*
cost of entry test, *124*	intellectual capital, *125*	
dynamic capabilities, *122*	intellectual property, *126*	

Study Questions

1. Choose your favorite firm in an industry that you like. Does the firm have resources or capabilities that give it a competitive advantage?

2. Perform a VRISA analysis for each of these resources. Which of the components of the VRISA analysis (value, rareness, imitability, substitutability, and appropriability) do you believe is the most critical to the competitive advantage?

3. Can any of the resources or capabilities in question 1 be extended to other markets? Why or why not?

4. In general, which of the attributes of a resource (value, rareness, imitability, substitutability, and appropriability) do you believe is the most important and why?

Endnotes

1. R. M. Grant, *Contemporary Strategy Analysis: Concepts, Techniques, Applications* (Oxford, England: Blackwell, 2002), p. 307.

2. Given the critical role that intangible resources play in market value, many firms are taking another look at their financial statement reporting. See, for example, T. A. Stewart, *Intellectual Capital: The New Wealth of Organizations* (New York: Currency/Doubleday, 1997).

3. C. K. Prahalad and G. Hamel, "The Core Competences of the Corporation," *Harvard Business Review,* May–June 1990, pp. 79–91.

4. The value, rareness, and imitability criteria are explored by Professor Jay Barney in J. B. Barney, "Looking Inside for Competitive Advantage," *Academy of Management Executive* 9 (1995), pp. 49–61. The substitutability and appropriability criteria are explored in D. J. Collis and C. A. Montgomery, "Competing on Resources: Strategies for the 1990s," *Harvard Business Review,* July–August 1995, pp. 118–128.

5. I. Dierickx and K. Cool, "Asset Stock Accumulation and Sustainability of Competitive Advantage," *Management Science* 35 (1989), pp. 1504–1513.

6. J. B. Barney, "How a Firm's Capabilities Affect Boundary Decisions," *Sloan Management Review* 40 (1999), pp. 137–145.

7. Collis and Montgomery, "Competing on Resources."

8. J. H. Dyer and K. Nobeoka, "Creating and Managing a High Performance Knowledge-Sharing Network: The Toyota Case," *Strategic Management Journal* 21, pp. 345–367.

9. A. N. Afuah, "Mapping Technological Capabilities into Product Markets and Competitive Advantage," *Strategic Management Journal* 12 (2002), pp. 171–179.

10. This section is based on a discussion with and suggestions from my colleague Prashant Kale of the University of Michigan.

11. S. C. Johnson and C. Jones, "How to Organize for New Products," *Harvard Business Review,* May–June 1957, pp. 49–62; E. B. Roberts and C. A. Berry, "Entering New Businesses: Selecting Strategies for Success," *Sloan Management Review* 26 (1985), pp. 3–17.

12. This section draws heavily on A. N. Afuah, *Innovation Management: Strategies, Implementation, and Profits* (New York: Oxford University Press, 2003).

13. W. Cohen and D. Levinthal, "Absorptive Capacity: A New Perspective on Learning and Innovation," *Administrative Science Quarterly* 35 (1990), pp. 128–52.

14. Afuah, *Innovation Management.*

15. Johnson and Jones, "How to Organize for New Products"; Roberts and Berry, "Entering New Businesses."

16. D. J. Teece, G. Pisano, and A. Shuen, "Dynamic Capabilities and Strategic Management," *Strategic Management Journal* 18 (1997), pp. 509–533; K. M. Eisenhardt and J. A. Martin, "Dynamic Capabilities: What Are They?" *Strategic Management Journal* 21 (2000), pp. 1105–1121; C. Helfat, "Know-How and Asset Complementarity and Dynamic Capability Accumulation: The Case of R&D," *Strategic Management Journal* 18 (1997), pp. 339–360.

17. Questions 1, 3, and 4 draw on Porter's "essential" tests for diversification. See M. E. Porter, "From Competitive Advantage to Corporate Strategy," *Harvard Business Review,* May–June 1987, p. 46. For question 2, see A. N. Afuah and C. L. Tucci, *Internet Business Models and Strategies: Text and Cases* (New York: McGraw-Hill/Irwin, 2003).

18. J. Nahapiet and S. Ghoshal, "Social Capital, Intellectual Capital, and the Organizational Advantage," *Academy of Management Review* 23 (1998), p. 242.

19. T. A. Stewart, *Intellectual Capital: The New Wealth of Organizations* (New York: Currency/Doubleday, 1997).

20. L. Edvinsson and P. Sullivan, "Developing a Model for Managing Intellectual Capital," *European Management Journal* 14 (1996), pp. 356–371.

21. Edvinsson and Sullivan, "Developing a Model for Managing Intellectual Capital"; H. Saint-Onge, "Tacit Knowledge: The Key to the Strategic Alignment of Intellectual Capital," *Strategy and Leadership* 2, March–April 1996, pp. 1014–1025.

22. Edvinsson and Sullivan, "Developing a Model for Managing Intellectual Capital."

23. Prahalad and Hamel, "The Core Competences of the Corporation."

24. Saint-Onge, "Tacit Knowledge."

25. Afuah, *Innovation Management.*

Chapter **Seven**

Executing a Business Model

A firm's business model, no matter how well conceived, designed, and planned, must be executed well if the firm is going to profit from it. Deciding what value to offer customers, what market segment to offer this value to, how to charge customers, what the sources of revenue should be, and which activities to perform, when to perform them, and how to exploit the firm's resources is one thing. Implementing these decisions can be quite another. *Implementation* entails organizing to carry out the decisions: determining who works for whom, how to measure and reward performance, how information should flow in the organization, whom to hire, and so on. Consider Wal-Mart in its early days. The firm offered low-cost products largely to rural customers in areas of the southwestern United States that it had saturated with its stores and distribution centers, it established strong capabilities in logistics and information technology, and it built a low-cost operation and organizational culture that its nonunion employees cherished. But to implement these elements of its business model, Wal-Mart had to structure its organization, establish the right systems to measure and reward performance, hire the right people, and so on. Making decisions as to what to do focuses on *doing the right things.* Implementing the decisions focuses on *doing things right.* This chapter is about doing things right. It examines the relationships between a business model's strategy, the structure of the organization that must execute the business model, the systems and processes that complement the structure, and the people who must carry out the tasks. We explore these relationships using a business model, structure, systems, people, and environment (BS²PE) framework.[1]

The idea behind the **BS²PE framework** is that some organizational structures, systems and processes, and people are more suitable for some activities than for others (Figure 7.1).[2] Thus, some organizational structures, systems and processes, and people are more suitable for some business models than for others, given the environments in which the business models must be executed. The objective, in executing a business model in a given environment, is therefore to find those structures, systems, and people that best fit the set of activities that a firm chooses to perform, how it performs them, and when it performs them. In this chapter, we define each component of the BS²PE framework and explore some of the relationships between them.

BUSINESS MODEL

Recall that a firm's business model is the set of activities *which* it performs, *how* it performs them, and *when* it performs them so as to offer its customers benefits that they want and to earn a profit. In other words, it is a framework for making

FIGURE 7.1 BS²PE Framework

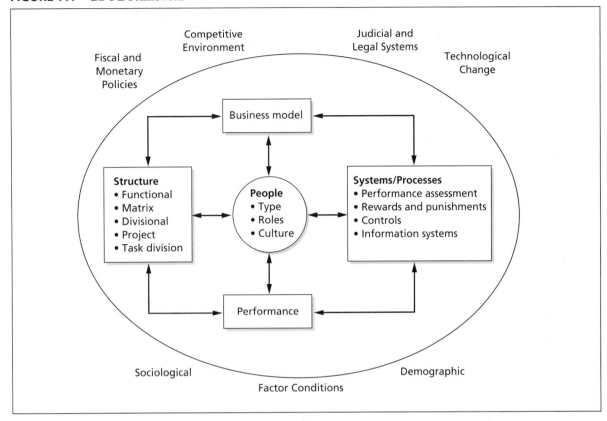

money by translating resources into products and services that customers want and appropriating the value. Also recall that a firm's business model consists of the performance-oriented aspects of its strategy and operational effectiveness. Throughout our discussion of the BS²PE framework, we assume that a business model drives the organizational structure and systems and, to a lesser extent, the people who are needed to execute the model.

STRUCTURE

While a firm's business model tells us what activities the firm wants to perform and how and when it wants to perform them, the firm's structure tells us who reports to whom and who is responsible for what activity. In deciding what structure is best for the implementation of a business model, it is important to keep in mind the following primary goals of an organizational structure.

1. *Differentiation* (in the organizational structure sense) *and integration:* For many industries, a firm's manufacturing and marketing groups are maintained as separate functions because each one necessarily has to specialize in what it does in order to be both efficient and effective in carrying out its activities. Manufacturing concentrates on building the product, while Marketing concentrates on pricing, positioning, and promoting the product. By concentrating on his or her area of expertise, for example, a manufacturing engineer who specializes in lean manufacturing at Toyota can do a better job at manufacturing than would be possible if he or she also had to worry about marketing. Likewise, a marketing

specialist can do a better job at pricing, positioning, or promoting the product. Thus it makes sense to have manufacturing personnel in one group and marketing personnel in a different group, with each group concentrating on what it does best and the personnel within each group learning from one another. This is **differentiation** in the organizational structure sense. However, to more efficiently and effectively develop and offer customers superior products, a firm's different functions often have to interact. That is, the value-adding activities of a firm's different functions must be integrated if its business model is going to perform well.[3] This is **integration** in the organizational structure sense.

2. *Coordination:* Interactions between groups often have to be coordinated. If an auto company wants the development and manufacturing of a car to be carried out efficiently, then by the time the design group of the company has finished designing the car, the manufacturing group should have had enough information from the design group to have all the necessary manufacturing capabilities in place. **Coordination** will ensure that this is the case. Thus a firm will more effectively and efficiently execute its business model if its different functions coordinate the value-adding activities that they perform.

The organizational structures that firms use to effect differentiation, integration, and coordination are variants of five major types: functional, multidivisional (M-form), matrix, project, and network.

Functional Structure

In the **functional structure,** employees are organized according to the function that they perform (Figure 7.2). Employees in Marketing or Sales report to supervisors or managers who are also in the marketing or sales function. Employees in Engineering and Manufacturing report to supervisors or managers who are also in Engineering and Manufacturing. And so on. Each of the functions or units— R&D, Manufacturing, Marketing and Sales, Engineering, and so on—which are also called *departments,* is usually a stage in a business system. Formal reporting and communications primarily occur within each department, usually up and down the organizational hierarchy. Each department gets its directions from corporate headquarters. That is, management responsibilities tend to be centralized. Effectively, people with similar functional skills, knowledge, and capabilities are grouped together. They usually also work in the same physical area, although digital networks such as the Internet can make that less necessary for some kinds of activities. In the sample functional organization in Figure 7.2, each vice president who heads one of the functional areas, from R&D to Marketing and Sales, reports to the chief executive officer (CEO). Each of these vice presidents also has managers reporting to him or her. These managers, in turn, have other people reporting to them. The number of people who report directly to a manager is called the manager's **span of control,** while the number of levels of management in the firm is called the **depth of the hierarchy.**

The functional structure has several advantages and disadvantages. First, since people with similar knowledge and skills are grouped together and are often located in the same physical location, they can communicate more often and are therefore more likely to develop in-depth knowledge of their functional area. That is, accumulation of functional skills and knowledge is likely to be fostered by a functional organization. A task that requires only the specialized knowledge of the area can be performed very effectively. Also, employees within a functional area can better monitor and help each other since they possess similar skills and

FIGURE 7.2
Functional
Organizational
Structure

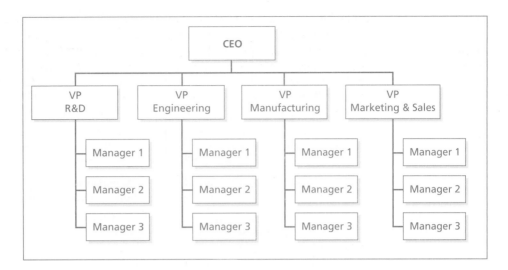

knowledge. Second, because employees are organized by function, there is a de facto division of labor that allows employees to specialize in the basic tasks of the function. Since they are also likely to have similar backgrounds and beliefs about what their function is and should be, employees are likely to perform function-specific tasks very well. However, they are likely to have rather subpar performance when tasks involve substantial coordination with other functions. This suggests that the functional organization may not be particularly suited for the effective and efficient design and manufacturing of products such as cars, which require coordination of many activities between functional units, especially since the allegiance of employees is to their functional departments. Until the late 1990s, Ford Motor Company had a functional organizational structure that exhibited some of the classic disadvantages of functional organization.

Third, since each department gets its overall direction from the managers at corporate headquarters, large firms with large functional units can present corporate management with some challenges. This is because giving effective directions requires that managers know not only about the functional areas but also about the different product lines, business units, and customers in different geographic regions that the firm must manage. Fourth, functional groups can be physically and virtually isolated from each other, making intradepartmental communications very difficult. Each of the functions may be housed in a different building, making interaction between employees more difficult. This can deprive functional units of critical information that could help them perform better. Functions can also be virtually separated in the way they perceive each other. For example, Manufacturing may view R&D as "those ivory tower academics,"[4] while R&D perceives Marketing as "those free-spending salesmen with Italian suits." Such prejudices can make information exchange very difficult. Fifth, given differences in their skills, experiences, and capabilities, functional departments may have goals that are not consistent with cooperating with other functions.

Multidivisional (M-Form) Structure

In the **multidivisional structure,** or **M-form structure,** employees are organized by divisions rather than by function (Figure 7.3).[5] These divisions can be organized by the type of product that each division sells (product line), by the type of customer (e.g., military or commercial), by the geographic regions that the firm

FIGURE 7.3
M-Form
Organizational
Structure

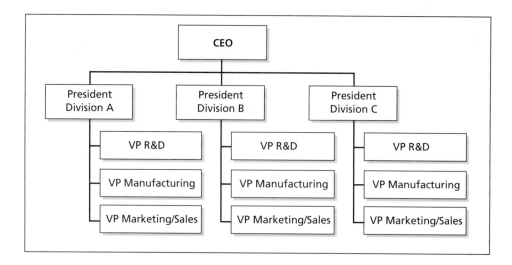

covers, or by the brand names that the firm offers. Each division usually acts as a business unit with profit and loss responsibility. That is, each unit generates some revenues and associated costs that are reported separately within the firm. Effectively, authority in the M-form structure is decentralized to the divisions, in contrast to the functional structure, where authority is centralized at corporate headquarters.

The multidivisional structure has several advantages. First, since management responsibility is not as centralized as it is in the functional structure, managers in the M-form structure need to focus their attention only on their specific divisions. This is a much more manageable task since each manager is likely to have the type of in-depth knowledge of the division's product line, brand, customers, or geographic region that he or she needs to better manage the business. Second, since each division has profit-and-loss responsibility, there is better accountability for each division's performance. That is, the firm can more easily tell which divisions are performing better than others and why. One disadvantage of the divisional structure is that firms may not be able to build as much in-depth knowledge of functional areas such as R&D as they would in a functional structure.

Matrix Structure

The **matrix structure** tries to capture some of the benefits of both the functional and the divisional structures. In one form of this structure, individuals from different functional areas are assigned to a project, but rather than reporting only to a project or functional manager, each employee reports to both a functional *and* a project manager (Figure 7.4). Effectively, many employees have one foot in a project group and another in a functional department. At a computer company, for example, key employees from Hardware Development, Software Development, Manufacturing, and Marketing and Sales, who are working on a project to develop a new product line, report both to the vice president in charge of the product line and to the managers of their functional areas. The idea here is to (1) achieve the cross-functional coordination that is critical for carrying out projects that require skills and knowledge from many functions, (2) maintain some performance accountability at the project level, and (3) allow project members to keep in close touch with their functional colleagues so as to benefit from the intrafunctional learning that takes place, especially in industries with fast-paced technological or market changes.

FIGURE 7.4
Matrix
Organizational
Structure

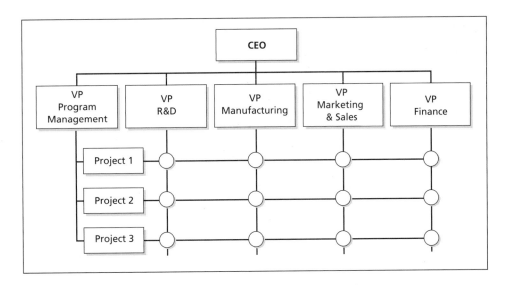

The matrix structure has several advantages. First, as we have seen, this structure is able to capture some of the benefits of both the functional and the divisional structures. Second, since employees have one foot in a project group and another in a functional area, they are able to bring to the project the latest thinking in their functional departments. They also have the opportunity to keep their knowledge of their functional areas up to date. Third, in some cases, an employee can work on more than one project, helping cross-pollinate not only functional knowledge but also project knowledge. Fourth, since the rate of change of technological or market knowledge is likely to vary from one function to another, employees can spend time on project management commensurate with the rate of change of the knowledge in their functional area. For example, if the rate of change of the underlying design technology is high while that of manufacturing is not, employees from Design can spend less time on the project while employees from Manufacturing can spend most of their time on the project and move to the project's location.

The matrix organization also has a number of disadvantages. First, since physical co-location with fellow project members can be critical to cross-functional coordination of activities and since physical co-location with functional colleagues can be critical to functional learning, employees in a matrix structure may have to physically co-locate in both their project and their functional areas. This can be costly. Moreover, an employee cannot be physically present in two different places at the same time. Second, having to report to both a functional and a project manager means having to manage two bosses at the same time. During times of conflict, it may not be easy for employees to decide where their allegiance should be. Third, the matrix structure can be more costly than the functional since it requires some duplication of effort. For example, it often requires both a functional and a project manager, whereas the functional structure requires only a functional manager.

Project Structure

In the **project structure,** employees are organized by the project that they are working on for the duration of the project. To develop a minivan, for example, employees from Marketing, Design, Manufacturing, Engineering, and other relevant functions are assigned to the project and work for the project manager, not their functional managers. Usually, the organization also has functional departments, but employees are pulled out of these departments to work on the project and report to the project manager during the duration of the project (Figure 7.5). During this time, their allegiance is to the project manager. Since members of a project team are usually located in the same physical location, they can more easily interact with each other and exchange information. The project structure has one major drawback: While working on a project, employees from functional areas whose underlying technological and/or market knowledge changes rapidly may not be able to keep up with the changes. That is, if the rate of change of the knowledge that underpins a functional area is high and the project's duration is long, employees may find their functional skills outdated. By the same token, being far removed from their functional areas means that employees may not be able to bring to the project the latest thinking in the functional areas.

Network Structure

Technological change has facilitated the emergence of a new kind of organizational structure—the **network structure,** or **virtual structure.**[6] In this structure, the firm outsources all the major value-adding activities of its business systems and acts more like a mediator (Figure 7.6). Such firms would contract a market research firm to perform market research for a particular product or idea, find a design firm to design the product, buy their components from suppliers, find another firm to manufacture the product, and find others to sell the product to customers. Nike performs some of its own marketing, but its structure is close to being virtual. One factor that has enabled the emergence of this structure is the proliferation of digital technologies such as the Internet. These technologies allow firms to coordinate and monitor from just about anywhere certain types of value-adding activities being performed all over the world. The network structure has two main advantages. First, a firm can avoid making large investments in assets since it outsources all the major value-adding activities of its business system. It can therefore have a relatively high return on assets. Second, in industries where the rate of change of technology is fast and often renders existing capabilities

FIGURE 7.5 **Project Structure**

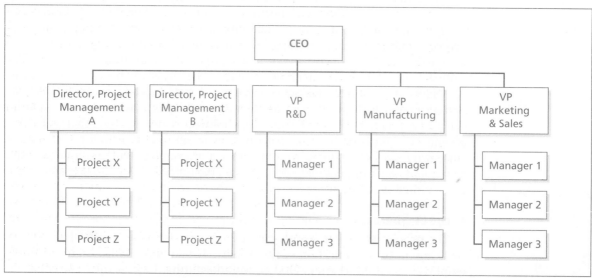

FIGURE 7.6
Network Structure

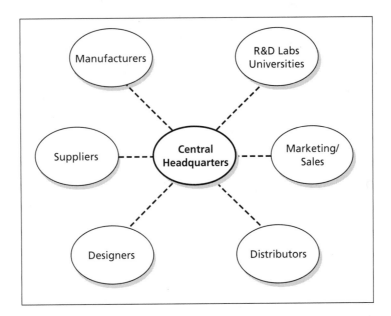

obsolete, having a virtual structure means that a firm does not have to worry about important assets being rendered obsolete by new technology. It can switch suppliers or manufacturers or distributors whenever it finds one that can better exploit the new technology.

The network structure also has two main disadvantages. First, it is difficult to have a competitive advantage when the firm does not perform major value-adding activities. However, whether this is a disadvantage depends on the type of valuable, rare, inimitable, nonsubstitutable resources or capabilities that a firm has. If a firm has a strong brand or architectural capabilities that are valuable, rare, inimitable, and nonsubstitutable, it can make money since, by definition, it can offer customers something that competitors cannot. *Architectural capabilities* are capabilities that allow a firm to integrate different activities. For example, a firm may be highly skilled at negotiating contracts with and monitoring suppliers, manufacturers, marketers, distributors, and designers. Second, contracting out all major activities deprives a firm of the cross-functional interaction, coordination, and communication that can be critical for product development projects and projects that may be more efficiently done within the same firm.

Functional or Project Structure?

The structure that a firm chooses is a function of many factors, including the type of industry in which a firm is competing, the firm's business model, the systems that the firm already has in place, and so on. Tom Allen, of MIT, offers a framework that can be used to explore when to have a project structure rather than a functional one. His framework is shown in Figure 7.7. The choice of a project structure over a functional structure depends on three factors: the rate of change of the technology that underpins the industry in question, the duration of the project, and the amount of interrelatedness of the different components or subsystems of the product being developed in the project.[7] If the project is very long and the rate of change of the knowledge in different functional departments that is brought to bear on the project is very fast, the firm may want to stay with the functional structure. If the project is of short duration and the rate of change of

FIGURE 7.7
Functional versus Project Structure

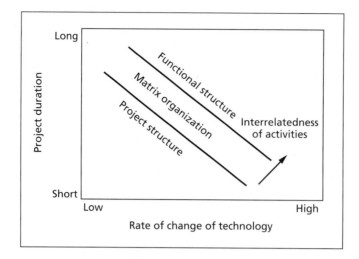

the knowledge needed from functional areas is slow, the firm is better off with a project structure. The more interrelated the different activities that must be performed during the project, the more coordination that is needed and therefore the more a firm may want to use the project structure. In the gray areas where it is not clear whether to use the project or functional structure, the matrix structure may be appropriate.

SYSTEMS AND PROCESSES

The primary goal of systems, in executing a business model, is to elicit the best performance from employees, given the structure that the firm is pursuing. Organizational structures tell us who reports to whom and does what, but they say very little about how to keep employees motivated as they carry out their assigned tasks and responsibilities in executing a business model.[8] **Systems** spell out how the performance of individuals, groups, functions, divisions, and organizations is monitored (especially feedback on how the organization's or group's members are doing), measured, rewarded, and punished. They also specify and facilitate the flow of information to the right decision makers at the right time. **Processes** are the "patterns of interaction, coordination, communication, and decision making [that] employees use to transform resources into products and services of greater worth."[9] The following quote from Donald Peterson, a former Ford CEO, illustrates some of the problems that firms can face if they do not have the right systems and processes in place.

> You dealt only with issues that the Statements of Authorities and Responsibilities said were yours. You learned real fast to stay inside your limits. . . . There was little or no interaction and no problem solving. What's more, the financial rewards were geared to results in managing your own chimney. Top management knew this was a problem, but there were historical barriers in the way. An entire layer of people at the chimney tops—the equivalent of divisional presidents—had come up through their respective chimneys and had enormous loyalty to their former colleagues. It was civil war at the top. The question was never, "Are we winning against the Japanese?" but rather, "Are we winning against each other?"[10]

Performance measures, rewards, and information flows vary from firm to firm and from industry to industry.

Firm-Level Performance Measures

Performance measures, especially when tied to incentives, are powerful weapons for getting individuals, groups, and organizations to carry out the execution of a business model. They allow management and shareholders to keep a pulse on the firm's health as it executes its business model. **Firm-level performance measures** can be financial or behavioral.

Financial Measures

Financial measures often include profits, gross profit margin, market share, cash flow, stock market price, earnings per share, return on investment, return on equity, and economic value added.[11] The major financial measures are explained below and summarized in Table 7.1.

TABLE 7.1   **Summary of Financial Measures**

Financial Measure	Definition	Calculation
Cash flow	The difference between the cash a company receives and the cash it pays out; a measure of cash that is available to fund activities or be paid out to shareholders	After-tax profits + depreciation
Earnings per share	The amount that is available to owners of common shares	$\dfrac{\text{Profits after taxes} - \text{preferred stock dividends}}{\text{Common stock shares outstanding}}$
Economic value added (EVA)	A measure of economic profit	After-tax profits − cost of capital
Gross profit margin	A measure of the extent to which revenues cover a firm's costs and then generate a profit	$\dfrac{\text{Sales} - \text{cost of goods sold}}{\text{Sales}}$
Market share	A firm's share of the revenues from a market (or of the units sold to the market)	$\dfrac{\text{Firm's total revenues from (or units sold to) a market}}{\text{Total revenues (units) of all participants in market}}$
Profits	Revenues minus the accounting costs of generating the revenues	Revenues − costs
Return on assets	The return on the assets that have been invested in the firm	$\dfrac{\text{Profits after taxes}}{\text{Total assets}}$
Return on equity	The return on the total shareholder equity in the firm	$\dfrac{\text{Profits after taxes}}{\text{Total shareholder equity}}$
Stock price	The present value of expected future cash flows	$\sum_{t=0}^{t=n} \dfrac{C_t}{(1 + r_k)^t}$ where C_t is the free cash flow at time t, and r_k is the firm's cost of capital. This discounting reflects the fact that money has a higher value today than it does tomorrow.

A firm's **profits** are its revenues minus its costs. This measure is regularly tracked by management and financial analysts alike. Sooner or later, a firm has to be profitable. It has to make money. Another measure that is tracked carefully by analysts and firms is **gross profit margin.** This is a measure of the extent to which a firm's revenues cover variable costs and contribute toward fixed costs and generating a profit. The higher the profit margins from a particular product, for example, the more of that product the firm will want to sell since the product covers not only product's variable costs but can contribute more (than products with lower profit margins) toward covering fixed costs and generating a profit. A firm's **revenue market share** is the firm's share of revenues from the market. This is usually measured as a percentage, that is, the firm's revenues from the market divided by the total revenues generated by all firms in the market. A firm's market share can also be measured in terms of the firm's share of units sold in the market, or its **unit market share**. As a percentage, this is the number of units sold by the firm to the market divided by the total number of units sold to the market. As we saw in Chapter 2, a high market share gives a firm economies-of-scale advantages. Under Jack Welch in the late 1980s and 1990s, General Electric would stay in a business only if GE had the number-one or number-two market share in the business. If its business did not come in first or second on this measure, GE sold the business.

When a firm writes checks to pay salaries, dividends, and other accounts payable, there should be cash available in deposits at a financial institution so that the checks can be redeemed for cash. Thus, it is important to make sure that cash inflows exceed cash outflows. **Cash flow** is a measure of the difference between cash inflows and cash outflows. Note that although profits are highly correlated with cash flows, a firm can be profitable and still have negative cash flows. Another measure of firm performance is its **stock price.** This is the present value of the firm's expected future cash flows. It is a reflection of how the market expects the firm to perform in the future. Firms and their CEOs are often assessed on the basis of their stock prices and therefore pay very close attention to their stock prices. Another measure is **earnings per share.** This is the after-tax profits that are available to holders of common shares for each share of the company that they own. The company usually reinvests this amount back into the company or pays it out as dividends to shareholders. Shareholders can use the earnings-per-share measure to gauge how well their investment in the company is doing. Creating the value for customers that generates profits usually requires investment in plants, equipment, inventories, and so on. **Return on investment (ROI)** is a measure of the extent to which the investment in capital is generating profits. Financial analysts can use ROI to compare how different firms use capital. A firm can use it to compare how well its strategy or business model is working relative to its competitors.

Economic value added (EVA), not to be confused with the customer value that we defined in Chapter 2 and use throughout this book, is another financial performance measure that has found favor at many firms since the early 1990s.[12] Proponents of this measure argue that the profits that are usually shown in financial statements do not fully account for the cost of the capital used to generate them. To reflect this cost, EVA is calculated by adjusting after-tax profits by the cost of capital. The rationale behind the measure is as follows: It takes money (capital) to buy the buildings, plants, equipment, inventories, and other tangible assets that are used to create customer value and generate profits. This capital consist of two types: borrowed and equity. Borrowed or *debt capital* is the money that firms borrow, and its cost, in the short term, is the interest that firms have to pay on the debt. *Equity capital* is the money that shareholders provide when they buy a company's stock. By investing their money in your company, for example, shareholders are forgoing earning opportunities elsewhere. Thus, your company's cost of equity capital is the price appreciation and dividends that your shareholders could have earned by investing in another asset (e.g., a portfolio of companies) that is as risky as your company. Effectively, since capital costs money, this cost should be taken into consideration when measuring how well a firm is performing as it uses capital to generate profits. A firm's EVA is therefore its after-tax profits adjusted by the cost of capital that is used to generate the profits:

$$\text{Economic value added} = \text{operating profits} - \text{taxes} - \text{cost of capital}$$

where

$$\text{Cost of capital} = \text{total capital used} \times \begin{array}{l} \text{weighted average cost} \\ \text{of debt and cost of equity} \end{array}$$

Financial measures sometimes do not reflect what is really going on in a company. They indicate nothing about what *drives* the financial performance that is being measured. For example, they may be measuring the outcome of activities or projects that were started months or even years earlier and may not reflect activities that are in the pipeline. Consider a pharmaceutical company that is making a lot of money today from drugs it discovered many years ago. Financial results will not tell us that the patents on these drugs, which have prevented competitors from imitating the drugs, are about to expire and that the firm has no other drugs in the pipeline. If managers depend on only financial measures, by the time they find out that there is something wrong with their company it may be too late to turn the firm around. To get a more realistic picture of a firm's situation, managers may be better off with behavioral measures that go deeper into the activities that underpin profitability.

Behavioral Measures

Two measures that examine the activities that underpin a firm's profitability are *components of a business model* and the *balanced scorecard.*

Components of a Business Model To use the components of a business model as a measure of performance, a firm has to appraise its components as detailed in Chapter 11. The advantage of component appraisal as a measure is that it enables a firm to determine which component, if any, has problems so that it can solve them at once and get its business model back on track before it is too late to do so.

Balanced Scorecard The **balanced scorecard** is a framework for measuring firm performance that was developed by Robert Norton and David Kaplan.[13] The framework's performance measures are a combination of financial measures and some of the organizational measures that drive financial performance.[14] Performance is measured from four perspectives: customer, internal, innovation and learning, and financial.

Customer perspective. In designing measures that take the customer's perspective, the firm must ask, How do customers see us? Depending on its industry, a firm may measure itself by the lead times of the new products that it introduces, conformance to customer requirements such as just-in-time delivery, performance of the products, and products' costs to customers.

Internal perspective. In this perspective, the firm asks, What must we excel in? If a firm performs well when measured from the customer perspective, this is likely the result of how it performs the activities of its business systems. Thus, a firm is better off putting in place performance measures for these internal business activities. For example, a firm may want to measure the activities that impact cycle time, quality, employee skills, and productivity.

Innovation and learning perspective. Here, the primary question for the firm is, Can we continue to improve and create value? Since markets and technologies change, a firm must have an ability to innovate, improve, and learn. Therefore, a firm needs performance measures that focus on its ability to innovate. Such measures include new product development cycle times, impact of new products on existing products, number of new products introduced, and percentage of annual revenues that comes from new products.

Financial perspective. In the financial perspective, the firm asks, How do we look to shareholders? Measures such as cash flow, sales growth, operating income, and return on equity have been used to measure performance from the financial perspective.

Group-Level Performance Measures

In the context of **group-level performance measures,** a group is a division, functional department, or project group of an organization that is implementing a business model. The entity could also be a subgroup within one of these larger groups. Many of the performance measures that are used at the firm level can also be used at the group level. When EVA is used at the division level, after-tax profits and cost of capital must be adjusted for divisional peculiarities. When used as a framework for measuring group-level performance, the balanced scorecard must also be adjusted for group-specific characteristics. Using nonfinancial performance measures at the group level is also common. At 3M, for example, the measure is that 25 percent of a division's sales in any year must be from products introduced within the previous five years.[15]

Another performance measure that is used at the group level is the operating budget. An **operating budget** details how employees and their managers plan to use organizational resources, especially money, to carry out, in the best way they can, activities that underpin a business model. A primary responsibility of managers is to make sure that they achieve the goals they negotiated with their bosses and do so below budget. A product development group may negotiate what the development time, quality, and reliability for a new product should be.

Individual-Level Performance Measures

Individual performance measures vary considerably by organization and depend very much on organizational and group goals. At the R&D laboratory of a pharmaceutical firm, for example, scientists might be measured by the number of science publications they generate each year. At a consulting or law firm, partners might be measured by the amount of business they bring in, while associates might be measured by how quickly and effectively they complete projects. Often these measures are arrived at by means of **management by objectives (MBO).** This is a system of evaluating individuals by their ability to attain goals that are usually jointly set by the individual and his or her manager. These goals are usually tied to group or company goals. A scientist at a start-up biotech firm may agree with his or her manager to be measured by the number of patents he or she files per year. Patents are an important asset for a start-up biotech firm, and therefore pursuing patents may be an important goal of a biotech firm.

In general, **individual-level performance measures** may be as different as jobs are different but should be tied to the overall goals of the individual's group or organization. In a customer service group, an individual may be measured by how courteous he or she is when answering the phone, by the number of e-mails that the individual can respond to, or by how accurately the individual portrays the company or its products. A manager's performance may be measured by the performance of his or her group or organization. A divisional or functional manager may be evaluated by his or her ability to get things done within budget. A CEO is usually measured by the financial performance of her or his organization.

Reward Systems

People often do something because they believe that it is the right thing to do. Many others, however, need incentives. Incentives can be offered on an organizational, group, or individual basis.

Firm-Level Measures

A common firm-level reward system is profit sharing. In **profit sharing,** a portion of the firm's profits is shared by employees. Firms such as Wal-Mart and Southwest Airlines have been using this reward system for a long time. Profit sharing encourages employees who are interested in the promised share of profits to pay more attention to the organizational activities that impact firm profits. Profit sharing at Wal-Mart has been credited with the very low levels of theft that the company experiences.[16] Another reward system used by firms is an **employee stock option plan (ESOP).** In an ESOP, the company allows employees to buy its stock at prices that are below market prices. Usually, the company buys the shares from shares outstanding or issues more shares. In any case, an ESOP costs money to establish and run. However, an ESOP can be beneficial to a company since employees who become shareholders are more likely to be motivated to carry out activities that increase profitability and shareholder value. If enough employees of a firm buy its stock, they may end up controlling it. Firms can also use *bonuses* to reward performance. In this case, an organization pays its employees some amount of money when a performance target is met. A firm may decide to pay each employee $500 if the company attains revenues of $10 billion or if certain cost reductions are attained. An investment bank may decide to pay bonuses to its employees when its revenues from merger and acquisition deals or from taking private companies public exceed a certain target.

Group-Level Rewards

One of the most common group-level performance rewards is the *group bonus.* A group that develops and launches an award-winning new product on time and below cost may be given a cash bonus. Another group may receive cash because it completed its own project well under the budgeted cost. Rewards are not always financial. A picture of a team that completed a key project for the company can be displayed on the home page of the company's website for visitors of the site to see. A firm can also have special occasions at which groups are publicly recognized for their achievements. For example, a team that discovered a new drug may be presented with medals in a company ceremony at which team members' families are present.

Individual-Level Rewards

Reward systems for individuals come in many shapes. By far the most common way to reward individual performance is to tie *pay raises* to performance and not to seniority. The better the individual's performance, the higher the pay raise that he or she receives. Superior performance can also be rewarded with a *promotion.* The idea here is that by tying pay raises or promotion to performance rather than seniority, a firm is giving employees an incentive to strive for better performance rather than encouraging so-called deadweight to hang around. In a *per-unit output plan,* an individual's pay is proportional to the number of units that he or she produces. Such a plan is used when the output can be objectively measured. For example, a tailor may be paid by how many shirts he or she sews and not the number of hours worked. Sales personnel are often paid a *commission* instead of or in addition to a salary. The sales *commission* is usually some percentage of the dollar value of the sales the person makes. As is the case with a per-unit output plan, commissions can be a good incentive for individual performance. A firm's key individual contributors, such as its chief executive officer (CEO), chief financial officer (CFO), and chief technology officer (CTO), can be singled out for *individual bonuses* when the company meets certain performance goals. Such key personnel may receive additional percentages of their salaries in the form of bonuses.

Individual rewards do not always have to be financial. Not everyone is motivated by money. This is why many companies have *nonfinancial awards.* Individuals may have their names included in a product that they helped develop so that every customer who buys the product will know who worked on it. In some software programs, for example, project members' names are written in the software's "Easter eggs" so that people who know where to look can find the names of the individuals who made key contributions to the program. At many workplaces, the picture of the employee of the week is displayed where employees and customers alike can see it. Employees of the week can bring their families to work to share in their joy. Sending e-mails to everyone in the company detailing the achievements of particular individuals is another means of recognition. The picture of a key contributor may also be displayed on the home page of the company's website with details of the individual's contributions. The 3M company has an award ceremony once a year on its "Oscar night" to honor its innovators.

Information Flows

It is important that firms have systems that allow information to flow in the shortest possible time to the right targets for decision making. For discussion purposes, we can group information flow systems into two types: (1) the information and communication technologies that allow electronic information to be exchanged and (2) the physical building layouts that facilitate in-person interaction. Digital networks such as the Internet make it possible for anyone in an organization to have access to some types of information anywhere within the organization.[17] For example, during product development, information on the status of the product, ideas for better products, and so on, are available to anyone with permission to access the company's intranet. If such information had to go through a functional department's hierarchy, its transmission would take much longer and might result in distorted information. Thus, information and communication technologies can be used to, for example, mitigate one of the shortcomings of a functional structure: the tendency for information to flow only up and down the hierarchy of each function.

While digital networks make distance a nonfactor as far as communication of some kinds of information is concerned, certain other kinds of information are best elicited or exchanged in person. For example, it is difficult to get the feel and smell of a new car over the Internet. Professor Tom Allen's research suggests that the physical layout of buildings can play an important role in the amount of communication that takes place between people and therefore can have a significant impact on innovation.[18] Many innovative ideas have been arrived at during unplanned encounters in a parking lot or at a water cooler. In such cases where there is still a need for physical, in-person communication, buildings that facilitate such interaction are necessary. If the marketing, R&D, and manufacturing groups of a company are located in the same area and eat in the same cafeteria, share the same restrooms, and bump into each other often, they are more likely to exchange new ideas than they would be if they were located in different buildings or regions.

Processes

Recall that *processes* are the "patterns of interaction, coordination, communication, and decision making" that firms use to perform the activities that transform their resources into customer value and position them to appropriate the value.[19] Communication, interaction, and coordination of the activities of a business system are critical to the execution of a business model. Desired patterns of communication, interaction, coordination, and decision making can be established by a firm through the choices it makes, or they can emerge from the firm's culture. For example, in a process it called "chemicalization," Sharp compulsorily transferred the top 3 percent of its scientists to different laboratories every three years.[20] At 3M, employees are expected to spend 15 percent of their time on anything they want, as long as it is product-related. And if an employee has a feasible idea, the employee can get a grant of up to $50,000 to pursue it.[21]

Popular processes such as benchmarking, total quality management (TQM), reengineering, and x-engineering can play important roles in the implementation of business models. A firm can benchmark best practices within and outside its industry by comparing financial measures (profits, gross profit margin, market share, cash flow, stock price, return on investment, return on equity, and economic value added), business model components, and balanced-scorecard measures. With this information a firm can decide whether it needs to reengineer all its processes or adopt TQM processes. Reengineering takes a new look at the activities that a firm performs and its patterns of communication, interaction, coordination, and decision making so that the firm can do better in areas where it fell short in the benchmarking. Adopting a TQM approach helps the firm perform its activities more accurately and keep improving.

PEOPLE

People are central to everything in a business model. They formulate and execute the business model. Whether employees of an organization are motivated by the performance and reward systems that it has put in place is a function of the organization's culture, the type of employees, and the roles that they play within the organization.

Culture

A key instrument that a firm can use in the implementation of a business model is its culture. Various definitions of **culture** exist, two of which are very relevant to our exploration of the implementation of business models. Professor Ed Schein, in his book on organizational culture, defines it as

> the pattern of basic assumptions that a given group has invented, discovered, or developed in learning to cope with its problems of external adaptation and internal integration, and that have worked well enough to be considered valid, and, therefore, to be taught to new members as the correct way to perceive, think, and feel in relation to these problems.[22]

Business journalists Bro Uttal and Jaclyn Fierman define organizational culture as

> a system of shared values (what is important) and beliefs (how things work) that interact with the organization's people, organizational structures, and systems to produce behavioral norms (the way we do things around here).[23]

If a firm's culture—that is, its employees' beliefs (how things work) and shared values (what is important to employees)—is in line with the firm's performance measures and rewards, the firm is more likely to have an easier time implementing its business model. Over the years, both Southwest Airlines and Wal-Mart have built organizational cultures that have allowed them to sustain very profitable business models. Employees at Southwest, for example, have come to consider themselves as a family, a community whose members put the community before themselves and therefore accepted low salaries so that the company could make money, some of which went into their profit-sharing plans. If people believe in frugality, it is easier to sell a low-cost strategy to them. That was the case at Wal-Mart, where Sam Walton, the company's founder, instilled a strong sense of frugality in most of its employees.

Culture is not always good. In some cases, a firm's culture can prevent it from adapting to necessary changes. It has been suggested that one reason IBM had difficulties profiting from personal computers was that its culture was more suited to mainframe computers, which had dominated the company for a long time, than to PCs. Many mergers and acquisitions fail because of the differences between the cultures of the acquirer and acquiree. For example, the failure of the acquisition of Digital Equipment Corporation (DEC) by Compaq has been attributed to the cultural differences between DEC, which had never grown out of its glorious past in which it made the key components that it needed (chips, hardware, and software) and kept its technology proprietary, and Compaq, which had grown by peddling IBM-compatible PC hardware. If a functional area has a very strong culture and the company decides to change its organizational structure from functional to, say, project or divisional, the functional group can offer enough resistance to damage the transition to the new structure. Ford Motor Company's efforts in the late 1990s to restructure its organization, systems, and processes met with considerable resistance from the functional fiefdoms. Finally, international cultural differences can be the source of friction during a cooperative effort that involves participants from different nationalities, as the following example shows.

Example:
International Culture Clash

The experiences of engineers from Siemens (a German company), IBM (an American company), and Toshiba (a Japanese company) while working on the development of a memory microchip in Fishkill, New York, illustrate some of the friction that can result from international cultural differences.[24] The Toshiba engineers did not like their American offices largely because each engineer had a private office. The Japanese engineers were used to working together in big rooms that look somewhat like classrooms. To these engineers, being in a large office with many other engineers allows for informal communications, which they considered important for work. It also allows them to overhear personal conversations, even family matters. Supervisors look over subordinates' shoulders. The private offices were okay with the Siemens engineers, but the Germans were appalled by the fact that the offices had no windows. How could an engineer in a company such as IBM have an office without a window to the outside? The offices had narrow panes of glass on the doors, which led to a hallway, so that visitors could see if occupants were busy before trying to enter. German and Japanese engineers sometimes hung their coats over the glass pane, blocking people from seeing inside the office, and this was very annoying to the IBM engineers. Another problem was IBM's strict no-smoking policy, which meant that Japanese and German engineers had to go outside in the severe winter cold to smoke.

Type of People

Not everyone is meant for every job. Nor is every reward system going to motivate every employee. Thus, in implementing a business model strategy, it is important to get the right people to perform the right tasks. This is usually the responsibility of the human resource function of most firms, and many managers spend sleepless nights worrying about what type of employees to hire. In general, they want to hire people with the best fit to the job and company. When Southwest Airlines hired people, for example, it was more interested in their attitude than in their skills.

Leadership Roles

Top management and firm leaders play a critical role in conceptualizing business models, shaping culture, defining performance measures and rewards, defining hiring criteria, and shaping the overall strategy of the firm. The organizational cultures that have allowed both Southwest Airlines and Wal-Mart to excel have been attributed to their leaders, Herb Kellerher and Sam Walton, respectively. In addition to the formal roles that top management plays, there are other, less formal roles—such as idea generator, boundary spanner, champion, sponsor, and project manager—that are also critical to business model implementation, especially when the model involves a new product or service.

Dominant Managerial Logic

Each manager brings to every business situation a set of biases, beliefs, and assumptions about the market that his or her firm serves, whom to hire, what technology to use to compete in the market, who the firm's competitors are, and what types of business models are successful in the industry.[25] This set of biases, assumptions, and beliefs is a manager's *managerial logic.* It defines the frame or mental model that a manager is likely to use as a basis in decision making. Depending on a firm's strategies, systems, technology, organizational structure, culture, and success, there usually emerges a **dominant managerial logic,** a common way of viewing how best to do business as a manager in the firm.[26] For a firm that does not face major change and whose key business model components remain relatively the same, dominant managerial logic serves the design and implementation of the business model very well and allows the firm to do very well. In the face of a radical change, however, dominant managerial logic can become a handicap. Managers may be stuck in the old ways of doing things, reinforcing old processes and not doing what they need to do to help their organizations change. Many of the problems that IBM had before the arrival of Lou Geshner as CEO are usually attributed to the fact that the company's top management was made up of managers from the company's mainframe division, whose managerial logic was very dominant.

Professor C. K. Prahalad and Gary Hamel argue that top management teams that have a "genetic mix"—that is, teams with managers drawn from different backgrounds (marketing, R&D, manufacturing, etc.) or from different national cultures—can better deal with change. Lou Geshner came from outside IBM and therefore did not suffer from the company's dominant managerial logic. This may have been a factor in his success at IBM.

Champions

In some cases, for a business model to be effectively implemented, it needs a **champion,** someone who will articulate a vision of what the business model is all about and how the activities that are performed will offer superior customer value and position a firm to appropriate the value.[27] By evangelically communicating his or her vision of the business model's potential to the different departments of the firm, a champion can help other employees understand the rationale behind the business model, especially how it will make money, thereby motivating and inspiring the employees who will carry out the activities of the business model. The firm may also need to champion its product to customers, complementors, suppliers, and investors. Sometimes, this is not easy. The first cell phone was the size of a suitcase and had to be wheeled around. Imagine trying to convince people at the time that cell phones would one day be carried around in purses. Now imagine trying to convince people that cell phones would make money.

Boundary Spanners

Information in some stages of a business system can be very localized in that it may be a strong function of the culture, language, needs, and history of the department or organization. An R&D department may have its own acronyms, scientific jargon, and culture that Marketing and Manufacturing do not understand. Marketing and Manufacturing may see R&D scientists as snobs that live in an ivory tower. **Boundary spanners** link the departments in a business system.[28] They understand the idiosyncrasies not only of their departments but also of other departments and can take department-specific questions, translate them into a language that other departments can understand, obtain answers, and translate them into terminology that their home departments can understand.

Sponsors

A **sponsor** of a new business model is a senior-level manager who provides behind-the-scenes support for it.[29] He or she is like a godfather or godmother who protects the new business model from political enemies. By acting as a sponsor, the person is sending a signal to political foes of the business that they will face the wrath of a senior manager and sponsor and is also reassuring the champion and other key individuals that they have the support of a senior manager.

Project Manager

Where a business model includes developing a new product, project managers can play important roles. A **project manager** is responsible for plotting out who should do what and when it should be done so as to complete a project in a way that meets or exceeds requirements. A project manager is to meeting schedules what a champion is to articulating a vision of the potential of a business model. He or she is the central nervous system of information that has to do with a project's personnel, tasks, timing, and progress. Project managers can be classified as heavyweight or lightweight on the basis of the managers' span of control.[30] A *heavyweight* project manager is one with extensive authority and responsibility for the project, from concept creation to design to manufacturing to marketing and making money. A *lightweight* project manager has less extensive authority and responsibility, authority usually limited mainly to engineering functions and with no authority or responsibility over concept creation and other market-related aspects of the product. Kim Clark and Takahira Fujimoto found that the use of heavyweight product managers helped reduce lead times and total engineering hours (and therefore cost, all else equal) and improved design quality in the automobile industry.[31]

ENVIRONMENT

A firm's competitive and macro environments also play a role in the type of structure, systems and processes, and people that the firm can choose when implementing its business model. In fast-paced industries where technologies and markets change rapidly, a firm needs to be able to maintain deep knowledge of the underpinning technology and of the markets that it must serve. In such industries, a good choice of structure is a matrix structure since it allows employees who are working on a project to have one foot in the project group and another in their functional groups. If a firm has to choose a functional structure in a fast-paced industry, its systems and processes must facilitate communication, interaction, and coordination across the different functions of the structure. In a country or region without a good telecommunication infrastructure, a network structure is difficult to implement. In countries where people identify with the firm that they work for, employees may be more willing to do whatever it takes for their company to win. If winning means these employees have to go out of their way to effect cross-functional interactions, they will do so, thereby compensating for the shortcomings of a functional structure. In countries where customers are very demanding, benchmarking and total quality control are more likely to be pursued irrespective of the type of structure that firms employ. Finally, it will be easier for a firm to find the employees it wants in a country with an educated workforce than in one without such a workforce.

Compensating Nature of BS²PE

Each component of BS²PE has some drawbacks. Thus, in implementing a business model, a firm may want to compensate for the disadvantages of each component through the choices that it makes in designing other components. Consider the primary disadvantage of a functional organization: inefficient and ineffective performance of tasks such as new product development that require frequent and detailed cross-functional interaction and coordination. Systems can be used to mitigate, but not eliminate, such disadvantages. For example, when a firm ties functional managers' salaries, bonuses, or other rewards to project outcomes, its functional departments are more likely to pay more attention to cross-functional projects. When a firm uses information technologies such as the Internet, information can move horizontally between functional departments instead of up and down each function's hierarchy. When a firm forces key personnel from functional departments to move around, it can better spread their functional expertise among different projects. Sharp's chemicalization program forces scientists to spread their knowledge within Sharp and learn in the process of doing so. Similarly, 3M's requirement that employees spend 15 percent of their time on product ideas encourages them to look outside their functional areas since products are usually the result of cross-functional activities. A company's processes may require that developers of a product move along with their design from R&D to Manufacturing and on to Marketing and Sales. This facilitates technology transfer.

The type of people in an organization can also mitigate the disadvantages of a structure or systems. A business model champion who articulates a vision of what the business model can do for the firm and for the people executing the model may inspire functional departments to take part in cross-functional activities. A sponsor's prestige and power can also force some functional managers to be more cooperative in cross-functional activities.

Summary

If a business model is going to give a firm a competitive advantage, it must be executed well. It is one thing to decide which activities a firm should perform, how to perform them, and when to perform them. It is quite another to execute these decisions well. That is, it is one thing to decide how to do the right things but quite another to do things right. Executing a business model requires an organizational structure, systems and processes, and people who can effectively carry out the activities of the model, given the environment in which the activities take place. By using the business model, structure, systems, people, and environment (BS^{2}PE) framework, a firm can explore how to organize to more effectively execute a business model. Each organizational structure—functional, M-form, matrix, project, and network—has advantages and disadvantages when used to carry out a specific activity. Designing the right systems and processes can mitigate some of the disadvantages and retain or reinforce the advantages. Hiring the right people or building the right culture can also mitigate the disadvantages of an organizational structure. The environment in which a firm executes its business model is a constraint that must be taken into consideration in implementing a business model.

The BS^{2}PE framework suggests that if a firm's business model changes radically—that is, if the activities which the firm performs, how it performs them, and when it performs them change radically—the way the business model is executed may have to be fundamentally altered. And if execution has to fundamentally change, the systems and processes usually have to change too. A firm that, in the face of radical change, pursues a different structure but leaves the systems and processes intact may be making a mistake.

Key Terms

Study Questions

1. What would be the differences between executing a business model for the Airbus 380 and one for a café such as Starbucks?

2. How would executing a business model for a start-up be different from that of an entrenched incumbent?

3. To what extent does the advent of the Internet change the way an automobile company might execute its business plans?

Endnotes

1. This section draws on A. N. Afuah, *Innovation Management: Strategies, Implementation, and Profits* (New York: Oxford University Press, 2003), chap. 5.

2. J. R. Galbraith, "Designing the Innovating Organization," *Organizational Dynamics* 10 (1982), pp. 5–25.

3. P. R. Lawrence and J. W. Lorsch, *Organization and Environments: Managing Differentiation and Integration* (Homewood, IL: Irwin, 1967).

4. T. J. Allen, "People and Technology Transfer," working paper 10-90, International Center for Research on Management of Technology, MIT, 1990.

5. A. D. Chandler, *Strategy and Structure: Chapters in the History of the Industrial Enterprise* Cambridge, MA: MIT Press, 1962).

6. R. E. Miles, C. C. Snow, J. A. Mathews, G. Miles, and H. J. Coleman, Jr., "Organizing the Knowledge Age: Anticipating the Cellular Form," *Academy of Management Executive,* November 1997, pp. 7–24; "The Virtual Corporation," *Business Week,* Feb. 8, 1993; W. H. Davidow and M. S. Malone, *The Virtual Corporation* (New York: HarperCollins, 1992).

7. T. Allen, *Managing the Flow of Technology* (Cambridge, MA: MIT Press, 1984).

8. C. W. L. Hill and G. R. Jones, *Strategic Management: An Integrated Approach* (Boston: Houghton Mifflin, 1995).

9. C. M. Christensen and M. Overdorf, "Meeting the Challenge of Disruptive Change," *Harvard Business Review,* March–April 2000, pp. 67–76, quotation is on p. 68.

10. M. Pelofsky and L. Schleisinger, "Transformation at Ford," Harvard Business School case 9-390-083, rev. Nov. 15, 1991, p. 11.

11. For an excellent treatment of firm performance, see J. B. Barney, *Gaining and Sustaining Competitive Advantage* (Reading, MA: Addison-Wesley, 1997).

12. S. Tully, "EVA, the Real Key to Creating Wealth," *Fortune,* Sept. 20, 1993, pp. 38–50; J. Stern, B. Stewart, and D. Chew, "The EVA Financial Management System," *Journal of Applied Corporate Finance* 8 (1996), pp. 32–46.

13. K. S. Kaplan and D. P. Norton, "Measures That Drive Performance," *Harvard Business Review,* January–February 1992; K. S. Kaplan and D. P. Norton, "Using the Balanced Scorecard as a Strategic Management System," *Harvard Business Review,* January–February 1996.

14. Ibid.

15. K. Labich, "The Innovators," *Fortune,* June 6, 1988, pp. 49–58; R. Mitchell, "Masters of Innovation," *Business Week,* Apr. 10, 1989, p. 58; K. Kelly, "3M Run Scared? Forget about It," *Business Week,* Sept. 16, 1991, pp. 59–62.

16. P. S. Bradley and P. Ghemawatt, "Wal-Mart Stores: Discount Operations." Harvard Business School case 387-018, 1996.

17. A. N. Afuah and C. L. Tucci, *Internet Business Models and Strategies: Text and Cases* (New York: McGraw-Hill, 2003); A. N. Afuah, "Redefining Firm Boundaries in the Face of the Internet: Are Firms Really Shrinking?" *Academy of Management Review* 28 (2003), pp. 34–53.

18. T. Allen, *Managing the Flow of Technology* (Cambridge, MA: MIT Press, 1984).

19. Christensen and Overdorf, "Meeting the Challenge of Disruptive Change."

20. T. Noda and D. J. Collis, "Sharp Technology: Technology Strategy," Harvard Business School case 9-793-064, 1993.

21. Kelly, "3M Run Scared?"

22. E. Schein, *Organizational Culture and Leadership* (San Francisco: Jossey-Bass, 1985).

23. B. Uttal and J. Fierman, "The Corporate Culture Vultures," *Fortune,* Oct. 17, 1983, pp. 66–73.

24. This fascinating case is detailed in E. S. Browning, "Side by Side: Computer Chip Project Brings Rivals Together, but the Cultures Clash; Foreign Work Habits Get in Way of Creative Leaps, Hobbling Joint Research; Softball Is Not the Answer," *The Wall Street Journal,* May 3, 1994, p. 1A.

25. R. A. Bettis and C. K. Prahalad, "The Dominant Logic: Retrospective and Extension," *Strategic Management Journal* 16 (1995), pp. 5–14.

26. G. M. Hamel and C. K. Prahalad, *Competing for the Future* (Boston: Harvard Business School Press, 1994).

27. The concept of champions was first developed by D. A. Schön in his seminal article, "Champions for Radical New Inventions," *Harvard Business Review* 41 (1963), pp. 77–86. J. M. Howell and C. A. Higgins, "Champions of Technological Innovation," *Administrative Sciences Quarterly* 35 (1990), pp. 317–341.

28. Allen, *Managing the Flow of Technology.*

29. E. B. Roberts and A. R. Fusfeld, "Staffing the Innovative Technology-Based Organization," *Sloan Management Review* 22 (1981), pp. 19–34.

30. K. B. Clark and T. Fujimoto, *Product Development Performance: Strategy, Organization, and Management in the World Automobile Industry* (Boston: Harvard Business School Press, 1991).

31. Clark and Fujimoto, *Product Development Performance.*

Chapter **Eight**

Innovation, Sustainability, and Change

The cornerstone of many profitable business models is innovation—innovation in delivering superior customer value and positioning the firm so that it can appropriate the value it has created. Firms that successfully innovate or exploit other firms' innovations can make great amounts of money. Change, especially technological change, often offers firms an opportunity to reinforce an existing advantage. It can also offer attackers an opportunity to erode advantages that incumbent firms have established using existing technologies and processes. In this chapter, we explore the roles that innovation and change play in the profitability of a business model and examine the strategies that firms can pursue to sustain competitive advantages. We start the chapter by defining innovation and discussing some of the factors that determine the ability of a firm to innovate and profit in doing so. We then discuss three generic strategies that firms use to sustain profitability from innovation. Finally, we discuss the impact that change can have on competitive advantage and explore how firms can take advantage of change by innovating.

INNOVATION

Innovation is the use of new knowledge to offer a new product or service that customers want.[1] It usually entails using new knowledge to perform some or all of the activities of a business system in new ways that result in better customer value or better positioning of the firm to appropriate the value created. The new knowledge can be knowledge of the technology that underpins the product or service, such as knowledge of components, linkages between components, methods, processes, and techniques that go into a product or service. It can also be knowledge of distribution channels, product applications, and customer expectations, preferences, needs, and wants. The process of innovation can be divided into invention and commercialization. An invention can be a new gadget that an engineer has created or a new chemical compound that a pharmaceutical company has discovered that can cure a disease. The term *invention* also refers to the new way of doing things that allowed the engineer to develop the new gadget or the pharmaceutical company to discover the new compound. That is, **invention** pertains to the use of new knowledge to create or discover new things. Very often, invention is not enough to make money. Inventions must be commercialized to make money. They must be marketed, distributed, and delivered to customers.

Invention

The process of invention usually includes the generation of new knowledge and the translation of that knowledge into new products or services. This is a searching, researching, and development process that can be an integral part of any stage of a business system, although it is often housed primarily, but not exclusively, in a separate R&D department. No matter where in a business system research and development activities are located, the process of knowledge generation and translation into products and services is determined by several factors.

Investment in R&D

Firms that invest heavily in R&D usually generate more inventions and patents per R&D dollar than those that do not.[2] They may not always make money from the inventions, but that is a different topic that we will explore later. The main point for now is that there are economies of scale and scope in R&D.

Communications and Interaction

The performance of a product development team increases when team members communicate frequently with each other, with members of related project groups, with employees in different functional groups within the firm, and with people outside the company at supplier, customer, competitor, or complementor firms or at universities.[3] While the bulk of such communication centers on the exchange of technical knowledge, some of it conveys information to managers, such as sponsors, who provide continued financial and moral support for team activities and thus need to be kept informed.[4]

Involvement of Multiple Functions

Market information during the research and development of a product can be useful in developing a product that meets customer needs. Thus, essential marketing personnel can be moved to the R&D group to work closely with the development teams. Having the designer of a product move with his or her product as it goes through the value chain from R&D to Manufacturing to Marketing and Sales can provide the designer with vital information that he or she can use when designing the next product.

The Right People

Having champions to articulate a vision of the benefits of the invention being developed can help in two ways. First, a clearer vision of an invention's benefits can motivate the employees who work on the project and the managers who must allocate some of the scarce resources to the project. Second, a project accompanied by a compelling articulation of benefits can be more convincing to outside investors than a project that has no such articulation. Boundary spanners facilitate communication between groups. Project managers, especially heavyweight project managers, can reduce development times and costs while improving final product quality.[5]

The Right Environment

Some environments are more conducive to invention than others. Those that are conducive usually have certain characteristics.[6] First, the existence of related industries, universities, and research institutions in a region or country plays an important role. The existence of related industries means the presence of people with related knowledge with whom a firm's R&D personnel can interact to exchange and build ideas. Moreover, suppliers, customers, complementors, and competitors can be sources of inventions.[7] Universities and related research institutions provide personnel with related R&D interests with whom a firm's R&D employees can interact, and they also train a pool of potential employees from which firms can choose. Many of these potential employees invent products and go on to found their own firms. From Yahoo! and Sun Microsystems, started by graduate students at Stanford, to Netscape, started by a Stanford professor and a University of Illinois student, examples abound.

Second, the presence of a system that provides financial support and rewards for innovation can motivate inventors. A well-developed venture capital system that provides money for start-ups and an initial public offering (IPO) system that allows firms to go public relatively early can motivate some inventors.[8] Third, a culture that tolerates failure allows individuals and firms to be more daring and therefore more likely to come up with breakthrough ideas and inventions.[9] Finally, government policies in a region or country also play an important role in the ability of firms to invent.[10] Governments that sponsor R&D often make it possible for firms to pursue certain projects that would not have been undertaken without such sponsorship. The benefits of some of these projects can be far-reaching for many industries and other countries. For example, the research efforts that led to the invention of the Internet and the discovery of DNA were sponsored by governments. Governments also train scientists at universities and other institutions. Laws protecting intellectual property encourage firms to invest in creating their own property rather than preying on that of others. Likewise, lower capital gain taxes that allow firms to keep more of what they make may encourage them to spend more on innovation.

Commercialization

Research and product development are only the first step in delivering superior value to customers. The next step is **commercialization** of the invention. One way of looking at the commercialization process is through the lens of the marketing mix, or the four P's of marketing: product, promotion, place, and price.[11] In the first P, *product,* the product that has been developed is given a brand name and packaged, and a decision is made as to which of its features to emphasize. In the next P, *promotion,* the firm makes decisions on sales promotion, advertising, the sales force, public relations, and direct marketing. In the third P, *place,* decisions are made about distribution channels, geographic market segments, inventory, and transportation. In the final P, *price,* decisions are made about pricing, including list price, discounts, allowances, payment period, and credit terms. Many of the factors that impact invention also impact commercialization. For example, there may be economies of scale and scope in advertising. Being located near customers can help a firm better understand which channels will serve customers best and how best to serve each channel.

Profiting from Innovation

Since the goal of a business model is to make money, the next question is, When does a firm make money from invention and commercialization? Not all firms make money from their inventions, and many firms make money from other firms' inventions. The question is, Why? The Inimitability and Complementary Assets model throws some light on this question.

Inimitability and Complementary Assets Model

Professor David Teece of the University of California at Berkeley was puzzled by why RC Cola invented both caffeine-free cola and diet cola, yet Coca-Cola and PepsiCo made most of the money from these products, and why EMI, the British record company, invented the CT scanner but GE made most of the money from this critical medical equipment, which won its inventor the Nobel Prize in medicine. Teece's research suggested that two things determine the extent to which a firm can profit from its invention or innovation: inimitability and complementary assets (see Figure 8.1).[12] **Inimitability** is the extent to which an invention or discovery cannot be copied or leapfrogged. High inimitability may be a result of the intellectual property protection of the invention or discovery, the failure of potential imitators to have what it takes to imitate, or the inventor's strategies to protect the invention. **Complementary assets** are all the other resources, apart from the invention or discovery, that a firm needs to enable it to offer customer value and appropriate the value. These assets include shelf space, distribution channels, brand, manufacturing, marketing, service, reputation, installed base of products, relationships with clients or suppliers, relationships with governments, and complementary technologies. Figure 8.1 shows the circumstances under which a firm can expect to profit from innovation or change.

Cell I: When inimitability is low, it is difficult for an inventor to make money in the long term if complementary assets are easily available or unimportant. This is because as soon as competitors find out that an invention is making money, they rush in to imitate the inventor. Since complementary assets are easily available or unimportant, competitors can quickly offer the same value to customers, thereby evaporating any prospects for profits.

Cell II: If complementary assets are tightly held and important—that is, rare, difficult to imitate or substitute, and valuable—the owner of the assets makes money. This is because even though many competitors can imitate the invention, few, if any, have the necessary complementary assets. In our example of the CT

FIGURE 8.1
**Inimitability/
Complementary
Assets Framework**

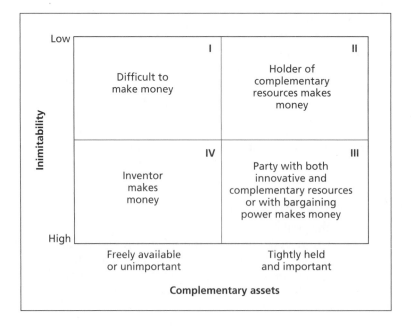

scanner, the inventor itself, EMI, lacked the complementary assets. General Electric ended up making most of the profits from the invention because GE had complementary assets such as distribution channels and the relations with U.S. hospitals that were critical to selling such expensive medical equipment. In the early 1970s when CT scanners were being marketed to U.S. hospitals, these assets were rare, difficult to imitate or substitute. and valuable. In our cola example, Coca-Cola and PepsiCo had brand-name reputations, shelf space, marketing, and distribution channels that were also rare, difficult to imitate, and valuable, and these assets allowed them to capture most of the profits from RC Cola's diet and caffeine-free cola inventions, which were easy to imitate.

Cell III: When inimitability is high and complementary assets are important and difficult to acquire, whoever has both the invention and the assets or the more important of the two stands to profit from the invention. This was the case in Pixar's interaction with Disney. Inimitability of Pixar's digital studio technology is somewhat high given the software copyrights Pixar holds and the combination of technology and creativity that it takes to deliver a compelling animation movie. However, offering customers movies made with that technology requires distribution channels, brand-name recognition, and financing, which are tightly held by the likes of Disney and Sony Pictures. Prior to the release of *Toy Story,* Disney had the bargaining power because it had all the complementary assets and the technology had not been proved. After the release and success of *Toy Story,* which proved that Pixar could combine technology and creativity—a combination that is more difficult to imitate than plain computer animation—Pixar was able to renegotiate a better deal.[13]

Cell IV: When inimitability is high and complementary assets are freely available or unimportant, an innovator stands to profit from its invention. For example, the inventor of the Stradivarius violin stood to profit from it because no one could imitate the violin, and complementary assets for it were neither difficult to acquire nor important.

Implication of the Model

One implication of this model is that a firm that has difficult-to-imitate, important complementary assets can make a substantial amount of money from inventions that are easy to imitate. Microsoft did not invent word processing, spreadsheets, or graphical user interface (GUI) operating systems. But it has profited immensely from these inventions largely because of its installed base of software on computers that use the Intel microprocessor architecture, starting with DOS machines.

Determining a Firm's Complementary Assets

If complementary assets can be as important as the Inimitability and Complementary Assets model suggests, a firm should identify its complementary assets. Since complementary assets are all the other resources, apart from the invention or discovery, that a firm needs to enable it to offer customer value and appropriate the value, one way for a firm to determine its complementary assets is as follows:

1. The firm analyzes and understands the competitive position—customer value, targeted market segments, prices, sources of revenues, and bargaining power—that it occupies or wants to occupy.
2. The firm determines which activities of its business systems allow it to attain the desired competitive position.

3. The firm determines what resources, other than the invention or discovery, are critical to performing those business system activities. The firm's complementary assets are all the other resources, in addition to its invention or discovery, that it needs to attain the competitive positions. Firms that attempt to determine their complementary resources usually end up generating a laundry list of resources. To avoid generating such a list, firms should perform the VRISA analysis (described in Chapter 6) for each complementary asset. By determining the extent to which its complementary assets make significant contributions to customer value and the extent to which they are rare, imitable, substitutable, and appropriable, a firm can weed out the not-so-valuable resources from the valuable ones.

GENERIC STRATEGIES FOR SUSTAINABILITY OF PROFITS

For a manager who is interested in making money from innovation, Figure 8.1 raises some interesting questions. Suppose a firm finds itself in cell I, where it is difficult to make money. That is, the firm has invented or discovered something that is easy to imitate, and complementary assets are easy to come by or unimportant. Is there anything that the firm can do to improve its situation? What should a firm do if its invention is easy to imitate but complementary assets, which it does not have, are tightly held and important? In other words, are there any strategies that a firm that finds itself in one of the cells in Figure 8.1 can pursue? The answer is yes. Depending on which cell the firm is in, it can pursue a *block, run,* or *team-up* strategy or a combination of these strategies. We describe each of these generic strategies below and then apply them in the context of the Inimitability and Complementary Assets model.

Block Strategy

One strategy that a firm can pursue in defense of its competitive advantage is the block strategy. In the **block strategy,** a firm takes actions that are designed to preserve the inimitability and nonsubstitutability of its valuable resources or that prevent entry into its product market space.

Preserving Inimitability

Preserving inimitability of resources can be achieved in two main ways. First, a firm can keep its know-how proprietary, thereby preventing rivals and potential imitators from duplicating the capability. For example, Coca-Cola moved out of India, a country of over 1 billion people, rather than reveal its secret cola formula to Indian government officials. Second, a firm can sue any party that attempts to violate its intellectual property rights or steal its trade secrets. In so doing, a firm may also be sending a signal to potential imitators that they will face retaliation. In the 1980s and 1990s, Intel did not hesitate to sue firms that illegally tried to copy its microprocessor microcode, a critical part of its microprocessors that is copyrighted.

Preventing Entry

A firm can prevent entry into its market space by signaling that postentry prices will be low. The rationale here is that firms will enter a market only if they believe that they will make money. If they believe that a firm already in the market will lower its prices when they enter, potential new entrants are less likely to enter. A firm can signal that postentry prices will be low in several ways.

1. It can establish a reputation for retaliating with lower prices against any firm that enters its product market space. For example, if an airline is known for cutting its fares on a particular route when another airline starts flying the same route, potential entrants in this route would think twice before entering. Of course, if a new entrant has a very attractive cost structure, it may still enter and do well.

2. A firm can invest in idiosyncratic assets in a market, signaling its commitment to stay in that market and fight when entry occurs or rivalry increases. An asset is *idiosyncratic* to a market if it cannot be profitably deployed elsewhere. For example, an aluminum smelter built in a remote area next to a cheap source of electricity and close to bauxite deposits is an idiosyncratic asset since it cannot be profitably relocated. A firm that invests in idiosyncratic assets is not likely to pick up and leave the market since moving its assets elsewhere would be unprofitable. It would probably stay and fight new entrants by, for example, offering lower prices, especially if doing so covers its variable costs and makes a contribution toward its fixed costs. Potential new entrants are likely to understand this and therefore not enter. In our example of the aluminum smelter plant, the owner cannot cost-effectively use the plant for something other than producing aluminum and is therefore likely to stay in the market and lower its prices, especially if doing so at least covers its variable costs.

3. A firm that has captured a large market share and therefore enjoys scale economies can profitably offer lower prices to its customers than can a new entrant with a very small market share, thereby potentially reducing new entry. This is particularly true in an industry with a large minimum efficient scale. As a firm produces more of a particular product, the cost per unit of the product usually falls. Beyond a certain volume, the decrease in unit cost stops. This volume is called the **minimum efficient scale (MES),** the minimum volume that a firm has to produce in order to attain the minimum per-unit cost possible in the industry. If a firm is already producing at the minimum efficient scale, an entrant must produce at least at this volume if it is going to enjoy the same economies-of-scale cost savings. But producing that much means adding that much more output to the market. The larger the MES and therefore the more of the product that a new entrant would have to bring into the market, the lower the prices would be. Thus, if the minimum efficient scale is large and industry firms are already producing at the MES, potential entrants are less likely to enter since they can expect prices to drop considerably given how much more they would have to add to the industry's capacity.

4. A firm may be in a market because exit costs are too high. For example, in a country where unions are very strong or government laws frown on laying off people, a firm may decide to stay in a market because its costs of exiting are higher than those of charging lower prices and losing money. Finally, a firm that is in an industry for reasons other than profit maximization may be willing to lower its prices to stay in the market. For example, if a firm is in a market because it wants to learn, it may not mind charging lower prices than its profit-maximizing rivals charge. Suppose Honda is in lawn mowers because it wants to learn more about small engines. Honda may decide to lower its prices when a new firm enters the lawn mower market if Honda believes that what it learns from lawn mower engines can help it in its search for a smaller and lighter fuel-efficient automobile engine.

As a strategy for sustaining a competitive advantage, blocking does not always work. One reason for the insufficiency of blocking is change. Regulation and deregulation, changes in customer preferences and expectations, or radical technological change can render valuable, inimitable resources less valuable. For example, the advent of the personal computer rendered IBM's skills in mainframe computers less valuable, taking away some of IBM's competitive advantage. Similarly, for a software developer whose access to distribution channels was a valuable, nonsubstitutable resource, the Internet has eroded this advantage since new entrants can now sell their products online.

Run Strategy

In a **run strategy,** a firm performs activities that allow it to keep innovating—using new knowledge to offer its customers better value that they want and improving its business model. In this way, by the time competitors have imitated the firm's existing innovations, it has moved on to newer and better ones. The run strategy accepts the fact that no matter how formidable the barriers to entry that a firm has erected may appear to be, they are still often penetrable, circumventable, or eventually defeatable. Sitting complacently behind such barriers gives competitors time to catch up to or leapfrog a firm that only blocks. In some industries, a firm that has a competitive advantage often has to run, constantly innovating so as to maintain its lead. Running entails changing some subset of components or linkages of the firm's business model or creating a whole new business model to offer customers better value and make money doing so. Dell Computer practiced the run strategy in a way, often introducing better ways of selling its PCs before its competitors copied its existing sales strategy. Often in running, firms may have to cannibalize their own existing products before competitors do. In the late 1980s and 1990s, Intel usually introduced a new generation of microprocessors before unit sales of its existing one had peaked. If it had not—and despite its microcode copyrights, which protect its microprocessors from illegal copying—other firms would have found it a little easier to catch up.[14]

Team-Up Strategy

Often, a firm just cannot do all it needs to alone, so it must team up with others through some kind of strategic alliance, joint venture, acquisition, or equity arrangement. The **team-up strategy** allows a firm to share in resources that it does not have and may not want to acquire or that it cannot acquire even if it wanted to. In some industries, running also requires teaming up, largely because the innovation to be undertaken is too complex or too expensive for one firm. For example, Intel and Hewlett-Packard had to team up to develop the very expensive and complex titanium 64-bit microprocessor chip, a project that not even Intel wanted to undertake alone.

Generic Strategies and the Inimitability and Complementary Assets Model

Now that we have explained the block, run, and team-up strategies, let's return to our earlier question: Is there anything that a firm can do if it finds itself in one of the cells in Figure 8.1? As Figure 8.2 shows, the firm can use one or more of the generic strategies, depending on the cell it is in.

Cell I: A firm that finds itself in cell I can pursue a run strategy. The idea here is that if a firm can keep innovating, then by the time its rivals have caught up with an existing innovation, the firm will have moved on to another, better innovation.

FIGURE 8.2
Block, Run, and Team-Up Strategies

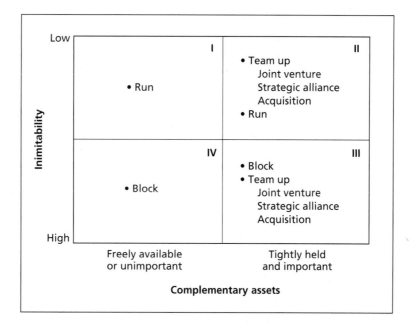

Cell II: The more frequently encountered case in many industries is that of cell II, where the invention is easy to imitate and complementary assets are tightly held and important. If, for example, a start-up company has the invention or discovery and an incumbent has the complementary assets, both can team up to profit from the innovation. They can form a joint venture, a strategic alliance, or a merger through acquisition. If a firm decides to team up, it must do so early, before its invention can be imitated or leapfrogged, so it can use the invention as a bargaining chip. An inventor with an imitable invention can also offer itself for acquisition by a firm that has the complementary resources if the owner of the assets wants the invention but does not have the time required to imitate the invention. For example, Soma.com, an online drug retailer, was bought by CVS, the drugstore chain. Soma.com had the Internet technology for online drug prescription fulfillment transactions, and CVS had the brand, retail stores, and relationships with the health care community. Very often, incumbents with difficult-to-imitate complementary assets choose to imitate the invention, while start-ups with inventions struggle to build complementary assets.

Cell III: A firm that finds itself in cell III can pursue one of two strategies: block or team up. If the firm that has the tightly held and important complementary assets also owns the high-inimitability invention, it can block rivals and potential new entrants from having access to either. If one firm has the invention while another has the complementary assets, both firms can team up. The pharmaceutical industry offers many good examples. In that industry, many start-up biotechnology firms develop new drugs whose patents limit imitability. However, they do not have the resources needed to carry out all the clinical testing that is critical for getting a new drug approved, by the U.S. Food and Drug Administration, for marketing in the United States. These start-ups usually do not have sales forces that call on doctors, marketing power, and brand-name reputations. As a result, the number of strategic alliances between large, established pharmaceutical companies and biotechnology start-ups is large. Teaming up is not limited, however, to the pairing of start-ups with established firms. Pfizer, a large, traditional pharmaceutical company, bought Warner-Lambert, another large, established company, because the latter had a drug (Lipitor) that was difficult for Pfizer to quickly imitate and Pfizer had the level of sales and marketing, which Warner-Lambert did not have, that was necessary to profit from the drug. Since most inventions or discoveries eventually get imitated, substituted, or leapfrogged, a firm that tries to protect either for too long risks losing any competitive edge that it may have had.

Cell IV: In cases where an invention or discovery is difficult to imitate but complementary assets are easy to come by or unimportant, a firm may be better off pursuing a block strategy, in which it tries to prevent others from imitating its invention or strategy.

CHANGE

Just about every firm, sooner or later, has to face change. In effect, change alters the way firms (1) create and offer customer value and (2) position themselves to appropriate the value. For most business models, change represents both a threat and an opportunity. It is a threat in that it can erode a firm's competitive advantage, and it is an opportunity in that a firm can use it to reinforce its advantage or leapfrog competitors.

Sources of Change

Change can be initiated by a firm or by any of its coopetitors—the suppliers, customers, rivals, new entrants, and complementors with whom it often cooperates and competes. It can also come from a firm's macro environment.

The Firm and Its Coopetitors

Firms and their coopetitors, whether incumbents or new entrants, are often the source of change, especially technological change. The invention and commercialization of the microprocessor by Intel and the processor's adoption by Intel's coopetitors spearheaded changes in the computer industry that eroded the competitive advantage of minicomputer and mainframe computer makers and allowed new computer and software companies to build new competitive advantages. Wal-Mart's decision to saturate contiguous small towns in the southwestern United States with its stores, build logistics systems, integrate information technology into its key activities early, and establish distribution centers to serve the stores changed the nature of discount retailing in the United States. The manufacturing methods that Ford introduced with its Model T changed the way goods are produced. Change can also come from a competitor that has found a way to introduce a better business model and erode the industry leader's advantage. By selling directly to end customers and, later, using a build-to-order model, Dell was able to erode Compaq's leadership position in the PC market. A firm that has a competitive advantage can also initiate change in a bid to increase its lead. For example, in the 1980s and 1990s, Intel usually introduced a new generation of microprocessor before the one being replaced had peaked in sales.

Macro Environment

Change can also come from a firm's macro environment: technological, political-legal, demographic, sociocultural, economic, and natural factors. Technological change can have a huge impact on business models. In the late 1990s, the Internet forced many companies to reexamine their business models. Through regulation and deregulation, legislation, and other policies, governments can be the source of changes that have significant consequences for business models. For example, deregulation of the airline industry in the United States and Europe forced many airlines to rethink their business models. Change can also be a confluence of both technological change and government regulation or deregulation. For example, from the mid-1980s to mid-1990s, each regional telephone company in the United States owned the copper wiring that connected residential homes and businesses in its region, and each therefore had local monopoly power over phone services. Today cell phone technology and regulatory changes are forcing many of these local companies to reexamine their business models.

The source of change can be demographic. For example, population shifts can result in changes in the tastes and preferences of the population in a market segment that a firm serves, forcing the firm to either change and offer the new value wanted by the segment's current population or be pushed out by attackers. Customers in a region that a firm once served with low-cost goods can become more affluent and want luxury goods. Economic growth or shocks can result in higher or lower incomes and therefore in more or less demand for certain kinds of products. Changes in the supply of a product or its complement can cause changes in the demand for the product and in the business models of suppliers. For example, the petroleum crisis of the 1970s increased the demand for vehicles with higher gas mileage than U.S. automakers could offer. This opened up an opportunity for Japanese car makers, whose cars were more fuel efficient than those of American competitors, to gain market share. Concern about the natural environment can prompt customers to look for different kinds of benefits in the products they buy. For example, customers who are concerned about air pollution may prefer cars with more emission control rather than less. Governments can legislate the pollution levels that are acceptable for products such as cars, thereby influencing manufacturers to supply products that meet the regulations. Concern about the natural environment can also cause firms to change the way they perform certain value chain activities. For example, many aluminum-can makers pursued more recycling to cut down on the problems caused by cans that are thrown away.

Change and Innovation

To take advantage of change, a firm has to innovate. That is, the firm has to use new knowledge from the change to invent or discover something that customers want, commercialize the product, or better position itself to appropriate the value that it creates for customers. For example, to take advantage of changes in the lifestyles of working families, frozen-food companies have had to develop and commercialize the types of food that these families want and can afford. To take advantage of changes introduced by the PC, Microsoft developed and commercialized new products such as Word, Excel, and Windows for the PC. Dell took advantage of the Internet to introduce its build-to-order process, in which customers use the Internet to tell Dell what they want in their PCs and Dell delivers the computers to them in a few days.

Firms whose competitive advantages have been eroded by change are those that were unable to innovate with the change and whose competitors did. For example, the mainframe and minicomputer makers whose advantages were eroded by PCs were unable to innovate. Whether a firm takes advantage of change to reinforce or gain an advantage or sees its advantage eroded by change is a function of the type of change.

Type of Change

Change can be classified as a function of whether it renders existing products noncompetitive, whether it creates different markets, or whether it renders existing resources and capabilities obsolete.[15] Using these classifications, we explore four models of change: incremental versus radical, disruptive, systemic, and dynamic. In this section, the words *innovation* and *change* are used interchangeably, reflecting the fact that change is usually exploited by using the new knowledge from it to innovate and innovation usually results in change.

Incremental versus Radical Change

One of the simplest but highly useful models of change is the *incremental versus radical change model.* Consider an industry whose firms, the incumbents, have developed resources and capabilities that allow them to offer superior customer value and appropriate the value. One can think of change as having an impact on the customer value offered by these incumbents or on the resources and capabilities that they use to offer customer value and appropriate it.

Impact on Customer Value If a change results in a new product that renders existing products noncompetitive—by virtue of the superior value that the new product embodies—it is said to be **radical in the economic sense.** Incumbents, whose current products give them an advantage, are usually reluctant to invest in such changes for fear of cannibalizing their existing products and eroding their advantages.[16] New entrants do not have a market position to defend and are therefore more likely to be first to embrace change that is radical in the economic sense. A good example of a radical change is the personal computer, which rendered minicomputers noncompetitive. Another is the electronic point-of-sale (EPOS) cash register, which rendered existing mechanical cash registers noncompetitive.

If a change results in enhancing existing products or allows them to remain competitive, it is said to be **incremental in the economic sense.** Since such a change does not threaten the customer value that incumbents offer and may even reinforce their market positions, incumbents have an incentive to invest in such changes and are therefore more likely to embrace incremental change than are new entrants. Examples of incremental changes include diet and caffeine-free colas, which allowed classic cola drinks to stay competitive in the market, and the electric razor, which allowed traditional, mechanical razors to remain competitive.

Impact on Resources and Capabilities In addition to impacting customer value, change usually impacts the capabilities that firms use to offer customer value and appropriate it. The resources and capabilities needed to exploit a change can be very different from existing incumbent resources and capabilities, thereby rendering the latter obsolete as far as exploiting the change is concerned. For example, the resources and capabilities required to offer electronic calculators were very different from those required to offer mechanical calculators. Offering mechanical calculators required resources and capabilities in connecting gears, ratchets, belts, and levers to produce calculations, while offering electronic calculators required resources and capabilities in using microchips and software technologies. Note that electronic calculators were also a radical change in the economic sense since they rendered mechanical calculators noncompetitive. But also note that not all changes that are radical in the organizational sense are radical in the economic sense. The electric shaver is a good example because it required radically different resources and capabilities from those used to make mechanical razors but did not leave the latter noncompetitive.

Disruptive Change

The *disruptive change model,* championed by Professor Clayton Christensen of the Harvard Business School, argues that the main reason incumbents fail to exploit disruptive changes is not that the change is radical to them, as suggested by the incremental versus radical model. Rather, incumbents fail because they spend too much time listening to and meeting the needs of their existing mainstream customers, who, initially, have no use for products from the disruptive change.[17] According to this model, **disruptive changes,** or technologies, have the following characteristics:

1. They create new markets by introducing a new kind of product or service.
2. The new product or service from the change costs less than existing products or services.
3. Initially, the new products perform worse than existing products when judged by the performance metrics that mainstream existing customers value. Eventually, however, the performance catches up and addresses the needs of mainstream customers.

To understand the model, suppose that an incumbent firm offers product A, which in year 1 more than meets the demand *B* as far as the key performance attributes that the firm's customers want in the product are concerned (Figure 8.3). Also suppose that in year 2 a new product, C, which costs less than A and meets the performance requirements *D* demanded by a new market, is introduced by new entrants. Initially, C's performance is inferior to that of A and clearly does not meet the performance requirements demanded by *B.* Given its investments in the technology, processes, and systems that underpin product A and the fact that its customers still want A, the incumbent continues to meet its customers' requirements by focusing on what has allowed it, in the past, to offer A and paying little attention to C. Meanwhile, new entrants keep improving the performance of product C. Eventually, say, in year 5, C's performance has improved to the point where it meets the needs of the market with demand *B* as well as that with *D.* Customers with demand *B* switch to product C (since C is cheaper and meets their needs), and new entrants now have both *B* and *D* markets. By this time, it is too late for the

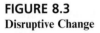
FIGURE 8.3
Disruptive Change

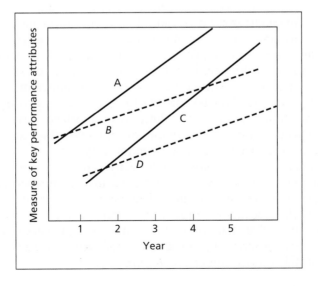

incumbent (producer of A) to shed its old processes, systems, and culture, which had served it so well with the old technology, to develop C and gain a product advantage in C.

The invasion of minicomputers and mainframes by PCs offers a good example of a disruptive change. Minicomputers (A in Figure 8.3) were in the market before PCs and satisfied the needs of many customers as far as speed, software, and memory capacity were concerned (*B*). When PCs (C) came along, their prices were much lower than those of minicomputers, and their speeds, memory, and software (C) were inferior to those demanded by many minicomputer customers (*B*) but met the needs of most of the computer enthusiasts and hobbyists who bought PCs (*D*). As the performance of personal computers increased, minicomputer makers kept listening to their customers, offering them minicomputers and not paying enough attention to PCs. Eventually, PC performance improved to the point where it more than met the needs of many minicomputer customers. By this time, it was too late for many minicomputer makers. New entrants to the computer market, such as Compaq and Dell, had already developed their resources and capabilities in PCs and captured most of the market share in the PC market.

To avoid being a victim of disruptive change, an incumbent can create a separate group within itself or form a separate entity outside the firm. Whether a firm responds to a disruptive change by pursuing innovation internally or externally depends on how much the systems, processes, values, and culture that are required to exploit the change differ from the ones that the firm already possesses. If the difference is very big, the firm should go outside; if not, it should stay inside and pursue the innovation via a separate internal group.

Systemic Change

The **systemic change model** argues that since customer value usually is a result of value-adding activities from coopetitors along a value system, it is important to think of change as **systemic change,** that is, to think of it in terms of its impact on all the coopetitors along the value system.[18] When faced with change, a firm should consider the impact of the change on its suppliers, customers, and complementors as well as on itself.[19] For example, in exploring the impact of the Internet on publishers, a publishing firm would be shortsighted not to also explore the impact on authors and on booksellers such as Borders. This is because a change can be incremental to a manufacturer but be radical to its customers and complementors and incremental to its suppliers. A firm that focuses only on itself could get the false illusion that all is fine. For example, the Dvorak Simplified Keyboard (DSK) arrangement that was meant to replace the QWERTY arrangement, which most of today's keyboards have, was competence-enhancing to its innovator, Dvorak, and other typewriter manufacturers: To manufacture the DSK, all they had to do was rearrange the position of the keys. But it was competence-destroying to customers who had already learned how to type with the QWERTY keyboard: To use the DSK, they would have to relearn how to touch-type.

For another example, consider the electric car. Such cars would be a radical change not only to automakers but also to suppliers of mechanical components for the internal combustion engine automobile, complementors such as gas station owners and oil companies, and some users of cars. Thus, according to the systemic model, an automaker that concentrates only on the impact of the electric car on automakers and neglects the impact on suppliers, complementors, and customers may be making a costly mistake.

Dynamic Change

The incremental versus radical, disruptive, and value system models of change are static because they say nothing about the fact that change usually evolves. Change usually has a life cycle, and, as such, can be viewed as **dynamic change.** *Dynamic change models,* or **technology life-cycle** models, have been used as frameworks for understanding the evolving impact of change on offering customer value and appropriating it after a change, as well as understanding the consequences for business models. According to one of these models, a change usually goes through three phases: fluid, transitional, and stable (Figure 8.4).[20]

1. *Emerging, or fluid, phase:* In the **fluid phase,** at the onset of a change, there is a great deal of uncertainty as to how to create, offer, and appropriate customer value. Firms are not quite sure which business system activities to pursue, how to pursue them, and when to pursue them. Customers may not know what they should value in the change. Product quality is usually low, and cost and prices are high, as economies of scale and learning have yet to set in. Market penetration is low and most customers are either **lead users**—customers whose needs are similar to those of other users except that they have these needs months or years before most of the marketplace—or high-income users. As the uncertainty about what value to create and offer and what activities to perform to do so decreases, profit-motivated entrepreneurs enter to exploit the change. Since product or service and market requirements are still ambiguous, there are very few failures. Early in the life of the Internet, for example, many firms did not fail. As more and more firms enter, there is competition to develop products or services. There is also competition for resources—for capital, for talented employees—and for customers and suppliers.

2. *Growth, or transitional, phase:* The change enters the **transitional phase** when some standardization of components, market needs, and product design features takes place and a standard or common framework for offering products or services emerges. The customer base increases from lead and high-income users to mass market during the growth phase. Many firms are unable to compete for customers, suppliers, and resources, and are forced to file for bankruptcy, be sold, or

FIGURE 8.4
Technology Life Cycle

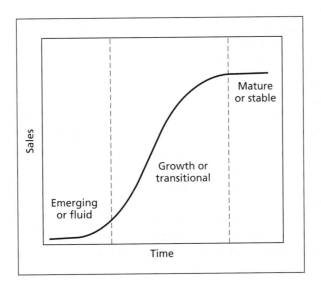

merge. The Internet bubble burst represented such a time for online firms. Thus the number of entries decreases drastically, while the number of exits increases tremendously.

3. *Mature, or stable, phase:* In the **stable phase,** products built around the common framework or standard proliferate. Products are highly defined, with differences fewer than similarities between competing products. Growth slows considerably, with most output earmarked to satisfy replacement needs. The total number of firms in each industry decreases considerably from the peak of the growth phase. In the U.S. automobile industry, for example, out of the hundreds of automakers that had entered the market at one time or another, only three firms remained during the stable phase. In this phase, a firm's strategies focus on defending its position and watching out for the next technological change that could start the life cycle over again.

One of the key points about the technology life-cycle model is that it applies to a firm's business model as well as to an innovation: both evolve through the same phases. The activities that a firm performs in the fluid phase can be very different from those performed in the stable phase. For example, in the fluid phase of the PC industry, customers needed a lot of hand-holding since they knew very little about computers. Thus, selling complete systems and having dealers was the way to go. In the stable phase, many customers do not need hand-holding and therefore can buy their PCs through the Internet.

When to Expect or Initiate Change

Given how important change is and the fact that there can be first-mover advantages in exploiting change, an important question is, How does a firm know when to expect change that is likely to impact its competitive positioning? A firm that scans its environment often for threats and opportunities from change can improve its ability to expect or initiate change.

Environmental Scanning

Environmental scanning for change consists of keeping an eye on potential sources of change—in both industry and macro environments. Through competitive intelligence, a firm can monitor its major coopetitors' business models for any movements that suggest change. Also, by monitoring its macro environment's technological, economic, political-legal, demographic, sociocultural, and natural elements, a firm can keep track of possible changes. Examples of macroenvironment variables that can be monitored are[21]:

- *Technological:* potential technological discontinuities, new products that have been introduced and the technologies that underpin them, intellectual property policy changes, government and industry spending on R&D, competitors' spending on R&D, and rate of obsolescence of industry products.
- *Economic:* currency movements, disposable incomes, interest rates, money supply, inflation, and unemployment.
- *Political-legal:* antitrust regulation, tax laws, foreign trade regulation, and employee protection laws.
- *Demographic:* population changes, age distributions, ethnic mixes, education levels, lifestyle changes, consumer activism, birthrates, life expectancies, and household patterns in cities, regions, and countries.
- *Sociocultural:* changes in beliefs, norms, and values.

- *Natural:* environmental protection laws and the objectives of key environmental organizations.

Timing

One problem that firms often face is how to predict when potential changes are likely to impact their business models, especially if no firm has adopted the changes in the firms' industry yet. This is a question that has challenged scholars of change for a long time. In the area of technological change, two ideas have been explored. The first was proposed by Richard Foster of the McKinsey company. He argued that the rate at which a technology advances is a function of the amount of effort put into the technology and follows the S-curve shown in Figure 8.5a.[22] Technological progress starts off slowly, then increases rapidly, and then diminishes as the physical limits of the technology are approached. Close to the physical limit, the return on effort becomes small. At this point, a new technology whose underlying physical properties allow it to overcome the physical limit of the old technology must be used. The automobile industry's effort to reduce emissions from automobiles is a good example. Over the years, automakers have improved the emissions from their internal combustion engine automobiles. However, the limit to how cleanly the internal combustion engine automobile can burn gasoline and the limit to the ability to control auto emissions are being approached. Investments in emission control equipment no longer produce much improvement in the level of emissions expelled. A new power source such as electricity results in a new S-curve with a different physical limit (Figure 8.5b). According to Foster, such diminishing returns in the results produced by efforts to improve physical parameters are a signal that changing to a new S-curve is imminent.

The second idea for predicting when a technological change is likely to impact a firm's business model is based on the fact that the core technology that underpins a product or industry often underpins other products or industries.[23] Thus, by paying attention to these other industries, and not just its own industry, a firm can better tell when to

FIGURE 8.5a
Foster's S-Curve

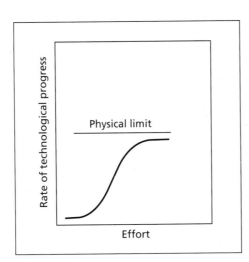

FIGURE 8.5b
Automobile S-Curves

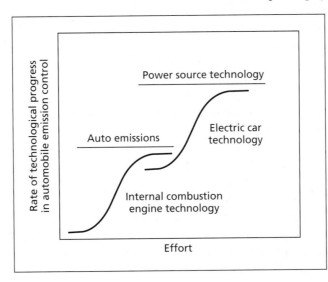

embrace a technological change—and this can be well before the old technology has reached its physical limit. For example, at one time or another, computers, calculators, cash registers, and watches used mechanical gears, ratchets, belts, springs, motors, and levers to perform calculations. These products were very limited in their ability to compute and were often very bulky and unreliable. The switch to electronics came at different times for each of these industries. Computers were the first to switch from mechanical to electronic technology, with the first general-purpose electronic computer (made from vacuum tubes) publicly revealed in 1946.[24] As electronic technology progressed—with transistors displacing vacuum tubes and then integrated circuits (microchips) replacing transistors—calculators, cash registers, and watches were also converted from mechanical to electronic. Thus, according to this second view, after seeing what happened in the computer industry, managers in the calculator, cash register, and watch industries should have known that the mechanical technologies that underpinned their products would have to change too.

Summary

One way for a firm to offer superior customer value and position itself to appropriate the value is to innovate. Innovation consists of both invention and commercialization. Turning an invention into value that customers perceive as superior and positioning a firm to profit from the value usually requires complementary assets. An invention that is difficult to imitate, substitute, or leapfrog can earn its owner profits. A firm that has valuable, rare, difficult-to-imitate or substitute complementary assets stands to profit from an invention that is easy to imitate. To sustain profits from their business models, firms usually pursue some combination of block, run, or team-up strategies. In a block strategy, a firm pursues activities that have the potential to prevent existing rivals and potential new entrants from imitating its business model. In a run strategy, a firm pursues activities that allow it to keep innovating or reinventing its business model and improving the model before competitors have had a chance to catch up with the old model. In a team-up strategy, a firm partners with coopetitors by entering into alliances, taking equity shares in ventures, forming joint ventures, acquiring another firm, or offering itself for acquisition.

No matter how successful a firm is in pursuing a block, run, or team-up strategy, it must face change sooner or later. Change offers incumbents with a lead an opportunity to extend their lead. It also offers attackers an opportunity to erode the advantages built by existing winners. Taking advantage of change usually means innovating—using new knowledge from the change to offer new products with superior customer value and positioning the firm to appropriate the value. How well a firm can take advantage of change is a function of the type of change. Change can be incremental, radical, disruptive, systemic, or dynamic. Determining what type of change may occur soon usually entails performing an environmental scan.

Key Terms

block strategy, *158*
commercialization, *155*
complementary assets, *156*
disruptive change, *165*
dynamic change, *167*

environmental scanning, *168*
fluid phase, *167*
incremental in the economic sense, *164*
inimitability, *156*

innovation, *153*
invention, *153*
lead users, *167*
minimum efficient scale (MES), *159*

Study Questions

1. Name five innovations in which complementary assets played a critical role in determining winners in the race to capture profits from the innovation.
2. Is the cell phone a disruptive technology? If so, to what?
3. Can an innovation that is incremental to a firm be radical to its customers? Give examples, if any. Why is this important?
4. What is the relationship between the complementary assets model explored in this chapter and the familiarity matrix of Chapter 6?
5. Should the dot-com boom and burst of the late 1990s and early 2000 have been expected?

Endnotes

1. A. N. Afuah, *Innovation Management: Strategies, Implementation, and Profits* (New York: Oxford University Press, 2003).
2. R. Henderson and I. Cockburn, "Scale, Scope, and Spillovers: The Determinants of Research Productivity in Drug Discovery," *Rand Journal of Economics* 27 (1996), pp. 32–59.
3. T. Allen, *Managing the Flow of Technology* (Cambridge, MA: MIT Press, 1984).
4. D. G. Ancona and D. F. Caldwell, "Bridging the Boundary: External Process and Performance in Organizational Teams," *Administrative Sciences Quarterly* 37 (1992), pp. 634–665.
5. K. B. Clark and K. Fujimoto, *Product Development Performance: Strategy, Organization, and Management in the World Automobile Industry* (Boston: Harvard Business School Press, 1991).
6. This section draws heavily on Afuah, *Innovation Management.*
7. E. Von Hippel, *The Sources of Innovation* (New York: Oxford University Press, 1988).
8. C. Farrell, "The Boom in IPOs," *Business Week,* Dec. 18, 1995, p. 64.
9. "Please Dare to Fail," *The Economist*, Sept. 28, 1996.
10. See Afuah, *Innovation Management,* chap. 16.
11. P. Kotler, *Marketing Management* (Upper Saddle River, NJ: Prentice-Hall, 2002).
12. D. J. Teece, "Profiting from Technological Innovation: Implications for Integration, Collaboration, Licensing and Public Policy," *Research Policy* 15 (1986), pp. 285–306; see also Afuah, *Innovation Management.*
13. C. Crane, W. Johnson, K. Neumark, and C. Perrigo, "PIXAR, 1966," University of Michigan Business School case, 1998.
14. By 2003, Advanced Micro Devices had made a lot of progress but was far from catching up with Intel in revenues and profits.
15. Parts of this section are reproduced from A. N. Afuah and C. L. Tucci, *Internet Business Models and Strategies: Text and Cases* (New York: McGraw-Hill, 2003), chap. 5.
16. R. Henderson, "Underinvestment and Incompetence as Responses to Radical Innovation: Evidence from the Photolithographic Alignment Industry," *Rand Journal of Economics* 24 (1993), pp. 248–269; see Afuah, *Innovation Management,* chap. 12.
17. C. M. Christensen, *The Innovator's Dilemma* (Boston: Harvard Business School Press, 1997); C. M. Christensen and M. Overdorf, "Meeting the Challenge of Disruptive Change," *Harvard Business Review,* March–April 2000, pp. 67–76.
18. A. N. Afuah and N. Bahram, "The Hypercube of Innovation," *Research Policy* 24 (1995), pp. 51–76.

19. A. N. Afuah, "Do Your *Co-opetitors'* Capabilities Matter in the Face of a Technological Change?" *Strategic Management Journal* 21 (2000), pp. 387–404.

20. J. M. Utterback, *Mastering the Dynamics of Innovation* (Boston: Harvard Business School Press, 1994); A. N. Afuah and J. M. Utterback, "Responding to Structural Industry Changes: A Technological Innovation Perspective," *Industrial and Corporate Change* 6 (1997).

21. Kotler, *Marketing Management;* also see J. D. Hunger and T. L. Wheelen, *Essentials of Strategic Management* (Upper Saddle River, NJ: Prentice-Hall, 2003).

22. R. Foster, *Innovation: The Attacker's Advantage* (New York: Summit Books, 1986).

23. See Afuah, *Innovation Management,* chap. 6. D. A. Levinthal, "The Slow Pace of Rapid Technological Change: Gradualism and Punctuation in Technological Change," *Industrial and Corporate Change* 7 (1998), pp. 217–247.

24. The first commercial general-purpose computer, the UNIVAC I, was delivered in June 1951 by Remington-Rand.

Analyzing the Cost of a Business Model

As we have argued throughout this book, the activities that a firm performs, how it performs them, and when it performs them in building and translating its resources into the right positions in its industry and markets determine the profitability of its business model. But it costs money to acquire and maintain resources, to perform the activities that enable a firm to attain and maintain desired positions in an industry, and to deal with industry competitive forces and macro-environment forces. Whether a firm is a low-cost producer or product differentiator, minimizing its costs (given the benefits that it wants to offer) is an important objective if the firm wants to have a long-term competitive advantage. Understanding what drives the cost of each activity is a good start. In this chapter, we discuss methods for analyzing the costs associated with a business model. We start the chapter by exploring the factors that drive a business model's costs. We then examine how firms can track the costs of value-adding activities and the products that they create. Finally, we explore the role that the quantity of output produced plays in the cost of products.

COST DRIVERS

Cost drivers are the basic factors that determine costs.[1] Thus, the cost drivers of a business model are the factors associated with the firm's resources, activities, positions, and industry that have a causal effect on the model's costs (Figure 9.1). In other words, all the things that a firm does to offer superior customer value and appropriate it cost money. A business model has four major cost drivers: industry drivers, resource drivers, activity drivers, and position drivers.

Industry Drivers

A firm's competitive, cooperative, and macro environments—its **industry cost drivers**—can have major effects on its costs.

Competitive Environment

If a firm's suppliers have bargaining power over it, the firm can end up either paying more for its supplies, being forced to take inputs of lower quality than their prices warrant, or both. Paying more means higher costs for the firm. Receiving lower-quality inputs may mean that the firm has to spend more to transform its inputs into the type of quality that its customers want. If the threat of potential

FIGURE 9.1
Cost Drivers of a
Business Model

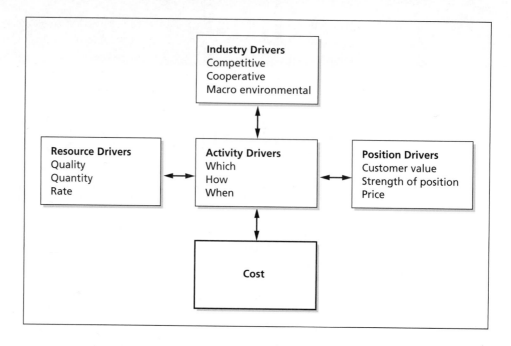

new entry is high, a firm may spend more trying to build barriers to entry. For example, a firm may advertise more to build brand loyalty. If rivalry in a firm's industry is high, the firm might decide to differentiate its products to reduce the effects of rivalry. This costs money. For example, Coca-Cola spends over 40 percent of its revenues from sales of concentrate on marketing and sales, much of which goes toward building its brand equity and distinguishing its brand from the other soda brands. If the threat of substitutes is high, a firm may have to take measures to make the substitutes less viable. Some of Coca-Cola's heavy expenses on marketing and sales go toward making its sodas more available in more places than many substitutes. It is not unusual to find Coke in parts of some developing countries where clean water, a viable substitute, is nowhere to be found. Finally, powerful customers can force a firm to add more features to a product than it should, given the prices that it is receiving for the products. Such additional features can be expensive.

Cooperative Environment

Cooperation in an industry can play an important role in the cost of the activities that firms in the industry perform. For example, in the 1980s and 1990s, part of the cost advantage that Japanese automobile companies had over their U.S. counterparts was attributed to the cooperative relationships that they had with their suppliers compared to the more adversarial relationships that U.S. automakers had with their own suppliers.[2] In the semiconductor industry, where R&D costs are very high, rivals often form alliances to share development costs. Since customers can be sources of innovation, cooperating with them can reduce the cost of exploiting such innovations.[3]

Macro Environment

A firm's overarching environment of government policies, fiscal and monetary policies, judicial and legal systems, and technological change can impact its costs.[4] For example, if a government imposes tariffs on certain imports, it is artificially raising the prices of these imports for the firms that use the imports as inputs. By imposing quotas on steel, the U.S. government is keeping the price of steel high and thereby increasing the cost to users of steel in the United States, such as automobile companies. If a government reduces the prime rate and therefore interest rates, it reduces the cost of borrowing money. A firm in a country where there are no intellectual property laws or where such laws are not enforced has to spend more money to pursue a block strategy than does a firm in a country where such laws exist and are enforced. Technological change has a dual role. It can decrease or increase a firm's costs. On one hand, for example, firms that use microchips as inputs have seen the costs per unit of microchip functionality decrease steadily over the past four decades. On the other hand, rapid technological change often means obsolescence of capabilities and the need to spend more on new capabilities. For example, the semiconductor firms that produce microchips often have to build newer and more expensive plants to keep up with technological change.

Resource Drivers

Recall that resources can be grouped into tangible, intangible, and human. Tangible resources include both physical (e.g., plants and equipment) and financial resources. No matter what form they come in, however, resources cost money. How much they cost is a function of their **resource cost drivers:** their quality, their quantity, and the prevailing rate charged.

Quality

Recall from Chapter 6 that resources that are valuable, rare, difficult to imitate or substitute, and appropriable can allow their owner to make money. Since a business model is about making money, we will say that resources that meet these conditions are of better quality than those that do not. That is, we can measure the quality of resources by performing a VRISA (value, rareness, imitability, substitutability, and appropriability) analysis. If a firm already owns high-quality resources, the resources can allow the firm to offer lower-cost products than those of competitors. However, resources can be very costly to a firm that does not already have them but wants to own them. For example, Southwest Airlines' network of uncongested or inner-city airports contributes to its ability to offer lower-cost service than its competitors offer. However, such a network would be very expensive, if not impossible, for a competitor to replicate. A firm that has a good reputation for performing well financially is likely to obtain debt at a lower interest rate than one that does not have such a reputation. However, attaining a good financial reputation is not easy. A firm that has good relationships with unions may be able to negotiate better concessions from the unions than one whose union relationships are adversarial.

Quantity

The cost of a resource can also depend on the quantity of the resource that the firm owns. For some resources, the more of the resource that a firm owns, the less the per-unit cost of the resource. This is an example of economies of scale, which we discussed in Chapter 2. For example, major pharmaceutical companies have extensive R&D capabilities and enjoy economies of scale and scope; therefore, their cost per patent is lower than that of firms with small-scale capabilities. However, building these capabilities can be very expensive. In pharmaceuticals, doing so means competing for smart scientists, building laboratories, generating and filing patents, and so on. Moreover, if a firm wants to expand its capabilities, the cost of adding more units of high-quality resources may become too expensive beyond the amount at which diseconomies of scale set in. Recall that high-quality units are those that are valuable, rare, difficult to imitate or substitute, and appropriable.

Rate

How much it costs a firm to acquire a certain quantity of high-quality resources is a function of the per-unit base rate in the market. This rate is usually a function of the macro environment. For example, the costs of acquiring human resources in a country depend on the level of wages in the country. The interest that a firm pays on debt is a function of interest rates in the country in question. How much a pharmaceutical company pays per patent is a function of how much the country in question charges per filing. How much a firm spends to replace capabilities that have been rendered obsolete by technological change depends on the rate of technological change.

Activity Drivers

As we explained in Chapter 5, the cost of activities that a firm performs in translating its resources into the positions that allow it to make money depends on which activities the firm performs, how it performs them, and when it performs them. Thus these three factors are the **activity cost drivers** of a business model.

Which

As we saw in Chapter 5, the types of activities that a firm performs or chooses not to perform have an impact on its costs. Many activities keep costs low; others, especially differentiation activities, can vastly increase costs. Semiconductor and pharmaceutical firms spend high percentages of their sales revenues on R&D every year developing new products and processes.

How

How a firm operates also impacts its costs. Firms that implement total quality management (TQM), reengineering, benchmarking, and other proven methods of doing things right can considerably reduce the costs of the activities they perform. A company that is poorly run can incur costs so high that they drive the company out of business.

When

Being the first to perform certain activities can mean incurring higher costs initially but can give a firm first-mover advantages that will translate into lower cost for the firm. For example, a firm that develops and launches a new product alone can make some initial costly mistakes such as offering customers the wrong value—mistakes that firms adopting the technology later can learn from. However, the first-mover firm can also learn from its mistakes and thus enjoy economies of learning. Moreover, by being first to offer the product, it can capture a higher market share and therefore also enjoy economies of scale. Of course, it may be less costly for a firm to enter a market later rather than earlier. Pharmaceutical companies that wait until drug patents have expired can offer generic versions of drugs, thereby keeping their costs low, but they are unable to earn the price premiums that patented drugs usually do.

Position Drivers

The types of activities that a firm performs, and therefore the firm's costs, depend on three **position cost drivers:** the type of value that the firm wants to offer the customers it targets, the relative positioning that the firm wants to attain vis-à-vis its suppliers, customers, rivals, potential new entrants, substitutes, and complementors, and the price that the firm intends to charge its customers.

Customer Value

A firm with a low-cost strategy usually pursues low-cost activities. One with a differentiation strategy pursues activities that allow it to distinguish its products from competitors' products, with the goal that the price premium from differentiation more than compensates for the extra cost of differentiation. In either case, costs incurred are likely to go up with the quality of benefits that a firm wants to offer customers. Such costs are likely to be higher if a firm wants to offer value that is superior to that from competitors. This is so partly because offering superior value may require resources that are valuable, rare, inimitable, nonsubstitutable, and appropriable and such resources can be expensive to acquire.

Strength of Position

Many of the things that a firm can do to better its position vis-à-vis suppliers, customers, rivals, and potential new entrants can be costly. Filing patents or taking other steps to defend intellectual property so as to raise barriers to entry costs money.

Price

To offer low prices and remain profitable, a firm must have costs that are lower than its competitors'. Thus, on the one hand, a firm that has pieced together a system of activities or built resources and capabilities that allow it to keep its costs lower than its competitors can offer lower prices to its customers and remain profitable. On the other hand, a firm whose market dictates that it compete on price has to piece together the type of system of activities or build the type of resources that will enable it to compete on price. If it cannot, it is likely to be forced out of the market.

MEASURING COSTS

A good way to start doing something about a business model's costs or begin understanding why they are low is to measure them. By measuring costs, a firm can pinpoint where they are lowest or highest and then it can determine why they are low or high by backtracking to the cost drivers. A firm's financial statement and its internal activity-based accounting systems can provide information for determining the magnitude and sources of costs.

Financial Statements

The data presented in an income statement, such as the Microchip Technologies statement shown in Table 9.1, can be extracted from a firm's financial statements. Such a statement contains useful cost information. The **cost of goods sold** (lines

TABLE 9.1
Income Statement of Microchip Technologies, Inc.

		Amount ($)	Lines
1	Revenues	430,000	
2	Cost of goods sold:		
3	Beginning finished goods inventory, Jan. 1, 2002	100,000	
4	Cost of goods produced	200,000	
5	Cost of goods available for sale	300,000	3 + 4
6	Ending finished goods inventory, Dec. 31, 2002	30,000	
7	Total cost of goods sold	270,000	5 − 6
8	Gross margin (gross profit)	150,000	1 − 7
9	Selling and general administrative expenses	100,000	
10	Operating income	60,000	8 − 9
11	Interest expenses	28,000	
12	Income before Taxes	32,000	10 − 11
13	Taxes	1,000	
14	Net income	31,000	12 − 13

2 and 7) is the total cost directly attributable to products whose manufacturing was completed during the period in question, whether manufacturing of the products was started during that period or not. These costs are made up of both direct and indirect costs. The **gross margin** or *gross profit* is the difference between revenues and cost of goods sold. **Selling and general administrative expenses** are the costs associated with the marketing and selling of the goods and with the general administration of the company. **Operating income** is the difference between gross margin and selling and general administrative expenses. **Interest expenses** are the interest paid on the debts that the firm owes; they are the cost of the money that the firm has borrowed.

From a cost point of view, two significant factors can be determined by comparative analyses of income statement data. First, a comparison of the firm's income statements, present and past, can indicate *trends*. It is important to track costs so that the firm knows whether they are increasing or decreasing and can then look into why they are doing so. Second, a comparison of the firm's income statement data with industry averages can reveal *differences* between the firm's costs and those of competitors. For example, if Microchip Technologies' cost of goods sold as a percentage of its sales is higher than its industry's average, this can mean that its cost of goods sold is too high or that its cost of goods sold is very low and it passes on some of its cost savings to customers in the form of lower prices. If Microchip Technologies' interest expenses are very high compared to its industry's average, it may be carrying too much debt compared to competitors. When such differences exist, the important thing is to find out why.

There are two major disadvantages of using cost data from income statements as a basis for tracking the sources of cost differences. First, the cost of many products is lumped into a single item, cost of goods sold. For a company that has hundreds of products, the overall cost of goods sold makes it difficult to tell the cost of each product and its contribution margin to the bottom line. For example, the cost-of-goods-sold figure in Boeing Corporation's income statement includes the cost of all the products Boeing finished during the period in question—different models of Boeing 737s, 747s, 777s, 767s, 757s, defense aircraft, and so on. Second, it is difficult to isolate the cost of each activity and therefore difficult to tell the role of each cost driver. An activity-based cost accounting method seeks to remove these disadvantages.

Activity-Based Cost Measurements

Since firms develop products by performing value-adding activities using resources, the objective of an **activity-based cost measurement** system is to track the cost of each product by tracking the cost of the activities that go into making the product and the resources that underpin each activity. There are two kinds of costs that must be tracked: direct and indirect costs. The **direct costs** of a product are the costs that can be easily traced to the product.[5] For example, the costs of the components, materials, and labor that go into assembling a Boeing 777 are its direct costs since it is easy to trace them to the plane in question. The **indirect costs** of a product are the costs that are related to the product but are difficult to trace to the product and therefore must be traced in an indirect way. For example, the costs of the computer aided design (CAD) tools and databases that maintain critical information on the designs of different planes cannot easily be traced to each of the different planes that Boeing builds each year. Since the costs of direct labor and direct materials are easy to trace, the problem in determining the costs of products and their underpinning activities lies in determining indirect costs. To do so, activity-based cost accounting draws on the fact that products are produced by performing activities and each activity uses resources whose costs are usually known. Figure 9.2 illustrates how the indirect costs associated with each of a firm's products can be tracked. In the figure, two resources are shared by four different activities that go into making two products, A and B. The direct costs for each product can be determined easily since the firm knows what components, materials, and labor go into each product.

Determining indirect costs takes advantage of two facts: that firms usually can estimate the cost of each resource used to perform value-adding activities and that the costs of resources add up to the firm's total spending. For example, the firm knows how much its plants and equipment cost, what the wages of indirect labor are, and so on. The problem, then, is how to allocate the costs of the different resources to the different activities and the costs of the different activities to the different products (Figure 9.2). In converting resource costs to activity costs, **resource-activity cost conversion drivers** are used. These are the factors that determine how much of a resource is used by an activity and therefore how much of the cost of the resource should be allocated to the activity. For resources that are not used up, such as human beings, the duration over which

FIGURE 9.2
Conversion of
Resource Costs into
Activity Costs and
into Product Costs

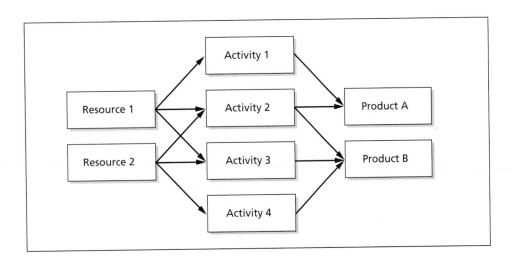

the resource is used by an activity determines how much of its cost is allocated to the activity.[6] For resources that are used up, such as electricity, the amount that is used by the activity is measured and allocated to the activity. Having determined the cost of each activity, the firm determines the cost of each product by using **activity-product cost conversion drivers.** These are the factors that determine how much of an activity goes into a product and therefore how much of the cost of the activity should be allocated to the product. These drivers include the frequency, duration, and complexity of the activities performed.[7]

Frequency of Activities

The more times that a firm performs a particular activity in adding value to a product, the larger the contribution of the activity to the cost of the product. For example, if manufacturing a product requires setting up a machine, setup costs go up with the number of times that the machine must be set up. A product that has been reworked costs more than one that has not. One reason for the higher costs is the fact that relevant resources have to be used more frequently and these resources cost money.

Duration of Activities

In addition to how many times an activity is performed, the length of time that it takes to perform the activity also impacts cost. The longer the duration of an activity, the more costly the activity is likely to be. For example, the longer it takes to rework a product, the more costly the product will be compared to products that need no rework. The higher costs are largely a result of the fact that resources have to be committed to the activity longer and resources cost money.

Complexity of Activities

Two activities can have very different costs even though they are performed with the same frequency and duration. This will be the case if the complexity of the activities differs, thereby requiring different resources. For example, a Boeing 767 is far more complex than a bicycle, and therefore repairs of the same duration and frequency on both systems cannot be expected to cost the same. Systems that are more complex cost more because they require a higher level of resources, in terms of the quality, quantity, or rate of resources.

TRACKING THE SOURCES OF COST DIFFERENCES

Suppose information from a firm's income statement or activity-based cost accounting shows that the firm's costs have been rising. The firm may want to reduce or eliminate this cost disadvantage. Suppose the information suggests that the firm's costs are lower than its competitors'. It may want to reinforce or defend this cost advantage. In either case, the firm will probably want to identify the sources of the disadvantage or advantage. One way to do so is to:

1. Identify the activities of the business model's business system—value chain, value network, or value shop.
2. Determine what drives the cost of each activity, and see if there is anything that can be done to improve the cost of the activity.

We use the example of firms in the PC industry to illustrate, below, how industry, position, activity, and resource cost drivers can influence the cost of each activity of a business system. The key points of the following discussion are summarized in Table 9.2.

Research and Development

Industry Drivers

Each PC firm's R&D costs depend in part on whether the firm is in the "Wintel" (*Win*dows In*tel*) or Apple camp. The Wintel camp is made up of microprocessor chip suppliers such as Intel and AMD, whose microprocessors are compatible with the Intel microprocessor architecture; PC makers whose PCs are compatible with the Intel architecture and Microsoft Windows operating system; and all the software suppliers that provide software for this architecture. The Apple camp is made up of Apple, the suppliers of the PowerPC microprocessor architecture that

TABLE 9.2   **Cost Drivers as Sources of Cost Differences: PC Industry**

Stage of Business System	Cost Drivers	
	Industry	**Position, Activity, and Resource**
Research and development	R&D spending depends on whether a firm is in the Wintel or Apple PC consortium. R&D spending in the Wintel camp is lower than that in the Apple camp and also depends on suppliers and complementors that have bargaining power.	It costs more to be a differentiator like Apple. Firms that choose to join the Wintel camp spend less on R&D. Emphasizing resources at the right points helps.
Product design	Sophistication and cost of designs depend on the camp a firm belongs to (Wintel or Apple) and on powerful suppliers of microprocessors and software.	Some business customers may require special features that can drive up costs. Cooperation with Wintel partners to release products on time keeps the cost of early product introduction low.
Manufacturing and operations	The rapid rate of change of the industry's technology, rapid drop in prices, and powerful suppliers of microprocessors and software mean inventory carrying costs can be a very high cost of manufacturing.	Location. Management of component inventory. Build to order more critical to keeping costs low.
Marketing and sales	Installed base decreases cost of advertising.	The commodity nature of the product suggests that PC firms may end up having to advertise more. Coopetitors in Wintel camp also advertise.
Distribution	The rapid change in technology and rapid drop in prices make it costly going through dealers. Customers are sophisticated enough to bypass dealers and go straight to manufacturers. The Internet helps reduce the cost of distribution.	Bypass distribution.

Apple uses in its PCs, and the complementors that offer software for this architecture. In 2002, the Wintel camp had close to 95 percent of the PC market share. While Apple develops its proprietary operating systems and hardware alone, Microsoft (on the operating system side) and numerous PC hardware firms such as Dell, HP, IBM, Sony, and Gateway (on the hardware side) perform R&D for the Wintel camp, thereby sharing R&D costs. Thus, R&D costs are considerably lower for each Wintel PC maker than for Apple. Also, since PC performance is driven largely by the microprocessor and operating system, and Intel and AMD perform the R&D for microprocessors, PC makers do not spend as much on improving processor performance.

Position, Activity, and Resource Drivers

Within the Wintel or Apple camp, there are many positions that firms can occupy. For example, firms can target the home or business computer market. In the business market segment, firms can offer low-end PCs, high-end PCs, or servers. Offering servers may require more R&D than offering low-end PCs. The more a firm wants to differentiate itself from other PC makers, the more the firm may have to spend on R&D to do so. Effectively, a firm's R&D costs depend on which market it wants to target. Firms that choose to join the Wintel camp spend less on R&D. Within the camp, each firm's R&D costs also depend on how much of its resources the firm wants to spend on R&D. In the 1990s, for example, Dell spent very little on R&D, choosing to take advantage of the innovations in microprocessor technology from Intel and in software from Microsoft. While Dell spent an average of 2 percent of sales on R&D, Apple spent an average of 6 percent.[8]

Product Design

Industry Drivers

Since designs in the Wintel camp have to be compatible with the Intel microprocessor architecture and the Microsoft Windows operating system, and the microprocessor and operating system are the primary drivers of a PC's performance, there is little variation in the design of PCs in the Wintel camp. This means that firms can quickly learn from each other through reverse engineering of designs. This keeps the cost of design down. The number of new models and frequency of design changes, which are also determinants of design costs, are influenced primarily by the frequency of introduction of microprocessors.

Position, Activity, and Resource Drivers

If a firm decides to be the first to offer a new PC when a new generation of microprocessors is introduced, it must design one without the benefit of learning from the trial, error, and correction that others usually make during the development of a new product. Therefore, it may incur higher costs than would be the case if it waited for someone else to be first. Moreover, since microprocessor prices drop rapidly, a firm that is the first to offer a product also must pay high microprocessor prices, further increasing its design costs.

Manufacturing and Operations

Industry Drivers

Since the PC industry is characterized by rapid increases in processor speeds and drops in prices, inventory holding costs during manufacturing can become a major part of manufacturing costs compared to those in other industries. Usually, inventory carrying costs are the opportunity costs of holding inventory—that is, the income forgone by tying up money in inventory instead of investing it in a money-making opportunity. In the PC industry, however, the situation is more demanding: If a PC manufacturer holds an inventory of microprocessors for more than six months, there is a chance that newer, faster, and cheaper versions of microprocessors will be introduced by chip makers, thereby rendering existing inventories obsolete. Thus, if the computer maker waits too long, it may lose more than the opportunity cost; it may have to write off some or all of the inventory over shorter periods of time than is the case in other industries. The problem in the PC industry may also be exacerbated when microprocessor suppliers such as Intel have the bargaining power. Powerful suppliers not only can extract high initial prices from PC makers but also can force PC makers to take newer and faster microprocessors before they want to. These suppliers can do so during bargaining or through advertising to end customers. For example, when Intel advertises a new microprocessor, end customers who want PCs with the new chip expect Dell and the other PC makers to have the new processor in their PCs right away.

Position, Activity, and Resource Drivers

To avoid inventory holding costs and other manufacturing costs, a PC maker is better off holding very little or no chip inventory and reducing manufacturing times. Dell Computer offers a very good example of how a firm can keep its inventory and manufacturing times to a minimum. With its build-to-order process, customers usually pay for their computers before Dell starts building them. It orders microprocessors and other components of the computer that a customer has ordered only after it has been paid for the computer. Thus Dell incurs few carrying costs. In fact, it makes money from the process since Dell takes its customers' money, invests it in other money-making opportunities, and pays its suppliers much later. It has also streamlined its manufacturing to the extent that once parts arrive, the actual manufacturing process takes so little time that chips cannot be rendered obsolete.

Marketing and Sales

Industry Drivers

Advertising and promotion costs depend on whether a firm belongs to the Wintel camp or the Apple camp. In the Wintel camp, advertising costs are shared somewhat by Intel, Microsoft, and the PC makers. Intel advertises and promotes all PCs that use its microprocessors. Microsoft advertises and promotes all PCs that use Windows. Some Wintel PC makers also advertise. Moreover, because the Wintel camp has more than 90 percent of the installed base of PCs, the installed base acts as a billboard for each customer who already has a Wintel PC and is thinking of buying a new one. Potential new buyers also have a higher likelihood of seeing a Wintel PC than seeing an Apple since the former are ubiquitous.

Position, Activity, and Resource Drivers

Since the basic features and functions of all Wintel PCs are similar, the switching costs for customers changing from one PC maker to another are low. Thus, one of the few ways in which PC makers can differentiate their products is through branding. This means they must spend more on advertising and promotion than they would if their products were differentiated. As we saw earlier, one negative effect of powerful suppliers such as Intel advertising to end customers is that PC makers may be forced to offer and promote a product when it is not cost-effective for them to do so. For example, PC firms may be forced to launch a campaign earlier than they would have liked to.

Distribution

Industry Drivers

Dealers offer a place where customers can go to experience a PC and then carry one home if they decide to buy one. However, dealers get a cut of the sales, thereby increasing the sales costs for a PC maker. Moreover, since PC technology improves rapidly and prices fall rapidly, PCs that remain with dealers too long can lose much of their value when newer PCs with better performance and lower prices are introduced. And while the PCs are on dealers' shelves, the PC maker may incur inventory carrying costs. The advent of the Internet offered PC companies the opportunity to bypass dealers and go directly to customers. The option of bypassing dealers has been made more attractive by the fact that while some PC customers may need hand-holding, most of them can order their own computers directly from PC makers without the help of a dealer. Large businesses have MIS departments or technical experts that can determine which computers meet the needs of their companies and can buy the computers directly from PC makers.

Position, Activity, and Resource Drivers

PC makers such as Dell have been quick to bypass dealers and sell directly to end customers.

ROLE OF FIXED COSTS AND DEMAND

In our discussion of costs thus far in this chapter, we have concentrated on inputs and said nothing about the impact of output on per-unit cost. As the number of units that a firm sells goes up, its per-unit cost drops. This drop is largely because total fixed costs do not increase no matter how much output is produced. This has implications for profitability that can be illustrated using the simple relationship that we introduced in Chapter 3:

$$\text{Profits} = \text{revenues} - \text{variable costs} - \text{fixed costs} \qquad \textbf{(9.1)}$$
$$= PQ - V_cQ - F_c = (P - V_c)Q - F_c$$
$$= \text{contribution margin} - F_c = (\text{contribution margin per unit})Q - F_c$$

where P is the price per unit of the product, V_c is the per-unit variable cost, Q is the total number of units sold, and F_c is the up-front or fixed costs. As we said in Chapter 3, the quantity $PQ - V_cQ$, or revenues minus variable costs, is the *contribution margin* and represents the amount over variable costs that contributes to recovering fixed costs. The quantity $P - V_c$, the difference between price and *per-unit* variable cost, is the *contribution margin per unit*.

Break-Even Analysis

If the contribution margin is positive, then, as the quantity sold goes up, a certain quantity is reached at which all the fixed costs have been recovered. This is the quantity at which revenues equal total costs, and it is called the **break-even**

point. It is the point where the firm has zero profits from the investment. This point can be determined by equating Equation 9.1 to zero since profits are zero. By doing that, we obtain

$$\text{Profits} = PQ - V_cQ - F_c = (P - V_c)Q - F_c = 0$$

From this,

$$Q = \frac{F_c}{(P - V_c)} \tag{9.2}$$

Since $P - V_c$ is the contribution margin per unit, the break-even quantity can be computed as

$$\text{Break-even quantity} = \frac{\text{fixed cost}}{\text{contribution margin per unit}} \tag{9.3}$$

Example 1

A microchip company has spent a total of $400 million on R&D, marketing, promotion, and other up-front fixed costs to offer a chip that it sells for $35 per unit. Each chip costs $15 dollars to produce. How many units must the company sell to break even?

Solution: There are two ways to determine the break-even point.

Method 1: Use Equation 9.3:

$$\text{Break-even quantity} = \frac{F_c}{(P - V_c)} = \frac{\text{fixed cost}}{\text{contribution margin per unit}}$$

$$= \frac{\$400,000,000}{(\$35 - \$15)} = 20,000,000 \text{ units}$$

The break-even quantity is 20 million units. That is, the microchip company has to produce 20 million units to recover its fixed costs.

Method 2: Calculate the contribution margin per unit as $35 − $15 = $20. That is, each microchip sold contributes $20 to recovering fixed costs. Since fixed costs are $400 million, the company would have to sell $400,000,000/$20 = 20 million units to cover all fixed costs and break even.

For several reasons, **break-even time,** the amount of time that it takes a company to break even, is also important. First, the longer it takes to break even, the longer resources may have to be tied up performing unprofitable activities, thereby causing the firm to forgo potentially profitable investment opportunities. Second, the longer it takes a firm to break even, the more time competitors have to catch up if they were behind or to increase their lead if they were ahead. Break-even time is obtained by dividing the break-even quantity by the sales rate. That is, break-even time (in years) is the break-even quantity divided by sales per year. Mathematically,

$$\text{Break-even time} = \frac{\text{break-even quantity}}{\text{sales rate}}$$

$$= \frac{F_c}{(P - V_c) \times (\text{sales rate})} \tag{9.4}$$

Example 2

A software company called PrintMoneySoft spent a total of $500 million on R&D, marketing, promotion, and other up-front fixed costs to offer a software package that it sells for $100 per copy. Since the company has posted the software on the Web for customers to download, each copy that it sells costs the company only $10 to produce and sell. Because of its huge installed base of customers, the company estimates that it can sell 25 million units per year. How long will it take for the company to break even?

Solution: There are two ways to determine the break-even time.

Method 1: Determine the break-even quantity, and then divide that quantity by the sales rate to get the break-even time:

$$\text{Break-even quantity} = \frac{F_c}{(P - V_c)} = \frac{\$500,000,000}{\$100 - \$10} = 5,560,000 \text{ units}$$

Since the sales rate is 25 million per year, the break-even time (in years) is 5,560,000/25,000,000 = 0.22 years

Method 2: Use Equation 9.4:

$$\text{Break-even time (years)} = \frac{\text{break-even quantity}}{\text{sales rate}} = \frac{F_c}{(P - V_c) \times (\text{sales rate})}$$

$$= \frac{\$500,000,000}{(\$100 - \$10) \times 25,000,000} = 0.22 \text{ years}$$

Illustrating the Significance of Resources

Break-even analysis can be used to illustrate the strategic significance of resources.

Example 3

Two firms, A and B, each developed a proprietary operating system for PCs in 2001 at an estimated cost of $1 billion. It cost each firm $15 to produce and deliver each copy of the operating system to customers. A's operating system is incorporated in each PC that PC makers sell, while B sells its operating system in the PCs that it makes. Because A has a huge installed base of customers and its operating system is incompatible with B's, A was able to sell 146 million copies of its operating system in 2001 at $55 each, while B sold only 3 million units of its own operating system. What are the break-even times for each firm? What is the strategic significance of each firm's installed base?

Solution: The break-even time for A (in years) is

$$\frac{\$1,000,000,000}{(\$55 - \$15) \times 146,000,000} = 0.171 \text{ years, or just over 2 months}$$

Break-even time for B (in years) if it sells its own operating system at $55 is

$$\frac{\$1,000,000,000}{(\$55 - \$15) \times 3,000,000} = 8.33 \text{ years, or just under 100 months}$$

Strategic implications: This simple calculation suggests two things: (1) If B wanted to break even in the same amount of time that it took A to break even (2 months), B would have to sell its operating system at $2,679.24 [(8.33/0.171) × $55] rather than $55. (2) During the 8.33 years that B is trying to break even, it is losing money while A is making money. The billions that A is earning while B is trying to break even can be reinvested in A's business to reinforce its existing positions in the market. Firm A can also invest the money in new businesses or pay it out to shareholders in the form of dividends.

A can also reduce its prices by as much as 50 percent and still make lots of money.

Sunk Costs and Competitive Position

When the costs of an asset have already been incurred and cannot be recovered because, for example, the asset has no equally valuable use elsewhere, such costs are called **sunk costs**.[9] For example, the costs of an aluminum plant built near a cheap source of electricity to smelter bauxite from a nearby mine are sunk because the plant has no equally valuable use outside of smelting aluminum. Sunk costs have some implications for barriers to entry, rivalry, and investment in technological change.

Barriers to Entry

If the investments made by existing competitors in an industry are sunk, these firms have to pay for the investments whether they exit the industry or not. Therefore, they are likely to stay in the industry and fight new entrants, even if they incur losses, as long as their prices are high enough to cover their variable costs and, maybe, make a contribution to recovering some of the sunk costs. Since profit-motivated potential new entrants will enter an industry only if they expect to make money, high sunk costs may act as a barrier to entry for new entrants. If fixed costs—both sunk and unsunk—are high, a new entrant also faces another potential problem: It must either capture a much higher share of the market to recover its investment in a timely manner or take too long to recover it. Such prospects can discourage some potential new entrants from attempting entry.

Rivalry

In bad times, rivals are more likely to lower their prices if most of their investments are sunk. This is because these incumbents have to pay the sunk costs whether they exit the market or not. Thus, each will be tempted to lower its prices as long as the prices at least cover its variable costs. If all rivals lower their prices in anticipation of at least covering their variable costs, this may amount to a price war, the last thing that they need.

Investing in Technological Change

In Chapter 8, we argued that the fear of cannibalizing its existing products may prevent a firm from investing in a new technology. Sunk costs can play an important role in a firm's willingness to invest in a new technology. Consider incumbents whose investments in an existing technology are sunk. In the face of a new technology, these incumbents weigh the costs of investing in the new technology versus the costs of staying with the existing technology, as well as the benefits from each technology. On the one hand, since the costs of the existing technology to incumbents are sunk, they are ignored. On the other hand, since investments have not yet been made in the new technology and are therefore not sunk, the costs of investing in the new technology are likely to be much more than the costs of staying with the old technology. Thus, unless the benefits of investing are compelling, a profit-motivated incumbent might not invest in the new technology, choosing to stay with the old one.

Fixed costs also play an important role in shaping the structure of the industry that emerges after a major technological change. This is best illustrated through an example.

Example 4

Six pharmaceutical companies sell a drug to patients whose doctors are very reluctant to change prescriptions from one company's drug to another's. The market shares of these companies are shown in Table 9.3. A new, genetically engineered version of the drug offers benefits so compelling that doctors want to switch to the new drug but prefer not to change pharmaceutical companies. To develop and market the drug, each firm must invest $200 million in up-front costs for R&D and marketing. Each daily dose is priced at $2.20 and costs $0.20 to produce. The technology is easy to imitate. The total market is $900 million per year. What impact will this technology have on market structure?

Solution: Since doctors do not want to switch pharmaceutical companies, it is difficult for firms to steal market share. Since the technology is easy to imitate, the problem boils down to one of investment—in particular, how long it will take each firm to recover its costs. The break-even times for the companies are shown in Table 9.3. On the basis of these times, A and B can recover their costs in a reasonable amount of time, while the smaller D, E, and F cannot. In

TABLE 9.3
Break-Even Times for Example 4

Pharmaceutical Company	Market Share	Sales Rate per Year = Market Share (millions)	Time to Break Even (years)*
A	40%	$360	2.8
B	30	270	3.7
C	15	135	7.4
D	7	63	15.9
E	6	54	18.5
F	2	18	55.6
		$900	

* = $200,000,000/[($2.20 − $0.20) × (sales rate)].

fact, it would take F an incredible 55.6 years to recover. Therefore, there is likely to be market consolidation in which smaller firms team up with larger ones. In fact, the larger ones are likely to buy the smaller ones.

The complementary assets model (discussed in Chapter 8) could also have been used to estimate what would happen. We are told that the technology is easy to imitate. Since doctors do not want to switch pharmaceutical companies, we can argue that relationships with doctors are important and tightly held complementary assets. Therefore, owners of complementary assets win. All firms have some relationships with doctors, but the larger firms deal with more doctors. So we can assume that the larger firms have more relationships with more doctors (more complementary assets). By teaming up, all the owners of complementary assets win, but the larger firms stand to gain more since they have more complementary assets.

Summary

Whether a firm's business model rests on a low-cost or differentiation strategy, it is still very important for the firm to understand the drivers of its costs. Each of the four major components of a business model—positions, industry factors, resources, and activities—generates costs that should be tracked. Annual financial statements are not enough. Activity-based cost accounting helps. In any case, tracking the drivers of the costs of a business model is critical. One way to analyze the cost of activities is to go through the value chain, value shop, or value network that underpins the business model and see how the major drivers of costs—positions, industry factors, resources, and activities—impact the cost of each activity that the firm performs. The text example of PC firms illustrates how this is done for a value chain.

Costs also vary with output. An exploration of how fixed costs vary with output can provide some interesting strategic insights.

Key Terms

activity-based cost measurement, *179*
activity cost drivers, *176*
activity-product cost conversion drivers, *179*
break-even point, *184*
break-even time, *185*
cost drivers, *173*

cost of goods sold, *177*
direct costs, *179*
gross margin, *178*
indirect costs, *179*
industry cost drivers, *173*
interest expenses, *178*
operating income, *178*
position cost drivers, *177*

resource-activity cost conversion drivers, *179*
resource cost drivers, *175*
selling and general administrative expenses, *178*
sunk costs, *186*

Study Questions

1. What is the difference between fixed costs and sunk costs?
2. Why is it bad for a company to carry too much debt?

Endnotes

1. There is a difference between how strategy scholars define the term *cost drivers* and how cost accounting scholars define it. The former focus on the factors that decrease costs, while the latter focus on the factors that allow them to measure costs. In this book, cost accounting cost drivers are called *cost conversion drivers*.

2. J. H. Dyer, "Specialized Supplier Networks as a Source of Competitive Advantage: Evidence from the Auto Industry," *Strategic Management Journal* 17 (1996), pp. 271–292; J. H. Dyer and K. Nobeoka, "Creating and Managing a High Performance Knowledge-Sharing Network: The Toyota Case," *Strategic Management Journal* 21 (2000), pp. 345–367.

3. E. Von Hippel, "Lead Users: A Source of Novel Product Concepts," *Management Science* 32 (1986), pp. 791–805.

4. M. E. Porter, *The Competitive Advantage of Nations* (New York: Free Press, 1990).

5. C. T. Horngren, G. Foster, and S. M. Datar, *Cost Accounting: A Managerial Emphasis* (Upper Saddle River, NJ: Prentice-Hall, 1999).

6. G. Cokins, *Activity-Based Cost Management: Making It Work—A Manager's Guide to Implementing and Sustaining an Effective ABC System* (Chicago: McGraw-Hill/Irwin, 1996).

7. R. S. Kaplan and R. Cooper, *Cost and Effect: Using Integrated Cost Systems to Drive Profitability and Performance* (Boston: Harvard Business School Press, 1998).

8. M. Kwak and D. B. Yoffie, "Apple Computer 1999," Harvard Business School case 9-799-108, 1999.

9. A. K. Dixit and R. S. Pindyck, *Investment under Uncertainty* (Princeton, NJ: Princeton University Press, 1994); D. Besanko, D. Dranove, and M. Shanley, *Economics of Strategy* (New York: Wiley, 2002).

Analyzing the Sources of Profitability and Competitive Advantage in a Business Model

There are many reasons that one may want to understand the sources of a firm's profitability or competitive advantage. Before investing in a firm, for example, an investor may want to go beyond the firm's profitability numbers and understand the underpinnings of the numbers. A firm may want to understand why it has a competitive advantage or disadvantage so that it can do something about it. It may also want to analyze the sources of its competitors' competitive advantage or disadvantage in order to take advantage of it. If you work for a consulting company, you may be hired by a firm to determine the sources of its competitive advantage or disadvantage and suggest what it should do to reinforce the advantage or overcome the disadvantage. In this chapter, we explore a method for analyzing the sources of a firm's profitability and competitive advantage. First, we explore the different components of the method. Then we perform an analysis of Southwest Airlines' competitive advantage to illustrate the method.

THE SEVEN C'S: AN INTEGRATIVE FRAMEWORK FOR ANALYZING THE SOURCES OF ADVANTAGE

Recall that a firm's profitability is determined by both industry and firm-specific factors. Because of differences in the nature of the competitive and macro-environment forces that act on different industries, some industries are, on average, more profitable than others. Within each industry, a firm makes more money than its rivals if its business model offers products or services at a lower cost than that of its rivals or offers differentiated products at premium prices that more than compensate for the extra cost of differentiation and the firm is well positioned vis-à-vis its coopetitors to appropriate the value. A firm has a **competitive advantage** if it earns a higher rate of profit than its rivals or has the potential to do so. A means for analyzing the sources of a business model's profitability or competitive advantage is the **seven C's framework.** The letter C stands for the first letter in each component of the framework: competitive position, connected activities, competitive and macro-environment forces, critical industry value drivers, capabilities and resources, change and sustainability, and cost of activities (Figure 10.1). The rationale for each of the C's is detailed below, but the underlying principle, briefly stated, is this: A business model makes money when it offers superior value to the right customers and is positioned well enough relative to its coopetitors to appropriate the value, and this includes charging prices that are close to customers' reservation prices. To do these things, a firm has to appropriately perform the activities of its business system. Performing these activities requires resources. In using resources to perform the activities, a firm has to keep its costs appropriately low, irrespective of whether it pursues a low-cost or differentiation strategy.

1. Competitive Position

For a firm to keep making money, customers must keep buying from the firm. For customers to keep buying from a firm, it must offer them something that they value and that its competitors cannot offer. That is, the firm must offer its customers superior value. This superior customer value comes in the form of low-cost or differentiated products or services. Usually, a firm does not offer the same value to all customers. The right customer value must be delivered to the right customer segments (demographic, geographic, etc.) with the right number of products or services that convey that value. Pratt and Whitney sells jet engines to both the U.S. military for use in military planes and to commercial airlines for use in their commercial jets. Within each market segment, a firm must determine which sources of revenue to pursue and which ones are more profitable. In the jet engine business, for example, there are two major sources of revenues: selling jet engines and servicing the engines, with the latter being the more profitable. How much a customer values a product also depends on the price of the product. Appropriating value entails pricing products well.

FIGURE 10.1

The Seven C's for Analyzing the Sources of a Firm's Profits and Competitive Advantage

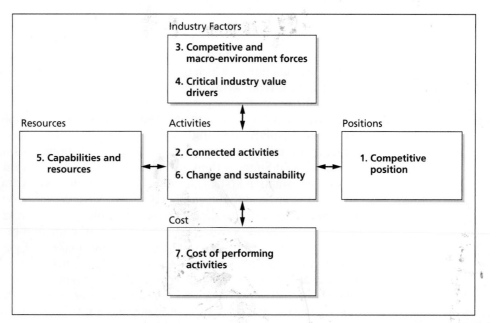

Thus, in analyzing the sources of a firm's profitability or competitive advantage, it is important to do the following:

1. Look for evidence of the firm's having a low-cost structure that allows it to pass on its cost savings to customers in the form of prices that are lower than those of competitors. If a firm's costs are low, there is usually some evidence of how its costs compare to those of rivals or its industry's average. For example, in 2002, Wal-Mart's rental, advertising, and payroll expenses as a fraction of sales were the lowest in discount retailing.[1] Such evidence is usually available from financial analysts, the firm's financial statements, and so on. The fact that a firm offers low prices does not always mean that the firm has low costs. Thus it is important not to jump to the conclusion that a firm has low costs just because it offers low prices.

2. Look for evidence of the firm's products or services being differentiated. Evidence of differentiation can be found in product features. For example, Pfizer's cholesterol drug, Lipitor, reduced bad cholesterol levels more than competing drugs. Such evidence can also be found in the customer rankings—such as those produced by JD Powers—of how satisfied customers are with a service or product. It can also be found in rankings of brands. Coca-Cola's superior worldwide brand-name reputation allows the firm to differentiate its cola drinks from competitors' colas, which are almost indistinguishable in taste from its colas.

3. Identify the market segments that the firm serves and the value that it offers to each segment.

4. Identify the sources of revenue within each segment and the profitability of each segment.

5. Identify the firm's pricing strategy.

6. Look for evidence of the firm's bargaining power over its coopetitors.

These details, and those of the other six C's, are summarized in Figure 10.2.

2. Connected Activities

Delivering the right value to the right market segments means performing the value-adding activities of a business system (value chain, value network, or value shop). How effective a firm is in offering better customer value than do its competitors is a function of which business system activities it chooses to perform and how and when it performs them. If the value that a firm offers customers is low cost, the activities that it performs should be designed to directly or indirectly lower costs. They should be **connected activities**.[2] For example, one reason Wal-Mart's rental, advertising, and payroll expenses are lower than those of its rivals in discount retailing is that it decided to saturate contiguous towns in the southwestern United States with many stores and build distribution centers and logistics and information systems to match. If the value that a firm offers is differentiation, the activities that it performs should be designed to directly or indirectly differentiate the firm. In the 1990s, for example, Coca-Cola spent as much as 43 percent of its revenues from concentrate on marketing and promotion as it built brand equity to keep differentiating itself from makers of generic sodas. Many U.S. pharmaceutical companies spend heavily on R&D in an effort to discover new drugs that are more effective in curing diseases. Each time such a firm discovers a new, effective drug and takes a patent on it, rivals have more difficulty trying to legally imitate it, thus allowing the firm to offer patients a valuable drug with one-of-a-kind benefits until the drug's patent expires.

FIGURE 10.2   Detailed Seven C's

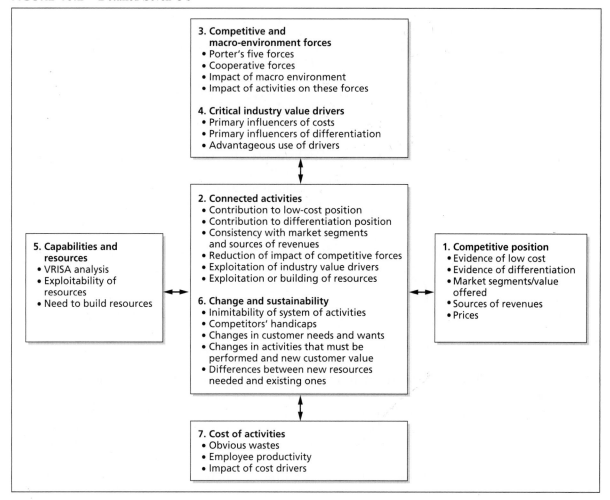

In choosing which activities to perform, it is important that a firm take advantage of critical industry value drivers—those characteristics of an industry that have the most impact on cost or differentiation (see the fourth C in Figure 10.1). In the airline industry, for example, turnaround time—the time that it takes to get a plane back in the air once it lands—is critical because planes make money when flying, not when waiting at a terminal. Thus airline activities that are designed to lower costs should also reduce turnaround time. For instance, not offering meals means that when a plane lands, it can be cleaned faster and does not have to wait for food to be loaded on before it can take off.

If the activities that a firm performs form a system that is difficult to imitate, they can give a firm a competitive advantage. Since customer value is sometimes not sufficient to give a firm a competitive advantage, the system of activities should also give the firm a favorable position vis-à-vis its customers, suppliers, complementors, and rivals (see the third C). Consider Wal-Mart again. By saturating contiguous towns with its stores and building distribution centers and logistics and information systems to match, it built a network of stores that reduce the power of customers within the network.

An activity that a firm chooses to perform can be performed internally or through an outside contractor. It can also be performed jointly through an alliance. A firm's choice of whether to perform an activity internally, through outsourcing, or through an alliance is a function of the extent to which the firm possesses superior core capabilities in performing the activity and the extent to which the capabilities are central to offering the right customer value to the right market segments (see the fifth C for more on capabilities). If a firm has superior capabilities in performing an activity and capabilities are central to offering the right value, the firm may want to perform the activity internally rather than outsource it. If not, it may want to outsource the performance of the activity to firms that have superior capabilities. For example, after experiencing several outages on its website in 1999, eBay decided to outsource its back-end technology to Abovenet Communications and Exodus Communications since both firms were more capable of running this technology than eBay was. Moreover, eBay's competitive advantage comes from its network of millions of registered clients and its brand name, not from Internet technology. By outsourcing this activity to two firms that had superior capabilities in performing the activity, eBay could focus on building some of its core capabilities: its network of registered users and its brand name.

An extremely important activity that is worth special treatment is pricing. Offering customers differentiated products or having a low-cost structure that allows a firm to be able to compete on price is one thing; likewise, having bargaining power over customers is one thing. Taking advantage of these positions and pricing products or services so as to maximize one's profits can be quite another. As we saw in Chapter 3, setting prices too high can drive away customers, while setting them too low leaves money on the table. A good pricing strategy carefully considers the customer value that the firm offers and its bargaining position versus customers. In the mid-1980s, for example, Wal-Mart's prices were 6 percent higher in locations where it had no direct competition from large discounters than they were in locations where it faced competition.[3]

In analyzing the sources of a firm's profitability and competitive advantage, one should try to identify the firm's *activities* that:

1. Directly or indirectly contribute to the firm's low-cost or differentiation advantage.
2. Are consistent with the market segments that the firm serves and its sources of revenues.
3. Directly or indirectly allow the firm to reduce the competitive forces exerted on it by suppliers, customers, rivals, potential new entrants, and substitutes (see the third C).
4. Take advantage of the firm's industry's critical value drivers in offering customer value or reducing the competitive forces exerted by suppliers, customers, rivals, potential new entrants, and substitutes (see the third and fourth C's).
5. Either (a) effectively use the firm's distinctive resources and capabilities in offering customer value or reducing the competitive forces exerted by suppliers, customers, rivals, potential new entrants, and substitutes, or (2) build these resources or capabilities (see the fifth C).

It is also important to examine the extent to which a firm's pricing strategy neither drives customers away nor leaves money on the table as a result of prices set too far above or below, respectively, customers' reservation prices.

3. Competitive Forces

As we saw in Chapter 2, an important determinant of the profitability of firms in an industry is the competitive forces from suppliers, customers, rivals, new entrants, and substitute products that act on industry firms. If suppliers have bargaining power over industry firms, they can extract high prices from those firms, thereby raising the firms' costs and lowering their profitability. Powerful suppliers can also force industry firms to take lower-quality inputs at prices that warrant higher quality. If industry firms are forced to take lower-quality inputs, they may have to incur additional expenses to improve the quality of the inputs or be forced to ship lower-quality outputs, which will fetch lower prices. Powerful customers can force industry firms to take lower prices for their products than the quality of the products warrants or can make them ship higher-quality products than the prices the customers pay indicate. High rivalry forces industry firms to lower their prices or spend more on advertising in an effort to differentiate their products. High threat of entry can force industry firms to spend more to raise barriers to entry or lower their prices to discourage new entrants. High threat of substitutes can force industry firms to lower their prices to keep customers from switching to substitutes. High threat of substitutes can also force industry firms to advertise or take other measures to differentiate their products without necessarily commanding a higher price.

The competitive forces that act on industry firms in so-called attractive industries are low, thereby making such industries more attractive on average. The competitive forces in so-called unattractive industries are high, thereby making firms in these industries less profitable on average.

The macro environment's technological, economic, political-legal, demographic, sociocultural, and natural factors can also influence industry and firm activities.

An analysis of the sources of a firm's profitability should include:

1. A Porter's five-force analysis of the firm's industry to determine what makes each of the forces high or low for the industry.
2. An identification of why the forces are high or low and what can be done to reduce the high forces and make the low ones even lower.
3. An identification of the extent to which the firm's actions (second C) have reduced the high forces and made the low ones even lower.
4. An identification of macro-environment forces of significance in the industry and how they can be influenced.
5. An identification of the extent to which the firm's actions (second C) have influenced macro-environment forces.
6. An identification of cooperative forces and how they can be influenced.

4. Critical Industry Value Drivers

In every industry, certain factors represent a significant percentage of cost or have a high potential for creating differentiation. These factors are the critical industry value drivers since they stand to have a significant impact on low cost and/or differentiation. A firm's actions (second C) should take advantage of these critical value drivers if the firm is to have a competitive advantage. In consulting, for example, wages constitute an extremely high percentage of a firm's expenses, and therefore utilization of consultants is critical. That is, a consulting firm wants its consultants to be engaged in client assignments at all times rather than be idle since every day not spent working on an assignment is a day of billings lost. Thus, for example, pursuing large accounts is a good activity (see the second C) since doing so reduces the frequency of terminating and starting new engagements and therefore reduces the chances of idling. In pharmaceuticals, performing R&D plays a major role in offering differentiated drugs. In choosing which activities to perform and which ones not to perform, a firm ought to pay careful attention to and take advantage of its industry's critical value drivers. As we will see later in the Southwest Airlines example, the company took advantage of the fact that turnaround times are critical value drivers in the airline industry.

In analyzing the sources of a firm's profitability and competitive advantage, it is important to:

1. Identify the industry factors that account for a significant percentage of cost or potentially can produce the most cost savings. Let's call these the *primary influencers of costs*.
2. Identify the industry factors that have a high potential for creating differentiation. Let's call these the *primary influencers of differentiation*.
3. Understand the objectives that the firm should pursue to take advantage of these factors in offering customer value or reducing the competitive forces exerted on the firm by suppliers, customers, rivals, potential new entrants, and substitutes.

5. Capabilities and Resources

To perform the value-adding activities that allow a firm to offer better customer value than offered by competitors and have an advantageous position vis-à-vis suppliers, customers, rivals, new entrants, and substitutes, the firm needs resources or assets (tangible and intangible) and capabilities. Firms that have resources or capabilities that are valuable, rare or unique, difficult to imitate, and nonsubstitutable can use them to gain a sustainable competitive advantage. The activities that a firm performs (second C) usually take advantage of any distinctive capabilities that it may have. They also help the firm build or protect such capabilities.

In analyzing the sources of a firm's profitability and competitive advantage, one should:

1. Identify the resources and capabilities that the firm has that are valuable, rare, inimitable, nonsubstitutable, and appropriable. This is done using a **VRISA** analysis.
2. Identify the extent to which the resources and capabilities can be used to offer customer value or reduce competitive forces exerted by suppliers, customers, rivals, potential new entrants, and substitutes.
3. Identify the extent to which the resources need to be built.

6. Change and Sustainability

If a firm has a competitive advantage, an important question is, Why can't competitors imitate the firm or leapfrog it? There are two major reasons that competitors may not be able to do so. First, there may be something about the firm and its activities that makes it difficult for others to imitate or leapfrog it. If a firm has resources or capabilities that are rare, valuable, nonsubstitutable, appropriable, and inimitable, competitors may find it difficult to erode the firm's competitive advantage. For example, Honda's ability to build light, efficient, high-performing engines is not easy to imitate or leapfrog. If a firm's activities form a system, competitors may be able to imitate some components of the system but may find it difficult to imitate the whole system. Imitating a system means not only imitating the components but also imitating the linkages between them. Second, there may be something about competitors that makes it difficult for them to successfully attack a firm with a competitive advantage. Prior commitments may prevent competitors from engaging in the activities that can allow them to imitate or leapfrog the leader. As we will see in the Southwest Airlines example on page 198, if U.S. airlines decided to fly only Boeing 737s, they would have to get rid of all the other kinds of planes that they used to fly (747s, 757s, 767s, A320s, A319s, etc.), renegotiate contracts with the pilots that used to fly these other planes or fire the pilots, and so on. This is not easy. And even if the other airlines were able to imitate this one component of the system, they would still have the other components *and* the linkages between the components to imitate. Competitors may also be prevented by their organizational systems, processes, cultures, and dominant managerial logic from being able to effectively imitate a firm with a competitive advantage.

The biggest threat to a firm's competitive advantage is change, and change can threaten a firm in three ways. First, what customers want can change either as a result of changes in their preferences or incomes or as a result of new products that offer them something different. Second, the type of activities that are used to offer customer value can change as a result of technological innovation, regulation or deregulation, or new game strategies. Third, the type of resources or capabilities that are needed can also change. If the change is radical, it can render existing capabilities obsolete. Most major changes usually pose some combination of the three different threats.

In analyzing the sources of a firm's profitability and competitive advantage, it is important to understand why the firm has or has not been able to sustain an advantage, especially in relation to how it deals with change:

1. Identify inimitability in the firm's activities—what it is about the firm's system of activities that makes the system difficult to imitate or leapfrog.
2. Identify inimitability and nonsubstitutability in the firm's resources and capabilities—what it is about the firm's resources or capabilities that is difficult to imitate or substitute. A VRISA analysis can be used.
3. Identify competitors' handicaps—what it is about competitors' prior commitments, systems and processes, or managerial dominant logic that makes it difficult for them to imitate the leader.
4. Determine the extent to which the value that customers want has changed and what this means to the firm. The change can be in customer needs, preferences, ability to afford the product, and so on.
5. Determine the extent to which the change requires performing very different activities from the firm's existing ones and the extent to which the resulting new customer value is superior to the value offered using existing activities.
6. Determine the extent to which the change requires very different resources and capabilities from the firm's existing ones and the extent to which the resulting new customer value is superior to the value offered using existing resources and capabilities.

7. Cost

In performing the activities of a business model, firms incur costs. Irrespective of whether a firm pursues a differentiation or low-cost strategy, its costs ought to be tracked and their drivers understood. For a low-cost strategy, many determinants of costs are usually identified in performing an analysis of the second C, connected activities. In any case, all the costs and cost drivers not analyzed in exploring the first six C's are analyzed now, under the seventh C. In addition to identifying any cost savings or losses that result from agency costs, economies of learning, and economies of scope and scale, it is also important to look for obvious waste. For example, a start-up with yearly sales of less than $1 million that has officers who each earn more than $1 million a year is wasting money even if the start-up is in a new economy. A discount retailer that has a lavish headquarters and private jets for its executives while the industry leader, Wal-Mart, has a very simple, low-cost headquarters and no private jets is wasting money. It is also useful to look for differences in productivity between the firm and its competitors. If a car company that has twice as many engineers as its competitors have (and that pays wages similar to those at competing firms) takes one year longer than its competitors to design a similar car, the company has problems.

In analyzing the sources of a firm's profitability and competitive advantage, it is important to:

1. Identify any agency costs.
2. Identify any obvious resource waste other than agency costs.
3. Look for employee productivity differences by, for example, benchmarking.

SAMPLE SEVEN C'S ANALYSIS

Case: Southwest Airlines in 2002

In 2002, when all the 2001 earnings numbers had been tallied, Southwest Airlines' earnings surprised many observers. While AMR (the parent company of American Airlines), United Airlines, and Delta Air Lines *lost* $1.76 billion, $2.145 billion, and $1.216 billion, respectively, Southwest Airlines astonished many by earning a *profit* of $511 million in a year that most airlines would rather forget (Table 10.1). At $10.8 billion, Southwest's market value was larger than that of all the other airlines combined. Its 2001 profits did not come as a total surprise to airline industry observers who knew that the company had posted profits every year since its incorporation in the early 1970s. Over the years, Southwest had won all kinds of airline industry awards for having the highest level of customer satisfaction.

TABLE 10.1   Earnings of Major U.S. Airlines, 2001

		Revenues		Profits		Profits as % of:		
Rank	Company	$, Millions	% Change from 2000	$, Millions	% Change from 2000	Revenues	Assets	Stockholders' Equity
1	AMR	18,963	−6	−1,762	−317	−9	−5	−33
2	UAL	16,138	−17	−2,145	−4,390	−13	−9	−71
3	Delta Air Lines	13,879	−17	−1,216	−247	−9	−5	−33
4	NWA	9,905	−13	−423	−265	−4	−3	N/A
5	Continental Airlines	8,969	−9	−95	−128	−1	−1	−8
6	US Airways Group	8,288	−11	−1,969	N/A	−24	−23	N/A
7	Southwest Airlines	5,555	−2	511 ·	−15	9	6	13
8	Alaska Air Group	2,141	−2	−40	N/A	−2	−1	−5
9	America West Holdings	2,066	−12	−148	−2,026	−7	−9	−28

Source: "Fortune 500," *Fortune*, Apr. 17, 2002.

Much of Southwest's success was attributed to a work culture that was the envy of major U.S. airlines. The company had assembled a workforce that worked "more productively, more flexibly, and more creatively."[4] Many employees regarded Southwest as a family. Potential employees were selected more for their attitude than for their skills, and once in the company, they were virtually assured of job security.[5] Its pilots were paid by the trip, rather than by the hour as at other airlines, and often flew 80 hours per month, compared to, say, United Airlines' pilots, who flew 50 hours a month.[6] A considerable portion of pilots' compensation was stock options. The base pay of Southwest flight attendants was considerably lower than that of attendants at competing airlines, yet they often worked as many as 150 hours per month compared to 80 hours at other airlines.[7] A base pay of $15 per hour at Southwest for a six-year veteran was not unusual, compared to $23 at competitors. The company was seen by some as having a familylike culture where people cared about each other and their company. In the words of a financial analyst, "The workforce is dedicated to the company. They are Moonies, basically. That's the way they operate."[8] Employees received profit sharing and had a relatively good union-firm relationship. They were flexible in performing their activities, and so it was not unusual to find a pilot helping out at a ticketing counter. Some observers attributed Southwest's success to the leadership of CEO Herb Kelleher, who had run the company for decades since its founding. It was not unusual to see Herb serving peanuts and drinks on flights, a job reserved for flight attendants at other airlines.

Like other airlines, the company offered a website (Southwest.com) that passengers could use to book their flights. Passengers could also call the airline or go through a travel agent to book their flights. However, Southwest's seats, schedules, prices, and other information required to book a flight were not available on major computerized reservation systems such as Apollo and Sabre; rather, the company depended on its own Southwest.com site. Apollo and Sabre were known to charge a fee of $2 per transaction. Since most travel agents used the Sabre and Apollo reservation systems, they had to call Southwest to book flights for their clients and charged Southwest a 10 percent commission for booking flights. Until 1992, travel agents booked only 55 percent of Southwest Airline's flights, compared to 90 percent for other airlines.[9]

Southwest operated largely out of the uncongested airports of smaller cities or out of the smaller airports of larger cities, such as Dallas's Love Field and Chicago's Midway. Operating out of such airports reduced the amount of time that Southwest's planes had to wait for takeoff and wait in the air for clearance to land. This saved the airline an average of 20 percent on flight time. The uncongested airports tended to have lower gate and landing fees, estimated to be $2.50 per passenger compared to between $6 and $8 at the more congested airports that most of Southwest's competitors used.[10] Southwest did not transfer passengers and baggage directly to other airlines' planes: Passengers from and to other airlines had to collect their bags and check in again. It offered frequent service to all the destinations that it served. To optimize the use of its gates, the company operated largely out of airports where it could schedule at least 20 flights per day. It usually scheduled eight or more one-way flights per day between two cities.

If Southwest's planes looked more alike than usual to a passenger who was flying Southwest for the first time, it was probably because the airline operated only Boeing 737 planes, unlike its competitors, who used all sorts of different planes.

In 1992, it operated 150 of these 737s, which flew a total of 1,500 trips per day. Southwest also had one of the youngest fleets of aircraft, and each of its planes cost $27 million and had an estimated life of 20 years.

Unlike other airlines, which offered business class in their flights, Southwest offered only coach and served no meals, choosing to serve only peanuts and drinks. In the early 1980s, when other airlines adopted "hub-and-spoke" systems, Southwest chose not to adopt the new system. Like most other airlines, however, Southwest had a frequent flyer program.

On new routes, Southwest could start out with prices that were as much as 60 percent below competitors' prices. Until the mid-1990s, most flights lasted an average of only 65 minutes.[11] Southwest's turnaround time—the time between arrival at and departure from the airport gate—averaged 15 minutes, compared to an industry average of 55 minutes. Turnaround time included the time in which arriving passengers got off the plane and departing ones got onboard, arriving baggage was unloaded and departing baggage loaded, and the aircraft was cleaned, tidied up, refueled, provisioned with food and drinks, and inspected. The events of September 11, 2001, had, however, resulted in changes in boarding security procedures that increased Southwest's turnaround time considerably and reduced its on-time arrivals, with as much as 22 percent of its flights not arriving on time.[12] It was estimated that adding 10 minutes to each of its short-haul flights would force the airline to add 40 planes to its 367 Boeing 737s.

In late 2002 United Airlines filed for bankruptcy, and in early 2003 there were rumors that AMR was considering filing for bankruptcy. Meanwhile, Southwest grew larger, but as it did so, many analysts wondered how long the Southwest formula and culture would hold. Would the company continue to have the type of stellar performance it had delivered for almost three decades? Would its costs continue to be considerably lower than those of competitors and allow it to continue charging lower prices than its competitors charge (Table 10.2)?

Analysis: Southwest Airlines' Sources of Profitability and Competitive Advantage

In 2002, Southwest Airlines was the only airline that had not lost money for over 30 years. In 2001 it earned $511 million, while every other airline lost money, with some losing billions. This is evidence that it had a competitive advantage in 2001. Its market value in 2002 was more than the combined market value of the other seven major U.S. airlines. This leads us to the all-important question: Why has the company done so well? To answer this question, we turn to a seven C's

TABLE 10.2   Major U.S. Airlines' Statistics, 2002

	Alaska	America West	American	Continental	Delta	Northwest	Southwest	United	US Airways
Cost per seat-mile (cents)	10.5	8.0	11.2	10.4	10.0	10.2	7.5	11.4	14.2
Aircraft hours per day	10	8.9	9.0	9.6	8.9	8.5	10.9	9.1	9.5

Source: Air Transport Association; *Time Magazine*, 2002.

analysis of the sources of Southwest Airlines' profitability and competitive advantage up to mid-2002. The analysis is outlined below and summarized in Figure 10.3.

1. Competitive Position

Low Cost Southwest Airlines' ability to keep its costs lower than competitors' costs is evidenced by its 2002 cost per available seat-mile of 7.5 cents, which is the lowest in the industry (Table 10.2). Its aircraft-hours-per-day figure is also the highest in the industry, suggesting that utilization of its planes is higher (Table 10.2). Planes make money when they are flying passengers, not when they are sitting on the ground. Thus, the higher the utilization, the lower the airline's costs for depreciation and employee wages per passenger-mile.

FIGURE 10.3 **Summary of Seven C's Analysis for Southwest Airlines**

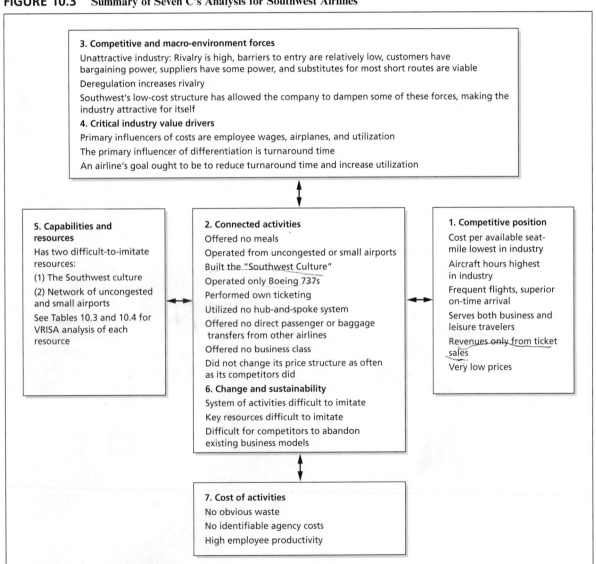

3. Competitive and macro-environment forces
Unattractive industry: Rivalry is high, barriers to entry are relatively low, customers have bargaining power, suppliers have some power, and substitutes for most short routes are viable
Deregulation increases rivalry
Southwest's low-cost structure has allowed the company to dampen some of these forces, making the industry attractive for itself
4. Critical industry value drivers
Primary influencers of costs are employee wages, airplanes, and utilization
The primary influencer of differentiation is turnaround time
An airline's goal ought to be to reduce turnaround time and increase utilization

5. Capabilities and resources
Has two difficult-to-imitate resources:
(1) The Southwest culture
(2) Network of uncongested and small airports
See Tables 10.3 and 10.4 for VRISA analysis of each resource

2. Connected activities
Offered no meals
Operated from uncongested or small airports
Built the "Southwest Culture"
Operated only Boeing 737s
Performed own ticketing
Utilized no hub-and-spoke system
Offered no direct passenger or baggage transfers from other airlines
Offered no business class
Did not change its price structure as often as its competitors did
6. Change and sustainability
System of activities difficult to imitate
Key resources difficult to imitate
Difficult for competitors to abandon existing business models

1. Competitive position
Cost per available seat-mile lowest in industry
Aircraft hours highest in industry
Frequent flights, superior on-time arrival
Serves both business and leisure travelers
Revenues only from ticket sales
Very low prices

7. Cost of activities
No obvious waste
No identifiable agency costs
High employee productivity

Differentiation Southwest's frequent flights, superior on-time arrival performance, and other performance rankings by JD Powers can be seen as evidence of service differentiation.

Market Segments Southwest serves both business and leisure travelers who would otherwise drive. All passengers receive the same service. There is no business class.

Sources of Revenues Southwest's only source of revenues is the income that it collects from selling airline tickets.

Prices Since Southwest's costs have been lower than its competitors' costs, it has been better able to pass on some of its cost savings to its customers in the form of lower prices.

2. Connected Activities

Offering No Meals Southwest offers no meals on its planes. If we assume that each meal costs an airline $4, then in 1992 when it flew 28 million passengers, it would have saved $112 million ($4 × 28 million) by not offering meals. Passengers do not miss the meals because many of its flights are short, lasting 55 minutes on average. (Besides, who wants to eat airline food?) Not offering meals also means that planes do not have to wait for provisioning with food and less time is needed for cleaning the planes, both of which reduce turnaround time.

Operating from Uncongested Airports Since gate and landing fees at uncongested airports are lower than those at more congested airports ($2.50 per passenger compared to between $6 and $8), Southwest saves about $5 per passenger. This means that, in 1992 for example, when it flew 28 million passengers, it saved $140 million. Operating out of uncongested airports also increases utilization of planes and pilots since planes do not have to wait as long for takeoff and landing. This also helps on-time arrival performance. It's also easier and cheaper for passengers to drive to and park at such airports than it is at the more congested ones. Finally, operating out of uncongested airports allows Southwest to expand and offer more frequent flights.

Building the "Southwest Culture" Southwest built and nurtured an organizational culture that has become the envy of competitors. The culture keeps employees so highly motivated and dedicated to the company that they are willing to accept low salaries and be flexible in the types of jobs that they can handle. In an industry where employee wages constitute such a high percentage of expenses (third C), it is important to keep wages lower than competitors' or get the best out of employees for the same wages. Southwest's culture, which is best captured by the quote "[Southwest's employees] work more productively, more flexibly, and more creatively," helps not only to keep wages low but also to inspire employees to work more flexibly and go the extra mile.

Getting employees to work more productively, more flexibly, and more creatively helps keep Southwest's costs lower than its competitors' costs. For example, by getting its employees to work almost twice as long as those of competitors without complaining—its pilots fly 80 hours per month compared to 50 hours by United's pilots; its flight attendants work 150 hours per month compared to 80 hours by competitors' attendants—Southwest employs fewer employees, thereby saving health insurance costs, hiring costs, office space, social security taxes, and so on. Getting employees to work more flexibly and productively also decreases turnaround time, thereby increasing on-time arrival performance. Paying pilots by the trip rather than by the hour inspires them to think of creative ways to get passengers to their destination on time, rather than burning the time in a lounge or waiting on the ground. Since a large portion of their compensation is stock options, pilots are likely to be more interested in finding creative ways to lower costs and boost profitability. Profit sharing also helps keep motivation high. Likewise, establishing good relationships with unions helps keep employees motivated and flexible.

Operating Only 737s   Operating only 737s has many advantages. Usually a pilot who is certified to fly one type of passenger jet plane must be certified again to fly another. For example, a pilot who is certified to fly a Boeing 737 cannot fly a 767 or an Airbus A300 without further training and certification. Thus, by flying only one type of plane, Southwest has more flexibility in assigning its pilots since any pilot can fly any of its planes. This potentially reduces costs since highly paid pilots are used more efficiently. It also potentially reduces turnaround time. Having only one type of plane means that the same type of spare part can be used on most of the company's fleet and the same mechanics can work on all of the company's planes. This not only keeps the cost of inventorying spare parts lower but also potentially reduces turnaround times. Usually, different types of planes require different gates for the boarding and disembarking of passengers. Having one type of plane means that an arriving plane does not have to wait for a specific gate to park at. Operating only 737s gives Southwest some bargaining power over suppliers of components and planes, since it buys very many of the same planes and spare parts.

However, operating only 737s also has some disadvantages. If there is a major problem with 737s that requires grounding the planes, Southwest will not be able to offer any service. Since Boeing is the only firm that makes 737s, it has more power over Southwest than it would otherwise have. Even so, Southwest has considerable bargaining power given the large number of planes that it buys.

Performing Own Ticketing   Performing its own ticketing allows Southwest to save the $2-per-transaction fee that other airlines have to pay Apollo or Sabre for each ticket sale. With the Internet, Southwest has its own reservation system. This has the disadvantage that the airline may be missing out on new customers who do not yet know about Southwest and its low fares.

Not Using Hub-and-Spoke   In a hub-and-spoke system, passengers heading to different destinations are flown from their departing city (a spoke) to a central location first (the hub) where they are combined with passengers from other spokes going to the same final destination and flown from the hub to that final destination. The main advantage of a hub-and-spoke system is that it increases load factor (how full a plane is), but passengers have to make an extra stop and take much longer to reach their final destination. Since Southwest's short-haul flights usually have high load factors, it does not need the hub-and-spoke. Another disadvantage of a hub-and-spoke system is that planes leaving from a hub to a final destination usually have to wait for passengers from different spokes to arrive. This increases the turnaround time. By not adopting a hub-and-spoke system, Southwest keeps its turnaround time low and on-time arrival performance high.

Disallowing Direct Passenger or Baggage Transfers from Other Airlines   By not allowing direct transfer of passengers or baggage from other airlines, Southwest avoids having its planes wait for other airlines' late planes. This keeps turnaround time low and on-time arrival performance high.

Offering No Business Class   By not offering business class, Southwest keeps service simple, which is consistent with its low-cost strategy.

Charging Low Prices Southwest usually offers promotion prices whenever it moves into a new area. Otherwise, its prices are generally lower compared to competitors' prices. It can afford to set its prices low because of its low-cost strategy.

3. Critical Industry Success Drivers

Recall that critical industry success drivers are those factors that have significant impact on cost or differentiation.

Primary Influencers of Costs At more than 30 percent of total expenses, labor costs account for a significant percentage of Southwest's costs. At $27 million per plane, planes and their maintenance also constitute a high percentage of the company's expense. Since a plane makes money for the airline when it flies and not when it is on the ground, utilization of planes and pilots is critical. That is, planes should be in the air taking passengers to their destinations, not waiting at a gate. Having high utilization of pilots and planes means their costs are expensed over more time spent making money and less time spent on the ground. High utilization is usually achieved by having short turnaround times. Recall from the case that turnaround time is the time between arrival at and departure from the airport gate. Improving employee productivity can also have an impact on cost since employee salaries constitute such a high fraction of expenses.

Primary Influencers of Differentiation Turnaround time is an influencer of differentiation. This is because shorter turnaround times usually mean better on-time arrival performance and more frequent flights.

Objectives Since utilization has a direct impact on low cost and differentiation, firms in the airline industry may want to pursue actions that maximize utilization (e.g., keeping turnaround time short, minimizing airplane mechanical problems and repair time, etc). Industry firms may also want to pursue actions that keep labor costs low.

4. Competitive Forces

Overall, the competitive forces that act on the airline industry in the United States are high. That is, on average, the U.S. airline industry is an unattractive industry. However, by taking the right actions (second C), a firm can still make money.

Customers For several reasons, customers have bargaining power. Switching costs for customers are still low despite frequent-flyer programs, which increase them. On many routes, customers have a choice of more than one airline. Service is highly undifferentiated.

Rivalry On most routes in the United States, airlines offer similar service to customers, who have very low or no switching costs (some minor switching costs result from frequent-flyer programs). In addition, these rivals are selling a perishable good since, once a plane takes off, empty seats on the plane are lost. For these reasons and more, rivalry is high.

Suppliers There are two major suppliers of passenger jet airplanes: Boeing and Airbus. Thus, although competition exists between the two to sell to the world's airlines, it may be less than it would be if there were more airlines. Given that employee wages are such a significant portion of expenses, employees and their unions can be seen as suppliers. Unions have collective bargaining power over many airlines.

Threat of New Entry Since potential new entrants can lease old planes, finding the planes needed to enter a new route is not difficult. However, it is difficult to find a network of airports with available landing slots and gates, which a new entrant will need to effectively compete with Southwest Airlines. Thus, entry is easy on some routes, but once in the industry, a new airline will not find it easy to grow and gain a competitive advantage.

Substitutes For short-haul routes such as the ones that Southwest operates, ground transportation and, in a few cases, rail are substitutes.

What Southwest's Actions Have Done

- By moving into uncongested airports, saturating them with frequent flights, and building a network of these airports and associated landing slots and gates, Southwest Airlines has reduced the extent to which new entrants can enter the industry and erode its competitive advantage. These actions also reduce existing rivals' ability to erode its competitive advantage.
- By establishing a cost structure that its rivals cannot match, Southwest has effectively reduced rivalry on the routes that it serves since rivals cannot offer the kinds of prices that it does.
- By having friendly relations with employees and unions, the firm is effectively removing the need for these suppliers to exercise their bargaining power.
- By having a low-cost structure that enables it to keep its prices low and by offering frequent flights, it is reducing the power of substitutes since travelers may find it just as convenient and inexpensive to fly Southwest as to drive.

5. Capabilities

Identifying Resources and Capabilities Two of Southwest's most valuable resources are (1) its network of uncongested airports with the associated landing slots and gates and (2) the "Southwest culture." As we saw in Chapter 6 and as repeated here in the VRISA analysis in Table 10.3, Southwest's network of uncongested airports is a valuable, rare, difficult-to-imitate, and difficult-to-substitute resource that Southwest has been able to appropriate. When Southwest moves into an airport, its low prices attract many passengers, allowing it to increase its number of flights out of the airport. The airport is added to its network. This network is one of the contributing factors in the firm's low-cost structure that enables it to offer customers lower prices. Although competitors fly to some of the same airports as Southwest, none of them has the network of uncongested airports—with associated gates and landing slots—that Southwest has. Competitors may be able to move into some uncongested airports, but it is difficult to duplicate the type of network that Southwest has built over the years. There are few substitutes for a network of uncongested airports as far as offering low-cost flights is concerned. As of early 2003, Southwest's suppliers and customers had some power over the firm, but their power was low enough for Southwest to be able to appropriate much of the value from its network of uncongested airports.

Southwest's culture, which has come to be known as the "Southwest culture," is valuable, rare, difficult to imitate, difficult to substitute, and appropriable (Table 10.4). The Southwest culture yields employees who are productive, flexible, motivated, and willing to accept a low base pay and work long hours. This contributes to the firm's low cost, frequent flights, and on-time arrival performance. Southwest is not the only airline with a culture, but only Southwest has employees who care so much about their company and what they do that they accept very low base salaries yet are very productive and flexible; work almost twice as long as and are more motivated than other airlines' employees; and would rather support the company than their union.

TABLE 10.3   **VRISA Analysis: Southwest Airlines' Network of Uncongested Airports, 2002**

Attribute	Key Question	Answer
Value	Does Southwest Airlines' network of uncongested airports provide customers with something that they value?	Yes. Planes can land and take off with fewer delays than occur at more congested airports, thereby offering passengers more frequent flights, which arrive on time, at low prices. Landing fees are lower. Passengers are more likely to find parking at such airports than at more congested ones.
Rareness (Uniqueness)	Is Southwest Airlines the only one with this capability? If not, is its level of the capability higher than that of competitors?	Yes. Other airlines fly to uncongested airports, but none has a network of such airports as large as Southwest's network. They do not have the associated landing slots and gates either.
Imitability	Is it easy for other firms to acquire Southwest Airlines' network of uncongested airports and associated gates and landing slots?	No. Competitors may be able to acquire access to a few uncongested airports, but to replicate Southwest's complete network is difficult.
Substitutability	Can another capability offer customers the same value that Southwest Airlines' network of uncongested airports does?	No. It is difficult to offer the type of low-cost, frequent flights that this network provides by any means other than the network.
Appropriability	Does Southwest Airlines make money from its network of uncongested airports?	Yes. Up to 2002, suppliers and customers did not have too much power over Southwest, so it was able to appropriate the value from its network.

For several reasons, duplicating this culture is likely to be difficult. First, although observers may think that they know exactly what makes Southwest employees so motivated, productive, flexible, and dedicated to Southwest, there may be a lot more that a firm needs to know to replicate the culture. In fact, it is possible that even Southwest itself does not know everything that underpins its enviable culture. It is difficult for a firm to duplicate something that it does not understand well. Second, building the Southwest culture may have involved a series of events during its life history that are difficult to re-create. For example, being in Dallas, going though deregulation when it did, having Herb Kelleher as its CEO when it did, and the demise of airlines such as Braniff and People Express may have had something to do with the type of culture that it built. These events may be impossible to re-create. Substitution is not easy because it is difficult to find other capabilities that give airlines the value that a productive, flexible, highly motivated workforce does in an industry where utilization is critical and wages constitute such a high fraction of costs. As long as there is no major change that diminishes the culture or reverses the relationships between Southwest and its suppliers and customers, Southwest should continue to appropriate the value from its extraordinary culture. One fear is that as the company grows larger, that sense of "family" that goes with a small company may disappear.

TABLE 10.4 **VRISA Analysis: the "Southwest Culture," 2002**

Attribute	Key Question	Answer
Value	Does the "Southwest culture" offer customers something that they value?	Yes. The culture results in employees who are productive, flexible, motivated, and willing to accept a low base pay and work long hours. This not only keeps costs down but also improves utilization and on-time delivery performance.
Rareness (Uniqueness)	Is Southwest Airlines the only one with this type of culture? If not, is the level of its culture higher than that of competitors?	Yes. Each airline has its own culture, but only the Southwest culture has inspired employees to care so much about their company that they accept very low base salaries yet are highly productive and flexible; work almost twice as long as and are more motivated than other airlines' employees; and would rather back the company than their union. The "family" at Southwest is just not found at other airlines.
Imitability	Is it easy for other firms to acquire this culture?	No. Duplicating this culture is likely to be difficult. Although other airlines may think they know what makes Southwest employees so motivated, productive, flexible, and dedicated, there may be a lot more that they need to know. It is difficult to duplicate something that is not well understood. Even Southwest itself may not know what makes it tick. Also, building the Southwest culture may have involved a series of events during its life history that are impossible for another firm to re-create (such as being in Dallas, going through deregulation when it did, having Herb Kelleher as its CEO when it did, and the demise of Braniff and People Express).
Substitutability	Can another capability offer customers the same value that the "Southwest culture" does?	No. In an industry where utilization is critical, it is difficult for another capability to give airlines the value created by a productive, flexible, highly motivated workforce.
Appropriability	Does Southwest make money from its unique culture?	Yes. Southwest's good position in relation to suppliers and customers enables it to appropriate the value from its extraordinary culture. Barring a major change that diminishes the culture or reverses the relationships, Southwest should continue to make money.

Using the Resources As already described, Southwest's culture and network of uncongested airports are used to lower its costs, improve on-time arrival performance, and facilitate frequent flights. They also help position Southwest well vis-à-vis suppliers, customers, rivals, and potential new entrants.

Building the Resources   Both the Southwest culture and its network of airports are resources and capabilities that it has built over the years as it has developed. As it grows larger, however, it is questionable whether Southwest will continue to have an environment that is conducive to its unique culture.

6. Change and Sustainability

Inimitability of Activities   Southwest's system of activities—operating from a network of uncongested airports, offering no meals, building and nurturing a difficult-to-imitate culture, operating only 737s, disallowing direct passenger or baggage transfers, performing its own ticketing, and offering no business class—is difficult to replicate. Existing rivals or potential new entrants may be able to replicate some of these activities, but replicating all of them is very difficult. They would have to imitate not only the components but also the linkages between the components. Moreover, even if they imitate Southwest, they cannot outdo Southwest at being Southwest.

Inimitability and Nonsubstitutability of Resources and Capabilities   Even if a firm wants to perform all these activities, it may not be able to acquire all the resources or capabilities that it needs. If a firm has money, it can buy all the 737s that it needs, but it may not be able to build a Southwest-type culture or a network of uncongested airports with the right number of gates and landing slots (see the fifth C and the VRISA analyses in Tables 10.3 and 10.4).

Competitors' Handicaps   Even if a competitor could duplicate Southwest's activities, it may not be able to get out of existing commitments. For example, operating only 737s may mean having to get rid of all the 757s, 767s, 747s, MD80s, DC-9s, A320s, A319s, A300s, and other airplanes that the airline has. Contracts with suppliers, pilots, and unions may make such a switch difficult. Operating only out of uncongested airports means abandoning existing gates at the congested airports that the competitor presently occupies. This may not be easy if the airline has contracts with unions and the municipalities that own the airports. Adopting a Southwest-like culture means abandoning the competitor's existing culture, and doing so may be very difficult. How does a firm change a 40-year-old culture to make people more productive, more flexible, and less pro union, as well as willing to work twice as many hours as they did before and have their base salaries reduced? It's difficult!

Several changes have impacted the airline industry since deregulation in the 1970s. The emergence and diffusion of the World Wide Web (WWW) helps Southwest. Prior to the Web, travel agents had to call Southwest to make reservations since Southwest did not subscribe to Sabre and Apollo, the reservation systems that travel agents used. With the Web, passengers themselves have access to Southwest's own reservation system and book their own flights. Travel agents can also access Southwest's reservation system if they want to. The events of September 11 prompted the U.S. government to make changes in passenger boarding procedures. These changes have seriously impacted Southwest's turnaround and on-time arriving performance. Because most of Southwest's flights are short, adding 10 minutes to each flight would necessitate adding an estimated 40 planes to its fleet of 367 Boeing 737s, as mentioned in the case. At $27 million per plane, the cost of the new planes would be extremely high, not to mention the costs of the extra pilots and other personnel that would need to be hired to operate the new planes. The 40 planes would also require extra gate space, landing slots, and so on. Southwest's biggest threat may be uncontrolled growth. As it grows, it may not be able to hang on to the culture that has been such an important source of advantage.

7. Cost of Activities

Since Southwest's strategy is primarily low cost, we have already explored many of the cost issues associated with the activities that the company performs. Here are a few more: With a base pay of $15 per hour for a six-year veteran compared to $23 at competitors, Southwest's flight attendants help keep its costs low, especially since they work an average of 150 hours per month compared to competitors' 80 hours per month. Since Southwest pays its pilots by the trip rather than by the hour, its pilots have an incentive not to idle around, thereby keeping costs down. The fact that Southwest Airlines' employees work longer for lower wages and excel in key measures such as airplane utilization and turn-around time suggests that the company has higher productivity numbers than those of competitors.

Conclusion

Southwest Airlines has a competitive advantage in the airline industry that comes from the system of activities that it performs and the valuable resources that allow it to perform these activities. This system of activities is consistent with its low-cost structure, frequent flights, and superior on-time arrival performance. The system takes advantage of critical industry value drivers and positions Southwest better than its competitors vis-à-vis suppliers, customers, rivals, potential new entrants, and substitutes. Although some of the activities can be imitated by competitors, it is difficult for competitors to replicate the whole system. Valuable and rare resources such as Southwest's culture and network of uncongested airports are also difficult to imitate or substitute. Competitors' prior commitments and their processes and systems make it difficult for them to imitate Southwest's profitable business model. As Southwest grows, however, there is some doubt as to whether the firm will continue to have the kind of culture that seems to be a key unifying factor in its system of activities.

Summary

Perhaps one of the most important but neglected exercises in strategy is analyzing why a firm is doing well or not doing well. Too often, firms spend time performing strategic planning without really understanding the reasons behind success or failure. What many firms and consultants call strategic analysis consists of anything from SWOT analysis to single-variable prescriptions in which the link to profitability is, at best, tenuous. The seven C's framework is a comprehensive approach to analyzing why a firm is profitable or unprofitable; it draws on strategy research to link drivers of revenues and costs to profitability measures. The analysis of Southwest Airlines' competitive advantage in 2003 is a good example of how the seven C's can be used.

Key Terms   competitive advantage, *190*   connected activities, *192*   seven C's framework, *190*

Study Questions

1. Refer to the case "eBay: Growing the World's Largest Online Trading Communities" at the end of this book. Why has eBay performed so well? (Hint: Perform a seven C's analysis of eBay.)

2. In question 2, separate the operational efficiency and strategic issues. Which ones dominate?

Endnotes

1. P. Ghemawat, "Wal-Mart Stores' Discount Operations," Harvard Business School case 9-387-018, 1986; "Change at the Check-Out: A Survey in Retailing," *The Economist,* Mar. 4, 1995.

2. The word *connected* in "connected activities" reflects the fact that activities that give a firm a competitive advantage are usually linked (connected) to each other and to the other components of a business model.

3. S. P. Bradley and P. Ghemawat, "Wal-Mart Stores, Inc." Harvard Business School case 9-794-024, 1996.

4. S. B. Donnelly, "One Airline's Magic," *Time Magazine,* Oct. 28, 2002, pp. 45–47, quote is on p. 46.

5. P. Dussauge and B. Garrette, "Mini-Case Southwest Airlines," internal memo, HEC, France, 1997.

6. Donnelly, "One Airline's Magic."

7. Ibid.

8. P. Elseworth, "Southwest Air's New Push West," *New York Times,* June 16, 1991.

9. R. H. Hallowell and J. L. Heskett, "Southwest Airlines: 1993 (A)," Harvard Business School case 9-694-023, 1997.

10. Ibid.

11. Ibid.

12. M. Trottman, "Vaunted Southwest Slips in On-Time Performance," *The Wall Street Journal,* Sept. 25, 2002.

Financing and Valuing
a Business Model

One of the assets that a firm needs to create value and be in a position to appropriate the value is money. The activities that a firm performs to create and offer customer value need to be financed. To finance an activity, an investor usually needs to be convinced that the investment will pay off. Thus, a manager who invests in a project needs to be convinced that the project will pay off. An investor who buys a stock needs to be convinced that the stock will appreciate or pay enough dividends to give the investor a return on his or her money. To determine whether an investment in an activity or an asset will pay off or not, one has to value the activity or asset. Thus, a firm values its potential projects to decide which one to invest in, and a venture capital firm values a start-up to decide whether to invest in it, and a potential buyer of a stock values the stock (or believes in an analyst's valuation) before investing in it. In this chapter, we explore how activities are valued and financed. We start with the different methods for valuing projects and business models. We then explore the sources of financing that are available to firms for their activities.

VALUATION OF A BUSINESS WITH EARNINGS

Firms can be grouped into publicly traded companies and privately held companies. Publicly traded companies are those whose shares are sold to the public. That is, anybody can buy shares of a publicly traded company. At any one time, each company has a certain number of shares outstanding. A firm's *outstanding shares* are the shares the firm has issued that are being held by people who bought them or that are in the market for anyone who wants to buy them. Owning shares of a company gives the owner of the shares the right to share in the profits that the company generates. The **market capital** or **market value** of a company is the price per share of its common stock multiplied by the number of shares outstanding. The market value of a firm at any one time reflects the expected profits that buyers of the stock believe the company will earn and the fact that the stock is a commodity whose price can move up or down as a result of the demand and supply for it. The means that are used to estimate what the market value should be include cash flow, price-earnings (P/E) ratio, price-earnings-growth (PEG) ratio, profitability-prediction measures, and intangible assets.

Cash Flow

During each accounting period, a firm receives money from its sources of revenues but must also pay out money to cover the costs that it incurs in offering value to its customers. The cash that the company generates is normally called *cash inflows,* while that which it consumes is called *cash outflows.* The excess of cash inflows over cash outflows is the amount that is available for the owners of the business to share or plow back into the business to expand it. Since owning a stock gives the stockholder the right to a share of the net cash that the company generates, we can expect the value of a firm to be related to the free cash flow that the firm generates. According to Warren Buffett:

> In the *Theory of Investment Value,* written over 50 years ago, John Burr Williams set forth the equation for value, which we condense here: The value of any stock, bond or business is determined by the cash inflows and outflows—discounted at the appropriate interest rate—that can be expected to occur during the remaining life of the asset.

Thus, the value of a business or firm is the **present value** of its future free cash flows discounted at its cost of capital. From this, the value V of a firm is[1]

$$V = C_0 + \frac{C_1}{(1 + r_k)} + \frac{C_2}{(1 + r_k)^2} + \frac{C_3}{(1 + r_k)^3} + \ldots \frac{C_n}{(1 + r_k)^n} \quad \textbf{(11.1)}$$

$$= \sum_{t=0}^{t=n} \frac{C_t}{(1 + r_k)^t}$$

where:

- C_t is the **free cash flow** at time t. This is the cash from operations that is available for distribution to claimholders—equity investors and debtors—who provide capital. It is the difference between cash earnings and cash investments.
- r_k is the firm's **discount rate.** This is the firm's opportunity cost of capital. It is the expected rate of return that could be earned by investing money in another asset instead of in the company. It reflects the **systematic risk**—that is, risk that is specific to the firm's business model and therefore cannot be eliminated by diversification. This can be estimated using a model such as the **capital asset pricing model (CAPM),** which states:

$$r_k = r_f + \beta_i(r_m - r_f) \quad \textbf{(11.2)}$$

That is, the discount rate consists of two parts: a risk-free rate, r_f, and a risk premium, $\beta_i(r_m - r_f)$. The **risk-free rate,** r_f, can be proxied with the interest rate on Treasury bills. The idea is that if a person invests money in U.S. Treasury bills, she or he would get a sure return since the government is always going to be there and will pay its debts. This interest rate is low since it is risk-free. The **risk premium,** $\beta_i(r_m - r_f)$, reflects the additional interest that should be expected, on top of the risk-free rate, since investing in a business is more risky than investing in Treasury bills. The risk premium is equal to the systematic risk, β_i, of the firm times the excess return over the market return r_m. The beta (β) of similar businesses (within or outside the firm's industry) is used.

A major drawback of the cash flow valuation method is that forecasting future cash flows accurately is extremely difficult. The further into the future, the more difficult it is to forecast cash flows. Equation 11.1 can be further simplified by assuming that the free cash flows generated by the firm being valued will reach a constant amount (an annuity) of C_f after n years. If we do so, Equation 11.1 reduces to

$$V = \frac{C_f}{r_k(1 + r_k)^n} \qquad \textbf{(11.3)}$$

If we further assume that the constant free cash flows start in the present year, then $n = 0$ and Equation 11.3 reduces to

$$V = \frac{C_f}{r_k} \qquad \textbf{(11.4)}$$

Another way to simplify Equation 11.1 is to assume that today's free cash flow, C_0, which we know, will grow at a constant rate g forever. If we do so, Equation 11.1 reduces to

$$V = \frac{C_0}{r_k - g} \qquad \textbf{(11.5)}$$

Strategic Implication of High Valuations

Although Equations 11.3 and 11.4 are very simple, they can help us ask some important questions about a business model. We will get to these questions by making some simple calculations. Consider the top 25 U.S. corporations, ranked by market value, in *Fortune* magazine's list of the top 500 in 2000 (Table 11.1). Cisco's market valuation on March 14, 2000, was \$453.88 billion; its profits in 1999 were \$2.10 billion. The question is whether Cisco was overvalued at \$453.88 billion. We can answer this question using Equations 11.3, 11.4, and 11.5. From Equation 11.4, the free cash flow that Cisco would have to generate every year, forever, for its \$453.88 billion valuation to be right is $C_f = \$453.88 \times r_k$ billion. If we assume that investors in Cisco expect a 15 percent return, Cisco would have to generate \$68.08 (\$453.88 $\times$ .15) *billion* in free cash flows every year to infinity. Since free cash flows are usually less than profits after tax, Cisco would have to make profits of more than \$68 billion to justify this valuation. Its profits in 1999 were just over \$2 billion. How can any company generate after-tax profits of more than \$68 billion a year forever? In particular, what is it about Cisco's business model that would make one believe that the company can quickly ramp its profits from \$2 billion to more than \$68 billion and maintain that advantage forever?

An analysis such as the one undertaken in Chapter 10 would help answer this question. Given the rate of change in Cisco's industry, it is doubtful that the company can reach such a high level of profits and sustain it forever. By the same token, Oracle's \$217.26 billion valuation suggests that it would have to generate \$32.59 billion in free cash flows forever. However, its 1999 profits were only \$1.29 billion. The question, then, becomes, What is there about Oracle and the software industry that would enable the company to very quickly increase its profits from \$1.24 billion to more than \$32.59 billion and maintain it at that level forever? Given the decrease in barriers to entry in software brought on by the Internet, reaching such high levels of profits will be difficult. The expected free cash flows of the other top 25 most highly valued U.S. firms in 2000 are shown in column 5.

Now assume that it will take Cisco some time, say, five years, to reach the constant free cash flows. Using Equation 11.3, $C_f = \$453.88 \times 0.15(1 + 0.15)^5 = \$136.94$ billion. That is, from 2005 on, Cisco should be generating \$136.94 billion

TABLE 11.1 **Expected Free Cash Flows and Growth Rates, 25 Most Valuable U.S. Firms, 2000**

1	2	3	4	5	6	7	8
Rank	Company	Market Value, 3/14/00 (billions)	Profits, 1999 (billions)	Expected Future Net Cash Flows 1* (billions)	2† (billions)	Expected Growth Rate $r_{k'} =$ 15%	Expected Growth Rate $r_{k'} =$ 10%
1	Microsoft	$492.46	$7.79	$73.87	$148.58	13.42%	8.42%
2	Cisco Systems	453.88	2.10	68.08	136.94	14.54	9.54
3	General Electric	417.18	10.72	62.58	125.86	12.43	7.43
4	Intel	391.82	7.31	58.77	118.21	13.13	8.13
5	ExxonMobil	268.60	7.91	40.29	81.04	12.06	7.06
6	AT&T	236.70	3.43	35.51	71.41	13.55	8.55
7	Oracle	217.26	1.29	32.59	65.55	14.41	9.41
8	Lucent Technologies	214.19	4.77	32.13	64.62	12.77	7.77
9	Wal-Mart Stores	212.67	5.34	31.90	64.16	12.49	7.49
10	International Business Machines (IBM)	193.81	7.71	29.07	58.47	11.02	6.02
11	Citigroup	167.53	8.97	25.13	50.55	9.65	4.65
12	Dell Computer	143.49	1.67	21.52	43.29	13.84	8.84
13	SBC Communications	143.03	8.16	21.45	43.15	9.29	4.29
14	America Online	140.90	0.76	21.13	42.51	14.46	9.46
15	Hewlett-Packard	140.21	3.49	21.03	42.30	12.51	7.51
16	Sun Microsystems	137.92	1.03	20.69	41.61	14.25	9.25
17	American International Group (AIG)	132.84	5.06	19.93	40.08	11.19	6.19
18	Merck	130.87	5.89	19.63	39.48	10.50	5.50
19	Texas Instruments	127.93	1.41	19.19	38.60	13.90	8.90
20	Pfizer	127.91	3.18	19.19	38.59	12.51	7.51
21	EMC	126.27	1.01	18.94	38.10	14.20	9.20
22	Home Depot	122.93	3.84	18.44	37.09	11.88	6.88
23	MCI Worldcom‡	122.23	4.01	18.33	36.88	11.72	6.72
24	Motorola	115.19	0.82	17.28	34.75	14.29	9.29
25	Time Warner§	112.13	1.95	16.82	33.83	13.26	8.26

*Annuities beginning immediately.
†Annuities beginning in 2005.
‡Filed for bankruptcy in 2002.
§Merged with America Online (line 14 above).
Source: *Fortune,* April 21, 2001.

in free cash every year to infinity. The question now becomes, What is it about Cisco's business model that will enable it to increase its profits from $2 billion in 1999 to more than $136 billion in 2005 and maintain the profits at that level forever? Oracle's $217.26 billion valuation suggests that, beginning in 2005, it would have to generate $65.55 billion in free cash flows forever to justify the valuation. The expected free cash flows of the other top 25 U.S. firms for annuities beginning in 2005 are shown in column 6. Using Equation 11.5, one can also calculate the growth rates that each firm would have to have to justify its valuation. Again, assuming a discount rate of 15 percent, Cisco would need to grow at 14.54 percent forever to justify its $453.88 billion valuation. Given that the U.S. economy has grown at less than 4 percent, Cisco's free cash flows alone should one day be larger than the U.S. economy to justify the valuation.

The February 13, 2003, market values of the firms in Table 11.1 and their corresponding expected free cash flows and growth rates are shown in Table 11.2. Cisco's market value has dropped to $96.67 billion. Using a 15 percent discount rate, the expected free cash flows from Cisco are now $14.5 billion for annuities that begin immediately and $29.17 billion for those that begin in 2005. The expected growth rates for discount rates of 15 and 10 percent are down to 11.78 and 6.78 percent, respectively.

Recall from earlier chapters that a system of activities that is consistent with low-cost or product differentiation, takes advantage of industry value drivers, builds and exploits resources, and keeps costs low can enable a business model to offer superior customer value and appropriate the value. Also, a firm that has valuable, rare, difficult-to-imitate or substitute resources can earn more profits

TABLE 11.2   Expected Free Cash Flows and Growth Rates, Selected Firms, 2003

1	2	3	4	5	6	7	8
		Market Value, 2/13/03 (billions)	**Profits, 2002 (billions)**	**Expected Future Net Cash Flows 1* (billions)**	**2† (billions)**	**Expected Growth Rate $r_{k'} =$ 15%**	**Expected Growth Rate $r_{k'} =$ 10%**
Rank	**Company**						
1	Microsoft	$251.70	$9.54	$37.76	$75.94	11.21%	6.21%
2	Cisco Systems	96.67	3.11	14.50	29.17	11.78	6.78
3	General Electric	220.30	15.10	33.05	66.47	8.15	3.15
4	Intel	103.40	3.12	15.51	31.20	11.98	6.98
5	ExxonMobil	221.80	11.50	33.27	66.92	9.82	4.82
6	AT&T	13.67	(13.30)	2.05	4.12		
7	Oracle	61.17	2.04	9.18	18.46	11.67	6.67
8	Lucent Technologies	6.41	(11.90)	0.96	1.93		
9	Wal-Mart Stores	209.40	7.70	31.41	63.18	11.32	6.32
10	International Business Machines (IBM)	128.90	5.33	19.34	38.89	10.87	5.87
11	Citigroup	160.50	13.40	24.08	48.42	6.65	1.65
12	Dell Computer	64.87	1.98	9.73	19.57	11.95	6.95
13	SBC Communications	74.94	7.47	11.24	22.61	5.03	0.03
14	America Online	46.15	(44.61)	6.92	13.92		
15	Hewlett-Packard	53.66	(0.92)	8.05	16.19		
16	Sun Microsystems	10.50	(2.37)	1.58	3.17		
17	American International Group (AIG)	128.08	7.49	19.21	38.64	9.15	4.15
18	Merck	120.70	7.15	18.11	36.42	9.08	4.08
19	Texas Instruments	26.46	(0.34)	3.97	7.98		
20	Pfizer	175.70	9.39	26.36	53.01	9.66	4.66
21	EMC	17.53	(0.12)	2.63	5.29		
22	Home Depot	48.38	3.69	7.26	14.60	7.37	2.37
23	MCI Worldcom‡						
24	Motorola	18.59	(2.48)	2.79	5.61		
25	Time Warner§						

*Annuities beginning immediately.

†Annuities beginning in 2005.

‡Filed for bankruptcy in 2002.

§Merged with America Online (line 14 above).

Source: Yahoo, Finance, http://finance.yahoo.com/, accessed 2/13/03.

than its rivals in the markets in which it competes. These facts lead to three interesting strategic questions for each of the firms in Table 11.1 as well as for investors: (1) What is it about the firm's system of activities and resources that would enable the firm to keep offering superior customer value and remain in a position to make such profits for so long, in spite of change and competitors? (2) Size can help when it comes to things such as economies of scale, but when do diseconomies of scale begin to set in? Profits or free cash flows of $69 billion may require close to half a trillion dollars of revenues per year for most firms. (3) What is it about competitors that prevents them from finding newer and better ways to capture a share of such revenues and profits? An analysis similar to the one we explored in Chapter 10 would suggest that sustaining such huge profits to perpetuity is going to be very difficult. Thus, the firms in Table 11.1 may have been overvalued.

One thing that an overvalued firm can do is use its high valuation as currency to pay for acquisitions and mergers that it might want to make.

Price-Earnings Ratio

The need to estimate future cash flows is avoided in the **price-earnings (P/E) ratio** or **earnings multiple** method of valuing firms. To estimate the value of a company, a P/E ratio for the firm is determined and multiplied by the firm's earnings to obtain its share price. The share price is then multiplied by the number of shares outstanding to obtain the market value. The P/E ratio is also called the **capitalization factor** and reflects investors' expectations of future earnings. Given how important this ratio can be, the question is, How is the P/E ratio determined for a particular company? Usually, analysts find firms whose systematic risks, and therefore beta coefficients, are similar to that of the firm in question. The P/E ratio of these firms is used as a base and adjusted for any differences between the firm and the reference group of firms. For example, if a firm is determined to be more risky than the reference group, the risk is adjusted upward and therefore the beta and P/E are also adjusted upward. The ratio is also adjusted for general conditions such as market conditions. For example, it is adjusted downward in a bear market and upward in a bull market.[2] It is only after all these adjustments have been made that the ratio can be multiplied by earnings to obtain the share price.

How do we know from a stock's P/E ratio if the firm is overvalued? It is very difficult to tell. Since systematic risk varies, we can expect P/E ratios to also vary.

Example

A biotech start-up that has just earned $5 million wants to go public. The company's investment bank suggests that it should issue 10 million shares. Other biotech firms in the same therapeutic area have a P/E ratio of 25. What should be the share price of the firm?

Solution: The biotech firm's earnings per share ($5/10) are $0.50 per share. Since the P/E ratio is 25,

$$\frac{P}{E} = 25 = \frac{P}{\$0.5}, \text{ from which } P = \$12.5$$

The price per share is $12.5, and the firm's market value is $125 million ($12.5 × 10 million).

Shortcomings

The P/E ratio has several shortcomings. First, it assumes that historical earnings are a predictor of future free cash flows. Earnings are not always a good predictor of future earnings, let alone a good predictor of free cash flows. Second, a P/E ratio says nothing about the scale and difficulty of activities that would have to be performed to earn the cash.

Price-Earnings-Growth Ratio

Like the P/E ratio method, the **price-earnings-growth (PEG) ratio** method also uses historical earnings to predict future free cash flows. However, the PEG ratio explicitly incorporates the role of growth. The P/E ratio is determined as described above and then adjustments are made for growth by dividing the P/E ratio by the growth rate. The rationale behind adding a growth rate is very simple: All else equal, a firm that is growing faster is more likely to have higher earnings and free cash flows than one that is not. One assumption is that the firm has a sound business model that allows it to grow and keep growing.

There is some debate as to what is considered a good PEG ratio. One rule of thumb argues that stocks with PEG ratios of less than 1.00 are reasonable while those with ratios of more than 1.00 are considered overvalued. There is no clear, empirical evidence for this rule. Such generalizations are no substitute for careful research that digests a firm's business model to understand why one can expect profits from the company down the line.

Example

Two biotech firms offer the same drug in the same therapeutic area and are considered to have the same systematic risk, but firm A is growing at 20 percent while firm B is growing at 50 percent. Both have a P/E ratio of 25. What is the PEG ratio of each?

Solution:

$$\text{PEG ratio} = \frac{P/E}{\text{growth rate}}$$

Therefore, firm A's PEG ratio is 25/20 = 1.25; Firm B's PEG ratio is 25/50 = 0.50. On the basis of the PEG ratios, firm A appears to be overvalued, while firm B does not.

Shortcomings

The shortcomings that plague the P/E ratio also impact the PEG ratio, but the latter also suffers from another problem. Consider two stocks, A and B, each with a PEG ratio of .8, which is considered to be good. However, A has a P/E ratio of 20 and a growth rate of 25 percent, while B has a P/E of 4 and a growth rate of 5 percent. These are clearly two very different firms, with one experiencing very high growth while the other is not. Lumping them in the same category may be tantamount to mixing apples and oranges.

VALUATION OF A BUSINESS WITH NO EARNINGS

Many start-ups lose money or have negative cash flows in their formative years, making it difficult to depend on earnings as a predictor of future cash flows. Since earnings themselves have their own predictors, we can use such predictors as proxies for earnings. These proxies include revenues, contribution margins, market share, and revenue share growth. Beyond that, we can also use measures of a firm's resources.

Profitability-Prediction Measures

Several **profitability-prediction measures** provide estimates of market value. They include the price-revenues ratio, contribution margin, and market share growth.

The **price-revenues ratio** or **revenue multiple** has been used to value businesses that generate revenues but not positive earnings. Value is estimated using the same procedures that are used to obtain value from the P/E ratio, but with revenues substituted for earnings. Just as PEG is used to adjust P/E for growth, a price-revenues-growth ratio can be used to adjust the price-revenues ratio for growth. Using the price-revenues-growth ratio is similar to using PEG. The primary shortcoming of using revenue multiples to value firms is that revenues are not always reflective of earnings. Using revenues leaves out the other critical component of earnings: cost. The revenues ratios should be adjusted for differences in cost structures.

Contribution margin and market share growth are predictors of profitability and have also been used to value firms. Recall that the contribution margin is the excess of revenues over variable costs that goes to cover fixed costs. A firm with negative earnings that has a high contribution margin and a high revenue market share growth rate potentially can have very high earnings in the future. This is because as its market share increases, it can cover more of its fixed costs. Once the fixed costs have been covered, the part of the contribution margin that went to cover fixed costs can now become profits. Thus, when combined, contribution margin and revenue market share growth can be good predictors of profitability and can be used in place of earnings to value a firm that is not yet profitable.

Critical Intangible Resources

Sometimes, there is a need to value a firm before it has produced any product. In that case, valuing the firm goes deeper than contribution margins, market growth rates, and revenues since the firm does not yet have any of these. In such a case, one can use measures of resources that industry analysts believe can lead to future profits. These are intangible assets and include intellectual property and human capital. In valuing a biotech start-up, for example, the number of important patents and reputable scientists with PhDs has been used to proxy future revenues.

VALUATION OF PROJECTS

One of the things that a firm must do to generate large-enough cash flows for its stock to be highly valued is invest in the right projects. Investing in the wrong projects has two bad effects. First, it wastes the initial investment in the project and may result in a loss of money with each unit of product sold if products from the project cannot even cover their variable costs. Second, by tying up money in a bad project, a firm may be forgoing outstanding projects that the money could have been used to sponsor. Thus, being able to choose the right project in which to invest can be critical. To commit funds to a project, management usually has to convince itself that the project is financially viable. One way to determine the financial viability of a project is to perform a **net present value (NPV) analysis.** First, the present value (PV) of the stream of cash outflows that are required to perform the activities of the project, and thus create, offer, and appropriate customer value, is calculated. Next, the PV of the expected cash generated (the cash inflows) by the value created is calculated. Management invests in the project if the present value of the cash generated is greater than that of cash outflows. In other words, if the present value of cash inflows exceeds the present value of cash outflows—that is, the net present value is positive—management can invest in the project.[3]

Discounted Cash Flows

A popular means for performing NPV analysis is the **discounted cash flow (DCF) model** shown in Equation 11.6. Expected cash flows, $E[C_t]$, for each period, t, are discounted back to the present using an appropriate discount rate, r_k, at each of the n periods:

$$PV = \sum_{t=0}^{t=n} \frac{E[C_t]}{(1 + r_k)^t} = C_0 + \frac{C_1}{(1 + r_k)} + \frac{C_2}{(1 + r_k)^2} + \frac{C_3}{(1 + r_k)^3} + \cdots \frac{C_n}{(1 + r_k)^n} \textbf{(11.6)}$$

This relationship for valuing a project is very similar to the one for valuing a firm that we explored in Equation 11.1. The discount rate, r_k, is the opportunity cost of capital for the project in question. It is the expected rate of return that the firm could earn from investing the money in another project of similar risk. It reflects the systematic risk—that is, risk that is specific to the project and therefore difficult to diversify by undertaking many projects of different risks.

As was the case with the relation for valuing a firm, the discount rate can also be estimated using the CAPM:

$$r_k = r_f + \beta_i(r_m - r_f)$$

In applying the CAPM to projects, however, the beta of similar projects (within or outside the firm) is used. Often, the beta of a specific project is difficult to measure, making it difficult to estimate the discount rate. Some firms proxy the discount rate with the *weighted average cost of capital (WACC)*—that is, the average of the discount rates of the firm's projects. This is a good approximation if the company's projects have similar betas.

Discounted Cash Flow and Business Models

For many reasons, DCF may not be a good tool for deciding whether or not to pursue business model projects that embody high uncertainty. First, DCF neglects the immense role that management plays in making strategic decisions as projects evolve and the uncertainty that underpins value-adding activities decreases. One reason DCF valuation is inappropriate for projects with high uncertainty is that it was designed for a different purpose.[4] It was developed for securities such as bonds and stocks. Investors in these securities are passive in that there is rarely much that they can do to improve the interest rate they get on bonds or the dividends they get on stocks. Thus applying DCF to a business model project assumes that management is going to be passive. But managers for most projects are anything but passive. They are constantly making decisions as technological and market uncertainties decrease, and they take advantage of the various options that come up as the uncertainty decreases. Following invention, they may decide, for example, that the invention is easy to imitate, and they may therefore recommend that their firm team up with another firm that has the necessary complementary assets rather than develop the assets internally as previously planned. Such a decision would change the project's risk and therefore its discount rate. But DCF assumes a constant discount rate.

Second, many projects, especially those that rest on radical or disruptive change, have no existing or past projects whose betas can be used as a substitute for estimating the systematic risk.[5] In the late 1970s and early 1980s, for instance, how could Apple determine what a good beta was for its personal computer projects? Using the betas from mainframe computer projects at IBM or minicomputer projects at DEC would have been a mistake since the PC business turned out to be very different from the minicomputer and mainframe computer businesses. Many of the projects undertaken during the Internet boom were not like any previous projects. For example, eBay's online auction projects have a lot to do with building a brand and an online community that can trade 24 hours per day. This is very different from the projects of a bricks-and-mortar auction house, where the focus is on inviting people to show up at a specific place and time for an auction at which individuals shout out prices. Even for incumbents who have pursued projects before, using a weighted cost of capital may not be a good idea if the new project is radically different from the firm's previous ones. Ford's fuel-cell car projects are not likely to have the same risks as its internal combustion engine car projects.

Third, the terminal value—the value of assets at the end of the period over which cash flows are discounted—is assumed to be zero. However, the value of many intangible assets such as copyrights, stocks of knowledge, and brands do not disappear at the terminal period. Moreover, some intangibles such as brands actually grow in value with time. Fourth, many intangible assets that can be extended to other applications or other markets where they can generate cash are not considered in DCF. A pharmaceutical company's sales force that is established to sell hypertension medication to cardiologists can also sell cholesterol drugs later when the firm has discovered one or formed an alliance with a company that has developed one.

Fifth, DCF does not take into consideration the consequences for the rest of the firm's business model of not pursuing a project. If a firm gave up research on liquid crystal display (LCD) technology in the 1970s because the project did not meet the firm's DCF criteria for producing calculators, what would happen down the line if other applications, such as notebook and desktop computers, need LCDs? Would the firm have the capabilities to compete in the new market? Sixth, DCF assumes that investments are reversible or, if irreversible, that the decision to invest is a now or never decision. Again, this is an artifact of the fact that DCF was designed for bonds and stocks, most of which can be resold. Unfortunately, cash outlays for many projects are sunk. Moreover, if a firm invests in R&D today, it does not have to invest in the manufacturing plant and marketing right away. The firm can wait until the outcome of the R&D is known.

Options Approach

Many of the shortcomings of DCF as an evaluation tool for business model projects with high uncertainty can be avoided by using an options approach. In an **options approach**, an investor makes an initial investment (buys an option) which gives the investor the right to decide later—when some of the underpinning uncertainty has been reduced—whether to invest more (exercise the option) or cut the losses incurred so far and not invest anymore (let the option expire). To explore how managers can use the options approach to decide whether to undertake projects or not, let us start with an explanation of what we mean by an option.

We will concentrate on the **call option** since it is the most relevant for our purposes. Suppose you believe that company A's stock, which presently sells for $50, will be selling for $100 five months from today. If you have the money, or can borrow it, to buy the stock, you can buy many shares of A and double your money in only five months. Rather than buy the stocks outright, you could buy a call option on the stock. That is, for a specific amount of money, you can obtain the right, but not the obligation, to buy a specific number of shares of A's stock at a specific price called the **strike price** (say, $60 in our example) on a specific date. If, on that date, the market price of the stock is $100, as you hoped, or even just slightly higher than the $60 price specified in the option contract, you can *exercise* the contract by buying the stock at the strike price of $60 and then sell it right away at its higher market price. If you were wrong in thinking that A's stock would perform well and, for some reason, its market value dropped below the $60 strike price to about $20, you can allow the contract to *expire* and limit your losses to just the option price, the amount that you originally paid for the right to buy the stock.

Some of the elements of a call option are shown in Figure 11.1. At $t = 0$, the option purchase date, you pay a price—the **option price, P_o**—for the right, but not the obligation, to buy shares at the *exercise price, P_e*, on the exercise date ($t = 1$). Between $t = 0$ and $t = 1$, the price of the stock is a random variable and can take any path. Three of the numerous possible paths are shown in Figure 11.1. If the price of the stock on the exercise date is below the contract price, the price at which you contracted at $t = 0$ to buy, you will lose money if you buy. For example, if the price of the stock took the path that led it to P_1, you do not want to exercise the option to buy the stock since the prevailing price is below the exercise price. However, if the stock's price took the path that led it to a price of P_3 at $t = 1$, you want to buy since the stock is now worth more than the exercise price and you can make money even after taking into consideration the option price, P_o, that you paid originally for the right to buy the stock. If the market value of the stock is P_2, you may still want to buy the stock even though the price is less than the sum of the exercise price and option price. The rationale is that the option price is a sunk cost and therefore a bygone. And bygones are bygones. If you decide not to exercise your option to buy, you are losing out on $P_2 - P_e$.

Now, the question is, What does a call option have to do with financing business model projects? Many of the projects are associated with high uncertainty. Consider an innovation process, for example. It involves both invention and commercialization, both of which usually consist of many steps that each have an uncertain outcome. A manager can invest in the first stage of a project. At the end of the first stage, some of the uncertainties surrounding the innovation are resolved, and more options open up in the second stage. Thus, the manager has a better idea as to whether it is worthwhile continuing with the project and

FIGURE 11.1
Some Elements of a Call Option

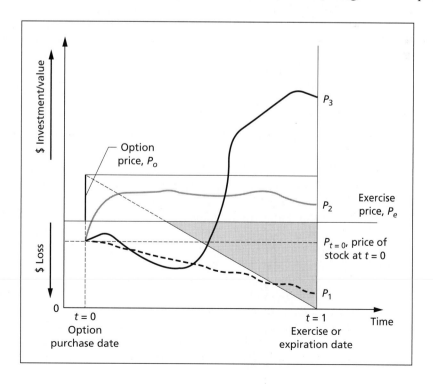

investing in the next stage or not. For example, when Intel invented the microprocessor in 1971, it had no idea that most of the profits from it would come from selling the processor for use in personal computers.

Investing in the first stage of a project is equivalent to buying a call option that gives a firm the right to invest in the second stage. The beginning of the first stage can be seen as the option purchase date and the investment as the option price. Purchasing the call option (investing in the first stage) gives the manager the right to any options that emerge during the activities of that stage: the technical possibilities, the market applications, and competitors' strategies. In Intel's case, one option that emerged after its invention of the microprocessor was the PC market. Investing in the first stage creates more options for a firm. At the end of that stage, the manager can decide whether to invest in the next stage or not. More important, she or he can decide which of the different opportunities that have opened up to invest in. Investing in the next stage is tantamount to exercising the *call option*. Not investing is letting the *call expire*. Investing in the second stage is equivalent to buying a call option for the right to invest in the third stage. At the end of the second stage, the manager can then determine whether to invest in the third, and so on. The downside is limited to the costs incurred in the first stage(s).

Options versus DCF as an Innovation Tool

The option characteristics we have explored suggest that firms with business model projects that are associated with high uncertainty are better off using the options approach for evaluating the financial viability of their projects. Most business model projects that involve innovation require attention from management and decision making at the various stages of the innovation process. The options approach facilitates these requirements; the DCF method does not. Many investments in innovation, such as R&D expenses, investment in a state-of-the-art semiconductor plant, or advertising for a particular drug, are sunk costs. The options approach assumes they are; DCF assumes they are not. DCF uses very high discounts when uncertainty is high, thereby resulting in lower NPVs. This suggests that the higher the uncertainty associated with a project, the less the firm should invest in the project. In contrast, the options approach views uncertainty as an opportunity for creating more value. With options, the higher the uncertainty, the greater the number of options and therefore the more the firm should think about investing.

The options approach allows managers to capture the value of resources developed at different stages of the innovation process.[6] If after invention, for example, a manager discovers that it will cost too much to commercialize the invention, he or she may decide not to invest in the commercialization. But the firm will have acquired some competences during the invention process that it can use later in other inventions. Thus, even if a pharmaceutical firm discovers a new chemical compound with little therapeutic value and decides not to pursue FDA approval for the drug, the firm may not have wasted the investment in the discovery. It has learned more about drug discovery. It has also taken a patent on the drug that it can license out to other firms. In addition, the compound may turn out to have some other therapeutic value that was not anticipated at the beginning of the discovery. Rogaine, which is used to treat male pattern baldness, was originally meant to be a drug to treat high blood pressure but it failed in that respect. DCF would not capture such effects since it calculates NPV only on the basis of cash flows.

The real options approach has one major disadvantage. Since a firm cannot invest in the next stage until the outcome of the previous one has been determined, it is difficult to take advantage of concurrent methods to speed the development and launch processes of a new product. Consider the case of a product for which the design takes two years and building the manufacturing plant takes one year. If building could start while the design is still under way, the manufacturing plant could be ready by the time the design is done. The options method requires that investing in the manufacturing plant cannot start until the outcome of the design has been determined. Waiting for the outcome of the design could delay the project by as much as a year.

The Real Options Price

An important question that we have not explored yet is, What should the price of an option be? How much should you pay today for the right, but not the obligation, to buy A's stock five months from now? In **real options** terms, how much should you invest in R&D for the right, but not the obligation, to commercialize whatever invention or discovery comes out of the R&D? The question of what a financial option is worth was answered by Fisher Black, Myrone Scholes, and Robert Merton. They determined the value of an option and expressed it in the now-famous Black-Scholes formula:

$$V_o = A\,N(d_1) - [Xe^{-r_f T}N(d_2)] \qquad \textbf{(11.7)}$$

where V_o = value of the option

X = exercise price of the option

A = value of the underlying asset

T = time to maturity

r_f = risk-free rate

$$d_1 = \frac{\ln(A/X) + r_f T}{s\sqrt{T}} + \frac{1}{2}s\sqrt{T}$$

$$d_2 = d_1 - s\sqrt{T}$$

where S^2 = variance in the price of the underlying asset

$N(d_1)$ = cumulative area of d_1 in a normal distribution

$N(d_2)$ = cumulative area of d_2 in a normal distribution

Since these variables are not as easily quantifiable in real options as they are in financial options, we use the formula here only as a guide to tell us which variables are important and whether they tend to increase or decrease the **option value**. First, the higher the value of the underlying asset at $t = 0$, the higher the value of the option will be. Second, the higher the exercise price, the lower the value of the option. That is, after a firm has invested in R&D, it would prefer not to invest heavily in manufacturing and marketing. Third, the higher the interest rate, the higher the value of the option. Fourth, the further the exercise date is from the option purchase date, the higher the valuation of the call option. Finally, the more volatile the underlying asset, the higher the valuation of the option.

Illustration of DCF and Options Approaches

The example below illustrates some of the differences between the DCF and the options approaches to evaluating business model projects.

Example

A firm is considering a project to design a revolutionary new cell phone microchip that recharges the battery using motion and sound from the cell phone user and solar energy. The chip uses new materials and is so good that cell phone batteries hardly ever have to be charged. Because of the revolutionary nature of the design and the types of materials required, the uncertainty about whether the chip will work or not is very high. There is also a lot of uncertainty as to how well received the product will be, whether to advertise it directly to the consumers who buy cell phones rather than to the makers of cell phones, who will be the ones to adopt the microchip for use in the phones they build.

The decision tree for the microchip and associated outcomes is shown in Figure 11.2. In the first stage, the firm has the choice of investing in the project or opting out. It costs $400 million to develop the product. With this investment, there is a 20 percent chance of an "excellent" outcome in that the chip will be the killer application that the company envisions. The project has a 50 percent chance of a good outcome in that the chip will reduce the need to charge the battery to about once a week instead of the targeted once a month. There is also a 30 percent chance that the design will fail. After the R&D process, the microchip must be manufactured and marketed. Building the state-of-the-art plant and marketing the chip will cost $1.5 billion. The payoff can be anything from $6 billion to −$6 billion, as shown in Figure 11.2.

DCF Approach: Using DCF, we can determine the NPV by taking into consideration the R&D and market uncertainties with the assumption that once the decision to invest in R&D has been made, the firm must commercialize the product. The R&D uncertainties are accounted for by the 0.5 probability, and marketing uncertainties by the 0.3 and 0.7 probabilities. In millions of dollars,

FIGURE 11.2
Cell Phone Chip Project

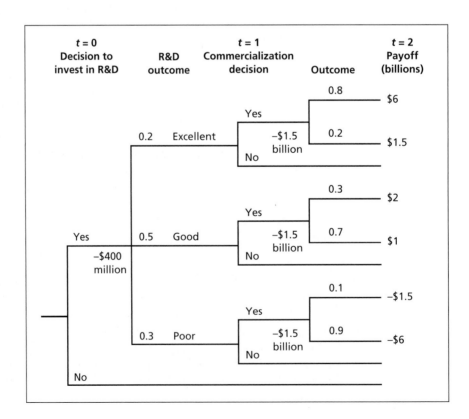

$$NPV = -400 - \frac{0.5 \times 1,500}{1 + 0.15} + \frac{0.5(0.3 \times 2,000 + 0.7 \times 1,000)}{(1 + 0.15)^2} = -561$$

Options Approach: In the options approach, the microchip firm sees the investment in R&D only as a call option that allows it to see what its alternatives at the end of that stage are. If the design works, the firm can proceed with building the plant and marketing. The firm can proceed only if the outcome is "excellent." No money is invested in the manufacturing plant or marketing until the outcome of the design is determined. Thus, the "excellent" path in Figure 11.2 is taken:

$$NPV = -400 - \frac{0.2 \times 1,500}{1 + 0.15} + \frac{0.2(0.8 \times 6,000 + 0.2 \times 1,500)}{(1 + 0.15)^2} = 110$$

Using the options method, the NPV is positive at $110 million, whereas using DCF, the NPV is negative at −$561 million.

SOURCES OF FINANCING

We explore below five sources of money for financing a business: retained earnings, working capital, debt, equity, and strategic collaboration.

Retained Earnings

A firm can do one of two things with the after-tax profits that it generates: It can pay them to shareholders in the form of dividends, or it can hold them back as **retained earnings** to be reinvested in the business. Since retained earnings can be used to finance more activities, a firm with a profitable business model does not have to seek outside financing.[7] By 2003, Microsoft had accumulated over $40 billion in cash or cash equivalents from all the earnings it had retained over its many profitable years. One view of finance argues that, rather than retaining profits to finance new activities, a firm should pay all after-tax profits as dividends to shareholders and let them decide where to invest their money. The assumption is that all investors are efficient at finding the right investment opportunities. There are two counterarguments to this view. First, as of 2003, dividends were taxed, and so the shareholder would be taxed twice on these funds (first as corporate earnings when the company's income is taxed and then as dividends when the individual's income is taxed). Moreover, small investors must pay transaction costs whenever they buy new stocks or bonds. For example, each time an individual receives dividends and wants to reinvest them, he or she has to pay a commission to buy stock or other assets. Second, if a company is making a great deal of money, the chances are that it will be difficult for an individual investor to find better investment opportunities than the one already paying the large dividends.

Strategic Implications

The extent to which a firm can earn profits and therefore have the option to use retained earnings to finance its activities is a function of the profitability of its business model. And the profitability of a firm's business model is a function of the extent to which the activities which the firm performs, how it performs them, and when it performs them enable the firm to offer superior customer value and be in a position to appropriate the value. Thus, only firms that have profitable business models have the option to use retained earnings as a source of financing.

Working Capital

A firm's **working capital** is its current assets minus current liabilities. *Current assets* are assets that can easily be converted into cash within a year. They include marketable securities, accounts receivable, inventories, and prepaid expenses as well as cash and cash equivalents. *Current liabilities* are liabilities such as short-term debt, accounts payable, and accrued liabilities that must be paid within a year. Working capital is a good source of financing for a firm if the firm can find a way to collect its accounts receivable from customers early but pay its creditors much later. It can use the money that it collects from customers to finance its activities during the period between the time it collects the cash and the time it pays suppliers. Also, by keeping its inventories low, a firm can use the money that would have been tied up in inventories to finance its activities. Both approaches are used by Dell Computer. Most customers who use the company's build-to-order system pay Dell when they place their computer orders. Dell collects the payments right away but does not have to pay the suppliers of the components that will go into the computers until much later. Because Dell builds the computers very quickly, it saves on inventories, thereby allowing the funds that would have been tied up in inventory to be used for financing other activities.

Strategic Implications

A firm's working capital and the extent to which it can be used as a source of financing is a function of the firm's position relative to its coopetitors and of the payment practices in its industry. To induce customers to pay right away for a product that they will receive later, a firm must offer them something that competitors do not or must have some power over them. To delay payments over and beyond industry standard times, a firm must have some kind of power over suppliers.

Debt

A firm can borrow money from a money-lending institution such as a bank or sell bonds or notes to raise money. In return for the money, the lender receives interest payments. Many lenders require some form of physical assets as collateral. **Debt financing** has several advantages.[8] First, in the United States and other countries, tax laws allow interest paid on debt to be deducted from a firm's income. Retained earnings and dividends do not enjoy such a break, and thus debt financing has an advantage over equity financing in this respect. The tax break means that debt financing will result in higher after-tax earnings and therefore higher valuation. The downside is that since lenders must pay higher tax rates because of the interest income they receive, they factor their higher taxes into the interest rates they demand; as a result, borrowers pay higher interest rates on debt.[9] If the capital gain tax and personal income tax rates are the same, however, the first advantage of debt financing holds. The second advantage of debt financing is that it forces management to be more prudent in spending and therefore create value more efficiently. The reasoning behind this concept is this: If a firm has equity rather than debt financing, the earnings that would have gone to pay interest will either be paid out as dividends to shareholders or be held back as retained earnings. If management has the retained earnings, it may decide to use them for projects that the company really does not need, wasting the money. CEOs have been known to use such free cash to buy company jets and other non-value-adding "toys." Under debt financing, since the firm is obliged to make interest payments, managers have fewer slack resources and are therefore more efficient in creating value.

The main disadvantage of debt is that if debt becomes too high, a firm may find itself in **financial distress**—the situation in which it cannot make the interest and principal payments on its debt. As a result, the firm may be forced to restructure its finances or declare bankruptcy. Either case can be very costly, possibly even resulting in the demise of the firm. It is very difficult for financially distressed firms to find new management talent, financing for new activities, and good suppliers and customers. In addition, financial distress may lead to haggling between shareholders and creditors that can end up in the courts, costing the company even more money.

Strategic Implications

Debt can be a good thing where the tax rates permit. But like most things in life, too much debt is not good. In formulating and executing a business model, it is important to keep an eye on tax rates and on how much debt is too much for a firm given the industry and country. Usually, a firm with a good business model should be able to generate enough cash to service its debts, but too much debt can stifle a company's efforts to deliver superior value, even when the firm has a viable business model.

Equity

A popular way of financing a business model is through equity. In **equity financing,** shares of a firm are sold to investors in return for money. Each investor is then entitled to a share of the firm's earnings that is proportional to his or her share of the company. There are two primary forms of equity: public and private (Figure 11.3).

Public Equity

In public equity, stocks are issued to the public via a stock exchange such as the New York Stock Exchange. When a firm issues public equity for the first time, it does so through an *initial public offering (IPO)*. In an IPO, anyone can buy shares of the company and, in return, is entitled to a share of the company's future free cash flows that is proportional to the percentage of shares outstanding that the person owns. A firm that already has shares outstanding can issue more shares to the public to raise money. Doing so dilutes the value of the shares since any earnings to be shared among shareholders must now be shared among more shareholders.

FIGURE 11.3
Types of Equity

Source: A. N. Afuah,
*Innovation Management:
Strategies, Implementation,
and Profits* (New York:
Oxford University Press,
1998).

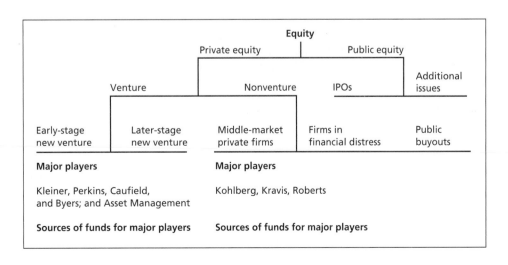

Private Equity

There are two major forms of private equity: venture and nonventure (Figure 11.3). *Venture equity* is usually issued by start-ups (new ventures) in the early or later stages of their life cycles. For part ownership of the venture, a venture capital firm or other financier can offer financing. Financing terms vary considerably. For example, financing can be in the form of debt that is convertible into equity. *Nonventure equity* is usually issued by three types of firms: private firms that want to raise money but want to remain private, firms experiencing financial difficulties, or groups that want to buy out other firms. In the United States, major players in this area include buyout groups such as Kohlberg, Kravis, Roberts (KKR).

The money used in private equity financing comes from a network of investors. The relationship between this network and issuers of private equity is shown in Figure 11.4.

Issuers Issuers of private equity include new ventures, middle-market private firms, and public firms.[10] New ventures that are not ready to go public and do not have the collateral assets, reputation, or cash flow that lenders typically require turn to the private equity markets, usually to venture capital firms or to "angels," private individuals who have money to invest in risky ventures. A middle-market private firm that needs money to expand, change its capital structure, or change ownership can also issue private equity. Private equity is not limited to private companies and new ventures. Public firms that want to go private—via, for example, a management or leveraged buyout—can also issue private equity. So can public companies that are in distress.

FIGURE 11.4 **Organized Private Equity Market**

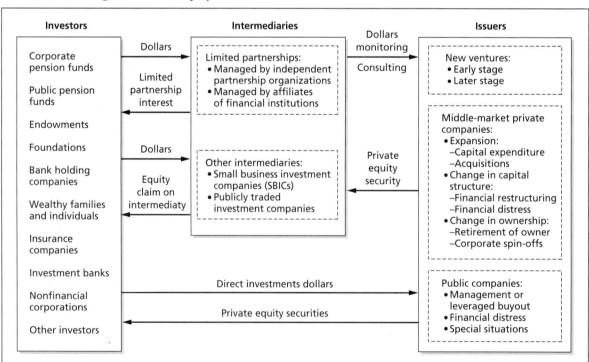

Source: Adapted from G. W. Fenn, N. Liang, and S. Prowse, "The Economics of Private Equity," Board of Governors of the Federal Reserve System, Washington, DC, December 1995.

Investors Investors are often organizations that have diversified investment portfolios and therefore can afford to invest part of their portfolios in very risky ventures. Some investors, the so-called angels, are individuals. The list of investors includes both public and private pension funds, foundations, investment banks, insurance companies, and wealthy families and individuals. Because these investors are often not very conversant with the knowledge that underpins the ventures or firms they are backing, they usually depend on intermediaries.

Intermediaries Intermediaries are venture capital firms and other investors that work directly with the issuers of equity. They usually specialize by industry, market, location, type of investments, and, sometimes, type of technology that underpins business models. Such expertise puts them in a better position than less knowledgeable investors to evaluate the equity issuer's business model and to monitor execution of the model. The money that they use is usually not theirs; they use money pooled from different investors. Their experience in managing high-risk investments provides them with the expertise and reputation that are critical in convincing investors to entrust them with the investors' money. They usually form limited partnerships with investors, in which the intermediaries serve as general partners responsible for managing the partnerships' investments. They contribute a very small fraction (1 percent in 1994) of the partnerships' total capital, while investors provide the rest. As general partners, intermediaries have unlimited liability. Investors, on the other hand, have limited liability, and therefore, at worst, they can lose their investment.[11] Business plans or other proposals from seekers of financing are first screened using the partners' internal, predetermined criteria. Proposals that survive this phase undergo further screening that includes archival computer searches for information on the investment, consultation with industry experts, and visits to the firm to interview key personnel.

The main advantage of equity financing is that shareholders, unlike creditors, are less likely to force a firm into bankruptcy, so equity financing is less risky in that respect. As we briefly mentioned above, when we discussed the advantages and disadvantages of debt financing, managers of firms with equity financing have more cash to work with since the firms do not have debt to service. These managers may therefore be tempted to use the money inefficiently.

Strategic Collaboration

Firms that seek financing usually need the money to buy assets. If a firm can gain access to the assets without having to buy them, it can eliminate the need for financing. A firm can accomplish this by teaming up with another firm. In the typical case, rather than trying to raise money to acquire assets, a firm that has an invention or discovery but no complementary assets teams up with a firm that has the assets. For example, when Pixar developed its first digital animation movie, *Toy Story I,* it teamed up with the Disney company to have access to Disney's resources in marketing, branding, distribution channels, and animation creativity. At the time, it would have been very difficult for Pixar to raise the amount of money that would have been needed to acquire such tightly held and important complementary assets.

Entrepreneurs and Financing

One of the many challenges that entrepreneurs face is obtaining financing. The primary reason for this predicament is uncertainty. There is usually considerable uncertainty about the activities for which an entrepreneur wants financing. From a financier's point of view, the worries about such uncertainty can be summarized in three questions:

1. Can the activities that the entrepreneur intends to perform actually be performed (by anyone) such that they deliver the type of superior value and profits that the entrepreneur claims they will?
2. If the activities can be performed, is the entrepreneur the one to perform them?
3. What assurances are there that, after getting the money, the entrepreneur will not change his or her mind and perform some other activities rather than the ones he or she contracted to perform?

Venture capital firms use different measures to tackle these problems. First, in specializing by industry, market, location, type of investments, and type of technology that underpins the entrepreneur's business model, a venture capital firm can better evaluate whether activities can be performed as claimed by an entrepreneur. This puts the venture capitalist in a better position to know if the entrepreneur is the one to perform the activities. Second, a venture capitalist finds out as much as possible about the people who will be managing the venture. This, coupled with the venture capitalist's expertise in the activities of the business model, allows the venture capitalist to better determine whether top management has the ability to oversee the activities or not.

Third, venture capitalists use some combination of the following measures to align management's interests with those of the venture capitalist, thereby alleviating problem 3:

- A significant fraction of a manager's compensation can be common shares of the venture, rather than large salaries.
- An "earn-out" arrangement can be instituted whereby managers can increase their share of stock as the venture meets certain performance measures.
- The venture capital firm can be issued convertible preferred stock. The idea here is that since, in the event of liquidation, preferred stockholders are paid before common stockholders, managers (who own common stock) are likely to work harder to make sure that the firm stays liquid.
- Employment contracts can include provisions for penalizing poor performance. Stock ownership incentives usually focus on the upside of performance and may encourage very risky undertakings. Establishing penalties for poor performance guards against that. Contracts can specify, for example, that managers can be replaced under certain conditions and their stocks bought back at a low price if their performance drops below a particular level.
- The venture capital firm can ensure that it is well represented on the board of directors of the firm it finances.
- The venture capital firm can control access to additional capital. This can be done by making sure that any promised funds are not released at once but, rather, are distributed over the life of the venture. Ventures usually get their financing in rounds, and partners can control when and how each round is released.
- Agreements can give partners the right to inspect the company's facilities and records and to receive timely financial reports and operating statements.
- Partners can try to maintain voting control of the firm.

Summary

To carry out the activities of a business model, a firm needs money. To invest in activities, an investor needs to value the activities. The means that have been used to value firms and their activities include free cash flow, price-earnings (P/E) ratio, price-earnings-growth (PEG) ratio, profitability-prediction measures, and intangible assets. No matter which measure is used, it is important to understand the strategic implications of the numbers. To value internal projects, a firm can use the discounted cash flow or options approach. Sources of financing include retained earnings, working capital, debt, equity, and strategic collaboration with coopetitors. Obtaining funds from any of these sources has strategic implications that must be carefully considered before going ahead with the financing. Sometimes, the "cheapest" source of money, as measured by interest payments, is not the best from a strategic point of view.

Key Terms

call option, *220*	market capital, *211*	price-revenues ratio, *217*
capital asset pricing model (CAPM), *212*	market value, *211*	profitability-prediction measures, *217*
capitalization factor, *216*	net present value (NPV) analysis, *218*	real option, *223*
debt financing, *226*	option price, *221*	retained earnings, *225*
discount rate, *212*	option value, *223*	revenue multiple, *217*
discounted cash flow (DCF) model, *218*	options approach, *220*	risk-free rate, *212*
earnings multiple, *216*	present value, *212*	risk premium, *212*
equity financing, *227*	price-earnings-growth (PEG) ratio, *217*	strike price, *220*
financial distress, *227*	price-earnings (P/E) ratio, *216*	systematic risk, *212*
free cash flow, *212*		working capital, *226*

Study Questions

1. Refer to Figure 11.1. Suppose that at $t = 1$, the stock price is between $P_{t=0}$ and P_e. Would you exercise the option to buy shares of A?

2. Why would negative working capital be a good thing?

3. Why might P/E and PEG be misleading?

4. What do we mean when we say that a firm is in financial distress? How does being in financial distress impact a firm's business model?

Endnotes

1. See, for example, R. A. Brealey and S. C. Myers, *Principles of Corporate Finance* (New York: McGraw-Hill, 1995).

2. M. J. Dollinger, *Entrepreneurship: Strategies and Resources* (Burr Ridge, IL: McGraw-Hill, 1995).

3. Net present value (NPV) estimations feature prominently in many finance texts. See, for example, Brealey and Myers, *Principles of Corporate Finance.*

4. Brealey and Myers, *Principles of Corporate Finance.*

5. The disadvantages of DCF outlined here are further explored in A. K. Dixit and R. S. Pindyck, *Investment under Uncertainty* (Princeton, NJ: Princeton University Press, 1994); Brealey and Myers, *Principles of Corporate Finance;* A. K. Naj, "Manager's Journal: In R&D, the Next Best Thing to a Gut Feeling," *The Wall Street Journal,* May 21, 1990.

6. R. McGrath, "Falling Forward: Real Option Reasoning and Entrepreneurial Failure," *Academy of Management Review* 24 (1999), pp. 13–31.

7. Which type of financing is best for a firm and how the firm should go about obtaining that financing are very important topics in corporate finance. See, for example, Brealey and Myers, *Principles of Corporate Finance.*

8. See, for example, K. G. Palepu, P. M. Healey, and V. L. Bernard, *Business Analysis & Valuation: Using Financial Statements* (Cincinnati, OH: South-Western Publishing, 2000).

9. M. Miller, "Debt and Taxes," *Journal of Finance* 32 (1977), pp. 261–276.

10. G. W. Fenn, N. Liang, and S. Prowse, "The Economics of Private Equity," Board of Governors of the Federal Reserve System, Washington, DC, December 1995.

11. Ibid.

Business Model Planning Process

Throughout this book, we have emphasized the fact that the activities which a firm performs, how it performs them, and when it performs them can enable the firm to offer superior customer value and appropriate the value (make money commensurate with the value). An important question that we have not yet explored is, How do firms make decisions about which activities to perform, as well as how and when to perform them, and link these decisions together to form business models or strategies?[1] In other words, what is the process for arriving at decisions and a business model? We explore this question in the first part of this chapter. Then, in the second part, we present a business model planning process that asks three questions: Where is the firm now (as far as its business model is concerned)? Where does the firm go next, and how does it get there? How does the firm implement the decisions to get there? We conclude the chapter with a reminder that a plan for a business model rarely is the result of a grand design that emerges from the office of the CEO; rather, it is usually the result of actions taken over some time by individual managers scattered throughout an organization, with a lot of help from the CEO's office.

BUSINESS MODEL– AND STRATEGY-MAKING PROCESSES

Since business models play such an important role for firms, an interesting question is, What is the process by which firms make the decisions about the activities that add up to a business model or strategy? Professor Henry Mintzberg proposed that the strategy-making processes that firms employ can be divided into three different modes: entrepreneurial, adaptive, and planning (Figure 12.1).[2]

Entrepreneurial Mode

In the **entrepreneurial mode** of strategy making and business model making, an organization focuses on identifying and pursuing opportunities, relegating problems to second place (Figure 12.1).[3] The organization's dominant goal is growth. The firm uses resources to actively pursue opportunities rather than passively waiting for problems to solve. Power is concentrated in the hands of one person, sometimes called the *entrepreneur,* who seeks out conditions of uncertainty in which his or her organization can make large gains. For example, he or she would rather go after technological discontinuities that can yield vast improvements

FIGURE 12.1
Strategy-Making Processes: Characteristics and Conditions

Source: H. Mintzberg, "Strategy Making in Three Modes," *California Management Review* 16 (Winter 1973), p. 49.

Characteristic	Strategy-Making Role		
	Entrepreneurial	Adaptive	Planning
Path of model	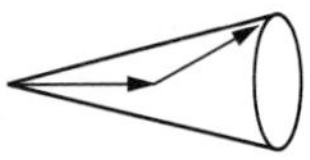	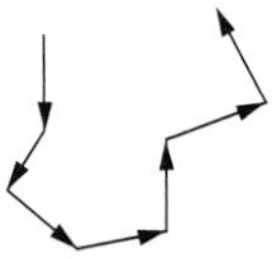	
Motive for decision	Proactive	Reactive	Proactive and reactive
Goals of organization	Growth	Indeterminate	Efficiency and growth
Evaluation of proposals	Judgmental	Judgmental	Analytical
Choices made by	Entrepreneur	Bargaining	Management
Decision horizon	Long term	Short term	Long term
Preferred environment	Uncertainty	Certainty	Risk
Decision linkages	Loosely coupled	Disjointed	Integrated
Flexibility of modes	Flexible	Adaptive	Constrained
Size of moves	Bold decisions	Incremental steps	Global strategies
Vision of direction	General	None	Specific
Condition of Use			
Source of power	Entrepreneur	Divided	Management
Objectives of organization	Operational	Nonoperational	Operational
Organizational environment	Yielding	Complex, dynamic	Predictable, stable
Status of organization	Young, small, or strong leadership	Established	Large

over existing technologies than go after incremental technological changes that yield minor gains. The environment that suits the entrepreneurial mode is one that the entrepreneur has control over. The business model that emerges is usually a reflection of the top manager or entrepreneur.

The entrepreneurial mode is therefore best for organizations such as start-ups that are young, small, and growth-oriented and have a very small amount of sunk costs. Organizations that are in trouble sometimes use the entrepreneurial mode for business model making since they have little choice other than to make large, bold moves in the attempt to get themselves out of trouble.

Adaptive Mode

In the **adaptive mode** of strategy and business model making, the firm has no clear goals and no one powerful person is in charge (Figure 12.1).[4] Rather, different powerful stakeholders (shareholders, top management, governments, unions, employees, and coopetitors) pull the firm in different directions, with each force having its own goals in mind. There is bargaining between groups, with different groups losing on some issues and winning on others. The bargaining can also be between functional managers who head departments within the firm. Rather than seeking opportunities to make big leaps, as an organization in the entrepreneurial mode would do, an organization in the adaptive mode is tied up reacting to problems. Because there are no clear goals and the organization reacts to problems, strategy and business model making is likely to be fragmented.

The adaptive mode is best for complex and dynamic environments. The business model of a firm that is in the adaptive mode usually emerges from the interaction of different actors and not from a grand design that came out of the CEO's office years earlier.

Planning Mode

An organization in the **planning mode** of strategy and business model making systematically pursues goals that are explicitly expressed in quantitative terms. Different scenarios for attaining the stated goals are systematically analyzed, with the benefits of each scenario carefully weighed against its costs. Developing the plan is largely the responsibility of an analyst who works with management. Such an analyst has the time and talent for the analysis, both of which the CEO usually does not have. Attention is given not only to the decisions and how they relate to attaining stated goals but also to the linkages between the goals. Effectively, all the major decisions that underpin a business model and the linkages between the decisions are designed at a specific point in time. Thus, the activities which a firm performs, how it performs them, and when it performs them are indicated by the analysis.

The planning mode is best in stable, predictable environments where goals can be stated in numbers. The firm must be large enough to afford the costs associated with formal strategic planning.

Combined Modes

Most organizations use combinations of the three modes. Different functional units within the same organization can have different decision-making modes. For example, the R&D department of a pharmaceutical company may employ the entrepreneurial mode, whereby the head of R&D has all the power as to pursuing R&D and setting the department's goals. At the same time, the company's marketing and manufacturing departments may use the planning mode since the market for most drugs and the technology for manufacturing them are relatively predictable.

The modes utilized can also vary over time. Consider the technology life cycle. As a technology evolves, the modes that firms use for business model and strategy making may also have to change. In the fluid phase, when there is still much uncertainty and many opportunities to make big leaps with the new technology, the entrepreneurial mode is probably best. In the transition state, when a dominant design is about to emerge, power is distributed among the different firms with competing technologies and the lead users, so the adaptive mode might be best. In the stable phase, when changes in the underpinning technology are incremental and the behavior of competitors, customers, suppliers, and other stakeholders is more predictable, the planning mode may be best.

Different divisions within a firm can also operate in different modes. For example, in 1980, when IBM decided to enter the personal computer business, it formed a separate unit whose orientation was more entrepreneurial than that of the mainframe and minicomputer divisions, which had more predictable markets and therefore utilized the planning mode.

BUSINESS MODEL PLANNING PROCESS

As we saw in Chapter 8, change is one thing that we can count on. Every business model, sooner or later, will face change. At some point, either the technology on which the business model rests will change, competitors will change their own business models, customer needs and expectations will change, or something in the overarching environment in which a firm is operating will change. Thus, irrespective of the business model– or strategy-making mode that a firm uses, it may be a good idea to periodically take a look at the business model by asking three very simple but important questions (Figure 12.2): Where is the firm now (as far as its business model is concerned)? Where does the firm go next, and how does it get there? How does the firm implement these decisions? We will call an exploration of these three questions a **business model planning process.**

Where Is the Firm Now?

The first step in a firm's business model planning process is to answer the question "Where is the firm now?" Determining the answer to this comprehensive question involves answering three other questions: (1) How well is the firm performing? (2) What is it about its business model that enables the firm to perform the way it has been performing? (3) Has anything changed that is a cause for concern or an opportunity to exploit?

Performance

Since a business model is a framework for making money, profitability measures can be used to assess how well a firm is performing. These include cash flow, earnings per share, economic value added (EVA), return on assets, and return on equity. Since profit margins, market share, and revenue growth can be indicators of profits, especially when a firm is in a young but growing market, these three can also be used to measure how well a firm is performing.

FIGURE 12.2
Business Model Planning Process

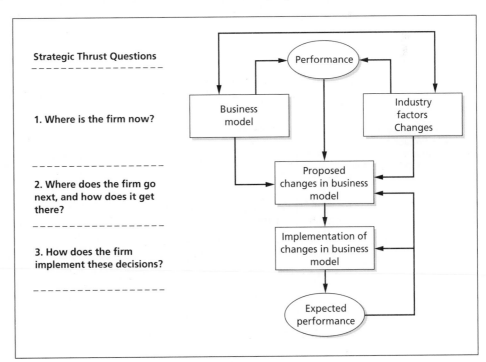

Strategic Thrust Questions

1. Where is the firm now?

2. Where does the firm go next, and how does it get there?

3. How does the firm implement these decisions?

Performance

Business model

Industry factors Changes

Proposed changes in business model

Implementation of changes in business model

Expected performance

Business Model

After determining performance, the next task is to find out what makes the firm perform well or not perform well. The question here—what it is about a firm's business model that makes the firm perform the way it has been performing—is what Chapter 10 was all about. Figure 10.2, which is reproduced here as Figure 12.3, summarizes the key points in that chapter that are relevant to this discussion.

Industry Environment and Change

Next, the firm scans both the competitive and macro environments to see if there is any change that threatens the firm or that offers it an opportunity to exploit.

Where Does the Firm Go Next, and How Does It Get There?

From an analysis of its performance, its business model, and industry factors and change, a firm can determine the weaknesses and strengths of its business model and the threats and opportunities of its environment. On the basis of these facts, the firm must determine where to go next and how to get there.

FIGURE 12.3   **Key Elements of the Seven C's**

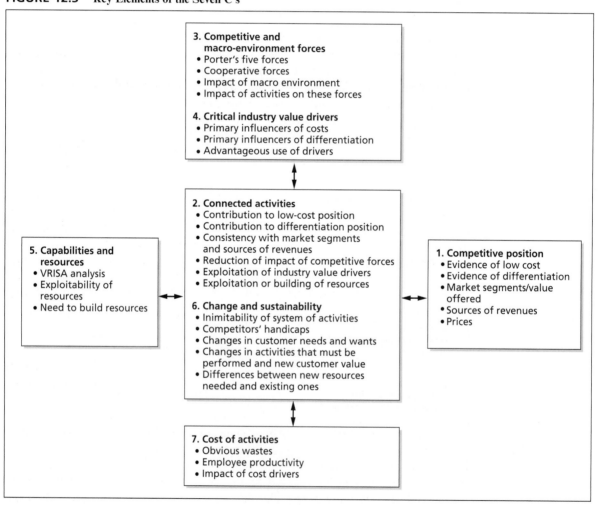

Where Does the Firm Go Next?

Where a firm decides to go next is a function of many factors, including the opportunities and threats that the performance analysis exposes and the strengths and weaknesses of the firm's business model. In particular, it is a function of (1) the extent to which the firm's resources and system of activities can be extended to exploit new market opportunities for offering and appropriating superior customer value or to defend against new threats uncovered in the analysis and (2) the extent to which a new system of activities or resources can be built so as to exploit new market opportunities or defend against new threats.

How Does the Firm Get There?

If a firm wants to use its existing system of activities or resources to exploit new opportunities, it may need complementary assets. To obtain these assets, the firm can either develop them internally or team up with a firm that has them. Which approach it chooses, as we saw in Chapters 6 and 8, is a function of the type of change that prompts the firm to alter its business model. The more unfamiliar the change, the more a firm may want to think about teaming up. Teaming up can involve a strategic alliance, joint venture, venture capital investment, or acquisition.

How Does the Firm Implement These Decisions?

Deciding where a firm should go and how to get there is one thing. Implementing these decisions is another. As we saw in Chapter 7, a firm needs the right strategy, structure, systems, people, and environment (S^3PE) to successfully implement changes in a business model. To pursue the right S^3PE fit, it is important for the firm to understand the following pitfalls that can stand in the way of any firm that faces change.

Dominant Managerial Logic

Recall that in a relatively stable environment, dominant managerial logic can be a good thing: Managers with the same managerial logic have the same beliefs, biases, and assumptions about the market their firm serves, whom to hire, what technology to use to compete, who the firm's competitors are, and how to develop and execute a business model.[5] However, if change requires that a firm perform a relatively different system of activities that necessitates different assumptions about the underpinning technology and market, a firm's dominant managerial logic may prevent the firm from effectively executing changes in its business model. Given their old ways of thinking, managers may have the tendency to think and act as if the situation were business as usual and may fight to maintain the status quo.[6]

Competency Trap

If a change in a business model requires new resources, there are two reasons that existing resources may act as a handicap to acquiring and using new ones. First, if existing resources are sunk investments, calculations of the cost of investing in new resources versus the cost of staying with existing ones will show that staying with existing resources is a cost advantage.[7] Second, the new resources and capabilities needed may be very different from existing resources and involve skills, knowledge, and routines that require *un*learning old ways of doing things.[8] Anyone who has had to break old personal habits or routines, especially those that have been practiced over a long period and have served him or her well, knows how difficult it is to unlearn old ways of doing things. This difficulty is known as the **competency trap.**

Fear of Cannibalization and Loss of Revenue

If changes required in a business model mean having to cannibalize existing revenue streams, a firm may hesitate to invest in the changes. This can make it more difficult to implement the changes.

Political Power

If a firm's top management consists of different political coalitions, each one formed to protect and enhance its vested interests,[9] some factions may want the changes in the business model while others may not. If changes are going to destroy the power of the power elite in a firm, the elite may work hard to impede adoption of the changes.[10]

Coopetitor Power

Coopetitor power can be a significant pitfall for a firm attempting to implement change. If coopetitors have power over a firm, they may delay changes in the firm's business model if such changes would alter their own business models in ways that they do not like. For example, if changes in a business model require that the firm offer a new product that its existing major customers do not want, the firm is unlikely to invest heavily in the new technology even though there may be new applications for the new product.[11]

BUSINESS PLAN

For many businesses, especially start-ups, one result of the business model planning process is a business plan. A firm's **business plan** is a reflection of the firm's business model at a point in time and spells out how the firm plans to make money. Table 12.1 summarizes the key elements of a business plan. Most of these elements follow from the seven C's of Figure 12.2.

Competitive Position

A firm's business plan should start with a clear statement of what it is that the firm intends to offer customers that competitors do not. If the value that the firm intends to offer is differentiation, the firm should clearly state what the differentiation benefits to customers will be. The firm should also clearly outline the market segments that it intends to target and the value that each segment can expect. This information should be followed by a statement on the firm's expected sources of revenues and relative positioning vis-à-vis its coopetitors. Finally, the firm should outline its pricing strategies.

Connected Activities

Since a firm can attain the right positions only by performing the right activities at the right times, a firm's business plan must spell out the activities that the firm performs or intends to perform. If the firm's plan is to offer lower-cost products than competitors do, the firm should clearly outline the system of activities that it will perform to allow it to offer the lower-cost products. If the plan is to offer differentiated products, the firm should clearly show how the system of activities that it intends to perform will:

1. Result in customer value (low cost and differentiation).
2. Be consistent with the market segments and sources of revenues that the firm targets.

TABLE 12.1 Elements of a Business Plan

1. Competitive position	a. What is the firm's value proposition? What does the firm offer its customers that competitors cannot or that is superior to what competitors can offer?
	b. What market segments does the firm offer value to, and what is the range of products that the firm offers to each segment?
	c. What are the firm's primary sources of revenues?
	d. How well positioned is the firm relative to its coopetitors?
	e. How does the firm price the products?
2. Connected activities	a. What activities does the firm perform to support its competitive position so as to make money?
	b. How are these activities consistent with low cost or differentiation, market segments, sources of revenues, and prices that the firm charges?
	c. How do the activities build and exploit resources?
	d. How do the activities exploit industry value drivers?
	e. How do the activities dampen industry competitive and macro-environment forces?
3. Competitive and macro-environment forces	a. What are the competitive forces that act on the industry, and how are they expected to change? How can an industry firm take advantage of these forces?
	b. What are the macro-environment forces that act on industry firms, and how are these forces expected to change? How can a firm take advantage of these forces?
4. Critical industry value drivers	a. What are the primary drivers of cost and differentiation in the industry? How can a firm take advantage of these drivers in the activities that it conducts?
5. Capabilities and resources	a. What resources does the firm have or plan to acquire that are valuable, rare, inimitable, and nonsubstitutable?
	b. Can the value from these resources be appropriated?
	c. Can these resources be extended to offer value in other markets and appropriate the value?
6. Change and sustainability	a. How difficult is it to imitate the system of activities that the firm performs?
	b. What is it about competitors that makes it difficult for them to imitate the business model?
	c. What changes (potential and existing) should the firm be worried about?
	d. What kinds of activities would the firm need to perform, given the changes?
	e. What kinds of resources does the firm need, given the changes?
7. Cost of activities	a. What are the key cost drivers?
	b. What is the firm's burn rate?
	c. How productive are employees?
8. Execution of the plan	a. What types of people does the firm need to run the business model, and can the people that the firm has execute the model?
	b. What types of structure, systems, processes, and culture does the firm need to execute the business model? Does the firm have all these?
9. Expected performance	a. Given the different elements of the business plan, how is the firm expected to perform over the years?
	b. How is its performance expected to compare to that of existing and potential competitors?

3. Be consistent with the prices that the firm intends to charge.
4. Reduce the impact of industry competitive forces.
5. Take advantage of industry value drivers in supporting the firm's competitive position.

Competitive Forces

A business plan should show the competitive and macro-environment forces in the industry in which the firm intends to compete. More importantly, it should detail the actions that can be taken to reduce the impact of these forces on industry firms and should specify the tactics that competitors are using to take advantage of the forces. Of the activities that can be performed to reduce the impact of competitive forces, the firm should identify which ones it is not performing and explain why.

Critical Industry Value Drivers

A business plan should detail the characteristics of the industry that have the most impact on cost and differentiation. It should also state what kinds of activities can be performed to take advantage of these value drivers in positioning the firm to offer superior customer value and appropriate the value. The firm should identify which of these activities it has chosen not to perform and explain why.

Capabilities and Resources

Since activities rest on resources and capabilities, it is critical that a business plan detail the firm's existing resources, its resource gaps, and the means by which the gaps will be filled. In particular, the firm should itemize the resources necessary for performing the activities detailed above, specifying which of these resources it has and which ones it needs to acquire. This should be followed by a VRISA analysis of the key resources. If resources must be acquired, an analysis of how they will be obtained should be undertaken. If a resource has to be used in more than one product market, a careful analysis of the extendability potential of the resource must be performed.

For a start-up, one of the most important resources is the people who will carry out the business plan. Thus, it is important that a start-up detail the backgrounds of top managers, explaining how their experiences and skills relate to the activities of the business plan.

Change and Sustainability

As we have seen, a firm's competitive advantage usually comes from the system of activities that it performs or the resources and capabilities that underpin the activities. It is important to explicitly state in the business plan:

1. The characteristics of the firm's system of activities and/or resources and capabilities that allow it to have a competitive advantage.
2. The characteristics of competitors (existing and potential) that prevent them from imitating and leapfrogging this system of activities and/or resources and capabilities.

Since most advantages are eventually eroded by change, the business plan should state what changes are anticipated and how the firm plans on dealing with them. The plan should be explicit about when the firm will pursue a run, team-up, or block strategy in response to anticipated change.

Cost

A business plan must contain a section that details how the firm will keep its costs low, even if the firm plans to pursue a differentiation strategy. For a start-up, its **burn rate,** the rate at which it spends cash relative to the amount of cash it has, should be carefully forecasted and monitored. If a firm spends its cash too quickly, it can run out of cash and be forced into a financial crisis, no matter how bright its future might otherwise be.

Execution

Since people are central to the execution of a business model, a business plan should include a list of the key people needed to execute the model and should note their backgrounds and capabilities. The relevance of their backgrounds to their jobs with the firm should be stated. An outline of the types of structure, systems, processes, and culture that the firm has or will put in place to execute the business model should also be included in the plan.

Performance

Finally, a business plan should contain a detailed forecast of how the firm expects to perform over the years. It should show how this performance is consistent with the positions, activities, resources, cost drivers, and environment (industry and macro) of the firm.

Summary

A firm's business model– or strategy-making process is usually a combination of the entrepreneurial, adaptive, and planning modes. Most business models and strategies are not the result of a grand design that emerges from the CEO's office and must be followed word for word as if it were a battle plan. Rather, business models are a combination of planned activities, activities that stemmed from the interplay of different employees with different levels of power, and some bold moves that resulted in important leaps.

Key Terms

adaptive mode, *233*
burn rate, *241*
business model planning
process, *235*

business plan, *238*
competency trap, *237*
coopetitor power, *238*

entrepreneurial mode, *232*
planning mode, *234*

Study Questions

1. What is the difference between a business model and a business plan?
2. In what industries would you expect each of the following business model–making processes to be most prevalent?
   1. Adaptive   2. Entrepreneurial   3. Planning

Endnotes

1. This question was asked by H. Mintzberg in his seminal paper "Strategy Making in Three Modes," *California Management Review* 16 (Winter 1973), pp. 44–53.
2. This section draws heavily on ibid.
3. P. F. Drucker, "Entrepreneurship in the Business Enterprise," *Journal of Business Policy* (1970), pp. 2–14.
4. R. Cyert and J. March, *A Behavioral Theory of the Firm* (Englewood Cliffs, NJ: Prentice-Hall, 1968).

5. G. M. Hamel and C. K. Prahalad, *Competing for the Future* (Boston: Harvard Business School Press, 1994); R. A. Bettis and C. K. Prahalad, "The Dominant Logic: Retrospective and Extension," *Strategic Management Journal* 16 (1995), pp. 5–14.

6. D. C. Hambrick, M. A. Geletkanycz, and J. W. Fredrickson, "Top Executive Commitment to the Status Quo: Some Tests of Its Determinants," *Strategic Management Journal* 14 (1993), pp. 401–418.

7. A. K. Dixit and R. S. Pindyck, *Investment under Uncertainty* (Princeton, NJ: Princeton University Press, 1994).

8. Bettis and Prahalad, "The Dominant Logic."

9. J. Pfeffer, *Managing with Power: Politics and Influence in Organizations* (Boston: Harvard Business School Press, 1992).

10. C. H. Ferguson and C. R. Morris, *Computer Wars: How the West Can Win in the Post-IBM World* (New York: Time Books, 1993).

11. C. M. Christensen and J. L. Bower, "Customer Power, Strategic Investment and Failure of Leading Firms," *Strategic Management Journal* 17 (1996), pp. 197–218.

Corporate Social Responsibility and Governance

In early 2000, Enron had what appeared to be a winning business model. Through its business model, the company had risen rapidly to the seventh position on the Fortune 500 list of the largest U.S. corporations in 2000, and it posted profits that seemed to be among the highest for a service company. On December 2, 2001, the company filed for bankruptcy. Thousands of Enron employees stood to lose their pensions, which had been invested in the company's stock. Millions of its shareholders stood to lose their investments in the company, whose share price had risen to more than $80 in 2000. Some of its top managers stood to be indicted for money laundering, conspiracy to defraud, and other offenses.[1] Its auditor, Arthur Andersen, was on the verge of bankruptcy largely as a result of the auditor's dealings with Enron and its decision to shred documents relating to Enron when word of Enron's wrongdoings came out. In another case, two officials of Tyco International were indicted in 2002 for stealing more than $170 million from Tyco and for illegally obtaining more than $400 million by selling shares of Tyco. The list goes on and on.

In performing the activities that allow a firm to offer superior customer value and appropriate the value, every firm must choose between legal and moral rights and wrongs. An insurance company that keeps its costs low by refusing to pay legitimate health insurance claims is being irresponsible and hurting the patients. Refusing to pay a legitimate health insurance claim is wrong. A firm may be tempted to illegally dispose of its toxic waste in a nearby river or in a developing country to avoid the extra costs of disposing of the waste legitimately. Doing so is wrong. Top management that manipulates its firm's accounting systems to report inflated earnings and thus be compensated for performance that never occurred or to hide poor performance is being irresponsible. Irresponsible actions can have important consequences not only for a firm but also for its **stakeholders**—the individuals and groups such as shareholders, employees, coopetitors, creditors, unions, local communities, and governments that can impact or are impacted by the firm's business model.[2]

In previous chapters, we explored how to *do the right things* and *do them right* to offer superior customer value and be in a position to appropriate the value. In this chapter, we explore the responsibilities of a firm to society that go beyond profitability. We explore how, in performing value-adding and value-appropriating activities, a firm can avoid doing things that are ethically or legally wrong and that usually hurt stakeholders. The chapter also examines how a firm can go beyond the legal and ethical responsibilities and help its community. We start the chapter by exploring the relationship between a firm and its stakeholders and by defining corporate social responsibility. This is followed by a discussion of the role of corporate governance in helping to meet the needs of stakeholders. We then explore the drivers of corporate social responsibility.

PROFITABILITY AND SOCIAL RESPONSIBILITY

A business model is about making money, and our discussion in this book thus far has been about profitability. In focusing on the activities which a firm performs and how and when it performs them, we have shown how these factors can enable the firm to create and offer its customers superior value and be in a position to make profits that are commensurate with that value. However, it has been argued that a firm's responsibilities go beyond profitability. According to Professor Archie Carroll, a firm has four types of responsibilities, namely, economic, legal, ethical, and discretionary, with the last two being its **social responsibilities** (Table 13.1).[3]

Economic Responsibilities

A firm's **economic responsibilities** are to create and offer superior value to customers and to put itself in a position to make money from the value so that it can pay its shareholders, creditors, and employees and meet its financial obligations in dealing with coopetitors and governments. A firm that does not make money is not likely to be able to fulfill social responsibilities such as making philanthropic donations to local communities.

Legal Responsibilities

Governments set laws and regulations that firms within their jurisdictions have to obey. A firm fulfills its **legal responsibilities** by obeying the laws in the areas where it operates. Firms fulfill their economic obligations within the framework of the laws and regulations of their environment. Firms that do not obey these laws can face punishments that range from simple fines to termination of the business. For example, in 2002, after being sued by the U.S. Securities and Exchange Commission (SEC), Xerox admitted overstating its profits by some $1.4 billion between 1997 and 2001. In April 2002, Xerox paid a $10 million fine to settle the case.[4] A company that keeps violating the law and paying fines may see its

TABLE 13.1
Firm's Responsibilities to Its Stakeholders

| | Responsibilities | | | |
| | Economic | Legal | Social | |
Stakeholders			Ethical	Discretionary
Shareholders	√	√		
Employees	√	√	√	√
Coopetitors	√	√		
Creditors	√	√		
Unions		√	√	
Local communities		√	√	√
Governments	√	√	√	

profits dwindle further as good employees avoid working for it and its coopetitors stop dealing with it. Many of the illegal activities that firms engage in occur while they are trying to meet their economic obligations to shareholders.

Ethical Responsibilities

Ethical and discretionary responsibilities are a firm's social responsibilities. A firm's **ethical responsibilities** consist of doing the things that its society values and believes are the right things to do even though they are not required by law. Since values within a society can vary considerably, it can be expected that what is considered ethical by some may not be by others. For example, between 1996 and 2001, Enron paid no taxes in four of the five fiscal years on profits of more than $1 billion, and was actually eligible for $382 million in tax refunds.[5] The company had created 881 partnerships in the Cayman Islands and other tax havens. This may have been legal but was considered by some to be unethical.

The ethical responsibilities of a firm are usually very ill defined. However, if enough people feel very strongly that something is ethical, they can convince the government to incorporate it into law, making it a legal responsibility for firms. Some activities that are forbidden by law in many developed countries are not illegal in some developing countries. Since such activities are likely to be considered unethical in developed countries, conglomerates or their contractors that engage in these activities in developing countries may be accused of being unethical. For example, child labor is forbidden in developed countries, and firms that use child labor in developing countries are likely to be considered unethical.

Although academic research has not yet established that doing ethical things increases firm profitability, many anecdotal examples suggest that there may be a link between ethical activities and firm profitability. For example, a firm can drive away customers who believe that it is being unethical by employing children in a developing country to manufacture its products.

Discretionary Responsibilities

A firm is fulfilling its **discretionary responsibilities** when it does good things for stakeholders that it is not obligated to do and that few people expect it to do. If a firm does not do them, the firm is not necessarily seen as unethical, although it may be seen as uncaring. When an oil company builds schools and health care centers in villages near the sites where it drills for and extracts oil, it is fulfilling a discretionary responsibility—a social responsibility. Contributing to the local football team for children is a discretionary responsibility. So is providing child care in some communities. If discretionary responsibilities become very popular, they may become ethical and eventually legal. For example, disability and retirement benefits, the eight-hour workday, and guaranteed work for at least 48 weeks per year are now laws in many countries. But they were discretionary activities when Procter and Gamble (P&G) pioneered them.[6] P&G introduced disability and retirement benefits in 1915, the eight-hour workday in 1918, and guaranteed work for at least 48 weeks per year in the 1920s. Henry Heinz was the first to introduce paid citizenship education for employees.

The Social Responsibility Debate

As we have defined them, a firm's social responsibilities are its ethical and discretionary responsibilities. However, not all scholars agree on whether a firm has any business taking on social responsibilities, in particular, performing discretionary activities. On one side of the debate are scholars who argue that a firm has no business performing socially responsible activities. One of the leading proponents of this view is Professor Milton Friedman, a Nobel laureate from the University of Chicago, who stated:

> In such an economy [a free economy], there is one and only one social responsibility of business—to use its resources and engage in activities designed to increase profits so long as it stays within the rules of the game, which is to say, engages in open and free competition without deception or fraud. Similarly, the "social responsibility" of labor leaders is to serve the interest of the members of their unions.[7]

The idea here is that shareholders and employees are part of society and management's responsibility is to them—to generate wealth for shareholders and pay the employees who generate the wealth. By using a firm's money or other resources to perform discretionary activities that benefit other stakeholders, so the argument goes, a manager is being socially irresponsible to shareholders and employees, the people that the manager is supposed to serve. The responsibility for stakeholders such as local communities rests with other institutions such as the government, which receives taxes from profitable firms. Thus, an oil company that extracts oil close to an African village would be acting irresponsibly by building a school or health care center for the village. The country's government, which receives taxes and royalties from the oil company, is responsible for building the schools and health care centers for such villages. The responsibility of the oil company is to its shareholders and employees, not to the villagers.

On the other side of the debate are scholars who insist that investing in socially responsible activities is a good strategy that can increase the value of a firm's stock. The leading proponent of this view was Professor Edward Bowman of the Wharton School of the University of Pennsylvania.[8] There are five supporting points for this argument:

1. There are many socially conscious individuals and institutional investors such as cities, states, universities, churches, and some mutual funds that invest only in socially responsible businesses.[9]
2. Investors see firms that are socially irresponsible as being more risky than socially responsible firms and are therefore more likely to invest in the latter.
3. Socially responsible businesses can build brand equity and loyal customers, thereby differentiating their products. Scholarly evidence as to whether being socially responsible improves financial performance is mixed: Some studies show that being socially responsible helps profitability; others see no relationship between the two.[10]
4. Being socially responsible builds trust, and trust can give firms an edge when dealing with customers, suppliers, employees, and regulators.[11]
5. Being socially responsible attracts good employees.

However, some studies have found that profitability enables firms to undertake discretionary activities,[12] rather than discretionary activities' leading to profitability.

PRINCIPAL-AGENT AND CORPORATE GOVERNANCE STRUCTURE

Stakeholders usually have some expectations of a firm as it performs its economic, legal, and social responsibilities. For example, shareholders expect a firm to increase shareholder wealth; employees expect a firm to treat them fairly and justly; governments expect a firm to pay its taxes, create jobs, and obey laws;

unions expect a firm to meet their demands; coopetitors expect a firm not to free-ride; villagers in an area where a logging company harvests timber may expect the company to replant trees; and so on. Meeting these expectations means performing legally and socially responsible activities that enable a firm to offer its customers superior value and appropriate the value.

Principal-Agent Relationship

Since it is impossible for stakeholders to physically oversee all the activities a firm performs, they usually depend on the firm's management to act on their behalf to ensure that their expectations are met responsibly. This stakeholder-firm relationship is a type of **principal-agent relationship:** the stakeholders, known as the *principal,* implicitly or explicitly delegate to the firm's management, known as the *agent,* the responsibility of making sure that their expectations are met. For example, shareholders delegate to management the task of ensuring that shareholder wealth is being increased legally and in a socially responsible way, governments delegate to management the responsibility of making sure that the firm obeys laws and regulations, and so on.

For several reasons, the agent does not always do what the principal wants. First, the agent's interests may be very different from those of stakeholders.[13] For example, management may be more interested in enriching itself in the short term than in creating long-term wealth for shareholders or doing what is morally and legally right. Monitoring management to make sure that it is doing the right things and doing them right can be very costly, and this is one reason that recalcitrant managers are usually caught when it is too late to prevent damage. Second, management may be cognitively limited and therefore does not have what it takes to deliver what stakeholders want in a responsible way. Because stakeholders can also be cognitively limited, the problem of monitoring is often exacerbated since cognitively limited stakeholders do not know what to monitor and how to monitor it. The average owner of Enron stock had no idea how Enron kept its books and how such books should be kept. The average villager in a developing country where oil companies drill for oil has no idea what his or her rights are as far as an oil company's activities in the village are concerned. Third, the stakeholder and firm may simply disagree on each other's expectations or may not even know that such expectations exist, especially if they are not based on laws or precedence. For example, a firm may not agree with a union's demands for huge increases in wages when union members already earn very high salaries and the firm is near bankruptcy. An oil company may not agree with villagers' demands that it spend 0.01 percent of its proceeds from the region's oil on educating children in the area or reclaiming damaged land.

Corporate Governance Structure

In the principal-agent model, shareholders and other stakeholders are the principal and top management is the agent. Since thousands of people can own shares in a company at any one time, it is difficult for every shareholder to monitor all the activities that a firm's CEO and managers are performing. Therefore, shareholders elect directors to represent them and protect their interests. These directors, together called a **board of directors,** have the responsibility of establishing corporate policies and the authority to monitor compliance with these policies by the CEO and other top management. The board also has the power to fire the CEO and other top managers. Top management's own responsibilities include setting the firm's strategy and formulating and executing the business model that will deliver the type of performance that the directors and shareholders expect. Thus, shareholders depend on the board of directors to ensure that their interests are being reflected by management. This overall process, in which shareholders, directors, and top management determine the direction and performance of a firm, is referred to as **corporate governance.** To effectively carry out their responsibilities, directors should have a good understanding of what is going on inside and outside the company.

At the top of a board of directors is the chairperson of the board. Directors can be from inside the company, in which case they are known as **inside directors** or **executive directors.** They can also be from outside the firm, in which case they are called **outside directors, nonexecutive directors,** or **independent directors.** Since the structure of a firm involves the relationships between different groups, who reports to whom, and who performs which tasks, two important concerns about the corporate governance structure of a firm are (1) the makeup (constitution) of the board of directors, in particular, how many outside directors relative to inside ones the board should have, and (2) the relationship between the CEO of the firm and the chairperson of the board, in particular, whether the CEO should also be the chairperson. The advantage of having outside directors is that they bring an independent view to the board and have less conflict of interest in monitoring management. In comparison, inside directors know much more about the company's activities and less about the outside environment, and they may be less objective in monitoring their own activities. The structure of boards varies from country to country. In Germany, for example, inside directors sit on one board, while outside directors sit on a separate board. The outside directors—who are stakeholders such as trade-union officials, bankers, and employee representatives—monitor the inside directors.[14] Boards in the United States, Britain, and Australia usually have both inside and outside directors meet as one group for board meetings. In 2001, 78 percent of the directors of U.S. companies were outsiders.[15]

It is not unusual for the chairperson of the board to also be the CEO of the company. However, since one of the main jobs of the board of directors is to monitor and sometimes fire the CEO, having the CEO serve as chairperson raises an important question: How can the chairperson be objective in watching himself or herself? In 2000, 80 percent of U.S. companies had CEOs who also served as chairperson of the board.[16] Another consideration that may affect a board member's ability is the number of other boards that the member serves on. In the 1980s and 1990s in the United States, it was not unusual to see the same people sitting on more than 10 boards. While being on many boards may enable a director to bring in useful outside perspectives, it may place too many demands on the director and sometimes leads to conflicts of interest because of his or her responsibilities to the different firms. Very few boards in the United States have members who are nonmanagement employees.

DRIVERS OF SOCIAL RESPONSIBILITY AND IRRESPONSIBILITY

Nine factors determine the extent to which a firm acts legally and socially responsibly or irresponsibly as it carries out the activities of its business model and interacts with stakeholders: information asymmetry, people, power, uncertainty, strategy, performance, organizational structure, systems, and environment (Figure 13.1).

FIGURE 13.1
Drivers of
Responsible Activities

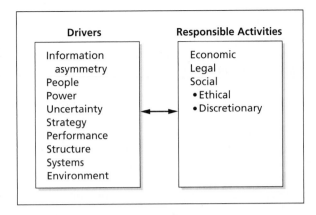

Drivers	Responsible Activities
Information asymmetry People Power Uncertainty Strategy Performance Structure Systems Environment	Economic Legal Social • Ethical • Discretionary

Information Asymmetry

In the principal-agent relationship, the primary way to know whether the agent is doing his or her job well is through the information that the agent provides to the principal. Such information is sometimes validated by a third party. For example, management provides information to stakeholders about the financial status of the company through a financial statement that has been validated by an auditor. However, a firm usually has an **information asymmetry** advantage over stakeholders. Party A has an information asymmetry advantage over party B if A has information that B does not have—information that is important to B in interacting with A. For example, a firm may have information about its costs, revenues, and profits that shareholders and the public do not have. A company may have more information on the work conditions in its overseas plants than workers' rights activists in its home country do. A start-up may keep silent about an impending lawsuit when it convinces an investor to take a major stake in it.

An information asymmetry advantage creates room for opportunism—room for a firm to lie, cheat, or act in other irresponsible ways. The inclusion of a third party such as an auditor is intended to reduce the level of opportunism. However, this does not always prevent irresponsible acts. Many of the corporate scandals that occurred around 2000 involved firms that irresponsibly took advantage of information asymmetry. Enron's fall started when the company removed liabilities from its balance sheet and assigned them to special-purpose entities without telling the public or shareholders what it had done. When Enron's auditing firm, Arthur Andersen, heard about the impending crisis, it allegedly shredded many important documents. In 2002, about 250 U.S. public corporations had to restate their financial accounts because of "mistakes" that had been made in preceding years.[17]

Information asymmetry can continue to exist between a firm and stakeholders even when the firm wants to eliminate the asymmetry. This is the case when the stakeholder cannot process and make sense of the information provided by the firm. The average shareholder does not understand all the nuances of a financial statement or all the information and processes that go into preparing financial statements. This is one reason that shareholders often depend on independent auditors to certify that the information in a financial statement was arrived at using approved methods.

People

Having an information asymmetry advantage is one thing. Acting irresponsibly by being opportunistic with the information usually takes a certain type of person. In the two years before his company went bankrupt, Global Crossing's boss made over $500 million from the sale of the company's stock.[18] When the company filed for bankruptcy, many of its shareholders, who by then held near-worthless shares, were not pleased with the CEO's actions. What type of person can be entrusted by stakeholders and then can act in a way that they see as irresponsible? Two factors shed light on the answers: morals and bias.

Morals

Top management's beliefs about what is wrong or right play an important role in determining how responsibly a firm can carry out its activities. If top management's beliefs stray from what society believes is right or wrong, trouble can arise for the firm. Basically, CEOs and directors who lack certain moral principles are not likely to be economically, legally, and socially responsible. Three such principles are honoring agreements, avoiding lying, and avoiding harm.[19]

Honoring agreements: This is one of the moral rules without which markets fail.[20] Markets fail when people cannot buy or sell goods and services. CEOs who do not honor agreements will quickly find out that few people want to sign agreements with them. The few firms that dare enter into agreements with a firm whose management does not honor such documents will try to protect themselves by including as many contingencies as possible when drawing up the agreements. They will also more carefully monitor and enforce compliance with the agreements. Since taking these extra measures is too costly for many firms that want to be competitive in their markets, they will simply refrain from doing business with a firm whose management cannot be trusted. This makes it more difficult for such a firm to fulfill its economic responsibilities. Not honoring agreements can also cause a firm to spend considerable time in court and therefore gain a reputation as being legally irresponsible.

Avoiding lying: This is the other moral rule without which markets fail.[21] If top management lies, it is difficult for potential investors to believe in the firm's financial statements. It is also difficult for suppliers or customers to believe the firm. Lying is irresponsible economically, legally, and socially.

Avoiding harm to others: This is the third moral rule for responsible behavior. A health insurance organization that refuses to pay legitimate claims may be able to argue its way through a court with good lawyers, but refusing to pay the legitimate claim harms someone who does not deserve to be harmed. An executive who wants to avoid harming stakeholders is more likely to strive to meet their expectations than is one who disregards harm.

People without these morals can turn a good system into a nightmare. For example, tying executives' salaries to firm profitability is a good idea, but doing so creates the temptation for irresponsible managers to overstate their earnings. Such compensation approaches should be used only if managers have the morals to report their earnings accurately and to not hurt coopetitors.

Bias

In performing certain activities, even honest people with very strong morals can succumb to unconscious bias. The effects of bias can be just as devastating as those of poor morals. Bias stems from the fact that people's desires have a very strong influence on the way they interpret information even when they want to be objective and impartial.[22] According to Max Bazerman, George Loewenstein, and Don Moore, "Without knowing it, we tend to critically scrutinize and then discard facts that contradict the conclusions we want to reach, and we uncritically embrace evidence that supports our positions." [23] Professors Bazerman, Loewenstein, and Moore argue that several conditions increase the prevalence of bias: ambiguity, approval, attachment, discounting, escalation, and familiarity.[24]

Ambiguity Wherever there is ambiguity, there is room for opportunism. For example, considerable ambiguity can exist in deciding whether something is an investment or an expense or when revenue should be recognized. Every year, *Money Magazine* sends the financial records of a hypothetical family to up to 50 professional tax accountants to figure out how much the family owes in taxes. In 1990, the answers ranged from $6,807 to $73, 247; in 1998, they ranged from $37,715 to $68,912. Thus, ambiguity can introduce a lot of room for bias.

Approval Many people are more likely to be biased when they are endorsing other people's judgments that match their own biases than when they have to make their own original judgments. If people keep telling a CEO that he is a good person, he is more likely to donate to charity than he would if no one told him that.

Attachment When person X equates his or her interests with Y's, X is more likely to interpret data to favor Y than would be the case otherwise. Thus, an auditor that is hired by a firm to approve its accounts is more likely to be biased toward going easy on the books than one that is hired by the tax division of the government to go over the firm's books.

Discounting Many people would rather respond to immediate consequences than to those in the future. The more uncertain the future consequences are compared to immediate ones, the more that such people prefer responding to the immediate ones. Thus, since the benefits of exercise are not immediately apparent but usually accumulate over time, many people postpone exercising because the immediate consequence—finding the time, place, and will to exercise—is a bother compared to the ease of sitting down to watch TV and talk.

Escalation To maintain a good image in the eyes of fellow employees, friends, family, and even strangers, some people may explain away or hide seemingly unimportant indiscretions. The problem in doing so is that even a small mistake can lead to significant negative effects. Suppose an employee mistakenly recognizes earnings earlier than he or she should have but, rather than correct the mistake, conceals it to maintain a good image. If it takes auditors two years to catch the mistake, what started out as a minor error in judgment may now look like a scandal.

Familiarity Many people are less willing to hurt people whom they know than to hurt strangers. For example, an auditor that has strong relationships with a firm is less likely to reject the firm's financial statements than one that has no such relations.

Power

Person X has power over Y in a transaction if Y's actions reflect more of X's interests than Y would like. If a firm has power over a potential stakeholder, the temptation to be opportunistic is greater. For example, an oil company that goes to a poor developing country to drill for oil has more power over the villagers and more information about the drilling's effects (both good and bad) on villagers than the villagers do. Such a firm can get away with a lot if it decides to be opportunistic. If a firm has a great deal of power over a stakeholder, the stakeholder is less likely to complain. For example, villagers in a developing country are less likely to fight against a big oil company that supplies 90 percent of their country's revenues. Finally, if a stakeholder is very uncertain about what to expect from a firm, the stakeholder is less likely to take action against the firm and win.

Uncertainty

Activities that are associated with uncertainty offer a firm more chances to be opportunistic. This is partly because more uncertainty means more opportunities for information asymmetry. For example, in using genetic engineering to produce new foods, organisms, or medicines, there is uncertainty as to what the exact outcome of some processes might be. A firm whose research produces undesirable results may decide not to reveal them, thereby making it difficult for stakeholders to know what really happened. As another example, if an oil company wants to start pumping oil near a village in a developing country, there is a lot of uncertainty about what the villagers can expect from the oil company and what the company can get out of the oil wells. Thus, there is more room for opportunism.

Strategy

Recall that a strategy is a commitment to one set of activities rather than another. Thus, a firm whose strategy specifically makes a commitment to performing socially responsible activities and devotes resources to doing so is more likely to be socially responsible than one that does not. Since strategy is usually the responsibility of top management, the extent to which a firm's strategy makes commitments to performing socially responsible activities is a function of the top management's moral convictions and commitment to social responsibility.

Performance

A firm's performance has an impact on the extent to which the firm can act responsibly. A firm that makes huge profits has more money to spend and can therefore fund more discretionary activities than its less profitable counterparts can.[25] On the other hand, a firm that is losing money may be tempted to hide its true financial situation by overstating its profits.

Structure

Recall that one of the responsibilities of a board of directors is to oversee the activities of top management. The board has the power to replace top management. Thus, if the CEO of a company is also the chairperson of its board, it is difficult for directors to be as objective in criticizing and punishing the CEO. Therefore, a CEO with bad morals or poor judgment is more likely to get the company into trouble when he or she is also chairperson of the board. The makeup of a board is also likely to have an impact on the extent to which the firm meets the expectations of different stakeholders. A board that consists mainly of inside directors is less likely to censure top management since such directors are usually top managers. Boards with union members are likely to pay attention to union issues, while boards with environmentalists are likely to pay attention to issues that concern the natural environment. However, most boards are elected by shareholders and therefore cater largely to the needs of shareholders, paying attention to the needs of other stakeholders only to the extent that doing so may enhance shareholder wealth.

Systems

At the corporate level, systems specify what constitutes performance for top management and directors and how that performance is monitored, measured, rewarded, and punished. A primary goal of systems is to reduce the principal-agent problems that exist between shareholders, directors, and top management by aligning management interests with those of directors and shareholders. For example, if a firm ties top management's performance and rewards to shareholder wealth creation, the managers are more likely to pay attention to creating wealth for shareholders. Indeed, a firm's executives are often measured by how well their company's stock performs. In the short term, other measures may be used. For example, a CEO who has been hired to turn a company around may be evaluated in his or her first few years by cost reduction, sales growth, profit margins, or any other measure that indicates whether the CEO has put the company back on the path to prosperity.

An important question is, What would encourage top management and directors to better meet performance goals? A popular incentive that firms use is options in the company. That is, the individuals are given the right, but not the obligation, to buy a certain number of shares of their company at some future time at a fixed, usually low, price. The idea is to give management an incentive to increase the share price: The higher the share price goes, the more money the managers will make when they exercise their options; and as the share price increases, so too does shareholder wealth. However, unscrupulous top managers with many stock options that are contingent on short-term performance measures might be tempted to alter financial statements to make the firm look better than it really is. Paying top management salary increases that are proportional to share price increases can also be an incentive that increases shareholder wealth. To align directors' interests with those of shareholders, paying the directors in stocks or stock options is a better incentive than paying them straight salaries for their work. For both top managers and directors, owning the company's stock rather than options can be a better incentive to work harder to increase share prices. Directors who use their own money to buy a substantial number of shares in a company are also more likely to work harder toward getting the company to meet its performance goals.

Environment

Carrying out economic, legal, and social responsibilities requires the right environments. In particular, the culture of a country or region, the existence of monitoring institutions such as auditors, the country's government and the extent to which laws are enforced, and technological change can impact a firm's ability to be socially responsible.

Culture

A region's or country's culture plays an important role in shaping the types of systems and structures that firms adopt. Recall that *culture* can be defined as a system of shared values (what is important) and beliefs (how things work). Thus, to the extent that values and beliefs vary from country to country and region to region, we can expect to see regional differences in the systems and structures used by firms as they pursue their economic, legal, and social responsibilities. For example, in the United States, a CEO is normally given free rein to run the company as she or he sees fit. The board of directors is there to occasionally check on the CEO, but very often the CEO is also the chairperson of the board. Europeans are less enthusiastic about having one person run the show; they believe that the temptation to act irresponsibly when handed such a powerful job can be too much for many individuals.[26] In Europe, the job of CEO is usually not combined with that of chairperson of the board.

In some countries, nepotism is rife. People are appointed to top jobs not so much because they are talented as because they are family members, relatives, friends or their family members, or members of a special group. If such appointees are inept, shareholders can suffer. In some countries, bribery is rife. In environments where almost everything is for sale, it is difficult to be economically, legally, and socially responsible.

Monitoring Institutions

During the Enron crisis in the United States, it quickly became clear that Arthur Andersen—the auditor that was supposed to audit Enron's books and issue an independent, unbiased report that the public could depend on—had failed the public. Since the average shareholder does not have the expertise to understand what goes into a financial statement, he or she depends on institutions that specialize in financial matters. Auditors help reinforce trust in financial statements. If auditors do their job well, firms are less likely to manipulate numbers, as they fear being caught in an audit. In countries where there are activists for specific causes, the activists function as monitors, bringing attention to the causes and related issues of responsibility. Without such activists, breaches of social responsibility can go undetected. For example, most developing countries in which excessive logging takes place do not have activists to point out where and when loggers go wrong.

Government and Laws

The role of government in a firm's economic, legal, and social responsibilities is critical. Governments write, monitor, and enforce the laws that underpin agreements between firms and their coopetitors, and therefore they can have a large influence on the economic responsibilities of a firm. We explored the impact of government on a firm's economic responsibilities in Chapters 1 and 5. Here, we focus on the legal and social responsibilities. Too many very restrictive laws can stifle business, but some managers, if left unchecked, act very irresponsibly. Thus, government laws can be used to influence not only the types of corporate structures and systems in a country but also the behavior of managers. For example, the Sarbanes-Oxley legislation, passed in July 2002, requires that U.S. firms have more outside directors who do not do business with the company they serve or with its top management.[27] It also "encourages" outside directors to meet separately from inside directors.

Enforcing laws influences top management by acting as a deterrent. If an executive bankrupts his or her company through illegal investments or accounting fraud and gets away with hundreds of millions of dollars, this sends the wrong message to other irresponsible managers. If a company can make $4 billion in profits and get away with paying no taxes, this tells other firms with irresponsible managers that it is okay to avoid paying their fair share of taxes. In contrast, if CEOs are imprisoned for fraud and serve sentences with other criminals, that may deter other top managers from attempting such crimes.

Globalization and Technological Change

A firm has a **global market** if the firm's performance in any particular country or region is a function of not only its activities in that country or region but also its activities worldwide. Firms that operate in global markets face more social responsibility challenges than those that operate only in a local market. First, the nature of responsibilities varies among countries. A discretionary responsibility in one country may be an ethical responsibility in another and a legal responsibility in yet another. Child labor is a good example. In the developed world, it is against the law to employ children in public businesses. In some other countries, no such laws exist, but people frown on the practice of employing children. In still others, children have to work to feed their families. Second, in trying to be progressive in developing countries, a firm often faces some interesting dilemmas. For example, Nike pays its workers in its shoe factory in Vietnam more money than the country's medical doctors make.[28] The question is, What is the social consequence of medical doctors' quitting their jobs to join Nike?

Technological changes such as the Internet help reduce information asymmetry;[29] a vast amount of information is now available to many people at low cost. For example, activists in a developed country can more easily obtain information about the work conditions at a conglomerate's plants in a developing country, sometimes with the click of a mouse. Thus, conglomerates may be more inclined to be socially responsible worldwide. While the Internet can facilitate the move toward social responsibility, biotechnology raises some interesting moral questions, particularly as to research on growing human organs and cloning human beings.

Summary

There are four kinds of responsibilities that a firm faces as it formulates and executes its business model: economic, legal, ethical, and discretionary. Of these, ethical and discretionary responsibilities are usually referred to as social responsibilities. There are two opposing views on the extent of a firm's responsibilities. One view is that a firm's only responsibility is economic and to shareholders. According to this view, firms exist to legally create shareholder wealth, not to serve as charities; social responsibility is the government's job. The other view argues that being socially responsible is not only a moral approach but also a good strategy that can increase shareholder wealth. Thus, according to this view, a firm's stakeholders include shareholders, employees, coopetitors, creditors, unions, local communities, and governments.

Responsibility for running a firm is usually delegated to top managers, irrespective of who the stakeholders are. In this firm-stakeholder relationship, stakeholders are the principal and top management is the agent. In the principal-agent relationship, top management does not always have the interests of stakeholders at heart. To look after their interests, shareholders usually elect directors to monitor top management to ensure that it is not pursuing its own interests. The makeup of the board of directors and the structure of the relationship between top management and the board play an important role in ensuring that shareholder interests are served. The systems that are put in place can align management's interests with those of shareholders. A firm with the best systems and structure may still get into trouble if top management's sense of what is right or wrong is very different from society's. The environment in which a firm operates plays an important role in determining the type of systems and structure that a firm has. In the end, it is people that matter. Top managers' beliefs about what is wrong or right, as well as their fear of or respect for government and laws, play a key role.

Key Terms

board of directors, *247*
corporate governance, *248*
discretionary responsibilities,
  245
economic responsibilities,
  244
ethical responsibilities, *245*

executive directors, *248*
global market, *254*
independent directors, *248*
information asymmetry, *249*
inside directors, *248*
legal responsibilities, *244*
nonexecutive directors, *248*

outside directors, *248*
principal-agent relationship,
  247
social responsibilities, *244*
stakeholders, *243*

Study Question

What is the impact of the Internet and digital networks on corporate social responsibility likely to be?

Endnotes

1. "Out to Catch the Big Fish," *The Economist* (Sept. 14, 2002), pp. 61–62.

2. R. E. Freeman, *Strategic Management: A Stakeholder Approach* (Boston: Pitman, 1984); R. K. Mitchell, B. R. Agle, and D. J. Wood, "Towards a Theory of Stakeholder Identification and Salience: Defining the Principle of Who and What Really Counts," *Academy of Management Review* 22 (1997), pp. 453–486; T. J. Rowley, "Moving beyond Dyadic Ties: A Network Theory of Stakeholder Influences," *Academy of Management Review* 22 (1997), pp. 887–910; J. E. Post, L. E. Preston, and S. Sachs, "Managing the Extended Enterprise: The New Stakeholder View," *California Management Review* 45 (Fall 2002), pp. 5–28.

3. A. B. Carroll, "A Three Dimensional Conceptual Mode of Corporate Performance," *Academy of Management Review* 4 (1979), pp. 497–505.

4. "Corporate America's Woes Continued," *The Economist* (Nov. 30, 2002), pp. 59–61.

5. D. C. Johnston, "Senate Finance Panel Wants Tax Information from Enron," *New York Times* (Jan. 24, 2002), p. C7.

6. "Special Report: Social Corporate Responsibility: Lots of It About," *The Economist,* Dec. 14, 2002, pp. 62–63.

7. M. Friedman, *Capitalism and Freedom* (Chicago: University of Chicago Press, 1963), p. 133; M. Friedman, "The Social Responsibility of Business Is to Increase Its Profits," *New York Times Magazine,* Sept. 13, 1970, pp. 126–127.

8. E. H. Bowman, "Corporate Social Responsibility and the Investor," *Journal of Contemporary Business* (Winter 1973), pp. 49–58.

9. C. W. L. Hill and G. R. Jones, *Strategic Management: An Integrated Approach* (Boston: Houghton Mifflin, 1998).

10. See, for example, K. E. Aupperle, A. B. Carroll, and J. D. Hatfield, "An Empirical Examination of the Relationship between Corporate Social Responsibility and Profitability," *Academy of Management Journal* 28 (1985), pp. 446–464; A. McWilliams and D. Siegel, "Corporate Social Responsibility and Financial Performance: Correlation or Misspecification?" *Strategic Management Journal* 21 (2000), pp. 603–609.

11. "Special Report: Corporate Social Responsibility."

12. S. A. Waddock and S. B. Graves, "The Corporate Social Performance–Financial Performance Link," *Strategic Management Journal* 18 (2000), pp. 303–319.

13. T. M. Jones and C. L. Hill, "Stakeholder Agency Theory," *Journal of Management Studies* 29 (1992), pp. 131–154; S. Ross, "The Economic Theory of Agency: The Principal's Problem," *American Economic Review* 63 (1973), pp. 134–139.

14. "The Fading Appeal of the Boardroom," *The Economist,* Feb. 2, 2001.

15. Ibid.

16. R. Carlsson, *Ownership and Value Creation: Strategies, Corporate Governance in the New Economy* (New York: Wiley, 2001).

17. "Corporate America's Woes Continued."

18. Ibid.

19. D. P. Quinn and T. M. Jones, "An Agent Morality View of Business Policy," *Academy of Management Review* 20 (1995), pp. 22–42.

20. C. McMahon, "Morality and the Invisible Hand," *Philosophy & Public Affairs* 10 (1981), pp. 247–277.

21. D. M. Hausman and M. S. McPherson, "Taking Ethics Seriously: Economics and Contemporary Moral Philosophy," *Journal of Economic Literature* 31 (1993), pp. 671–731.

22. D. M. Messick and M. H. Bazerman, "Ethical Leadership and the Psychology of Decision Making," *Sloan Management Review* (Winter 1996); M. H. Bazerman, G. Loewenstein, and D. A. Moore, "Why Good Accountants Do Bad Audits," *Harvard Business Review* (November 2002), pp. 97–102.

23. Bazerman, Loewenstein, and Moore, "Why Good Accountants Do Bad Audits."

24. Ibid.

25. Waddock and Graves, "The Corporate Social Performance–Financial Performance Link."

26. "Corporate America's Woes Continued."

27. C. Hymowitz, "How to Fix a Broken System: A Rush of New Plans Promises to Make Corporate Boards More Accountable; Will They Work?" *The Wall Street Journal,* Feb. 24, 2003.

28. "Doing Well by Doing Good," *The Economist,* Apr. 4, 2000, pp. 65–68.

29. A. N. Afuah, "Redefining Firm Boundaries in the Face of the Internet: Are Firms Really Shrinking?" *Academy of Management Review* 34 (2003), pp. 34–53.

Part **Two**

Cases

Case 1

Viagra: A Hard Act to Follow

In the late 1940s, Percy Spencer stopped in front of a magnetron (the power tube that drives a radar set) while touring one of his laboratories at the Raytheon Company. Suddenly, he realized that the chocolate bar in his pocket had begun to melt. His curiosity piqued, the surprised inventor fetched a bag of unpopped popcorn and held it up to the magnetron. To Spencer's delight, the kernels quickly exploded and the microwave oven was born.[1]

"Serendipity" is defined as, "The faculty of finding valuable or agreeable things not sought for."[2] From dynamite to penicillin, many of history's greatest technological advances have been the result of fortunate accidents. However, realizing that an event is noteworthy and then finding commercial value in that discovery requires more than just luck. Nick Terrett, the Pfizer chemist credited with piecing together the puzzle that led to the discovery of Viagra (sildenafil citrate), comments:

> The story that the media have promoted is that the discovery [of the drug] is serendipitous, but fortune favors the prepared mind that is alert to exploit new findings. The result is that we have a high-quality drug, and erectile dysfunction was the home where that drug could have the most impact. This just reflects an investment in basic research.[3]

If "basic research" is all that is required to make a billion dollar per year drug, why was Pfizer the first pharmaceutical company to bring the drug to market and how will the company remain ahead of its competitors? How can other pharmaceutical companies apply the lessons learned from Viagra to ensure that they discover and commercialize the next blockbuster prescription drug?

THE DRUG DISCOVERY AND DEVELOPMENT PROCESS

The drug discovery process is a challenging, resource-intensive, and risky endeavor. It can take as long as 15 years to bring a compound from the researcher's laboratory to the market, often with development costs of over $500 million.[4] The Research and Development (R&D) process used by the major pharmaceutical companies can be divided into pre-clinical research, clinical research, and submission/approval.

Pre-clinical Research

Target Identification The first step in drug discovery is the establishment of disease-relevant targets upon which a potential drug will act. Ideally, these targets are associated with chronic diseases afflicting a large number of individuals. To date, all of the pharmaceutical drugs ever developed have targeted approximately 500 known physiologic targets, primarily proteins involved in diseases.

The selection and examination of specific biological targets have been greatly enhanced by recent technological advances in genomics and proteomics. With the sequencing of the human genome completed and an improved understanding of the specific proteins for which these genes code, pharmaceutical researchers will soon have access to information on thousands of protein targets and their respective roles in human disease.

Assay Development Once the target is established, pharmaceutical researchers design artificial biochemical systems known as "target assays" based on the target protein and its function within the body. Several assays are designed, each providing a realistic human physiologic environment within which to test potential compounds.

Generating Leads Chemical compounds that produce desired outcomes when tested in the assays are considered for "lead compound" status. Due to the potential for failure, it is necessary to select multiple lead compounds. With the advent of high-throughput screening technologies, the number of compounds and speed of assessment have significantly increased. Lead compounds can also be licensed from other institutions in exchange for cash and/or various agreements based on potential development milestones and revenues.

Optimizing Leads Lead compounds are biochemically altered to enhance their therapeutic properties. This practice relies heavily on a process innovation

Jeff Kreick, Richard Mitschke, Corey Peak, Lee Susen, and Wade Warren prepared this case under the supervision of Professor Allan Afuah as a basis for class discussion rather than to illustrate either effective or ineffective management. Creative liberties have been taken in developing the introductory and concluding paragraphs of the case.

known as "rational drug design" (see Exhibit 1). Chemical leads usually possess many, but not all, of the properties required for ultimate success. Chemists and biologists work in tandem to optimize the lead's structure in order to add needed characteristics to the compound.[5]

Clinical Research

If a compound passes pre-clinical testing, an application is filed with the relevant governmental regulatory authority requesting permission for human clinical testing. Historically, it has taken approximately 100 different research projects to produce just one candidate for clinical trial. Of those that are tested on humans, less than 10% actually receive final approval and become marketable drug therapies. Researchers continue to apply new process innovations in an effort to improve the odds of success.[6]

Phase I clinical trials: Testing usually involves a small number (20 to 80) of healthy volunteers. These trials are conducted to determine dosage levels and to study the drug's safety profile, including any potential side effects.

Phase II clinical trials: The drug is given to a larger number (50 to 500) of patients diagnosed with the disease of interest. Phase II studies confirm the safety profile within the relevant patient groups and measure the drug's effectiveness.

Phase III clinical trials: The final studies involve many more people and are much larger in scale and expense. The main focus is the generation of substantial evidence about the drug's safety and effectiveness in the intended patient population. Phase III trials are one of the last and most important steps in obtaining FDA approval for commercialization.[7]

Submission and Approval

Governmental regulatory agencies are presented with all of the relevant data from pre-clinical and clinical trials as part of the pharmaceutical company's official request for marketing authorization. This report is known as a New Drug Application (NDA) in the United States and a Marketing Authorization Application (MAA) internationally. The regulatory agencies review the document to determine whether the scientific research supports the request. If, and when, the application is approved, the company receives permission to market the drug,

but only according to the specific indication(s), or disease(s), for which it has been approved.[8]

PFIZER, INC.

With approximately $30 billion in revenues, Pfizer was arguably the dominant global pharmaceutical company in 2002.* Not only did Pfizer have the largest R&D budget in the industry ($4.4 billion in 2000),[9] but it was also well known for its massive sales force and its marketing prowess. Analysts believed Pfizer had had the highest earnings growth rate in the industry (25%) for 2000–2002 due to its stable of blockbuster drugs, a strong drug pipeline, and merger-related cost savings. Among all major pharmaceutical firms, Pfizer had the lowest risk of market share loss due to generic drug sales because less than 15% of its 2000 pharmaceutical sales would be exposed to generic cannibalization before 2005.[10]

History

In the mid-1840s, Charles Pfizer and his cousin, Charles Erhart, immigrated to the United States from Germany. Charles Pfizer was a chemist by trade, while Erhart was a confectioner. The two united their skills in 1849 and formed a chemical firm, Charles Pfizer and Co., in Brooklyn, New York. Initially, they established a competitive advantage by manufacturing specialty chemicals that were not otherwise produced domestically.

The cousins' initial breakthrough marked the first of many medical innovations for Pfizer. They transformed an existing intensely bitter treatment of parasitic worms (santonin) into a more palatable agent by mixing it with almond-flavored toffee and shaping it into a candy cone. The product was immediately successful and, within a decade, Charles Pfizer and Co. produced over a dozen other chemicals and medicines. As a result of the company's growth during the Civil War, Pfizer opened new corporate offices in the Wall Street district of Manhattan in 1868.

The company was thrust into the modern drug business in 1941 when it developed a cost effective method for mass-producing penicillin. In fact, Pfizer saved countless lives by supplying over half of the "miracle drug" used by the Allied forces during World War II. With the capital raised through penicillin sales, Pfizer increased its research and development expenditures. In 1950, the first drug from the

---

*This argument is based on the number of top selling drugs, total revenues, and R&D spending. See Exhibit 2 for Pfizer's financial performance.

company's discovery program, Terramycin, a broad-spectrum antibiotic, became Pfizer's first pharmaceutical drug. Pfizer also opened operational facilities throughout the United States and internationally during this period, including the Sandwich, England, facility responsible for the production of Viagra. Worldwide sales surpassed $200 million in the mid-1960s and then reached the billion dollar mark in 1972.

Mergers and Acquisitions

Pfizer's impressive growth came from both continuous new product launches (including polio vaccines and antibiotics) and an aggressive acquisition strategy. In 1953, Pfizer bought drug maker Roerig. In the 1960s, the company moved into consumer products with the purchase of BenGay, Desitin, and cosmetics maker Coty. It also bought a hospital products company and a heart-valve manufacturer.[11] In 1997, Pfizer began marketing Lipitor, the cholesterol-lowering drug discovered by Warner-Lambert. The blockbuster drug grabbed 13% market share within its first four months on the market. Later in 2000, Warner-Lambert, which also makes popular products such as Listerine, Rolaids, and Sudafed, merged with Pfizer.[12]

Product Portfolio

As of 2002, the company had four operating groups: Consumer Health Care, Animal Health, Pharmaceuticals, and Research & Development. The Consumer Health Group represented many of the most trusted over-the-counter brand names in the industry, including Benadryl, Sudafed, Listerine, Rolaids, Visine, Schick, and Dentyne. Pfizer's Animal Health Group produced anti-infectives, anti-parasitics, anti-inflammatories, vaccines, and other medicines for more than 30 animal species. These capabilities made Pfizer an acknowledged global leader in improving the health of pets, livestock, and poultry. The Pharmaceuticals Group was a recognized leader as well; Pfizer produced five of the top 20 best-selling medications (Exhibit 3). The major pharmaceutical categories included cardiovascular, infectious diseases, central nervous system disorders, arthritis, erectile dysfunction, allergies, and diabetes. Pfizer's global R&D division was created after the merger with Warner-Lambert and was the world's largest private biomedical R&D operation.[13] (Exhibit 4 details many of Pfizer's products.)

ERECTILE DYSFUNCTION

Erectile dysfunction (ED), also known as impotence, is defined as the inability to achieve or maintain an erection sufficient for satisfactory sexual performance. ED does not address issues related to libido, fertility, premature ejaculation, or orgasm. While most men experience erectile problems at some point in their lifetime, ED is a chronic disorder. Estimates range from 30 to 50 million affected men in the United States, and older men are more likely to suffer from ED than younger men (65% of men over 60). Before the advent of orally administered drugs, less than 10% of men suffering from ED sought medical solutions.[14]

Erectile dysfunction can be categorized as either functional (psychological) or organic (physical), although the disorder is rarely either purely functional or organic in origin. In the 1960s, the sex researchers Masters and Johnson declared that impotence was primarily a psychological problem,[15] but health experts now believe that 80% of ED is "organic" in nature. Causes of ED include a number of disorders and diseases, age, medication, and recreational drug use. Amongst diabetics, for example, ED occurs in up to 40% of men.[16]

Prior Treatments

Before the release of Viagra, the American Urology Association recommended three basic treatments for impotence: vacuum therapy, injection and intraurethral therapy, and surgical implants.

Vacuum therapy was the least invasive of the recommended treatments and involved placing a vacuum cylinder over the penis to increase blood flow into the organ. A tension ring would then be placed on the base of the erect penis to maintain rigidity. While the device had success rates of 90%, many patients found the devices difficult to use. The costs ranged from $150 to $400, and leading brands included ErecAid, Post-T-Vac, and VED.

Injection therapy caused an immediate erection through the injection of a mixture of drugs into the base of the penis. While the results were instant, the therapy was often described as "painful" and had the potential to form scar tissue at the point of injection. A newer method involved the placement of a suppository an inch into the urethra. The drugs used in both of these treatments could induce prolonged erections, a condition known as priapism, which caused tissue destruction if not corrected within hours. Costs averaged $20 for a single injection or urethral insert.

Surgical implants were the riskiest treatment and required a surgeon to insert inflatable cylinders into the penis, a pump in the scrotum, and a reservoir either in the scrotum or abdomen. While sensation, ejaculation, and orgasm usually were not affected, implants were only 20% effective and had been associated with postoperative infections, mechanical failure, silicon particle shedding, and the risk of the initial surgery. The surgery and equipment cost up to $20,000 and required a short hospital stay. Leading vendors for these prosthetics were American Medical Systems and Mentor Urology.[17]

Vascular surgery and hormone treatments served a very small percentage of ED patients and were rarely administered. Vascular surgery was used for young patients who had pelvic or perineal trauma, and hormone treatments were given to patients with extremely low levels of testosterone.[18]

Many alternative remedies have been used to combat impotence, but these products tend to suggest an aphrodisiac effect (help with the loss of sexual desire) rather than improvement with impotence. Alternative treatments range from the "potency wood" of South America to the penis of the tiger in China. Foods that some people claim have aphrodisiacal qualities include chilies, chocolate, licorice, lard, scallops, oysters, olives, and anchovies. No evidence exists to support these claims.[19]

VIAGRA DEVELOPMENT

Pfizer's Sandwich, England, facility was the largest pharmaceutical research operation outside of the United States. Serving as Pfizer's European research center, it employed 3,500 people, almost half of them in research and development. Prior to the development of Viagra, drugs developed at the Sandwich facility were responsible for nearly 40% of Pfizer's total pharmaceutical sales.[20] Dr. Peter Ringrose, Senior Vice President of Worldwide Discovery and Medicinal Research and Development until 1997, believed that the facility's success was linked to its distinctive trans-Atlantic chemistry—British irreverence combined with its parent's American entrepreneurship.[21]

Nick Terrett, a Pfizer chemist at the Sandwich research facility, joined a project in 1986 to help develop a lead compound for the treatment of cardiovascular disease. Terrett began by studying hypertension, but he soon shifted his focus to angina, a type of chest pain caused by poor blood flow to the heart. Terrett decided to target known inhibitors of the phosphodiesterase enzyme (PDE) for drug development, reasoning that a PDE inhibitor could lead to relaxation of smooth muscle cells in the kidney and blood vessels, thereby increasing blood flow and lowering blood pressure.

Terrett's team employed a recent innovation in drug discovery known as "rational drug design" (see Exhibit 1) to efficiently improve upon the structure and subsequent efficacy of these previously established PDE inhibitors. Approximately 1,500 chemical compounds were created, tested, and screened during the four-year discovery process. The compound that would ultimately become known as Viagra, UK-92,480, was first synthesized in July 1989. While it was not the most selective of the compounds they had synthesized, it had the best overall performance in pre-clinical testing.

Unfortunately, UK-92,480 proved less efficacious in clinical trials than Terrett had hoped. It passed phase I safety tests in healthy volunteers, but the data on changes in blood pressure and cardiac output were discouraging. Then, in 1992, several critical events occurred that offered new hope to Terrett and his team. While results from the phase II trials in angina patients indicated that UK-92,480 had poor efficacy, a clinician who was running a late phase I dosage study on normal men noted that erections were occurring as a side effect of the drug. Participants did not report the erections until they were well into the 10-day trial period, and the finding alone did not cause the strategic shift in the drug's development. "The decision to do the pilot studies [in erectile dysfunction patients] wasn't that obvious. Erections hadn't been reported until the 4th or 5th day, and there were other side effects as well," said Ian Howard Osterloh, global candidate team leader for Viagra's research and development group.[22]

At the same time, nitric oxide (NO) was receiving a great deal of research attention because of its recently discovered physiological effects, including the regulation of such diverse functions as blood pressure, nerve firing, and immune responses.* More

---

*The three scientists, Robert Furchgott, Louis Ignarro, and Ferid Murad, responsible for this discovery won the 1998 Nobel Prize in Physiology or Medicine.

importantly for Pfizer, there were also reports that NO served as a mediator in penile erections. Terrett recognized that the mechanism of action of UK-92,480 (suppression of PDE) would amplify the effects of NO, and he hypothesized that it could therefore potentially alleviate the underlying chemical shortcoming behind erectile dysfunction (see Exhibit 5). He reported, "So these three came together: There was anecdotal evidence of erections in the drug trial, reports in the literature about nitric oxide's effects on blood vessels, and evidence that erectile function is related to nitric oxide."[23]

The Erectile Dysfunction Trials

Pfizer faced several difficult challenges when deciding whether to pursue UK-92,480 as a drug to combat erectile dysfunction rather than as an angina treatment. "The observation was made in healthy volunteers, but only those taking 3 doses a day for 10 days. None of the single-dose studies had shown erections, so it wasn't clear that it would be of clinical use," said Michael Allen, a clinical trial leader for Pfizer. Moreover, the diagnostic criteria, efficacy instruments, and regulatory guidelines necessary to conduct clinical trials did not exist for the disorder.

However, there appeared to be a very strong market opportunity. "Based on survey reports, we were thinking that about 1 in 20 men aged greater than 40 suffered from erectile dysfunction," said Allen. Those estimates would prove to be significantly lower than the actual market size, due primarily to the fact that affected men were not reporting the disorder to their doctors. Pfizer took two years to assess the market need for an erectile dysfunction medicine and to prepare for new clinical trials. By 1994, they had decided to pursue phase II testing with men suffering from ED.

Unlike injection therapies, Viagra would cause erections only in the presence of sexual stimulation. This characteristic was viewed as positive for the patient, but it presented a challenge to the design of the clinical trials. "There was no point in analyzing the effect unless there was sexual stimulation, and the quality of the sexual stimulation was going to be important, so obviously any assessment in a laboratory was bound to be artificial. The real test had to be in the home setting," said Osterloh. He decided to ask his patients to document their erections and the ensuing sexual experience through a diary. In some cases, supporting evidence was also drawn from the entries of the patient's partner. "Fortu-

nately, the regulatory authorities bought into using these questionnaires as the main marker of efficacy," said Osterloh.

The results of the trials were immediately encouraging, and the drug's efficacy proved to be far superior to injection therapies. 88% of the patients reported improved erections compared with 39% of the patients who were given placebos. 90% of the patients indicated that they wished to continue treatment. As patients flocked to enroll in the trials, the original market forecast began to look understated. "That made it clear that there were a lot of patients out there seeking help," said Allen.

Government regulations required that all medications distributed to patients during clinical research be accounted for at the end of the trials. As patients were asked to turn in their unused pills, the research team heard excuses like, "Oh, I flushed them down the toilet." When trial participants were informed that Viagra would not be available until after regulatory approval was obtained, many patients wrote Pfizer to express their despair.

Excerpts of Two Letters from Patients in the
Viagra Clinical Trials[24]

Before I took part in this study, I was heavily depressed. I was continually arguing with my wife and generally making life hell for her and my children . . . Entering the study saved our family from much grief . . . It probably saved my marriage and possibly my life.

The drug has proved very effective in enabling me to engage in sexual activity . . . Despite my age (91 on 24th Oct.), I am able to function as well as men many years my junior.

Osterloh said, "We've never had the level of patient response that we've had in this program."[25]

COMMERCIALIZATION— BRINGING VIAGRA TO MARKET

Pfizer took some calculated risks in anticipation of FDA approval of Viagra. Rather than waiting for final FDA approval, they began preparing for large-scale manufacturing while the drug was still in early testing. This aggressive move allowed Pfizer to meet the anticipated market demand for the drug at its launch. Another strategic maneuver used to expedite the Viagra launch focused on conducting more than half of the necessary clinical trials with smaller partner firms in order to complete the research faster.* Once the product was approved by the FDA, Pfizer's sales force of 4,500 sales representatives (the largest for any U.S. pharmaceutical firm) was ready to take the message to the prescribing doctors.[26]

Pfizer believed that it had a blockbuster in the making and filed an application with the FDA for Viagra to receive a priority review on September 29, 1997. Viagra received rapid FDA approval and was available for sale in early April, 1998. By its second week on the market, Viagra had captured 79% of the ED market, making the launch the largest in history.[27] After Pfizer racked up a record 300,000 prescriptions per week by early May, some particularly enthusiastic analysts predicted that sales could eventually be as high as $10 to $20 billion a year worldwide.[28] Dr. John Stripling, an Atlanta urologist, wrote so many Viagra prescriptions that he decided to start using a rubber stamp.[29]

Direct-to-Consumer Advertising (DTC)

Pharmaceutical promotional spending grew from $9.2 billion in 1996 to $15.7 billion in 2000 and has become one of the fastest growing categories of advertising. Direct-to-consumer (DTC) advertising of prescription medicines informed consumers about new medical treatments, provided a valuable resource for patients to obtain information about specific diseases, conditions, and treatments, and helped to initiate a dialogue between patients and doctors. 86% of people that viewed DTC ads said the ads helped increase their awareness of new drugs, and 62% said the ads helped them to have better discussions with their physician about their health.[30]

There was also a growing acceptance of DTC advertising by doctors. 64% of doctors believed that DTC advertising helped to "educate and inform" their patients, and 40% of doctors believed the ads increased patient compliance.[31] Critics of DTC advertising claimed that it unnecessarily drove up pharmaceutical expenditures and misled consumers into believing that they needed drugs that might be inappropriate for them. Proponents countered that, after the relaxation of DTC advertising rules and the launch of Viagra, it was discovered that for every million men who asked for the medicine, an estimated 30,000 had untreated diabetes, 140,000 had untreated high blood pressure, and 50,000 had untreated heart disease.[32]

In 1990, 10 different medicines were advertised directly to consumers. In 1997, that number climbed to 79, as the FDA relaxed restrictions on DTC ads and as more pharmaceutical companies recognized the value in raising awareness levels of their medicines with patients.[33] DTC advertising expenditures increased at an exponential rate and topped $2.2 billion in 2000, an increase of over 53% per annum since 1995.[34] The 50 most heavily DTC-advertised drugs in 2000 represented 95% of all DTC spending. Vioxx, an antiarthritic drug, topped the chart at over $160 million. DTC advertising expenses for Viagra in 2000 were $89 million, making it the 6th most advertised drug to consumers. (Exhibit 6 shows a list of DTC spending for the top 10 in 2000.)

Pfizer used a variety of DTC advertising to reach Viagra's target audience. Bob Dole, former U.S. Senator and 1996 Republican Presidential Nominee, was selected by Pfizer to participate in advertisements and speaking engagements focused on raising awareness about impotence and men's health.[35] Pfizer also sponsored a NASCAR racecar driven by Mark Martin that featured the Viagra logo on its hood. The NASCAR audience was predominately men (62%) and had proven to be brand loyal, with 72% of the fans supporting advertiser's products (compared to around 37% of fans of the NBA, NFL, and Major League Baseball).[36] NASCAR's television ratings were second only to the NFL in 1998 and increased 40% while other major sports remained unchanged or declined during the same period. The great 1970s Hall of Fame hockey player Guy LaFleur was a spokesperson for Pfizer Canada, directly targeting the Canadian male audience.[37]

Other forms of pharmaceutical promotion included "detailing" (which was a one-to-one sales call from a pharmaceutical representative), medical journal advertising, and meetings and events targeted towards physicians. Total promotional expenditures for the industry in 2000 were $15.7 billion, with DTC advertising contributing nearly $2.5 billion (15.9%).

Lifestyle Drugs

The rise of DTC advertising in the United States coincided with the development and marketing of a new class of drugs called "lifestyle drugs." One definition of "lifestyle drugs" stated that they " . . . are attractive to the popular media; they enhance quality

---

*Some firms, such as Merck, prefer to do most of their important clinical trials in-house.

of life; they often address problems of a social or cosmetic nature; they are not conducive to reimbursement." This term was somewhat contentious for pharmaceutical companies since it implied that there was not a medical necessity for the drugs they were marketing.[38]

Other diseases besides ED that were widely classified as lifestyle diseases included obesity, depression, hair loss, social anxiety, and allergies. Some of these diseases were basic side-effects of aging and, as the large "baby boomer" portion of the U.S. population continued to grow older, treatments for these age-related diseases were predicted to increase in popularity.

Reimbursement/Insurance Issues

Although controversial, many formularies defined Viagra as a reimbursable prescription with a stated maximum amount allowed. An example health plan would reimburse for up to 6 tablets per month provided that the patient was male, over 18 years of age, and had been diagnosed with ED. Ninety days was the normal prescription length (18 tablets). Some health plans dropped Viagra from the formulary, claiming that it was a lifestyle drug. In 1999, there were 12 states that were allowed to exclude Viagra on formularies. Many states cited "black market" sales of the drug as support for their argument against inclusion. As of 2002, the Department of Veterans' Affairs (VA) did not support the drug, but nationwide Medicaid did. Approximately 72% of health plans had the drug on formulary and 98% of these had restrictions. The restrictions limited quantity (64%), required medical necessity (19%), and/or required patient co-pay or additional premiums (11%).[39]

Internet Sales

The fact that Viagra was available only with a doctor's prescription didn't stop the drug from being sold online by several vendors. Online pricing for the drug varied, but averaged close to $10 per 100mg pill (very close to brick-and-mortar drugstore prices). There was also a consultation fee of approximately $75 and shipping costs of approximately $18. The typical order quantity was 60 pills, and refill quantities varied from vendor to vendor. The total average price on the Internet was $715 for a 12-month supply.

International Expansion

Viagra was available with a prescription in more than 100 countries and, as of October 2001, 40% of the worldwide revenue for Viagra came from outside the United States.[40] In January 2000, India approved production of a Viagra generic, which would sell for $1.60. The patent laws in India protect the production process of a drug, but not the drug itself. In July of 2000, Viagra was launched successfully in China. In September 2001, Germany's health ministry reported that 616 people worldwide had died after using Viagra, but cautioned against attributing blame for the deaths to the drug. Pfizer responded by saying that the drug was safe when used as prescribed. "Many patients taking Viagra have underlying cardiovascular disease, such as hypertension. Erectile dysfunction is a symptom of those conditions, so they already have risk factors for heart attack."[41]

VIAGRA: "A BLOCKBUSTER"

One month after the drug's debut, Wall Street analysts initially estimated that sales of Viagra would easily hit $5 billion, and some optimistic projections topped $11 billion.[42] In 1998, Pfizer reported Viagra sales of $788 million.[43]

Drugs termed "blockbuster" generally have sales that exceed the $1 billion mark. In 1999, its first full year on the market, Viagra crossed this threshold with sales of $1.02 billion. Sales increased 32% to $1.3 billion in 2000[44] and to $1.5 billion in 2001 (an increase of 15%). Viagra represented one of eight drugs in the Pfizer portfolio that exceeded this $1 billion sales mark in 2000. As of October 2001, Pfizer reported that more than 45 million Viagra prescriptions had been written by more than 500,000 physicians for more than 16 million men worldwide.

One commonly cited statistic was that half of American men between the ages of 40 and 70 suffer from ED to some extent, but it's not clear how many men would actually prove to be regular customers. If just 16 million people used it once a week, annual sales could hit $5.8 billion, but doctors were predicting that the average rate of use would likely be closer to a dozen times a month.[45] In the U.S. alone, there were an estimated 30 million affected men.

THE FUTURE OF VIAGRA

Pfizer's patent on Viagra is set to expire in 2011, potentially allowing for another decade of high revenue opportunities for Pfizer before generics hit the market. However, competition looms on the horizon for Viagra. Eli Lilly, in partnership with ICOS Corporation, submitted an NDA for Cialis in June 2001, and Bayer announced plans to submit an NDA for Vardenafil in late 2001. Both of these drugs would be oral ED treatments targeting the same population as Pfizer's Viagra. Other treatments in development include Nastech Pharmaceutical's apomorphine HCl, TAP Pharmaceutical's Uprima, and Zonagen's Vasomax.

Can Pfizer continue to grow the market for ED treatment and reach the $5 billion sales mark, projected when the drug was launched? How will these new competitive treatments affect Viagra's growth, and how should Pfizer react?

EXHIBIT 1
Rational Drug Design Background Information
Source: Direct Excerpt: "What Is Bioinformatics?" *Bioplanet;* Direct Excerpt: "Rational Drug Design." ABC Online.

BIOINFORMATICS

Bioinformatics is the application of computer technology to the management of biological information. Computers are used to gather, store, analyze, and integrate biological and genetic information, which can then be applied to gene-based drug discovery and development. The need for Bioinformatics capabilities has been precipitated by the explosion of publicly available genomic information resulting from the Human Genome Project.

The science of Bioinformatics, which is the melding of molecular biology with computer science, is essential to the use of genomic information in understanding human diseases and in the identification of new molecular targets for drug discovery. In recognition of this, many universities, government institutions, and pharmaceutical firms have formed bioinformatics groups, consisting of computational biologists and bioinformatics computer scientists. Such groups will be key to unraveling the mass of information generated by large scale sequencing efforts under way in laboratories around the world.

RATIONAL DRUG DESIGN

So let's take a closer look at this idea of "rational drug design," which it's said is the way of the future for finding new medications. It's a high-tech, knowledge-intensive approach, the basic idea being that if you know exactly which gene, and which protein, is the culprit for an illness, you can tailor-make a drug to combat it.

The key is to understand the shape of the chemicals involved. Because in every chemical reaction, and your body is going through hundreds, even thousands, right now, a molecule of a very specific shape is interacting with another molecule of a very specific complementary shape. The molecules can interact only if they literally fit together, and pharmaceuticals work by interfering with this highly specific interaction.

In the past, finding out what drugs worked for any particular disease was basically trial and error. But increasingly, researchers are beginning with an understanding of the mechanism of the disease, and building a molecule to get in its way. One way of doing that is by modeling the molecules on a powerful computer and doing a series of 3D jigsaw puzzles.

EXHIBIT 2 Pfizer Financial Performance*
Source: Pfizer 2000 Annual Report, Case Team Analysis.

Income Statement
(all numbers in millions)

	Fiscal Year Ending December 31, XXXX		
	2000	**1999**	**1998**
Revenue	$ 29,574	$ 27,376	$ 23,231
Cost of sales	4,907	5,464	4,907
Gross profit	24,667	21,912	18,324
SG&A expense	11,442	10,810	9,563
Research and development	4,435	4,036	3,305
Merger-related costs	3,257	33	—
Other expenses/(income)	(248)	88	1,059
Earnings before taxes	5,781	6,945	4,397
Provision for income taxes	2,049	1,968	1,163
Minority interests	14	5	2
Income from continuing operations	3,718	4,972	3,232
Discontinued operations	8	(20)	1,401
Net income	3,726	4,952	4,633

Balance Sheet

	2000	1999
Current assets	$17,187	$16,311
Noncurrent assets	16,323	15,061
Total assets	33,510	31,372
Current liabilities	11,981	11,896
Noncurrent liabilities	5,453	5,526
Total liabilities	17,434	17,422
Shareholders' equity	16,076	13,950
Total liabilities and shareholders' equity	33,510	31,372
Profit Margin (%)	12.6%	18.1%
Effective Tax Rate (%)	35.4%	28.3%
Return on Equity (%)	23.2%	35.5%
Return on Assets (%)	11.1%	15.8%
Growth Rates		
5-Yr Annual Earnings Growth		12.12%
5-Yr Annual Div Growth		15.58%
5-Yr Annual Revenue Growth		23.39%
% Chg EPS YTD vs Last YTD		155.6%

*Financial data have been restated to reflect the merger with Warner-Lambert Company, accounted for as a pooling of interests.

EXHIBIT 3 Top 50 Branded Pharmaceuticals in 2000 (U.S. Retail Sales and Market Share)
Source: Scott-Levin SPA.

Product	Manufacturer	Sales (000)	Market Share
Prilosec	AstraZeneca	4,102,195	3.70%
Lipitor	**Pfizer/Parke-Davis**	**3,692,657**	**3.40%**
Prevacid	Tap	2,832,602	2.60%
Prozac	Eli Lilly	2,567,107	2.30%
Zocor	Merck	2,207,042	2.00%
Celebrex	**Searle/Pfizer**	**2,015,508**	**1.80%**
Zoloft	**Pfizer**	**1,890,416**	**1.70%**
Paxil	SmithKline Beecham	1,807,955	1.60%
Caritin	Schering-Plough	1,667,347	1.50%
Glucophage	Bristol-Myers Squibb	1,629,157	1.50%
Norvasc	**Pfizer**	**1,597,091**	**1.50%**
Augmentin	SmithKline Beecham	1,584,397	1.40%
Vioxx	Merck	1,517,993	1.40%
Zyprexa	Eli Lilly	1,418,411	1.30%
Pravachol	Bristol-Myers Squibb	1,203,474	1.10%
Premarin tablets	Wyeth-Ayerst	1,146,808	1.00%
Neurontin	Parke-Davis	1,131,678	1.00%
Oxycontin	Purdue Pharma	1,052,771	1.00%
Cipro	Bayer	1,023,657	0.90%
Zithromax Z-Pak	**Pfizer**	**961,579**	**0.90%**
Risperdal	Janssen	959,707	0.90%
Wellbutrin SR	Glaxo Wellcome	850,934	0.80%
Zestril	AstraZeneca	833,359	0.80%
Effexor XR	Wyeth-Ayerst	815,816	0.70%
Allegra	Hoechst Marion Roussel	810,001	0.70%
Viagra	**Pfizer**	**809,377**	**0.70%**
Ambien	Searle	798,858	0.70%
Depakote	Abbott	758,329	0.70%
Levaquin	Ortho-McNeil	753,711	0.70%
Imitrex	Glaxo Wellcome	747,631	0.70%
Zyrtec	**Pfizer**	**739,543**	**0.70%**
Celexa	Forest	737,487	0.70%
Prempro	Wyeth-Ayerst	711,798	0.60%
Fosamax	Merck	704,289	0.60%
Singulair	Merck	676,515	0.60%
Synthroid	Knoll	649,256	0.60%
Flovent	Glaxo Wellcome	647,980	0.60%
Accutane	Roche	636,246	0.60%
Flonase	Glaxo Wellcome	618,714	0.60%
Avandia	SmithKline Beecham	617,629	0.60%
Ortho Tri-Cyclen	Ortho-McNeil	616,997	0.60%
Ultram	Ortho-McNeil	601,465	0.50%
Plavix	Bristol-Myers Squibb	599,512	0.50%
Biaxin	Abbott	599,366	0.50%
Vasotec	Merck	584,418	0.50%
Pepcid	Merck	568,684	0.50%
Actos	Takeda	550,674	0.50%
Accupril	Parke-Davis	500,793	0.50%
Enbrel	Immunex/Wyeth-Ayerst	500,363	0.50%
Claritin D 24-hour	Schering-Plough	493,420	0.40%

EXHIBIT 4   **Major Pfizer Products, March 2001**
Source: SG Cowen Securities Corporation.

Cardiovascular
Lipitor
Norvasc
Cardura
Accupri
Tikosyn
Lopid
Minipress XL/Minipress
Procardia XL

Anti-Infectives
Zithromax
Diflucan
Viracept
Unasyn IM/IV/Oral
Sulperazone
Unasyn/Sulperazone
Vfend
Rescriptor
Cefobid
Trovan

Central Nervous System
Zoloft
Neurontin
Geodon
Relpax
Pregabalin
Aricept
Dilantin
Cerebyx
Cognex

Metabolic
Exubera
Glucotrol Line
FemHRT
Rezulin

Animal Health
Nemex
Coxistac
Mecadox
Stafac
Dectomax
Revolution
SBH Animal Health

Anti-Inflammatory
Celebrex
Ponstel
Feldene

Consumer Care Products
Schick/Wilkinson
Listerine/Cool Mint
Tetra
Sudafed
Zantac 75
Lubriderm
Benedryl
Neosporin
Visine
Actifed
Plax
Rolaids
Desitin
Unisom
EPT
Benylin
Barbasol
Nix
Listerine Toothpaste
Polysporin
Sinutab

Confectionary
Halls Line
Trident
Dentyne
Certs
Clorets Line
Bubbaloo
Chiclets

EXHIBIT 5
Nitric Oxide and the
Molecular Basis of an
Erection
Viagra acts by
inhibiting PDE 5 and
thereby raising the
concentration of
cGMP. This in turn
results in an erection.

MOLECULAR BASIS OF AN ERECTION

Nitric Oxide (NO) was receiving a lot of research attention because of its role as a signaling molecule. NO acts as an intercellular messenger. It has a wide range of physiological effects, including vasodilation, antiplatelet activity, modulation of neurotransmission, and immune defense against pathogens. Importantly for Pfizer, there were reports that NO also plays an essential role in penile erection. NO, like ANP, activates secondary signaling via cGMP. That suggested a hypothesis for how UK-92,480 might help impotent men: In men with erectile dysfunction, sexual stimulation released insufficient NO from the penile nerves. As a result, cGMP was not building up to sufficient levels to relax the vascular muscles in the penis. Those muscles constrict the blood vessels used to fill the erectile chambers of the penis. When the muscles relax, the vessels dilate sufficiently for blood to fill the erectile chambers, causing an erection. If the NO deficiency hypothesis was true, it followed that by preventing PDE 5 from converting cGMP to GMP, UK-92,480 would cause cGMP in the penis to increase until the vascular muscles relaxed, blood flowed, and an erection resulted.

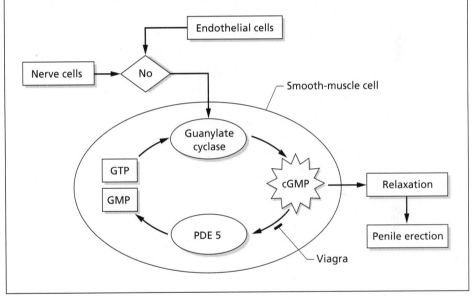

EXHIBIT 6   Top Ten Drugs Sorted by 2000 DTC Advertising Spending
Source: "Prescription Drugs and Mass Media Advertisement, 2000." *NIHCM*, Nov. 2001.

Rank	Name	Type	2000 DTC Spending (millions)
1	Vioxx	Antiarthritic	$160.80
2	Prilosec	Antiulcerant	$107.50
3	Claritin	Oral Antihistimine	$99.70
4	Paxil	Antidepressant	$91.80
5	Zocor	Cholesterol Reducer	$91.20
6	**Viagra**	**Sex Function Disorder**	**$89.50**
7	Celebrex	Antiarthritic	$78.30
8	Flonase	Respiratory Steroids	$73.50
9	Allegra	Oral Antihistimine	$67.00
10	Meridiaa	Antiobesity	$65.00

Endnotes

1. "Microwave Oven and Percy Spencer." About.com, October 2001.

2. *Webster-Merriam Online,* October 2001.

3. Robert Cooke, "A Potent Pill for the Endangered?" *Newsday,* October 20, 1998.

4. "The Cost of Pharmaceuticals." Pfizer.com, September 2001.

5. "Drug Innovations and Approval." Aventis.com, October 2001.

6. David McGibney, "The Future of the Pharmaceutical Industry," Pfizer.com, February 2, 1999.

7. "Drug Development and Review Definitions." Center for Drug Evaluation and Research.

8. "Drug Innovations and Approval," Aventis.com, October 2001.

9. "Great American Companies," Salomon Smith Barney Access, November 2001.

10. Ibid.

11. "Pfizer, Inc.," Hoover's Online, November 2001.

12. Noelle Knox, "Pfizer, Warner-Lambert Agree to Merge," *St. Louis Post-Dispatch,* February 8, 2000.

13. "Collaborative Lab Designed to Ratchet Up Productivity," *Drug Discovery & Development,* August 2000.

14. "Erectile Dysfunction Treatments," Bandolier.

15. John Leland, "A Pill for Impotence?" *Newsweek,* November 17, 1997.

16. "Erectile function and dysfunction," About.com, October 2001.

17. "Impotence Treatment Options," *Viagra Impotence Pill.*

18. "Erectile function and dysfunction," About.com, November 2001.

19. "Impotence (Erectile Dysfunction)," *Medscape Health.*

20. Paul Durman, "Pfizer's UK Labs Find Way from TCP to Viagra," *The Times,* August 17, 1998.

21. Stephen D. Moore, "Pfizer's English Site is Research Boon," *The Wall Street Journal,* September 6, 1996.

22. "Viagra History," *Viagra Impotence Pill.*

23. Robert Cooke, "A Potent Pill for the Endangered?" *Newsday,* October 20, 1998.

24. Jim Kling, "From Hypertension to Angina to Viagra," *Modern Drug Discovery,* 1998.

25. "Viagra History," *Viagra Impotence Pill.*

26. Amy Barrett, "The Formula at Pfizer: Don't Run with the Crowd," *Business Week,* May 11, 1998.

27. "Number of Viagra Prescriptions Sets Launch Record," *Los Angeles Times,* April 21, 1998.

28. Langreth and Petersen, "Drugs: The Morning After: Sales of Viagra Cool Down," *Wall Street Journal,* October 15, 1998.

29. "Number of Viagra Prescriptions Sets Launch Record," *Los Angeles Times,* April 21, 1998.

30. "DTC Advertising Informs Patients About Untreated Diseases, New Treatments, PhRMA Tells Senate Subcommittee," *PhRMA,* July 24, 2001.

31. Ibid.

32. "Backgrounders and Facts: Direct-to-Consumer Advertising," *PhRMA.*

33. Ibid.

34. "Prescription Drugs and Mass Media Advertisement, 2000," *NIHCM,* November 2001.

35. Barbara Lippert, "The Subject Is Erectile Dysfunction, and Media-Happy Bob Dole Is Talking Shop," *Ad Week,* March 8, 1999.

36. NASCAR.com, November 2001.

37. Mike Ulmer, "Lafleur Deal to Push Viagra Is Just the Tip of the Iceberg," *Toronto Sun,* September 7, 2001.

38. "The Lifestyle Drugs Outlook to 2005," InPharm.com, February 1999.

39. Barrueta, Campen, Levine, & Millares, "Kaiser Permanente's Prescription Drug Benefit," *Health Affairs,* May 2000.

40. "2001 Third Quarter Earnings Release," Pfizer.com, October 17, 2001.

41. "Germany Probes Viagra Deaths," *BBC News,* September 10, 2001.

42. Barrett, Laderman, Mandel, Weber, "The New Era of Lifestyle Drugs," *Business Week,* April 30, 1998.

43. Pfizer 1999 Annual Report.

44. Pfizer 2000 Annual Report.

45. Barrett, Laderman, Mandel, Weber, "The New Era of Lifestyle Drugs," *Business Week,* April 30, 1998.

Case 2

Eclipse: The Next Big Thing in Small Aircraft

I applaud the Eclipse team, our investors, suppliers and partners for their steadfast dedication to realizing our dream of changing the way people travel. What we accomplished today is now part of aviation history. Today we stand together, more certain than ever that the Eclipse 500 will forever change the landscape of transportation.[1] (Vern Raburn, CEO, Eclipse Aviation, August 26, 2002)

Vern Raburn, CEO of Eclipse Aviation, stood on the tarmac next to the sleek Eclipse 500 jet a few hours after it had completed its first successful test flight. This was a momentous day for Eclipse Aviation. With break-through design and technology, the Eclipse 500 seemed destined for marketplace success. The test flight had proven the viability of all three pivotal components: revolutionary new engine, ground-breaking friction stir welding design, and advanced avionics instrumentation. These new and untested technologies, developed with key strategic partners, had just demonstrated that they could work together in a single aircraft system. Although many hours of testing still remained, Federal Aviation Administration (FAA) certification for the aircraft was on the horizon for December 2003. In spite of the recent economic downturn and the decline in air travel and aircraft purchasing, the company booked 2,072 pre-orders with an aggressive delivery commitment for January 2004.

INDUSTRY OVERVIEW

Aircraft History

The commercial aircraft industry was born on December 27, 1906, when French emissary Arnold Fordyce purchased one flying machine from the Wright Brothers for $200,000.[2] For the next 40 years, airplanes were almost exclusively in the domain of the military and mail delivery. In the 1930s, United Airlines began operations utilizing the first commercial airliner. Over the next 30 years, several major technological innovations contributed to the development of the airplane as a viable mode of transportation.[3] Radio was used by pilots to avoid storms, and later radio beacons were installed throughout the country to allow pilots to navigate at night and in poor visibility. Pressurized cabins allowed pilots to operate in the inhospitable, oxygen-poor environment above 10,000 feet of elevation. The jet engine, when finally combined with a fuselage that could handle the added stresses, pushed airplanes to previously unattainable speeds and distances. Radar was developed to help locate enemy aircraft, but later would allow radar operators to control air traffic at commercial airports. These innovations, combined with a post-war economic boom, resulted in a huge expansion in commercial aviation during the 1950s when more than one million passengers crossed the Atlantic by plane in a single year, surpassing those traveling by steamship. In 1952 the small plane industry was born with the introduction of the Cessna XL 19B, the world's first turboprop light plane.

Among the most significant nontechnological changes to affect air travel was the 1978 Airline Deregulation Act.[4] Prior to the act, the industry was controlled by the Civil Avionics Board, which determined routes and set prices. With the influence of market forces, the industry experienced escalating airline competition, lower prices, and a sharp increase in the number of available flights. The effect was a huge jump in air travel.

Hub-and-Spoke System

Deregulation left another lasting impact on the industry, the hub-and-spoke system.[5] It became common practice for airlines to select large hub airports to act as transfer points for passengers and cargo. There was a resulting decrease in the number of large carriers servicing small communities and regional airports. In 2002, there were 142 hub airports, accounting for an estimated 80% of U.S. air travel.[6] Four hundred larger nonhub airports, more than 5,000 public, and thousands of private airports handled the remaining 20%. Siphoning the majority of air traffic through a few hub airports contributed to growing congestion and delays. It was estimated that door to door travel time for trips less than 500 miles was roughly the same for air as automobile.

Sarah Davis, Michael Garceau, Victor Gonzalez-Maartens, Jeff Huebner, and Gonzalo Mannucci prepared this case under the supervision of Professor Allan Afuah as a basis for class discussion rather than to illustrate either effective or ineffective management. Creative liberties have been taken in developing the introductory and concluding paragraphs of the case.

Regional Airlines

The air service gap vacated by the hub-and-spoke system had largely been filled by regional airlines.[7] The FAA categorized airlines into: major airlines, such as US Airways and Delta, with greater than $1 billion in revenue and offering national or worldwide service; national airlines, such as Midwest Express and Hawaiian Air, with $100 million to $1 billion in revenue and typically serving particular regions or cities with a mix of large and mid-size jets; and regional airlines, with less than $100 million in revenue and typically serving one region and providing service between one large city and the small cities surrounding it. Regional airlines had a boom in sales and profitability in the years following airline deregulation.

Regional carriers were further subdivided according to size.[8] Large regionals, with operating revenues of $20 million to $100 million, typically utilized aircraft that seat more than 60 passengers, so they held Department of Transportation fitness certificates and had to comply with various FAA operating requirements. Medium regionals, with operating revenues under $20 million, operated similar to large regionals, but on a smaller scale.

Small regionals, often called commuters, were not defined by revenue, but could be identified by the small aircraft that they operated.[9] As all the aircraft they operated had 60 or fewer seats, they were not required to hold a Department of Transportation fitness certificate. Contrary to what the name might suggest, small regionals were the single largest segment of the Regional Airline market.

A survey conducted in 1998 revealed that, in aggregate, regional airline fleets were 65% turboprop, 23% piston-engine, and 12% jet, and averaged 28 seats per aircraft.[10]

Many of the smaller aircraft operated by regional airlines were defined under the General Aviation Manufacturers Association (GAMA) as "general aviation aircraft." [11] These aircraft ranged from small, single-engine planes to mid-size turboprops to the larger turbofans capable of nonstop trans-Pacific flights. The purchasers of these aircraft included individuals, companies, state governments, universities, and others who were interested in quickly and efficiently reaching the more than 5,000 small and rural communities in the United States not served by commercial airlines.

The manufacture of business and regional jets, those with less than 100 seats, was an estimated $18 billion industry in 2001.[12] Roughly fifteen major players shared this revenue, with five in particular dominating the landscape. By far the largest business and regional aircraft manufacturer in the world was Bombardier Inc., owning 26% of the global market. Gulfstream, a General Dynamics subsidiary, was next with an 18% market share. The top five were rounded out by Cessna, a Textron Incorporated division, with 17% market share; Embraer S.A. with 14% market share; and Raytheon Company's business jet division with 10% market share. In general, business jets are classified by the number of passengers they carry and the type of engine: piston, turboprop, turbofan/turbojet.

Aircraft Manufacturing

Aircraft manufacturing is a highly capital-intensive endeavor, requiring large up-front investments in production equipment, continued expenditure throughout the long product development cycle, and heavy research and development investments, which all contribute to one of the highest barriers to entry of any industry.[13] The make-up of the business jet segment, however, demonstrates that these dynamics do not hold true throughout the entire industry. The small business jet segment was highly fragmented with new competitors from entrepreneurs, armed with only venture capital dollars and their own passion, to large diversified manufacturers continuing to enter the industry.

INDUSTRY TRENDS

Security

The tragic events of September 11, 2001, fundamentally changed the commercial aviation industry in the U.S.[14] Heightened government and customer fears made flying commercially a greater hassle for consumers. With more intense security requirements, customers became subject to longer lines at check-in and security and greater restrictions on baggage, particularly carryon luggage. Even after negotiating check-in and security, passengers could even be subject to additional "random" searches prior to boarding the aircraft.

The increased security proved to be one of many burdens that the commercial airline industry was forced to bear following the attacks.[15] Although the government took control of security screeners and the wages associated with those employees, commercial airlines still incurred higher costs as a result of new security requirements. Federal mandates stipulated that commercial airlines secure cockpit doors, purchase equipment costing up to $1 million per machine to screen checked baggage, and pay federal surcharges and airport charges for security screening. These additional costs contributed to decreased profits for major airlines. It could only be assumed that the costs would ultimately be passed to the consumer.

Major Commercial Airlines in Trouble

Customer apprehension also caused industry load factors (the percentage of airline seats actually sold) to hit historically low levels following September 11, 2001.[16] The industry load factor plummeted to 56.2% in September 2001 from 76.2% in August 2001. As a result of this large decrease in demand, commercial airlines cut capacity sharply by reducing flight schedules, laid off 80,300 employees, retired airplanes from service, and cancelled or deferred orders for new airplanes. Additionally, many commercial airlines decreased service to small airports in money-losing markets.[17] Approximately a dozen communities saw service reduced by at least 50%, while ten airports lost commercial service altogether. To compound the issue of decreased demand, average commercial airline prices declined drastically as well.[18] By June 30, 2002, the average one-way domestic fare for a thousand-mile journey had fallen to $118.50, compared to $131.31 a year earlier and $146.52 in January 2001.

Between the events of September 11, 2001, and the ensuing drop in customer demand, commercial airlines were faced with a growing liquidity crisis.[19] Commercial airlines experienced a cash crunch following the four day shutdown imposed by the government on September 11. To prevent some of the major carriers from immediately declaring bankruptcy, Congress passed the Air Transportation Safety and Stabilization Act on September 22, 2001, to give immediate aid to cash-strapped commercial airlines and to provide up to $10 billion in loan guarantees to the industry. Although this act temporarily saved commercial carriers in the most precarious positions, it only postponed the inevitable: US Airways declared bankruptcy on August 11, 2002, while other major carriers remained perilously close to insolvency. Industry-wide, the liquidity crisis constrained commercial airlines' ability to increase capital expenditures and add to flight service networks, thus limiting future growth opportunities and expansion.

Labor

Labor disputes within the commercial airline industry threatened the future of regional service in the U.S.[20]

Scope clauses in existing labor contracts limited the ability of commercial airlines to expand regionally, as pilots who flew large jets for major carriers sought to protect their high salaries by limiting the number of small aircraft in their employers' fleets. Yet the biggest emerging segment of the regional jet market consisted of 70 to 100 seat aircraft. Given the existing scope clauses, some major airlines could be forced to continue operating only large aircraft unsuitable for expansion into regional markets.

Small Aircraft Transportation System (SATS)

The aforementioned hub-and-spoke congestion caused NASA, the Department of Transportation, local aviation and airport authorities, and manufacturers like Eclipse to pursue an alternative to the large airliner, hub-and-spoke system that dominated air travel.[21] SATS was created to make use of the 5,000 public-use airports in the country, within a 20 mile drive of 98% of the U.S. population. NASA believed that these grossly underutilized airports, which supported less than 50 million take-offs and landings in 2000, could, with some minor investment, support up to 500 million. If low-cost air travel technologies and efficient regional air service operators could be identified, SATS could lead to more routes, greater scheduling flexibility, shorter travel times, fewer delays, and lower prices without compromising safety or security.

ECLIPSE AVIATION

Eclipse Aviation was an emerging player in this growing market for smaller aircraft. The firm was founded in 1998, and based in Albuquerque, New Mexico, at Sunport International Airport.[22] Eclipse had over 200 employees, 125 of whom were engineers. CEO Vern Raburn had been with the company since its inception. Raburn had 25 years experience in the information technology industry and held senior executive positions at Microsoft, Lotus Development, Symantec, Slate, and the Paul Allen Group. As a pilot, he amassed almost 5,000 hours of flight time and earned type certificates in aircraft ranging from four-engine airliners to World War II bombers to modern executive jets.

The company was created to design, certify, and manufacture a new line of economical jet aircraft by applying revolutionary manufacturing, engine, and electronics systems to its aircraft.[23] Eclipse intended to sell these aircraft at a third the price of its competitors. The company wanted to provide commercial air passengers with an alternative that allowed more affordable, direct travel between "non-hub" cities.

THE ECLIPSE 500

Although Eclipse Aviation officially launched in 2000, development of the Eclipse 500 had been in progress for two years (see Exhibit 1 for a progress and development timeline). Superior product performance within the small aircraft class was a key point of differentiation for the Eclipse 500. The design, construction, and materials selection of the Eclipse 500 optimized the essential elements of airplane performance: thrust, drag, weight, lift.

Four components go into the engineering of all airplanes: lift, thrust, drag, and weight. Lift is balanced against the other three factors. There is a critical balance between the engine power, overall airplane weight (including body, passengers, fuel, baggage, etc.), aerodynamics, and lift. The challenge of aviation engineers since the first flight has been to design and build airplanes which can continually improve performance characteristics while maintaining affordable costs of operations.

The central consideration for a superior small aircraft product is the requirement of carrying small groups over a relatively short distance in the best possible time. As of 2002, light aircraft (twin-propeller aircraft and light jets) could meet these requirements but at an initial cost of multiple millions of dollars.[24] Additionally, the annual and hourly operating costs were significant for these airplanes.

Eclipse Aviation believed it could radically change this industry by offering a light jet at an affordable price. The proposed jet, the Eclipse 500, was touted as being able to meet all of these requirements at a fraction of the initial and ongoing operating costs. Needless to say, there were doubters to Eclipse's success. Eclipse believed that these skeptics were all following the same logic, WCSYC, which stood for "we couldn't, so you can't."[25]

Eclipse Aviation guaranteed that it could have a light jet certified by December 31, 2003, with the following performance characteristics:[26]

- The guaranteed price of the Eclipse 500 would be $837,500 (+5%) (in June 2000 U.S. dollars).
- The guaranteed performance of the Eclipse 500 would be a maximum cruise speed of 355 knots (+/− 2.5%), a stall speed of 62 knots (+/− 4%), a range with four occupants of 1,300 nautical

miles (+/− 5%), and a useful load of 2,000 pounds (+/− 2.5%).

- The guaranteed standard equipment included:

Full IFR capability	Dual mode S transponder
3 large EFIS displays PFDs & MFD	Dual GPS, IFR enroute & approach certified
Flight management system	Dual AHRS with air data computer
3-axis auto pilot	Dual pitot static system
Color weather radar	Certified for known icing
Dual VHF com	Air conditioning
Dual VHF nav	Standard interior with five seats
Dual localizer and glide slope	Standard paint scheme

Eclipse Aviation hoped to achieve these performance objectives by incorporating three significant design and manufacturing capabilities into the Eclipse 500: friction stir welding, integrated avionics, and advanced turbine technology.

Friction Stir Welding: A Disruptive Technology in Aircraft Manufacturing

Designers of the Eclipse 500 decided early on to use aluminum for the structural components of the aircraft rather than more expensive and hard-to-produce composite materials. Raburn believed that composites offered no substantial weight or strength advantages over aluminum.[27] With a lower-cost aluminum as a base, Eclipse was the first to implement an advanced manufacturing process known as friction stir welding in the assembly of thin-gauge aircraft aluminum. To do so, Eclipse had to petition the FAA for a friction stir welding specification, which they received in May 2002 (one year ahead of schedule).[28]

Friction stir welding was used to produce the main structures of the Boeing Delta family of rockets. The process was also used in the shipbuilding and maritime industries. Eclipse was pioneering the use of friction stir welding for thin materials used in the construction of the Eclipse 500. It was an advanced, high-speed manufacturing process for joining aluminum, which replaced labor-intensive riveting in more than 60% of the Eclipse 500. This technology was highly automated and significantly faster than other structural joining processes. Moreover, it enabled a drastic reduction in aircraft assembly time and eliminated the need for thousands of rivets, resulting in reduced assembly costs, better quality joining, and stronger, lighter joints.[29]

Eclipse partnered with MTS Systems Corporation and the Alcoa Technical Center to develop, validate, certify, and implement the friction stir welding process.[30] Eclipse planned to construct a 50,000 square foot facility that would house the friction stir welding operation. The facility would have enough capacity to support friction stir welding for the company's planned rate of up to 1,500 aircraft per year.

Avio Intelligent Flight System: Innovation in Flight Avionics

The Eclipse 500 was expected to fully integrate its avionics and electronics into the cockpit of the airplane.[31] Traditionally, airplane cockpits were characterized by an endless dashboard of dials, gadgets, and gauges. The Eclipse 500 cockpit combined many of these tools into a pilot-friendly display, the Avio Intelligent Flight System, to promote ease of use and safety. Eclipse used an open architecture of low-cost displays and modular, digital systems to meet these criteria. Eclipse expected that this method would greatly reduce the avionics and electronics costs (see Exhibit 2 for a summary of features).

Tests of the initial Avio avionics and electrical system were scheduled to begin in December 2002 when the fourth Eclipse 500 test aircraft joined the FAA certification program. Raburn was aware that the key challenge for Avio might not be technological, but rather financial. With Avio's unprecedented functionality, it was both a potential source of cost savings, and if glitches and/or other problems arose, a cost inflator. With the Eclipse 500 so fundamentally driven by reduced costs, the success of the program could depend on the performance and acceptance of the Avio system.[32]

The Eclipse Engine: Williams International

Using advanced turbine technology, the engine of the Eclipse 500 was expected to provide a thrust-to-weight ratio that was more than two times that of the state-of-the-art business engine.[33] This technological improvement enabled the airplane to have better overall performance characteristics. The initial engine, called the FJX-2 turbo fan, was devel-

oped by Williams International of Walled Lake, Michigan, and encouraged by funding from NASA's General Aviation Propulsion (GAP) initiative. The goal was to create a highly efficient low-cost turbo fan engine for use in light aircraft.[34]

The Williams EJ22 was the first commercial version of the FXJ-2 engine developed by Williams and NASA under the GAP initiative.[35] The Williams International EJ22 turbofan weighed about 85 pounds each and provided 770 pounds of thrust at sea level, the highest thrust-to-weight ratio of any commercial turbofan engine ever produced. These engines were thought to be the secret weapon of the Eclipse 500 because of their excellent performance, light weight, and power. Moreover, Eclipse partially funded the engine's development and had exclusive rights to it for five years.

Federal Aviation Administration Approval Process

A significant factor in all aircraft design, manufacture, and flight was the FAA and its regulatory processes. Typically, an airplane needed to be certified by the FAA prior to complete manufacturing and sale to customers. For airplanes that used existing technologies and processes, the certification process could be fairly straightforward. However, airplanes such as the Eclipse 500 needed to be "type certified" (an original design approval) before they could be put into production. This process was quite involved and could take numerous years to complete.

The FAA design approval process for type certification was comprised of six phases that needed to be completed:[36]

- *Phase I:* Partnership for Safety Plan
- *Phase II:* Conceptual Design and Standards
- *Phase III:* Refined Product Definition and Risk Management
- *Phase IV:* Certification Project Planning
- *Phase V:* Certification Project Management
- *Phase VI:* Post Certification

By following these steps, Eclipse Aviation hoped to achieve the type certification necessary for the Eclipse 500. This certification essentially allowed pilots to be trained and then insured to fly the plane. Therefore, it was critical for the process to be followed closely and completed. Eclipse had promised its initial purchasers that the Eclipse 500 would be certified by December 31, 2003—a confident yet bold projection.

COMPETITORS

A Crowded Field of Small Business Jet Manufacturers

Eclipse was faced with a formidable competitive landscape consisting of large, established manufacturers such as Bombardier (see Exhibit 3 for a list of the major players in the General Aviation industry) and enthusiastic entrepreneurial startups like Adam Aircraft. These manufacturers offered a range of models to cater to needs and uses of their various clients (see Exhibit 4 for a breakdown of the performance and pricing of competitive models). In the late nineties, a new breed of aircraft manufacturers began emerging to compete with Eclipse for who would be the leader in the next generation of business jets.

Cirrus Design Corporation

Cirrus Design Corporation was founded by lifelong flying enthusiasts, Alan and Dale Klapmeier, in 1984 to design and manufacture kit aircraft.[37] Cirrus soon graduated to full certified commercial aircraft with the SR20, a four-seat single engine luxury jet. One of the unique aspects of the plane was its Cirrus Airframe Parachute System (CAPS), a parachute system that brought the plane down safely in the event of emergency. Just a few years later, Cirrus began selling the SR22, which was similar to the SR20 but with a more powerful engine and extended range. Additional developments in their pipeline included the SR21, powered by a turbo diesel engine, and an all-electric version of the SR20.

Safire

In 2002, Safire was still testing its first commercial airplane, The Safire Personal Jet, a twin-turbofan engine jet that was expected to sell for about $1,000,000.[38] Called S-26, this innovative aircraft was largely dependent upon Agilis Engine Inc.'s development of the TF800 engine. The engine, also still being tested, was designed to produce 900 pounds of thrust, which would be necessary to meet the ambitious performance specifications. Safire was in the process of obtaining additional capital from private investors or possibly debt financing. Given a successful round of funding, Safire predicted that it would be funded well through prototyping and into full production. Nonrefundable pre-orders were said to number more than 900. This aircraft represented the Eclipse 500's most direct competitor.

Adam Aircraft

Founded in 1999, Adam was another company with a breakthrough jet on the verge of commercial sale.[39] The first flight of its A500, in July 2002, demonstrated that its unique twin-engine, center thrust design could be a viable alternative to single engine turboprops, and at a price of $850,000. Further on the horizon was the A700, which would fly higher and faster than the A500. The A700 was projected to be test-flown in 2003 and had an estimated price of $1,995,000.

Lancair

Founded in 1984, Lancair was another kit manufacturer, having sold more than 2,000 units.[40] Building upon manufacturing and design expertise, Lancair introduced its first certified commercial airplane, the Columbia 300, several years later. One of the company's most recent product introductions, the Columbia 350, was an all-electric version of the 300 and was expected to complete certification in late 2002. The company also planned to begin production of its new turbocharged airplane, the Columbia 400.

Another Competitor?

In late 2002, Honda Motors made major waves in the General Aviation industry by revealing the ongoing development of fuel-efficient aircraft engines, which it planned to some day incorporate into its own "Honda Civic of the sky."[41] The airplane was projected to be about the size of a twin-engine Citation and to have an expected maximum cruising altitude of 33,000 feet. At the time, the company planned to sell its still uncertified engine to aircraft manufacturers, with industry expectations that it would log engine flight hours and develop production knowledge for the eventual inclusion of the engine in a fuselage of its own design and manufacture. Given Honda's presumed engine superiority, low-cost manufacturing expertise, deep pockets, and marketing capabilities, its role remained unclear but of significant concern to the industry.

CUSTOMERS

The air transportation industry was undergoing many changes and so were the customer profiles of those who purchased aircraft. Distinct customer segments were evolving among purchasers and operators of smaller aircraft like the Eclipse 500. These "customers," or buyers, of aircraft each served a unique "consumer," or traveler. The aircraft product they purchased had to meet both the firm's business operating requirements and the needs of the travelers they served. Operating costs, performance, and safety were key considerations in the firm's purchase decision. Additionally, the aircraft operator had to consider the safety, speed, and comfort of the aircraft as product features desired by the passengers they serviced.

In the current aircraft market, there were three key customer targets for small jets like the Eclipse 500.

1. Fractional Ownership Operators

Fractional ownership operators administered corporate shared ownership programs.[42] They served companies seeking the benefits of lower ownership costs (purchase and maintenance), while still enjoying the flexibility and access privileges of a corporate jet. A "big three" had emerged among fractional ownership operators: NetJets, Bombardier Flexjet, and Flight Options/Travel Air (see Exhibit 3). NetJets, the industry leader and a business unit of Warren Buffett's Berkshire-Hathaway, was already profitable.

As of July 2002, fractional companies operated 19% of all business aircraft flown (750 out of 3,900 total aircraft units).[43] The fractional aircraft in operation were maturing: the average age of all fractionally owned aircraft was 5.2 years. The fractional programs were structured to turn over (sell or trade) equipment every five to ten years.[44] Fractional aircraft were flown more hours per year than most corporate aircraft: 800 to 1,100 hours annually versus 400 to 600 hours a year for traditional corporate aircraft.

In early 2002, the fleet of the three operators numbered 642 aircraft and 5,156 participating shareholders.[45] The aircraft purchases of NetJets alone totaled more than $19 billion over the past 6 years. More and more corporations were purchasing fractional ownership shares, rather than buying a wholly owned jet. Fractional ownership operators were emerging as a powerful customer buying segment. In fact, they accounted for the largest single source of business jet sales for Cessna Aircraft, Gulfstream Aerospace, and Raytheon Aircraft.

2. Charter Flight Operators

Charter flight operators provided private "air taxi" service that originated at both hub and smaller, local airports. Among the leaders in this field were Skyjet, FlightTime, and eBizJets. The majority of their passengers were corporate travelers who flew less than 50 hours per year. Much of the growth in charter

flights was fueled by the major airlines' low satisfaction ratings and long waits, exacerbated by increased security and wait times following September 11th.[46] The charter companies mainly operated smaller or "light" jets. Light jets were the most frequently used category of airplane among charter passengers, and they had a high rate of attracting first-time customers. Half of the light jet operators saw growth of at least 50 percent.

The main benefit of charter flights to the passenger were flexibility of the timing and purchase of air travel. Many of the charter operators had formed extensive partnerships and networks. If one charter company did not have aircraft or a flight available, they could arrange for the passenger to fly with a partner operator in the network.

3. Commercial Airlines

The large commercial airlines were presently not the main target customers for small jets such as the Eclipse. However, the potential existed for the airlines to "fill the gap" in the service routes to smaller, local airports not presently served by the major airlines. The airlines were ceding this "air taxi" business to regional airlines. These shorter routes represented a considerable business opportunity: 20% of total U.S. air travel.

One major commercial operator, UAL, the parent of United Airlines, created a new operating division in the spring of 2001 offering fractional shares in business jets, corporate shuttles, charters, and aircraft management services.[47] For this new venture, UAL had plans for a mixed fleet of 200 aircraft. That full spectrum of aircraft to be purchased would include six to eight models ranging from small business jets up to larger models such as the Gulfstream.

THE VALUE PROPOSITION

Raburn was determined to produce the world's most affordable personal jet without cutting corners. The Eclipse 500 was a luxurious six passenger, twin-engine aircraft that cost about one-fourth of the price of available private jets (by comparison, the Cessna CJ1 Citation cost more than $3.7 million).[48] Moreover, on July 26, 2000, Eclipse announced its price, performance, and equipment guarantee that helped generate a healthy pipeline of orders. The guarantee specified that the deposit on the Eclipse 500 would be refundable if the performance specifications were not met at a price less than 5% higher than that originally quoted.[49]

By September 2002, early market demand for the Eclipse 500 had exceeded expectations with the order book reaching 2,072 orders. The order book was made up of 1,357 firm orders and 715 options, allowing Eclipse to secure more than $65 million in nonrefundable deposits for the Eclipse 500. With the first customer deliveries scheduled to occur in January 2004, these orders represented the first two-and-a-half years of aircraft production. Raburn's pride was best reflected in his announcement, "[To] our knowledge, the Eclipse 500 order book is greater than that of any single civilian jet in the history of aviation."[50]

Customers also would derive value from the lower operating costs of the Eclipse 500. The company estimated that the direct operating costs (DOC), including fuel and maintenance, would be as low as $0.56 per mile (see Exhibit 5).[51] In comparison, that was about one-fourth the operating cost of a King Air and half that of a Baron.

ELEMENTS OF THE BUSINESS MODEL

Managing Production Costs

Eclipse Aviation sought to deliver a distinctive product at a competitive price. To achieve its goal of low-cost jet aviation, Eclipse pursued innovative technologies and manufacturing methods with various partners. Friction stir welding was a key innovation in the Eclipse 500 that lowered manufacturing costs. In addition to friction stir welding, Eclipse planned to achieve high volume production with precisely machined parts, a modular assembly approach, and modern supply chain management practices. Once production began, the company expected to deliver 140 aircraft in 2004, 500 aircraft in 2005, and 900 aircraft in 2006. The full production rate of 1,500 per year would be reached in 2007.[52]

Strategic Collaboration: Avio Intelligent Flight System

Eclipse created Avio by collaborating with Avidyne Corporation, BAE (British Aerospace) Systems Aircraft Controls Inc., General Dynamics, and Williams International. The Avidyne Corporation led the avionics industry with innovative products that enhanced pilots' situational awareness during all phases of flight, while BAE Systems had a respected history of producing flight proven military and commercial control systems.[53]

Avio was a comprehensive avionics and aircraft management suite that delivered a high level of integration and reliability. The fully computerized avionics and operating systems, which included digital displays in lieu of analog instruments, were a key source for cost savings. According to Raburn, "You couldn't get this functionality for much less than $1 million if you went to the OEMs." [54]

Strategic Alliance: Williams International

Williams International Inc. manufactured the turbofan engine for the Eclipse 500, thus creating what many industry observers consider a disruptive technology in jet engines. The engines were key components for the aircraft to meet the price and performance guarantees Eclipse Aviation promised to its clients in early 2000. These engines would allow the Eclipse 500 to have a range of 1,300 nautical miles, reach cruising speeds of 408 mph, and a cruising altitude of 41,000 feet. Some found it hard to believe that an engine roughly the size of a bongo drum could provide all of this power.[55]

THE SKIES AHEAD

Vern Raburn stared in near-disbelief at the Eclipse 500 and remembered his words to the media just a few weeks ago:

> [We] have accomplished more in a shorter period of time than any other company [in the industry] in the past 40 years.[56]

Indeed, Eclipse had come a long way, very quickly. What he wanted now were clear skies for the coming launch into the marketplace.

EXHIBIT 1 Eclipse Aviation Progress & Development Timeline

Source: Eclipse Website <http:www.eclipseaviation.com>.

May 1998	Company founded
June 1999	$60 million in initial funding raised
June 1999	Aircraft development program began
March 2000	Primary wind tunnel testing completed
May 2000	Launch of Eclipse 500 purchase programs
May 2000	Platinum purchase program sold out
July 2000	Announced guaranteed performance, price, and equipment specifications
August 2000	Second round of wind tunnel testing completed
September 2000	Completion of preliminary design review
October 2000	Type certification filed to FAA for Eclipse 500
December 2000	Funding totals $120 million
January 2001	Third round of wind tunnel testing completed
March 2001	Began expansion of manufacturing and assembly facility in Albuquerque, NM
May 2001	Critical design review began
July 2001	Over 170 employees dedicated to Eclipse 500 program
September 2001	First metal cut for Eclipse 500
February 2002	Third round of financing secured, $100 million. To date Eclipse Aviation has secured private equity funding of $220 million.
June 2002	FAA approved friction stir welding process specification
July 2002	Eclipse 500 Rolls out. It secured fourth round of funding for $18 million. Funding to date is $238 million.
August 26, 2002	Eclipse 500 First Flight

EXHIBIT 2 Avio Intelligent Flight System

Source: Eclipse Website, <http://www.eclipseaviation.com/500jet/avio.htm>.

The two primary flight displays (PFDs)—the smaller screens on each end—and the multi-function display (MFD) in the center provide pilot with high-resolution display of all flight parameters, engine and system performance data, and total system control. Pilot and co-pilot keyboards are standard equipment.

Summary of Features

Flight Guidance and Control.
- Dual channel, 3-axis autopilot
- Flight management system
- Aircraft performance computer
- Auto-throttle

Situational Awareness.
- Weather radar
- Traffic information services (TIS)
- Automatic dependent surveillance broadcast — B (ADS-B)
- Terrain avoidance warning system — B (TAWS-B)

Communication and Navigation.
- Dual VHF com/nav
- Dual localizer and glidescope
- Dual mode S transponder
- Dual global positioning system (GPS)
- Dual attitude and heading reference system (AHRS) with air data computer
- Active route moving map
- Flight path predictor
- Emergency locator transmitter (ELT)
- VNAV and LNAV
- Data loader

(continued)

EXHIBIT 2   **Avio Intelligent Flight System** (*continued*)

Operational Capability.
- Reduced vertical separation minimum (RVSM) capable

Autopilot Functions
- Auto-throttle (ATS)/airspeed capture hold, thrust hold (MCT, T/O)
- Yaw damper
- Pitch/roll flight director
- Heading select and heading hold
- Altitude capture and hold
- Pitch synch
- Tactical control steering (TCS)
- Vertical speed hold
- Lateral and Vertical nav (LNAV and VNAV)
- Approach (LOC, G/S, LNAV, LNAV+VNAV)

The Avio Architecture

The streamlined glass cockpit, comprehensive avionics, and extensive electronic support available to the Eclipse 500 pilot are the result of an integrated electronics architecture that extends to every part of the Eclipse 500 jet. Avio displays one integrated picture of what the aircraft is doing, instead of many little pieces of data that must be assimilated and correlated by the pilot. Utilizing digital technology, Avio distributes intelligence throughout the Eclipse 500, which is controlled through redundant aircraft computers. Data buses allow large volumes of data to be shared among Avio's components.

Electronic Systems Control. Avio's system management provides electronic control of the major systems on the aircraft, including full authority digital engine controls (FADEC), flight management system, communications, autopilot, auto-throttle, flaps, trim, landing gear, and environmental systems. Flight controls and brakes are conventional.

Health Monitoring. Avio captures health-monitoring data from the Eclipse 500's systems, creating a history of the performance of each system. This allows potential problems to be identified and corrected well before a system actually malfunctions.

Redundant Systems. Because of the high level of redundancy in all subsystems, Avio provides the pilot with knowledge and situational awareness even if an electronic component fails. All critical functions are duplicated, the components physically separated and powered by separate power buses and sources.

Circuit Breakers, Switches, Actuators. Avio uses electronic circuit breakers almost exclusively, delivering higher reliability and tighter tolerances than traditional mechanical circuit breakers. Extensive use of proximity switches instead of antiquated micro switches and the use of smart actuators further enhance Avio's reliability.

Future Expansion. Eclipse will provide enhancements to Avio, which can be incorporated easily and inexpensively via software installations.

Avio Major Components

Electric Power Distribution System (EPDS).
- Electronic circuit breakers
- Bus configuration contactors
- Fault detection
- Current and voltage monitors

Avionics and Pilot Information and Control.
- Primary flight display, including integrated radio controls
- Multifunction display
- Air data computer and inertial references
- GPS

Aircraft Integrated Electronics Unit (AIEU).
- Engine controls (two FADEC channels for each engine)
- Sensor systems (e.g., fuel level, secondary engine sensors, and ECS/VCS)
- Autopilot/auto-throttle/yaw damper/roll boost
- Systems control (flaps, landing gear, external lighting, ECS/VCS, etc.)
- Health detection, redundancy management

EXHIBIT 3 **General Aviation Manufacturers**
Source: Hoovers.com Company Capsules, as of December 10, 2002; for Pilatus: Pilatus Aircraft Company, December 8, 2002, <http://www.pilatus-aircraft.com>.

Bombardier

Location	Montreal, Quebec, Canada	*Employees*	74,879 Corporate-wide
Product	Commercial airliners	*Sales/Income*	2001 Sales—$13.6B (up 27%)
Description	Canadair and de Havilland		2001 Net Income—$246M
	regional aircraft		(down 62%)
	Challenger and Learjet business jets		

Company Description: Through its Aerospace subsidiary (65% of total company sales) Bombardier was the world's #3 manufacturer of commercial airliners behind Boeing and Airbus; the #1 regional aircraft maker; and #1 maker of business jets. Its Learjet business is a pioneer in the industry, and one of the most famous names in business jets. Like much of the industry, 2001 was a bad year for Bombardier, resulting in job cuts and a temporary halt in business jet production. Bombardier was also involved in railway equipment, snowmobiles, all-terrain vehicles, and personal watercraft. The firm was publicly held, but controlled by the Bombardier family.

Gulfstream Aerospace Corporation

Location	Savannah, Georgia, USA	*Employees*	7,800
Product	Intercontinental business aircraft	*Sales/Income*	2001 Sales—$3.2B (up 7.8%)
Description	used to transport executives,		
	wealthy individuals, and		
	government heads of state.		

Company Description: This General Dynamics subsidiary was the world's #2 manufacturer of business jets. The company's Gulfstream Financial Services unit offered a number of services to help customers purchase its jets, such as fractional ownership, leases, and third-party financing. The company also sold used aircraft and offered aftermarket maintenance services.

Dassault Aviation SA

Location	Paris, France	*Employees*	11,000
Product	Falcon business jets	*Sales/Income*	2001 Sales—$3B (down 6.4%)
Description	Military Aircraft—Mirage and		
	Rafale jet fighters, and		
	unmanned aerial vehicles		

Company Description: Dassault Aviation, the world's #3 business jet manufacturer, manufactured a number of aerospace products, with the Falcon family of business jets providing the majority of sales. Although publicly traded, the Dassault family owned 49.9% of the company and Aerospatiale Matra owned about 46%.

Cessna Aircraft Company

Location	Wichita, Kansas, USA	*Employees*	n/a
Product	Citation business jets	*Sales Income*	2001 Sales—$3B
Description	Caravan utility turboprops used		
	for freight, amphibious and		
	commercial aviation		
	Small single-engine planes for		
	personal and small-business		
	purposes		

Company Description: Textron subsidiary Cessna was the world's #4 business jet manufacturer and one of the most famous names in small planes. Cessna made a variety of models of its famous Citation jet and also offered shared ownership for its business jets.

(continued)

EXHIBIT 3   **General Aviation Manufacturers** (*continued*)

Fairchild Dornier Corporation

Location	Wessling, Germany	*Employees*	4,300
Product	728Jet for regional airlines	*Sales/Income*	2001 Sales—$701 M (up 9%)
Description	Envoy 3 Corporate Shuttle for		
	corporate customers		
	328, 728, and 928JetSMA for		
	government customers such		
	as the U.S. Air Force		

Company Description: Fairchild is the world's #3 regional aircraft maker. The privately held company was still operating, but had declared bankruptcy in early 2002.

Pilatus Aircraft

Location	Stans, Switzerland	*Employees*	1,000
Product	PC-12 personal aircraft	*Sales/Income*	n/a
Description			

Company Description: Pilatus Aircraft Limited, founded in 1939, became a pioneer in small aircraft industry with the development of the legendary PC-6 Porter, "The Jeep of the Air," a single-engine turbo-prop plane. In 1996, Pilatus established its Business Aircraft division in Colorado. PC-12, a turboprop airplane introduced in 1994, had sold 300 units (70% in North & South America). In a feature entitled "The Best Private Planes," which appeared in Forbes.com on October 22, 2001, the PC-12 was selected as the "Best Turboprop."

Raytheon Aircraft

Location	Wichita, Kansas, USA	*Employees*	11,800
Product	Hawker, Horizon, Beechjet, and	*Sales/Income*	2001 Division Sales—$2.5B
Description	Premier business jets		(down 20%)
	Baron and Bonanza personal aircraft		
	1900D regional airliners		

Company Description: This division of Raytheon Company owns and operates some famous names in business jets. Raytheon Aircraft also sells used aircraft, and offers fractional ownerships and aircraft charter, management, and maintenance services. It was rumored that Raytheon was looking to sell the division, which accounted about 15% of Raytheon's total sales, but lost money on the whole.

Mooney Aerospace Group, Ltd.

Location	Long Beach, California, USA	*Employees*	n/a
Product	Jetcruzer and Stratocruzer	*Sales/Income*	n/a
Description	business jets		

Company Description: With its roots in Wichita, Kansas, in the 1950s, Mooney is a cost-based competitor, offering low price business jets and personal aircraft.

EXHIBIT 4   Comparison of Business Jet Models

Sources: General Aviation Manufacturers Association, *2001 General Aviation Statistical Databook* (Unit Sales); Manufacturer Websites (Model, Engine, Speed, Passengers, Price, Range, Altitude, Operating Costs); *World Aircraft Sales Monthly* (Price); Aviation Research Group Inc., *2002 Operating Costs Guide* (Operating Costs).

Model	Engine	2001 Unit Sales	Speed (ktas)	Passenger Seats (not including crew of 2)	Price	Range (nautical miles)	Altitude (feet)	Operating Costs (per flight hour)
Adam Aircraft								
A700	Twin-Turbofan	n/a	340	4	$1,995,000	1,400	41,000	n/a
A500	Twin-Turbofan	n/a	250	4	$850,000	1,150	25,000	n/a
Boeing Business Jets								
BBJ	Twin-Turbofan	14	528	18	$47,000,000	6,200	41,000	$2,597.23
Cessna Aircraft								
750 Citation X	Twin-Turbofan	37	586	8	$18,615,000	3,900	51,000	$1,305.13
Sovereign	Twin-Turbofan	n/a	457	12	n/a	2,679	47,000	
560XL Citation Excel	Twin-Turbofan	79	431	7	$9,732,000	2,080	45,000	$988.29
560 Citation Encore	Twin-Turbofan	6	427	7	$7,304,000	1,970	45,000	$787.38
550 Citation Bravo	Twin-Turbofan	54	402	7	$5,434,000	1,900	45,000	$670.37
CJ3	Twin-Turbofan	n/a	417	6	n/a	1,900	45,000	n/a
CJ2	Twin-Turbofan	8	410	6	$5,305,000	1,738	45,000	$601.00
CJ1	Twin-Turbofan	56	380	4	$3,700,000	1,475	41,000	$536.63
Mustang	Twin-Turbofan	n/a	340	4	n/a	1,300	41,000	n/a
Cirrus Design								
Cirrus SR20	Single Turboprop, 200hp	95	160	4	$207,000	800	17,500	n/a
Cirrus SR22	Single Turboprop, 310hp	n/a	180	4	$289,000	1,000	17,500	n/a
Commander Aircraft								
270	Single Turboprop, 260hp	n/a	164	2	$515,000	1,005	16,800	n/a
270TC	Single Turboprop, 270hp	n/a	197	2	$565,000	870	25,000	n/a
Eclipse Aviation								
Eclipse 500	Twin-Turbofan	n/a	355	4	$835,000	1,300	41,000	$204.52 (projected)
Gulfstream								
G100	Twin-Turbofan	n/a	459	7	$12,350,000	2,700	45,000	$881.15
G150	Twin-Turbofan	n/a	459	8	n/a	2,700	45,000	n/a
G200	Twin-Turbofan	n/a	459	10	$18,750,000	3,600	45,000	$1,036.00
Lancair								
Columbia 300	Single Turboprop, 310hp	5	190	4	$379,000	1,320	18,000	n/a
Columbia 350	Single Turboprop, 310hp	n/a	190	4	n/a	1,320	18,000	n/a
Columbia 400	Single Turboprop, 310hp	n/a	230	4	n/a	n/a	18,000	n/a
Learjet								
31A	Twin-Turbofan	27	477	6	$6,525,600	1,455	43,000	$722.83
40	Twin-Turbofan	n/a	457	4	n/a	1,803	51,000	n/a
45	Twin-Turbofan	71	457	8	$9,420,400	2,098	51,000	$797.90
60	Twin-Turbofan	35	491	10	$11,968,300	2,510	51,000	$989.31

(continued)

EXHIBIT 4   Comparison of Business Jet Models (*continued*)

Model	Engine	2001 Unit Sales	Speed (ktas)	Passenger Seats (not including crew of 2)	Price	Range (nautical miles)	Altitude (feet)	Operating Costs (per flight hour)
Mooney Aircraft								
Eagle 2	Single Piston Engine, 244hp	n/a	180	2	$299,950	1,200	18,500	n/a
Ovation2	Single Piston Engine, 280hp	n/a	192	2	$349,950	1,240	20,000	n/a
Bravo	Single Piston Engine, 270hp	n/a	220	2	$399,950	1,070	25,000	n/a
Pilatus								
PC-12	Single Engine Turboprop	n/a	270	9	$2,700,000	2,261	30,000	$322.80
Raytheon Aircraft (Beechcraft)								
Premier I	Twin-Turbofan	n/a	451	6	$5,258,015	1,490	41,000	$648.78
King Air 350	Twin-Turboprop	n/a	312	9	$5,499,720	1,786	35,000	$563.26
King Air B200	Turboprop	n/a	292	6	$44,481,230	1,755	35,000	$507.85
King Air C90B	Twin-Turboprop	n/a	246	5	$2,931,000	1,276	30,000	$414.86
Beechjet 400A	Twin-Turbofan	n/a	468	7	n/a	1,735	45,000	n/a
Beech Baron 58	Twin Piston Engine	n/a	200	4	n/a	1,569	20,688	n/a
Safire Aircraft Company								
Safire S-26	Twin-Turbofan	n/a	340	5	$1,000,000	1,400	37,000	n/a
The New Piper Aircraft								
Meridian	Single Engine Turboprop, 500hp	n/a	262	4	$1,619,391	1,018	30,000	$242.52
Mirage	Single Engine Turboprop, 350hp	n/a	213	4	$929,900	1,548	25,000	n/a
Seneca V	Single Engine Turboprop, 220hp	n/a	204	4	$583,900	935	18,500	n/a
Saratoga TC	Single Engine Turboprop, 300hp	n/a	194	4	$470,200	1,090	20,000	n/a
Saratoga HP	Single Engine Turboprop, 300hp	n/a	166	4	$440,800	988	15,588	n/a
Archer III	Single Engine Turboprop, 180hp	n/a	133	4	$195,000	444	14,100	n/a

Note: This information was collected from various sources, sometimes with conflicting information. This is meant to be used for case analysis, not for making purchase decisions.

EXHIBIT 5
Estimated Direct Operating Cost (DOC)
Source: Eclipse Aviation Website.

Fuel ($2.00/gallon)	$89.21
Maintenance	
Labor ($60.00/manhour)	$15.79
Parts, Airframe, Engine, Avionics	$63.52
Engine Reserve	$36.00
TOTAL DOC per Flight Hour	**$204.52**
Total DOC/statute mile	$0.56

Notes: Costs based on 500nm stage length; engine reserve provided by Williams International; fuel and labor costs vary by location.

Endnotes

1. "Eclipse 500 Jet Achieves First Flight," Eclipse Aviation press release, http://www.eclipseaviation.com, August 26, 2002.

2. American Institute of Aeronautics and Astronautics, *History of Flight,* http://www.flight100.org/history_intro.html, December 9, 2002.

3. Airline Transport Association, *The Airline Handbook—Online Version,* Chapter 1: Brief History of Aviation, http://www.airlines.org/public/publications/display1.asp?nid=961, December 10, 2002.

4. Airline Transport Association, *The Airline Handbook—Online Version,* Chapter 2: Deregulation, http://www.airlines.org/public/publications/display1.asp?nid=962, December 10, 2002.

5. Airline Transport Association, *The Airline Handbook—Online Version,* Chapter 1: Brief History of Aviation, http://www.airlines.org/public/publications/display1.asp?nid=961, December 10, 2002.

6. U.S. General Accounting Office, *Commercial Aviation: Air Service Trends at Small Communities Since October 2000,* March 2002, pp. 10–19.

7. Airline Transport Association, *The Airline Handbook—Online Version,* December 10, 2002, Chapter 3: Structure of the Industry, http://www.airlines.org/public/publications/display1.asp?nid=963.

8. Airline Transport Association, *The Airline Handbook—Online Version,* December 10, 2002, Chapter 3: Structure of the Industry, http://www.airlines.org/public/publications/display1.asp?nid=963.

9. Airline Transport Association, *The Airline Handbook—Online Version,* December 10, 2002, Chapter 3: Structure of the Industry, http://www.airlines.org/public/publications/display1.asp?nid=963.

10. Regional Airline Association, presented by Debby McElroy, "The Regional Jet Service Debate," November 1, 1999, http://www.aviationtoday.com/reports/crnews1199.ppt.

11. General Aviation Manufacturers Association, *2001 General Aviation Statistical Databook,* revised October 21, 2001, p. 1.

12. Standard & Poor's, *Industry Surveys: Aerospace & Defense,* October 31, 2002, p. 4.

13. Standard & Poor's, *Industry Surveys: Aerospace & Defense,* October 31, 2002, p. 19.

14. Standard & Poor's, *Industry Surveys: Airlines,* September 26, 2002, pp. 3, 9.

15. Standard & Poor's, *Industry Surveys: Airlines,* September 26, 2002, p. 3.

16. Standard & Poor's, *Industry Surveys: Airlines,* September 26, 2002, pp. 1, 2.

17. B. De Lollis and B. Hansen, "Airlines abandon small cities; 10 lose all commercial flight service as pinched companies slash spending," *USA Today,* October 23, 2002, p. B1.

18. Standard & Poor's, *Industry Surveys: Airlines,* September 26, 2002, p. 4.

19. Standard & Poor's, *Industry Surveys: Airlines,* September 26, 2002, pp. 2, 9.

20. S. Arnoult, "A question of scope: ALPA's vigorous defense of scope clauses has frustrated airlines but also left some regional pilots wondering whether the union can represent their interests fairly," *Air Transport World,* June 1, 2002, p. 20.

21. J. Fallows, "Free Flight: From Airline Hell to a New Age of Travel," *PublicAffairs,* 2001.

22. Eclipse Aviation Company, http://www.eclipseaviation.com.

23. Eclipse Aviation Company, http://www.eclipseaviation.com.

24. See source information for Exhibit 4.

25. *Twin & Turbine,* "Flying in the Face of Convention," October 1, 2000.

26. Presentation by Don Taylor, VP Safety, Training and Flight Operations at Eclipse, April 15, 2002.

27. Eclipse 500 Jet, Performance, Eclipse Aviation, November 28, 2002, http://www.eclipseaviation.com.

28. Eric Adams, "15th Annual Best of What's New: Aviation and Space Grand Award Winner," *Popular Science Magazine Online,* December 2002.

29. AIN Alerts, "FAA Approves Eclipse 500 Assembly Process," June 2002.

30. "Eclipse Aviation Breaks Ground for Friction Stir Welding Center," Eclipse Aviation press release, http://www.eclipseaviation.com, November 6, 2002.

31. Presentation by Don Taylor, VP Safety, Training and Flight Operations at Eclipse, April 15, 2002.

32. "Eclipse Aviation Breaks Ground for Friction Stir Welding Center," Eclipse Aviation press release, http://www.eclipseaviation.com, November 6, 2002.

33. *Twin & Turbine,* "Flying in the Face of Convention," October 1, 2000.

34. Presentation by Don Taylor, VP Safety, Training and Flight Operations at Eclipse, April 15, 2002.

35. Frances Fiorino, "Eclipse 500 Rolls Out in Face of Skepticism," *Aviation Week & Space Technology,* July 22, 2002.

36. Federal Aviation Administration website: www.faa.gov, specifically http://www1.faa.gov/certification/aircraft/, November 4, 2002.

37. Cirrus Design Company, http://www.cirrusdesign.com, December 8, 2002.

38. Safire Aircraft Company, http://www.safireaircraft.com, December 8, 2002.

39. James Wynbrandt, "Adam Is Airborn," *EAA Airventure Today,* Volume 3, Number 8, July 29, 2002.

40. Lancair Company, http://www.lancairusa.com, December 8, 2002.

41. Norihiko Shirouzu, "Coming Model from Honda Sprouts Wings, Will It Fly?" *The Wall Street Journal,* December 3, 2002.

42. David Esler, *Special Report: The State of Fractional Ownership,* http://www.aviationnow.com, September 2002.

43. Robert W. Moorman, *A Fraction of the Business,* http://aviationnow.com, October 2002.

44. Robert W. Moorman, *A Fraction of the Business,* http://aviationnow.com, October 2002.

45. David Collogan, *Business Aviation Outlook Remains Strong Heading into New Year,* December 28, 2001, http://www.aviationnow.com.

46. Kerry Lynch, *Charter Bookings Weather Slow Economy,* http://www.aviationnow.com, March 6, 2002.

47. Kerry Lynch, *UAL to Launch Charter Service with Embraer Legacy,* http://www.aviationnow.com, June 13, 2001.

48. Sally Donnelly, "For Sale: a Jet, Under $1 Million," *Time Magazine Online,* Time 100 Innovators, http://www.time.com/time/Innovators/Travel/profile_raburn.html, January 2002.

49. Eclipse 500 Jet, Guarantees, Eclipse Aviation, http://www.eclipseaviation.com, November 28, 2002.

50. "Eclipse 500 Order Book Tops 2,000," Eclipse Aviation press release, http://www .eclipseaviation.com, September 9, 2002.

51. "Eclipse 500 Order Book Tops 2,000," Eclipse Aviation press release, http://www .eclipseaviation.com, September 9, 2002.

52. "Eclipse Aviation Breaks Ground for Friction Stir Welding Center," Eclipse Aviation press release, http://www.eclipseaviation.com, November 6, 2002.

53. "Eclipse 500 Order Book Tops 2,000," Eclipse Aviation press release, http://www .eclipseaviation.com, September 9, 2002.

54. Guy Norris, "The Eclipse 500's Innovative Avio Avionics and Systems Management Suite Is a Key Element of the Personal Jet," *Flight International,* July 30, 2002.

55. Frances Fiorino, "Eclipse 500 Rolls Out in Face of Skepticism," *Aviation Week & Space Technology,* July 22, 2002.

56. David Collogan, *Eclipse Rolls Out No. 1 Aircraft, First Flight Expected Soon,* http://www.aviationnow.com, July 15, 2002.

Case 3

Salton, Inc. and the George Foreman Grill

On a clear December day in 1999, as he was preparing to make his final decision on whether to offer former boxer George Foreman the wealthiest celebrity endorsement contract of all time, Salton, Inc. CEO Leon Dreimann chuckled. His thoughts had drifted to how he might write his current situation into a sales pitch for one of his company's famous infomercials:

> Believe me—you're not going to find a more successful small appliance than the "George Foreman Lean, Mean Fat-Reducing Grilling Machine" on the market today! (wait for applause) In fact, over just a few years, this grill has become the most successful new product ever introduced in the history of the industry. And a lot of the credit for that has to go to our endorser . . . George Foreman! (wait for applause)
>
> We think the grill is just the beginning. We have many more ideas for new products that will provide the same convenient, healthy cooking style you've been asking for . . . for example the Foreman outdoor grill shown right here. In fact, we're so confident you'll like our new Foreman products that we're betting the farm on it! (wait for gasps from the audience) That's right, we're going to give our friend George here $138 million for the permanent rights to his name!!! (wait for applause) George is here to stay—and all for the low, low price of $138 million. I mean, you just can't find a better deal than this, folks.

Focusing on his current situation, Dreimann wondered if his company's success with the Foreman Grill was extendable to other products. Was the "busy American"/healthy living lifestyle here to stay, or would customers' needs change? Was the indoor grill a one-time purchase, or would it become a staple product in the kitchen, perhaps the next KitchenAid? Could the Foreman concept sell outside the U.S.? And was the 50-year-old former boxer really this valuable to selling a grill?

He had many other related questions going through his head, but he kept coming back to one: was the George Foreman line really "here to stay"?

SALTON BACKGROUND

Based in Lake Forest, Illinois, Salton, Inc. (NYSE: SFP) was a designer, marketer, and distributor of a wide range of quality kitchen, home, personal, and beauty care appliances. The Salton brand was first introduced in 1947 and was tightly associated with the Salton Hotray product, a warming tray designed to keep food warm at the dinner table. Over time, products under the Salton umbrella came to include several licensed and brand names including Melitta, Sasaki, Farberware, White-Westinghouse, and Block China.[1]

In the late 1980s, Dreimann led a $6 million management buyout and injected new vitality into a company struggling to earn modest annual revenue and income in a congested small household appliance market. Dreimann's move sparked immediate growth and led Salton to increase revenues to a record $13 million in 1989. Along with warming trays, shower radios and espresso/cappuccino machines collectively drove sales growth. By 1991, Dreimann had led the company to the public markets, where it opened on the NASDAQ (the company ultimately moved its shares to the NYSE in early 1999). Salton initially struggled, earning only modest sales and incurring losses over the next three years. In 1993, the company boldly purchased the existing product lines of "Juiceman" and "Breadman"—brands whose groundbreaking use of "infomercials" had helped to catapult their joint sales to more than $45 million annually[2] (See Exhibit 1, which illustrates Salton's income statements and balance sheets from 1995—1999, and Exhibit 2, which shows Salton's market share leadership by 1999).

Salton operated on the premise that owning manufacturing meant lower margins. As such, throughout its history under Dreimann, the firm resisted acquisitions or business extensions that relied on domestic manufacturing. Instead, it outsourced production, component sourcing, and factory labor. Implied in this dedication to outsourcing were strong relationships with suppliers. Salton relied on these relationships as a source for both product innovation and development. All of Salton's products were sourced

Diana Alpert, David Aznavorian, Alice Boswell, David Lowy, and Amy Percy prepared this case under the supervision of Professor Allan Afuah as a basis for class discussion rather than to illustrate either effective or ineffective management. Creative liberties have been taken in developing the introductory and concluding paragraphs of the case.

from overseas locations in Asia (Hong Kong, China, and Taiwan primarily), where the company drew on 50 different suppliers. Despite this diversification, the company relied on one supplier—Markpeak Ltd. based in Hong Kong—for 38% of its products. The company resisted entering into long-term supplier contracts, emphasizing instead the value of competitive bidding for individual purchase orders as a means of maximizing its margin position. Upon shipment and delivery into Salton's warehouses, merchandise was quality controlled by Salton associates, who enforced the company's high standards for design and engineering.[3] In contrast, Salton's competitors were slow in sourcing from outside the U.S. Even among those competitors who did source from overseas, Salton was able to purchase at a lower overall cost due to its volume (See Exhibit 3).

Salton's strategy of outsourcing allowed it to concentrate on sales and marketing. Along with the reduction of resources implied in ownership of manufacturing assets, the company was also able to offer retailers attractive margins at price points similar to its competitors.[4] Products were marketed and sold in the United States through an internal sales force and a network of approximately 300 independently commissioned sales representatives. The customer-driven focus of the company was personified by its use of an advanced electronic data interchange (EDI) that was offered to qualified customers. The system allowed Salton to track sales, receive customers' orders, and transmit shipping and invoice information electronically.

Salton's distribution network was wide and varied, focusing on mass merchants (54% of company revenue), department stores (16%), specialty stores (6%), and warehouse clubs (5%).[5] Key customers included Wal-Mart (13.3%), KMart (12.4%), Sears (8.4%), Target/DHF/Mervyn's (7.5%), Federated Department Stores (4.8%), and May Department Stores (3.0%).[6]

In addition to these traditional distribution partners, Salton also sold its products directly to consumers through infomercials (accounting for 6% of company revenue). Infomercials—television commercials presented in the form of a short documentary or "talk show"—were typically 30 minutes in length and aired on television networks during off-peak viewing hours early in the morning, late at night, and throughout the day on weekends.

With such a diversified distribution system in place, Salton management argued that it was able to shift merchandise around to the most profitable channels as warranted by the needs of the market.

THE SMALL HOUSEHOLD APPLIANCE INDUSTRY

By 1998, consumers were reported to be spending more than $11.5 billion on small household appliances.[7] The small household appliance industry was a sub-segment of the larger housewares industry (with $58.4 billion in sales in 1998) and was known for its intense competition. The market was fragmented with prices that were extremely sensitive, and as a result the industry was known to offer relatively low profit margins.

Industry experts effectively identified two critical drivers for success:[8]

Product Innovations: A manufacturer's continuous innovation was required to retain its shelf space and add margin. New products were not known to displace competitors' products, but to simply replace an older incarnation of the same company/branded category offering. Unwarranted price increases on an already existing product typically led to a decrease in market share and retailer favorability.

Retailer relationships: Distribution partners included all national and regional chains as well as the emerging category of virtual retailers such as Amazon.com.

Two primary trends were also driving change within the industry:

Concentration of sales:[9] In spite of widespread distribution, the concentration of sales skewed toward specialty, discount, and department stores, with discount/supercenter merchandisers representing the majority of sales. Discount merchandisers were emerging as the largest distribution outlet for housewares and appliances, boasting more than three times the sales of the nearest competitive channel. The declining market share of full-price department stores was putting further pressure on houseware and appliance makers' margins. Partly bucking this trend was the performance of the premium-priced Williams-Sonoma franchise, which had recently earned a popular position among consumers by offering high-end appliances—inspiring manufacturers to reconsider possibilities that might exist for recovering increased profits at retail. Although lacking an extensive track record, in 1999 the Internet also presented a new and viable sales channel.

On-line stores such as Amazon.com offered consumers universal access to a discount center in the virtual retail space.

Concentration of vendors:[10] Given that retailers were constantly working to retain their margins, many looked to consolidating their vendor bases. With most small appliance firms holding full product portfolios, it was rapidly becoming conventional for retailers to simply choose two to three main brands from an individual manufacturer to stock on their shelves. As firms tried to manage this shift, smaller franchise acquisitions, mergers, and consolidations were becoming more common as a way of dealing with the trend. The behavior of many leading manufacturers reflected this: Applica was exploring the possibility of purchasing Black & Decker's household products division in a multi-million dollar deal; Libbey was poised to make an offer for Oneida; and Salton had just purchased the Toastmaster franchise of kitchen appliances and time products.

Consumer Push toward Healthier and More Convenient Foods

As a growing trend throughout the early 1990s, consumers were learning more about the effects of diet and nutrition on their health. The stringent government regulations that detailed the nutritional content of all food products sold in the U.S., combined with an increasing awareness of dietary-related health issues, prompted consumers to demand healthier foods for their busy lives.[11] Coinciding with this trend was ongoing experimentation by consumers to find new ways to modify their eating habits in order to lose weight. One particular diet, with increasingly popular appeal, was an all-protein diet. As part of its dietary doctrine, it encouraged consumers to eat meats, vegetables, and fish at the expense of what were perceived to be fat-inducing carbohydrates.

In response to consumers' preferences, food companies began to launch educational campaigns focusing on providing new and healthier dietary alternatives. The newly appointed CEO of Kraft Foods, one of the largest and most influential food and beverage companies in the world, validated this trend by stating that "[Kraft's] priority is to build sales growth with new products focused on the areas of health and nutrition."[12]

At the same time that consumers were showing interest in healthier eating, they were also learning more about healthier cooking practices. A cable television franchise called "The Food Network" was developing programming (and strengthening ratings) based on young, exciting chefs such as Emeril Legasse and Bobby Flay. These food connoisseurs, each of whom had gained popularity by cooking in the kitchens of some of America's finest restaurants, were quickly becoming household names. Incrementally, they were also beginning to license their names to the sales of cookware and specialty food items.

While consumers were seeking healthier and more exciting styles of cooking, their schedules were making it difficult for "the busy American" to find time to cook fresh food. According to industry research group NPD Food World, from 1996 until the end of 1999, sales of frozen dinners climbed 22%. Only 52% of Americans used their stoves daily, down from almost 70% in 1985. Consumers were also spending less money on groceries and less time cleaning their pots and pans.[13] They were spending more time and money eating out, carrying out, or having food delivered than ever before.

The trade-offs made by consumers in deciding between healthy eating and convenience did not go unnoticed by the small household appliance industry or retailers in the space. Representatives of the national retailer Service Merchandise described the issue:

> [The healthy cooking concept] is real hard to describe to the consumer. A lot of what we sell—any non-stick cooking equipment—could be labeled "healthy cooking." But I don't think consumers really buy into it . . . we've done surveys on why people like non-stick and the majority of respondents alluded to its convenience because pots and pans are so easy to clean up. These reasons came out way ahead of "because you don't need to use oil, so it's more healthy."[14]

While the nascent concept of indoor grilling was recognized for having the potential to fit the dietary needs of a healthy consumer who also valued convenience, its use as a gourmet culinary instrument did not receive high marks from key influencers within the industry, including celebrity chef Flay. As host of The Food Network's televised program "Hot off the Grill with Bobby Flay," and author of the best-selling cookbook "Boy Meets Grill," Flay boldly stated, "I don't recommend electric grills . . . period. Most of the time they don't get hot enough . . . and when they do, they don't impart much flavor."[15]

Flay's point was not lost on the consumer market. It was commonly accepted that the major advantages of cooking on an outdoor grill were its convenience for cooking and cleaning. Many consumers were also deferential to the crust and smoky flavor that came from cooking on an outdoor grill.[16] In the highly publicized burger wars of the late 1980s and early 1990s, Burger King had capitalized on such salient points with consumers in its differentiating strategy from McDonald's. To the pleasure of many consumers who switched their fast-food allegiances, Burger King was valued for its superior quality hamburger largely based on its "flame broiled" taste.

Competitive Landscape

Salton competed with a number of firms in the small household appliance industry in each of its principal product categories:

> *Kitchen and small electrical appliances*—Hamilton Beach, Rival, Krups, Rowenta, Black and Decker, Windmere-Durable, Sunbeam-Oster.
>
> *Tabletop products*—Mikasa, Lenox, Miller Rogaska, Villeroy Boch, Waterford Crystal, Baccarat Crystal.
>
> *Personal care products*—Conair, Vidal Sassoon, Windmere Durable, Helen of Troy, Andis.[17]

Internally, Salton recognized more than 40 competitive manufacturers vying for market share in the esteemed kitchen and small appliance space alone. Many of the competitors within the crowded category were among the most well-known and well-capitalized home appliance brands in the world, including Sunbeam-Oster, Hamilton Beach/Proctor-Silex, Black & Decker, West Bend, Helen of Troy, Krups, Cuisinart, Rival, Tefal, Braun, Waring, and KitchenAid.

Other than Salton, the top three firms in the category were Sunbeam, Nacco Industries (which owned the Hamilton Beach–Proctor Silex brands), and Applica. The three firms accounted for over 23% of sales.

Sunbeam

The brands of Sunbeam included Oster, Sunbeam, and Mr. Coffee. The franchise commanded significant market share within the fragmented small household appliance industry; however, the company also had a history of financial challenges and difficulty. Many insiders felt that Sunbeam was near bankruptcy and industry experts were strongly encouraging management to stabilize the franchise. In spite of such turmoil, the company remained active in small household appliances, commanding a leading share of market position of 7.7%. Sunbeam's household kitchen appliance group represented 36% of company revenue. At one time, its portfolio of products had included indoor grills, although the franchise chose to quickly exit the category after repeated failure in attempts to gain efficient market entry and secure product sell-through.

Contributing to its spotty record, in 1993 Sunbeam had voluntarily recalled 4,500 electric indoor grills due to concerns of grease fires that were sparked during initial operation of the product. The 1,000-watt grill, following its recall, was immediately discontinued. The product was then replaced with an 800-watt version that, as of 1994, had yet to prove itself at retail. Sunbeam had also offered a Carousel Rotisserie Cooker that was made available under the Oster brand.

In its emerging product releases, Sunbeam had begun to show improved strengths in innovation and, to this end, was poised to file more than 70 new patents. Rumors were circulating that Sunbeam was in the early stages of launching a new line of household appliances known as "smart" appliances— home units that would "talk" with one another through an installed home electrical system. Industry experts were bullish on Sunbeam's prospects if it was able to carry out such an innovative launch successfully. Such a move would constitute a significant shift in the household appliance space and might ultimately threaten every household appliance manufacturer across product categories and offerings.

NACCO Industries

NACCO Industries was a large holding corporation that owned the Hamilton Beach/Proctor Silex line. As a consolidated entity, NACCO was substantially larger than Salton in revenue with sales of $2.6 billion in 1999. The Hamilton Beach/Proctor Silex division alone represented more than $400 million of these top-line sales.

Hamilton Beach/Proctor Silex manufactured appliances for both the home and commercial kitchen segments of the market. The Hamilton Beach product portfolio included almost every type of small household kitchen appliance imaginable, including blenders, coffee makers, food processors, mixers, indoor grills, kettles, knives, roasters, and toasters.

Within the indoor grill category specifically, Hamilton Beach featured the largest catalog with nine SKUs available for purchase. The franchise's grills ranged in price from $20 to $70. Alternatively, the Proctor Silex division of indoor grills was generally targeted to the more price-conscious consumer. They were commonly found at retail priced anywhere between $14 to $20.

Applica

Applica was the kitchen appliance division of Windmere-Durable Holdings. It manufactured and marketed products under licensed brand names, its own brand names (Windmere), and other private-label brands. Applica's interests to acquire Black & Decker were well known within the industry. If the acquisition were to be approved and successful, the Black & Decker division was targeted to quickly rise in prominence and serve as Windmere-Durable's largest business group.[18] To compete in the indoor grill category, Applica intended to launch a grill product under the Black & Decker brand. The grill was expected to be sold at a $50 price point.

GEORGE FOREMAN "ENTERS THE RING"

1993 marked the latest in Salton product innovation with its introduction of an indoor grilling product to the U.S. small household appliance market. The grill was purchased outright from inventor Michael Boehm, the head of Intellection (a developer of consumer electric, photo, and houseware goods). Given its strengths in marketing and distribution, Salton anticipated that the appliance would be an instant success and chose to launch it at the food industry's annual Gourmet Show. The product, however, generated little interest. Disappointed by its lukewarm response, Salton opted to temporarily "shelve" it, choosing to refocus on several other products in development.

As Salton set its sights elsewhere, George Foreman—the famous boxer of the 1970s (who by the 1990s had become a popular celebrity endorser)—was searching to put his name on a consumer product. Long before he had pursued endorsement deals, Foreman had established his career as a world heavyweight boxer. He eventually earned the title of world heavyweight champion after debuting with a gold medal performance at the 1968 Olympics. In spite of his glorious achievements, several highly publicized episodes had tainted his reputation within the sport, including his alleged association with boxing "bad boy" Sonny Liston. Foreman's brute strength in the ring also made him a surprisingly "un-sellable" fighter; leading promoter Don King was reputed to have steered away from promoting Foreman out of concern that he knocked out his opponents too early in fights. An antagonistic relationship with the public and press only further undermined Foreman's popularity. Even during his rise to the heavyweight

title in 1973, Foreman maintained an unfavorable reputation in the eyes of many. By 1974, when he faced and lost to Mohammed Ali in the renowned "Rumble in the Jungle" match in Zaire, his career had started a steep decline. Depressed and distraught, Foreman retired from the ring in 1977, turning to religion and family to set his life back on track.

While in retirement (and pursuing a second career as a minister), Foreman's weight increased from 215 to 315 pounds. Over time, he realized he needed to regain control of his health. Foreman chose to come out of retirement and box again. As part of his comeback, he focused on healthy living—including healthy eating and physical exercise. In 1987, he officially re-entered the ring to renew his career. Over the course of the next ten years, he went on to fight 34 more times, winning the heavyweight title again at age 45. In 1997, he chose to retire for a second time—and this time, for good.

His resurgence in the ring, his dedication to his family, his distinct, gregarious personality, and his happy-go-lucky demeanor made George Foreman one of the more likeable public personalities in the 1990s. Capitalizing on this, he pursued endorsement contracts and appeared in television advertisements for both Meineke Mufflers and Doritos Chips. Still, by the mid-1990s, he was looking for his own product to endorse.

Given Foreman's interest in healthy eating, his lawyer looked to find products that would match Foreman's passion for fitness. In his search, he came upon Salton's grill and ordered one for Foreman to try out. After seeing and using it, Foreman was excited and approached Dreimann to discuss a deal. When Dreimann and Salton accepted, a joint venture was formed.

The original arrangement offered Foreman 45% of the profits from grill sales, while Salton received the balance. No specific endorsement fees were paid to Foreman up front, as he only made money as grills were sold. At the time of the deal, Foreman envisioned himself making approximately $1 million. Neither Salton nor Foreman had any real expectations for how successful he might be as a pitchman for a small kitchen appliance.

BRINGING THE GEORGE FOREMAN GRILL TO MARKET
The Product

The indoor grill's launch ushered in a new era for the Salton franchise. In recognition of the firm's aggressive push into health, "Innovative Products for a Healthy Today and Tomorrow" was adopted as the company's new tagline.

Prior to introduction, several critical marketing elements were defined and clarified. Before formalizing the relationship with George Foreman, Salton's marketing team had named the grill "The Mean Machine," an allusion to the team of convicts who played football in the 1974 Burt Reynolds' movie "The Longest Yard." Seeing the potential market awareness and visibility that Foreman's name implied, the marketing team recognized that choosing the right name was critical. The team eventually settled on "George Foreman Lean Mean Fat-Reducing Grilling Machine." In much the same way that Cuisinart had become inextricably linked to the category of food processors, and KitchenAid had become linked to the category of small mixers, so too did Salton hope that George Foreman and grills would become a tightly correlated association.[19]

Along with the product's branding, it was internally emphasized that its features and benefits were clearly related to the consumer. In order to capitalize on the "busy American" phenomenon, and address the needs of those consumers who described their schedules as "too hectic for cooking," it was important that the grill be known for making cooking easier.[20] To this end, Salton wanted to communicate that the grill was fast, reliable, and versatile. It wanted a dummy-proof product.

In most every way, it was. Like a waffle iron or sandwich griddle, the George Foreman Grill was designed to cook from both the lid and the bottom, effectively squeezing the food between two heating surfaces that would reach 350 to 400 degrees in approximately five minutes. The squeezing process made cooking fast: a two-inch Halibut steak would cook in six minutes; a steak or burger, four minutes; shrimp, ninety seconds. Users could also grill vegetables such as onions, portabella mushrooms, or broccoli. The Teflon-coated metal was nonstick, reducing the need for oil or spray. Cleaning could be done simply and quickly with the wipe of a paper towel. The gravity and weight of the top plate was also key to the grill's fat-reducing mechanics. All dripping followed the 3-inch tilt drains of the grill's interior and trickled down into a dish. Unlike the process of frying, Foreman grilling left no pool of fat crackling at the bottom of the pan during cooking—an attractive benefit to the consumer seeking healthier food preparation.[21]

Production

The production team turned to its relationship with Markpeak, Ltd. and established it as a sole supplier given its demonstrated expertise and experience in the small appliance space. Although Markpeak dealt with ten other manufacturers, the team felt there were no other foreign suppliers who could match Salton's margin interests and meet its quality and delivery expectations.

Advertising, Pricing, and Distribution

Previously in 1991, Salton's sales of its "Sandwich Maker" had leveraged the then-nascent vehicle of infomercials: thirty-minute "advertorials" that ran during off-peak hours. For its "Sandwich Maker" advertorials' success had come as a lucky accident. Struggling to gain retailer and consumer awareness in an unfamiliar product niche, Salton went on-air with its message and sold more than three million units in the ensuing 15 to 16 months. At the time, the company springboarded from a modest $18 million franchise to a $52 million operation.[22]

Where Salton's "Sandwich Maker" success had revealed infomercials' capacity for creating consumer awareness and interest in a new product, Salton's more recent "Juiceman" launch had illustrated the value of infomercials in pricing and retailer relationships. Also released via infomercial, Salton launched its professional "Juiceman" at a $199 price point. To the retail market, months after its introduction, Salton introduced a more consumer-friendly version of "Juiceman" at $79.99 (with about half as many features and benefits as the professional version). Regardless of channel—whether the retailer represented a mass merchant or department store—the price stayed the same. One retail price carried across all channels. Leveraging the weight that infomercials could bring to educating consumers about a product's features, the "Juiceman" product sold well in retail channels at premium price points. Unlike other small household appliances that were generating less than 25% retail margins, the "Juiceman" earned more than 35%.

With such a pre-existing track record, the Salton management team felt confident that it could use infomercials to effectively educate consumers about George Foreman Grills, create residual demand with retail partners, and gain more retail partners through profit maximization. For all these "brass rings," it was still unclear as to how Foreman's presence would either add to or detract from its strategy.

Feeling comfortable with the formula, the marketing team established an original grill price of $79.99 and chose to also introduce a smaller, consumer-friendly version at $39.99. Building upon key learnings from the "Juiceman," it felt confident that consumers would gravitate to the smaller, lower-price point offering. Prior to market launch, however, several market research reports trickled in which spoke to overall product favorability mixed with apprehension about price. Armed with this new information, the marketing team quickly changed course. Price points were reduced to $59.99 and $29.99 respectively prior to the grill reaching retail channels.

From its introduction in mid-1994 through 1995, the Foreman Grill's infomercial ran every day as a vehicle for generating top-line consumer awareness. The marketing message in the infomercials helped to convey that it was a product that could be used daily. With everyday usage, Salton hoped that the grill's replacement cycle would be three years (as opposed to a cycle of six years for toasters or ten years for mixers)—an outcome that would ideally increase consumer turnover and perpetuate the product's longer desired life cycle in the market.[23]

Eventually, as planned, retail partnerships began to complement the infomercial/direct sales approach about 6–12 months later. Carefully selected partnerships with QVC (a television shopping network), Sears, Target, and Federated Department Stores, Inc. ensured broad retail coverage. Although there was some concern about potential discounted pricing practices, the Salton team felt confident that its universal pricing strategy would be both enforceable and attractive to retailers so long as demand created by the infomercial was sustained. As an insurance policy to inspire higher consumer demand in the market, Foreman grills were distributed to retailers on allocation.

Contrary to the expectations of the marketing team, the larger Foreman grill outsold the smaller version 3.5:1 through its infomercial. Lessons learned, as well as presence on the QVC network, enabled Salton to shift strategy once again and inform retail partners about what would make an effective retail mix—stressing that retailers should carry, and dedicate premium shelf space to, the *larger* Foreman grill even at its elevated price point. Recognizing the 40–60% margin that the larger unit presented, retailers complied.

Early Success

Within one year of the grill's launch, the proof was in the numbers: Salton sold 200,000 units in an abbreviated first year of sales. By 1996, sales rose to 1 million units. Within three years, sales had skyrocketed to 4 million units a year.

While the grill was successful with many retailers, it was also profitable via infomercial. When asked in an interview, Dreimann commented on what had been internally identified as a self-perpetuating market effect, "The infomercial business has not only been a support business for our retail, it's become a totally profitable business all by itself. The more we sell on television, the more we sell at retail. And the more we sell at retail, the more we spend on TV."[24]

Akin to the somewhat surprising sales mix, the consumer demographics for Foreman grill purchases was also surprising to the Salton marketing team. 40% of the purchasing audience was male, far higher than the average percentage that purchased small appliance products. More than 50% of the consumer base was over 50 years old. The user demographic also skewed to low- and middle-income households with 38% of buyers falling into income brackets between $15,000 and $34,999 annually.

"Ironically, it's exceptionally popular among single people and elderly people," Dreimann commented. "It's a very skewed demographic."[25]

In spite of its early success, many industry experts felt they had seen the "Foreman Phenomenon" before. The grill's rapid success was not new to many pundits. While occasionally products did get "hot," projected life cycles were known to be short. Bread machines, for example, had been big sellers in the U.S. in the early 1990s, but peaked only a few years later and then dropped off. Sales of espresso makers had leveled off as well in the mid-1990s as consumers discovered that the coffee café environment was what drew them to espresso consumption, and not the actual drink.[26]

Defying skeptics' prognostications, and offering validation to the Salton's team market launch strategy, the George Foreman Grill stayed red hot. By 1998, indoor grills were accounting for more than $300 million in total retail sales.[27] Within the Salton cachet, the grill displaced former leading product divisions including toasters and juice makers, and jumped to over 40% of overall company sales.[28]

1999 would be recognized as a landmark year for Salton and the George Foreman Grill. In a year that included the unfortunate passing of original company founder, Lewis Salton, there was also much for Salton insiders to celebrate. Overall kitchenware sales had grown 7.1% to $6.1 billion. The Foreman Grill was recognized as being largely contributory to this. Foreman grills were also accountable for the growth of the indoor grill category to more than 9.8 million annual units.[29] Salton, meanwhile, was recording annual sales of $506 million with net income of $90 million. The George Foreman Grill division was credited for delivering approximately $205 million of this sales total.[30]

The Salton management team determined that it was an opportune time to leverage the Foreman brand into other sectors. Plans went into motion for the launch of an outdoor grill. While this product was not considered part of the small household appliance category and would be sold into retail channels other than those where small appliances were sold, many industry insiders felt that it would be sold out before it even hit the shelves.[31] The George Foreman Outdoor Grill was scheduled to launch in 2000 into the $2.5 billion market for outdoor grills at a $199–$599 price range. Plans were also developing for a George Foreman Indoor/Outdoor Electric Grill with two SKUs of $99 and $149. Analysts expected this would quickly become a $40 million business[32] (see Exhibits 4 and 5).

Rather than bash the Foreman franchise, competitors candidly lauded the Salton team's efforts:

> The characteristics of the market have changed quite a bit with the continued success of the George Foreman line. That has moved a lot of retailers out of opening price-point grills into much higher price points: as high as $99. Such a climb is unusual for a small-electrics product. One of the really interesting things that Salton has been able to do to help grow the category, however, is to move price points up dramatically. It appears retailers have been able to maintain margins on the product as well. (Rob Moser, president of Maverick Industries and the Healthy Griller product)

ANOTHER "RUMBLE IN THE JUNGLE"?

As the company approached 2000, Foreman grills were showing some vulnerability in their defenses.

In the trade, *Consumer Reports* had issued a report on the original George Foreman Grill that put it through its paces. In December 1999, the magazine did a comparative test where identical burgers were cooked from 80% lean ground beef on the Foreman grill and then on a regular pan. Contrary to Salton infomercial claims that Foreman burgers had 4% less fat than pan burgers, the *Consumer Reports* test "found no significant difference in fat reduction."[33]

Lawsuits were also beginning to surface in objection to Salton's pricing strategies. Three multimillion dollar suits were brought on behalf of more than forty states, including Washington, D.C., and Puerto Rico. Although Salton denied any wrongdoing, many industry insiders speculated that the company was guilty of price-fixing and had coerced retailers into deals at the expense of competitors, whose products were tagged for removal from retailers' shelves.

Questions were also forming about the potential of the Foreman Grill in international markets. While the company's sales were almost exclusively based in the U.S. and Canada, the Salton team had begun to explore equity positions in South Africa with Amalgamated Appliance Holdings, Ltd. On the table was also the potential acquisition of British-based appliance company Pifco Holdings plc. In France, appliance distributor Look for Group was eager to formalize an agreement with Salton. Given its historical track record, the Salton management team was unsure as to whether these potentially costly acquisitions would prove fruitful. Recalling images of the mighty Foreman who entered Zaire in 1974 for the "Rumble in the Jungle" with Mohammed Ali, only to come away beaten and disgraced, Foreman grills faced an uncertain future outside the United States.

Bob Messenger, editor of *Food Trends Newsletter* in Chicago, summarized what many in the industry were speculating:

> The George Foreman Grill just exemplifies where the food industry is going. So that you and I, and our wives and girlfriends—and even our mom—don't have to put in the time to cook. I suspect that George Foreman is going great guns, but it will be history in two years. Something else will evolve.[34]

CAN FOREMAN GO A FEW MORE ROUNDS?

Dreimann's daydream about the "new" Foreman infomercial ended abruptly as he looked down and saw the revised contract that lay before him. "$138 million . . . wow," he thought to himself as he ran through even more questions in his mind.

Salton had already paid Foreman $60 million—was another $138 million worth it? Would this turn out to be another home run like baseball great Joe DiMaggio going to bat for Mr. Coffee, or had George scored a knockout too quickly like he had in so many fights early in his career? Was the George

Foreman line of products and the Foreman brand destined to slump? Or, did the aging spokesman still have some "spring in his legs" to carry over into other products in other small appliance categories? Was Salton becoming overly reliant on the Foreman line to drive its performance? Would this deal fundamentally change the way Salton ran its business?

He remembered what Salton President William Rue had mentioned to him during a recent round of golf about the evolving relationship with George, "We have never regretted our deal with Foreman at all. Without doing this, we won't be able to expand the brand. Foreman is a brand to us. It's not a grill."

EXHIBIT 1   Salton Financial Information[35] (dollars in millions, except per share data)

Income Statement

	FY Ends in June					
	FY99	**FY98**	**FY97**	**FY96**	**FY95**	**FY94**
Net sales	506.1	305.6	182.8	99.2	77.0	48.8
Cost of sales	285.5	179.4	121.6	66.9	55.6	37.3
Distribution expenses	21.6	12.3	7.8	5.9	4.6	3.4
Gross profit	199.0	113.9	53.4	26.4	16.9	8.0
SG&A expenses	129.6	84.2	42.9	21.3	13.1	8.5
Operating income	69.4	29.7	10.5	5.1	3.8	−0.5
Interest expense	−15.5	−5.3	−4.1	−3.9	−3.1	−2.0
Costs associated with refinancing	0.0	−1.1	0.0	0.0	0.0	0.0
Realized gain on sale of securities	0.0	9.0	0.0	0.0	0.0	0.0
Class action lawsuit expense	0.0	0.0	0.0	0.0	0.0	0.5
Income before tax	53.9	32.3	6.4	1.2	0.7	−2.0
Income tax expense	19.3	12.2	2.0	−3.5	0.0	0.0
Net income	34.6	20.1	4.4	4.7	0.7	−2.0
EPS, diluted—reported	2.37	0.99	0.22	0.46	0.07	−0.39
EPS, diluted—continuing operations	2.37	0.99	0.22	0.46	0.07	−0.39
Depreciation & amortization	7.3	4.3	3.1	2.2	2.0	1.6
EBITDA	76.7	34.0	13.6	7.3	5.7	1.1
COGS/sales	56.4%	58.7%	66.5%	67.5%	72.2%	76.5%
Distribution/sales	4.3%	4.0%	4.3%	5.9%	5.9%	7.0%
Gross margin	39.3%	37.3%	29.2%	26.6%	21.9%	16.5%
SG&A/sales	25.6%	27.6%	23.5%	21.5%	17.1%	17.4%
Tax rate	35.9%	37.9%	31.3%	−301.0%	3.0%	0.0%
Net margin	6.8%	6.5%	2.4%	4.6%	80.0%	−60.0%
D&A/sales	1.4%	1.4%	1.7%	2.2%	2.6%	3.2%
EBITDA margin	15.2%	11.1%	7.4%	7.3%	7.4%	2.3%

Balance Sheet

	FY99	FY98	FY97	FY96	FY95	
Cash	11.2	0.7	2.6	0.0	0.0	
Accounts receivable, less allowances	96.2	43.2	25.6	15.9	13.5	
Inventories	144.1	76.5	42.0	28.3	19.4	
Prepaid expenses and other current assets	6.4	2.9	3.7	1.9	1.0	
Federal income taxes refundable	0.0	0.0	1.1	0.0	0.0	
Deferred income taxes	3.1	4.6	1.7	1.9	0.0	
Total current assets	261.0	127.9	76.7	48.0	33.9	

(*continued*)

EXHIBIT 1 Salton Financial Information[35] (dollars in millions, except per share data) (*continued*)

	FY99	FY98	FY97	FY96	FY95
Property, plant, & equipment	24.7	8.3	8.3	6.2	3.6
Intangibles, net of accum. amort.	42.6	5.1	4.9	3.7	3.6
Noncurrent deferred income taxes	0.0	0.0	0.2	1.6	0.0
Investment in Windmere common stock	0.0	0.0	12.2	0.0	0.0
Total assets	328.3	141.3	102.3	59.5	41.1
Revolving line of credit	32.2	50.5	38.0	24.1	17.8
Accounts payable	41.0	19.0	17.4	10.1	5.4
Accrued expenses	0.0	7.2	2.8	1.2	0.6
Income taxes payable	0.0	6.5	0.1	0.0	0.0
Current portion, subordinated debt	0.0	0.0	0.5	0.4	0.6
Other current liabilities	21.9	0.0	0.0	0.0	0.4
Total current liabilities	95.1	83.2	58.8	35.8	24.8
Long-term debt	182.3	0.0	0.0	0.5	0.9
Noncurrent deferred income taxes	0.2	0.5	0.0	0.0	0.0
Due to Windmere	0.0	0.0	4.9	3.2	0.0
Total liabilities	277.6	83.7	63.7	39.5	25.7
Common stock	0.2	0.2	0.1	0.1	0.1
Unrealized gain on securities avail. for sale	0.0	0.0	1.3	0.0	0.0
Additional paid in capital	91.9	53.4	53.0	29.3	29.3
Treasury stock—at cost	−90.8	0.0	0.0	0.0	0.0
Less note rec. from stock issuance	0.0	−10.8	−10.8	0.0	0.0
Accumulated other comprehensive income	0.0	−0.1	0.0	0.0	0.0
Retained earnings	49.4	14.9	−5.0	−9.4	−14.0
Total stockholders equity	50.7	57.6	38.6	20.0	15.4
Total liabilities & stockholders' equity	328.3	141.3	102.3	59.5	41.1

EXHIBIT 2
Salton's Market Share Leadership[36]

	Rank	Market Share
Juicers	#1	66%
Indoor Grills	#1	30–50%
Breadmakers	#1	26%
Toasters	#2	30%
Griddles	#1	40%
Waffle Makers	#1	35%
Toaster Ovens	#2	18%
Buffet Ranges	#1	—*

*Data for sufficiently small product categories is unavailable.

EXHIBIT 3
Operating Margins for Comparable Companies[37]

Company	FY99 Operating Margin
General Housewares	9.8%
Global-Tech Appliances	6.4%
Helen of Troy	12.3%
Libbey	18.3%
National Presto	16.8%
Oneida	12.9%
Premark (Consumer Products Group)	9.6%
Royal Appliance	1.9%
Salton	13.7%
Sunbeam	nmf
Windmere-Durable	5.7%

EXHIBIT 4
Small Household Appliance Category Sizes[38] (millions of U.S.D.)

Category	Estimated Market Size
Toasters	110.0
Indoor Grills	360.0
Outdoor Grills	2,500.0
Juice Extractors	52.5
Breadmakers	30.0
Waffle Makers	20.0
Griddles	NA*
Buffet Ranges	NA*

*Data for sufficiently small product categories is unavailable.

EXHIBIT 5
Foreman Future Revenue Growth Estimates[39] (millions of U.S.D.)

	FY2000E	FY2001E	FY2002E
Product Line			
Foreman Indoor/Outdoor Grill	—	40.0	35.0
Foreman Outdoor Grill	—	12.0	25.0
Product			
Foreman Indoor Grill	—	−45.0	−42.0

Endnotes

1. Peter Schaeffer and Jasmine Koh, "Branded Consumer Products: Salton, Inc.," Donaldson, Lufkin & Jenrette, May 17, 1999.

2. Peter Schaeffer and Jasmine Koh, "Branded Consumer Products: Salton, Inc.," Donaldson, Lufkin & Jenrette, May 17, 1999.

3. John Baugh and Scott Miller, "Floorcoverings/Furnishings/Household Products: Salton, Inc," First Union Securities Inc., May 29, 2001.

4. James McAree, "Consumer Products: Salton, Inc.," Lazard Freres & Co. LLC, October 12, 1999.

5. James McAree, "Consumer Products: Salton, Inc.," Lazard Freres & Co. LLC, October 12, 1999.

6. John Baugh and Scott Miller, "Floorcoverings/Furnishings/Household Products: Salton, Inc," First Union Securities Inc., May 29, 2001.

7. Peter Schaeffer and Jasmine Koh, "Branded Consumer Products: Salton, Inc.," Donaldson, Lufkin & Jenrette, May 17, 1999.

8. John Baugh and Scott Miller, "Floorcoverings/Furnishings/Household Products: Salton, Inc," First Union Securities Inc., May 29, 2001.

9. John Baugh and Scott Miller, "Floorcoverings/Furnishings/Household Products: Salton, Inc," First Union Securities Inc., May 29, 2001.

10. Peter Schaeffer and Jasmine Koh, "Branded Consumer Products: Salton, Inc.," Donaldson, Lufkin & Jenrette, May 17, 1999.

11. Holly Werner, "Those Tricky Trends: Translating Consumer Preferences into New Products Is a Tough Business," *HFN,* December 15, 1997.

12. Holly Werner, "Those Tricky Trends: Translating Consumer Preferences into New Products Is a Tough Business," *HFN,* December 15, 1997.

13. Pooja Bhatia, "What, Me Cook?—With U.S. Kitchen IQs Falling, Makers Push Smart Appliances; The $90 Frozen-Pizza Heater," *The Wall Street Journal,* March 1, 2002.

14. Holly Werner, "Those Tricky Trends: Translating Consumer Preferences into New Products Is a Tough Business," *HFN,* December 15, 1997.

15. Charles Passy, "Catalog Critic: Grill Trouble—Indoor Grills Can't Make Us Forget Backyard Barbecues; Our Beef? There's Sizzle but No Smoke," *The Wall Street Journal,* August 25, 2000.

16. Douglas Hanks III, "The Foreman Phenomenon; Doesn't Your Countertop Have a Lean Mean Grilling Machine?" *The Washington Post,* June 14, 2000.

17. Peter Schaeffer and Jasmine Koh, "Branded Consumer Products: Salton, Inc.," Donaldson, Lufkin & Jenrette, May 17, 1999.

18. James McAree, "Consumer Products: Salton, Inc.," Lazard Freres & Co. LLC, October 12, 1999.

19. Company Records, Internal Powerpoint Presentation Presented to Sales Distributors.

20. Douglas Hanks III, "The Foreman Phenomenon; Doesn't Your Countertop Have a Lean Mean Grilling Machine?" *The Washington Post,* June 14, 2000.

21. Douglas Hanks III, "The Foreman Phenomenon; Doesn't Your Countertop Have a Lean Mean Grilling Machine?" *The Washington Post,* June 14, 2000.

22. Steven Dworman, "Salton-Maxim Solutions," *ADWEEK Eastern Edition,* June 30, 1997.

23. Alice Beebe Longley and Jason Horowitz, "Salton, Inc: Prospects Hinge Largely on Foreman Grills," Credit First Suisse Boston, April 16, 2002.

24. Leon Dreimann in interview with Steven Dworman, "Salton-Maxim Solutions," *ADWEEK Eastern Edition,* June 30, 1997.

25. Douglas Hanks III, "The Foreman Phenomenon; Doesn't Your Countertop Have a Lean Mean Grilling Machine?" *The Washington Post,* June 14, 2000.

26. Shirley Leung, "Foreman Scores with Salton Deal—But Will the Ex-Champion Deliver the Punches for the Grill Maker?" *Asian Wall Street Journal,* February 5, 2001.

27. Thyra Porter, "Indoor Grills Heat Up; Consumers Bring Outdoor Flavor Inside with Electric Grills," *HFN,* August 16, 1999.

28. Michelle Leder, "A Hot Grill Cools Off, Salton Feels Pressure," *The New York Times,* January 28, 2001.

29. Shirley Leung, "Foreman Scores with Salton Deal—But Will the Ex-Champion Deliver the Punches for the Grill Maker?" *Asian Wall Street Journal,* February 5, 2001.

30. John Baugh and Scott Miller, "Floorcoverings/Furnishings/Household Products: Salton, Inc," First Union Securities Inc., May 29, 2001.

31. "Off the Record: Household Products and Personal Care," *The Wall Street Transcript,* June 19, 2000.

32. John Baugh and Scott Miller, "Floorcoverings/Furnishings/Household Products: Salton, Inc," First Union Securities Inc., May 29, 2001.

33. Douglas Hanks III, "The Foreman Phenomenon; Doesn't Your Countertop Have a Lean Mean Grilling Machine?" *The Washington Post,* June 14, 2000.

34. Douglas Hanks III, "The Foreman Phenomenon; Doesn't Your Countertop Have a Lean Mean Grilling Machine?" *The Washington Post,* June 14, 2000.

35. James McAree, "Consumer Products: Salton, Inc.," Lazard Freres & Co. LLC, October 12, 1999.

36. Peter Schaeffer and Jasmine Koh, "Branded Consumer Products: Salton, Inc.," Donaldson, Lufkin & Jenrette, May 17, 1999.

37. James McAree, "Consumer Products: Salton, Inc.," Lazard Freres & Co. LLC, October 12, 1999.

38. John Baugh and Scott Miller, "Floorcoverings/Furnishings/Household Products: Salton, Inc," First Union Securities Inc., May 29, 2001.

39. John Baugh and Scott Miller, "Floorcoverings/Furnishings/Household Products: Salton, Inc," First Union Securities Inc., May 29, 2001.

Case 4

Satellite Digital Audio Radio Service (SDARS):
Beyond AM, Beyond FM . . . Radio Takes a Serious Step Forward

Let us be clear, we believe this is the [terrestrial] radio stations' game to lose—they have a huge advantage in installed radios; they dominate the listener ratings; they have the ability to do local programming; they have great research departments, smart programmers and strong management teams; and their service is free. (Robertson Stephens Inc.—The Satellite Radio Industry, 2002)

A recent CNN poll of 7,159 listeners reported that 73% of all respondents thought music radio was "terrible" compared with only 2% that described it as great. (Cable News Network, 2002)

January 10, 2003—it was a cold, windy Friday night (like all winter nights in Michigan) as Hugh Panero, the CEO of XM Satellite Radio, rolled up to the private "who's-who in the auto industry" black-tie charity ball marking the opening of the North American International Auto Show. The valets scampered about as the door of his GM-provided Cadillac limousine opened to the red carpet at Detroit's Cobo Center. He exited to the flash of media cameras while his lovely date took escort by his side. As was typical, just a few cars behind, Joseph Clayton, CEO of Sirius Satellite Radio, rolled up in his Ford-provided Lincoln Town Car. The icy Detroit wind cut through his Armani tuxedo, he shivered thinking back to his glory days on the beach as vice chairman of the now bankrupt Bermuda-based Global Crossing.

The two men, now just a couple hundred yards from each other, shook a few hands and slapped a few backs as they made their way toward their respective corporate displays. After each had finished a drink, single malt scotch for Mr. Panero and a dry martini for Mr. Clayton, they turned from their guests, their brows furrowed and eyes squinted as they caught each other's glare across the crowd. The Sirius and XM displays lay just within eyeshot.

Radio hadn't substantively changed in over 30 years. Each knew they had a fighting chance to ride a technology wave with potential to sweep the country.

In a room full of potential automotive customers the two began to wonder: Did they have the right alliances? Were their revenue models correct? Could they acquire sufficient funding? Did they have adequate product distribution capability? Would the technology function as planned? Will the service be compelling enough to drive consumer adoption? In short, they had both been invited to the bowl game. The question was—would the tickets sell out and who had the winning game plan?

THE HISTORY OF RADIO

The Early Years

In 1877, Thomas Edison recorded the first sound, "Mary had a Little Lamb," on mechanical cylinders. A decade later, Heinrich Hertz proved that electricity could travel through space in waves.[1] By 1895, Guglielmo Marconi successfully transmitted the first radio signal one mile across his family's estate.[2] The following year, elated with his success, Marconi took his radio transmission system to England. British officials, unfamiliar with this device, believed Marconi was a spy and destroyed Marconi's invention. After receiving patent approval in 1896, Marconi improved upon the system's capabilities and established the Wireless Telegraph and Signal Company, known today as Marconi plc. His work led to the first trans-Atlantic wireless signal communication on December 12, 1901.[3]

Radio technology progressed rapidly over the next two decades to include commercial applications. As the quality and distance of radio transmission improved to include human voices, American commercialism began to take note. In 1919, General Electric established the Radio Corporation of America (RCA) for the purpose of capitalizing on this

Jim Callahan, Shelly Cropper, Jed Hunter, Rebecca Kucker, and Angela Mitzel prepared this case under the supervision of Professor Allan Afuah as a basis for class discussion rather than to illustrate either effective or ineffective management. Creative liberties have been taken in developing the introductory and concluding paragraphs of the case.

technology.[4] Technological advances increased further when the three main American radio companies, GE, RCA, and AT&T, agreed to share all radio patents.[5] In 1922, WEAF in New York City became the first radio station to offer airtime to advertisers, which led to radio's first paid commercial.[6]

The Radio Rush

At the onset of the First World War, all radio patent protection was suspended to slow private technology investment and reduce the threat of espionage. Then, in 1920, with just five operational stations, the first ever broadcast of election results began an era known as the "radio rush." In 1924, the amplitude modulation (AM) band was established, setting a broadcasting standard for the radio industry. With this standard, the number of radio stations in the U.S. grew to over 1,400, while the number of home radio sets was estimated at 3 million. "Pay radio," a radio vending machine that charged a nickel for five minutes of radio time, helped to further widen consumer awareness.[7] With national interest brewing in 1926, the National Broadcasting Company (NBC) was formed through the combined efforts of RCA, Westinghouse, and GE. Not to be outdone, a second radio network, Columbia Broadcasting System (CBS), was established in 1927.[8] The first factory installed automotive radios were offered in 1932. These early car stereos required the driver to stop the car to put up an antenna.[9]

Congress passed The Communications Act of 1934 to form the Federal Communications Commission (FCC), "for the purpose of regulating interstate and foreign commerce in communication by wire and radio so as to make available, so far as possible, to all the people of the United States a rapid, efficient, nation-wide, and world-wide wire and radio communication service with adequate facilities at reasonable charges. . . ." This independent government agency was directly responsible to Congress and had jurisdiction covering the 50 states, the District of Columbia, and U.S. possessions.[10] It would be another year before the successful demonstration of frequency modulation (FM) radio in 1935.

Radio set sales peaked in 1947, the same year the transistor was developed leading to smaller and less expensive sets. Thanks to additional innovations like Hi-Fi stereo records, eight-track tapes, and the silicon integrated circuit, radio sales grew from 7 million per year in 1955 to near record levels of 11 million per year in 1960. After the authorization of FM broadcast in 1961, the manufacture of portable AM/FM radios grew by 750% between 1960 and 1965.[11] By 1977, the number of FM receivers had exploded to 205 million, penetrating 95% of U.S. households.[12] Because of its superior sound quality and clarity, FM radio surpassed the previously dominant AM radio in number of broadcasting stations.

Satellite Digital Audio Radio Service (SDARS) Emerges

By the mid-90s there were nearly 600 million traditional terrestrial based radio receivers in use worldwide and the FCC had recently abolished limits on the number of radio stations one entity could own. This led to massive industry consolidation and, though tested, terrestrial digital broadcast radio was not growing as many experts had predicted.

In 1995, a new radio frequency spectrum was allocated between 2310 and 2360 megahertz for use by nationwide satellite radio providers. Two years later, the FCC held the first SDARS frequency auction, granting only two licenses from the four original applications. American Mobile Radio Corporation (now XM Radio) and Satellite CD Radio (now Sirius Satellite Radio) established themselves in a regulated duopoly by bidding $89.9 and $83.3 million, respectively.[13] See Exhibit 4 for key dates timeline.

In response to the emergence of SDARS, the FCC was quoted as saying it "could not entirely rule out the possibility of a major adverse impact" to traditional local broadcasters.[14] Consequently, less than three years later, the FCC approved the $23 billion merger of terrestrial radio operators AMFM and Clear Channel Communications to create the largest terrestrial broadcast network owning over 1,000 stations.[15]

SDARS TECHNOLOGY

SDARS Provider Equipment Requirements

Since the first satellite was launched in 1957—the Soviet Union's Sputnik 1—four main companies have emerged in communication fixed satellite services: Intelstat, PanAmSat, SES Global, and Loral Space and Communications. Independent of maker, however, all satellite systems share three basic components: the satellite, the uplinks, and the downlinks. Communication satellites use three main orbits: low earth orbit (less than 3,100 miles above the earth), medium earth orbits (6,200–12,400 miles), and geostationary earth orbits (22,237 miles above the earth).[16]

Satellites travel in either a circular or elliptical orbit balancing the earth's gravity against the satellite's centrifugal inertia. One type of circular orbit, geostationary, follows a path around the equator at an orbit rate of once every 24 hours (~7,000 mph). Since the earth also revolves every 24 hours, a satellite in geostationary orbit appears to stay in the same position relative to the earth's surface. High orbits, such as geostationary, offer a better vantage point than low orbits and thus require fewer satellites to cover a specific area; however, they typically have flatter "look" angles and therefore are more subject to terrestrial-based signal blockage. Lower orbits offer favorably steeper "look" angles and faster signal response (less latency from physical signal travel delay) with lower power requirements, but require more satellites to cover the same footprint.[17]

As opposed to ground-based regional antenna towers required for traditional broadcasting, satellite radio allows a subscriber to receive a radio signal from an earth-orbiting satellite. Programming content is sent from studios through terrestrial uplinks to two or three satellites orbiting the earth. The satellites then retransmit the same signal back to thousands of ground-based downlinks in subscribers' vehicles or homes. The transmissions are known as "line-of-sight." Terrestrial repeaters are installed to boost the signals around or through earth-based obstacles such as tall buildings or tunnels. Systems with flatter "look" angles typically require more repeaters and correspondingly have more repeater maintenance cost. Weather does not deteriorate SDARS signals due to the attenuation free frequency range on which SDARS transmits.[18]

Consumer Equipment Requirements

Eventually, the majority of SDARS receivers will be factory-installed units that seamlessly incorporate satellite radio functionality into the car, alongside the current range of features. In the interim, there are primarily three different types of aftermarket units consumers may purchase to receive satellite radio signals: an in-dash unit capable of receiving AM/FM and satellite transmissions, an FM modulator that receives the SDARS signal and then retransmits it to the existing FM stereo from a trunk mounted device, and finally a "plug-and-play" device, which is a portable unit that may be used in both the automobile and the home.

In all three cases, the consumer must purchase a tuner ($250–$400) and antenna ($50–$100) and typically pay an installation fee ($60–100 except for "plug-and-play" units). The SDARS companies and equipment manufacturers jointly subsidize the equipment prices and incentives to position SDARS receivers at the premium end of existing traditional radio equipment. As satellite radio equipment becomes an option in new vehicles, the incremental costs for factory installations over traditional two band receivers are estimated at $100–150 and are expected to be largely overlooked in the price of a new car.[19]

The two SDARS companies have aligned with leading electronics manufacturers to provide brand name equipment consumers know and trust. See Exhibit 1. Currently, only one set of proprietary chips is included in each receiver. This means that consumers must choose a satellite radio provider at the point of equipment purchase and cannot switch providers without the purchase of new equipment. However, under mandate of the FCC license requirements, both XM and Sirius have signed an agreement to develop an interoperable standard as early as 2004—meaning any given receiver will include chip sets allowing consumers to choose either satellite radio service.[20] Although satellite radio providers may not be motivated to move toward interoperability, this feature would provide more flexibility and is likely to be supported by electronics equipment manufacturers and consumers.

THE SATELLITE RADIO INDUSTRY

Satellite radio was founded on the basis of four main benefits over terrestrial-based networks:[21]

- *Broader programming variety*—SDARS provides 100 unique channels nationwide, with wider variety, brand name programming, and a real-time music data display (title, artist, album, genre, etc.).
- *Minimal or no commercial spot load*—Traditional commercial load averages 15 minutes per programming hour—SDARS is expected to average six minutes per hour. (Note: Both XM and Sirius offer at least 30 commercial free channels.)
- *Nationwide coverage*—Flexibility to listen to the same station nationwide on extended road trips.
- *Digital quality*—SDARS utilizes digital broadcast quality vs. analog signals for the majority of current terrestrial radio.

The FCC controls the number of satellite broadcast licenses and has currently limited the players, via auction, to XM Radio and Sirius Satellite Radio. Startup costs for new entry to this market are currently estimated at $1 billion.[22]

Competitors

Terrestrial Radio Networks With little threat from new entrants, satellite radio will experience the biggest threat from traditional terrestrial radio. The terrestrial radio networks present the biggest obstacle to SDARS's success due to five key advantages:

- Enormous existing install base.
- Local programming like weather, news, traffic, sports, etc.— without the need to manually switch between local and satellite reception.
- Large and well established management teams with excellent market research.
- User base resistance to change.
- Free service.

As dominant as their position is, today's radio operators lack digital broadcast sound quality and continue to have significantly higher commercial loads—15–16 minute commercial loads per hour in many markets. Also, the variety of formats on terrestrial radio has become so limited that an increasing number of listeners are unable to find programming that interests them—the Radio Advertising Bureau estimated that 14 formats represent over 99% of all U.S. radio stations.[23]

To defend their position, radio operators have begun to fight back with digital radio, also called in-band on-channel (IBOC) radio. iBiquity, the developer and licensor of this technology, promises improved sound quality over existing AM and FM signals, better reception of weak signals, and even wireless data services.[24] The required investment in new-generation technology is estimated at under $100,000 per station. Broadcasters supporting the launch of IBOC technology include radio industry heavyweights Clear Channel Communications and Infinity Broadcast, among others. Hardware on the receiving end must also change. The first factory-installed and aftermarket digital receivers for automobiles are expected in 2003. Digital systems are expected to cost consumers about $100 more than comparable radios.[25]

Traditional radio operators are divided on the threat of satellite radio. Yet, terrestrial-based digital radio also requires a significant investment for both the network and the consumer. In response, several existing traditional radio networks have begun substantial upgrades to bring their networks up to digital standards, while simultaneously hedging their exposure with equity investments in SDARS. Meanwhile, nearly half of the existing stations simply refuse to air commercials for SDARS in an attempt to block what they clearly see could be a potential threat.[26]

Other Competitors Alternatively, digital recordings such as MP3s and CDs also pose a threat to satellite radio but come with their own drawbacks in substantially limited access to content as well as added complexity, especially in the case of MP3s. Digital cable brings comparable service into the home; however, it lacks the mobility of SDARS.

Distribution

Satellite radio receivers are available through two main distribution channels: factory installation through automotive original equipment manufacturers (OEMs) and aftermarket installation through mass and consumer electronics retailers. Both XM and Sirius have been aggressively forging alliances with OEMs and retailers. See Exhibit 1.

Aftermarket sales, averaging 11 million traditional units per year,[27] will comprise the primary source of early subscribers. However, with 17.2 million new cars sold annually, the OEM channel is expected to become an increasingly significant subscriber base, with leading OEM alliances playing an important role in capturing initial subscriptions. If radio receivers become interoperable, this will deteriorate the importance of company specific equipment installations but will underline the significance of service packaging options direct from the OEM. OEM dealers will play a critical role in selling the actual SDARS receiver unit and service packages, and then including the monthly service/installation fee into the financing package of the car.

Revenue and Cost Models

The existing industry revenue model relies primarily on monthly subscriber fees. XM and Sirius charge monthly fees of $9.95 and $12.95, respectively, for their service. Additionally, each company charges a one-time activation fee approximately equal to one month's service fee. Advertising revenues serve to offset added expense for talk programming on both XM and Sirius, while XM also extracts incremental advertising revenue for a portion of its music channels. Both companies will likely offer premium channels for small additional monthly fees (approximately $3–$5). Advertising revenue forecasts are highly uncertain but are generally expected to contribute a diminishing portion of overall revenue, representing a mere 9% by 2010.[28]

SDARS providers face initially crushing costs. The ongoing costs can be viewed in three buckets:

those required to operate the system, those to acquire customers, and those in revenue sharing with OEM partners. The operating costs include satellite and repeater system overhead and maintenance, internal studio operating costs, music producer royalty fees (7–8% of revenue vs. 4–5% for terrestrial broadcasters), and customer service support. The subscriber acquisition costs include advertising, hardware subsidies to offset equipment costs, and dealer incentives to encourage retail sales staff. Finally, the OEM revenue sharing costs, while not publicly disclosed, are estimated at 9–15% of subscriber fee revenue. The OEM agreements were established to encourage car manufacturers to include SDARS units as options in new vehicles. Initially the costs are expected to completely consume profits; however, by 2010 analysts predict EBITDA margins to be near 50%, roughly equivalent to traditional broadcasters.[29]

XM SATELLITE RADIO

Beyond FM: XM Explodes onto the Market

Founded approximately two years after Sirius, XM Satellite Radio has emerged as the first-mover in the SDARS race. XM achieved this leading position through the combination of Sirius' technical and management setbacks and XM's consistent execution of several strategic decisions formulated to differentiate its product offering. While this early lead does not ensure long-term success, XM has positioned itself for growth through a framework of strategic alliances with key industry players in manufacturing, programming, and sales.[30]

XM launched its nationwide service on November 12, 2001—seven months before Sirius—with a massive advertising campaign. Television images of basketballs falling from the sky and rock stars like David Bowie crashing through rooftops caught viewers' attention, but industry experts say these ads failed to show consumers exactly how satellite radio works.[31] Even so, the tag lines of "Beyond AM. Beyond FM." and "Radio to the Power of X" began to clue consumers into the benefits of XM's service offering. The company spent almost $100 million in sales and marketing efforts in 2001. In addition to the huge advertising campaign, promotions were conducted at concerts, NASCAR events, and various retail outlets.

The company broadcasts its programs from a 150,000-square-foot broadcast center and corporate headquarters in Washington, D.C. The XM broadcast center includes 82 broadcast studios and a 2,600-square-foot performance studio for live recordings and broadcasts. The XM signal is beamed from two earth-station antennas to the company's two satellites, affectionately named "Rock" and "Roll." These geostationary satellites are positioned 22,000 miles above the Earth.[32]

The satellite system was built with the help of several technology partners. Boeing Satellite Systems built the two HS 702 high-power satellites and a third spare satellite. In September 2001, Boeing advised XM of a progressive degradation problem with the solar output power of its 702-class satellites. XM management adjusted the estimated useful life of "Rock" and "Roll" to 6.75 years, thus having to replace the satellites around years 2007–2008.[33] Alcatel provided the communications payload equipment. The telemetry and tracking system was provided by Telesat Canada. Hughes Electronics Corp. and LCC International designed and deployed the terrestrial repeater network, which consists of 800–900 high- and low-power units. The chip set used to decode the XM signal was designed and developed by STMicroelectronics.[34]

Programming

XM offers 70 music channels and 30 channels of news, talk, sports, and entertainment. The company provides original programming including live artist performances along with programs produced by leading content providers such as CNBC, Fox News Channel, ESPN, and The Weather Channel. See Exhibit 2 for detailed program listings. XM has chosen to differentiate some of its music programming through arrangements with several programming partners, including Viacom's MTV and VH1 and terrestrial radio behemoth Clear Channel Communications.[35] Clear Channel provides XM with some rebroadcasts of radio stations in major metropolitan areas, and XM is clever about integrating the content so listeners cannot easily tell what is original broadcasting and what is not. The company intends to compensate some partners by selling advertising on partner-affiliated channels and sharing 50% of the proceeds.[36]

Revenues

As mentioned in the industry section, revenues are generated from advertising, activation fees, and subscription fees. XM sells advertising on about 40 of its 70 music stations and all 30 of its news, talk, and information stations. Commercial programming is limited to no more than six minutes per program hour on commercial-loaded music stations. In 2002, analysts estimate that advertising revenue will be $3.2 million or 14% of XM's total revenues. Over the next five years, advertising revenue is anticipated to contribute approximately 20–25% to total revenues.[37] See Exhibit 3 for financial and operating data.

Subscriber-based revenues include both activation fees and monthly subscription fees. Subscribers may order XM service either over the phone or through the company's website. The initial activation fee is $9.99 for subscriptions ordered over the company's website or $14.99 for those ordered over the phone. In 2002, activation fees are estimated to be $1 million or 5% of total revenues. Over the next five years, activation fees are estimated to contribute approximately 3–5% of total revenues. The primary source for company revenues is monthly subscriber fees. The monthly subscription fee for XM's service is $9.99. The company recently added a premium adult channel, Playboy Radio, which can be activated for a one-time charge of $4.99 and an additional monthly service charge of $2.99 over the standard monthly fee. In 2002, subscription fees are estimated to be $17.9 million or 79% of total revenues. Over the next five years, the contribution from subscription fees is estimated to grow to 88% of total revenues.[38]

General Motors: Distribution & Strategic Partner

XM's most significant partner is General Motors, the largest U.S. automotive manufacturer, producing 28% of new cars and light trucks sold in the U.S. in 2000. In July 1999, GM became a strategic investor in XM by purchasing $50 million of convertible notes. GM will also be a significant source of revenue for XM through an exclusive distribution agreement. Beginning in fall 2003, GM offered XM satellite radios as a factory-installed option in 25 of its 2003 models, representing over 55% of all GM cars currently being sold. Consumers will have the option of having the monthly subscription fee for XM service included in their vehicle lease or financing, so they will have to pay only one bill. In return for GM's partnership, XM has agreed to pay GM $35 million spread over the first four years of the agreement.[39]* In addition, XM has agreed to help subsidize the cost of the radios, pay GM a percentage of subscription revenue earned through the agreement, and place in-dealership promotional kiosks to aid awareness of the XM service.

The Future of XM

XM is expected to have 350,000 subscribers by the end of 2002. This number is far from the 4 million subscribers needed to break even; however, it is far ahead of Sirius' subscriber base. XM is currently funded through the first quarter of 2003. And while the availability of venture capital is never guaranteed, GM's financial and strategic support appears to be an important "safety net." This resolute support from GM is viewed to remain strong as the large auto manufacturer attempts to use XM as a competitive advantage to drive floor traffic and incremental sales after several seasons of 0% financing offers and deep product discounts in response to decreased demand in new autos after the September 11th terrorist attacks and subsequent economic recession.[40] XM estimates that it will need approximately $350 million in total funding until the company can self-support its operations.

SIRIUS SATELLITE RADIO
Overcoming Setbacks

On May 17, 1990, Sirius Satellite Radio was incorporated as Satellite CD Radio. With a successful bid for one of the two available FCC satellite broadcasting licenses, Sirius took an early lead in the SDARS race. In 1998, the company signed an agreement with Lucent Technologies to develop the chip sets to be used in radios sold to consumers. The company originally agreed to pay $9 million to Lucent, but paid significantly more as the production date was postponed several times.[41]

Senior management was shaken up after these delays, including the resignation of then CEO David Margolese. The new management team, headed by CEO Joe Clayton, former vice chairman of now bankrupt Global Crossing, and CFO John Scelfo, made strides to renew investor confidence by consistently hitting key milestone dates. In fall 2001, the company hired Michael Ledford as its new senior VP of engineering to manage the chip set project. Ledford was previously with Intel and Ford and brought significant expertise to Sirius. Under Ledford, the company completed the development of its chip set and launched nationwide by the revised schedule date of July 1, 2002. Final costs attributed to the chip set delays are estimated at about $100 million.[42]

Sirius broadcasts its programs from a 90,000-square-foot broadcast center and corporate headquarters in New York City. This broadcast center

---

* If interoperability should negate this exclusive agreement, XM will not be required to make any further payments.

includes 76 production facilities, performance spaces, and a comprehensive digital library with the capacity to store 2 million pieces of music. The Sirius signal is beamed to three satellites moving in elliptical orbits. Sirius made the decision to change from geostationary to elliptical orbits to provide its satellites better elevation angles and a maximum amount of time to travel over the U.S. This decision required the use of a third satellite but reduced the number of terrestrial repeaters to about 100.

The company outsourced the construction of its satellite systems and continues to outsource the transmission of its broadcasts. Loral Space and Communications built Sirius' satellites. These model FS-1300 satellites have a 15-year life expectancy. The company's terrestrial repeaters were constructed and deployed by Black & Veach, a Kansas City construction firm. Globecomm Systems, Inc. designed and developed Sirius' digital broadcast equipment and deployed some of its terrestrial repeaters.[43]

Programming and Marketing Efforts: "100% Commercial Free . . . Music"

Sirius broadcasts 60 music channels and 40 channels of sports, news, and entertainment. Much like competitor XM, Sirius has formed agreements with various programmers to broadcast third-party programming on its channels. Sirius offers programming from various outside sources, including Bloomberg, CNBC, Discovery Networks, Hispanic Radio Network, The Weather Channel, and an exclusive agreement with NPR.

The company has made several strategic programming decisions in order to differentiate its service offering from XM. One of the most significant decisions is to offer original music content that is commercial free. To accompany this original music content, the company has hired popular entertainment personalities as hosts for specific genres, including comedians Dan Akroyd and Jason Alexander, rapper Grandmaster Flash, country music favorite Randy Travis, and sports commentator Michael Feinstein, to name just a few. The company has also entered into a programming and marketing partnership with House of Blues Entertainment, Inc. Through a multiyear agreement, Sirius will market its service at House of Blues concerts as well as develop ongoing programs with the House of Blues, such as the Sirius Emerging Artist program and Sirius Second Stages, where up and coming bands are featured in advance of featured performers.[44]

Sirius' other marketing efforts include the largest spectator sport in the U.S.—NASCAR. Through an agreement with ISC Motorsports, Sirius plans to reach NASCAR fans on a number of different levels, including direct-to-consumer promotions, at-track activation at ISC venues, and co-marketing opportunities with local retail partners, all designed to drive new subscribers for Sirius' service. Sirius' partnership with ISC also includes title sponsorship of two NASCAR Winston Cup Series events—the Sirius Satellite Radio 400 at Michigan International Speedway and the Sirius Satellite Radio at The Glen at Watkins Glen International.[45]

Revenues

Because of Sirius' decision to keep music programming commercial free, 95% of revenues are expected to be generated from subscriber activation fees and monthly service fees over the next few years.[46] Sirius charges $12.95 per month for service and a one-time activation fee of $15 if activated by phone and $5 online. Total revenue in 2002 is expected to be $12.7 million. In 2002, it is estimated that less than 2% of this revenue will be generated from advertising while the other 98% will be derived from subscriber and activation fees.[47] See Exhibit 3 for financial and operating data.

Multiple Partners Aligned for Distribution

Sirius has signed exclusive distribution agreements with automotive OEMs Ford, DaimlerChrysler, and BMW North America, representing just over 41% of the new cars and light trucks sold in the United States in 2000. In return for installing Sirius radios in new vehicles, each auto manufacturer receives a portion of subscription revenue, a subsidy for advertising and equipment costs, and warrants to purchase Sirius shares.[48]

The company has also signed a partnership with rental car company The Hertz Corporation. Beginning December 1, 2002, Hertz and Sirius will provide radios in approximately 20,000 Ford vehicles at major airport locations in California and Florida. These satellite-radio equipped vehicles will cost renters $5 extra per day.[49]

The Future of Sirius

On October 17, 2002, Sirius announced a major debt-restructuring plan, converting debt and preferred stock into common stock, eliminating virtually all debt from its balance sheet. Sirius is currently funded through year 2003 and estimates that it will need approximately $75 million more in total funding.[50] Sirius is estimated to have 35,000 subscribers by 2002 year end, and while this number is only 10% of XM's year-end subscriber base, industry analysts project an almost 50-50 dead heat by year 2007.

CONSUMER DEMAND FOR SDARS

The primary market for SDARS technology is mobile (auto/truck) radio listeners. At the writing of this case there were approximately 222.4 million registered cars in the U.S., and each year radio manufacturers sell over 29 million car radios (17 million original equipment radios, 11 million aftermarket radios, and 1.2 million CD changers).[51] These numbers are expected to grow about 3% year over year through 2007. The average commute per motorist was 45 minutes, and 75% of the population listened to radio daily, with 95% listening weekly.[52] Research reveals the overwhelming dissatisfaction listeners have toward current terrestrial radio programming.

The SDARS market can be divided into luxury (cars greater than $35k), non-luxury, and long-haul (typically truckers driving more than 500 miles per day). Initial adopters are expected to come from the luxury and long-haul segments. Gizmo-loving luxury buyers are expected to be less adverse to the monthly service price and equipment complexity while long-haul drivers are expected to be more cognizant of the value-added nationwide programming.[53] As penetration for SDARS in the long-haul market grows from 2% currently to 48% by 2007, it is expected this market will balloon to 1.6 million subscribers. The long-haul market is estimated to represent 7.3% of the total 22 million potential SDARS subscribers in 2007.[54]

While the primary initial market is mobile, there is a complementary market for in-home users. Sony makes a "plug-and-play" XM radio for use both in the car and home. The company also reports that 1.5 million Sony home stereos sold in 2000 and 2001 are XM-capable. Sirius is expected to follow suit with in-home capable equipment.

Analysts estimate subscriptions could grow to 38 million by 2010 (15% of all radios sold between 2002–2010).[55] However, one of the biggest challenges the SDARS companies face is to provide a compelling enough reason to lure consumers into a subscription plan when they are accustomed to receiving terrestrial radio broadcasts for free. A 2001 survey showed that 69% of consumers will not pay monthly fees at the level currently charged by XM and 85% will not pay at the level charged by Sirius. See Exhibit 5.

The Fourth Quarter . . .

As the night wound down and the final token schmoozing came to an anti-climactic end, the crowd of elegant evening gowns and dapper black tuxedos began to thin. Mr. Panero's and Mr. Clayton's eyes caught each other's focus once again as they made their way to the coat check. It was inevitable; their paths were bound to cross. They stood silent and awkward next to each other in line waiting to overtip the staff for mediocre coat storage service.

In such close proximity both began to think silently: Was the SDARS market mass or niche? Could they both exist? How would interoperability impact their businesses? Were their alliances as important as they thought? Who are the truly important partners? How would they market their service B2B and B2C? Did they have enough funding to reach critical mass? Could they work together to jointly enlarge the market for each other's benefit? Would they ultimately join forces?

The coats finally came, and as each quickly put distance between the other, the tension painfully subsided. Mr. Panero eased out of the circular drive in his Cadillac, but as he looked back at the halogen lit red carpet he caught Mr. Clayton's stare one last time in the rearview mirror just as he too was entering his Lincoln. Mr. Clayton smirked while Mr. Panero confidently sped away.

EXHIBIT 1   Hardware Manufacturer and Retail Company Alliances
Source: SkyReport Web site <www.skyreport.com> & Sky Trends 2001.

XM		Sirius
National Retailers		
Best Buy	Sears	Best Buy
Circuit City	Wal-Mart	Circuit City
Regional Retailers		
Al & Ed's		Al & Ed's
CarToys		CarToys
Cowboy Maloney's		Cowboy Maloney's
Crutchfield		Crutchfield
Good Guys		Good Guys
Magnolia Hi-Fi		Magnolia Hi-Fi
Mobile-One		Mobile-One
Sound Advice		Sound Advice
Tweeter		Tweeter
Ultimate Electronics		Ultimate Electronics
Marine Audio		Marine Audio
LiveTV		LiveTV
		Pana-Pacific
Consumer Electronics Manufacturers		
Alpine		Alpine
Antenna Specialists		Antenna Specialists
Blaupunkt		Blaupunkt
Eclipse-Fujitsu Ten		Eclipse-Fujitsu Ten
Pana-Pacific		Pana-Pacific
Panasonic		Panasonic
Pioneer		Pioneer
Sanyo		Sanyo
Sony		Sony
Audiovox		Audiovox
Clarion		Clarion
Delphi		Delphi
Mitsubishi		Mitsubishi
Visteon		Visteon
Terk		Terk
Bontec		Jensen
Hyundai Autonet		Kenwood
Motorola		BMW
Sharp		DaimlerChrysler
General Motors		Dodge
Pontiac		Jeep
Cadillac		Mercedes Benz
Buick		Ford
GMC		Jaguar
Chevrolet		Lincoln
Saturn		Mazda
Saab		Mercury
Isuzu		Freightliner
Suzuki		Sterling
Freightliner		Porsche
Peterbilt		Nissan
Porsche		Volkswagen
Nissan		Volvo
Volkswagen		

EXHIBIT 2   Programming
Source: <www.sirius.com>. Accessed December 2002.

Sirius	XM
Music	
Decades—4 channels	Decades—6 channels
Pop/Hits—4 channels	Pop/Hits—11 channels
Rock—11 channels	Rock—12 channels
Country—6 channels	Country—6 channels
R&B/Urban—8 channels	Urban—8 channels
Dance—4 channels	Dance—4 channels
Jazz, Blues and Standards—8 channels	Jazz and Blues—7 channels
Latin (Spanish)—5 channels	Latin (Spanish)—5 channels
Classical—3 channels	Classical—3 channels
Christian—2 channels	Christian—2 channels
Reggae, World, New Age, Other—4 channels	World—5 channels
News	
ABC News and Talk	ABC News and Talk
BBC World Service News	BBC World Service News
Bloomberg	Bloomberg
CNBC	CNBC
CNN Headline News	CNN Headline News
C-SPAN Radio	C-SPAN Radio
Fox News Channel	Fox News Channel
The Weather Channel Radio	The Weather Channel Radio
BBC Mundo (Spanish)	CNN (Spanish)
La Red Hispana (Spanish)	CNET Radio
NPR Now	CNN
NPR Talk	
PRI's Public Radio Channel	
Real Sirius	
Sirius Talk	
World Radio Network	
Sports	
ESPN Radio	ESPN Radio
ESPN News	ESPN News
Sports Byline USA	The Sporting News
Speed Channel Radio (NASCAR, F1, CART)	NASCAR Radio
OLN Adventure Radio	Fox Sports Radio
Radio Deportivo (Spanish)	
Entertainment	
Radio Disney	Radio Disney
Sirius Kids	XM Kids
Buzz Sirius	Buzz XM
Discovery Channel Radio	Discovery Channel Radio
E! Entertainment	E! Entertainment
Radio Classics	Radio Classics
Sirius Trucking Network	Open Road (Trucking)
A&E Satellite Radio	Extreme XM (24 hr. morning shows)
Sirius Comedy	XM Comedy
Sirius Entertainment	Laugh USA
WSM Entertainment	Sonic Theater (Audio books, radio dramas)
The World Network (Urban ministries and gospel)	Ask!
TWC Radio Network, Central, East, West—3 channels	XM Live
Wisdom Radio (Health)	The Power (African American Talk)
YAK! (Guy Talk)	Family Talk
Radio Amigo & Radio Mujer (Spanish)	Premium Channel: Playboy Radio

EXHIBIT 3 Financial and Operating Data ($ in millions)

Source: Robertson Stephens estimates.

XM

FY December	2001	2002E	2003E	2004E	2005E	2006E	2007E	2008E	2009E	2010E
Total Subscribers	27,773	348,307	1,011,053	2,779,301	4,982,440	7,487,512	9,888,503	12.439M	15.039M	17.857M
Subscription Revenue	.2	7.9	78.3	225.8	493.4	831.7	1,214.6	1,631.7	2,104.2	2,639.2
Activation Fee Revenue	0.0	3.7	7.4	20.5	28.6	36.4	40.9	49.1	57.0	67.9
Advertising Revenue	0.3	1.0	2.0	8.8	31.8	69.8	124.6	210.4	273.1	342.8
Total Revenue	**0.5**	**22.6**	**87.8**	**255.2**	**553.9**	**937.9**	**1,380.2**	**1,891.2**	**2,434.3**	**3,049.9**
Subscription Revenue (%)	45.4%	79.4%	89.3%	88.5%	89.1%	88.7%	88.0%	86.3%	86.4%	86.5%
Activation Fee Revenue (%)	6.7%	16.2%	8.5%	8.1%	5.2%	3.9%	3.0%	2.6%	2.3%	2.2%
Advertising Revenue (%)	47.9%	4.4%	2.2%	3.5%	5.7%	7.4%	9.0%	11.1%	11.2%	11.2%
Total Expenses	240.2	282.2	313.8	473.6	590.9	768.7	900.3	1,103.3	1,304.1	1,538.6
EBITDA	(239.6)	(259.6)	(226.1)	(218.4)	(37.0)	169.2	479.9	787.9	1,130.2	1,511.3

Sirius

FY December	2001	2002E	2003E	2004E	2005E	2006E	2007E	2008E	2009E	2010E
Total Subscribers	0.0	132,175	685,124	2,391,373	4,809,936	7,605,145	10.331M	13.266M	16.322M	19.642M
Subscription Revenue		10.3	61.2	240.2	592.2	1,064.9	1,603.8	2,200.0	2,883.9	3,667.9
Activation Fee Revenue		2.2	8.8	28.5	44.5	57.5	65.4	79.4	93.7	112.1
Advertising Revenue		0.2	1.9	9.9	33.6	67.7	112.8	180.9	226.8	275.7
Total Revenue		**12.7**	**71.9**	**278.6**	**670.3**	**1,190.1**	**1,782.0**	**2,460.3**	**3,204.4**	**4,055.7**
Subscription Revenue (%)		81.1%	85.2%	86.2%	88.3%	89.5%	90.0%	89.4%	90.0%	90.4%
Activation Fee Revenue (%)		17.1%	12.2%	10.2%	6.6%	4.8%	3.7%	3.2%	2.9%	2.8%
Advertising Revenue (%)		1.9%	2.6%	3.6%	5.0%	5.7%	6.3%	7.4%	7.1%	6.8%
Total Expenses	139.5	229.8	285.5	446.3	600.4	758.3	898.7	1,102.6	1,351.3	1,650.7
EBITDA	(139.5)	(217.1)	(213.6)	(167.6)	69.9	431.8	883.3	1,357.7	1,853.1	2,405.0

EXHIBIT 4
Timeline of Key Milestones since Inception
Source: Bear, Stearns & Co. Inc.

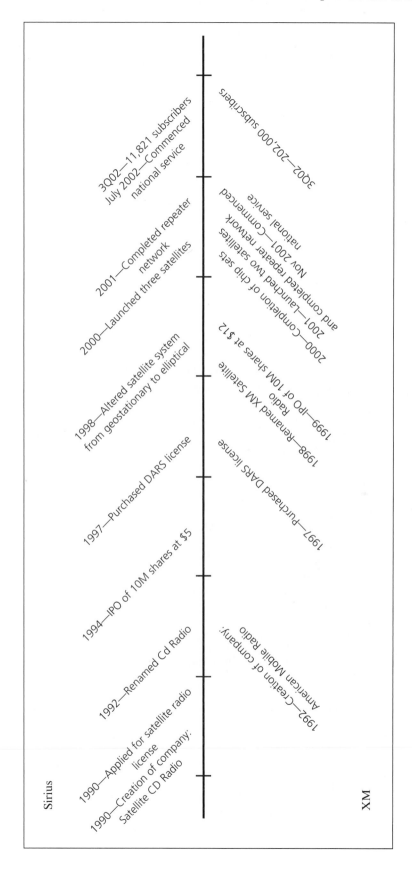

Sirius

3Q02—11,821 subscribers
July 2002—Commenced national service

2001—Completed repeater network

2000—Launched three satellites

1998—Altered satellite system from geostationary to elliptical

1997—Purchased DARS license

1994—IPO of 10M shares at $5

1992—Renamed Cd Radio

1990—Applied for satellite radio license

1990—Creation of company: Satellite CD Radio

XM

3Q02—202,000 subscribers

2001—Completed repeater network
Nov 2001—Commenced national service

2000—Completion of chip sets
2001—Launched two satellites and completed repeater network

1999—IPO of 10M shares at $12

1998—Renamed XM Satellite Radio

1997—Purchased DARS license

1992—Creation of company: American Mobile Radio

EXHIBIT 5
Consumers'
Willingness to Pay
for SDARS
Source: CEA Market
Research, *Digitizing
the Airways: The
Conversion to Digital
Radio,* 4/01.

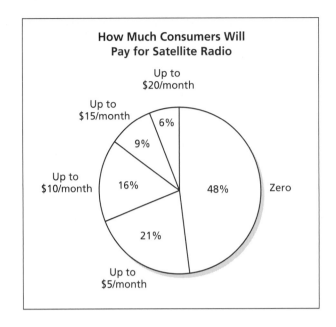

How Much Consumers Will Pay for Satellite Radio

- Up to $20/month — 6%
- Up to $15/month — 9%
- Up to $10/month — 16%
- Up to $5/month — 21%
- Zero — 48%

Endnotes

1. www.northwinds.net/bchris/, December 2002.
2. www.marconi.com/html/about/marconihistory.htm.
3. Ibid.
4. www.northwinds.net/bchris/, December 2002.
5. Ibid.
6. Ibid.
7. Ibid.
8. Ibid.
9. Ibid.
10. www.fcc.gov, December 2002.
11. www.northwinds.net/bchris/, December 2002.
12. Ibid.
13. James Marsh, Rory Maher, and David Murphy, "Satellite Radio Industry Report," Robertson Stephens, Inc., April 29, 2002.
14. www.northwinds.net/bchris/, December 2002.
15. Ibid.
16. James Marsh, Rory Maher, and David Murphy, "Satellite Radio Industry Report," Robertson Stephens, Inc., April 29, 2002.
17. Ibid.
18. Ibid.
19. Ibid.
20. Ibid.
21. Ibid.
22. Robert Peck and Shlomi Yedid, "Satellite Industry Report," Bear Stearns, June 2002.
23. James Marsh, Rory Maher, and David Murphy, "Satellite Radio Industry Report," Robertson Stephens, Inc., April 29, 2002.
24. www.ibiquity.com, December 2002.

25. John Slania, "A Battle for the Airwaves: Crossed Signals," *Crain Communications,* Inc., 2002.

26. James Marsh, Rory Maher, and David Murphy, "Satellite Radio Industry Report," Robertson Stephens, Inc., April 29, 2002.

27. Ibid.

28. Ibid.

29. Ibid.

30. Ibid.

31. Alex Markels, "100 Channels, but Where Are the Subscribers?" *The New York Times,* Nov. 3, 2002.

32. www.xmradio.com, December 2002.

33. Morgan Stanley 3Q02 Meeting Notes, November 15, 2002.

34. James Marsh, Rory Maher, and David Murphy, "Satellite Radio Industry Report," Robertson Stephens, Inc., April 29, 2002.

35. www.xmradio.com, December 2002.

36. James Marsh, Rory Maher, and David Murphy, "Satellite Radio Industry Report," Robertson Stephens, Inc., April 29, 2002.

37. Ibid.

38. Ibid.

39. Ibid.

40. Marc E. Nabi and Ryan D. Brown, "XM Satellite Radio Holdings, Inc.: The Second Coming Is Close at Hand," Merrill Lynch, October 8, 2002.

41. James Marsh, Rory Maher, and David Murphy, "Satellite Radio Industry Report," Robertson Stephens, Inc., April 29, 2002.

42. Ibid.

43. Ibid.

44. www.sirius.com, December 2002.

45. Ibid.

46. James Marsh, Rory Maher, and David Murphy, "Satellite Radio Industry Report," Robertson Stephens, Inc., April 29, 2002.

47. Vijay Jayant and David T. Veal, "Sirius Satellite Radio: Restructuring Plans Announced but Risks Remain," Morgan Stanley, October 21, 2002.

48. James Marsh, Rory Maher, and David Murphy, "Satellite Radio Industry Report," Robertson Stephens, Inc., April 29, 2002.

49. Hertz press release on Sirius Satellite Radio corporate website, "Hertz Gets Sirius for Car Rental Customers," November, 2002.

50. William Kidd, "Sirius Satellite Radio," Lehman Brothers, October 18, 2002.

51. Robert Peck and Shlomi Yedid, "Satellite Industry Report," Bear Stearns, June 2002.

52. www.xmradio.com, December 2002.

53. James Marsh, Rory Maher, and David Murphy, "Satellite Radio Industry Report," Robertson Stephens, Inc., April 29, 2002.

54. Robert Peck and Shlomi Yedid, "Satellite Industry Report," Bear Stearns, June 2002.

55. James Marsh, Rory Maher, and David Murphy, "Satellite Radio Industry Report," Robertson Stephens, Inc., April 29, 2002.

Case 5

Segway: Segue to . . .

If enough people see the machine, you won't have to convince them to architect cities around it. It'll just happen. (Steve Jobs, CEO, Apple Computer)

I had been sure that (I) wouldn't see the development of anything in (my) lifetime as important as the World Wide Web—until I saw "IT." This could be the fastest product to reach $1 billion in sales. (John Doerr, Partner, Kleiner Perkins Caufield & Byers)

It is a product so revolutionary, you'll have no problem selling it. [This should be] the most famous and anticipated product introduction of all time. (Jeff Bezos, Founder and CEO, Amazon.com)

INTRODUCTION

Late one evening in the fall of 2002, Dean Kamen went on a longer than usual helicopter ride. He passed on taking his smaller chopper over his Westwind Estate in rural Manchester, New Hampshire, and instead piled into his turbine-driven Enstrom and headed toward the city lights of downtown Boston. As he approached, the car lights coming from the traffic-jammed streets below illuminated the night sky, and Kamen breathed easy. Seeing the packed cars below in the city streets again reminded him of the urgency of his most ambitious invention yet, the Segway HT (Human Transporter). Like his prior inventions, including the AutoSyringe drug delivery device and the *i*Bot stair-climbing wheelchair, Kamen was confident the Segway would revolutionize the way people performed certain tasks. But *unlike* the AutoSyringe and *i*Bot, the Segway could potentially impact every person in the world for generations. Kamen reflected on the various milestones achieved and the challenges ahead.

BACKGROUND

The Inventor

Dean Kamen was an inventor known for both his eccentricity and his ability to invent items that revolutionized industries. A self-taught physicist and engineer, Dean Kamen's history of innovation went back to his undergraduate days, when he developed the world's first wearable infusion pump. After dropping out of school, he founded AutoSyringe Inc. in 1976 to manufacture and market pumps. Following the sale of AutoSyringe to a division of the Baxter Healthcare Corporation, he founded DEKA Research & Development Corporation. [1]

DEKA Research & Development Corporation

Kamen founded DEKA Research & Development Corporation to provide an infrastructure for bringing his ideas to fruition. Since its inception in 1982, DEKA's mission was to "foster innovation" and to utilize technology to enhance the quality of human life. To accomplish this goal, the company recruited innovative people across a variety of fields, including engineering. All of this talent was placed into a flat organization, with limited formal structure, so that the best ideas would freely cross-pollinate throughout the company. With such a small organization (less than 200 employees), and a lack of "handbook-style" management, the true driving force of DEKA was Kamen's strong personality. Though he demanded excellent results from the small DEKA staff, Kamen also provided freedom and encouraged creativity. How the staff got its results and created solutions was up to them, and this made DEKA an organization with exceptionally high morale. [2]

Many firms reward success and punish failure. This was not the case at DEKA Research. Although no one was deliberately trying to come up with bad ideas that would put the company out of business, engineers involved in the development of the Segway Human Transporter (HT) were encouraged to come up with outlandish ideas. Doug Field, Vice President of Product Development at Segway LLC and former development engineer at DEKA, said,

The whole purpose is to stimulate thinking, because the best way to come up with a good idea is to have lots to choose from. This philosophy forms the foundation of the way Dean and DEKA

Christopher Cho, Mike Koziol, Kelly Mao, Travis Narum, Rachey Peten, and Steven Van Metre prepared this case under the supervision of Professor Allan Afuah as a basis for class discussion rather than to illustrate either effective or ineffective management. Creative liberties have been taken in developing the introductory and concluding paragraphs of the case.

works. Dean says, "You have to kiss a lot of frogs to find a prince." And he's always pushing us for more and different ideas rather than settling on one too early.[3]

Supporting this "let's throw wet spaghetti against a wall and see what sticks" philosophy was one of several specific features of the DEKA organization and culture. Engineers were encouraged to learn to use the company's in-house machine shop so that they could directly create and test some of the crazier ideas. Kamen presented an annual "frog award" to the engineer who came up with the "off-the-wall" and most spectacularly failed idea. Multiple small projects were run at once, and engineers were encouraged to participate and contribute to several projects at once, stimulating the flow of information. Furthermore, each engineering team meeting was designated as either "ideation" (idea generation) or "execution," so that the team knew what it should be focused on and could move good ideas quickly through development. Small execution teams also helped keep projects focused and on track. The company was also not afraid to outsource components of its designs that, while critical, were not the true source of product innovation.[4]

This somewhat entropic approach to R&D had a strong track record of success. Projects at DEKA typically fell into two categories: contract research and development projects for healthcare corporations such as Baxter and Johnson & Johnson and Kamen's personal projects on innovative technologies. The contract research and development projects were typically derived out of a need that a medical device company or other corporation had encountered yet did not have a solution for.[5] As stated by Baxter's former chairman, "If you've got a tough problem, there's only one place to go."[6] Projects[7] that had grown out of these partnerships included:

- *iBot* (aka "Fred"): A patented DEKA invention, the *i*Bot was a mobility machine developed for Independence Technology (a division of Johnson & Johnson). The *i*Bot looked like a wheelchair but was capable of a lot more. The *i*Bot enabled its user to climb up and down stairs and over uneven surfaces. It was full of gyroscopes, electric motors, and computers. While the *i*Bot was currently tied up in the FDA approval process, it was expected to be priced at $20,000.
- *Homechoice dialysis machine:* Designed for Baxter and awarded Design News' 1993 Medical Product of the Year, Homechoice was a peritoneal dialysis machine that gave patients with chronic renal failure the freedom to travel far from home. Homechoice was a compact machine that could easily be taken on an airplane or in a car. Previous models of these machines were bigger and difficult to travel with.
- *Hydroflex irrigation pump:* In partnership with Davol Inc. (a medical devices company), DEKA designed, developed, and manufactured the Hydroflex pump. Hydroflex was a high performance irrigation pump used in laparoscopic and arthroscopic surgeries.
- *Intravascular Stent:* DEKA developed this Intravascular Stent in conjunction with Johnson & Johnson. The stent helped prevent blockage in arteries and was an alternative to open heart surgery.
- *Therakos UVAR XTS system:* Working with Therakos (a division of Johnson & Johnson), DEKA developed this system that aids in the treatment of skin manifestations of cutaneous T-cell lymphoma (CTCL), a malignancy of T cells that invades the skin. The system measures, pumps, and routes fluid.

While medical device corporations funded the innovations in medical field technology, they also paid DEKA handsome fees for these developments. These contracts more than paid the bills; they also made Kamen a wealthy man, and enabled him to privately fund his personal and often more risky projects. These projects primarily stemmed from Kamen's thoughts on how to cure some of society's ills. These projects tackled everything from environmental issues to personal mobility. According to Kamen, "Sometimes we crash and burn. It's better to do it in private. I'd rather lose my own money than someone else's."[8]

THE SEGWAY HUMAN TRANSPORTER

The Product and Technology

One of the highest profile projects of DEKA's "personal" projects was the Segway HT, which arose in part from the technology developments of the *i*Bot Mobility System and in part from Kamen's deep desire to create an alternative form of transportation to compete with the automobile. The development teams at DEKA thus created the Segway HT, a two-wheel, self-balancing, electric-powered transporter. (See Exhibit 1 for a picture of the Segway HT.) From the beginning, the goal with the device was to address the problem of moving people and products relatively short distances more efficiently. The product was thus designed to enhance productivity by: increasing the distance and speed a person could travel and the amount they could carry; taking up no more room than a pedestrian (its footprint measured 19 inches by 25 inches); and using less energy per mile than a person walking.

To accomplish this, the Segway HT used redundant electric and mechanical systems in order to enable easy operation and navigation. The Segway HT features included: a "power assist mode" to move the product up and down stairs; a lowering control shaft that allowed it to fit in a car trunk; a set of keys encoded with a 64-bit security ID to prevent theft; and openings in the fender and wheels that could be used with a variety of security devices. Generally speaking, the Segway HT consisted of three electronic and control subsystems, which were concealed within an aluminum frame that many in the media called "a cross between a pogo-stick and a push lawnmower."[9] In brief (see Exhibit 2 for more details), these subsystems were:

Sensor and input subsystem: Five intertial solid-state gyroscopic sensors, optical footpad sensors, two tilt sensors, motor encoders, and steering sensors, which combined to collect data on the Segway's and the rider's speed, momentum, and rate of change. The sensors gathered data for yaw, pitch, and roll, and fed it to the control subsystem, which in turn provided the propulsion system with the appropriate power adjustments to stabilize the machine.

Control subsystem: Two microprocessor controller boards, each of which processed momentum and balance calculations. These calculations then fed adjustments in power and torque to the wheel motors and balance servos. The control subsystem also processed information from the rider controls (steering and speed).

Propulsion subsystem: Took torque output from the motors and converted it into propulsion for the gearboxes, wheels, and tiers. The unique brushless motor design with hemispherical windings and integrated heat management increased the torque output of the propulsion system, which in turn improved the ability of the Segway to stabilize itself.[10]

The revolutionary part of the Segway HT was its "dynamic stabilization" technology, which used solid-state gyroscopes, a complicated network of sensors and microprocessors, and electric servomotors to keep the transporter balanced. This web of interrelated components determined the exact position and momentum of the Segway and its rider and made up to 100 tiny adjustments per second to keep the machine effectively balanced. This in turn enabled the Segway HT to use a design with a much higher center of gravity and smaller base while still providing a stable, nontippable ride.[11]

Two models of the Segway HT were offered, the i Series and the e Series:

- The i Series was offered to both personal and business customers. The first model, the i167, featured a powerful battery for extended speed and range, as well as large wheels and low-pressure tires for enhanced performance in variable terrain. The i Series had a maximum speed of 12.5 miles per hour and a range of 15 miles per charge. The transporter weighed 83 pounds, had a payload capacity of 250 pounds, and sold for $4,950.

- The e Series was equipped with large storage bags and cargo racks, which increased carrying capacity and thus offered enhanced adaptability for commercial customers. It featured the same performance attributes as the i Series, with several additions that enhanced its value for commercial applications. First, it had been equipped with an "e-stand"—an electronic parking stand that allowed the unit to balance unattended. This unique feature allowed the user to transition on and off the device in the workplace with maximum efficiency. Second, the cargo carrying capacity included three separate storage compartments that allowed a user to handle up to an additional 75 pounds of cargo, such as tools, supplies, packages, or equipment. This version sold for between $7,000 and $9,000.

In addition, a smaller, lighter version, dubbed the p Series, was expected to come to market in early-to-mid 2003, and be priced between $2,000 and $3,000.

Development of the Segway HT

As mentioned, part of the stimulus for the Segway was the technology behind the *i*Bot wheelchair. Kamen and the DEKA development team recognized the potential of applying the core balancing technology to a device for people without mobility impairments. The *i*Bot project was also the source of Ginger's mysterious code name, as Kamen explained:

> Watching the *i*Bot, we used to say, "Look at that light, graceful robot, dancing up the stairs"—so we started referring to it as Fred Upstairs, after Fred Astair. After we built Fred, it was only natural to name its smaller partner Ginger.[12]

The DEKA team knew that its critical contribution was the dynamic stabilization technology and the overall configuration of the Segway HT, and these were the primary areas in which Kamen and his team filed numerous patents.[13] The company was thus comfortable in working with a group of outside development partners with other areas of expertise. This critical group of supply partners contributed both product expertise and money to the development process, helping to ensure that specs and deadlines were met. This group of partners (see Exhibit 3 for additional information) included:

Silicon Sensing Systems—the world's leading provider of silicon micro-machined sensors; collaborated on the Segway's gyro and tilt sensor systems, key components of the machine's self-balancing capability.

Pacific Scientific—manufacturer of high performance electric motors and drive systems; designed Segway HT's compact, brushless, electric servo motor.

Delphi Automotive Systems—manufacturer of integrated circuits, smart sensors, and software algorithms for the transportation and aerospace industries; assisted in the development of the integrated circuit boards to meet the standards used for automotive reliability levels in extreme environments.

Axicon—leading designer and developer of quiet gear systems; developed the quiet helical gear systems and was the exclusive supplier of the Segway HT transmissions.

In addition to the development funds contributed by the supplier partners, the Segway HT project received over $75 million in capital from CSFB Private Equity Fund, Kleiner Perkins Caufield & Byers (a leading venture capital firm), and Kamen's own personal contributions.[14] Kleiner Perkins partner John Doerr's personal stake was reputed to be as high as $30 million for a 7% stake in the company. In total, more than $100 million was put behind the human transporter project.[15]

COMPETITION

Kamen believed the Segway HT filled a gap where no other products competed at the time. The Segway developers hoped customers who required a simple, efficient mode of personal transportation would adopt the product en masse. According to Kamen and his team, one attractive feature of the Segway was its ability to provide a more rapid mode of transportation than walking without the size constraints of larger vehicles, especially cars, carts, and bicycles. Another proposed benefit was that the vehicle was significantly more efficient than an automobile for short personal transportation and did not rely on fossil fuels. The objective was for these benefits to draw consumers interested in the Segway for personal transportation and businesses, as well as government agencies interested in the transporter for commercial, industrial, and municipal use. However, contrary to Kamen's belief, several products did exist that were potentially competitive depending on the right market conditions.

"Smart cars" or small, electric powered vehicles had been available for years, but up to that point proved unable to gain mass appeal in the United States. Due to increasing pollution restrictions in America, companies such as General Motors resorted to giving these "smart cars" away in order to bring its fleet emissions down.[16] Ford abandoned its electric-vehicle division in August 2002.[17] However, these smaller, more energy efficient vehicles reached wider penetration in Europe and Asia, where cities were more congested and air pollution restrictions were more stringent. Furthermore, new types of alternative fuel source cars, such as fuel cell and gasoline-electric hybrids, could further dampen enthusiasm for the Segway as an environmentally friendly substitute for the auto. Motorcycles and mopeds were also a competing alternative. Due to their smaller size, these vehicles helped reduce traffic congestion, and were also popular in congested European and Asian cities. Smart cars, even the smallest of the "minis," typically carried 2–3 passengers in addition to the driver, and even motorcycles and larger mopeds were equipped for up to 2 people. Furthermore, smart cars (whether powered by electricity, fuel cells, or gasoline-electric hybrid engines), motorcycles, and mopeds were all "street legal," and thus had a competitive advantage over the Segway HT in this respect.

Although it was usually not "street legal," the golf cart was another source of potential competition. Golf carts typically used electric motors (or more infrequently internal combustion engines), carried 2–4 people, and had space for cargo (or golf bags). Companies, organizations, and individuals frequently used such carts for a variety of tasks, from sports teams using them to carry gear, to employees using them for travel across corporate campuses, to shift supervisors using them to travel within large manufacturing facilities. College campuses had also adopted the golf cart. For example, the University of Nevada at Las Vegas had seen a proliferation of golf cart use on its campus, primarily as a result of students and faculty finding better ways to deal with the extreme heat and the increased distances they had to travel across the expanding desert campus.[18] Even retirees in Florida took to using personal golf carts for routine errands within the retirement community.

When it came to analyzing the competitive landscape for the Segway HT, nothing could be ruled out. Even a child's motorized scooter could be considered a competing product to the Segway HT. Razor USA, manufacturer of the Razor scooter, sold millions of the E-Electric and XLR8R battery-powered versions of the child's toy. This company and others in the same sector sold products that ranged in price from under one hundred to several hundred dollars and which, apart from the complexity of the dynamic stabilization, offered some of the same benefits and product features as the much more expensive Segway.

Exhibit 4 presents market data on these potentially competitive products including total worldwide market size and typical product price ranges.

SEGWAY LLC
From DEKA to Segway LLC

Unlike other products in DEKA's portfolio, Kamen decided the Segway HT should not be licensed for other companies to sell. Instead, a separate company, Segway LLC, was founded in 1999 to bring the Human Transporter to market. The first reason behind this decision was Kamen's belief that the combination of science, engineering, and vision embodied in the Segway HT was truly revolutionary and that it could be used to improve people's daily lives and transform transportation and city planning.

> Today, 3.2 billion people live in cities. More than half the human population lives in cities. If we could give them an attractive, productive alternative to using great big vehicles to get around

at speeds of seven or eight miles an hour, which is the average speed of a taxicab in the 20 largest cities on the planet, it would by itself be a huge, huge solution to the congestion and pollution and energy demand problems the world is facing today.[19] (Dean Kamen)

Furthermore, Kamen believed that few, if any, existing companies could effectively turn this vision into a reality. While auto companies might know transportation, the Segway HT would be priced more like a consumer electronics product or appliance. However, these firms would know nothing about the transportation industry and the regulations needed for wide Segway adoption. Kamen was also afraid that another company might not take the Segway HT seriously, and it would end up as just another toy or fad. "I can't work on something that's just about that," he says. "I want to make a product that really has a serious impact on the environment, that can bring energy back to our inner cities."[20]

In addition, Kamen, an inventor with no small amount of business sense, recognized that if his vision for the Segway HT materialized, then the potential profits would be tremendous. In addition to adding to his already considerable personal wealth, the success of Segway LLC could, like the contract projects at DEKA, continue to fund a host of pet projects, including a portable electric generator/water purifier, based on the concepts of a 19th century Scottish minister, Robert Stirling, which Kamen hoped could revolutionize third world development.[21] It was partly for this reason that Kamen chose to incorporate Segway as a limited liability company. This newer and more complex form of organization placed limitations on the rights of investors in the firm. And unlike most start-ups, the ownership stakes in an LLC could go up or down, according to other partner agreements and how well the company did.

The Organization

Management Team   After deciding that a separate company was required and having incorporated Segway as an LLC, Kamen began to build the company by recruiting an impressive management team with diverse executive experiences from companies including Subaru, Enstrom Helicopter, Johnson and Johnson, SPX, Cabletron, Iridium, and Gillette. George Muller, former President of Subaru America, was named President of Segway LLC and was responsible for all aspects of the business, including sales and marketing, product development, operations, finance, and human resources. Other key executives included Robert Tuttle, Vice Chairman of Segway LLC, and Douglas Field, a former DEKA development engineer, who was Segway's VP of Development and Operations. A list of Segway executives can be found in Exhibit 5.

Organizational Structure Segway's small number of employees was organized into 16 functional and development teams.

- Development teams included 36 employees in: User Interface Design, Power Base Design, Embedded Design, Industrial Design, Dynamics, Mechanical Integrity, and Electrical Integrity teams.
- Operational teams included 33 employees in: Supply Chain, Manufacturing, and Technical Service teams.
- Functional teams included several dozen employees in: Regulatory, Marketing, Sales, Information Technology, Human Resources, and Finance teams.

Like DEKA, Segway LLC, according to engineer John Morrell, who had no official job title, was "a very flat organization. Everyone here is your colleague, no matter what your responsibilities are. It's a real jeans-and-sneakers kind of place."[22] Furthermore, given its small size (approximately half the size of DEKA), Segway LLC relied on the DEKA development resources in addition to its own for improvements to the Segway HT product line.[23]

MARKET ENTRY STRATEGY

Kamen proclaimed the Segway "will be to the car what the car was to the horse and buggy."[24] Certainly, the large amount of press that the product generated while known as "IT" and "Ginger" was testament to its ability to capture the public's imagination. And while the Segway HT may not have lived up to the pre-release hype and speculation (said Kamen, "but what possibly could have?!"), Kamen and his invention were still prominent in the public eye. Nevertheless, Kamen was not naïve to think that the free publicity alone would change the world's, and especially America's, love affair with the automobile. Furthermore, while Segway LLC did not recognize any true competitors to the human transporter, the company did understand the challenges of bringing the revolutionary product to market. Kamen and his company realized that it was not a simple case of "build it and they will come," and thus they adopted a very specific product launch plan.

Strategic Relationships

The first part of the plan was to work with large, established institutions in order to jointly test the Segway HT under practical conditions. Some of the institutions that Segway LLC partnered with included:

Government agencies: U.S. Postal Service, National Parks Service, U.S. Department of Defense, Police Departments of Boston, Chicago, and the Capitol, Cities of Atlanta, Palo Alto, and Toledo, San Francisco International Airport, California Department of Transportation.

Corporations: Amazon.com (in order to improve "picking efficiency" in the distribution warehouses, commented its founder Jeff Bezos), GE Plastics, and Walt Disney Company.

Universities: Stanford University

There were three main benefits to working with these types of organizations. First, these large, reputable institutions created a fertile testing ground for the Segway—over 50,000 hours of "product testing" had been logged with these different partners. Second, many of the institutions were "high-profile," professionally run, and well-respected. Thus, the belief was that if they adopted the Segway, then average consumers would begin to view the product more as a serious productivity tool and less as a toy. Furthermore, the risks of regulatory hurdles could be mitigated by convincing government agencies of the ease of use and safety of the product. Finally, these large institutions could easily afford the approximate $8,500 price tag of the Segway.

Concurrent with working to develop these corporate and government partnerships, Kamen used his reputation as a brilliant and prolific inventor to bring business and technology luminaries—such as Jeff Bezos (Founder and CEO of Amazon.com), John Doerr (Partner of Kleiner Perkins Caufield & Byers), Steve Jobs (CEO of Apple Computer), John Chambers (CEO of Cisco Systems), and Andy Grove (Chairman of Intel)—among the fold of Segway devotees. These luminaries acted as champions of the product, and in doing so created greater consumer interest and helped to influence regulatory decisions.

Regulatory Environment

The regulatory aspects were critical, for if the Segway HT was to become a successful, widely adopted consumer product in the United States, then the transportation laws had to be in place to support its use. Being too slow and too small to compete for road space with trucks and cars, the Segway HT was best suited for sidewalks and other pedestrian paths. However, in the United States, 41 states had laws preventing the use of motorized vehicles on pedestrian walkways.[25] Segway LLC pursued a regulatory blitzkrieg strategy with the hope that it could change these laws. In the United States, each state legislature ruled on matters that affected streets and sidewalks throughout its state. By December 2002, due to the direct campaigning of Segway's regulatory organization, the publicity created by its partnerships, and the efforts of its product champions, 32 states had passed laws to make Segway legal on streets and/or sidewalks. Laws could be comprehensive and specific, but often states made broad rulings pertaining to pedestrian traffic or granted local governments such as municipalities and townships the power to regulate the time, place, and manner for using transportation devices, including the power to outright ban them from certain areas. California was one such state to do so in the fall of 2002. Furthermore, local governments could in turn divvy up power among local districts to decide regulations on a per street basis. Both states and localities took cues from federal regulatory bodies that assessed the safety of vehicles. The Consumer Product Safety Commission (CPSC), which began reviewing the Segway HT in May of 2002, is one example. Its initial reviews were positive. One senior CPSC official stated,

> The Segway has safety features that are far more substantial than we normally see in a consumer product—features closer to those associated with medical devices.[26]

All this made for a complex regulatory environment in which proponents and opponents squared off to decide the fate of the urban landscape. Those involved ranged from overarching supporters to groups demanding outright bans. Governor Gray Davis of California belonged to the former group. In the fall of 2002 he stated,

> This new and innovative means of individual transportation will allow people to move throughout urban environments without pollution, significant levels of noise, or massive parking areas.[27]

Most, however, fell somewhere in between. For example, Bruce Livingston, lobbyist for elderly rights in San Francisco, stated,

> This is a great new technology in search of a place to be put. That doesn't mean it should be allowed everywhere.[28]

In the United States, the Segway HT was relatively successful in overcoming regulatory hurdles. Its quick acceptance was somewhat unprecedented given that laws pertaining to scooters and other such devices typically entailed numerous bills and took several years to pass. Further, Segway LLC had a minuscule two-person regulatory staff and a relatively small budget. Its strategy entailed fanning out to approach state governments by hiring local lobbyists in most states and providing Segway HT samples to lawmakers. The result in most cases was a slew of photo opportunities as legislators smilingly rode Segways around their offices. The company also provided samples to potential opponents, including special interest and advocacy groups.

The regulatory environment in Europe and Asia differed from the United States. In Europe, although its traditions of law were similar to those in the United States, opposition was not as stiff. Generally, Europeans were more open to alternative modes of transportation and trying out new things, and governments for the most part supported this. In Asia, although more difficult to generalize due to the heterogeneity of culture and economics across different countries, many developing countries embraced such alternative transportation modes as a way to deal with burgeoning populations that needed more efficient means of travel in crowded urban areas. Further, the legislative infrastructure in developing Asian countries was usually not as developed and did not generally specifically address these smaller issues. One exception was Singapore where the government closely monitored and regulated all transportation. Japan was more similar to the U.S. and Europe.

Marketing Strategy

Given this background, Segway's marketing chief Gary Bridge said,

> We're very, very interested in the consumer market in Europe, because you have a denser population. And you have, as you've seen, bike trails everywhere, sidewalks that connect to bike trails, a tradition of walking, taking bikes on trains, intermodule, so all of the infrastructure is here that we look for.[29]

Bridge further explained Segway LLC targeted the consumer, military, and industrial markets in Europe and Asia, where there existed fewer regulatory hurdles than in the United States. Kamen reiterated this strategy stating that Europe was way ahead of America in terms of its readiness for the Segway HT. Said Kamen,

> They are greener, the cities are smaller, there's more mass transit and people are more accustomed to walking. Society in Europe is more likely to embrace the Segway.

Kamen believed Asia represented a strong potential long-term market, as many Asian cities were young and could still incorporate urban planning designed specifically around the Segway HT.

The total number of Segway HTs sold had been limited. This fact could have been a result of pursuing a strategy of corporate/institutional partner-testing and regulatory negotiations, which itself appeared to be laying the groundwork for a large push into the consumer market. DEKA and Segway continued to develop the product to make it ready for a consumer launch. They cut costs in the production of the dynamic stabilization unit and developed a lighter, less expensive consumer version (the p Series). In anticipation of March 2003 deliveries, a 77,000-square-foot factory with manufacturing capacity of 40,000 units per month was built near the company's headquarters in New Hampshire, and Segway LLC planned to hold training classes in February in various cities around the country. How many orders the company had received was a secret, but a spokesperson for DEKA said they were "very hapapy" with the number of orders.[30] Nonetheless, the company had not yet announced how consumer or industrial users would service the product, apart from suggesting in product literature that "authorized service representatives" would be available. Further, no decisions had yet been announced suggesting whether the product would be made available through auto or motorcycle dealers, retail stores, or other channels.

In fact, the only channel partnership announced was a marketing partnership with Amazon.com, in which the online retailer would be used as an exclusive consumer sales channel. On November 18, 2002, Amazon.com began taking orders for the HT product. According to Kamen, Segway's decision to partner with Amazon.com "just makes sense. Who better to bring the first Segway HTs to the public? Amazon.com is the world's largest Internet retailer, trusted by its customers to deliver the hottest, hard-to-find products. This venture with Amazon.com is a great way to reward fans of both our companies."[31] At the same time, the company's significant (and to great extent free) publicity continued to position the Segway HT for consumer launch. During its December 2001 launch campaign, Segway generated 758 million impressions, valued in the $70 million to $80 million range, the company said, followed by similar levels in January and February. The company planned a much smaller ad campaign to occur sometime between late 2002 and mid-2003 in order to back the brand's consumer launch. But Segway's publicity kept paying dividends, Mr. Bridge noted. The Segway HT made prominent appearances in NBC's *Frasier* and the season finale of CBS's *The Education of Max Bickford* and was planned to appear in upcoming movies. The ultimate success of the consumer campaign, both in the U.S. and abroad, remained unclear.

CONCLUSION

Developed at a cost of more than $100 million, the Segway was a complex bundle of hardware and software that mimicked the human body's ability to maintain its balance. Reviews were mixed, ranging from the glowing endorsement from Andy Grove, the chairman of Intel, to the harsh review in Business 2.0's report "101 Dumbest Moments in Business History" that summarized the Segway as "a product that costs 30 times what a bicycle does yet makes a rider look like a total dork who's too lazy to walk." Despite the skeptics, Segway LLC had conducted field tests with prominent partners such as the United States Postal Service, the National Park Service, and the Cities of Atlanta, Chicago, and Boston, and staged roll-outs were being planned. But Kamen had grander ambitions in mind for the consumer market. In his heart, Kamen believed the Segway would be to the car what the car was to the horse and buggy. He smiled at the thought of his response to a reporter's question about the likelihood of its mass adoption, "Cars are great for going long distances, but it makes no sense at all for people in cities to use a 4,000-pound piece of metal to haul their 150-pound asses around town."

As he hovered over Boston, Kamen contemplated how he would accomplish his goal. Should Segway LLC first focus on a particular segment of the consumer market and then branch out, or target the entire market out of the gate instead? Once that was decided, how should the Segway be marketed and distributed? How would regulations in the U.S., Europe, and Asia impact sales? Further, how would the transportation industry react to this alternative mode of transportation?

EXHIBIT 1

The Segway Human Transporter
Dean Kamen on the Segway HT

EXHIBIT 2 **Segway Human Transporter Core Technology Description**
Source: How Stuff Works website, <www.howstuffworks.com>.

The Segway HT utilizes a technology called "dynamic stabilization" that uses solid-state gyroscopes, tilt sensors, high-speed microprocessors, and powerful electric motors to keep the transporter balanced. These systems sense the rider's center of gravity, instantaneously assess the information, and make minute adjustments one hundred times a second. Below are excerpts from a description of Segway's technology by www.howstuffworks.com.

The Segway HT has five gyroscopic sensors, though it needs only three to detect forward and backward pitch as well as leaning to the left or right (termed "roll"). The extra sensors add redundancy, to make the vehicle more reliable. The primary sensor system is an assembly of gyroscopes. Segways use a special solid-state angular rate sensor constructed using silicon. Additionally, the Segway has two tilt sensors filled with electrolyte fluid. Like your inner ear, this system figures out its own position relative to the ground based on the tilt of the fluid surface.

All of the tilt information is passed on to the "brain" of the vehicle, two electronic controller circuit boards comprising a cluster of microprocessors. The Segway has a total of 10 onboard microprocessors. Normally, both boards work together, but if one board breaks down, the other will take over all functions so that the system can notify the rider of a failure and shut down gracefully.

The Segway requires this much brain power because it needs to make extremely precise adjustments to keep from falling over. In normal operation, the controller boards check the position sensors about 100 times per second. The microprocessors run an advanced piece of software that monitors all of the stability information and adjusts the speed of several electric motors accordingly. The electric motors, which are powered by a pair of rechargeable nickel metal hydride (NIMH) batteries, can turn each of the wheels independently at variable speeds.

When the vehicle leans forward, the motors spin both wheels forward to keep from tilting over. When the vehicle leans backward, the motors spin both wheels backward. When the rider operates the handlebar control to turn left or right, the motors spin one wheel faster than the other, or spin the wheels in opposite directions, so that the vehicle rotates.

EXHIBIT 3   Segway HT Supplier and Developer Partners
Source: DEKA Research and Development website, http://www.dekaresearch.com.

The Segway HT development required several key supply partners.

Silicon Sensing Systems is the world's leading provider of Silicon Micro-Machined sensors to the automotive, commercial, and aerospace sectors. The company collaborated on development of the HT's gyro and tilt sensor systems, for the self-balancing capability.

Michelin is a recognized leader in innovative mobility solutions. Michelin engineers created the Michelin Balance tire, which has the proper compound, unique tread design, rolling resistance, and handling to function on the Segway HT.

Pacific Scientific, a Danaher Motion company, manufactures high performance electric motors and drive systems for precision automation applications. The company designed the Segway HT's compact, brushless, electric servo motor.

Delphi Automotive Systems manufactures integrated circuits and smart sensors for the transportation, aerospace, and other industries. Delphi assisted in the development of integrated circuit boards for use in the HT control subsystem.

Saft, a leader in the worldwide marketplace for self-contained energy solutions, created rechargeable, self-contained NiCd and NiMH batteries that require no external charger.

Magnetek engineers systems that supply and control power for both home and industrial applications and designed the power supply/battery re-charger for the HT.

Axicon is a leading designer and developer of quiet gear systems and collaboratively developed the helical gear systems and is the exclusive supplier of HT transmissions.

GE Plastics provided Segway LLC with a host of durable and environmentally friendly materials for the Segway HT.

Microprocessor Designs (μPD) is a product design and development firm specializing in embedded microcomputer hardware and firmware and collaborated on the subsystem's hardware, firmware design, integration, and testing.

IBM and the Center for IBM e-business Innovation created the Segway HT website to express the product vision and serve the needs of the HT customers.

Appshop developed enterprise application solutions for Segway LLC's e-commerce, customer care, supply chain, manufacturing, and finance processes.

Jager Di Paola Kemp Design (JDK) worked with Segway LLC to create a brand platform, identity, business papers, packaging, and marketing/promotional materials and collaborated with the development team on product color, graphics, and finishes.

EXHIBIT 4   Worldwide Market Sizes of Competing Products

Source: Thompson Corporation Tablebase (Euromoney Publications PLC). Hoover's Online company and industry profiles (various). Case writer estimates.

	Thousands of Units in Use at the End of:		
Area	**2000**	**2003 (E)**	**2006 (E)**
United States:			
All-Battery Electric Vehicles	4	10	25
Hybrid Electric	10	45	110
Fuel Cell Vehicles	0.1	15	50
Golf Carts (personal vehicles)	400	600	800
Industrial Vehicles	600	800	1,000
Mopeds	45	125	300
Electric Bikes	100	400	985
Electric Scooters	1,500	1,700	1,750
Worldwide:			
All-Battery Electric Vehicles	20	34	58
Hybrid Electric	45	90	180
Fuel Cell Vehicles	0.45	30	150
Golf Carts (personal vehicles)	890	1,350	1,750
Industrial Vehicles	650	825	1,050
Mopeds	300	1,000	1,875
Electric Bikes	2,000	6,000	8,545
Electric Scooters	2,000	2,100	2,200

Notes: Price comparisons for several of the products are given below, along with estimated manufacturers net margin (in parentheses).

Hybrid Electric Cars: $20,000–25,000 (1–2.5%)
Golf Carts: $4,000–8,000 (4–5%)
Mopeds: $3,000–5,000 (3–5%)
Electric Bicycles: $500–1,000 (7–8%)
Electric Scooters: $100–500 (8–10%)

EXHIBIT 5
Segway LLC
Executive
Management Team

George T. Muller, President

Robert Tuttle, Vice Chairman

J. Douglas Field, Vice President, Development and Operations

Drew Ladau, Vice President and General Manager, U.S. Business

Scott Frock, Director, Finance

Brian Toohey, Vice President, Regulatory & International

Patrick Zilvitis, CIO

Endnotes

1. www.dekaresearch.com, November 2002.
2. Scott Kirsner, "Breakout Artist," *Wired Magazine.* www.wired.com/wired/archive/8.09/kamen.html?pg=1&topic=&topic_set, September 2000.
3. Karen Auguston Field and John Lewis, "Balancing Act," *Design News.* March 25, 2002.
4. Ibid.
5. www.dekaresearch.com, December 2002.

6. Scott Kirsner, "Breakout Artist," *Wired Magazine.* www.wired.com/wired/archive/8.09/kamen.html?pg=1&topic=&topic_set, September 2000.

7. www.dekaresearch.com, December 2002.

8. Scott Kirsner, "Breakout Artist," *Wired Magazine.* www.wired.com/wired/archive/8.09/kamen.html?pg=1&topic=&topic_set, September 2000.

9. Rob Zaneski, "New Scooter Spurs Interest as Police Tool," *The Capitol Times.* www.madison.com/captimes/opinion/column/zaneski/34222.php, October 16, 2002.

10. Karen Auguston Field and John Lewis, "Balancing Act," *Design News.* March 25, 2002.

11. Ibid.

12. John Heilemann, "Reinventing the Wheel," *Times Magazine online edition.* www.time.com/time//business/article/0,8599,186660,00.html, December 2, 2001.

13. *Delphion Intellectual Asset Management,* www.delphion.com/cgi/bin/patsearch, December 2002.

14. Brian Dumain, "Profile of an Entrepreneurial on a Roll: Dean Kamen," *Fortune Small Business.* July/August 2002.

15. Matt Marshall, "Kleiner Perkins Hopes Segway Scooter Gets on a Roll," *The Mercury News.* http://www.siliconvalley.com/mld/siliconvalley/business/columnists/3638932.htm, July 10, 2002.

16. *United States: GM Spreads Risk with Diverse New Investment Plans,* World Market Research Center. August 16, 2002.

17. Danny Hakim, "Automakers Look beyond Electric," *The New York Times.* September 22, 2002.

18. Jonathan Marguiles. "A la Cart," *The Chronicle of Higher Education.* September 27, 2002.

19. The Great Inventor, *60 minutes II transcript.* www.cbsnews.com/stories/2002/11/12/60/ii/main529070.shtml, November 13, 2002.

20. Ibid.

21. Scott Kirsner, "Breakout Artist," *Wired Magazine.* www.wired.com/wired/archive/8.09/kamen_pr.html, September 2000.

22. Rick Lockridge and Barbara Moffatt, "The IT Guy: Inventor Dean Kamen Does More Than Human Transporters," *abcnews.com.* http://abcnews.go.com/sections/scitech/TechTV/kamen020731.html, July 31, 2002.

23. Tom McNickol, "Why 6-Legged Bots Rule," *Wired Magazine.* www.wired.com/wired/archive/10.11/bots.html, November 2002.

24. John Heilemann, "Reinventing the Wheel," *Time Magazine online edition.* www.times.com/times/business/article/0,8599,186660,00.html, December 2, 2001.

25. Seven, primarily agricultural, states had no such regulations.

26. John Heilemann, "Reinventing the Wheel," *Time Magazine online edition.* www.times.com/times/business/article/0,8599,186660,00.html, December 2, 2001.

27. Richard Shim, "Segway Faces Regulation in California," *Cnet news.com.* October 2, 2002.

28. Mark Sappenfield, "Every City Makes Way for Segway: Except One," *Christian Science Monitor.* www.segwaychat.com/forum/topic.asp?topic_id=566, December 2, 2002.

29. The Great Inventor, *60 minutes II transcript.* www.cbs.com/stories/2002/11/12/60ii/main529070.shtml, November 13, 2002.

30. Leander Kahney, "Segway Owners a Small, Happy Club," *Wired News.* www.wired.com/news/print/0,1294,568814,00.html, December 12, 2002.

31. http://www.segway.com/aboutus/press_releases/pr_111802.html, December 2002.

Case 6

LEGO Bionicle: The Building Blocks to Core Competency?

It's kind of odd that LEGO is trying to make action figures. Unless they come up with some brilliant idea, I think they should stick to what they know. (Raymond, 9-year-old LEGO customer[1])

In December 2001, with the launch of LEGO Bionicle, Kjeld Kirk Kristiansen, President & CEO of LEGO Company, undertook the largest product launch in LEGO's history. The new LEGO Bionicle line was controversial in many ways. The Bionicle figures were not made from the company's proprietary plastic blocks nor were they meant for "open play,"* both foundations for the company's long-standing success. LEGO Bionicle was also created along multiple entertainment platforms, meaning that the line would include action figures, video games, fast food toys, and comics, as well as other multimedia aspects (including clothing and a movie). LEGO Bionicle represented a considerable departure from tradition for the company.

Kjeld Kirk Kristiansen had recently presented LEGO's vision for the 22nd century at a company gathering. Many long-standing and well-respected employees expressed concerns about the Bionicle launch during the question-and-answer session that followed: Did the Bionicle launch represent a new strategy for LEGO? Were all of the elements of the launch in place in order to ensure its success? Was the Bionicle line merely a response to a fad that would lead the company falsely away from its competencies? Did the launch of Bionicle threaten to cannibalize LEGO's other new products, for which the company had paid large licensing fees?

These were all issues Kjeld Kirk Kristiansen hoped to answer.

THE TOY INDUSTRY

Overall Industry

The toy industry is a mature and competitive one. The global market for toys is roughly $70 billion (including video games).[2] Sales in the U.S. make up almost half of that figure. In 2000, U.S. industry revenues were approximately $29.4 billion.[3] Prior to 2000, industry growth was typically 5% per year.[4] However, in 2000, overall wholesale sales slipped 1.4%.[5] Simultaneously, "Smart Toys," those incorporating computer chips, experienced a 98% increase in sales (refer to Exhibit 1 for more information concerning industry sales).[6]

Unique Aspects of the Industry[7]

The toy industry exhibits the following characteristics:

- Time to market is critical.
- Constant product innovation is required.
- Product turnover is vital.
- Product life cycle is short.
- There are well-defined selling seasons.
- Significant reductions in price are taken at the end of season.
- The majority of manufacturing is done in Southeast Asia.
- There are high cannibalization rates.
- Demand is sensitive to product safety issues.

These attributes make the aging industry a challenging and risky one to operate in. Therefore, the introduction of a new toy line can be either rewarding or financially devastating to a toy manufacturer (refer to Exhibit 2 for more information on industry specific risks).

INDUSTRY PLAYERS

Manufacturers

In 1998, the top 5 manufacturers held approximately 40%[8] market share of the U.S. toy industry. The two largest of these manufacturers were Mattel and Hasbro, with approximately $4.67 billion and $3.8 billion[9] in revenues respectively. Each company underwent major consolidations between 1995 and 2000. Hasbro acquired Tiger Electronics, Galoob, Oddzon, Cap Toys, Atari, and Micropose. Mattel acquired

---

Ena Sinha and Courtney Loveman prepared this case under the supervision of Professor Allan Afuah as a basis for class discussion rather than to illustrate either effective or ineffective management. Creative liberties have been taken in developing the introductory and concluding paragraphs of the case.

* Free-form play that is derived from and inspires the imagination.

Learning Company, Pleasant Company, and Tyco. As of 1998, LEGO held a third place share of the U.S. toy market.

Major manufacturers in the industry possessed many advantages. Economies of scale and significant financial resources allowed these large companies to create "big" brands, supported by good distribution networks and marketing leverage. The larger manufacturers were also able to secure lucrative licensing agreements and enter into international alliances with other companies. In 1999, Mattel entered into an alliance with Bandai, the number one manufacturer of toys in Japan. With this alliance, the two companies, able to market each other's toys, gained access to new core competencies; Mattel benefited from Bandai's technological strengths and Bandai benefited from Mattel's global market reach. Hasbro had a similar alliance with Tomy Co., the second largest manufacturer in Japan.

Smaller manufacturers, on the other hand, had the ability to usurp power in the industry by bringing unique products to market more quickly. Market share tended to have less significance in the toy industry since trend-seeking consumers were characterized by fickle purchasing habits. There was always the opportunity for a new star to emerge in the industry. For example, companies such as Ty (Beanie Babies) and Larami (Super Soakers) were able to create hit products that turned them into major players, despite their relatively small firm sizes. Razor USA, a small manufacturer and the maker of the Razor Scooter, was another phenomenon; the company's product ranked among the top 5 selling toys in 2000 (#3). Razor USA made approximately $550 million in 2001 alone.[10]

Manufacturers, regardless of size, faced many product and supply risks in the toy industry. Capacity issues, supply disruptions, and currency fluctuations were just a few of the considerations. To address these risks, manufacturers often employed alternative means of managing production and distribution (refer to Exhibit 2 for more information).

Retailers

In 1998, the top 5 toy retailers held 54% share of the market.[11] Discount retailers in the U.S., such as Wal-Mart, held a significant position. E-tailing was considered a growth area for the industry. Only $50 million was spent on toys over the net in 1998; that figure jumped to $350 million in 1999.[12] Approximately $1.2 billion was spent, in 2002, for online toy purchases.[13] In 2000, Toys "R" Us and Amazon joined forces to become the largest toy distributor on the Internet.

Retailers were wary of product demand risks in the industry. Toys tended toward short product life cycles (one year or less), suffered from seasonality, and were subject to fad volatility. Another important issue was that 50–60% of all toys were sold in the last quarter of the year.[14] Therefore, retailers sought out toys that they believed would have some imperviousness to consumer trends. Barbie, by Mattel, was a quintessential example; the line was created over forty-two years ago and, yet, ranked consistently among top sellers (refer to Exhibit 3 for more on top-selling toys).

Consumers

4% of the world's children resided in North America and, yet, those children accounted for roughly 45% of all toy purchases.[15] In spite of the fact that children significantly influenced the purchase, adults were most often the actual "purchasers." The traditional core group of toy consumers was 14 years and younger; the 14-and-under age group is expected to grow 3.5% from 1995 to 2010.[16] A 1996 study showed that American children between the ages of 5 and 14 spent $27 billion on toys and directly influenced the spending of $117 billion. In 2001, this age group was expected to spend $67 billion and influence spending of $144 billion (refer to Exhibit 4 for further consumer spending information).[17] The demographics of this core group were also changing. According to census data, 39.1% of children in the U.S. were minorities. Hispanic children became the largest minority group in 1998.[18] The second fastest growing demographic for children was among the Asian population. In 2001, approximately 3.4% of children in the U.S. were of Asian descent.[19] Companies were reacting to this shift by producing more toys with Hispanic or Asian themes.

Another growing consumer trend was "gray power"; grandparents were spending more on toys, although they continued to represent a price and value conscious consumer set.[20] Their toy purchases are expected to grow to $100 million by 2010.

TRENDS IN THE INDUSTRY
Licensing

It is estimated that, in 2000, $5.8 billion was generated from the licensing of entertainment icons from films, television, and video games.[21] This was a 4.4% increase over the prior year.[22] In 2001, some important licensing properties included Star Wars, Harry Potter, Lord of the Rings, and Monsters Inc.

Interactivity

The sale of "smart toys" increased 98% to approximately $1 billion in 2000 (while video game sales fell 6% over the same period).[23] Robotic pets led the way for these computerized toys; the sale of these "animals" jumped from $5 million to $159 million in 2000.[24]

Pat Feely, chairman of the Toy Industry Association, Inc. (formerly, the Toy Manufacturers of America), offered this insight: "Kids are becoming more involved with technology and the industry is responding aggressively. When you consider that more than 60% of American households with children have computers with Internet access, you can begin to see the importance technology will have in the future of toys."[25]

The Action Figure Segment

According to the Toy Industry Association, action figure sales were down 26.7% in 2000.[26] The typical consumer for this segment was either a young boy who bought the figure for entertainment purposes or an older male who bought the figure for an existing collection. The most important attributes, for a collector, were the intricacies of the figure and the number of lifelike details.

COMPETITORS

[The toy market] is extremely volatile. When I was growing up, a fad lasted a lot longer than it does these days. (T. K. MacKay, toy analyst, Morningstar Inc.[27])

There are some fantasy-based, story-driven toys that are worthy of mention either because they posed a threat to the long-term success of the Bionicle line or because they illustrate the dangers associated with investing significantly in fad products.

Pokemon

Although "fad" toys are generally much maligned after their time has come and gone, no one can dispute the force with which Pokemon entered the toy market. Pokemon focused on one hook—collectibility.[28]

To introduce and hype this Japanese product to North American children, the company used 14-minute teasers that were sent to 1.2 million households. The teasers explained the toy concept and introduced the video game to new users.

The "toy" was a multi-platform concept that melded trading cards with action figures, TV shows, and video games. Full licensing (bought by Hasbro) and merchandising were utilized. Children began wearing Pokemon clothing and accessories. The trading cards were particularly popular because their low price point offered younger consumers the opportunity to purchase them with allowance money.

Those beyond the core market, including older children, young pre-schoolers, and girls, also got in on the Pokemon craze. Increased demand, coupled with marketing-induced supply limitations, caused a shortage and, thus, a black market emerged. As of 1999, the Pokemon craze had grossed $7 billion worldwide.[29] One place where people had surely been buying was the massive 10,000-square-foot Pokemon Center in Manhattan (built in 2001)—an interactive, free-admission wonderland, offering a game room with new Pokemon games, a Pokemon distributing machine (by which kids can come in with their Game Boy cartridges and capture rare Pokemon), an educational Pokedex machine (with vital information on all 251 characters), and retail sections vending video games, plush, movies, card packs (including rare and collectible). "Four of the top video games in 2001 were Pokemon. It's an incredibly strong property. This is a brand that will be around for 20, 30, 40 years and the Pokemon Center shows our commitment,"[30] said Bruce Loeb, Pokemon USA VP of marketing.

Harry Potter

Harry Potter, the protagonist in the series of books written by British author J. K. Rowling, is an orphaned boy who learns he is a sorcerer, fighting evil while attending a boarding school dedicated to the study of magic. Although the books were originally intended for an elementary school audience, the author's crystalline imagery, her sophisticated writing style, and her use of the universal themes of good and evil appealed to readers of all ages. The books, as of January 2002, had sold 116 million copies worldwide.[31]

Merchandise related to the books would prove to be very popular among children 6–12 years old. On November 15, 2001, Warner Brothers released the first Harry Potter movie. *Harry Potter and the Sorcerer's Stone* raked in a record-breaking $90.3 million during its opening weekend (Nov. 16–18).[32] As of December 9, 2001, it had earned more than $239 million dollars.[33] To hype Harry Potter during the holiday season, there was a full merchandising and marketing campaign. Interestingly enough, LEGO was part of that merchandising campaign, creating limited-edition Harry Potter building sets.

According to industry analysts, though, Harry Potter merchandise was in shorter supply for the 2001 holiday season. Since the licensed products did not sell as well as predicted in 2000, retailers reduced order quantities. "Then the excitement with the movie started," said Jim Silver, publisher of *Toy Wishes* magazine, "and the only way to describe what's happened with Harry Potter toys is that it [was] like a light switch suddenly got flipped on."[34]

Yu-Gi-Oh!

In 2002, a new game from Japan called Yu-Gi-Oh! took over wish lists for boys ages 8 to 16. Yu-Gi-Oh! (pronounced yoo-ghee-oh) is a teenage character with yellow hair that resembles lightning bolts. In an example of its popularity, Yu-Gi-Oh! made it on the top 10 list of the most-searched-for topics by the lycos.com Web search engine. It ranked just below Harry Potter and Lord of the Rings, but above Playstation 2 and Spider-Man.

"Yu-Gi-Oh!, a successor to Pokemon, [was] a cartoon aimed at younger kids, accompanied by a card game with addictive properties similar to crack cocaine. Trust my wife, it is the bane of every second grade teacher's existence," wrote the Lycos 50 columnist Aaron Schatz.[35] "Yu-Gi-Oh! first showed up on our radar in April 2002, and has been on the Lycos 50 ever since."

Pokemon plummeted 57% in 2002 and, in April, fell off the Lycos 50 for the first time ever. In 2001, Pokemon had 145 times as many searches as Yu-Gi-Oh!; 12 months later, Yu-Gi-Oh! got three times as many searches as Pokemon.

Other products available included two home videos, T-shirts, action figures, puzzles, comic books, and an animated TV series based on the ever-expanding cast of characters. Yu-Gi-Oh! trading cards came out in the spring of 2002, but Konami, the maker of Yu-Gi-Oh!, released translated cards to stores only a few at a time in order to heighten the demand for the trend. Versions of the Yu-Gi-Oh! game have also been adapted for play on Game Boy Advance and PlayStation.

LEGO—THE FOUNDATION

The basis of all LEGO products and activities is our belief that children and their needs must be taken seriously. We see it as our most important task to stimulate children's imagination and creativity and to encourage them to explore, experience and express their own world—a world without limits. (LEGO.com)

Both *Fortune* magazine (1999) and the British Association of Toy Retailers (2000) named the LEGO brick "Toy of the Century." In winning such awards, LEGO exemplified its meaning (derived from the Dutch words for "play well"). The LEGO Company aimed for a global approach, having LEGO pieces represent the rainbow of colors of the world. According to Lincoln Armstrong, Brand Manager for LEGO, "[The company] develops products for all children regardless of race or nationality."[36]

The legacy began in 1932. Ole Kirk Christiansen was a carpenter who began making wooden toys in Billund, Denmark. In 1947, Ole made a daring move that would forever transform the business. He brought plastic injection molding to Billund. By 1958, the patented version of the LEGO Block was created. In 1954, Godtfred Kirk Christiansen, Ole's son, developed the "LEGO system of play." This system emphasized the importance of free form, or "open," play and would characterize LEGO for the next thirty years.

Company Values

The LEGO mission was to "Nurture the child in each of us." The company viewed children as role models because "they are curious, creative, and imaginative. They embrace discovery and wonder. They are natural learners. These are precious qualities that should be nurtured and stimulated throughout our lives."[37]

Based on these beliefs, in 1963, Godtfred Kirk Christiansen formulated the LEGO System of Play, defined by the following 10 characteristics:

All play materials must:

1. Have unlimited play possibilities.
2. Be unisex.
3. Be for all ages.
4. Have an opportunity for year-round use.
5. Offer stimulating and absorbing play.
6. Offer endless hours of play.
7. Help stimulate imagination, creativity, and development.
8. Multiply play value (through new products).
9. Always be topical.
10. Be leaders in safety and quality.

LEGO drew on their mission, values, and "play principles" to create blocks that were always backwards-compatible (i.e., a block purchased in 1970 could still be incorporated into a set purchased in 1995). The product was characterized by its "clutch power" (indicating superior hold) to deliver high technical, consumer, and development quality. Many psychologists praised LEGO blocks because of their durability and their capacity to allow children to further develop their imaginations.

LEGO "sets" followed the creation of the blocks themselves. These "sets" enabled children to build according to a theme; they were a successful extension for LEGO. However, they did represent a departure from the core of free-form toys. Some consumers and industry insiders criticized the new direction that LEGO was taking.

LEGO—THE NEXT GENERATION

> [LEGO] needs to be reminded what its core values are all about. LEGO is about imagination and construction, teaching hand-to-eye coordination in a fun way. In a recent press release, LEGO says it has got to focus on the core business, and then, in the next breath, talks about tie-ins with Disney and Harry Potter. What has that got to do with the core product? (Ian Madeley, Managing Director, Logistix Kids[38])

In 1998, LEGO was in the red for the second time in its 60-year history. In 2000, it sustained a DKr 831 million loss (refer to Exhibit 5).[39] The firm hadn't had a top-selling toy in 7 years. The world of toys had changed. Toys with hot licensing properties and/or hi-tech components sold well in the late 90s and continued to outpace the market into the new millennium. In 1997, LEGO offered neither licensed products nor hi-tech gadgetry. In 1998, however, they signed an agreement to sell LEGO Star Wars kits. Despite the fact that this set turned out to be LEGO's best-selling line, heavy royalties apparently affected overall profitability. LEGO did not disclose the cost of the "Star Wars" license, but it has been reported that Hasbro (LEGO's only major competitor in the "Star Wars" toy market) paid $600 million to renew its own license. The "Star Wars" agreement was followed by agreements with Disney (Winnie the Pooh) and HIT Entertainment (Bob the Builder); both met with only moderate success.

In 1998, LEGO also made a daring move into the world of technology when it launched LEGO Mindstorms. LEGO Mindstorms represented the culmination of many years of research at MIT. The products were a group of complex robots assembled from bricks embedded with chips and lights. The robots were subsequently programmable, by the consumer, to perform various actions. The product was cost-prohibitive and never reached a large audience of children; a basic set cost $199.99. With this product, though, LEGO managed to reach an adult segment for the first time in their history. After the launch, Mindstorm communities sprang up on the Internet. Users were sharing information on how to reprogram the LEGO operating system. In an unprecedented move, LEGO officially recognized the communities and their reprogramming efforts in 2001. The company encouraged co-creation of programs for the Mindstorm operating system. Although Mindstorms was thought to be a success by many industry experts, LEGO was still unable to turn a profit in the years following Mindstorms' launch. Thus, executives envisioned yet another way to join the top ranks of the toy elite: Create a multiple-platform technology-related experience for children.

BIONICLE—SIX HEROES, ONE DESTINY

> Once a paradise, Mata Nui has become a place of darkness and fear, ruled by the deadly Makuta. Now six mighty heroes, the Toa, have come to gather the masks of power and challenge the Makuta. Explore the island . . . learn the legends . . . and begin to solve the mystery of Bionicle. (Excerpt from LEGO.com, December 2000)

In December 2000, the first bit of information about Bionicle was released on the Internet. "Bionicle" (a word which originates from the words "biological" and "chronicle") was a multi-dimensional experience; it would incorporate a slowly unfolding story of good and evil on an exotic island.

The Experience

LEGO had previously gone down the multi-dimensional platform road with the RoboRiders and Throwbot lines. These products, however, did not have an associated evolutionary story component. With Bionicle, LEGO created in-house, character-driven story lines to support the platforms. The Bionicle entertainment platforms included: easy-to-build action figures, trading cards, T-shirts, comic books, soundtrack, Internet games, video games, and a major motion picture.

In order to make the multi-dimensional experience a reality, LEGO partnered with:

- Electronic Arts, the world's leading interactive entertainment software company, to co-publish software titles.
- Universal Music, to create music and multimedia CDs.
- Upper Deck, to create trading cards.
- Nintendo, to develop software for the GameBoy platform.
- DC Comics, to create three comic books based on Bionicle characters.
- Walt Disney–owned production studio Miramax, to develop a film (slated for release in 2003–2004).

The Product

Essentially, Bionicle consisted of 7-inch plastic extraterrestrial figures (with attachable weapons and parts) whose battles were played out in legends on the Internet. This was an entirely different approach to themed toys for the company. Firstly, the figures were not independent of the story and could not be deconstructed. Secondly, they snapped together in a "non-LEGO" manner, without the use of modular plastic blocks.

This product heralded the first time that LEGO had engaged in story creation. In-house story development was executed in an effort to eliminate royalty payments, allowing LEGO to keep all of the profits. The plan was to update the online story monthly. According to Colin Gillespie, a marketing manager for Bionicle in the United States, "[Children] understand media. If they are spoon-fed everything at the start, it is a bit of a turnoff. If you build up too much energy right at the front end and tell the whole story, people might be tired of it by the end."[40] The action figures came accompanied by password codes on the inside of their packages to allow the consumer to access the website in order to obtain recent story information. In 2001, the website was averaging 2 million hits per month.[41]

Target Consumer

Bionicle was aimed at 5–12 year olds. With only one female character, the toys were geared largely toward boys. This target market contradicted the age group that industry experts had focused on for "action figure" play; experts had determined that interest in action figures peaked at age 4 and then decreased significantly from there, topping out at approximately 8 years old. The "tween market" (6–12) continued to favor the video game market; this presented a significant challenge to traditional toy manufacturers.

Viral Marketing

LEGO implemented an aggressive viral marketing strategy for the launch of this product. The company spent $15 million to create a "buzz" about the line. Six Nissan Frontier pickup trucks (each themed after one of the robotic heroes in the series) embarked on a 12-week tour of 50 cities. Their destinations included skateboard parks, BMX tracks, baseball courts, and little league fields. The vehicles were interactive and allowed interested participants to experience the Bionicle story line first-hand. LEGO had also signed sponsorship and endorsement deals with skateboard venues and stars.

In the summer and fall of 2001, LEGO ran ads in the kids space on MSN's gaming site, mailed 1.5 million free comic books to LEGO club members, handed out trading cards at comic book stores, and provided 3 million free book covers and locker posters to schools.

Traditional Marketing

LEGO did not abandon traditional media completely during the launch. Print ads were run in magazines, including *Boys Life,* DC Comics, *Nickelodeon,* and *Sports Illustrated Kids.* TV commercials were aired on Cartoon Network, Fox Kids, WB, Fox Family, and Nickelodeon. Bionicle also aired a movie trailer before screenings of *The Mummy Returns, Shrek,* and *Planet of the Apes.* McDonald's exclusively featured Bionicle in Happy Meals in September 2001.

Distribution and Production

In addition to being sold at brick-and-mortar toy retailers, the Bionicle experience was web-integrated to allow for online purchasing. For Christmas 2001, KB Toys complained that Bionicles were in short supply; LEGO increased production as a response. The company was estimating retail sales of over $80 million by the end of the 2001 holiday season.[42]

Economic Climate in December 2001

The holiday season offered Bionicle's best chance for success. However, in December 2001, the United States was preoccupied with terrorism, recession, and the possibility of an impending war. Consumer confidence had fallen to its lowest level in 44 years.[43] The National Retail Federation predicted that shoppers would be more discriminating during the holiday season. Despite this, Melissa Williams, Toy Analyst for Gerard Klauer Mattison, echoed the sentiment that "parents continue to spend money on kids, even in difficult economic times. The toy business depends more on the product offerings than the economy."[44]

Financial Outlook

The Bionicle toy line was comparably priced to similar action figure and hi-tech products. The action figures ranged from $2.99 to $6.99. Complex remote control operated figures cost approximately $69.99. Full engagement in the game, through ownership of all of the components, however, required significant consumer investment.

Toy insiders said that the company's predicted sales of more than $80 million in the first year was a very ambitious target, especially since blockbusters such as Teenage Mutant Ninja Turtles and Power Rangers made only half of that amount.[45]

KB Toys, Toys "R" Us, and Playdate media predicted Bionicle to be a top seller in the 2001 holiday season. Traffic on the website confirmed that young boys would be the biggest purchasers of Bionicle. According to Juniper Media Metrix, in June 2001, Bionicle received 40.8 million impressions at their site (Amazon was second with 18.1 million impressions).[46]

The Story/Game[47]

The Great creator Mata Nui (the name of both a great spirit and the island itself) kindly watched over its inhabitants. His evil brother, Makuta, grew jealous of the worship from the common villagers, called Tohunga, and cast a sleeping spell on Mata Nui. He then took control of the universe. The villagers believe that six heroes, called Toa, will save them from their dark existence. The Turaga are the village leaders who use masks and weapons to protect the villagers. Each also protects the legend of a Toa.

Six heroes (Toa) duel against Makuta's henchmen to regain control of the island of Mata Nui. Each hero has a specific skill and can precipitate cataclysmic events to fight off their enemies. The heroes must work together to collect the masks of power (Kanohi) in order to ultimately defeat the Makuta. Three Toa can be combined to make a large one. The Turaga aids a Toa in the quest. Each Toa, Turaga, and Tohunga is aligned with the natural forces of air, fire, earth, ice, or stone. The Toa are larger than the Tohunga or Turaga.

The Makuta henchmen are evil due to the infected masks (Rahi) they wear. They can be tamed if the masks are removed. Removing a mask is equivalent to vanquishing an enemy in Bionicle.

The Toa, Turaga, and Tohunga all use the masks of power (Kanohi) to aid them in their quest. There are twelve basic mask shapes, six of which are noble masks of power, while the other six are the great masks of power. Each mask comes in a variety of colors that can be interchanged among the various characters. The Makuta henchmen try to capture the masks from the heroes since the masks of power increase the skills of the Toa.

Each Toa must collect six great masks of power in his/her own color before challenging Makuta. Mask sets include two randomly packed masks, plus a head and pole for display. Each mask also has a code that allows the consumer to access information on the Website. Noble masks do not possess as much energy as the great masks. Both the Toa and Turaga can wear them. Each dimension of the game (Internet, trading card, or video game) is integrated with the story and involves collecting the masks and engaging in battle.

THE DECISION

Did the Bionicle launch represent a new strategy for LEGO? Were all elements of the launch in place to ensure its success? Was the Bionicle launch a progressive move for the company or a panicked response to a fad, thus leading the company astray from its competencies? Did the launch of Bionicle threaten to cannibalize the launch of LEGO's other large licensing agreements (e.g., Harry Potter, Star Wars)?

Kjeld Kirk Kristiansen prepared to address the questions posed by his employees. He was mindful of the need to link the company's heritage to its future and was cognizant of the risks the company has taken on with launch of LEGO Bionicle. Would LEGO be able to make its mark in a high-tech society?

EXHIBIT 1 Industry Sales

Source: Website of the International Council of Toy Industries, http://www.toy-icti.org/publications/wtf&f_2001/05.html, adapted from The NPD Group Worldwide.

	Key Figures, 2000		
	Total Toy Markets incl. Video Games (Million U.S. $)	Child Population (Million)	Average Expenditure per Child (U.S. $)
World	**69,493**	**1,658**	**32**
North America	30,949	67	328
Europe*	16,059	126	100
Asia	16,942	1,038	13
Latin & South America	2,768	165	15
Middle East	972	3	243
Oceania	1,370	6	187
Africa	433	253	2

		Million U.S. $		
		1998	1999	2000
World	**Traditional Toys**	54,898**	55,645	54,742
	Video Games	14,533**	15,445**	14,752

* Includes Eastern countries.

** The 2001 World Toy Facts & Figures analysis process reflects the most current data available; as a result, some 1998 and 1999 figures may have been restated.

EXHIBIT 2 **Industry Risks**

Source: "Learning from Toys: Lessons in Managing Supply Chain Risk from the Toy Industry," M. Eric Johnson; *California Management Review,* by the Regents of the University of California, Volume 43, Number 3, spring 2001.

Product Demand Risks	
Risk	**Alternative Means of Managing Risk**
Seasonal Imbalances	Using licensed products in off-season events
	Adding alternative channels, such as McDonald's
	Developing collector markets (Beanie Babies)
Fad Volatility	Channel release strategies for licensed products such as image protection
	Keeping store inventories lean to prevent saturation
	Developing collector markets
New Product Adoption	Starting long life products in specialty channels
	Developing product extensions/branding for existing toys
	Licensing as awareness, imagery, and hype continue to build
Short Product Life	Managing variety by rolling the mix and creating collector markets

Product Supply Risks	
Risk	**Alternative Means of Managing Risk**
Manufacturing Capacity	Outsourcing—improves economies of scale and asset utilization
	Combining off-setting seasonal products (i.e., snowsleds and swimming pools)
Logistics Capacity	Consolidation—larger volumes create economies of scale
	Supplemental Outsourcing—surge capacity in peaks outsourced
	Electronic Supply Chain—improves knowledge of demand at retail
	Product diversion
	Channel Coordination—moving excess to alternative or overseas markets
	Retail Ready—pre-distribute to reduce time to shelf
Currency Fluctuations	Financial Hedging—contracts in stable currency and forward contracts
	Diversification of suppliers in different countries
	Operational Hedging—Several plants in different countries
Supply Disruption	Diversification of suppliers in different countries

EXHIBIT 3   2000 Top-Selling Toys by Dollar Sales (w/o video games)
Source: NPD TRSTS Toys Tracking Service; information provided by Toy Manufacturers of America, Inc.

Rank	Item Description	Manufacturer	Retail Price
1	Hot Wheels Basic Cars	Mattel	$0.86
2	Poo-Chi Robotic Dog	Tiger Electronics	$22.51
3	Leap Pad	Leapfrog	$43.11
4	Barbie Cruisin Jeep	Fisher-Price	$218.69
5	Tekno Robot Dog	Manley Toy Quest	$35.10
6	Celebration Barbie	Mattel	$28.74
7	Pokemon Series #2	Wizards of the Coast	$3.16
8	Who Wants Be a Millionaire	Pressman	$22.93
9	Pokemon Rocket Booster	Wizards of the Coast	$3.23
10	Barbie Cash Register	Kid Designs	$38.49
11	Kawasaki New Ninja	Fisher-Price	$174.55
12	Barbie Wizard of Oz Asst	Mattel	$15.08
13	Hw 5 Car Gift Pack	Mattel	$4.42
14	Hd Motorcycle	Fisher-Price	$184.98
15	Furby Asst	Tiger Electronics	$15.47
16	Magna Doodle	Fisher-Price	$13.66
17	Diva Starz Doll Asst	Mattel	$27.37
18	Easy Bake Oven/Snack Ctr	Hasbro	$16.68
19	Barbie & Krissy Mermaids	Mattel	$22.40
20	Bop It Extreme	Hasbro Games	$20.94

EXHIBIT 4   Spending Information: Average Expenditure per Child (Ages 0–14)
Source: Website of the International Council of Toy Industries, <http://www.toy-icti.org/publications/wtf&f_2001/05.html>.

	Traditional Toys (U.S. $)	
	1999	**2000**
World	**27****	**27**
North America	270**	271
Europe*	119**	84
Asia	11	11
Latin & South America	14	14
Middle East	160	206
Oceania	172	159
Africa	1	1

* Includes Eastern countries.

** The 2001 World Toy Facts & Figures analysis reflects the most current data available; as a result, some 1999 figures may have been restated.

EXHIBIT 5   LEGO Financials

LEGO Company
Financial Statements
Years Ending 1999 & 2000

	Profit & Loss Account (DKr m.)			
	2000	**%**	**1999**	**%**
Net Sales	9.467	100	9.808	100
Operating Costs	−10.145	−107	−8.615	−87.8
Manufacturing Costs	−191	−2	−555	−5.7
Operating Results	−869	−9	638	6.5
Financial Items	−201	−2	−122	−1.2
Results before Tax	−1070	−11	516	5.3
Tax for the Year	239	2	−242	−2.5
Results for the Year	−831	−9	274	2.8

	Balance Sheet (DKr m.)			
	2000	**%**	**1999**	**%**
Fixed Assets	6.620	53.9	6.035	47.8
Current Assets	5.660	46.1	6.659	52.2
Total Assets	12.28	100	12.694	100
Equity	6.262	51	6.976	53.0
Minority Interest	4	0	4	0
Provisions	442	3.6	435	4.1
Long-term Debt	1.866	15.2	1.992	15.4
Short-term Debt	3.706	30.2	3.287	27.5
Liabilities & Equity	12.28	100	12.694	100

	Financial Key Figures (%)			
	2000	**1999**		
Profit Margin	−8.8	2.8		
Return on Equity	−13.3	3.8		
Solvency Ration	51	55		

Endnotes

1. Martha Mendoza, "Lego's New Action Figure Disappointing to Parents, but Fun for the Kids," Associated Press, September 25, 2002.

2. www.toy-icti.org.

3. Ibid.

4. Eric Johnson, "Learning from Toys: Lessons in Managing Supply Chain Risk from the Toy Industry," *California Management Review,* Volume 43, Number 3 (Spring 2001), p. 106–122.

5. Deborah Porterfield, "Tech Toys Computer Chips Power Newest in Electronic Fun," *Detroit News,* February 19, 2001, p. 1.

6. Ibid.

7. Eric Johnson, "Learning from Toys: Lessons in Managing Supply Chain Risk from the Toy Industry," *California Management Review,* Volume 43, Number 3 (Spring 2001), p. 106–122.

8. Ibid.

9. Doug Olenick, "Toy Biz Blames Economy for Slump," *Twice,* February 26, 2001: Volume 16, Issue 5, p.1.

10. Maria Weiskott, "Shifting Shares: Whims and Trends Impact Manufacturer's Share of Market," *Playthings,* August 1, 2001.

11. Eric Johnson, "Learning from Toys: Lessons in Managing Supply Chain Risk from the Toy Industry," *California Management Review,* Volume 43, Number 3 (Spring 2001), p. 106–122.
12. Doug Olenick, "Traditional Toys Tops in Tech Environment," *Twice,* February 21, 2001, Volume 15, Issue 5, p. 38.
13. *Children's Business,* February, 2002.
14. Eric Johnson, "Learning from Toys: Lessons in Managing Supply Chain Risk from the Toy Industry," *California Management Review,* Volume 43, Number 3 (Spring 2001), p. 106–122.
15. Ibid.
16. Ibid.
17. Ibid.
18. "Growing with the Hispanic Market: Targeting a Burgeoning Segment of the U.S. Population," *Playthings,* January 1, 2001.
19. "Census Sense: As the Asian-American Population Grows, so Does the Marketplace," *Playthings,* September 1, 2001.
20. "There's Nothing Drab about Gray Consumers," *Playthings,* April 10, 2001.
21. "Popularized Entertainment Icons Continue to Dominate Licensing," *DSN Retailing Today,* July 9, 2001, 4.
22. Ibid.
23. Deborah Porterfield, "Tech Toys Computer Chips Power Newest in Electronic Fun," *Detroit News,* February 19, 2001, p. 1.
24. Ibid.
25. Ibid.
26. "Armed & Ready: After Drop in Sales, Action Figures Attempt Comeback at Retail," *Playthings,* September 1, 2001.
27. Krissah Williams, "Lego Plots a Comeback," *The Washington Post,* August 19, 2001, p. H1.
28. Susan Fournier, "Pokemon: Gotta Catch 'Em All," Harvard Business School Case (June 19, 2001).
29. Ibid.
30. Toy Fair Preview, Fairchild Publications, February 2002.
31. "'Potter' Is Off to a Flying Start; Hollywood Puts Magical Spin on London Premiere," *USA Today,* p. D1.
32. "Moving on Up," *Publishers Weekly,* New York, December 3, 2001: Issue 49, p. 25.
33. www.yahoo.com.
34. "Lots of Competition for 2001's Hit Toy," *New York Times,* November 22, 2001, p. C1.
35. Lisa Kranz, *Ventura County Star,* December 15, 2002, p. E1.
36. "Growing with the Hispanic Market: Targeting a Burgeoning Segment of the U.S. Population," *Playthings,* January 1, 2001.
37. LEGO Investor Relations Kit & "Why Can't LEGO Click," *Fast Company,* Issue 50, p. 144–157.
38. "A Brick Too Far," *Marketing Week,* March 15, 2001, p. 26.
39. Ibid.
40. Krissah Williams, "LEGO Plots a Comeback," *The Washington Post,* August 19, 2001, p. H1.
41. Ibid.
42. Cheryl Cornacchia, "Bionicle Blitz," *Windsor Star,* November 10, 2001, p. F6.
43. "11 Years Ago in Time," *Time,* December 17, 2001, Volume 158, Issue 26, p. 19.
44. "Toy Sellers Bet on Holiday Boost," *Detroit News,* October 10, 2001, p. 1.
45. "LEGO Leaps into Action with Fantasy-Based Toys," *Wall Street Journal,* February 2, 2001, p. B1.
46. "Bionicle Web Chronicle," *Advertising Age,* Volume 72, Issue 33, August 2001, p. 21.
47. About.com.

Case 7

KPN Mobile and the Introduction of i-Mode in Europe

On December 10, 2002, NTT DoCoMo decided that it would not exercise its right to purchase more KPN Mobile stock. This meant that after the issue of the new shares by KPN Mobile to its parent, Royal KPN, NTT DoCoMo's stake in KPN Mobile would be lowered from 15% to 2.2%. The issue of the shares had been an attempt to raise funds as part of a debt-to-equity swap.[1]

Back in Tokyo, NTT President Norio Wada wondered how everything went wrong. NTT's mobile subsidiary, NTT DoCoMo, had already posted losses of 307.8 billion yen (US$2.54 billion) in the first half of fiscal year 2002 from its three overseas investments.[2] mMode, its joint venture with AT&T, was failing to offer what American users wanted. It was too early to see whether its services through KG Telecom in Taiwan were successful. The performance of KPN Mobile, a provider of i-mode services in Germany, Belgium, and the Netherlands (a company in which NTT held a 15% equity stake), was not up to expectations. NTT DoCoMo had already lost three quarters of its 1.9 trillion yen (US$15.6 billion) investment in less than three years, and was contemplating whether to continue investing overseas, despite the fact that i-mode launches were coming up in France and Spain.[3]

When the revolutionary wireless web service i-mode was launched in 1999 in Japan, it was wildly successful, attracting over 1 million new customers every month for the first two years. DoCoMo had the right business model, the right technology, the right partnerships, and the right target segment. By December 2002, the book value of DoCoMo's investment in KPN Mobile had dropped to virtually nothing from 410 billion yen (US$3.4 billion).[4]

KPN CEO A. J. Scheepbouwer was even more worried than Wada. Without the financial resources of NTT DoCoMo, KPN Mobile and thus its parent Royal KPN would lose its credibility with other investors. Moreover, without an international strategic partner, it was stuck with an i-mode license but no

technical and strategic support. Scheepbouwer sat back and wondered what the future of i-mode services for KPN Mobile was.

MOBILE COMMUNICATIONS IN EUROPE

Overview

In 2001, Europe constituted the biggest market for mobile communications in the world. A successful standardization process had largely facilitated the impressive growth rate that the market experienced over the nineties. Backed by a recommendation by the Commission of the European Communities (December 1986), the major European operators joined forces to establish a common network standard operating on digital technology. The goal was to substitute the existing, outdated, local analog networks that suffered from incompatibility between each other, lacked reliability, and were unfit to cope with the increasing demand for connectivity. The new standard, GSM (Global System for Mobile Communication), was identified as a 2nd Generation (2G) technology, to distinguish it from the previous analog standards (1st Generation—1G). Soon after becoming operational, GSM rapidly substituted the previous technology, as it proved to be more reliable and allowed roaming between the different European sovereign states. The availability of a wider selection of handsets and the promotional support of the operators further enhanced the rapid introduction of GSM in Europe.[5]

Between 1995 and 2001 the number of mobile users in Europe skyrocketed to 306 million from 23 million. However, adoption was unevenly distributed across Europe, with 6 countries (Germany, UK, France, Italy, Spain, and the Netherlands) accounting for 78% of all revenues. Market penetration had, in a few years, reached 80% from a mere 6% in 1995,[6] a sign that mobile phones had become a part of every European's life. All mobile operators

Marcos Almeida, Rob van Dale, Prasanth Menon, Pier Paolo Noventa, Nicola Saraceno, and Benjamin H. Wong prepared this case under the supervision of Professor Allan Afuah as a basis for class discussion rather than to illustrate either effective or ineffective management. Creative liberties have been taken in developing the introductory and concluding paragraphs of the case.

across Europe targeted both the consumer and business segments, offering two payment solutions—contracts and prepaid.

Voice Traffic

The market seemed to be approaching saturation in the last several years. It started displaying several signs of maturing as a market, including the decrease in the number of new entrants. Rather than competing over attracting new users, incumbents shifted their focus to retaining the existing customer base and increasing the revenues generated per customer, measured by monthly Average Revenue per User (ARPU). In Europe, ARPU generated by voice traffic experienced a sharp decrease over the years, and stabilized at 29 Euros/month (US$29.9) in late 2001.[7] The potential for generating revenue growth resided heavily on the data transmission (see Exhibit 1).

Messaging

Short Messaging Services (SMS) had experienced outstanding growth in the last several years. Their low cost (0.12 Euros/US$0.123 on average) served as a substitute for short calls and mobile e-mail service. Inter-operability, favorable demographics of mobile ownership (SMS appealed to young people in particular), and positive publicity have resulted in its huge popularity. In 2001, SMS traffic constituted 14% of total revenues for mobile operators, with an annual growth rate of 95%.[8] Voice traffic had become essentially a commodity and SMS messaging was seen to be at the forefront of a plethora of new data communication services operators could offer to maintain a sustained growth rate. European operators upgraded their messaging services and introduced Enhanced Messaging Services (EMS) that allowed the transmission of instant pictures, photography, and advertising. The ultimate goal was to upgrade mobile messaging services to equal that of e-mail and to integrate Multimedia Messaging Services (MMS) that allowed the user to send and receive audiovisual messages.

Additional Services on the GSM Network

Apart from messaging, the technology had the potential to offer a wider range of services. Most analysts considered Internet browsing, gaming, and mobile commerce as the most promising applications. The first attempt in this direction was the offering of Wireless Application Protocol (WAP), a set of open protocols to develop applications that also had basic browsing capabilities. Operating on the existing GSM network, WAP offered access to websites developed in Wireless Markup Language (WML), the equivalent of Hypertext Markup Language (HTML) when the Internet was accessed through fixed line devices. Because WAP operated on GSM, a circuit-switched network, WAP users had to establish a dial-up connection with the provider and were charged for the use of WAP services on a per-minute basis—with the proceeds going in full to the telecom operator.[9] The cost of using the services depended on the speed of connection at the particular location and time the user was connecting. The most popular services among WAP users were e-mail, news, sports, and music. Although over 50% of handsets in use in 2001 were WAP-enabled, these services failed to deliver the expected results in terms of revenues and market penetration. In April 2002, the ARPU generated by WAP services was only 0.03 Euros (US$0.03), as opposed to 2.7 Euros (US$2.8) generated by SMS. Market penetration was only 6% by this time.[10]

Network Improvements

In order to avoid the drawbacks of the circuit-switched network, the majority of European operators enhanced their GSM network to adopt packet-switched technology. This allowed the transmission of data as packets, similar to that of Internet Protocol (IP). This enhanced network, named General Packet Radio Services (GPRS), provided users with "always-on connectivity" as well as increased transmission rates. Most importantly, GPRS made it feasible to charge users based on data volume rather than on a time basis. GPRS allowed connection speeds up to 115 Kbps compared to the maximum of 9.6 Kbps that GSM offered. GPRS was considered to be an intermediate solution toward the introduction of a totally new network technology—the so-called 3rd Generation (3G) standard. Also known as the Universal Mobile Telecommunication System (UMTS), it was a digital packet switching technology that would maintain the advantages of GPRS, increasing quality and speed of data transmission (up to 2 Mbps).[11]

The expected increase in revenue generated through data transmission services inflated the price of UMTS licenses, awarded on a national basis by all European governments between March 2000 and September 2001. In Germany, for example, the

UMTS licenses were awarded at the record price of 7.7 billion Euros (US$7.9 billion). The total cost of licenses to run 3G services in Europe was approximated to be 175 billion Euros (US$180 billion)—around 70 Euros (US$72) per person in Europe. In addition to obtaining a license, UMTS operators would have to incur the capital expenditure to install the network, considered to be at least as much as the cost of the license.[12]

Financial Pressures

While it was not certain whether the public would accept the new high-margin services, these new services did require substantial investments. The expenditures due to the UMTS licenses, the numerous mergers, and the economic recession put all operators under financial pressure, which limited their ability to raise resources for these new projects. In 2002, all operators had significant amounts of debt on their balance sheets and saw their credit ratings plummet, making it costly to issue new debt. At the same time their valuations had substantially decreased between 2000 and 2002—thus impeding access to the stock markets to raise new capital (see Exhibit 2).[13]

While new technologies and applications were potentially able to offer new revenue streams and increase customer retention, mobile operators were increasingly concerned about their operating costs. They focused on cost savings, involving selling bandwidth capacity (roaming) and developing agreements to share a common infrastructure. Another method used to increase operating efficiency was to consolidate. The number of mergers increased significantly over the years, and by 2002, a handful of operators dominated the entire market (see Exhibit 3). Among these, Vodafone showed a dominant presence. With 64 million subscribers in 13 countries, the company appeared to be the best positioned to take advantage of the future opportunities the market offered. Along with its various local subsidiaries the company had access to 11 UMTS licenses across Europe.[14]

Opportunities

Mobile operators were increasingly under pressure to counter the decrease of voice revenues and recover the high investments in new network technology by growing nonvoice revenues dramatically, including a) Nonvoice access charges (e.g., for data transmission) and b) Nonaccess charges including (i) Subscriptions, (ii) Transaction fees, and (iii) Advertising.

Analysts had stated that based on the previous experience, the key criteria considered necessary for mass-market uptake for any new data transmission applications were a) Good terminals offering a simple interface, b) Fast, always-on connections, c) Proven security, d) Wide range of relevant applications, e) Reliable, high quality information, f) Good quality customer and technical support and, g) Full mobility, including cross-border operation.[15]

KPN

History

In many European countries, including the Netherlands, the dominant player in the telecommunications industry (fixed line telephone and telegraph) was a government-owned entity. The history of KPN goes back to the time when the government started to build public telegraph lines for commercial and governmental services in 1852. This Post Telephone and Telegraph (PTT) company remained a government-controlled entity until 1994. To make the post and telecom divisions more competitive and to raise capital in the stock market, the mail and telephone activities were split in 1998. The Royal KPN remained the telecom company, while the post services merged with the Australian TNT into TNT Post Group (now called TPG). At this time, the telecom industry in the Netherlands was liberalized, enabling competitors to enter the fixed and mobile telecom industry. The former European state-owned companies now were competition to each other, requiring a big change in the way business was done.[16]

Company Profile

The former state-owned Dutch Koninklijke PTT Nederland (Royal PTT Netherlands, KPN) was a monopolist in the mail and telephone industry of the Netherlands until 1998. Since then, all of KPN's mobile voice, data, and Internet services have been provided by its wholly owned subsidiary, KPN Mobile, a company with 7,400 employees. This separate entity allowed the group to focus its activities in the mobile telecommunications market. The KPN Mobile Group operated in three countries. E-Plus was the third largest mobile operator in Germany, with approximately 7.5 million subscribers. BASE in Belgium had 1.0 million subscribers, and KPN Mobile had 5.2 million subscribers, which made it the largest mobile operator in the Netherlands. KPN Mobile acquired UMTS (3G) licensees in the Dutch,

German, and Belgian markets and a 15% stake in Hutchinson 3G UK Ltd. It began offering GPRS services in 2001, and in early 2002 it offered in Germany and the Netherlands a service that had revolutionized the Japanese mobile market and caught the fancy of mobile operators all over the world, *i-mode*.

Strategy for the Mobile Communication Market

KPN Mobile offered its first mobile network in the Netherlands and was without competition before 1998. As a result, the early users of mobile telecommunications, largely companies, had developed long-term relationships with KPN. The combined offering of data, fixed, and mobile services to corporations was an important factor in KPN's ability to retain these customers.

E-Plus and BASE weren't as established, with BASE being one of the youngest companies in the industry in Europe. BASE was started as KPN Orange in 1999 as a 50/50 joint venture between KPN Mobile and Orange plc. However, in February 2001 KPN bought out Orange's 50% stake and the name of the company was changed to BASE. In 1999 KPN Mobile bought 77.49% of the shares of the German E-Plus from BellSouth. It bought the remaining 22.51% in March 2002. BellSouth decided that a European mobile network did not fit into their strategy, while KPN Mobile was expanding and consolidating its activities at the time.[17]

The consolidation of the German and Belgian markets fit well with KPN Mobile's strategy. The company also sold its minority stakes in mobile operators in countries such as the Czech Republic and Indonesia. The revenues from these sales went toward reducing the already enormous debt in its books and its consolidation efforts in West Europe. After having initially harbored ambitions of becoming one of the biggest pan-European operators, KPN realized that it had to focus on the Belgian, Dutch, and German markets, which had comparable customer usage and culture.

Business Model

In all three of its markets, KPN Mobile offered both prepaid and post-paid subscriptions. Prepaid users bought a certain amount of minutes to call, while post-paid subscribers received bills after the calls. As of December 2002, the company faced troubles with a high percentage of its users being from the prepaid category (see Exhibit 3).[18] These users called very lit-

tle, and some of them actually didn't use their phones. If prepaid users didn't upgrade their prepaid phones for six months, KPN cancelled their subscriptions. The economic downturn had increased the number of subscribers who didn't use their phone anymore, and in the 3rd quarter of 2002, KPN closed out accounts of 177,000 prepaid users, compared to an average of 150,000 in previous quarters.[19] KPN tried to increase the level of post-paid subscribers by offering more value-added services to these subscribers. This strategy also had its drawbacks, as it eliminated from its target market the huge prepaid customer base.

KPN's margins varied greatly in different countries, from 43% in the Netherlands to 29.1% in Germany to 8.4 in Belgium.[20] The primary reason for this huge range is that the target customers in these markets were different. In the Netherlands a lot of the customers were businesses and corporations, while in both the other markets, particularly Belgium, most of the users were private subscribers.

NTT

History

Nippon Telegraph and Telephone Corporation (NTT) is Japan's largest telecommunications company. The company was modeled after the United States' telecom behemoth, AT&T. Until 1967, the government of Japan wholly owned NTT. Since then, it has been partially privatized and as of December 2002, only 46% of the company was owned by the state.[21] In 1999, the company was broken up into five separate companies, and NTT Group (now referred to as NTT) became the holding company for these companies. NTT's influence on the telecommunications industry in Japan covers the whole spectrum of telecommunications. Its subsidiaries include two monopoly local phone carriers (NTT East, NTT West), a long distance carrier (NTT Communications), a systems-integration company (NTT Data), and the leading mobile telecommunications provider in the country (NTT DoCoMo).

NTT DoCoMo

NTT DoCoMo (DoCoMo) was Japan's number one mobile telecommunications company in December 2002. The company was committed to providing users with cost-effective, high quality services. Its business model was geared to achieving these goals and obtaining a competitive advantage. Anticipating quick changes in the market, DoCoMo had increasingly invested in research and development and technology. These efforts resulted in the development of *i-mode,* a highly successful, groundbreaking service. After its success in Japan, its new projects and plans for the future included the adoption of its services worldwide and the advancement of mobile telecommunications technologies.

i-Mode in Japan

I-mode was a service that allowed users of i-mode-compatible handsets to obtain access to wireless web services. It was an enhancement of SMS, which was then the leading nonvoice mobile service. It was first introduced in Japan in February 1999. At this time, Japan's market for mobile telephony had almost matured. A new service was needed if NTT was to remain the leader in the telecommunications industry in Japan. The launch of i-mode proved to be extremely timely since users were in search of a new service. It also opened the opportunity of mobile multimedia services, unheard of at the time. In addition, it generated new streams of revenue for NTT. It was so successful that by November 2002, there were more than 35.6 million subscribers to the service with an ARPU of approximately 1,700 yen (US$14.16).[22] I-mode allowed its users to access a myriad of value-added services. Users were able to perform banking transactions and ticket reservations, check e-mail, view local news and stock quotes, and access telephone directories and restaurant guides. They were able to access more than 60,000 websites with the list growing daily. NTT DoCoMo also considered practicality and convenience while creating i-mode, introducing user-friendly, attractive i-mode handsets, which allowed easy access to its services.

DoCoMo believed that i-mode was a superior platform to WAP, the most widely used wireless Internet service in Europe at the time. I-mode used compact HTML (c-HTML), a subset of HTML, which enabled content providers to easily compile their HTML websites into i-mode-usable c-HTML. In contrast, WAP used WML, which was not as friendly to HTML programmers. I-mode had an entertainment focus, with its fun and simple services targeted toward adolescents; WAP's focus, on the other hand, was toward the business users, who make up a small population of wireless web users. In addition, i-mode mobile phones were small and had

large screens. DoCoMo created the portal *i-menu,* and it allowed easy access to all these services by pressing one button on the phone. The same could not be said for WAP. WAP users would have to navigate through many menus before being able to access wireless services. The most important advantage of i-mode was that it was packet-switched. I-mode users were charged by the volume of data transmitted. In contrast, WAP users were charged by the time they were connected.

COMPETITORS

As of December 2002, KDDI was the number two telecommunications company in Japan. It was known as DDI until it acquired IDO and KDD in 2000. Like NTT, the company provided fixed line access and long distance services as well as wireless Internet services, called EZweb and au. With 11.5 million EZweb and au users,[23] it was the second largest provider of wireless Internet access.

J-Phone was the third largest telecommunications company in Japan and offered its J-sky service, attracting over 11.3 million users. Like KDDI, it lagged behind i-mode because it did not have the network and brand reputation that NTT had established throughout the country. In all, the market size for wireless web services exceeded 58.9 million users in Japan in December 2002.

Business Model

DoCoMo had an attractive pricing strategy to ensure quick penetration into the market. Users paid monthly access charges of 300 yen (US$2.48). In addition they paid fees ranging from 0.3 yen (US$0.002) for a packet (128 bytes) of information to 60 yen (US$0.50) for transferring funds. Users also paid between 100 yen (US$0.83) and 300 yen (US$2.48) for each site they subscribed to. DoCoMo would take a 9% commission from these website subscription fees before transferring the remainder to the content providers. This pricing strategy allowed for increased revenues with increased usage. All these charges were consolidated with the other mobile phone service charges for the subscriber's convenience. As can be seen, the charges were relatively inexpensive as well. In comparison, dialup access could cost around 2,000 yen/month (US$16.67) with a 10 yen/minute (US$0.08) access charge, while broadband access could cost around 3,000 yen/month (US$24.80).[24] This was very much unlike other countries such as the U.S. where wireless access would cost more than fixed line access. A reason for this could be that since NTT controlled both the fixed and mobile markets, it could adopt pricing strategies to favor one type of access over another.

DoCoMo created strategic alliances worldwide all along the value chain. These partners included Internet Service Providers—ISPs (e.g., AOL, MSN), Content Providers (e.g., CNN, Dow Jones), Mobile Carriers (e.g., KG Telecom, KPN Mobile, AT&T), and Equipment Manufacturers (e.g., Ericsson, Toshiba). These alliances enabled DoCoMo to deliver an extremely cost-effective yet high quality service. Quality control for websites was crucial. DoCoMo had four requirements for content providers. First, the information provided needed to be the most current possible. This information needed to be comprehensive, and users would be able to directly connect to related content. Content had to be attractive, to increase traffic, and, finally, to be highly readable and easily retrieved. Considering the limitations of Internet access on a mobile phone, analysts believe that these were very important quality considerations.

Strategies

DoCoMo released its 3rd Generation (3G) technology for mobile phone technology in May 2001. FOMA (Freedom Of Multimedia Access) operated on the 2GHz band of the radio spectrum, allowing for transfer rates of 384 Kbps, compared to 64 Kbps of the then existing 2.5G technology. However, the company continued to face implementation problems even in December 2002, and these problems were preventing the new technology from leaping over i-mode. While i-mode popularity had created high switching costs, the large amount of power these mobile devices required for operation was also a stumbling block. The Japanese market for mobile telecommunications was quickly becoming saturated, and DoCoMo felt the need to expand internationally. With its lack of experience with the telecommunications industry outside of Japan, DoCoMo and NTT needed established local partners in these new markets, which had the capabilities to make the global expansion of i-mode a reality. At the same time, KPN Mobile was looking for ways to offer new services to its subscribers. It looked like a joint venture was in the making.

THE PARTNERSHIP

Preparation for the Launch (September 2001 to March 2002)

In September 2000, KPN Mobile and DoCoMo signed a memorandum of understanding to consider establishing a joint venture, which would provide mobile Internet services in Europe based on i-mode's technology and business model. Earlier, DoCoMo had invested in KPN Mobile by taking a 15% equity position in the company.[25] DoCoMo signed the joint venture agreement with KPN Mobile in order to accelerate its expansion in the European market.[26] In January 2001, DoCoMo, Telecom Italia Mobile (TIM), and KPN Mobile signed a memorandum of understanding to consider establishing a joint venture that would provide early deployment of mobile multimedia services in Europe.[27]

On November 7, 2001, DoCoMo and KPN Mobile announced the introduction of mobile Internet services in Europe. DoCoMo licensed the key technologies needed for these services to KPN Mobile. A similar agreement was also negotiated between DoCoMo and E-Plus.[28] As in Japan, i-mode in Europe would be based on an open platform with KPN Mobile. Content providers would offer certified i-mode content sites via the i-mode portal. I-mode would be launched in Europe under the same name as in Japan with the corresponding logo.[29]

Internet i-mode services would be offered through the mobile networks of GPRS (Global Packet Radio Service) and, later, third-generation (UMTS) mobile networks. DoCoMo would provide KPN Mobile with the know-how and technical specifications for network servers and interface applications, as well as i-mode-compatible mobile phone handsets. The first i-mode handset had been developed and manufactured for the European market by NEC based on Japanese designs. The first model was the N2li. Distinctive features of this handset were a much larger screen, color display, and improved sound quality. Users could also send and receive e-mails containing up to 1,000 characters and SMS messages up to 160 characters. The handset was GPRS (and therefore GSM) compatible. The built-in i-mode browser enabled users to read both i-mode-compatible HTML and WML content. Users could access to all i-mode services with this handset in addition to mobile telephone calls, SMS messages, and e-mail.[30]

It is crucial to encourage content providers to create high-quality content . . . By ensuring maximum cohesion in the development of handsets, networks, Internet gateways, portal sites and mobile content, we have created a so called value chain that offers maximum satisfaction for users . . . The success of these efforts is very evident in Japan. (Takeshi Natsuno, Managing Director, i-Mode Strategy Department, NTT DoCoMo)

KPN planned to carry out the market introduction of i-mode in a step-by-step fashion. Once the basic infrastructure was in place and handsets and services were available, it planned to begin with a "friendly user period," where i-mode would be tested by a limited group of users. The next step would be taken in the first months of 2002 when a few hundred customers would be invited to join KPN Mobile initiatives in gaining further i-mode usage experience. Once both steps had been successfully completed, KPN Mobile would introduce i-mode market wide.

By November 2001, negotiations with over 100 content providers were at an advanced stage. Content was developed in cooperation with multiple leading European content providers. The development process was based on the successful "content governance model" and business model developed by DoCoMo. Handsets were also tested to guarantee reliable delivery of i-mode content in Germany, the Netherlands, and Belgium. Content providers included the Royal Dutch Automobile Association (ANWB), the daily newspaper De Telegraaf, VI Planet Voetbal (soccer news), Belbios (cinema), 9292 OV Travelinfo, Intermediair (job vacancies), TMF, Rabo Bank and Photoplay (gaming), VI Michelin, Meteoplaza (WNI), Spiegel online (news magazine), Kicker online (soccer news), Deutsche Bahn (German railways), Phenomedia (gaming), and Falk online (route planner and city router.)[31] Both certified providers and noncertified providers had the opportunity to offer services via independent sites. These sites could be offered by consumers, companies, or organizations wishing to do so and could be accessed freely. Based on experience in Japan, it was expected that there would be a significant number of independent sites on offer.

The Beginning of the European Launch (March 2002)

KPN Mobile introduced i-mode in Europe on March 4, 2002. For KPN, this introduction marked the dawn of a new era. Following the model used by NTT DoCoMo in Japan, i-mode gave users quick and easy access to information they desired at any time, for business or for leisure. After having entered their personal preferences to customize their list of favorite sites, users would find i-mode even easier to use.[32]

I-mode was first launched in Germany, where customers of KPN Mobile's subsidiary E-Plus could buy an i-mode handset and subscription starting March 8. E-Plus announced that the NEC i-mode handset, the N21i, would sell at 249 Euros (US$255). A monthly i-mode subscription cost 3 Euros (US$3.1). The price of services provided by content partners would range from 0 to 2 Euros (US$2.1) per month. Later that month, KPN Mobile signed an agreement with Toshiba for the supply of a new i-mode handset for the European market—the TS21i. The first Toshiba handsets were expected to be released in the second half of 2002.[33] The TS21i was a compact phone incorporating a large color screen suitable for the graphics-based mobile services available via i-mode as well as access to all other i-mode services.

Competition

Meanwhile, Vodafone, one of the major European mobile data providers, was preparing to react to the threat of i-mode, which was competing head-on against its D2 and Libertel franchises in Germany and the Netherlands. Reports suggested that Vodafone, the world's largest carrier by proportionate subscriber ownership, was prepared to launch a faster version of its Vizzavi portal in the near future. The improved service suite would be accessible via an xHTML browser. XHTML was technically similar to i-mode's c-HTML, and was expected to facilitate interoperability with the Internet Protocol from the fixed line environment. The entire industry (including KPN Mobile) seemed determined to provide the converged browser technology called WAP 2.0 (WAP-Next generation)—a hybrid technology combining the best of the WAP (WML) and i-mode (c-HTML) characteristics. WAP 2.0 used the xHTML standard, which would allow the same content to be optimized for presentation on the different display structures.[34] KPN Mobile was monitoring other potential entrants offering GPRS-based systems. T-Mobil, for example, had indicated that it would introduce Ericsson's MMS system in Germany following the successful launch in Hungary by Westel.

Launch of i-Mode in the Netherlands (April 2002)

KPN Mobile began offering mobile data services using i-mode in the Netherlands on April 18. At launch, i-mode was available at 340 Primafoon, Bel-Company, and Phonehouse retail sites across the Netherlands. More retail chains were soon expected to offer i-mode subscriptions.[35]

In the Netherlands, the N21i handset from NEC was sold in combination with a voice and data subscription and was available starting from 199 Euros (US$204), depending on the type of voice subscription selected. The i-mode subscription included access to i-mode (3 Euros/US$3.1 per month) and a GPRS data bundle. The 200 Kb basic data bundle cost 2 Euros (US$2.1), which meant that customers could use i-mode for as low as 5 Euros (US$5.2) per month. Data bundles ranging from 1 Mb and 25 Mb were also available. The pricing structure meant that 25 Mb of data transmission could be obtained at over a 90% discount over the 200 Kb unit price.[36] See the table below for the pricing scheme.

Data Bundles (Kb)	Price (Euros)	Subscription Fee (Euros)	Total Cost (Euros)	Price per Kb (Euros)
200	2	3	5	0.0250
1,000	10	3	13	0.0125
5,000	15	3	18	0.0040
10,000	25	3	28	0.0035
25,000	45	3	48	0.0023

Source: www.i-mode.nl.

The basic data bundle (200 Kb) allowed the user the following:

- About 130 incoming/outgoing e-mails, length comparable to an SMS (150 characters).
- 80 incoming/outgoing e-mails of 1,000 characters.
- 40 5 Kb page views.
- 30 6 Kb image downloads.
- 25 8 Kb ring-tone downloads.

The usage of these services was expected to accelerate with increasing penetration, and with users exchanging more e-mails to discuss the sites they have visited (the so-called "network effect"). Analysts predicted that the average active i-mode user would not be able to get through a month with his 200-Kb bundle unused. Analysts also forecasted that favorable early use experiences could drive usage

straight up to the 15 Euros (US$15.4) per 5 Mb level for early adopters/corporate users. On average, it was expected that a non-corporate user would consume 2 to 3 of the 200 Kb bundles per month.

While the price for content ranged from 0 to 2 Euros (US$2.1) per month, a proportion of the content would always be free of charge. Some providers provided their services for free for an initial period, before going back to a combination of premium and free services. At launch, approximately 50% of services were free. KPN Mobile also offered i-mode customers a free e-mail service, with customers paying only for the data they send and receive. KPN Mobile charged content providers 14% of revenues to provide billing and credit risk to the customers, similar to the revenue model used by DoCoMo in Japan. Analysts in the telecom market believed the commission was low enough to encourage new sites to offer services. While the company closed negotiations with 50 content partners that had created 65 official sites, it was hoped that the growth in unofficial sites would trigger additional growth in subscriber take-up of the service, similar to the case in Japan. The sites were constantly checked for quality, ease of use, and customer service. I-mode customers also had access to numerous so-called "open" sites, which were both easy to develop and easy to access. The number of "open" i-mode sites was expected to increase rapidly in the Netherlands.

KPN was an established company in the fixed line Internet services in its home market. E-Plus in Germany was not an established company in fixed line Internet, while T-Mobile and T-Online had overwhelming leadership positions in their respective markets, which made them the partners of choice for content providers trying to enter the mobile content market. Like many other markets in Europe, the Netherlands had seen a steady increase in ARPU (Average Revenue per User) over the past three quarters. In Belgium, subsidiary KPN Mobile planned to launch KPN Orange, which would offer i-mode in June after re-branding the service offer to BASE.[37]

First Results of the Launch (August 2002–December 2002)

On August 15, 2002, KPN Mobile announced that it had signed up 100,000 i-mode subscribers in Germany and the Netherlands, approximately twice what it had in mid-June. The percentage of voice traffic generated by i-mode users was below 1% in both Germany and the Netherlands, less than half of what DoCoMo had achieved over the same period in

Japan (2.1% after five months). However, DoCoMo's growth was accelerating from that moment. With only 25,000 new subscribers per month, the target of 1 million i-mode subscribers within one year appeared rather aggressive. Ironically, the hurdle set for Europe was not very high. One million subscribers would equal only 8% of voice subscriptions. In comparison, Japan had reached 12% in the same time period. On this basis, it was not a surprise when KPN Mobile's subsidiary E-Plus lowered handset prices by 50% with a two-year contract and extended its discount "data" pricing scheme. More aggressive moves were expected especially in relation to handset prices. Content creation appeared to be the positive aspect with 90–100 menu services for both E-Plus in Germany and KPN Mobile in the Netherlands. By December 2002, unofficial content sites numbered approximately 7,000.[38] The ten most profitable sites as of this date consisted of four ring tones sites, two news sites, one weather, one erotic, one traffic, and one soccer site.

At the end of the 2nd quarter of 2002, KPN Mobile reported 71,000 users in Germany and 20,000 in the Netherlands, showing a decrease in the rate of growth. KPN Mobile announced that the subscriber addition would accelerate with the arrival of the more compact handset from Toshiba. According to analysts' estimates, the 1 million subscribers target implied that KPN Mobile would have needed to quadruple its previous monthly growth rate to 52,000 new subscribers per month in order to reach that goal by the end of 2003.

Customers and i-Mode Usage

According to KPN, the characteristics of the product users in Germany were the following:

- Over 82% of i-mode users were everyday users of the Internet via other media, 83% used e-mail, and 90% used SMS.
- 74% of users had personalized handset settings.
- 54% of business users made use of e-mail in business applications and 38% used i-mode services for business travel planning.
- 92% said they would recommend the product to others; 25% of current users were identified as newcomers to the network and cited the unique features of i-mode as the main reason for subscribing to the service.
- KPN Mobile claimed that Vodafone had suffered the worst defection rates—16% of i-mode users are claimed to have moved from Vodafone D2.

The characteristics of the product users in the Netherlands were reported to be:

- Majority of users were in the 20–35 age group.
- Private users 82%.
- 72% of users used between 200 Kb and 5 Mb of data per month; 28% used more than 5 Mb per month.

At the time, it was not apparent whether i-mode usage stimulated or depressed voice usage or SMS revenues. It was also not clear how the spending pattern of an i-mode subscriber would evolve over time, because of the lack of historical data.[39] However, data usage had been low and users were reported to be limiting the amount of usage on i-mode until they had a better idea how much it cost. Most users subscribed to the lowest-use package. Together with an average subscription to three sites (e.g., news, sports, ring-tones), average customer spending on i-mode services was roughly 13 Euros (US$13.4) per month (see Exhibit 4).

Promotion

From a marketing perspective, reports suggested that the typical i-mode display stands were prominent but lacking literature. Retailer chain sales personnel who were interviewed expressed the opinion that the NEC N21i looked too big compared to other handsets in the market and that it could discourage potential subscribers. However, they were optimistic that the introduction of the smaller Toshiba model would address some of these concerns. Reports suggested that there was a lot of experimentation going on to determine the main triggers for a subscriber to commit to i-mode. Analysts thought that KPN Mobile's promotions during August suggested that the situation in the Netherlands was reaching a level of urgency.

Challenges

> The success of i-mode is extremely important for the confidence of the telecom industry and the investor community. If it takes off, it will be a big boost. If it does not spread to the general population, it will deal the industry another blow. (Michelle de Lussanet, Telecom Analyst, Forrester Research, Amsterdam)

The telecom industry and investors were watching KPN Mobile's ability to replicate the DoCoMo's success story in Japan. The reason for the success in Japan was that services came at a time when mobile phones had just become mainstream. They were also introduced to a market in which personal computers weren't very popular—two conditions absent in Europe, where most people already had mobile phones and PCs. In addition, huge cultural differences could affect the acceptance of i-mode's value to the European customer. For example, a typical Japanese customer would be more tech-savvy than one from Europe and would be more receptive to new technologies. Long commutes to work in Japan also facilitated the quick adoption of entertainment services. The quick pace lifestyle of the Japanese put importance on convenience.

> We do not expect the same runaway success in Europe that the service received in Japan. Certain of the applications used in the Japanese market (photo transfers & gaming in particular) are successful owing to the characteristics of that market and we do not believe that this success will necessarily transfer into the European market. (BNP Paribas Analyst)

Indeed, there were still many significant hurdles to overcome. Even after the agreement with Toshiba, there was still a lack of variety of handsets—only two Japanese-made handsets in a market still dominated by Nokia. There were also some technical difficulties in developing i-mode on top of GPRS networks, which was not the platform used in Japan. Furthermore, although the number of sites had increased rapidly, more applications for European users needed to be developed urgently in order to reduce consumers' willingness to access competitors' WAP platform. Finally, cultural differences raised doubts about immediate adoption of the new applications.

The proportion of prepaid subscribers—66% in the Netherlands—was a key challenge to the development of a mass-market i-mode service, in contrast to the Japanese market landscape. This was a concern from the standpoints of both customer price sensitivity and billing. Many customers preferred prepaid phone service as a way to control costs. Prepaid users used their phones only about 42 minutes per month and spent about 13 Euros each; this was drastically less than that of a contract user (267 minutes/month and ARPU of 72 Euros). KPN Mobile would have to persuade these customers to start subscribing to its services, which could be extremely difficult. However, the company claimed to be addressing this issue, and some analysts expected to see a new prepaid product by early 2003. I-mode would also need to take a more aggressive approach to penetrate the market. Currently, the number of subscribers covered by the five

announced i-mode areas of deployment in Europe accounted for only 12.9% of the total pan-European mobile user base of 287 million. The areas where service has already been launched covered only 4.4% of the total. In the Dutch and German markets, i-mode's direct competitors were offerings from Vodafone, Orange, and DT, including MMS, a medium currently not available over i-mode.[40]

In September, the launch of i-mode in Belgium—originally planned for June—was delayed till later in the year. On November 12, 2002, KPN Mobile launched the second i-mode handset, the Toshiba TS21i, alongside the NEC N21i introduced earlier. The compact Toshiba TS21i was easy to operate and had a bright 256-color screen and integrated antenna. Depending on the subscription taken, KPN Mobile would offer the Toshiba TS21i starting from 0 Euros. Customers could use i-mode for free for the first three months (up to 10 Mb per month). The Toshiba handset came complete with an extra battery to guarantee permanent availability.[41] In December 2002, following the notice from KPN Mobile on November 15, 2002, for subscription of new shares, NTT DoCoMo decided not to exercise its right to subscribe to new shares of KPN Mobile as the company was about to issue new shares to Koninklijke KPN N.V. (KPN). As a result, NTT DoCoMo's voting interest decreased from 15% to approximately 2.2% at the issue of new shares.[42]

The Future

The plan that had earlier seemed perfect was not looking so good. KPN Mobile was not meeting expectations, and NTT DoCoMo, with its plan to not invest further in KPN Mobile, set them back even more. They were now stuck with an i-mode license with no support from NTT DoCoMo. KPN Mobile knew it had to implement i-mode, having already paid for it and spent millions of Euros implementing it in parts of Western Europe. But how would they go about doing it now?

DoCoMo's success in Japan came from the fact that they had power as well as good relations all along the value chain. Was this not true of KPN Mobile as well? If not, could this be the reason that KPN Mobile wasn't performing? Perhaps European users did not really need i-mode with all the services that it offered since voice traffic was already so inexpensive. Something needed to be done to stimulate usage. Should KPN Mobile target consumers and provide affordable i-mode services to prevent them from switching over to WAP? Or should it target suppliers and comple-mentors by having them supply better content and equipment? Or, was something else needed to be done?

KPN Mobile may not have won the battle, but could it win the war in the end? Who were the opponents they had to be wary of? What should they

know about the battlefield and the rules of engagement? Scheepbouwer thought about this for a moment, and then set off to the war room to plan for the next battle.

EXHIBIT 1
European Mobile ARPU: Voice vs. Data

Source: CSFB, 2002.

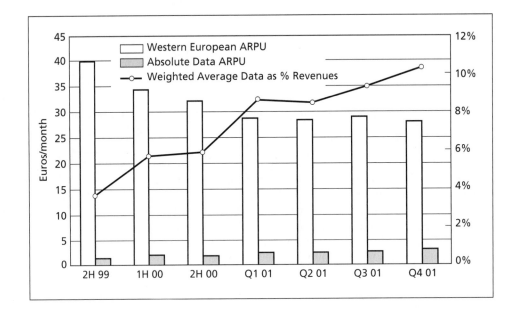

EXHIBIT 2 Summary of Financials of Key European Telecom Operators*
Source: Datastream, <www.datastream.com>, December 2002.

Company	Net Debt (2002)	Debt/ EBITDA	Market Cap (2001)	Market Cap (2002)	Percent Drop
KPN	15.3	4	N/A	N/A	
British Telecom	12.2	2.2	37.4	35.2	6%
Telia	16.1	1.6	9.9	9.2	7%
Telefonica Mobiles	26.7	2.1	36.5	29.5	19%
Deutsche Telekom	62.6	3.9	90.3	51	36%
TIM	24.4	2.3	62.9	39.6	37%
Vodafone	N/A	N/A	219.8	118.9	46%
Orange	N/A	N/A	54.4	27.9	49%
France Telecom	59.7	4.5	88.7	24.2	73%

*All figures in billions of Euro (except ratios).

EXHIBIT 3 Overview of the Mobile Telecommunications Market in Europe
Source: *HSBC,* September 2002.

Country	Population (M)	Mobile Subs (M)	Penetration (%)	Prepaid (%)	ARPU (2002)	ARPU (2004)	3GSM Operators
Austria	8.10	6.87	85	70	32	34	Mobilkom Maxmobil Connect Manesmann Hutchison
Belgium	10.10	7.78	77	62	33	37	Mobistar Proximus BASE
Denmark	5.30	4.02	76	58	27	28	TDC, Sonofon Mobilix, Telia
Finland	5.18	4.10	79	N/A	41	42	Sonera, DNA Radioilina
France	58.90	38.81	66	54	41	42	Orange, SFR Bouygues
Germany	82.02	55.52	68	55	24	29	DT-Mobile Manesmann E-Plus, Viag Mobilcom
Ireland	3.70	3.00	81	70	38	39	Eircell Digiphone Meteor
Italy	57.53	53.11	92	71	28	29	TIM, Omnitel Wind
Netherlands	15.86	12.18	77	79	28	29	KPN, Libertel Dutchtone Telfort, Ben
Norway	4.49	3.73	83	58	33	34	Telenor Netcom, Tele2
Portugal	10.01	8.99	90	71	33	34	TMN, Telecel Optimus Oniway
Spain	39.47	31.52	80	66	30	31	Telefonica Airtel, Amena
Sweden	8.87	7.19	81	67	30	32	Telia, Comviq Europolitan
Switzerland	7.17	5.71	80	68	54	56	DiAX Swisscom Orange
UK	59.50	48.29	81	68	54	56	Orange T-Mobile Virgin Mobile Vodafone

EXHIBIT 4 i-Mode Assumptions and Estimated Impact on KPN Group Revenues
Source: Daiwa Institute of Research, September 24, 2002.

Assumptions	Netherlands	Germany	Belgium	Incremental Group Revenue
2002				
Q4 monthly additions (k)	18	18	15	
Ending subs (k)	111	147	75	
Q4 ARPU	13	13	13	
i-mode revenue (Euros, M)	**4.87**	**8.38**	**2.67**	**0.13%**
2003				
Q4 monthly additions (k)	21	30	21	
Ending subs (k)	363	471	15	
Q4 ARPU	15	15	15	
i-mode revenue (Euros, M)	**42.66**	**53.87**	**34.50**	**1.05%**
2004				
Q4 monthly additions (k)	25	35	26	
Ending subs (k)	645	876	603	
Q4 ARPU	18	18	18	
i-mode revenue (Euros, M)	**108.05**	**144.59**	**98.10**	**2.78%**

Endnotes

1. "NTT DoCoMo, Inc. Does Not Make an Additional Investment in KPN Mobile N.V.," NTT, company press release, December 10, 2002.
2. The exchange rate (US$1.03 = 1 Euro) used was based on rates from December 18, 2002.
3. "The Globalization of i-Mode," *Daiwa Institute of Research,* September 24, 2002.
4. "The Globalization of i-Mode," *Daiwa Institute of Research,* September 24, 2002.
5. "The History of GSM," http://www.gsmworld.com/about/history, November 2002.
6. "European Mobile and Wireless Communications: Country and Operator Profiles," *IDC,* June 2001.
7. "GPRS 2002," *Credit Suisse First Boston,* March 2002.
8. "Mobile Tariffs—A Pan-European Survey," *HSBC,* September 2002.
9. "NTT DoCoMo's Strategy for Europe, and the Implications for European Operators," *HSBC,* July 17, 2000.
10. "Mobile Tariffs—A Pan-European Survey," *HSBC,* September 2002.
11. "3G Portal Study: A Reference Handbook for Portal Operators, Developers and the Mobile Industry," *UMTS,* October 16, 2001.
12. "UMTS Report—An Investment Perspective," *Durlacher Research,* March 2001.
13. "Too Many Debts; Too Few Calls," *Economist,* July 18, 2002.
14. "Vodafone Group," *Credit Suisse First Boston,* December 2002.
15. "UMTS Report—An Investment Perspective," *Durlacher Research,* March 2001.
16. www.kpn.com, December 2002.
17. www.dft.nl, December 11, 1999.
18. "European i-Mode Fixes the Mobile Net Experience," *Forrester Research,* April 22, 2002.
19. www.nu.nl, December 10, 2002.
20. "The Globalization of i-Mode," *Daiwa Institute of Research,* September 24, 2002.
21. "Nippon Telegraph and Telephone Corporation Profile," *Hoovers Online,* November 2002.
22. www.nttdocomo.com, December 16, 2002.

23. www.tca.or.jp, November 2002.

24. www.ocn.ne.jp, November 2002.

25. www.kpnmobile.com, January 31, 2003.

26. "NTT DoCoMo Signs MoU with KPN Mobile," *NTT*, company press release, September 29, 2001.

27. "NTT DoCoMo, TIM, and KPN Mobile Memorandum of Understanding," *NTT*, company press release, January 18, 2001.

28. "Introduction of i-Mode in Final Phase," *KPN*, company press release, November 11, 2001.

29. "KPN Mobile Group Starts Practical i-Mode Tests," *KPN*, company press release, December 17, 2001.

30. "KPN Mobile Group Starts Practical i-Mode Tests," *KPN*, company press release, December 17, 2001.

31. "KPN Introduced i-Mode in Europe," *KPN*, company press release, March 4, 2002.

32. "i-Mode Available in the Netherlands from April 18," *KPN*, company press release, April 4, 2002.

33. "KPN Mobile: Toshiba Second i-Mode Handset Supplier," *KPN*, company press release, March 12, 2002.

34. "Mobile Data: Introduction of i-Mode in the Netherlands," *Dresdner Kleinwort Wasserstein*, April 4, 2002.

35. "i-Mode Available in the Netherlands from April 18," *KPN*, company press release, April 4, 2002.

36. "Weekly PTT Pulse," *Daiwa Institute of Research Europe*, April 26, 2002.

37. "KPN Introduced i-Mode in Europe," *KPN*, company press release, March 4, 2002.

38. "European i-Mode Subscribers Hit 100,000," *Dresdner Kleinwort Wasserstein*, August 15, 2002.

39. "The Globalization of i-Mode," *Daiwa Institute of Research*, September 24, 2002.

40. "The Globalization of i-Mode," *Daiwa Institute of Research*, September 24, 2002.

41. "KPN Launches New i-Mode Handset," *KPN*, company press release, November 12, 2002.

42. "NTT DoCoMo, Inc. Does Not Make an Additional Investment in KPN Mobile N.V.," *NTT*, company press release, December 10, 2002.

Case 8

Lipitor: At the Heart of Warner-Lambert

INTRODUCTION

November 1999 was a tense month in the Morris Plains, New Jersey, headquarters of Warner-Lambert Company. On November 3, Warner-Lambert and American Home Products (AHP) announced an ambitious merger that would create the world's largest pharmaceutical company, with over $26 billion in combined annual revenues. The following day, Pfizer, Inc. announced an unsolicited $80 billion stock offer for Warner-Lambert, the largest hostile takeover attempt in the history of the pharmaceutical business.

Late on November 29, Warner-Lambert President and CEO Lodewijk J. R. de Vink settled in to read Pfizer's response to his latest move, a legal suit seeking to terminate the co-marketing agreement between Warner-Lambert and Pfizer for the wildly successful cholesterol-lowering drug Lipitor. Pfizer's short news release called Warner-Lambert's lawsuit the latest in "a series of desperate defensive measures designed to deny its shareholders the opportunity to consider a superior offer from Pfizer."[1] As de Vink reread the Pfizer statement and contemplated his next move, he recalled the chain of decisions that made Lipitor the engine of Warner-Lambert's recent success and the key prize in the ongoing merger battle.

PHARMACEUTICAL INDUSTRY OVERVIEW

The pharmaceutical industry is a critical element of health care delivery around the world. In 1998, sales of ethical pharmaceuticals reached $103.5 billion in the U.S. alone.[2] The U.S. is the single largest purchaser of prescription drugs, representing approximately 36% of the worldwide market.[3] As illustrated by the fact that in 1998 the largest pharmaceutical company captured only 6.5% of U.S. pharmaceutical sales, the industry is fragmented (Exhibit 1).[4]

The economics of the pharmaceutical industry are different from those in many other industries. Figure 1 breaks down the major expenditures of a drug company as a percentage of sales. Marketing and sales demands translate into the single largest expense incurred by the industry. Sales forces have nearly doubled in the past five years to more than 62,000 field representatives.[5] During the same period, federal regulations were eased, enabling drug companies to promote their products more like consumer goods. This has spurred the industry's onslaught of direct to consumer (DTC) television and print advertisements. In total, DTC spending was an estimated $1.2 billion in 1998.[6] Drug manufacturing costs are relatively low at only 17% of sales, but research and development investments are a higher percentage of sales than in virtually any other industry, including the electronics, aerospace, and automobile industries.[7]

FIGURE 1
Drug Company Functions as a Percent of Sales[8]

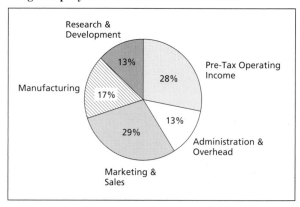

Pharmaceutical companies must invest heavily in research and development (R&D) to bring a new drug to market. R&D investment has steadily increased over the past two decades and is expected to reach $24 billion in 1999.[9] The entire process of discovering and developing a new drug is long and complex (Exhibit 2). It is estimated that only one out of nearly 10,000 chemically synthesized molecules investigated as drug candidates actually becomes an approved drug. During the 1990s, the average length of time required for drug development and government approval reached 15 years in the U.S.[10] As the length time to bring a

Matthew Leafstedt, Amy Marta, Jitendra Marwaha, Philip Schallwig, and Reka Shinkle prepared this case under the supervision of Professor Allan Afuah as a basis for class discussion rather than to illustrate either effective or ineffective management. Creative liberties have been taken in developing the introductory and concluding paragraphs of the case.

drug to market has increased, so have the costs, economic risks, and uncertainties. One study estimates the pre-tax cost of developing a drug introduced in 1990 to be $500 million.[11] This approximation is inclusive of the cost of research failures as well as successes. Moreover, most pharmaceutical companies continue to invest in research even after a drug has been introduced because additional clinical trials enhance the therapeutic knowledge and commercial potential of currently marketed drugs.

The costs of drug development are further intensified because of increased competition in the pharmaceutical marketplace, which has led to shorter exclusivity periods. The time during which the first drug in a therapeutic class is the sole drug on the market is shrinking. For example, Mevacor, the first drug in the groundbreaking cholesterol-lowering class of drugs called statins, was launched in 1987, but the second compound in this drug class, Pravachol, was not on the market until 1992. Mevacor enjoyed an almost four-year exclusivity period. This is in contrast to Invirase, the first in a new class of AIDS drugs called protease inhibitors, which entered the market in November 1995, only to have two competitors, Norvir and Crixivan, approved less than four months later. The time that companies have to recoup development costs to fund future R&D efforts has been severely compressed. Drug companies were traditionally concerned only about the effective patent lives (time on the market before patent expiration) of their drugs, which have averaged between 11 and 12 years over the past decade.[12] But patent life can no longer be used as a sole indicator of how long a product has to reap returns in the marketplace. Patent protection for drugs remains in effect, but comparable or superior drug substitutes are available quicker than they have ever been.

Another area of concern for pharmaceutical companies is the generic drug market. Generic drugs are low cost copies of products no longer patent protected. Once a drug loses patent exclusivity, other companies are free to petition the FDA for approval to manufacture and market generic substitutes. On average, generics are discounted 86% versus full price, branded drugs.[13] This discounted pricing is economically feasible because the generic manufacturers do not have significant development and marketing investments to recover. With cost-containment pressures increasing in the health care arena, market share of generic drugs has more than doubled in the past decade; they accounted for 41% of all prescriptions written in 1998.[14,15]

To combat the growing cost of R&D, shorter life cycles, and cost-containment pressures, pharmaceutical companies are forming more strategic alliances. The total number of alliances grew from 121 in 1986 to 627 in 1998.[16] In addition to alliances, mergers and acquisitions have also become larger and more frequent since the mid-1980s.[17] Pharmaceutical industry experts often debate the merits of these types of relationships, but experience says that these relationships can allow pharmaceutical companies to leverage others' research expertise, as well as bring products to market quicker and more effectively.

WARNER-LAMBERT COMPANY HISTORY

Warner-Lambert Company has evolved considerably throughout its history to become one of the world's leading pharmaceutical companies. A Philadelphia pharmacist, William Warner, laid the foundation of the current company in the early 1850s when he created a process to coat tablets of harsh tasting medications with a sugar shell. Over the years, the company expanded through many mergers and acquisitions to become an international competitor in several businesses. Today, Warner-Lambert is focused on three primary business segments: consumer health care products, confectioneries, and prescription pharmaceuticals (Exhibit 3).

The consumer health care products business is comprised of over-the-counter (OTC) medications, shaving products, and pet care products. The company owns the well-known Rolaids, Lubriderm, Benadryl, Listerine, Schick, and Tetra brands. The confectionery business consists of a broad line of chewing gums, bubble gums, breath mints, and cough drops including the Trident, Chiclets, Certs, and Halls brands.

The prescription pharmaceutical business segment is certainly the most substantial contributor to Warner-Lambert's bottom line, not only representing 57% of all sales, but also having the highest profit margin (Exhibit 3). Warner-Lambert has always been involved in medicine, but it reinforced its commitment in 1970 through the acquisition of Parke-Davis, a company with a rich past in prescription pharmaceuticals. Parke-Davis was responsible for developing a system for standardization of medicines before the turn of the century and it also created the first organized, systematic method for clinical testing of new drugs. In the 1950s, Parke-Davis was considered the biggest drug company in the U.S.

Unfortunately, Parke-Davis did not maintain its preeminence under the Warner-Lambert umbrella. Warner-Lambert spent the early 1990s recovering from a series of misfortunes in its pharmaceutical business that earned the company bad press and poor ratings from industry analysts. Warner-Lambert's confectionery and consumer health care businesses carried the pharmaceutical division. In 1993, Lopid, the company's leading drug, lost patent protection and the planned successor did not receive Federal Drug Administration (FDA) approval, so the company was left with nothing in position to mitigate the revenue loss from Lopid. That same year, the FDA cited Warner-Lambert for lack of regulatory compliance at two Puerto Rico manufacturing facilities. Eight drugs were recalled and manufacturing came to a halt while the plants were brought into compliance. The early 1990s also saw proposals for sweeping changes in the U.S. health care system—changes that threatened pharmaceutical companies. The industry reacted by down-sizing work forces and shrinking R&D budgets. Warner-Lambert laid off employees throughout the organization, including employees at the Parke-Davis research facility in Ann Arbor, Michigan, and reined in funding for R&D.[18] The situation was so dismal that industry analysts were questioning whether Warner-Lambert could survive as a serious pharmaceutical competitor. In May 1994, David Lippman of Prudential Securities concluded that the Warner-Lambert pharmaceutical business had "no growth potential," and that the R&D pipeline was "not sufficient to put the company back in the prescription drug game."[19]

Warner-Lambert has several therapeutic areas of interest for drug development including cardiovascular disease, central nervous system disease, diabetes, women's health, and anti-infectives/antivirals. Research in cardiovascular disease led to the discovery and development of a powerful cholesterol-lowering agent marketed under the brand name Lipitor (chemical name atorvastatin).

CORONARY ARTERY DISEASE

Coronary artery disease is the leading cause of death in the United States. Each year more than a million Americans suffer a heart attack, of which about half are fatal. A leading cause of coronary artery disease is the buildup of plaque in the blood vessels, which leads to blockage, heart attacks, and strokes. Frequently, this plaque buildup results from excessive cholesterol, which is transported in the bloodstream from the liver by low-density lipoprotein (LDL) and returned to the liver for elimination by high-density lipoprotein (HDL). In addition, new scientific data shows that when levels of another type of cholesterol, triglycerides, are elevated, plaque buildup can also result. Cholesterol is produced naturally by the body, in addition to being ingested through many foods. Efforts to lower LDL-borne cholesterol and triglycerides and raise HDL-borne cholesterol can have major benefits in reducing the risk of heart disease and improving overall cardiovascular health. As many as 50 million Americans are thought to have excessive LDL cholesterol levels; however, only an estimated 6 to 8 million are treated.[20]

Role of Statins in Coronary Artery Disease Treatment

Patients with high LDL cholesterol were historically treated with medicines that broke down cholesterol regardless of whether it was naturally produced by the body or from ingested food. While somewhat effective, these medicines did not prevent more cholesterol from being produced by the body. In addition, they caused side effects such as stomach pain and nausea.

The discovery of statins, a new therapeutic drug class, revolutionized the treatment of high cholesterol. Drugs known as statins have a unique method of action: they inhibit a key enzyme in the body from producing cholesterol. Rather than waiting for cholesterol to be produced and then attempting to reduce the overall levels, statins directly intervene in the body's production of cholesterol. As a result, this makes statins much more powerful than the older medications. In addition, statins are more convenient to use because they are dosed as tablets rather than liquids and cause few side effects, making them easier and safer for patients to take.

More than 45 years of research led to the discovery, development, and the 1987 Merck launch of the first statin, Mevacor. On the coattails of Mevacor's success, three more statins entered the marketplace. The market shares for the statins available just prior to the launch of Lipitor are listed in Figure 2.

LIPITOR RESEARCH AND DEVELOPMENT

The challenges faced by Warner-Lambert in the early 1990s resulted in reduced resources for R&D. Ron Cresswell, Chairman of Pharmaceutical Research, chose to focus his limited resources on a small number

FIGURE 2   U.S. Market Shares of Cholesterol-Lowering Drugs, January 1997[21]

Drug Name	Manufacturer	Launch Year	Market Share
Mevacor	Merck	1987	14%
Pravachol	Bristol-Myers Squibb	1991	21%
Zocor	Merck	1992	32%
Lescol	Novartis	1994	14%

Note: Market shares are based on the entire cholesterol-lowering drug market (not only statins).

of promising molecules. One of the chemical compounds retained for development was a statin now known as Lipitor. At the time, Cresswell's decision was viewed by some as "selling out" the company's future, because he neglected products in early stages of development, future revenue-generators, in favor of late stage products that could soon earn money for the ailing pharmaceutical division.

The retention of the statin Lipitor was contentious at times since it appeared to be a "me-too" product that would enter a crowded market dominated by products from some of the most powerful pharmaceutical companies in the world. But a Phase I study conducted in 1992 provided Warner-Lambert with an inkling that Lipitor could be a powerful cholesterol-lowering agent. LDL levels decreased nearly 50% in a trial involving healthy volunteers.[22] This was only the first phase of tests in a long series of expensive clinical trials that Warner-Lambert needed to complete to gather data for the FDA (Exhibit 2). Additional evidence supporting the power of Lipitor was gathered in a 1994 Phase II trial that demonstrated that the drug could reduce cholesterol levels by more than 60%, exceeding the established capabilities of all competing products.[23] By the time Lipitor was ready for Phase III trials, Warner-Lambert researchers were confident that their drug was differentiable from existing statins because of its superior ability to lower cholesterol levels.

A large drug development hurdle that Lipitor faced was to get through the rigorous and lengthy FDA regulatory review process as quickly as possible. The time it takes the FDA to complete a drug review varies, but on average the agency completes them in 12 months.[24] But, if a new drug treats a serious or life-threatening condition or addresses an unmet medical need, the FDA will consider it for a fast track review (approval decision generally expected within six months). Warner-Lambert was under pressure to get its drug to market quickly, and data from a Phase II study led to a pivotal fast track

strategy. In addition to conducting Phase III trials with people suffering from typical high cholesterol, the company decided to also run trials for familial hypercholesterolemia, a fatal hereditary condition resulting in exceptionally high cholesterol. A small minority of people suffer from this condition, and it was not clinically addressed by any of the competitive statins. "'There wasn't much of a downside risk,' reported Robert Zerbe, Senior Vice President Worldwide Clinical Research, 'If it didn't work it [Lipitor] wouldn't be any different than any of the others.' And if it did, he said, 'It would open up the possibility of priority review.'"[25] The results of the hypercholesterolemia trials justified an expedited review by the FDA and approval was granted for Lipitor (atorvastatin) just six months after submission of the New Drug Application (NDA).

As another part of Lipitor's development strategy, Warner-Lambert carried out head-to-head clinical trials against the leading commercial statins at the request of the marketing group. This tactic is rarely seen in the drug industry because if a new product fails to show significant superiority to competitors, it will be very difficult to persuade physicians to switch their patients to the new drug. Incontrovertible evidence of superiority is, however, an extremely desirable asset. Fortunately, Lipitor was found to be superior to all commercialized statins. In the head-to-head trials, Lipitor reduced elevated LDL cholesterol 40% to 60% across the full dose range (10mg to 80mg) and reduced triglycerides by 19% to 40%. The best selling competitive cholesterol reducer on the market, Zocor, decreased LDL cholesterol by only about 40%.[26,27,28]

Yet another motive for the aggressive push to market was the fact that Merck's Mevacor was expected to lose patent protection and go generic in 2001. Warner-Lambert needed as much time as possible to shift patients and physicians to its "new generation" drug, Lipitor, before generic Mevacor was available at much lower prices.[29]

After his 1988 arrival at Warner-Lambert, Ron Cresswell launched several initiatives instrumental in the development of Lipitor. Cresswell sought, in many ways, to bring the research organization into the modern world of pharmaceutical development and lay the foundation for a strong future. He increased the emphasis on biotechnology, hired talent, and built an experienced management team. Moreover, Cresswell integrated regulatory affairs and clinical research into the R&D organization with the intention of improving packages of documentation submitted to the FDA. Cresswell also sought to involve marketing earlier in the new drug development process. "Both R&D and marketing had a clear sense of the product's [Lipitor's] potential long before it received approval." In addition, Cresswell noted, "At the manufacturing level, we recognized some demanding parts of the chemical synthesis and were able to build the kind of relationship early with manufacturing that allowed us to make sure that the demands of that part of the process didn't hold the overall transition [Lipitor market entry] back."[30] Lastly, Warner-Lambert management developed a new compensation plan that uncapped performance incentives, thereby improving overall employee morale.[31]

Based on the organizational improvements and specific development strategies executed by Cresswell, Warner-Lambert gained FDA approval in December of 1996 for Lipitor, launching the product more than a full year ahead of many analyst predictions. Cresswell's, and others', efforts contributed to a turnaround in the Warner-Lambert pharmaceutical R&D organization.

BRINGING LIPITOR TO MARKET

Lipitor Marketing Challenges

Warner-Lambert faced serious challenges in bringing Lipitor to market. Although clinical results indicated superior efficacy for Lipitor, the fact remained that it would be the fifth statin available to patients and physicians. One of Lipitor's biggest challenges was to overcome the perception that it was a "me-too" product. Merck and Bristol-Myers Squibb, the incumbents, had proven products in the market. The companies marketing Zocor, Mevacor, and Pravachol enjoyed strong relationships with key medical "opinion leaders" such as cardiologists and possessed large and experienced sales forces. How could

Warner-Lambert, a smaller company, overcome the strong market positions held by the competitors?

Furthermore, Warner-Lambert was expecting to launch another major drug, Rezulin, at the same time as Lipitor. Many pharmaceutical companies view the first six months after a drug launch as the most critical time in a product's life cycle. The initial adoption rate by physicians can often make or break a new product. A successful launch is critical to a product's overall lifetime performance. To effectively launch one drug is a challenge, but to simultaneously launch two, both with blockbuster potential, was daunting. How could Warner-Lambert successfully launch and market Lipitor?

Alliance with Pfizer

Warner-Lambert wanted to employ a "saturation" approach to selling Lipitor. This was essential because Lipitor faced a marketplace with millions of untreated patients and a medical community largely content with the drugs already available to treat high cholesterol. The intent of the "saturation" strategy was to have as many sales representatives as possible contacting physicians. As Anthony Wild, Warner-Lambert Pharmaceutical Sector President, explained, "The more soldiers you have out there, the more guns, the more likely you are to achieve your ends." Warner-Lambert clearly understood that the sales force was a key success factor in any drug's performance, but a 1995 sales force deployment study conducted by consultants ZS Associates revealed that the company's sales force was inadequate in size and focus to effectively launch Lipitor.[32]

Executives at Warner-Lambert decided that a partnership was necessary to address its constrained sales and marketing resources. They were faced with balancing the need for sales and marketing assistance with immediate demands to generate profits for the floundering pharmaceutical business. To find a suitable partner, Warner-Lambert focused its search on companies that did not have a competing cholesterol-lowering product. Of the five companies the field was narrowed to, Pfizer and Hoffman-LaRoche were the top two choices. Competition in the negotiation process improved the likelihood that Warner-Lambert would get a more favorable deal. At one point in the negotiations, a Warner-Lambert fax intended for Hoffman-LaRoche accidentally ended up in a Pfizer fax machine, which helped convince Pfizer that it needed to make a great offer in order to get the Lipitor deal. In the end, Pfizer was chosen by Warner-Lambert because of its marketing prowess, experience, contacts, and credibility in cardiovascular medicine as well as recent successful drug launch experience. Moreover, unlike Hoffman-LaRoche, Pfizer was not then seen as a potential hostile acquirer.[33,34]

Details of the co-marketing agreement (Exhibit 4) state that Pfizer paid $205 million in up front money and milestone payments for the rights to sell Lipitor. Pfizer also committed to splitting all future product expenses including advertising, promotion, sampling, and sales force. Furthermore, Pfizer agreed to pay for half of any ongoing and planned clinical trials, which were reported to number more than 100 and involve 100,000 patients. In return, Pfizer would receive variable payments based on sales targets established in the agreement. Given the annual sales that Lipitor has reached, the arrangement indicates that Pfizer has been receiving 48% of net sales.[35]

Product Positioning

Lipitor was first and foremost marketed with a message of superior cholesterol-lowering capability. Drug companies are restricted to discussing only therapeutic benefits of their drugs that have been approved by the FDA in what is termed an "indication." The head-to-head clinical trials proved that Lipitor was the most potent statin on the market for reducing elevated total cholesterol, LDL cholesterol, and triglycerides over a range of comparable doses. Lipitor was the first statin approved for reducing triglycerides as well as the more common LDL cholesterol, making it an ideal drug for a broad range of patients. Although Pravachol and Zocor are effective at lowering high triglycerides, neither Bristol-Myers Squibb nor Merck possessed the triglyceride indication at the time of the Lipitor launch. Pravachol and Zocor promoted the fact that they were proven to reduce the risk of heart attacks, and Zocor had the added indication of reducing deaths related to heart attacks. These were very powerful marketing messages that Lipitor could not exploit. Use of Lipitor most likely also prevents heart attacks and saves lives, but data proving this fact did not exist. Instead, Lipitor relied on the medical community perception that all statins possess the same capabilities to reduce heart attacks and death through their cholesterol-lowering capabilities.[36]

The second piece of the Lipitor positioning message revolved around its ease of use. Determining a patient's optimal dose was not simple for physicians to accomplish with existing statins. This entailed selecting a starting dose, re-testing the patient's cholesterol after the drug has been used for a period of time, adjusting the dose, and repeating the cycle until the proper dose was identified. The process is inconvenient and time consuming. Fortunately with Lipitor, 72% of patients reach their target LDL cholesterol goal at the starting 10-milligram dosage, thereby eliminating the need for repetitive tinkering.[37,38] As Carl Seiden, an analyst from J. P. Morgan, put it, "The beauty of Lipitor's positioning is that physicians can remain 'lazy' by using the starting dose and then forgetting about it, but the goals achieved with Lipitor will be greater than with any other statin."[39]

Pricing Strategy

Warner-Lambert made the already convincing Lipitor value proposition even better with a moderate pricing strategy. The product was positioned with a message of therapeutic superiority and ease of use, but priced lower than the market leading competitors. Figure 3 compares the average prescription price for each of the statins at the time Lipitor entered the market. Even after the incredibly positive reception and adoption of Lipitor after launch, Warner-Lambert has maintained Lipitor average prescription prices below its primary competitors' prices.

FIGURE 3   Statin Average Prescription Pricing Structure[40,41]

Drug Name	1997 Average Prescription Price	1999 Average Prescription Price
Lescol	$52	$50
Lipitor	**$84**	**$91**
Pravachol	$93	$105
Zocor	$95	$125
Mevacor	$125	$137

Promotional Tactics

An assortment of promotional tactics were implemented by a marketing and medical team specifically dedicated to Lipitor to build as much awareness in the medical community as possible. Pre-launch efforts included a national cholesterol education program in conjunction with the American Heart Association. The intent was to educate physicians and patients that cholesterol needed to be treated more aggressively than it was; they needed to "go for the goal" established in guidelines set by the national cholesterol education program. The campaign positioned Lipitor as the drug best suited for attaining these targets. Additionally, Lipitor was publicized in medical journals and at major medical conventions with pre-market comparative efficacy data. Medical opinion leaders were also recruited to use free samples of Lipitor immediately after the drug was approved, but before it was formally launched. These pre-marketing efforts succeeded—a week before Lipitor was officially introduced, it already claimed 3% of all new cholesterol-lowering drug prescriptions.[42,43,44]

Sales Force

Warner-Lambert and Pfizer outgunned the competition with the largest statin sales force. Between Warner-Lambert and Pfizer, more than 2,200 sales representatives were believed to be selling Lipitor during its launch in the United States.[45] Lynn Alexy, Vice-President of Warner-Lambert Cardiovascular Disease Team, described their physician selection. "In total, we targeted about 91,000 key prescribers—physicians either in the cardiology area, internists and general and family practitioners—who had shown a track record of writing cholesterol-lowering agents."[46] By the end of the launch year, a total of 831,000 medical community contacts had been made on behalf of Lipitor, translating into a 29% share of voice in sales details, which has been upheld through 1998.[47] (See Figure 4.) A sales detail is simply a sales call on a doctor that results in the sales representative discussing the merits of a particular drug.

The sales force further supported the Lipitor campaign through the distribution of free product samples. Warner-Lambert and Pfizer implemented an aggressive sampling program, distributing 7.3 million samples to physicians in the first year of launch for a share of voice of slightly over 23%.[48]

FIGURE 4
Cholesterol-Lowering Drug Physician Details 1997[49]

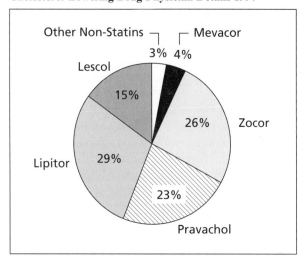

Lipitor Success

Lipitor is a blockbuster. Warner-Lambert and Pfizer have bragging rights to one of the most successful launches in the history of the pharmaceutical industry. After launching in January 1997, Lipitor reached $1 billion in domestic sales within its first 12 months on the market.[50] By the end of 1998, Lipitor was available for sale in 50 countries. Lipitor claimed U.S. market share leadership in the statin drug class in October 1997 with a 30% share of all new statin prescriptions (Exhibit 5).[51] Lipitor has continued to take share, finishing 1998 with 34% of the entire cholesterol-lowering new prescription market (Exhibit 6).

Hemant Shah, President of HKS & Company, a health care analysis firm, reiterated the sentiments of many when he said, "In my two decades of experience within the pharmaceutical industry, I have never witnessed the launch of a fifth comparable drug to treat a non-symptomatic disease take off as rapidly as Lipitor has."[52] The drug's success even caught Warner-Lambert by surprise. Manufacturing executives admitted that the market demand was so strong that they exhausted what they thought was a 3-month drug supply virtually overnight. The company was forced to purchase a fully operational manufacturing facility just months after Lipitor was launched in an effort to keep up with demand.[53] Industry analysts reported that Warner-Lambert's internal first year Lipitor sales expectations were set at only $100 million just prior to launch.[54]

LIPITOR NEXT STEPS

Future Lipitor Strategies

To date, Lipitor has benefited from the DTC advertising campaigns of its competitors. Both Merck and Bristol-Myers Squibb have spent tens of millions of dollars in DTC advertising for Zocor and Pravachol only to find that they were driving more patients to physicians but they were getting prescriptions for Lipitor. Warner-Lambert is now dropping its hat into the DTC ring with Lipitor as a means of expanding the entire statin market. Print and television ads were introduced in February 1999. Using the tagline, "The lower numbers you are looking for," Warner-Lambert is expecting to encourage patients to have their cholesterol checked with the hope that they will eventually be prescribed Lipitor.[55]

Warner-Lambert and Pfizer have been leveraging their relationship in an effort to identify Lipitor extensions. One concept is for a single product that concurrently treats high cholesterol and hypertension. The combination pill would include Lipitor and Pfizer's calcium channel blocker, Norvasc. Although this potential extension was publicly shared, the recent merger battles bring into question whether this is still a viable joint development program.[56]

Finally, Warner-Lambert has quietly admitted to examining the regulatory hurdles in selling Lipitor over-the-counter. A conversion from prescription to over-the-counter (OTC) rarely happens before a drug has lost patent protection. However, it appears that Warner-Lambert may be interested in pre-empting its patent expiry since protection will continue through 2010 for Lipitor.[57]

Future of Lipitor

Pharmaceutical industry analysts widely interpreted Pfizer's hostile attempt to take over Warner-Lambert as motivated by concern over the AHP merger's potential to affect the Lipitor co-marketing agreement. Worldwide Lipitor sales for 1999 are approaching $4 billion, only three years after introduction. Figure 5 illustrates one analyst's Lipitor sales projections through 2003, but sales are predicted to reach $10 billion before 2010 when patent expiration is expected.[58] Pfizer claims almost half of the drug's annual profits, making Lipitor an invaluable part of Pfizer's drug portfolio today and in the future.

As industry analysts hotly debated the fight for Warner-Lambert through the media, the players in the competition jockeyed to better position themselves for the impending contest. For de Vink to be battle-ready he needed to solidify his position on some important questions. Can Warner-Lambert continue to sell Lipitor on its own or does Pfizer still have something unique to provide? How much is Lipitor worth?

FIGURE 5 **Lipitor Worldwide Sales Projections[59]**

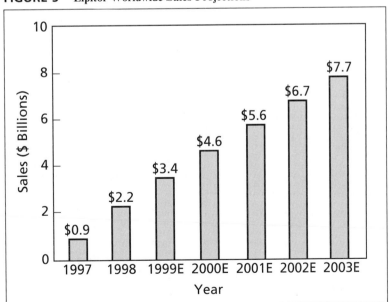

EXHIBIT 1 U.S. Market Share, Top 20 Pharmaceutical Companies, 1998
Source: U.S. Prescription Product Market, Year In Review 1998, IMS Health.

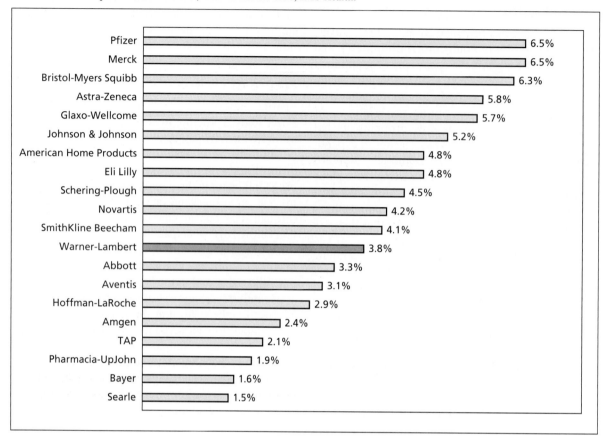

EXHIBIT 2   **U.S. Drug Development Process**
Source: Direct Excerpt: Pharmaceutical Industry Profile 1999, PhRMA.

DISCOVERY AND DEVELOPMENT

In the discovery phase, pharmaceutical companies employ thousands of scientists to search for compounds capable of affecting disease. While this was once a process of trial and error and serendipitous discovery, it has become more rational and systematic through the use of more sophisticated technology. But safety remains the paramount concern. Pharmaceutical companies and Federal Drug Administration (FDA) take extraordinary measures to ensure the safety of all approved prescription drugs. From discovery through post-marketing surveillance, drug sponsors and FDA share an overriding focus to ensure that medicines are safe and effective.

Once an entity has been identified as a potential drug candidate, FDA and industry follow elaborate scientific procedures to evaluate the safety and efficacy of the candidate. The procedures are divided into four specific stages: pre-clinical safety assessment, pre-approval safety assessment in humans, safety assessment during FDA regulatory review, and post-marketing safety surveillance.

PRE-CLINICAL ASSESSMENT

The relative safety of newly synthesized compounds is initially evaluated in both in vitro and in vivo tests. If a compound appears to have important biological activity and may be useful as a drug, special tests are conducted to evaluate safety in the major organ systems (e.g., central nervous, cardiovascular, and respiratory systems). These pharmacology studies are conducted in animals to ensure that a drug is safe enough to be tested in humans.

An important goal of these pre-clinical animal studies is to characterize any relationship between increased doses of the drug and toxic effects in the animals. Development of a drug is usually halted when tests suggest that it poses a significant risk for humans—especially organ damage, genetic defects, birth defects, or cancer.

PRE-APPROVAL ASSESSMENT IN HUMANS

A drug sponsor may begin clinical studies in humans once FDA is satisfied that the pre-clinical animal data does not show an unacceptable safety risk to humans. It takes many years for a clinical development program to gather sufficient data to prepare a New Drug Application (NDA) seeking FDA regulatory review to market a new drug.

Every clinical study evaluates safety, regardless of whether safety is a stated objective. During all studies, including quality-of-life and pharmacoeconomic studies, patients are observed for adverse events. The average NDA for a novel prescription drug is based on almost 70 clinical trials involving more than 4,000 patients—more than twice the number of trials and patients for the NDAs submitted in the early 1980s. Clinical studies are conducted in three stages:

Phase I: Most drugs are evaluated for safety in healthy volunteers in small initial trials. A trial is conducted of a single dose of the drug, beginning with small doses. If the drug is shown to be safe, multiple doses of the product are evaluated for safety in other clinical trials.

Phase II: The efficacy of the drug is the primary focus of these second-stage trials, but safety also is studied. These trials are conducted with patients instead of healthy volunteers; data are collected to determine whether the drug is safe for the patient population intended to be treated.

Phase III: These large trials evaluate safety and efficacy in groups of patients with the disease to be treated, including the elderly, patients with multiple diseases, those who take other drugs, and/or patients whose organs are impaired.

(continued)

EXHIBIT 2   U.S. Drug Development Process (*continued*)

FDA REVIEW

A sponsor submits an NDA to the FDA for approval to manufacture, distribute, and market a drug in the United States based on the safety and efficacy data obtained during the clinical trials. In addition to written reports of each individual study included in the NDA, an application must contain an integrated summary of all available information received from any source concerning the safety and efficacy of the drug.

The FDA usually completes its review of a "standard" drug in 10–12 months. One hundred and twenty days prior to a drug's anticipated approval, a sponsor must provide the agency with a summary of all safety information in the NDA, along with any additional safety information obtained during the review period.

While the FDA is approving drugs more expeditiously, the addition of 600 new reviewers made possible by the user fees paid by pharmaceutical companies has enabled the agency to maintain its high safety standards. Over the years, the percentage of applications approved and rejected by FDA has remained stable. Two decades ago, 10–15 percent of NDAs were rejected—the same as today.

POST-MARKETING SURVEILLANCE

Monitoring and evaluating a drug's safety becomes more complex after it is approved and marketed. Once on the market, a drug will be taken by many more patients than in the clinical trials, and physicians are free to use it in different doses, different dosing regimens, different patient populations, and in other ways that they believe will benefit patients. This wider use expands the safety information about a drug.

Adverse reactions that occur in fewer than 1 in 3,000–5,000 patients are unlikely to be detected in Phase I–III investigational clinical trials, and may be unknown at the time a drug is approved. These rare adverse reactions are more likely to be detected when large numbers of patients are exposed to a drug after it has been approved.

Safety monitoring continues for the life of a drug. Post-marketing surveillance is a highly regulated and labor-intensive global activity. Even before a drug is approved, multinational pharmaceutical companies establish large global systems to track, investigate, evaluate, and report adverse drug reactions (ADRs) for that product on a continuing basis to regulatory authorities around the world.

EXHIBIT 3   Warner-Lambert Sales by Business Segment, 1998
Sources: PaineWebber Drug Universe, October 11, 1999; SG Cowen Pharmaceutical Industry Pulse, March 1999.

Business Segment	% Worldwide Sales	Worldwide Sales ($ Millions)	U.S. Sales ($ Millions)	% Profit Margin
Pharmaceuticals	57%	$6,191	$4,232	22%
Lipitor	**20%**	**$2,184**	**$1,645**	—
Consumer Products	25%	$2,721	$1,475	18%
Confectioneries	17%	$1,889	$661	11%
Total		$10,801	$6,368	

EXHIBIT 4   **Warner-Lambert Summary of Lipitor Agreement with Pfizer Inc.**
Source: Warner-Lambert.

SUMMARY OF KEY TERMS OF LIPITOR ARRANGEMENTS

- Covers most major countries other than Japan & France; primarily co-promotion; 10 year term from launch
- $205 million from Pfizer in upfront & milestone payments for rights to Lipitor (already received)
- One quid pro quo product from Pfizer, chosen from among three listed in agreement, on terms to be negotiated; $30 million payable at rate of $6 million per year beginning in 2002 if no quid selected
- U.S. payments to Pfizer tied to baseline sales:

Agreement Year	Baseline Sales
1	$263 million
2	$337 million
3	$457 million
4	$541 million
5	$588 million
6	$612 million
7	$651 million
8	$688 million
9	$763 million
10	$753 million

Note: Agreement Year 1 ended March 31, 1998.

	% of Net Sales ("Standard" Definition)		
	Up to 50% of Baseline	50% to 100% of Baseline	Over Baseline
Years 1 through 5	13.35	31.15	48.00
Years 6 and 7	13.35	31.15	44.50
Year 8	13.35	22.25	31.15
Year 9	13.35	13.35	31.15
Year 10	8.90	8.90	31.15

- Pfizer pays 50% of all Product Expenses for years 1–7 and 35% of all Product Expenses for years 8–10. Product expenses include the following:

   Marketing, A&P, sampling
   Training and communications materials
   Product Lifecycle Plan Studies (clinical, pharmacoeconomic, etc.)
   Regulatory filings
   Net detailing (each party performs and pays for its own details)
   Net cost of goods or distribution

(continued)

EXHIBIT 4 **Warner-Lambert Summary of Lipitor Agreement with Pfizer Inc.** (*continued*)

- In International co-promotion countries, % of Net Sales payable to Pfizer ranges from 26.4% up to 44% (when market share hits 38%)
- In International co-promotion countries, Pfizer pays 50% of all Product Expenses and performs/pays for 50% of details (except Germany: 2/3 Warner-Lambert, 1/3 PFE)
- In International license countries, Warner-Lambert sells bulk tablets to Pfizer at 28% of Net Sales (and Pfizer covers all of its other costs)

TERMINATION PROVISIONS

- Both U.S. and International co-promotion arrangements can be terminated at the option of Warner-Lambert at the beginning of Agreement Year 6 (or at the beginning of Agreement Year 4 upon a Change of Control of Warner-Lambert)
- One year advance notification
- Any or all territories
- If terminated . . .

> Pfizer continues to fund its portion of covered Product Expenses
> Pfizer withdraws sales force support
> Warner-Lambert pays Pfizer 75% of the amount due under the agreements
> Pfizer is not obligated to pay annual quid option cash payments; years 6-10 $6MM each year

Both parties have the right to terminate for material breach (and above provisions not applicable) This summary is intended to provide readers with a brief, clear explanation of the agreement's most salient points. The full texts of the five agreements are available at www.warner-lambert.com.

EXHIBIT 5
U.S. Statin Market Share of New Prescriptions, 1991–1999
Source: Salomon Smith Barney, Scrip Picture Book, October 8, 1999; adapted from IMS, U.S. prescription market, retail only.

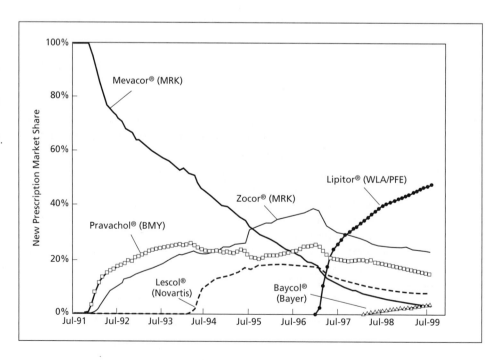

EXHIBIT 6   **Cholesterol-Lowering Prescription Drug Market Share, 1998**
Sources: J.P. Morgan, Prescription Pad, November 18, 1999; Morgan Stanley Dean Witter, Novartis: Keeping the Faith, February 3, 1999.

Drug	U.S. New Prescription Market Share (%)	Worldwide Sales ($ Millions)
Lipitor	34%	$2,185
Baycol	1%	$125
Zocor	24%	$3,945
Mevacor	6%	$745
Pravachol	16%	$1,643
Lescol	8%	$612
Other Non-Statins	12%	

Note: Baycol launched by Bayer/SmithKline Beecham in 1998.

Endnotes

1. "Pfizer Says Warner-Lambert Actions Represent 'A Desperate Act' to Deny Its Shareholders Superior Offer from Pfizer," Pfizer Press Release, November 29, 1999.
2. Retail Sales Estimates and Trends from 1991–1998, U.S. Department of Commerce.
3. Pharmaceutical Industry Pulse, SG Cowen, January 1999.
4. U.S. Prescription Product Market Year-In-Review 1998, IMS Health, January 1999.
5. Barrett, Amy, et al., "Addicted to Mergers?: Dealmaking May Not Be the Right Prescription for Drugmakers," *Business Week,* December 6, 1999.
6. Competitive Media Reporting, 1999.
7. Pharmaceutical Industry Profile, PhRMA, 1999.
8. Barrett, Amy, et al., "Addicted to Mergers?: Dealmaking May Not Be the Right Prescription for Drugmakers," *Business Week,* December 6, 1999.
9. Pharmaceutical Industry Profile, PhRMA, 1999.
10. Ibid.
11. Ibid.
12. Ibid.
13. Specialty Pharmaceuticals Industry, Warburg Dillon Read, May 5, 1999.
14. Ibid.
15. Specialty Pharmaceuticals Industry, Warburg Dillon Read, May 5, 1999.
16. Pharmaceutical Industry Profile, PhRMA, 1999.
17. Ibid.
18. Madell, Robin, "Banking on Blockbusters," *Pharmaceutical Executive,* August 1997.
19. Longman, Roger, "Warner-Lambert: The Virtues and Costs of Focus," *In Vivo,* April 1997.
20. Pfizer Annual Report, 1998.
21. Seiden, Carl, "Pfizer, Inc.," JP Morgan, October 8, 1997.
22. Gibson, D. M., et al. "Pharmacokinetic Characteristics of CI-981 as a Function of Morning versus Evening Dosing in Healthy Volunteers." Presented at the 8th Annual Meeting of the American Association of Pharmaceutical Scientists; November 14–18, 1993; Lake Buena Vista, Florida.
23. Nawrocki, J., et al., "Reduction of LDL-C by More than 60% with an HMG-CoA Reductase Inhibitor." Presented at the 10th Annual Symposium on Atherosclerosis; October 9–14, 1994; Montreal, Canada.
24. Pharmaceutical Industry Profile, PhRMA, 1999.
25. Longman, Roger, "Warner-Lambert: The Virtues and Costs of Focus," *In Vivo,* April 1997.

26. Grom, Taren, "Reaching the Goal," *PharmaBusiness,* May 1999.
27. Mincieli, Gary, "Make Room for Lipitor," *Med Ad News,* June 1997.
28. "Lipitor," *R&D Directions,* March 1997.
29. Longman, Roger, "Warner-Lambert: The Virtues and Costs of Focus," *In Vivo,* April 1997.
30. Madell, Robin, "Banking on Blockbusters," *Pharmaceutical Executive,* August 1997.
31. Longman, Roger, "Warner-Lambert: The Virtues and Costs of Focus," *In Vivo,* April 1997.
32. Ibid.
33. Warner-Lambert Annual Report, 1998.
34. Longman, Roger, "Warner-Lambert: The Virtues and Costs of Focus," *In Vivo,* April 1997.
35. Ibid.
36. "Lipitor's Dominant Position," *Med Ad News,* November 1998.
37. O'Reilly, Brian, "The Pills That Saved Warner-Lambert," *Fortune,* October 13, 1997.
38. Grom, Taren, "Reaching the Goal," *PharmaBusiness,* May 1999.
39. Seiden, Carl, "Pfizer, Inc.," JP Morgan, October 8, 1997.
40. National Prescription Audit, IMS, January–December 1997.
41. Price Probe Pricing History Report, 1992–1999.
42. Lorge, Sarah, "The Prescription for a Product Launch," *Sales and Marketing Management,* July 1997.
43. Grom, Taren, "Reaching the Goal," *PharmaBusiness,* May 1999.
44. "Lipitor," *R&D Directions,* March 1997.
45. Grom, Taren, "Reaching the Goal," *PharmaBusiness,* May 1999.
46. Ibid.
47. "Business Watch," *Medical Marketing and Media,* May 1998.
48. "Business Watch," *Medical Marketing and Media,* May 1998.
49. Seiden, Carl, "The Prescription Pad," JP Morgan, October 14, 1999.
50. Koberstein, Wayne, "Master Launchers," *Pharmaceutical Executive,* May 1998.
51. "Saturated, but Rapidly Growing," *R&D Directions,* January 1998.
52. Mincieli, Gary, "Make Room for Lipitor," *Med Ad News,* June 1997.
53. Warner-Lambert Annual Report, 1998.
54. Eisinger, Jesse, "New Entrant in Drug Market Causes a Stir—Lipitor for Cholesterol Seems to Be Pressuring Merck, Bristol-Myers," *Wall Street Journal,* March 31, 1997.
55. Spain, William, "Despite Small Ad Budget, Lipitor Is No. 1 in Category," *Advertising Age,* March, 15, 1999.
56. "Warner-Lambert, Pfizer Expand Lipitor Marketing Pact," *Drug Store News,* July 19, 1997.
57. Silverman, Edward, "Warner-Lambert Considers Wider Market for Cholesterol Drug," *Star-Ledger,* July 13, 1999.
58. Winslow, Ron, "Companies Struggle over Blockbuster Drugs," *Wall Street Journal,* November 8, 1999.
59. ING Baring Furman Selz, LLC, April 12, 1999.

Case 9

eBay: Growing the World's Largest Online Trading Community

They found the one kind of business you can run on the Internet where you can really just mint money. (Adam Cohen, author of *The Perfect Store: Inside eBay*[1])

eBay remains in rapid growth mode; there were a lot of skeptics who said they couldn't sustain it, but, so far, [the company] has proven them wrong. (Safa Rashtchy, VP, US Bancorp Piper Jaffray[2])

eBay CEO Meg Whitman drove into the company parking lot in her black Jeep Cherokee, parked in her usual spot, and proceeded quickly toward the office. Today was another special day for the popular e-tailer; eBay had surpassed its internal targets on all metrics, showing that it had truly matured from an online flea market to a bona fide holiday shopping destination. While the rest of the retail industry had suffered a downturn, eBay continued its impressive growth rate during this prolonged economic slowdown.

When she arrived at her office, there was already a pile of folders awaiting her on the desk. She glanced first at the selected list of comments from eBay's message boards that were compiled every morning to provide her with the pulse of the eBay community. However, her mind was squarely focused on the upcoming conference call with analysts to discuss the 2002 year-end results. Once again, the company had beaten analyst expectations, yet Whitman recognized that this was a critical time for the venture. In 2000, she'd confidently declared her goal of hitting $3 billion in revenue by 2005.[3] Although some pegged her "Herculean" goal as "too aggressive," the company had mushroomed from a community of 2 million users at the end of 1998 to 62 million registered users just 4 years later. "How can eBay continue to maintain its personal feel in spite of its staggering growth?" The company had outlined a strategy toward that end, but Whitman knew that success in pioneering new markets was far from guaranteed. One year ago, eBay shuttered its Japanese operations after performing far below expecta-

tions. In addition, it sold its traditional auction house, Butterfield's, and an offline car auction company, Kruse, when it realized that those acquisitions were not properly aligned with their long-term focus.

BACKGROUND

On Labor Day weekend in 1995, a ponytailed French-Iranian immigrant computer programmer named Pierre Omidyar launched a small, person-to-person, online trading service, called Auction Web, in his living room to help his fiancée expand her Pez dispenser collection. His first item sold was a $15 broken laser pointer. Initially, Omidyar was reticent to charge a fee, but added one in 1996 to cover the cost of his monthly Internet bill. As friends referred other friends, a group spirit and philosophy that espoused honesty and respect emerged. An example of this attitude was illustrated by the occasions when sellers shipped items even before receiving payment.

When Omidyar secured $8 million in venture capital in 1997, the company was relaunched as eBay and became the largest and most popular person-to-person trading community on the Internet. Benchmark Capital was hired to draw in managerial talent with the necessary credentials and, subsequently, an infusion of capital. In May 1998, Meg Whitman joined the company as president and CEO after serving as an executive for the Hasbro toy firm. Later that year, at the height of the dot-com boom, eBay went public; its subsequent meteoric rise in stock price made its top three executives instant billionaires (see Exhibit 1 for absolute and comparative stock price performance). The company rapidly expanded, post-IPO, by launching a national ad campaign, entering into strategic partnerships with America Online and WebTV, and making several acquisitions in 1999. These acquisitions included Alando (online auction company in Germany), Billpoint (online credit-card technology), and Butterfield & Butterfield (an upscale auction house). Despite experiencing a major server outage in 1999

Scott M. Tang prepared this case under the supervision of Professor Allan Afuah as a basis for class discussion rather than to illustrate either effective or ineffective management. Creative liberties have been taken in developing the introductory and concluding paragraphs of the case.

that caused management to realize the importance of bulletproofing their technology investments, the number of registered users continued to grow exponentially (see Exhibits 2–4 for number of registered users, items listed, and gross merchandised sales). By the end of 2002, in stark contrast to most of its other startup peers, eBay had not only survived the dot-com crash, but had emerged in a financial position unrivaled by its competitors (see Exhibit 5 for income statement).

Business Model

eBay operates as a fully automated commerce site (in both its historical auction format as well as its more recent fixed-price formats) for buying and selling a wide variety of items using its topically arranged website. Sellers list items and provide descriptions on the site, often with photographs. They also submit a starting price, set the length of the individual auction, the bidding increments, and an optional reserve price. Reserve price is the minimum price that the seller predetermines he would be willing to accept for the item. Potential buyers input a maximum price they are willing to pay; eBay will automatically bid just enough to outbid the previous high-bidder up to the maximum price listed by the seller. After the auction ends, eBay notifies the seller and the winning bidder and provides the necessary details for completion of the sale.

eBay's virtual marketplace uses a transaction-based revenue model. Buyers can browse for free; eBay makes its monies off of fees from sellers. eBay collects a small insertion fee from sellers listing each item and then charges a separate fee that is determined by the final sales price, if the auction was successful (see Exhibit 6 for a description of sample listing fees). eBay upsells additional marketing fees, which help the purveyor gain additional visibility on the website. These "feature fees" include the addition of supplementary photographs, bold-highlighted listings, and special-section displays. While eBay facilitates the transactions, it does not hold inventory nor does it provide logistics such as shipping or certification of the items being sold (it offers these services via independent partners). As a result, eBay carries no associated cost for these normal retail services (e.g., warehouses) and claims to have no liability for the sale. This low cost structure allowed the company to be profitable from the very outset. eBay enjoys an operating profit margin of 84% in contrast to Amazon.com's profit margin of 25%.[4]

eBay's product mix has shifted from primarily collectible items (such as Beanie Babies and Pokemon cards) to a mix that includes more practical everyday items such as consumer electronics, household goods, and clothing. eBay's product listings span 18,000 categories. The company has also expanded into several vertical channels such as industrials and automobiles that have helped raise the average selling price of goods sold on eBay, which translates to higher revenues for eBay. Today it trades everything from Prada handbags to Business Planning services to Gulfstream jets.

The company has developed a critical mass of buyers, sellers, and listings; this has created a cycle that enables eBay to continuously grow its user base. With 62 million registered users, eBay has 27.7 million "active" users[5]—those on the eBay platform who have bid, bought, or listed over the previous twelve months (at approximately $500 worth of merchandise per active user).[6] Buyers want access to the greatest selection of goods, while sellers want access to the market with the most buyers. eBay has both. There is also an intrinsic entertainment value in the medium of auctions—which company officials note as the "thrill of the hunt" and "joy of discovery" of bargain goods—that has enabled it to appeal to a very broad audience. Given the ability to monitor listings growth and closed auctions, eBay's business model also offers a unique level of transparency to Wall Street to help it spot weaknesses in the fundamentals.

Community

> eBay exists because of the strength and spirit of our community. (Meg Whitman, eBay President and CEO[7])

Even as its user base has grown from individual consumers to merchants, global corporations, and governmental agencies, eBay strives to cultivate a strong sense of community among buyers and sellers; this is a cornerstone of its business model. It has tapped into the basic human desire for belonging in its quest to become and remain the largest and most loyal online trading community on the Internet.

Trust and Safety One of eBay's founding values is the belief that "people are basically good."[8] To bolster this philosophy, eBay developed proactive measures for building trust in its community. In 1996, eBay introduced the Feedback Forum. The Forum created a file for each buying or selling member that enables other buyers and sellers who have engaged in transactions with that particular member to post compliments, criticisms, and other comments. In this way, every member's reputation becomes public record. This public record has evolved into such a powerful business tool that individuals have sued eBay for defamation of character due to the company's unwillingness to remove negative feedback that members felt was unjustified.[9] A member who has established a positive reputation over time will have a corresponding color-coded star symbol placed next to his/her name. One positive feedback receives one point, a neutral feedback receives zero points, and one point is deducted for each negative feedback posted. The feedback ratings are used as indicators of credibility and help to overcome the hesitancy of new members to transact with unknown trading partners. Historically, users have not been allowed to advertise their ratings on other commerce sites. When a group of former eBay members attempted to sell merchandise on Amazon.com and, accordingly, posted their eBay ratings, eBay successfully applied legal pressure to Amazon.com in order that the feedback claims be removed.[10]

eBay's members are further protected from unscrupulous sellers through the Buyers Protection Program. This program provides insurance for the first $200 (with a $25 deductible) of every transaction. Through partnerships with outside vendors, eBay offers additional services such as escrow assistance for higher priced transactions, item authentication (e.g., sports autographs, original paintings, etc.), warranty services, online dispute resolution, and seller identity verification. The company has borrowed fraud models from the financial service industry to proactively monitor potential fraud behavior and has cooperated with law enforcement agencies to investigate trading offenses. It boasts three former federal prosecutors on its fraud team.[11]

Community Feel eBay recognized that it was advantageous to connect members with one another directly in order to promote a "small-town" community feel. The company understood that people like to rally around common experiences and, thus, they encouraged this socialization online via thirty-four different chat rooms, sixty-five discussion boards, a monthly newsletter, a "giving board" for charitable donations to user-identified causes, and the opportunity to create personal home pages (free of charge) through eBay's "About Me" service. In 2002, the company started its annual eBay Live Community Conference, bringing thousands of community members to Anaheim, California, for three days to learn auction tips, to rub elbows with company executives, and to swap stories with other eBay members having similar interests.

Member Input From the outset, founder Omidyar sought to solicit input from the community about how eBay should run its business. When the company first started, members could send their thoughts and opinions to Omidyar directly. Today, eBay has several staff-moderated chat rooms and discussion boards dedicated to improving the quality of the eBay experience. In addition, day-long focus groups (dubbed *Voices*), culled from a spectrum of active eBay users, enable the company to receive detailed feedback on the state of the site and to gain input on upcoming proposed services. Early on, eBay found that it could not afford to make important decisions apart from its user base. An example of this fact occurred when the company tried to change the color of the feedback stars without consulting the user community; the resulting uproar on the message boards forced the staff member who was in charge of community strategy to alter her course.[12]

Education Realizing that those who are familiar with the "ins" and "outs" of eBay are apt to do more business on the site, eBay has created a number of educational features on its pages (such as interactive tours, tutorials, and electronic boards dedicated to "newbies") to help educate new users rapidly and efficiently. Offline events, such as eBay University, also enable the company to provide both education and networking opportunities for its community. eBay University is a series of seminars across the country, taught by eBay experts, that are designed to help novices and advanced users increase comprehension of the finer points of conducting eBay transactions.

GROWTH STRATEGY

When eBay started its IPO roadshow, it had estimated that its addressable market was $100 billion in collectibles. However, as eBay began to expand and as it witnessed the popularity of newly added categories, the addressable market figure was adjusted to $1.8 trillion: $200 billion in new/scarce products, $100 billion (of $2 trillion) in in-season retail, $500 billion in end-of-life products, and $1 trillion in used/vintage items.[13] Online commerce has been steadily gaining momentum with consumers: Jupiter

Research (a market tracking firm) predicted that 2003 numbers will top $51 billion, after posting $40 billion in sales in 2002 and a mere $12 billion in 1999.[14] To capture these markets, eBay set upon a four-prong growth strategy: (1) category expansion, (2) format expansion, (3) user expansion, and (4) auxiliary business expansion, all while maintaining both a high degree of financial discipline and consistent profitability.

Category Expansion

eBay has 23 subsites in categories such as Clothing, Travel, and Real Estate and has focused on category expansion as its main growth driver.[15] At the end of 2002, eBay had five categories that each generated more than $1 billion in gross merchandised sales (GMS). GMS is one of eBay's most important performance metrics since it reveals the level of trading activity across the site.

eBay established eBay Motors in 2000 when it noticed that cars were increasingly listed under the "miscellaneous" category. With 20,000 cars listed at any given time, eBay has become the largest seller of used cars[16] and the most popular automotive site on the Internet.[17] With growth that has surprised even the management team, eBay Motors sold $4.3 billion worth of vehicles and parts in 2002[18]—doubling the number from the previous year and posting the highest GMS of all eBay categories. Meg Whitman comments,

> With 20/20 hindsight, it's [the success of eBay Motors] not that surprising because it was an inefficient market that didn't have a lot of trust and didn't have a lot of transparency. It does on eBay . . . In some ways it's not that different from our original markets.[19]

In a deal that blends content with commerce, the company announced (early 2003) an exclusive partnership with Kelley Blue Book's kbb.com, the leading automotive pricing information site. Through the relationship with kbb.com, automotive shoppers who use kbb.com for research and pricing information will have direct access to the relevant vehicle listings on eBay Motors. Consumers who want to sell their used vehicles and are looking for content and pricing information on kbb.com will also be able to easily link to eBay Motors to list their used vehicle for sale. Additionally, this agreement will allow thousands of franchise dealers nationwide who use KarPower, Kelley Blue Book's dealer inventory management software, to more easily list inventory on eBay Motors.

Other subsites have also begun to appear. Partnerships with brand name players in each segment have been important in order for eBay to gain credibility within each category. eBay Sports, for example, has partnered with organizations such as the NFL and PGA Tour to offer licensed gear and unique sports experiences (e.g., behind-the-scenes views of charity tournaments). eBay Sports was ranked as the number one sports commerce site on the Web by Media Metrix and Nielsen/NetRatings,[20] generating $1.2 billion worth of sports-related items in 2002.[21] That year, eBay's Consumer Electronics and Computer category generated $1.8 and $1.9 billion worth of business respectively.[22] eBay Travel partnered with Priceline.com to offer airline tickets and, in the Real Estate category, the company bought HomesDirect, which operated an online marketplace for the sale of foreclosed properties. A piece of land is sold on eBay every 45 minutes.[23]

With three main subareas that include vertical industries (e.g., metalworking, industrial supplies, and restaurant and food service), office technology, and wholesale lots, eBay launched eBay Business in 2003, its foray into B2B online retailing. The company noted that existing corporate users were already using eBay to find other corporate buyers and sellers: eBay's business and industrial category had grown more than 90% per year in 2001 and 2002.[24] Those numbers were helped by earnings from eBay's first initiatives in B2B: selling business surplus with a subsidiary in Germany and buying an investment in Tradeout.com.[25]

eBay's category structure, with its dedicated category managers, allows eBay to understand the needs of a particular segment and to subsequently expand the category. Each category is decorated with an appropriate theme and features Top 10 and popular search lists as well as links to related community boards. eBay's category structure allows each category to act as if it were a profit center and enables eBay to take proactive measures against niche competitors.

Format Expansion

In 2000, collectibles comprised two-thirds of the goods sold on eBay. By 2002, that percentage had shrunk to 20%.[26] According to Whitman, auctions are more suitable for hard-to-find items such as antiques and collectibles. In contrast, the fastest emerging categories at eBay were mass-market items like consumer electronics and computers.[27] As a result, the company has undertaken a strategy to expand its formats to extend its reach to mainstream shoppers who tend to buy these "practical" goods (such as DVDs and books) via fixed pricing.

eBay explored its first non-auction format with the acquisition of Internet retailer Half.com in 2000. Half.com allowed individuals and merchants to pay for previously owned and new mass-market goods at a fixed price. Through Half.com, eBay has made inroads to rival Amazon.com's books and CD business and has initiated a fixed price service across the platform.[28] eBay created the "Buy-It-Now" (BIN) format option that has enabled buyers to immediately win an auction when they select an option to pay the seller's pre-established BIN selling price. eBay has also created a pure fixed price option. In mid-2001, eBay created eBay Stores dedicated to individual merchants. eBay Stores, in contrast to the individual auction listings, are standalone virtual storefronts where vendors can list their inventories together in one place in either auction or fixed price formats. While eBay promoted the increased opportunity for merchants to build their brand with eBay Stores, one disadvantage to date has been that the main eBay search function will not search for items listed in eBay Stores. However, searches may be conducted within a storefront.

The new fixed price formats have attracted buyers who would prefer not to wait or to participate in the often uncertain and somewhat risky auction format. For sellers, this option allows them to move inventory more quickly. The higher turnover has translated to an increased rate of sales and revenue for eBay. Fixed price trading is catching on with eBay members: Buy-It-Now represents 34% of U.S. listings, 35% of Germany listings, and 22% of U.K. listings.[29] Worldwide, fixed price formats comprise 24% of total GMS, primarily through the Buy-It-Now option.[30]

Marketing and Customer Acquisition

eBay has one of the most powerful brand names on the Internet. Whitman's background as a seasoned marketer at Hasbro and Procter & Gamble helped eBay to focus on building brand awareness and interest and then leveraging that brand equity to attract a critical mass of buyers and sellers to the eBay service. To attract new users, eBay uses partnerships, online advertising, PR, direct messaging via e-mail, word-of-mouth, and traditional advertising in areas where they can reach their target audience. On eBay, demand drives supply which, in turn, drives eBay.

In March 1999, eBay entered into a historic 4-year, $75 million joint marketing and development deal with American Online (AOL); this is one of the largest strategic partnerships to date.[31] Co-branded auction sites were developed for AOL and each of its other online brands (including CompuServe, Netscape's NetCenter, and the ICQ instant messaging service). The agreement gave eBay a "prominent presence" on AOL's various properties, which meant exposure to the biggest pool of Internet users on any single service. In return, AOL was promoted on eBay as its "preferred online service" and received $75 million over the contract period as well as ad revenues that would be generated through their co-developed sites. AOL's sales force would also be the third-party sales force for the limited advertising sold on eBay's website.[32]

In another major partnership deal, eBay joined forces with Microsoft in 2001 to incorporate eBay's auctions in MSN properties like the CarPoint shopping service and bCentral small business portal for small businesses. The arrangement lets eBay programmers use Microsoft web-design tools that could help bring eBay's auctions to pagers, web-connected TVs, and personal digital assistants such as Palm.[33]

Word-of-mouth is extremely important to eBay. More than half of its new customers come from referrals.[34] "If you just do the math off our quarterly financial filings, you see that we're spending less than $10 to acquire each new customer. We are being driven by word-of-mouth."[35] eBay found that referred customers tend to use the people who referred them as sources of advice and guidance rather than using eBay's own customer support; this, in essence, lowers eBay's customer service support costs.[36]

Noticing that its most avid users were also its best spokespeople, eBay created the PowerSellers membership program ("Aspire to be a PowerSeller," "Recognized, Respected & Rewarded"), offering extra services and recognition to community members who reached stringent monthly sales and positive feedback targets. The PowerSellers levels start at $1,000/month for Bronze and go to $150,000/month for Titanium. For their contributions to eBay, PowerSellers receive tips, invitations to company events, and additional customer service via e-mail and phone support. The highest PowerSellers also receive a dedicated eBay Account Manager. eBay began offering health insurance in 2002 to its PowerSellers through a third party vendor in recognition of the fact that many people earn their livelihoods from eBay.[37]

eBay also exploits the power of stories through effective public relations to drive word of mouth. In addition to consistently publicizing the success stories of eBay entrepreneurs, noteworthy items listed on eBay show up regularly in news reports across the country. In 2002, people saw coverage of the first actual "town"—a fixer upper in Northern California—being sold on eBay,[38] a Mig 21 fighter jet complete with spare engine and rocket pods and FAA license,[39] and a Mongolian barbecue franchise that was set to sell in first quarter 2003.[40] A luxury house (built in a former Atlas F nuclear missile silo in upstate New York) that sold on eBay brought international television news coverage from "20/20," "The Today Show," and on Japanese, Russian, and Canadian TV.[41] This free advertising and PR are the stronghold of its grassroots marketing efforts. Additionally, promotional events (such as eBay's annual "Free Listing Day") help engender member loyalty and generate more business.[42]

eBay has evolved from an e-commerce brand to a pop culture icon. To drive this phenomenon further, eBay signed an agreement with Sony Pictures television to co-produce an hour-long syndicated television show that will combine aspects of "Entertainment Tonight," "Ripley's Believe It or Not," and the "Antiques Roadshow."[43] The series will provide a one-minute local cutaway segment for affiliates, designed to promote the station's website as well as the market's hot auctions of the day. Local stations that pick up eBay-TV would earn $6 for every person that registers with eBay and, in addition, a commission on all eBay items sold through the station's site.

For the 2002 holiday season, eBay spent $14 million to support its latest customer acquisition strategy, its first major television ad campaign created to reposition the site as a holiday shopping destination.[44] The integrated marketing campaign also featured print ads and organized social parties to educate potential new users. These parties were essentially history lessons on the company's evolution. Since 40% of toys posted during the holidays were new merchandise,[45] the company identified the top 20 new toys that they believed would be in short supply during the holiday period and actively worked with PowerSellers to promote those items on their site.[46] Whitman had hinted at making merchandise demand information available, in the future, to provide valuable market research data to merchants.

Geographic Expansion

Regional Expansion eBay has local sites in 60 regional markets in the United States. After a successful pilot in Los Angeles,[47] local sites have been rolled out in cities from Honolulu, to Oklahoma City, to Miami. These regional eBay sites allow users to find items located near them and browse through items of local interest (e.g., concert tickets) or difficult-to-ship items (e.g., major appliances and boats). After initial plans to give the sites a regional flavor, eBay has subsequently opted to standardize these pages to give them a common look and feel. With its foray into fixed-pricing goods, eBay has fundamentally ventured into the $1.2 billion online classified industry, an industry that is expected to grow to $2.3 billion by 2007.[48] Regional expansion has been spurred on through partnerships such as AOL's Digital City,[49] a service that provides online city guides and regional newspapers.[50]

International Expansion Users on eBay represent countries from all over the world. With eBay's vision and global business strategy, the company continues to expand its service and brand abroad. Currently eBay has presence in 27 countries: the United States, Canada, Argentina, Brazil, Chile, Colombia, Ecuador, Mexico, Uruguay, Venezuela, Austria, Belgium, France, Germany, Ireland, Italy, Netherlands, Spain, Switzerland, Sweden, United Kingdom, Australia, Korea, New Zealand, Singapore, Taiwan, and China. It has entered these countries either by building from the ground up (e.g., United Kingdom, Canada, Austria, Switzerland), acquiring an existing online auction house (e.g., Germany, France, Taiwan), or investing in a partner (e.g., Korea, Latin America, China). eBay is the number one e-commerce site in 6 of these countries and is the market leader in 17 countries. eBay Germany represents 38% of all e-commerce in the third largest online market in the world.[51] Due to its rapid growth overseas, eBay's international operations have grown from 7% of total revenues to 25%. In a note to analysts, executives commented that international revenues might eventually overtake U.S. revenues.[52]

There are several factors that have enabled eBay to extend its success beyond North American borders. First, structural inefficiencies have lent themselves to the eBay value proposition: bringing buyers and sellers together. Fragmented markets, longer inventory cycles, underdeveloped retail options (i.e., shorter store hours, less selection), and wholesale channels help eBay make those markets more efficient. At the same time, structural efficiencies in certain markets (i.e., smaller geographies for faster shipping, faster adoption of electronic payments) create a better e-commerce environment. eBay, with its established business model, also faces less competition in these international markets.

Learning from its failure in Japan, where it allowed Yahoo! to develop a dominant position before entering the market, eBay recognized the need to have both a strong management team and first-mover advantage. eBay's strategy was to focus on building new user and listing growth to achieve market leadership quickly. This was accomplished by offering sellers minimal or no listing fees and through heavy promotional marketing. Once it reached critical mass, the company would then ramp up monetization. eBay's take rate on international GMS was 6.4% in third quarter 2002.[53] While the take rate was lower than in the United States, eBay plans to increase fee options to bring it closer to the 7.3% take rate found in the States.

Business Customer Expansion

To maintain its aggressive growth targets, eBay realized it needed to move beyond small-time merchants and to begin actively courting large companies. Blue-chip companies such as Motorola are discovering that they can get 40% to 50% more for their surplus inventory—45 cents on the dollar instead of 15 to 20 cents[54]—on eBay than they would through liquidating the merchandise themselves.[55] At least 71 large companies, including Bloomingdale's, Dell Computer, Sprint, The Sharper Image, IBM, Disney, and Sears, have been using eBay Stores as an alternate sales channel and/or for selling excess inventory, discontinued and refurbished products.[56] Even state governments are finding that they can auction off their surplus vehicles.[57] Large inventories of mass-produced goods benefit eBay: these items produce more listings, which in turn generate greater revenues for the company. Big business currently accounts for only 5% of total GMS for eBay.[58] While some eBay entrepreneurs believe these mass merchants depress prices and provide subpar customer service, others appreciate the increased traffic that the big retailers bring to the site.[59]

To help provide infrastructure to these larger businesses, eBay has partnered with several service providers (i.e., Accenture and Escrow.com). Accenture Connection to eBay was launched in 2002 to provide inventory management, product listings, warehousing, and logistics to midsize and large businesses (such as HP[60]) that sell on eBay.[61]

Recognizing that 70% of B2B commerce occurs in local markets, eBay established a core group of business Trading Assistants taken from its national network of 16,000 voluntary assistants to help business sellers trade in local markets.[62] The Trading Assistant service allows users to hire an experienced eBay member to sell for them for a fee. Since many business sellers do not want to deal with the Internet and do not have the time and expertise to coordinate listings, answer e-mails, and ship items, the Trading Assistant program broadens these sellers' reach.

Auxiliary Expansion

PayPal   To increase its nonauction revenue sources, eBay acquired Internet payment provider PayPal in October 2002 for $1.4 billion in stock.[63] While PayPal was initially conceived with the intention that people might pay each other back for dinner bills and such, the service was perfectly suited to the needs of eBay members; it freed anonymous buyers and sellers from the hassles of sending checks or money-order payments. The relationship between eBay and PayPal was symbiotic; at the time of the merger, eBay members closed 40% of their auctions with PayPal while rejecting Billpoint, eBay's own money-losing billing payment service.[64] Conversely, about 60% of PayPal's $2.14 billion payment volume business came from eBay.

Many users appreciated the relative safety and convenience of using PayPal. They also recognized that the 3.25% transaction rate[65] was lower than a merchant credit card account. The acquisition was "community approved" and emphasized the complementary missions of both organizations to help build small businesses.

PayPal allows money to be sent to anyone with an e-mail address, eliminating the need for sellers trying to process their own credit card payments. The process is as follows:[66] (1) A buyer purchases an item online and chooses to pay the seller via PayPal. Both buyer and seller must be registered with the company for the transaction to be completed. (2) The buyer chooses a method of payment, such as a bank or credit card account, from which the payment will be drawn, providing the seller's e-mail address and payment amount to PayPal. (3) PayPal subsequently transfers the funds to the seller's account while shielding the buyer's confidential financial information. Basic usage for the buyer is free; business accounts are charged a nominal fee. PayPal receives about 50% of the 3.25% transaction revenue rate after subtracting for transaction expense and loss rate.[67]

Since the acquisition, PayPal has grown even faster. In its first quarter under eBay management, PayPal was able to deliver net revenues of $74.7 million in 4Q 2002, up 86% from the previous year.[68] PayPal also increased the velocity of trade on eBay due to a faster and easier payment process, while allowing global transactions (currently used in 38 countries) for individual and small businesses. Company officials noted that PayPal's nonauction business accounted for about 30% of total payment volume and is growing at a much faster rate than the auction side.[69]

Off-line Auctions eBay acquired traditional classic car auctioneer Kruse International Automotive in 1999 for roughly $150 million in stock.[70] At the time, the company thought it could grow the market for collectible cars. However, it sold the subsidiary back to its former owner in 2002 to focus on online sales.[71] While Kruse never took off, the sale did help the company establish eBay Motors. In a similar fashion, eBay bought high-end fine art and antique auction house Butterfield & Butterfield in 1999, but sold the company in 2002 after its off-line sales plummeted.[72] eBay had bought Butterfield's when it looked like online auctions were headed "upscale." As with Kruse, the company did not grow rapidly enough to meet expectations. That experience, though, led to eBay's partnership with Sotheby's, who would use eBay as their fine auctions web portal. Sothebys.com was eBay's third attempt at creating an online marketing place for high-end collectibles.[73] Sotheby's announced, less than a year later, that it will cease its online auctions through the joint site. It will, however, continue to use eBay's live auction technology to allow its customers to bid online simultaneously with its traditional auctions.[74] Analysts believe that the inability to incorporate these premier off-line ventures demonstrates the fact that high-end bidders have been reluctant to alter their methods of buying and selling art and antiques, and, furthermore, that the buyers for high-end markets are well-known and specialized enough that Internet sales do not expand the market.[75]

Cost Discipline

Unlike many of its dot-com brethren during the Internet heyday, eBay eschewed expensive television marketing, insisting that word-of-mouth endorsements from its growing clan of eBay bargain hunters were its best promotion. It has maintained that cost-cutting focus. Costs per listing fell from $1.45 in 2000 to $1.25 in 2002.[76] Cost of site operations as a percentage of revenue similarly fell from 9.5% in 2001 to 6% in 2002.[77] In customer service, the company has managed to maintain the same number of customer support contacts while listings have doubled.[78]

CHALLENGES

Competition

eBay dominates the online auction market with 85% to 90% market share.[79] However, competitors are beginning to show signs of revitalization as they take note of the attractive economics of various segments of the online marketplace. The "Big Three" in auctions—Amazon.com, Yahoo! and eBay—have seen their product offerings beginning to converge.

Amazon.com, the largest single online shop, has seen rapid growth in its Amazon Marketplace.[80] After lackluster results for its own auction service (and with zShops, which is similar to eBay Stores), Amazon began to give small sellers the ability to list items side-by-side with Amazon's own offering of books, electronics, and other goods.[81] This has allowed sellers to place their products on Amazon's millions of highly trafficked Web pages as opposed to posting on the fringes of the Amazon site (where zShops and auctions were previously located). Amazon has the largest unique audience for a shopping destination, as rated by Nielsen's NetRatings.[82]

The Internet's second largest online auction, uBid, pulled out of consumer-to-consumer auctions in late 2002; this effectively eliminated 75% of the products available on its site.[83] uBid had only 4 percent of eBay's monthly visitors at the end of 2002. To retrench, the company focused on selling computers and consumer electronics. Unlike eBay, uBid owns all of the items on its site, buying excess inventory from manufacturers and other parties, thus allowing them to offer new products with warranties and customer service.[84] It has also opened a "Buy-It-Now Superstore" with the latest technological offerings as well as lower-cost goods (i.e., DVDs and CDs) to drive repeat visits.

As the Web's largest portal, Yahoo! also revamped its e-commerce options. In October 2002, Yahoo! integrated its auction, shopping, classifieds, and new "warehouse" site so that Internet users would be able to search the entire Yahoo! Shopping portfolio at one time and move easily between the sites by links found at the top of each page.[85] Yahoo! Warehouse includes an area where individuals and companies can sell used and overstocked merchandise with no listing fees.

AOL, the world's biggest online service, has announced (as of 2003) that it will develop a new marketplace that allows small and medium size businesses to sell to its enormous 76 million[86] unique audience base.[87] AOL will not offer auctions since it is prohibited in its partnership agreement with eBay. Instead, it will focus on offering overstocked consumer goods in a fixed-price format. Previously, it charged "rent" fees for providing retailer space on the AOL shopping site. As retailers have become increasingly hesitant to pay the rental fees associated with being in AOL's mall, AOL has changed its model, hoping that revenues from its new shopping service will counter slumping online ad sales.

Niche companies that specialize in particular market segments have taken note of eBay's category success and are offering auctions in addition to their traditional services. For example, AutoTrader.com, the online auto classified site, introduced its own auction in 2003 after ending a marketing partnership with eBay that began in 2000.[88] The company hopes to draw sellers away from eBay by leveraging its brand in off-line classified ads, charging no completed sales fee (but raising the initial listing fee to $50 from $40), and allowing for bid winners to inspect a vehicle before purchasing it.[89]

Potential Tension between Enterprise Sellers and Smaller Sellers

Some of eBay's small sellers feel alienated by the company's get-big initiatives. While eBay's push to bring in larger enterprises should attract more mainstream customers, this trend could anger eBay's core group of small and very vocal merchants who fear that the large retailers' lower prices and brand recognition will undermine their businesses. Many of them feel that because they have helped eBay become what it is today, they should be a priority focus for the company. In many ways, they feel eBay is *their* company.

Fraud

Although incidences of fraud registered less than 0.01% at eBay,[90] fraud remains a perennial concern for the company; the large number of listings on its site requires continual diligence in identifying and eliminating fraud. The FBI's Internet Fraud Complaint Center reported that online auction fraud was the most reported offense in 2001, consisting of 20,000-plus complaints, or 43% of all online fraud.[91] There are a number of popular auction scams. The most prevalent form is when a seller collects money for a purchase but does not send the item.[92] Other schemes include employing several bidders to artificially drive up the cost of an item, account identity theft, and setting up fake online escrow services.

Internet Tax

A factor that might impact eBay and the rest of online commerce is if the current ban on Federal and State taxes on online services is not renewed in November 2003. State governments have argued that the Internet Tax Non-Discrimination Act caused them to forgo $13 billion in potential tax revenue in 2002.[93] If Congress lifts the tax moratorium in 2003, consumers will shift some purchasing back to brick-and-mortar stores rather than pay taxes online.

Managing Growth in Stock Price

Some wonder if eBay can maintain its present growth rate to sustain its stock price.[94] eBay has a price-earning ratio of 87 based on 2002 earnings, compared to number one retailer Wal-Mart, which has a P/E ratio of 27. It would take several years for the company's price-to-earning ratio to fall to Wal-Mart levels assuming that the stock price remains at 2002 levels.[95]

Going Forward

Meg Whitman scanned the sheet of comments from members reacting to a new home page redesign. "Love the new simplified look," wrote one. Whitman remembered the first day she visited eBay when she was still a marketing executive at Hasbro. She recalled that she was struck by how the company had created an entirely new market on the Internet (a market that could not be replicated off-line) and by the strength of the emotional connection between eBay users and the company. So far the business model had worked. But, as the company continued to expand at such a rapid pace, how would the company perform its delicate balancing act, having large and small merchants operating side-by-side? How would trends in fixed pricing affect the auction side of the business? Would there eventually be any channel conflict? What if macroeconomic conditions were to stall future international growth? Where would the future growth drivers be?

As she looked out the window over her Jeep Cherokee, she couldn't help but think of the car that her son had purchased on the site and of how that symbolized eBay's growth during her tenure at the company.[96] She had said before: "Prioritization and focus are the key. My motto is that it's better to do five things at 100 percent than 20 things at 65 percent."[97] She contemplated the myriad of initiatives eBay was undertaking to support its aggressive growth targets. "Are we still focused on the right things?" she wondered as she left her office to take the analyst conference call.

EXHIBIT 1   **Stock Price (closing February 4, 2003)**
Source: BigCharts.com.

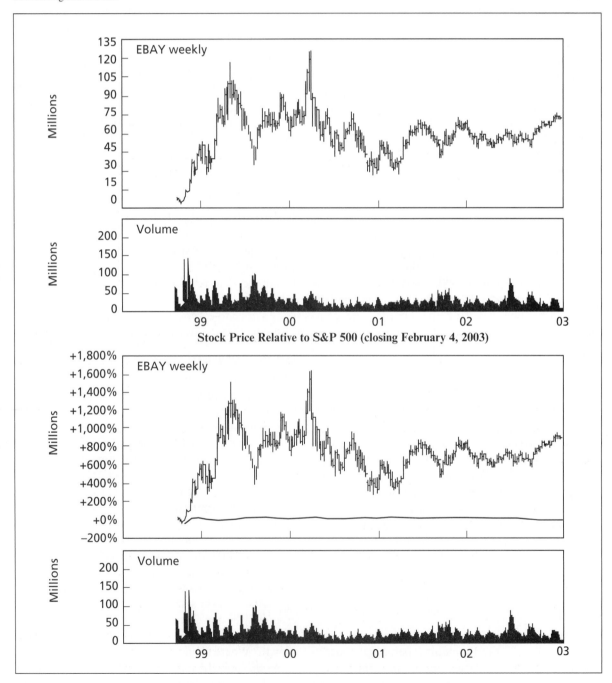

EXHIBIT 2
Number of Registered Users (thousands)
Source: Annual Reports, AP Newswires.

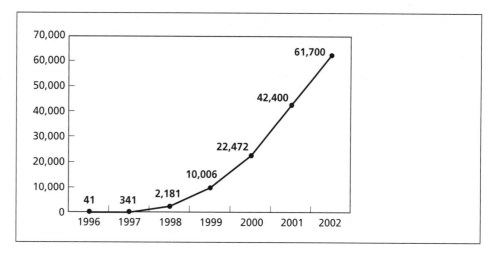

EXHIBIT 3
Number of Items Listed (thousands)
Source: Annual Reports, AP Newswires.

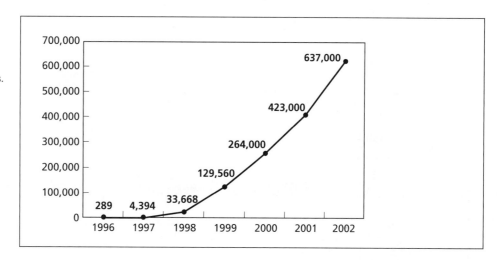

EXHIBIT 4
Gross Merchandise Sales ($ thousands)
Source: Annual Reports, AP Newswires.

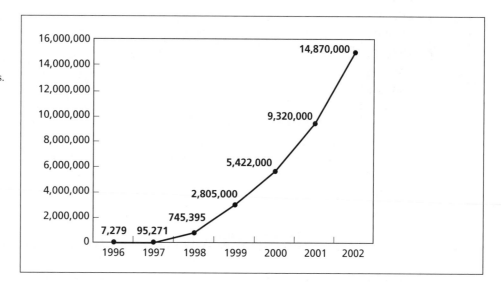

EXHIBIT 5 Consolidated Income Statement ($ in millions, year ending December 31)
Source: MSN Money.

Annual Income Statement (Values in Millions)	12/2001	12/2000	12/1999	12/1998	12/1997
Sales	748.8	431.4	224.7	47.4	5.7
Cost of Sales	81.7	51.7	33.3	2.3	0.7
Gross Operating Profit	667.1	379.7	191.4	45.1	5.0
Selling, General & Admin. Expense	437.0	298.0	162.9	33.5	3.5
Other Taxes	0.0	0.0	0.0	0.0	0.0
EBITDA	230.1	81.7	28.5	11.6	1.5
Depreciation & Amortization	89.7	45.2	25.4	5.4	0.1
EBIT	140.4	36.5	3.1	6.2	1.4
Other Income, Net	41.6	46.3	23.6	0.9	0.1
Total Income Avail. for Interest Exp.	165.8	81.2	22.3	7.1	1.5
Interest Expense	2.9	3.4	1.9	0.0	0.0
Minority Interest	−7.5	−3.1	0.3	0.0	0.0
Pre-tax Income	162.9	77.8	20.4	7.1	1.5
Income Taxes	80.0	32.7	9.4	4.6	0.7
Special Income/Charges	−16.2	−1.6	−4.4	0.0	0.0
Net Income from Cont. Operations	90.4	48.3	10.8	2.4	0.9
Net Income from Discont. Opers.	0.0	0.0	0.0	0.0	0.0
Net Income from Total Operations	90.4	48.3	10.8	2.4	0.9
Normalized Income	106.6	49.9	15.2	2.4	0.9
Extraordinary Income	0.0	0.0	0.0	0.0	0.0
Income from Cum. Eff. of Acct. Chg.	0.0	0.0	0.0	0.0	0.0
Income from Tax Loss Carryforward	0.0	0.0	0.0	0.0	0.0
Other Gains (Losses)	0.0	0.0	0.0	0.0	0.0
Total Net Income	**90.4**	**48.3**	**10.8**	**2.4**	**0.9**
Dividends Paid per Share	0.00	0.00	0.00	0.00	0.00
Preferred Dividends	0.00	0.00	0.00	0.00	0.00
Basic EPS from Cont. Operations	0.34	0.19	0.05	0.03	0.01
Basic EPS from Discont. Operations	0.00	0.00	0.00	0.00	0.00
Basic EPS from Total Operations	0.34	0.19	0.05	0.03	0.01
Diluted EPS from Cont. Operations	0.32	0.17	0.04	0.01	0.01
Diluted EPS from Discont. Operations	0.00	0.00	0.00	0.00	0.00
Diluted EPS from Total Operations	0.32	0.17	0.04	0.01	0.01

EXHIBIT 6 Sample eBay Fees

Source: Company website.

Listing Fees	$0.30 for $0.01–$9.99 value item (opening/minimum bid, BIN price, reserve price) $0.55 for $10–$24.99 value item $1.10 for $25–$49.99 value item $2.20 for $50–$199.99 value item $3.30 for $200+ value item $40 for cars/$25 for motorcycles $50 for real estate timeshare, 3–10 day listing $75 for real estate timeshare, 30 day listing
Reserve Auction Fees (refundable if item sells)	$0.50 for $0.01–$24.99 value item $1.00 for $25.00–$199.00 value item $2.00 for $200+ value item
Optional Feature Listing Fees	$99.95 for special featured section on home page and category views $19.95 for special featured section in category view $5.00 for colored band in group listing and search results $2.00 for boldface item title in group listing $0.25 for adding photo next to listing and putting into "Gallery" view $0.25 for adding a gift box graphic to signify gift idea purchase $0.10 for 10-day maximum length auction duration $0.10 for starting listings at any time up to 3 weeks in advance $0.05 for "Buy-It-Now" capability
Final Value Fees (paid only if auction was successful) Buy-It-Now price = Final Value	5.25% of closing value up to $25 Same as above + 2.75% remaining closing value up to $1,000 Same as above up to $1,000 + 1.5% on remaining closing balance $25 for motorcycles $40 for cars
eBay Stores Fees	$9.95/mo. Basic $49.95/mo. Featured: highlighted in category directory pages $499.95/mo. Anchor: showcased with own logo, top page
PayPal Fees	Free for Personal Account (but cannot receive credit cards) 2.9% + $0.30 (standard)/2.2% + $0.30 (merchant)

Endnotes

1. Jack Boulware, "eBay bid for global domination," *The Hamilton Spectator,* November 30, 2002.

2. Keith Regan, "EBay shatters Q4 Targets, joins billion-dollar club," www.Ecommerce-Times.com, January 17, 2002.

3. Deborah Asbrand, ". . . And eBay shoots too high," *The Industry Standard,* September 22, 2000.

4. Verne Kopytoff, "The eBay logic: Even in a sagging economy, people have time to buy and sell," *The San Francisco Chronicle,* December 1, 2002.

5. EBay Press Release, "eBay Inc. announces fourth quarter and year end 2002 financial results," January 16, 2003.

6. EBay 2002 Analyst Day Presentation, October 30, 2002.

7. Company Press Release, "eBay to celebrate its people and passion at eBay live 2002 community conference," March 13, 2002.

8. eBay company website.

9. "California man to drop libel claim," *Reuters News,* January 27, 2003.

10. Nick Wingfield, "Are you satisfied? eBay's battle against fraud rests primarily on a simple concept: customer feedback," *The Wall Street Journal,* September 16, 2002.

11. eBay (2002).

12. Jason Black, "Lean on me: Companies on the web are learning that paying attention to users who call the shots makes good sense for them," *Internet World,* May 15, 2001.

13. Total market universe now included new/scarce items, in-season retail, end-of-life, used/vintage (source: eBay 2002 Analyst Day).

14. Pete Barlas, "Online buying could top $51 bil this year—54% of U.S. residents online," *Investor Business Daily,* January 7, 2003.

15. "Q3 2002 eBay earnings conference call—final," Fair Disclosure Wire, October 17, 2002.

16. Jonathan Fahey, "Wheels of fortune: eBay Motors is showing that people will buy or sell anything at an online auction—even used cars," *Forbes,* January 6, 2003.

17. E-commerce technology briefing, "eBay and Autotrader will end partnership early," *The New York Times,* December 10, 2002.

18. eBay (4Q Financial Results).

19. Jonathan Weber and Miguel Heft, "Meg Whitman Speaks," *The Industry Standard,* August 6, 2001.

20. "PGA Tour launches golf auctions on eBay Sports," Market News Publishing, January 23, 2003.

21. eBay (4Q Financial Results).

22. eBay (4Q Financial Results).

23. "EBay finds more real estate buyers looking for land," *Reuters News,* September 4, 2002.

24. Kate Maddox, "eBay bids on B-to-B business: Internet giant to launch site for buyers and sellers," *B to B,* December 9, 2002.

25. Neil Cavuto, "eBay CEO interview," *Fox News: Cavuto Business Report,* January 27, 2000.

26. Patrick Seitz, " Auction king bets on fixed price," *Investor Business Daily,* June 25, 2002.

27. Ibid.

28. "Half.com emerges as primary threat to Amazon.com; success in retail requires improved targeting of customers and constant refinement of tactics say Compete," *Business Wire,* August 28, 2001.

29. Reuters Newswire, "Update 1: eBay rises on bullish analyst note," December 16, 2002.

30. eBay (4Q Financial Results).

31. George Anders, "eBay forms AOL marketing alliance, announces sale of $1 billion in stock," *The Wall Street Journal,* March 26, 1999.

32. Shannon Henry, "AOL, eBay team up to develop auction sites," *The Washington Post,* March 26, 1999.

33. "Microsoft, eBay join forces," *The Cincinnati Post,* March 13, 2001.

34. Frederick Reichheld and Phil Schefter, "E-loyalty: Your secret weapon on the web," *Harvard Business Review,* July–August 2000.

35. Ibid.

36. Ibid.

37. Ina Steiner, "eBay announces health insurance for its PowerSellers," *Auctionbyte Newsflash No. 343,* June 24, 2002.

38. Ann Oberthur, "eBay bid for California town closes at $1.8M," *AP Online,* December 29, 2002.

39. Nick Farrell, "Mig jet touches down on eBay," *VNUnet Newswire,* November 18, 2002.

40. Devlin Smith, "You bought what on eBay?!" *Entrepreneur Magazine,* January 2003.

41. Hart Seely, "Hidden lair in missile silo goes for $2.1 million," *The Post-Standard Syracuse,* November 16, 2002.

42. "Online auction site eBay holds free listing day," *Reuters News,* December 26, 2002.

43. Don Kaplan, "Bidding ends on eBay," *New York Post,* January 23, 2003.

44. Saul Hansell, "eBay profits rose sharply in 4th quarter," *The New York Times,* January 17, 2003.

45. "eBay plays toy industry barometer," *The Washington Post Online,* November 26, 2002.

46. Nick Wingfield, "How eBay spurred sellers to grab hot toys," *The Wall Street Journal,* December 13, 2002.

47. George Anders, "eBay plans regional Internet marketplace," *The Wall Street Journal,* October 1, 1999.

48. Robyn Greenspan, "Online ad gain led by classifieds," http://cyberatlas.internet.com/markets/advertising/article/0,,5941_1492151,00.html, October 31, 2002.

49. "America Online, eBay forge expanded four-year marketing deal," *Dow Jones Business News,* March 25, 1999.

50. "Star Tribune and eBay launch newspaper classifieds to drive more buyers to sellers," Star-Tribune Press Release, May 3, 2001.

51. eBay (2002).

52. Ibid.

53. Ibid.

54. Brian Grow, "Excess inventory? eBay to the rescue," *BusinessWeek,* September 9, 2002.

55. Alan Cohen, "Is this any place to run a business?" *Fortune Small Business,* November 1, 2002.

56. Grow (2002).

57. John Sanko, "State's used car sales go online: Colorado uses eBay to auction off fleet of surplus vehicles," *Rocky Mountain News,* December 12, 2002.

58. Ibid.

59. Ibid.

60. Amy Rogers, "HP unveils partnership with eBay," *Computer Reseller News,* December 2, 2002.

61. Ibid.

62. Patricia Fusco, "eBay business means business," *Ecommerce News,* January 30, 2003.

63. Nick Wingfield, "EBay completes PayPal deal, gaining web-payments heft," *The Wall Street Journal,* October 4, 2002.

64. Paul Abrahams, "Whitman finds a new pal to bill customers," *Financial Times,* July 9, 2002.

65. eBay (2002).

66. Verne Kopytoff and Benjamin Pimentel, "eBay's friendly takeover," *The San Francisco Chronicle,* July 9, 2002.

67. eBay (2002).

68. "PayPal volume rises (online payment service reports fourth quarter financial results)," *Cardline,* January 24, 2003.

69. eBay (2002).

70. David Shabelman, "eBay continues 'real world' retreat," *The Daily Deal,* October 4, 2002.

71. "Former owner buys back auto auction company from eBay," *Associated Press Newswires,* December 19, 2002.

72. Joelle Tessler, "eBay sells auction business Butterfields," *San Jose Mercury News,* August 2, 2002.

73. Troy Wolverton, "eBay's bid for high-end auction fails," TheStreet.com, February 4, 2003.

74. Bambi Francisco, "Sotheby's, eBay mend partnership," CBS.MarketWatch.com, February 4, 2003.

75. Wolverton (2003).

76. eBay (2002).

77. Ibid.

78. Ibid.

79. Mary Chao, "Entrepreneurs collect income using eBay," *Chicago Sun-Times,* October 6, 2002.

80. Rob Hof, "Is eBay's stock too hot to touch? It has a dizzying p-e ratio and appears priced for perfection, a promise that the online auctioneer may not be able to fulfill," *Business Week Online,* November 19, 2002.

81. Nick Wingfield, "The other eBay: Amazon is winning over small vendors," *The Wall Street Journal,* July 22, 2002.

82. "New Yahoo! Shopping network ranked the no. 2 online shopping destination by Nielsen//netratings," *Business Wire,* January 2, 2003.

83. Rob Kaiser, "Online auction site uBid returns to roots in technology," *Chicago Tribune,* January 12, 2003.

84. Ibid.

85. "Yahoo revamps site to include a section for used merchandise," *The Wall Street Journal,* October 16, 2001.

86. "Top 25 parent companies—December 2002," Nielsen//netRatings, http://pm.netratings .com/nnpm/owa/NRpublicreports.toppropertiesmonthly.

87. Julia Angwin and Nick Wingfield, "AOL enters eBay's turf with online shopping service," *The Wall Street Journal,* October 2, 2002.

88. Jonathan Fahey, "Wheels of fortune: eBay Motors is showing that people will buy or sell anything at an online auction—even used cars," *Forbes,* January 6, 2003.

89. Scott Leith, "Autotrader.com to start online sales to allow inspections," *Atlanta Journal—Constitution,* December 17, 2002.

90. Jon Swartz, "Fighting back: dissatisfied online shoppers take action," *USA Today,* September 19, 2002.

91. Tim Lemke, "Going, going, gone: thousands lose big money to online auction fraud," *The Washington Times,* October 21, 2002.

92. Nick Wingfield, "Are you satisfied? eBay's battle against fraud rests primarily on a simple concept: customer feedback," *The Wall Street Journal,* September 16, 2002.

93. Michael Totty, "E-commerce: the rules," *The Wall Street Journal,* January 27, 2003.

94. Robert Hof, "E-tail stocks: 'tis the season to be wary," *Businessweek,* December 30, 2002.

95. Ken Brown, "Analysts: still coming up rosy—over optimism on growth rates is rampant, and the estimates help to buoy market's valuation," *The Wall Street Journal,* January 27, 2003.

96. Christa D'Souza, "One dotcom that's still full of beans: Meg Whitman is the driving force behind eBay," *The Daily Telegraph,* August 13, 2002.

97. Michele Pepe, "No. 5—Meg Whitman," *Computer Reseller News,* November 18, 2002.

Case 10

Borders: Responding to Change

INTRODUCTION

In April 2001, Borders Group, Inc. seemed to have effectively given up on the Internet dream. Borders had operated its online retail site, Borders.com, since 1998. Despite winning considerable critical acclaim for its services, the company had been unable to make the operation profitable. A series of alliances and cooperative ventures had failed to bring Borders.com into the black. Borders now looked to work with the true heavyweight of online retailing, Amazon.com.

The Borders alliance with Amazon was seen by industry-watchers as more of a customer relations exercise than a strategic move to impact revenues. Bear, Stearns & Co. analyst Jeffrey Fieler commented:

> Basically, it's an incrementally positive [move] for both companies. Borders gets out of what seemed to be an interminably long path to profitability, and Amazon consolidates its market-leading position.[1]

By ceding complete operational control of their online retailing service, it appeared that Borders had turned away from the Internet in a move that Forrester analyst Carrie Johnson termed "Borders gives up on the future."[2] Having tried and failed to achieve positive results through cooperative ventures, it seemed this latest alliance was an escape route rather than a new direction.

One year later, on April 23, 2002, Borders Group Inc. and Amazon.com jointly announced a new development in their alliance. No longer would visitors to Amazon's website have to wait for delivery of their orders; they would be able to pick up their orders from their neighborhood Borders store. A partnership that had begun with Borders apparently ceding the online market was evolving into something more strategic and innovative.

BORDERS GROUP OVERVIEW

Ann Arbor Origin

The origin of Borders dates back to 1971, when two brothers, Louis and Tom Borders, founded an independent used bookstore in Ann Arbor, Michigan,

along with a book wholesaling business called Book Inventory Systems.[3] In 1985, after several years of gradual regional expansion, Borders opened the first book superstore. This new retail format had a dramatic and lasting effect on the bookselling industry. By 1988, Borders Books and Book Inventory Systems combined to produce sales of over $32 million.

National Growth and the Superstore

In 1989, Robert DiRomualdo, a graduate of Harvard Business School, was named president and chief executive of Borders. Taking advantage of a period of unprecedented growth in book retailing, DiRomualdo opened a further 14 stores in the next three years, and by 1992, Borders had quadrupled its size. In October of that year, Borders became a wholly owned subsidiary of Kmart. In 1993, sales from operations reached $224.8 million, up nearly 16 percent over the previous year. In August 1994, Borders and Waldenbooks formed a new company called Borders Group, Inc. In May 1995, a public offering of stock enabled a complete break with Kmart.[4] DiRomualdo was installed as the chairman of Borders.

The newly independent Borders superstore format combining books, music, and a coffee bar proved highly popular. Borders' coffee bars, which began as almost an afterthought to book sales, brought in profits in excess of $20 million.[5] Borders superstores were significantly larger than those of major rival Barnes & Noble, averaging almost 200,000 book, magazine, and music titles. Using a sophisticated computer inventory management system, Borders achieved the highest sales-per-square-foot ratio in the industry.[6] Borders' system of category management, treating each product category as a separate business unit, was an innovative approach to keep customer needs in focus while enabling inventory levels to be managed efficiently.

Industry Challenges

The late 1990s and early 2000s posed significant challenges to the book industry in general, and Borders specifically. Stock prices were down, and distribution

---

Ivan Gataric, Jon Gilbert, James Green, Iain Kennedy, William Lewallen, and Yosuke Sumita prepared this case under the supervision of Professor Allan Afuah as a basis for class discussion rather than to illustrate either effective or ineffective management. Creative liberties have been taken in developing the introductory and concluding paragraphs of the case.

and marketing challenges with online retailing brought both financial losses and shareholder disillusionment. Furthermore, a group of independent booksellers brought legal action, claiming that Borders and other major chains had made illegal deals with publishers.[7] Borders was eventually ordered to pay the American Booksellers Association $2.5 million in damages. In November 1999, Borders announced that Greg Josefowicz would succeed DiRomualdo as president and chief executive: Josefowicz would become Chairman of the Board in January of 2001.[8]

Borders in 2002

In April 2002, Borders Group was the second largest bookstore chain in the United States, based on sales and number of stores. It operated over 400 stores in the United States under the name Borders Books and Music.[9] The superstores featured books and music as well as special events, including live music, and guest appearances by artists and authors. The Borders Group subsidiary, Waldenbooks, was the largest mall-based book business in the world, with approximately 800 stores in malls and airports. Borders Group had a global presence with stores in the United Kingdom, Australia, Singapore, New Zealand, and Puerto Rico.

THE ECONOMICS OF SPECIALTY RETAILING

Overview

Retailing is traditionally a high-volume, low margin business. Trimming costs to the bone and aggressively driving sales are essential to profitability and survival. By its very nature, the industry is biased in favor of retailers that have more scale and greater cost efficiencies than their competitors.

In the 1990s the specialty retail landscape was increasingly populated by superstores, such as Barnes & Noble, Bed Bath & Beyond, Home Depot, and Toys "R" Us.[10] These specialty superstores, also known as "category killers" because of their dominance of particular merchandise categories, are larger than traditional retailers, and offer lower prices and a wider assortment of products.

The Category Killer

The category killer business model allows retailers to offer a larger assortment of products at lower prices than traditional retailers. Depending on the industry segment, category killer outlets range from 25,000 square feet to more than 100,000 square feet. These retailers offer five to ten times more stock-keeping units in their category than do department stores and mom-and-pop stores.[11]

Due to several factors, category killers typically have lower cost structures than traditional retailers. The stores are usually located at stand-alone sites or in shopping centers, with lower occupancy costs than malls or downtown locations. Initially, superstores were large warehouses operated as self-service outlets. Operating expenses were minimized and the savings were directly passed through to consumers. As the category killer retailers opened more stores, however, they realized savings from increased buying power and were able to lower prices even further. In recent years, many category killers have leveraged those savings to enhance their offering by increasing service levels and enhancing merchandise displays in an effort to attract more upscale customers.

In book retailing, superstores carry 50,000 to 175,000 individual titles. In contrast, the average bookstore chain or independent bookseller usually carries no more than 20,000 titles.[12] A sector-based view of title popularities is included as Exhibit 1. While these giant retailers may not provide the highly personalized attention that customers find at some smaller booksellers, they do maintain sufficient service levels and product knowledge.

Many book superstores also offer large selections of music and videos, often featuring extensive selections of prerecorded music, with an emphasis on hard-to-find recordings and categories such as jazz, opera, classical, and foreign music. The video section offers a broad assortment of titles, often with an emphasis on classic movies and unique titles. Music departments feature more than 50,000 titles, and video departments carry in excess of 10,000 titles.

Espresso bars, snack bars, listening stations, reading areas, and restrooms are also common features. In addition, a store may sponsor community events such as storytelling hours, poetry readings, discussion groups, and author appearances.

The New Landscape

By the mid-1990s, the rapid growth of superstores had dramatically altered the book retailing landscape. From only a handful in the mid-1980s, the number of book superstores rose to 210 in 1992, with sales totaling $526 million. By the end of 1997, the number of superstores had climbed to 924 with total sales of $4.04 billion.[13]

THE INTERNET'S IMPACT ON BOOKS AND MUSIC RETAILING

The Internet Comes of Age

Prior to the rapid growth of the Internet in the early 1990s, eCommerce was a term associated with the use of Electronic Data Interfaces (EDI) by and between manufacturers, suppliers, and distributors. Although a successful supply-chain tool, EDI lacked the ability to interface with a large customer base; it was inflexible and expensive to manage. The Internet, however, provided the ubiquitous and scalable network necessary for multiple layers of data communication, not only between segments of the value chain, but also with a large and rapidly evolving customer base. As such, analysts were predicting the expected growth in Internet usage (see Exhibit 2) to enable millions of consumers to conduct commerce online (see Exhibit 3).

The Internet promised a fundamental edge over traditional retailing: constrained neither by shelf space nor physical location, Internet retailers could be infinitely big, offering an exhaustive selection to online shoppers. The Internet could also eradicate many of the inconveniences of off-line retail shopping: getting to the store, looking for a book, waiting to be helped, waiting to pay, and paying higher prices to fund the physical and personnel infrastructures that added little value to the end customer. With the creation of the virtual shopping experience, some analysts were predicting that Internet commerce would lead to the demise of traditional retail stores.

In just a few years, as the Internet has grown in popularity, the volume of books sold online has exploded. In 1997, analysts were forecasting that total online book sales would exceed $550 million in 1998, up from an estimated $205 million in 1997 and less than $20 million in 1996.[14] Combined online sales of books, music, and videos were expected to grow from $835 million in 1998 to over $5.8 billion in 2002, a compound annual growth rate of 62.5 percent.[15] These forecasts were predicated on the entry of three major book and music retailers into the online space.

The Competitive Landscape of 1998

Barnes & Noble In 1997, Barnes & Noble was the leading U.S. bookstore in total number of stores and was the major brick-and-mortar competitor to Borders. In March 1997, Barnes & Noble launched their service as a channel on AOL. The company's own site, barnesandnoble.com, went online in May 1997 and offered access to 400,000 titles available for next-day delivery to customers' homes from a 350,000 square foot New Jersey warehousing facility. Its first-year sales were $14.6 million. In August 1998, Barnes & Noble announced its intent to spin off barnesandnoble.com to the public, hoping to raise up to $100 million in order to bolster its Internet operations in the face of serious competition.[16]

Bertelsmann Bertelsmann, a privately-held German conglomerate, was the second largest media company in the world behind Disney, with annual revenues of DM25 billion. Its interests include books with Doubleday and Random House, magazines, television, music, and the Internet via its 50 percent stake in AOL Europe. Its first foray into online bookselling was in November 1997. Boulevard Online, launched in Bertelsmann's home market, offered approximately 290,000 titles mainly in German.[17] Several months later, Bertelsmann announced the creation of Books-Online, which it planned to launch in the United States and Europe. After a proposed partnership with Amazon failed to materialize, Bertelsmann opted to pursue its U.S. strategy by teaming with barnesandnoble.com. The German company bought a 50 percent interest in the service in October 1998 for $200 million.[18]

Amazon.com Amazon.com was the brainchild of former Wall Street banker Jeff Bezos. Working in 1994 as a hedge-fund manager at D. E. Shaw, Bezos observed that the Internet was growing at 2,300 percent a year. In amazement, he set out to build a business that "would make sense in the context of that growth." Bezos drew up a list of 20 potential products and from this list selected books as the first product to sell online. His choice was based on the large existing market and large number of SKUs (1.5 million in print), as well as the suitability of computers to search such a huge selection, the fragmented nature of the existing market, and a highly inefficient distribution network.[19] Amazon presented a number of key differentiators and strengths very soon after its entry:

- *First Mover.* For all intents and purposes, Amazon defined online book retailing (even online retailing in general) with the launch of their virtual storefront in July 1995. Bezos's strategy was to use the Internet as a tool to remove the activities and expenses that were not adding value to the customer's experience. The benefit of this strategy was that Amazon could offer its books at a price point reflective of a 20 to 30 percent discount to traditional book retail prices. Bezos, however, recognized that price alone would not be enough to create superior, lasting value for customers.

- *Extensive Search Capability.* Not only did Amazon offer a huge assortment of titles; it allowed browsers to search by author, title, subject, or keyword. Users could also browse through predefined topic-based areas such as history, technology, and biographies.
- *Value-Added Content.* When titles were located, customers would often find access to a brief synopsis of the book as well as reviews—both from leading sources, such as *The New York Times* or *The Chicago Tribune*, and from other readers.
- *Personalization.* Amazon encouraged readers to sign up for a personal notification service called Eyes. Once signed up for the service, they would receive regular e-mails with reviews or recommendations of what Amazon's editors considered "exceptional" books.
- *Customer Service.* Bezos knew that superior customer service was necessary to the success of Amazon. Employees were encouraged to spend as much time, energy, and resources on building customer relationships as they did on selling products. When a customer needed help, the customer service reps took over—20 percent of Amazon's staff was dedicated to answering queries from customer email. In Bezos's own words, Amazon spent "money on things that matter to customers."[20]
- *1-Click Technology.* Amazon's 1-Click feature allows returning customers to purchase items by simply pressing the mouse button once. This technology saves the consumer time, as people do not have to re-enter shipping addresses or credit card numbers, and offers enhanced privacy and security. According to Forrester Research, consumers cite privacy and credit card fraud as the top two reasons why they do not shop online more frequently.

As Internet use increased, Amazon, through aggressive positioning and marketing, catapulted ahead of its competitors. From net sales of $511,000 in 1995, Amazon's revenues grew to $15.7 million in 1996, then to $147.8 million in 1997. Sales in the first half of 1998 were $203 million.[21] Amazon offered over 2.5 million titles of books and more than 200,000 CDs, twenty-five times the average physical music store. Details of the key differences in Amazon's business model relative to land-based bookstores are provided as Exhibit 4.

BORDERS ONLINE ENTRY

The Initial Website of 1995

Before launching its eCommerce website in 1998, Borders spent several years attempting to establish a revenue-generating presence on the Internet. In 1995, Borders.com included corporate information, store locations, and several daily product reviews. In November 1995, Borders began to build its Internet presence by announcing its sponsorship of SALON, a new online magazine that was devoted to books, the arts, and contemporary issues. Visitors to the SALON site were able to read book reviews and order featured titles through Borders' website. As part of the sponsorship, Borders and Waldenbooks displayed "Sneak Peek" titles in retail outlets and promoted the SALON website by handing out bookmarks displaying the SALON Internet address.

Borders Universe Enables Transactions

Soon after the formation of the SALON partnership, visitors to Borders.com were able to order titles reviewed through the website. At this time, however, transactions were "not the objective of the site," according to David Mackool, vice president of Borders Universe.[22] Borders Universe was an online inventory system that connected the company's retail outlets. Through this system, customers were able to order out-of-stock titles from other Borders store locations. Like the online orders, these in-store orders had to be picked up in the store. In December 1996, Borders announced that it would provide content to Open Sesame, a website that provided personalized information on books, music, and video.

1997 Brings Acclaimed Strategic Relationships

For Borders, 1997 brought the formation of additional strategic relationships with online content providers and search engines. By the end of the year, Borders had forged agreements with:

- CNET, the Internet's leading online content provider focused on technology, and all CNET-owned/operated sites, including SNAP! Online, its Internet service provider arm.

- Infoseek, a highly regarded search engine (rated #2 in terms of unique visitors on the Internet) that has a distinctive approach to integrating content into its search capability.
- Harvest, the world's leading out-of-print book search company.
- IBM, the company's main technology partner.[23]

With many strategic alliances in place at the end of 1997, Borders announced that its own Internet initiative was scheduled for launch in January 1998.

Borders.com Launches in 1998

Borders' target date of January 1998 came and went without a launch. At the time, Borders officials said the site needed additional testing, but later the delay was attributed to the need to establish its fulfillment center. By May 1998, Borders' fulfillment center in Nashville, Tennessee, was ready for business. The center was dedicated to Borders.com orders and housed "54 miles of inventory offering over 10 million books, CDs and videos in stock, competitively priced and available for immediate shipping."[24] On May 7, 1998, three years after Amazon.com launched, the new Borders.com went live with a public preview that allowed customers to browse, shop online, and give feedback to Borders before the site's grand opening later that summer.

The Borders.com site was organized into six departments: Books, Music, Video, Children's, Computer Books, and Borders NetCafe. See Exhibit 5 for details on the site organization. Borders heralded the site's product breadth and features, specifically noting:

Selection and Content

- Only online retailer with a comprehensive in-stock selection of three media categories: books, music, and video.
- Largest multimedia database on the Internet, with nearly three million book, video, and music titles.
- Largest in-stock multimedia selection of any online retailer, with more than 10 million books, CDs, and videos available for immediate shipping.
- Nearly 60 book, music, and video department sections, with 400 subsections.
- Streaming audio samples available from more than 380,000 songs on 42,000 albums.
- Thousands of Borders.com recommendation lists integrated throughout departments, sections, and subsections.

- Exclusive content from *Jazz Times, Rough Guides,* and *SALON Magazine.*
- Thousands of exclusive reviews from Borders book, music, and video experts.

Service

- Largest in-stock multimedia selection means fast delivery to customers' doorsteps and fewer split orders.
- Dedicated information desk lets visitors personally interact via e-mail with Borders.com staff.
- Live telephone support available 24 hours a day, seven days a week.
- Out-of-print book search available through Borders.com's exclusive partnership with Harvest Booksearch.[25]

IBM developed the front-end technology infrastructure for the Borders.com site, but Borders also employed the services of other technology firms to integrate the infrastructure. Level 8 Systems, a software company, provided Distributed Object Technology/Transactional Messaging technology.

In its effort to provide an online community, Borders partnered with Talk City. Talk City provided Borders with the technology for community-building chats and events. Talk City brought access to more than four million users of its Internet Community services. Chat room topics soon included Borders NetCafe, Kidz Korner, Reel Talk, Literatzi-Lobby, and Sci-Fi.[26]

TROUBLES FOR BORDERS.COM

Original Views of the Internet

The Internet gives us the opportunity to bring the traditional Borders advantages—a diverse selection, a dedication to customer service and an ability to foster community—to customers around the world," said Rick Vanzura, senior vice president of eCommerce and fulfillment for Borders.[27]

In 1998, Vanzura planned to use the website to "foster our international branding and to get the message out about our integrated approach to books, music and videos."[28] But even as Borders pushed further into cybersales, the company insisted in its annual report that it was not placing all of its eggs in the eCommerce basket, stating that they were "committed to remaining focused on building and enhancing our core retailing business. Our stores are the foundation of our company, and we will not compromise their standing as we respond to the opportunity of eCommerce."[29] Added Scott Wilder, director of online services for Borders.com, "We see the website as a way to extend our brand. Twenty-five percent of our business is coming from overseas, and we're already expanding the bricks-and-mortar business in places like Singapore and the U.K. We see the website as another vehicle to expand."

Struggles in 1998 and 1999

Before the end of 1998, the Borders.com site had to be upgraded twice and underwent a third upgrade in the beginning of 1999. Still, users were giving the site positive reviews. In the fall of 1998, *Money.com* magazine chose Borders.com as one of its "Best of the Internet" selections for the site's aesthetics, choices, and timeliness. In January 1999, Borders was named "one of the top 10 most trusted brands on the Internet and in other settings, and the single most trusted brand of any online book and music retailer" by a Cheskin Research study. Borders.com was also rated number one in customer fulfillment by a J. P. Morgan 1999 study.

However, Borders.com's online point of differentiation—selling books, music, and video together on the Internet—was quickly copied by competitors Amazon and barnesandnoble.com.[30] To strengthen its online presence, Borders continued to build alliances and increase its marketing efforts. In 1999, Borders enlarged its marketing budget fivefold, to an estimated $20 million.[31] Borders also formed an alliance with About.com to build individual co-branded bookstores on the many sections of About.com's network. Borders also partnered in 1999 with a content production company that provided live and archived webcasts on Borders.com, such as interviews with actors, performances by musicians, and readings by authors. In 2000, Borders selected E.piphany to create "a private database that gathers customer-supplied information on personal preferences and interests and ultimately delivers a highly individualized shopping experience that the customer controls."[32]

Continued Losses

But in 1998, Borders.com posted losses of $10.5 million on $4.6 million in sales. Those results, combined with Borders' late online entry, caused Borders stock to take a beating on Wall Street in 1999. According to one portfolio manager:

> Although Borders superstores are thriving, helping the company reap record-setting earnings last year of $92.1 million, its stock is currently trading around $14, near its 52-week low. That's down from a high

of $41.75 last July [1998]. Adding insult to injury, Amazon, which has never made a dime, trades around $175, with a market capitalization 27 times greater than the Ann Arbor, Mich.-based chain. The first-mover advantage is staggering and decisive.[33]

An Improved Borders.com for 2000

In February 2000, Borders closed its website for a weekend to upgrade content and commerce capabilities. These technological upgrades were intended to offer customers a host of specific improvements, including a streamlined order process that would be quicker, simpler, and smarter. Shoppers at Borders.com would no longer be required to register before moving through the order process or even checking out, though customers may, of course, continue to store their shipping and credit information online for easy retrieval. In addition, online shoppers would immediately notice the new graphic design of the site, including an updated color scheme and page layouts, as well as new editorial features designed to deepen the Borders.com browsing experience.[34]

The changes paid off in the near term. In Forrester Research's Fall 2000 PowerRankings, Borders.com edged in front of Amazon to take first place in the rankings. The results suggested that Amazon's lead might have been shrinking:

> In customer service, the attribute that consumers rank most important, and one that Amazon won across the board in the spring, Amazon was overtaken in all three categories. In Books, Amazon's spring Rankings lead of 2.2 points in customer service was reduced to a 1.1 point loss to barnesandnoble.com. While shopping for books at Amazon, the Forrester shopper endured average email response times of 19 hours and phone hold times of up to five minutes, which hurt Amazon, a site that claims to offer great customer service from the desktop to the doorstep.[35]

Borders.com online sales continued to increase through 2000; by 289.1 percent and 53.1 percent in 1999 and 2000 respectively. Net losses also continued to sharply increase. Borders.com underperformed in website visits as well. The site's 864,000 unique visitors in December 1999 paled in comparison with Amazon's 15.9 million and barnesandnoble.com's 5.9 million unique visitors.[36]

A New Direction for Borders.com

In 1999 and 2000, Borders executives began switching from an eCommerce focus to a "retail convergence strategy" that focused on the intersection of the Internet and retail outlets, or "clicks-and-mortar." According to Rick Vanzura, senior vice president of Borders.com, "Folks are so focused on the stand-alone eCommerce business, which is estimated to reach roughly 15 percent of the market eventually. We could be the dominant force for the other 85 percent, when you bring the site together with the compelling physical superstore experience."[37]

In 2000, Borders began installing in-store Internet kiosks, called "Title Sleuths," that enabled customers to locate books, music, and videos in the store or online and check availability and prices. Borders hired AltaVista Company, an Internet search provider, to provide the search engine in its in-store kiosks. Borders' 2000 website upgrade also provided "a platform for expansion and evolution of Borders across all channels including the new version of Title Sleuth."[38] This was a new strategy for the online book, music, and video market.

In February 2001, Borders spokeswoman Ann Blinkley stated that the company had determined that its "direct consumer online business will not generate profits in the foreseeable future and we're not investing more funds toward it."[39] The news came just days after Amazon.com announced that it would lay off 1,300 employees in a cost-cutting measure.

One month later, in March 2001, Borders announced a fulfillment agreement with Ingram Book Group. Under the agreement, Ingram became the provider of book fulfillment services for Borders online sales and in-store special orders. In the transaction, Ingram also received a large amount of inventory from Borders' fulfillment center in Tennessee. Borders' Josefowicz asserted, "The change will assure a continued high level of service to customers while allowing Borders Group to reduce its operating costs, a key aspect of driving improved future earnings."[40]

BORDERS AND AMAZON.COM ALLIANCE OF 2001

Motivations for Alliance

Following three years of increasing losses and a lack of interested acquirers for its online unit Josefowicz announced a strategic partnership with Amazon on April 11, 2001.[41] In addition to its poor financial performance in the past, Borders did not believe their online unit would become profitable in the future. According to Ed Wilhelm, Borders CFO and senior VP, "We didn't see our site becoming profitable in

the foreseeable future, but we did have a large group of customers that wanted to shop online."[42]

Not only did the alliance provide Borders with a means of refocusing efforts on its traditional brick-and-mortar business, but it also teamed them with a pure play Internet player. "This alliance allows Borders to offer our customers the convenience of an online shopping option with the added benefits that will emerge through our new association with Amazon.com, the world's recognized eCommerce leader," said Josefowicz. "While our customers' needs are met online by the people who do it better than anyone else, we will provide them with what we do best—the books, music and movies they love to explore in an engaging shopping atmosphere."[43] Josefowicz appeared to be the driving force behind the strategic alliance. "Clearly, the idea rested with our CEO," Wilhelm says, with the belief that the Internet "is definitely part of the future, and the choice is to build capabilities on your own or partner with someone who has already developed them."[44]

Details of the Deal

As outlined in the agreement, Amazon and Borders re-launched Borders.com as a co-branded site selling books, music, and DVDs in August 2001. Amazon ran the site separately from their main online store, handling customer service, inventory, and filling orders. The new site offered several features unique to the Borders site, namely store location information and in-store event calendars. At the time of the site launch, Borders and Amazon discussed the possibility of letting customers reserve titles to be picked up at local Borders stores, but this feature was not included at launch time.[45] In addition, Amazon incorporated its patented 1-Click ordering technology into the new site.

The exact terms of the Borders.com deal were not disclosed. However, an Amazon spokeswoman revealed that Borders would pay Amazon a onetime site development fee and the two companies had reached an agreement on revenue sharing. Amazon recognized the gross revenue, while the two companies shared net revenue.

Neither Borders nor Amazon changed its financial guidance following the announcement of the deal. However, Josefowicz stated the deal would help Borders Group deliver on their prior corporate target of 20 percent earnings growth over 2001. Borders also reduced 70 positions at Borders.com from a staff of approximately 100 as a result of the alliance with Amazon.[46]

THE BRICKS-AND-MORTAR-FOCUSED BORDERS OF APRIL 2002

A New Strategy

By the Spring of 2002, Borders' business strategy was well defined, "to continue its growth and increase its profitability through expanding and refining its core superstore business, driving international growth by leveraging infrastructure investments and expanding established markets, leveraging strategic alliances and in-store Internet-based commerce technologies which enhance the customer experience, and maximizing cash flow by containing costs."[47] And the strategy appeared to work exceptionally well. Borders superstore operations achieved annual growth in net sales and net income for the year ended January 27, 2002, of 6.0 percent and 27.6 percent respectively.[48] Its average sales per superstore were higher than the comparable figure of any publicly reporting book superstore operator.

Troubles at Waldenbooks

The Waldenbooks segment, however, experienced decreased comparable sales percentages for the past few years primarily due to the overall decrease in mall traffic and the impact of superstore openings. As a result, Borders developed a plan for the optimization of the Waldenbooks store base in order to improve net income and cash flow. This plan resulted in further store closing costs. The company expected these initiatives to support consolidated annual sales growth of 8 percent to 10 percent and consolidated annual earnings growth of 13 percent to 15 percent for the Borders Group.[49] Throughout the plan's implementation, careful monitoring and analysis will demand a significant level of attention from the senior management team of Borders.

International Expansion

Beyond the core Borders stores and Waldenbooks group, the third element of the Borders Group's business is its international initiative, which began in 1997. In just five years, the company has expanded its international operations to establish a presence on four continents. Borders believes it has a competitive advantage due to the depth of its system-driven assortment and level of service. In 2001, international sales increased 14.8 percent to $251.7 million. Currently, four of the ten highest volume Borders superstores are international stores. The international opportunity continues to be viewed as a substantial component of Borders' future success.[50]

EXTENDING THE PARTNERSHIP

Borders-Amazon Alliance of 2002

With all wheels turning in the bricks-and-mortar world, Borders' online business received another jolt on April 23, 2002. Borders and Amazon announced a multi-year extension of the original agreement. This announcement marked significant broadening and deepening of the alliance. A key element of the agreement was Amazon's offering Borders.com customers the option of picking up books, CDs, and DVDs at one of more than 365 Borders stores throughout the United States. The companies also announced an agreement to launch the new Amazon-powered Waldenbooks.com in time for the 2002 holiday season. The new site offered customers the benefits of Amazon's eCommerce platform, such as personalization and 1-Click ordering. The new Waldenbooks.com was intended to appeal to the three million members of Waldenbooks' Preferred Reader loyalty program who were able to earn points with every purchase made through the co-branded site. In addition, boutiques on romance and science fiction genres, high interest areas for the Preferred Reader audience, were featured on the site. The multi-year agreement had terms similar to those of the 2001 alliance, with all sales originating through the new site recorded by Amazon and a percentage of sales going to Borders. Inventory, fulfillment, and customer service continued to be provided by Amazon.[51]

Borders received a boost in 2002 from book releases by a number of best-selling authors, as well as from strong DVD sales. Music sales weakened and the sluggish economy weighed heavily on store traffic. Operating expenses trended lower, despite the lack of sales leverage, in part due to the company's cost-control and category management initiatives. Borders' relationship with Amazon has eliminated its Internet costs by shifting the fulfillment responsibility for Internet sales to Amazon in exchange for a fee.[52]

"This agreement is an important next step in the extremely successful alliance we've experienced with Amazon," said Josefowicz. "Customers overwhelmingly indicate a desire for the convenience of in-store pick up and we're delighted to offer it to the world's largest online audience of book, music, and movie lovers."[53]

"We're pleased to build on the success of our original alliance with Borders and now offer customers the option of picking up thousands of books, music and DVD products at their neighborhood Borders store," said Bezos. "Together, we're combining the convenience of online shopping with the speed of in-store pick up at a best-of-breed Borders store."[54]

Amazon's Position in April 2002

On the same day as the alliance announcement, Amazon reported a net loss of $23 million for the first quarter of 2002. Amazon Chief Financial Officer Warren Jenson said a combination of price cuts and free shipping attracted more business.[55]

While the new arrangement with Borders offered Amazon customers a different shipment method, one of the early criticisms of online retail, Amazon admitted that it was unclear to what extent the move would affect sales. "Borders accounts for a very small fraction of our sales under any scenario," Bezos told analysts.[56]

Regardless of the percentage impact on sales, the partnership extension allowed Amazon to offer its wide range of goods to Borders' online customer base, and to some extent use Borders stores for promotional purposes. Borders, meanwhile, hoped its customers would use the website and the 335 superstores and 900 Waldenbooks stores it operates interchangeably. Ideally for Borders, customers would use the Internet to see if their local Borders store has a book they want, reserve it online, and drive down to the store to pick it up, perhaps sitting in on a reading and buying a mocha latte while they are visiting.

It was clear that Amazon viewed the partnership as a winning proposition, as they recorded their first net profit in the fourth quarter of 2001. The move into the black came after Amazon made several high-profile alliances in 2001, as it abstained from acquisitions in favor of partnerships. Amazon had used acquisitions, strategic investments, in-house build-outs, and partnerships to evolve from a mere vendor of books and CDs to a diversified retailer. According to David Schehr, research director with Stamford, Conn.–based Gartner G2, change was forced on Amazon when the priority for Internet companies switched from growth to profitability. To support this goal, the company struck partnerships with mainstream retailers such as electronics giant Circuit City and discounter Target. The first Borders partnership and the subsequent extension were viewed as contributors to Amazon's profitability and provided a success story to fuel Amazon's partnering strategy.[57]

THE FUTURE OF BORDERS.COM

Although the extension of the Amazon-Borders partnership was received well by analysts and publicly applauded by each firm's CEO, select investors questioned whether this partnership was the best long-term solution for Borders.com. Borders was positioned to grab market share domestically and in several major overseas arenas with combined estimated market values of $3 billion, as it added to its base of productive book and music superstores. In 2002, 41 superstores opened in the U.S., while eight foreign units were unveiled. The aggressive expansion effort was expanded to continue in the years ahead, resulting in increased economies of scale and greater expense leverage. The continued downsizing of the mall-based Waldenbooks division was expected to result in increased productivity, especially after the store base drops to a manageable 700 units. But would these bricks-and-mortar activities be enough to propel Borders forward, or is a greater level of involvement in their online operations necessary to achieve its growth targets and capture its full potential?[58]

EXHIBIT 1
Domestic Book Market Sectors Forecast
Source: Veronis, Suhler & Associates, Wilkofskt Gruen Associates, Book Industry Group.

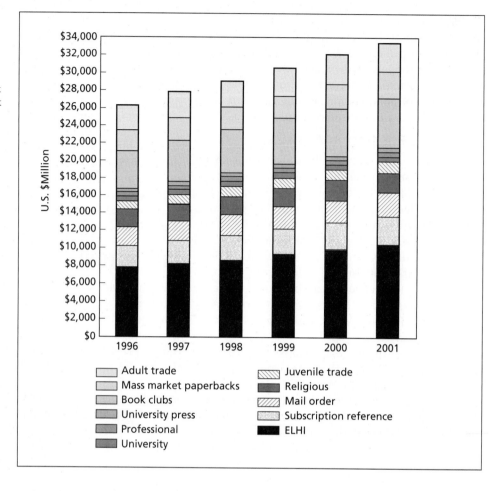

EXHIBIT 2
Worldwide Internet Forecast
Source: International Data Corporation.

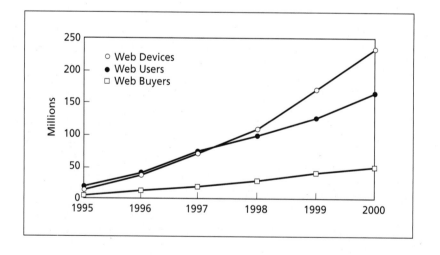

EXHIBIT 3
Worldwide Internet Commerce Forecast
Source: International Data Corporation.

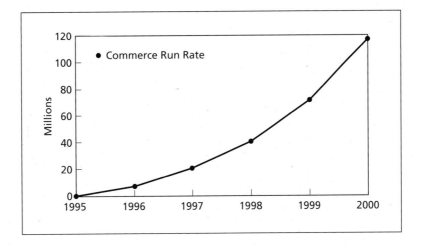

EXHIBIT 4   **Business Model Comparison**
Source: DMG Technology, Barnes and Noble's public information.

	Land-Based	Amazon
Superstores	439	1
Titles per superstore	175,000	2,500,000
Occupancy costs (% of sales)*	12%	4%
Sales per operating employee	$100,000	$300,000
Inventory turnover	3–4x	50–60x
Capital requirements	High	Low
Cash-flow characteristics	Poor	Great

*Includes rental, depreciation, amortizations, and pre-opening expenses.

EXHIBIT 5
Borders.com Site Organization

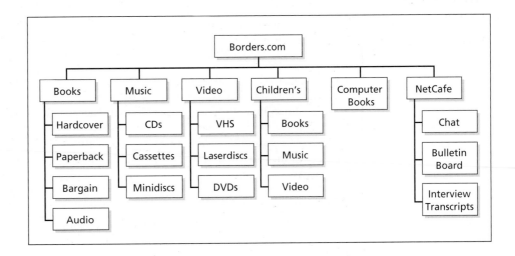

EXHIBIT 6 **Borders.com 1998–2000 Profit/Loss Report ($ in M)**
Source: Borders Group, Inc. Annual Reports.

	2000	**1999**	**1998**
Sales	$27.4	$17.9	4.6
Net loss	29.7	17.2	10.5
Net loss as a % of sales	108.4%	96.1%	228.3%
Depreciation expense	7.8	5.5	1.9
Interest expense	5.8	4.4	2.7

EXHIBIT 7
Combined Online Book, Music, and Video Sales, 2002E ($ in M)
Source: Jupiter Communications and Salomon Smith Barney.

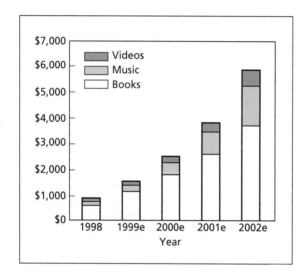

Endnotes

1. Bob Keefe, Cox News Services, San Diego, April 11, 2001.
2. Carrie A. Johnson, "Borders Cuts and Runs—Backwards," Forrester Brief, April 11, 2001.
3. *International Directory of Company Histories,* Vol. 43. St. James Press, 2002. Investext Plus Business and Company Resource Center, Gale Group Databases, December 2, 2002.
4. Matt Roush, "Borders Buys Rest of Its Stock: Move Aids Kmart Too," Crain's Detroit Business, pg. 4, July 24, 1995, and "Borders Group, Inc. Initial Public Offering Begins," P.R. Newswire, May 25, 1995.
5. *International Directory of Company Histories,* op cit.
6. *International Directory of Company Histories,* op cit.
7. David Kirkpatrick, "Smaller Bookstores End Court Struggle Against Two Chains,"*New York Times,* Section A, Page 1, Column 2, April 20, 2001.
8. Borders Group Press Release, "Borders Group Names Greg Josefowicz President and CEO," November 15, 1999, and Borders Group Press Release, "Borders Group Appoints Josefowicz Chairman of the Board," January 15, 2001.
9. Corporate Profile, Borders Investor Relations, http://www.bordersgroupinc.com, November 29, 2002.
10. Ray Lam, Standard & Poor's Retailing: Specialty Industry Survey, pg. 17, October 1, 1998.
11. Ibid.
12. William H. Donald, Standard & Poor's Publishing Industry Survey, pg. 16, October 29, 1998.
13. Ibid.

14. William H. Donald, Standard & Poor's Publishing Industry Survey, pg. 13, October 29, 1998.

15. Richard Zandi and Mark Rowen, Salomon Smith Barney, Equity Research: Amazon.com, pg. 26, April 21, 1999.

16. "Barnes & Noble to Sell Shares of Its Online Unit," *Los Angeles Times*, August 21, 1998.

17. "Internet Bookshop Opened by Bertelsmann," *Wall Street Journal Europe,* February 17, 1998.

18. William H. Donald, Standard & Poor's Publishing Industry Survey, pg. 13, October 29, 1998.

19. J. William Gurley, Deutsche Morgan Grenfell, "Amazon.com: The Quintessential Wave Rider," pg. 14, June 9, 1997.

20. Lucy Kellaway, "Billionaire Nerd with His Own Bandwidth," *Financial Times*, November 13, 1998.

21. William H. Donald, Standard & Poor's Publishing Industry Survey, pg. 12, October 29, 1998.

22. "With Eye Toward 'Virtual Store,' Borders Partners with Open Sesame," December 16, 1996.

23. "Borders Group Pre-Announces Third Quarter Results, Internet Plans," PR Newswire, November 4, 1997.

24. "Borders Group Unveils Public Preview of Borders.com," PR Newswire, May 11, 1998.

25. "Borders Group Unveils Public Preview of Borders.com," PR Newswire, May 11, 1998.

26. "Borders.com Adds ECommerce," *Advertising Age,* May 11, 1998.

27. "Borders Group Unveils Public Preview of Borders.com," PR Newswire, May 11, 1998.

28. "Borders Online at Last with Books, CDs, Videos," *Publishers Weekly,* May 18, 1998.

29. "Borders Online at Last with Books, CDs, Videos," *Publishers Weekly,* May 18, 1998.

30. "The Internet: Borders Struggles to Find Sales Edge in Cyberspace," *The Wall Street Journal Europe,* February 25, 1999.

31. Warren Cohen, "At Last, an Internet Strategy for Borders Online Front Lines," *U.S. News & World Report,* April 12, 1999.

32. "Borders Advances Retail Convergence Strategy Through Integrated Technology That Individualizes Customer Relationships," PR Newswire, May 24, 2000.

33. Warren Cohen, "At Last, an Internet Strategy for Borders Online Front Lines," *U.S. News & World Report,* April 12, 1999.

34. "Borders.com to Unveil 'Enhanced Shopping Experience,'" PR Newswire, February 9, 2000.

35. Forrester Research's PowerRankings, Fall 2000.

36. Louis Trager, "Borders.com Not a Best Seller," Interactive Week from ZDWire, February 28, 2000.

37. Warren Cohen, "At Last, an Internet Strategy for Borders Online Front Lines," *U.S. News & World Report,* April 12, 1999.

38. Sherman Fridman, "Borders.com Closes the Books on Its Old Website," Newsbytes News Network, February 9, 2000.

39. Jennifer Bott, "Borders Pronounces Online Sales a Drag," Knight Ridder Tribune Business News, February 1, 2001.

40. "Borders Group Forms Alliance with Ingram Book Group for Fulfillment Services," PR Newswire, March 15, 2001.

41. Christine Gordon, "Amazon.com Inc. Allies with Borders.com," *ECommerce,* April 11, 2001, http://www.Internetnews.com/ec-news/article.php/4_739981, December 1, 2002.

42. Cheryl Rosen, "Large-Scale Strategic Alliances Spell Disaster for Some Companies, but Amazon.com Has Made More than One Work," *InformationWeek,* June 4, 2001, http://www.informationweek.com/840/amz_online.htm, December 1, 2002.

43. "Amazon.com to Run Borders.com Website," *The Write News,* April 13, 2001, http://www.writenews.com/2001/041301_borders_amazon.htm, December 1, 2002.

44. Cheryl Rosen, "Large-Scale Strategic Alliances Spell Disaster for Some Companies, but Amazon.com Has Made More than One Work," *InformationWeek,* June, 4, 2001, http://www.informationweek.com/840/amz_online.htm, December 1, 2002.

45. Joelle Tessler, "Amazon Absorbs Borders' Online Bookselling Operations," Knight Ridder Tribune Business News, April 2, 2001, *Factiva,* December 1, 2002.

46. Molly Prior, "Amazon to Operate Borders.com," Discount Store News, May 1, 2001, *Factiva,* December 1, 2002.

47. Borders Annual Report 2001, December 1, 2002.

48. Borders Annual Report 2001, December 1, 2002.

49. Borders Annual Report 2001, December 1, 2002.

50. Borders Annual Report 2001, December 1, 2002.

51. Borders Group Press Release, "Borders Group and Amazon.com Extend Alliance with In-Store Pick Up at Borders Stores Nationwide for Amazon.com Customers and New Waldenbooks Teamed with Amazon.com Site," Borders Group, Inc., Ann Arbor, MI, April 23, 2002.

52. Maurice Levenson, "ValueLine Profile Summary Report for Borders Group, Inc.," Value Line, Inc., New York, NY, November 15, 2002.

53. Borders Group Press Release, "Borders Group and Amazon.com Extend Alliance . . ."

54. Borders Group Press Release, "Borders Group and Amazon.com Extend Alliance . . ."

55. George Tibbits, "Amazon.com Reports Loss of $23 Million, Beats Expectations," Associated Press Newswires, April 23, 2002.

56. Monica Soto, "Amazon.com's Cost-Conscious Strategy Works; Loss Narrows, Sales Rise as Customers Save More," *The Seattle Times,* April 24, 2002.

57. David Shabelman, "Amazon Shuns Deals for Alliances," The Deal, The Daily Deal, http://www.thedeal.com/, January 22, 2002 (November 19, 2002).

58. Maurice Levenson, "ValueLine Profile . . ."

Index